THE BEDFORD READER

Fourteenth Edition

X. J. Kennedy

Dorothy M. Kennedy

Jane E. Aaron

Ellen Kuhl Repetto

bedford/st.martin's
Macmillan Learning
Boston | New York

To Dorothy M. Kennedy, 1931–2018

FOR BEDFORD/ST. MARTIN'S
Vice President, Editorial, Macmillan Learning Humanities: Edwin Hill
Executive Program Director for English: Leasa Burton
Senior Program Manager: John E. Sullivan III
Executive Marketing Manager: Joy Fisher Williams
Director of Content Development, Humanities: Jane Knetzger
Developmental Editor: Cara Kaufman
Content Project Manager: Louis C. Bruno Jr.
Senior Workflow Project Manager: Jennifer Wetzel
Production Coordinator: Brianna Lester
Media Project Manager: Allison Hart
Media Editor: Daniel Johnson
Senior Manager of Publishing Services: Andrea Cava
Assistant Editor: William Hwang
Project Management: Lumina Datamatics, Inc.
Composition: Lumina Datamatics, Inc.
Permissions Manager: Kalina Ingham
Text Permissions Editors: Arthur Johnson and Mark Schaefer, Lumina Datamatics, Inc.
Photo Permissions Editor: Angela Boehler
Photo Researcher: Krystyna Borgen, Lumina Datamatics, Inc.
Director of Design, Content Management: Diana Blume
Cover Design: William Boardman
Cover Image: Malvern (acrylic on board)/Powis, Paul/PAUL POWIS/Private Collection/
    Bridgeman Images
Printing and Binding: LSC Communications

Manufactured in the United States of America.

2   3   4   5   6   24   23   22

For information, write: Bedford/St. Martin's, 75 Arlington Street, Boston, MA 02116

ISBN 978-1-319-19560-1 (Student Edition)
ISBN 978-1-319-28402-2 (Loose-leaf Edition)
ISBN 978-1-319-25653-1 (Casebound)
ISBN 978-1-319-26614-1 (Instructor's Edition)

ACKNOWLEDGMENTS
Text acknowledgments and copyrights appear at the back of the book on pages 719–22, which constitute an extension of the copyright page. Art acknowledgments and copyrights appear on the same pages as the art selections they cover.

Methods for Achieving Your Purpose in Writing

The Bedford Reader centers on common ways of thinking and writing about all kinds of subjects, from everyday experiences to public policies to scientific theories. Whatever your purpose in writing, one or more of these ways of thinking—or methods of development—can help you discover and shape your ideas in individual paragraphs or entire papers.

The following list connects various purposes you may have for writing and the methods for achieving those purposes. The blue boxes along the right edge of the page correspond to tabs on later pages where each method is explained.

PURPOSE	METHOD
To tell a story about your subject, possibly to enlighten readers or to explain something to them	Narration
To help readers understand your subject through the evidence of their senses—sight, hearing, touch, smell, taste	Description
To explain your subject with instances that show readers its nature or character	Example
To explain or evaluate your subject by helping readers see the similarities and differences between it and another subject	Comparison and Contrast
To inform readers how to do something or how something works—how a sequence of actions leads to a particular result	Process Analysis
To explain a conclusion about your subject by showing readers the subject's parts or elements	Division or Analysis
To help readers see order in your subject by understanding the kinds or groups it can be sorted into	Classification
To tell readers the reasons for or consequences of your subject, explaining why or what if	Cause and Effect
To show readers the meaning of your subject—its boundaries and its distinctions from other subjects	Definition
To have readers consider your opinion about your subject or your proposal for it	Argument and Persuasion

PREFACE FOR INSTRUCTORS

"A writer," says Saul Bellow, "is a reader moved to emulate." From the beginning, the aim of *The Bedford Reader* has been to move students to be writers, through reading and emulating the good writing of others.

Like its popular predecessors, this fourteenth edition pursues that aim both rhetorically and thematically. We present the rhetorical methods realistically, as we ourselves use them — as instinctive forms that assist invention and fruition and as flexible forms that mix easily for any purpose a writer may have. Further, we make numerous thematic connections among selections, both to spark students' interest in reading and to show how different writers tackle similar subjects with unique results.

Filling in this outline is a wealth of features, new and enduring.

NEW FEATURES

ENGAGING NEW READINGS BY REMARKABLE WRITERS   As always, we have been enthralled with freshening the book's selections. In searching for works academic yet lively, we discovered exceptional rhetorical models that will, we trust, also capture students' interest. The twenty-six new selections balance pieces by established favorites such as Paul Theroux and Sandra Cisneros with rising stars such as Scaachi Koul and Derek Thompson. Three new essays by exemplary college writers are part of the mix, assuring students that beginners, too, can produce writing worth reading.

EXCITING LITERARY DIMENSION   A highlight of the new selections is the addition of literature. Long known for showcasing exceptional prose by legends such as Langston Hughes and Louise Erdrich, *The Bedford Reader* now presents their art as well. Every chapter of readings includes a short story, a poem, or a script that demonstrates the rhetorical methods at play in forms we tend to read for pleasure. We are thrilled to introduce students to eleven works classic and contemporary—ranging from the canonical poetry of Emily Dickinson to the experimental science fiction of Ted Chiang—and have no doubt they will enjoy reading them as much as we have.

A STRONGER FOUNDATION IN READING AND WRITING   More than ever, *The Bedford Reader* puts students on solid footing as they learn and practice the interrelated processes of critical reading and academic writing. With the encouragement of instructors who use the book, we have restructured Part One, breaking the material on the writing process into three distinct chapters—on discovery and drafting, reviewing and revising, and editing—allowing for ease of comprehension and reference while following student writer Rosie Anaya from rough idea to finished essay as she models the stages of writing in response to reading.

- **A focus on reading to write.** As before, Chapter 1 stresses the connections between reading and writing and offers more guidance on active and critical reading than any other rhetorical reader. And the revised Chapter 2, on discovery and drafting, features new material on responding to a text, developing and organizing ideas, and integrating source material into students' own writing.

- **A new emphasis on peer review and collaborative writing** throughout starts with a new discussion of reviewing a draft and sample feedback comments in Chapter 3, reinforced with ten reworked revision checklists that now do double duty as peer review worksheets in each of the introductions to the methods (Chaps. 5–14).

- **A separate chapter on editing** (Chap. 4) highlights information on recognizing common errors and learning how to fix them, making this important reference material easier to find and to use.

- **An updated appendix** offers a brief overview of the research process and includes dozens of recent models for documenting sources in MLA and APA style. Both styles continue to be illustrated by annotated student research papers, and ten additional examples of documented writing, two of them new, are spread throughout the book.

ENHANCED VISUAL APPEAL   The fourteenth edition of *The Bedford Reader* also provides more support for media-savvy students, helping them to understand the methods by visualizing them at work.

- **New graphic organizers.** For each rhetorical chapter an innovative "How to Organize . . ." flowchart sketches out how that method is typically structured—for example, chronological order for narration and process analysis, spatial order for description, or climactic order for example and argument. Distilling the information in the method introductions into an easily digestible format, these simple organizers show at a glance how writers can use the methods to best effect.
- **More annotated essays.** Complementing the notes alongside Nancy Mairs's "Disability" and Rosie Anaya's response in Part One and the annotated student case studies in Part Two, two newly annotated essays help students follow the methods and hone their critical-reading skills. In Part Two's closing chapter on argument, new marginal notes alongside the text of Linda Chavez's "Supporting Family Values" illustrate the strategies the author uses to achieve her purpose. And in Part Three, new annotations with Joan Didion's "Earthquakes" highlight the writer's use of multiple methods.
- **Fresh images.** Emphasizing the visual as well as the verbal, each rhetorical chapter opens with a striking image, a third of them new—a photograph, a cartoon, an ad—with updated text and questions to invite students' critical reading. And several of the book's selections, five of them new to this edition, either take images as their starting points or include illustrations to explain or highlight key ideas.

TRADEMARK FEATURES

VARIED SELECTIONS BY QUALITY AUTHORS   All of them models of exceptional writing, the essays and literary works in *The Bedford Reader* vary in authorship, topic, even length and format. We offer clear and interesting applications of the methods of development by noted writers such as Amy Tan, N. Scott Momaday, Firoozeh Dumas, and David Sedaris. Half the selections are by women, and half touch on cultural diversity. They range in subject from family to science, from language to psychology, from food to politics.

FOCUS ON STUDENT WORK   Featuring more student writing than any other textbook of its kind, *The Bedford Reader* presents twenty-three models of exemplary college work (five of them new to this edition): multiple drafts of a student's critical reading and response to an essay; ten annotated examples of student writing in academic genres such as lab reports, field observations, and policy proposals; ten essays in the rhetorical methods given the same treatment as the professional writing; and two annotated research papers.

UNIQUE COMMENTS BY THE WRITERS ON WRITING After their essays, more than half of the book's writers offer comments on everything from reading to grammar to how they developed the particular piece we reprint. Besides providing rock-solid advice, these comments—seventeen of them new—prove that for the pros, too, writing is usually a challenge. For easy access, the "Writers on Writing" are listed in a Directory under the topics they address. Look up *Purpose*, for instance, and find that Chitra Divakaruni, Roxane Gay, and Brent Staples, among others, have something to say about this crucial aspect of the writing process.

REALISTIC TREATMENT OF THE RHETORICAL METHODS *The Bedford Reader* treats the methods of development not as empty forms but as tools for inventing, for shaping, and, ultimately, for accomplishing a purpose.

- **A practical guide.** The chapters on reading and writing in Part One and the introductions to the rhetorical methods in Part Two are simple and clear, with many explanations and suggestions distilled into bulleted lists and boxed guidelines so that students can easily follow and use the book's advice on their own. Each chapter introduction links the method to the range of purposes it can serve and gives step-by-step guidance for writing and revising. (For quick reference, the purpose/method links also appear inside the front cover, where they are keyed to the marginal page tabs that appear in each chapter introduction.)

- **A "Focus" box in every rhetorical chapter** highlights an element of writing that is especially relevant to that method—for example, verbs in narration, concrete words in description, parallelism in comparison and contrast, and tone in argument and persuasion. To show these elements in context, most selections include a question about them.

- **An emphasis on mixing the methods** takes the realistic approach even further. We show how writers freely combine methods to achieve their purposes: Each rhetorical introduction discusses how that method might work with others, and at least one "Other Methods" question after every selection helps students analyze how methods work together. Most significantly, Part Three provides an anthology of works by celebrated writers that specifically illustrate mixed methods. The headnotes for these selections point to where each method comes into play.

- **Careful attention to genre** shows students how they can apply the methods in their other courses. Integrated discussions throughout Part One introduce the concept of genre and explain how purpose, audience, and convention affect a writer's choices. And in each rhetorical chapter in Part Two, a "Student Case Study" offers brief guidelines for writing different kinds of projects — such as a critical review or an essay exam — and annotates a student-written document to demonstrate a specific application of method to genre. Two of these documents — a nursing student's résumé and job-application letter — are new to this edition.

EXTENSIVE THEMATIC CONNECTIONS   *The Bedford Reader* provides substantial opportunities for topical class discussion and writing. A pair of essays in each chapter addresses the same subject, from the ordinary (embarrassment) to the controversial (privilege). Three of those pairings are new, and the thoroughly refreshed chapter on argument now includes two new casebooks on current issues. At least one "Connections" writing topic after every selection suggests links to other selections in the book. And an alternate table of contents arranges the book's selections under more than three dozen topics and academic disciplines (five new).

ABUNDANT EDITORIAL APPARATUS   As always, we've surrounded the selections with a wealth of material designed to get students reading, thinking, and writing. To help structure students' critical approach to the selections, each one is preceded by a headnote on the author and a headnote on the selection itself, outlining the selection's cultural and historical contexts. Each selection is followed by sets of questions on meaning, writing strategy, and language and at least five writing suggestions. One writing suggestion encourages students to explore their responses in their journals; another suggests how to develop the journal writing into an essay; and others emphasize critical writing, research, and connections among selections.

Besides the aids provided with every selection, the book also includes additional writing topics at the end of every rhetorical chapter, a Glossary of Useful Terms that defines key terms used in the book (all those printed in SMALL CAPITAL LETTERS), and a comprehensive index that alphabetizes not only authors and titles but also all important topics (including the elements of composition).

COMPREHENSIVE INSTRUCTOR'S MANUAL   Available online on the book's catalog page at **macmillanlearning.com** or bound into the instructor's edition, *Notes and Resources for Teaching The Bedford Reader* suggests ways to integrate journaling and collaboration into writing classes; discusses uses for the book's chapters on critical reading, academic writing, and research and documentation; provides tips on using visuals and multimedia selections in a writing course; and offers sample syllabi for courses taking either a rhetorical or a thematic approach. In addition, *Notes and Resources* discusses every method, every selection (with multimedia resource suggestions and with possible answers provided for all questions), and every "Writers on Writing" commentary.

TWO VERSIONS   *The Bedford Reader* has a sibling. A shorter edition, *The Brief Bedford Reader,* features forty-eight readings instead of seventy-nine, omitting the student case studies and literary works and including five selections (rather than eight) in Part Three.

ACKNOWLEDGMENTS

Hundreds of teachers and students over the years have helped us shape *The Bedford Reader.* For this edition, the following teachers offered insights from their experiences that encouraged worthy changes: Megan Anderson, Limestone College; Pamela Arlov, Middle Georgia State University; Matthew Ayres, County College of Morris; Sarah Bane, Carl Albert State College; Shaindel Beers, Blue Mountain Community College; Janice Bellinghiere, Grossmont College; Andrei Belyi, Eastern Florida State College; Britt Benshetler, Northwest Vista College; Rhona Blaker, Glendale Community College; Floyd Brigdon, Trinity Valley Community College; Edison Cassadore, Tohono O'odham Community College; Phillip Chamberlin, Hillsborough Community College; Carla Chwat, University of North Georgia; Richard Costa, Bristol Community College; Syble Davis, Houston Community College; Christina Marie Devlin, Montgomery College; Meredith Dodson, Olivet College; Marie Eckstrom, Rio Hondo College; Rebecca Fedewa, Wisconsin Lutheran College; Dorothy Fleming, Curry College; Deirdre Frank, Peninsula College; Robert Giron, Montgomery College; Timothy Grams, Muskegon Community College; Eric James Hazell, Central Texas College; Mathew Hodges, Bristol Community College; Lisa Hoffman-Reyes, Tacoma Community College; Tia Hudson, Olympic College; Christine Kervina, Northern Virginia Community College; Neva Knott, Centralia College; Kevin Mackie, Austin Community College; Annette McCreedy, Nashville State Community College; Angela Mellor, Western Technical College; Agnetta Mendoza, Nashville State Community College; Amanda Meyer, Carroll Community College; Joseph O'Connell, Austin Community College; Barbara Parsons, Tacoma Community College; Steven Penn, Morehead State University; Sarah Peterson, Olivet College; Shakil Rabbi, Bowie State University; Ki Russell, Blue Mountain Community College; Maureen Salzer, Pima Community College; Vicki Samson, San Diego Mesa College; Jasna Shannon, Coker College; Katherine Simpson, Lord Fairfax Community College; Pamela Solberg, Western Technical College; Andrea Trapp, Cincinnati State Technical and Community College; John Valliere, Eastern Florida State College;

Summer Vertrees, Cumberland University; Gail Watson, County College of Morris; Brian White, Northeastern Illinois University; Nicole Wilson, Bowie State University; Dianna Woods, Northeast Texas Community College; and Marta Wozniak, Southwestern Oregon Community College.

We owe, as ever, countless debts to the creative people at and around Bedford/St. Martin's. Edwin Hill, Leasa Burton, John Sullivan, and Joy Fisher Williams contributed insight and support. Cara Kaufman, developing the book, was an eager collaborator and coconspirator: She helped to plan and implement the revisions, fresh features, and new reading selections; researched and drafted some of the apparatus; and gently prodded us along while keeping a calm hand on the controls. William Hwang assisted, running the review program and expertly coordinating the many details that went into this project. William Boardman created the refreshing new cover. Arthur Johnson and Mark Schaefer fought the permissions battle with grace and aplomb. Louis Bruno cheerfully planned and oversaw the production cycle, even as the schedule slipped. And Subramaniam Vengatakrishnan ably transformed the raw manuscript into the finished book you hold.

Finally, we wish to extend a note of gratitude to X. J. Kennedy and Dorothy M. Kennedy, the original authors of *The Bedford Reader* and its continuing benefactors. Although the Kennedys have been retired from active involvement with the book for some years now, their spirit guides every move we make, from reading selections to twists of phrase. And so it is with admiration and deep affection that we dedicate this edition to Dorothy's memory. We hope she'd be pleased with it.

BEDFORD/ST. MARTIN'S PUTS YOU FIRST

From day one, our goal has been simple: to provide inspiring resources that are grounded in best practices for teaching reading and writing. For more than thirty-five years, Bedford/St. Martin's has partnered with those in the field, listening to teachers, scholars, and students about the support writers need. We are committed to helping every writing instructor make the most of our resources.

HOW CAN WE HELP *YOU*?

✔ **Our editors** can align our resources to your outcomes through correlation and transition guides for your syllabus. Just ask us.

✔ **Our sales representatives** specialize in helping you find the right materials to support your course goals.

✔ **Our *Bits* blog** on the Bedford/St. Martin's English Community (**community .macmillan.com**) publishes fresh teaching ideas weekly. You'll also find easily downloadable professional resources and links to author webinars on our community site.

To learn more, contact your Bedford/St. Martin's sales representative or visit **macmillanlearning.com**.

PRINT AND DIGITAL OPTIONS FOR *THE BEDFORD READER*

Bedford/St. Martin's offers a choice of formats. Pick what works best for your course, and ask about our packaging options that offer savings for students.

Print

✔ **Paperback editions.** Choose between the full version of *The Bedford Reader* or a more concise option, *The Brief Bedford Reader*. To order the complete edition, use ISBN 978-1-319-19560-1; for the brief edition, use ISBN 978-1-319-19561-8.

✔ **Loose-leaf edition.** This format does not have a traditional binding; its pages are loose and hole-punched to provide flexibility and a lower price to students. It can be packaged with our digital space for additional savings. To order the loose-leaf packaged with Achieve, use ISBN 978-1-319-33563-2.

✔ **Instructor's edition.** *Notes and Resources for Teaching The Bedford Reader* is available bound into the back of the print book in limited quantities. Ask your sales representative or order your copy at the book's catalog page on **macmillanlearning.com**.

✔ ***A Student's Companion for The Bedford Reader.*** Available for students who could use a little extra support in the composition classroom, this guide offers additional support for students in ALP or co-requisite courses and helps beginning college writers develop on-level skills.

Digital

✔ **Innovative digital learning space.** Bedford/St. Martin's suite of digital tools makes it easy to get everyone on the same page by putting student writers at the center. For details, visit **macmillanlearning.com/college/us/englishdigital**.

✔ **Popular e-book formats.** For information about our e-book partners, visit **macmillanlearning.com/ebooks**.

✔ **Inclusive Access.** Enable every student to receive course materials through your LMS on the first day of class. Macmillan Learning's Inclusive Access program is the easiest, most affordable way to ensure all students have access to quality educational resources. Find out more at **macmillanlearning .com/inclusiveaccess**.

YOUR COURSE, YOUR WAY

No two writing programs or classrooms are exactly alike. Our Curriculum Solutions team works with you to design custom options that provide the resources your students need. (Note that the options below require enrollment minimums.)

✔ ***ForeWords for English.*** Customize any print resource to fit the focus of your course or program by choosing from a range of prepared topics, such as Sentence Guides for Academic Writers.

✔ **Macmillan Author Program (MAP).** Add excerpts or package acclaimed works from Macmillan's trade imprints to connect students with prominent authors and public conversations. A list of popular examples or academic themes is available upon request.

✔ ***Bedford Select.*** Build your own print handbook or anthology from a database of more than 800 selections, and add your own materials to create your ideal text. Package with any Bedford/St. Martin's text for additional savings. Visit **macmillanlearning.com/bedfordselect**.

INSTRUCTOR RESOURCES

You have a lot to do in your course. We want to make it easy for you to find the support you need—and to get it quickly.

Notes and Resources for Teaching The Bedford Reader is available as a PDF that can be downloaded from **macmillanlearning.com**. In addition to chapter overviews and teaching tips, the instructor's manual includes sample syllabi for courses taking either a rhetorical or thematic approach, suggested multimedia resources, and possible answers to the reading questions for each selection.

COUNCIL OF WRITING PROGRAM ADMINISTRATORS (WPA) OUTCOMES STATEMENT FOR FIRST-YEAR COMPOSITION

The following chart provides detailed information on how *The Bedford Reader* helps students build proficiency and achieve the learning outcomes that writing programs across the country use to assess their students' work: rhetorical knowledge; critical thinking, reading, and writing; writing processes; and knowledge of conventions.

WPA Outcomes	Relevant Features of *The Bedford Reader*, 14e
RHETORICAL KNOWLEDGE	
Learn and use key rhetorical concepts through analyzing and composing a variety of texts	• The organization of *The Bedford Reader* supports students' understanding of key rhetorical concepts. **Part One** explores in detail the reading and writing strategies most often required of college students. **Part Two** makes up a rhetorical reader, with ten comprehensive **chapter introductions** that explain how the strategies suit authors' purposes, and multiple readings that illustrate each method. • In Chapter 1, **Critical Reading**, students learn how to assess **context** and how to read critically, using annotation to analyze written and visual texts (pp. 9–26). • Chapter 2, **The Writing Process: Discovery and Drafting**, shows students how to identify their own **purpose**, **audience**, and **thesis** (pp. 27–40) through an understanding of the rhetorical situation. • All selections in Part Two are followed by questions on **Meaning**, **Writing Strategy**, and **Language**. A question labeled **Other Methods** highlights how writers use multiple rhetorical strategies to convey their messages. • **Journal Writing** prompts and **Suggestions for Writing** following each reading and **Additional Writing Topics** at the end of each chapter encourage students to write using the rhetorical method focused on in that chapter.
Gain experience reading and composing in several genres to understand how genre conventions shape and are shaped by readers' and writers' practices and purposes	• Chapters 5–14 are **organized by rhetorical method**, with at least four essays and one work of literature per chapter to give students experience and practice. • Ten **Student Case Studies**—one in each rhetorical chapter—present brief guidelines for writing in distinct academic genres, such as lab reports and field observations, with annotated samples of student writing. • **Seventy-nine reading selections** and **eleven standalone visual texts** span a variety of topics, disciplines, and genres. • The readings are accompanied by a **robust apparatus** that guides students through analyzing texts and writing for a variety of purposes and in a range of styles.

WPA Outcomes	Relevant Features of *The Bedford Reader*, 14e
Develop facility in responding to a variety of situations and contexts calling for purposeful shifts in voice, tone, level of formality, design, medium, and/or structure	• Detailed chapter introductions in Part Two explain how each rhetorical method can be used to achieve an author's purpose. • Students are introduced to the importance of structure in Chapter 2 and in the introductions to Chapters 5–14 in graphic organizer features labeled **"How to Organize . . . ,"** and critical reading questions following every reading selection highlight the writer's uses of method and language. • Chapter 4, **The Writing Process: Editing** (p. 56), and a boxed **Focus on Tone** feature in Chapter 14 (p. 496) provide guidance to help students adopt the appropriate voice and level of formality in their writing. • Chapter 4 on **Editing** presents thorough advice, with examples, on how to achieve clear and effective language and sentence structure.
Understand and use a variety of technologies to address a range of audiences	• The book assumes that most students compose in digital spaces, and instructions in a number of Suggestions for Writing and other prompts reflect and encourage this use of digital space. • Instructions for researching and collecting notes on sources in the Appendix, Research and Documentation, take as a given that students are working mostly with technology, so the advice offers strategies and a checklist for **evaluating sources** found online.
Match the capacities of different environments (e.g., print and electronic) to varying rhetorical situations	• Research coverage in the **Appendix: Research and Documentation**, gives instruction specific to research and project planning, from taking notes to finding and evaluating sources, in both print and online spaces.
CRITICAL THINKING, READING, AND COMPOSING	
Use composing and reading for inquiry, learning, critical thinking, and communicating in various rhetorical contexts	• Chapter 1, **Critical Reading**, gives students tools to read critically and as writers, so they can understand the **rhetorical context** and the writer's choices and then apply those tools to their own writing. • Chapter 2, **The Writing Process: Discovery and Drafting**, presents writing as **inquiry**, as a process of **gathering ideas and exploring topics**. • A **Journal Writing** prompt and a set of critical reading questions and writing suggestions after each reading encourage students to **write to learn** through informal writing and through composing full essays using any of the ten rhetorical methods.

WPA Outcomes	Relevant Features of *The Bedford Reader*, 14e
Read a diverse range of texts, attending especially to relationships between assertion and evidence, to patterns of organization, to the interplay between verbal and nonverbal elements, and to how these features function for different audiences and situations	• A lively collection of **seventy-nine classic and contemporary selections** from professional and student writers provides outstanding models carefully chosen to engage students and to clearly illustrate the rhetorical strategy at work in each chapter. • Each chapter features **at least one annotated text to show the rhetorical choices** writers make to achieve their purposes. • This book's **organization** offers the flexibility to teach it rhetorically, thematically, or a mix of the two. More than twenty **images** within and among the readings capture students' interest and encourage them to analyze the relationship between **visual and verbal elements**. • Chapter 14, **Argument and Persuasion**, provides thorough coverage of making and **supporting claims**, and the Appendix, **Research and Documentation**, provides information on **integrating sources responsibly**.
Locate and evaluate (for credibility, sufficiency, accuracy, timeliness, bias, and so on) primary and secondary research materials, including journal articles and essays, books, scholarly and professionally established and maintained databases or archives, and informal electronic networks and Internet sources	• The Appendix, **Research and Documentation**, reviews the skills involved in research and synthesis, with dedicated sections on Conducting Research (p. 648) and Writing with Sources (p. 652). It also includes extensive documentation models and two sample research papers, in MLA and APA style. • Helpful **checklists and directories** in the Appendix make useful **reference tools**: Questions for Evaluating Sources (p. 649), a directory to MLA Parenthetical Citations (p. 657), a directory to MLA List of Works Cited (p. 662), a directory to APA Parenthetical Citations (p. 677), and a directory to APA Reference List (p. 681). • Writing suggestions following many of the reading selections direct students to locate and integrate appropriate source material on focused topics.
Use strategies—such as interpretation, synthesis, response, critique, and design/redesign—to compose texts that integrate the writer's ideas with those from appropriate sources	• The chapters in Part One offer clear advice on **Analyzing Written Works** (p. 18), **Responding to a Text** (p. 32), and **Integrating Evidence** (p. 45), stressing the importance of marshalling sufficient **evidence** and **support** to develop an original idea. • The chapter introductions, reading questions, and writing prompts that accompany the selections in Parts Two and Three ask students to **interpret, respond to,** and **critique** the readings and the writers' choices, engaging in academic **conversation**. • Chapter 3 on **Reviewing and Revising** and the Appendix on **Research and Documentation** model strategies for evaluating sources; taking effective notes; using signal phrases to **integrate** quotations, summaries, and paraphrases smoothly; synthesizing sources; and avoiding plagiarism. • See also the previous section, "Locate and evaluate. . . ."

WPA Outcomes	Relevant Features of *The Bedford Reader*, 14e
PROCESSES	
Develop a writing project through multiple drafts	• Part One, Academic Reading and Writing, leads students through the process of writing an essay in four chapters on **Critical Reading**, **Discovery and Drafting**, **Reviewing and Revising**, and **Editing** while following the development of a student essay in multiple stages: Rosie Anaya's reading notes (p. 13), first draft (p. 39), revised draft (p. 51), editing (p. 61), and final draft (p. 62). • Helpful **checklists**—for **Critical Reading** (p. 17), **Analyzing a Written Work** (p. 18), **Examining an Image** (p. 23), **Peer Review and Revision** (p. 42), and for **Reviewing and Revising** an essay in each method—serve as reference tools during the writing process.
Develop flexible strategies for reading, drafting, reviewing, collaborating, revising, rewriting, rereading, and editing	• The chapter introductions, graphic organizers, checklists, and focus boxes in Part Two take students through the steps of **reading**, **forming a thesis**, **organizing**, **drafting**, **reviewing and revising**, and **editing** an essay using particular rhetorical methods (e.g., "Narration," pp. 67–115).
Use composing processes and tools as a means to discover and reconsider ideas	• A detailed section on **Discovering Ideas** in Chapter 2 (p. 30) covers keeping a journal, freewriting, using the methods of development, and responding to a text. • The reading apparatus includes questions for journaling, discussion, and homework, to guide students to **use writing to discover new ideas and writing topics**.
Experience the collaborative and social aspects of writing processes	• A discussion of **Peer Review** in Chapter 3 (p. 42) offers guidelines for collaborative work. • The journal response, critical reading questions, and writing topics that accompany each reading can be used for **group discussion and writing**.
Learn to give and to act on productive feedback to works in progress	• **Questions for Peer Review and Revision** in Chapter 3 and method-specific revision checklists in Chapters 5–14 provide useful benchmarks for **peer review** workshops. • A **sample essay in progress** by Rosie Anaya is shown in stages through Chapters 2, 3, and 4, illustrating a student's process during drafting, revising, and editing—and presenting a low-stakes opportunity for students to practice critiquing another student's drafts.
Adapt composing processes for a variety of technologies and modalities	• The book assumes that most students compose in digital spaces, and instructions in a number of writing topics and other prompts reflect and encourage this use of digital space. • Instructions for research and collecting notes on sources in the Appendix, Research and Documentation, assume that students are working mostly with technology, so the advice offers strategies and a checklist for **evaluating sources** found online.

WPA Outcomes	Relevant Features of *The Bedford Reader*, 14e
Reflect on the development of composing practices and how those practices influence their work	• **Journal Writing** prompts following each reading ask students to discover and apply their prior knowledge in response to the reading selection. • **Writers on Writing** commentaries accompanying more than half the readings discuss the writers' composing practices in their own words and link their reflections back to instructional content in the book.
KNOWLEDGE OF CONVENTIONS	
Develop knowledge of linguistic structures, including grammar, punctuation, and spelling, through practice in composing and revising	• Chapter 4, **Editing**, covers common grammar and mechanics errors and presents clear examples of corrections. Coverage includes sentence fragments, run-ons and comma splices, subject-verb agreement, pronouns, misplaced and dangling modifiers, parallelism, and more. • **Focus boxes** in Chapters 5–14 guide students as they survey their drafts for editing opportunities especially relevant to each method, such as verbs in narration and shifts in process analysis.
Understand why genre conventions for structure, paragraphing, tone, and mechanics vary	• Chapter introductions for the rhetorical strategies in Part Two explain how each strategy serves a writer's **purpose**. • An emphasis on combining strategies throughout, especially in reading questions labeled **Other Methods** and in Part Three, **Mixing the Methods**, further emphasizes the flexibility of rhetorical strategies and their variations.
Gain experience negotiating variations in genre conventions	• In addition to the support in chapter introductions and **Student Case Studies** mentioned above, **Additional Writing Topics** at the end of every chapter in Part Two encourage students to apply the rhetorical strategies to real-world genres and situations and use them in their writing.
Learn common formats and/or design features for different kinds of texts	• Model student writing is presented throughout the book with annotations highlighting **formatting conventions**. The Appendix features fully formatted examples of student research papers in **MLA style** and **APA style**.
Explore the concepts of intellectual property (such as fair use and copyright) that motivate documentation conventions	• The Appendix, **Research and Documentation**, explains why outside sources can help writers articulate their position in a conversation and extend their own ideas, and how doing so requires **thoughtful documentation** when **integrating** quotations, paraphrases, or summaries. • Two dedicated sections, **Integrating Source Material** (p. 653) and **Avoiding Plagiarism** (p. 655), further explore these concepts.
Practice applying citation conventions systematically in their own work	• The Appendix, **Research and Documentation**, offers detailed guidance on taking notes to avoid plagiarism as well as **model citations in MLA and APA style**.

CONTENTS

A writer with multiple sclerosis thinks she knows why the media carry so few images of people like herself with disabilities: Viewers might conclude, correctly, that "there is something ordinary about disability itself."

Inspired by reading Nancy Mairs's "Disability" (Chap. 1), a student writer argues that television should "portray psychological disability as a part of everyday life, not a crime."

The writer recalls her teenage angst when the minister and his cute blond son attended her family's Christmas Eve dinner, an elaborate Chinese feast.

Newly arrived in San Antonio, a pair of friends thought they were visiting an art exhibit. Their mistake was nothing short of mortifying.

An emergency medical technician responds to a 911 call, and a stand-off ensues.

6   DESCRIPTION: Writing with Your Senses   117

Visual Image: *Under the Passaic Falls,* photograph by Todd R. Darling

PAIRED
SELECTIONS

PAIRED
SELECTIONS

PAIRED
SELECTIONS

"What happens to a dream deferred?" One of the most influential leaders of the Harlem Renaissance imagines the possibilities.

Talking behind someone's back is bad. Or is it? A columnist brings in researchers and psychologists to refute a common assumption.

A specialist in economics and culture examines the delicate balance between familiarity and novelty that influences consumers to "like what they like."

Visual Image: *Raymond Loewy*, illustration by Mark Weaver, with photographs by Bernard Hoffman, Jack Garofalo, and Sherman Oaks Antique Mall

A respected journalist draws on scholarly research to explain why going to the "best" college or university might not be the best choice, especially for students who intend to study science, technology, or math.

Forcing developing countries to stop child labor might not be the cure-all it seems. The children themselves, asserts this writer, could suffer fates worse than working.

PAIRED
SELECTIONS

Americans who use illegal drugs harm more than just themselves, argues a student writer in this carefully researched essay. Consider the plight of Miguel, a South American boy victimized by the drug trade.

PAIRED
SELECTIONS

PART THREE

MIXING THE METHODS   567

After giving up meat and dairy, a student finds from her research that "a vegetarian diet could be 'just what the doctor ordered' for our global health."

For a writing seminar, a pre-med student investigates some "startling" discoveries in neuroscience—and is deeply encouraged by what he learns.

CONTENTS BY THEME AND DISCIPLINE

COMMUNICATION AND LANGUAGE

COMMUNITY

CRIME

DEATH

DIVERSITY

EDUCATION

ETHICS

FAMILY

HEALTH AND DISABILITY

HISTORY

HUMOR AND SATIRE

MARRIAGE

MYTH AND LEGEND

THE NATURAL ENVIRONMENT

PHILOSOPHY

POLITICS

POPULAR CULTURE

PSYCHOLOGY

READING AND WRITING

SCIENCE

SELF-DISCOVERY

SOCIAL CUSTOMS

SPORTS AND LEISURE

TECHNOLOGY

VIOLENCE

WAR AND CONFLICT

WORK

HOW (AND WHY) TO USE THIS BOOK

Many prophets have predicted the doom of words on paper, and they may yet be proved correct. Already, many of us are reading books and magazines mainly on mobile devices and communicating mostly by text messages. But even if we do discard paper and pens, the basic aims and methods of writing will not fundamentally change. Whether in print or on screen, we will need to explain our thoughts to others plainly and forcefully.

Our aim with *The Bedford Reader* is to provide you with ample and varied resources that will help you develop your skills as a reader and writer. In this academic toolbox, you'll find not only interesting models of good writing but also useful advice, reference guides, ideas for writing, and practical strategies that you can apply to your own work.

THE SELECTIONS

Readings

In this book, we trust, you'll find many selections you will enjoy and want to discuss. *The Bedford Reader* features work by some of the finest writers of nonfiction and literature.

1

The selections deal with more than just writing; they cut broadly across a college curriculum. You'll find essays, short stories, poems, and even a play that touch on science, history, business, culture, technology, sports, and politics. Some writers recall their childhoods, their problems and challenges. Some explore academic concerns such as the goals of education and the search for life in outer space. Some touch on matters likely to spark debate: free speech, class privilege, race relations, child labor. Some writers are serious; others, funny. In all, these selections mirror the kinds of reading you will meet in your other courses. Such reading is the intellectual storehouse of well-informed people with lively minds—who, to be sure, aren't found only on college campuses.

We have chosen the reading selections with one main purpose in mind: to show you how good writers write. Don't be discouraged if at first you find an immense gap in quality between Joan Didion's writing and yours. Of course there's a gap: Didion is an immortal with a unique style that she perfected over half a century. You don't have to judge your efforts by comparison. The idea is to gain whatever writing techniques you can. If you're going to learn from other writers, why not go to the best of them?

Student Examples

You can glean many skills by reading the work of seasoned writers, but you can also learn from your peers. Students, too, produce writing worth studying, as proved by Brad Manning, Koji Frahm, Laila Ayad, and many others. Throughout the book, you'll find student pieces among the professional selections, many of them annotated to show you how the writers' strategies work. These examples vary in subject, PURPOSE, and approach, but every one of them shows how much student writers can achieve with a little inspiration and effort.

Visuals

The selections in *The Bedford Reader* go beyond the written word. Much of what we "read" in the world is visual information, as in paintings and drawings, or visual-with-verbal information, as in advertisements and cartoons. In all, we include twenty-one visual works. Some of them are subjects of writing, as when a writer analyzes a photograph or a billboard. Other visual works stand free, offering themselves to be understood, interpreted, and perhaps enjoyed, just as prose and literature do. To help you get the most from these images, we offer advice on reading visuals, with a sample analysis of a photograph, in Chapter 1.

We combine visual material with written texts to further a key aim of *The Bedford Reader*: to encourage you to think critically about what you see, hear, and read. Like everyone else, you face a daily barrage of words and pictures. Mulling over the views of the writers, artists, and others represented in this book—figuring out their motives and strategies, agreeing or disagreeing with their ideas—will help you learn to manage, digest, and use in your own writing whatever media you encounter.

THE METHODS OF DEVELOPMENT

The selections in *The Bedford Reader* fall into distinct sections. In Part Two, the heart of the book, each of ten chapters explains a familiar method of developing ideas, such as NARRATION, DESCRIPTION, EXAMPLE, CAUSE AND EFFECT, or DEFINITION. These methods are extraordinarily useful tools for achieving your purpose in writing, whatever that purpose may be. They can help you discover what you know, what you need to know, how to think critically about your subject, and how to shape your ideas.

An introduction to each chapter outlines the method, explains its uses, and shows how you can apply it to your own writing. The reading selections that follow illustrate the method at work. Examining these selections, you'll discover two important facts about the methods of development. First, they are flexible: Two people can use the same method for quite different ends, and just about any method can point a way into just about any subject in any medium.

The second fact about the methods of development is this: A writer never sticks to just one method all the way through a piece of writing. Even when one method predominates, you'll see the writer pick up another method, let it shape a paragraph or more, and then move on to yet another method—all to achieve some overriding aim. Part Three offers an anthology of classic and contemporary selections that illustrate how, in most writing, the methods work together.

THE PRACTICAL GUIDANCE

Overviews of Reading, Writing, and Research

The selections in *The Bedford Reader* are meant to be enjoyed, but also to give you ideas for your own writing. We include four chapters in Part One to help you build your critical reading and writing skills as you work with the readings. You might want to read these chapters straight through as a general guide or turn back to them as necessary for reference, or both.

Chapter 1 explains the connection between reading and writing, outlines the goals of CRITICAL READING, and provides concrete advice for approaching written and visual works with an open, questioning mind. To demonstrate what academic reading entails, we include a sample essay and accompany it with one student's notes and with our own interpretations of the writer's meanings and strategies.

In Chapters 2, 3, and 4 we walk you through the stages of the writing process: drafting, revising, and editing. Like the first chapter, these three feature bulleted points and boxed checklists to help you find the information you need. They address in particular the challenges of ACADEMIC WRITING, whether in responding to individual selections or developing an idea with reference to multiple works, all the while following one student writer as she works from rough idea to final draft.

The Appendix goes over the basics of finding and using sources in academic writing. It offers dozens of citation models for both MLA and APA styles and includes two annotated student research papers.

Reading Questions and Writing Prompts

Following every reading selection in *The Bedford Reader*, you'll find a battery of questions that can help you analyze the work and respond to it. First, a suggestion for responding in your JOURNAL to what you've just read encourages you to think about the writer's themes and your reactions to them. Next, you'll find critical reading questions that can help you read beneath the surface of the work, teasing out the elements that contribute to the writer's success and even those that don't. (You can see a sample of how these questions work when we analyze Nancy Mairs's essay "Disability," starting on p. 12.)

After these questions are at least four suggestions for writing, including one that proposes turning your journal entry into an essay, one that links the selection with one or two others in the book, and one that asks you to read the selection and write about it with your critical faculties alert. Additional suggestions for writing appear at the end of each chapter. We intend these prompts not as rigid taskmasters but as helpful guides. Certainly you can respond to them exactly as written, but if they spark other insights for you, by all means pursue your inspiration. Writing is always best when it comes from a real interest in the subject and a desire to write about it.

Glossary and Index

In this introduction and throughout the following chapters, certain words appear in CAPITAL LETTERS. These are key terms helpful in discussing both the selections in this book and the reading and writing you do. If you'd like to see such a term defined and illustrated, you can find it in the Glossary of Useful Terms on pages 693–707. The Glossary offers more than just brief definitions. It is there to provide you with further explanation, examples, and support.

You can also find the help you need by consulting the Index, located at the back of the book. Say you're revising a draft and your instructor has commented that your essay needs a clearer thesis, but you're not sure what that means or what to do. Look up THESIS, and you'll discover exactly where in *The Bedford Reader* you can find advice for clarifying and expressing your main idea.

THE WRITERS ON WRITING

A final word. The writers represented in this book did not produce their readable and informative texts on the first try, as if by magic, leaving the rest of us to cope with writer's block, awkward sentences, and all the other difficulties of writing. As proof, we visit their workshops. Following more than half the selections are comments by their writers, revealing how they write (or wrote), offering their tricks, setting forth things they admire about good writing. Accompanying the comments are tips on how you can apply the writers' insights to your own work, and a directory at the back of the book points you toward their advice on such practical matters as drafting, finding your point, and revising. No doubt you'll notice some contradictions in these comments: The writers disagree about when and how to think about readers, about whether outlines have any value, about whether style follows subject or vice versa. The reason for the differences of opinion is, simply, that no two writers follow the same path to finished work. Even the same writer may take a left instead of the customary right turn if the writing situation demands a change. A key aim of providing the writers' statements is to suggest the sheer variety of routes open to you, the many approaches to writing and strategies for succeeding at it.

Let's get started then.

PART ONE

ACADEMIC READING AND WRITING

1

CRITICAL READING

Learning from Other Writers

Reading and writing are interconnected. Deepen your mastery of one, and you deepen your mastery of the other. The experience of carefully reading an excellent writer, noticing not only what the writer has to say but also the quality of its saying, rubs off (if you are patient and perceptive) on your own writing. For any writer, then, reading is indispensable. It turns up fresh ideas; it stocks the mind with information, understanding, and examples; it instills critical awareness of one's own surroundings.

Whatever career you enter, reading will be an integral part of your work. You may be trying to understand a new company policy, seeking the truth in a campaign ad, researching a scientific development, or looking for pointers to sharpen your skills. Such reading, like writing itself, demands effort. Unlike the casual reading you might do to pass the time or entertain yourself, CRITICAL READING involves looking beneath the surface of a text, seeking to understand the creator's intentions, the strategies for achieving them, and their effects. This book offers dozens of selections that reward critical reading and can teach you how to become a better writer. To learn from a selection, plan to spend an hour or two in its company. Seek out some quiet place—a library, a study cubicle, your room. Switch off the music and the phone. The fewer the distractions, the easier your task will be and the more you'll enjoy it.

How do you read critically? Exactly how, that is, do you see beneath the surface of a work, master its complexities, gauge its intentions and techniques, judge its value? To find out, we'll model critical-thinking processes that you can apply to the written and visual selections in this book, taking a close look at an essay and a photograph for examples.

READING ACTIVELY

Previewing

Critical reading starts before you read the first word of a piece of writing. You take stock of what's before you, locating clues to the work's content and the writer's biases. Whenever you approach a written work, make a point of assessing these features beforehand:

- **The title.** Effective titles do more than lure readers in; they also hint at what to expect from a work. Often the title will tell you the writer's subject, as with Anna Quindlen's "Homeless." Sometimes the title immediately states the main point the writer will make: "Gossip Is Good." Some titles suggest the method a writer proposes to follow: "How to Write an A Paper." And the title may reveal the writer's attitude toward the material, as "Live Free and Starve" does.

- **The author.** Whatever you know or can learn about a writer—upbringing, special training, previous publications, outlook, ideology—can often help you predict something about a work. Is the writer a political conservative or a liberal? a feminist? an athlete? an internationally renowned philosopher? a popular comedian? By knowing something about the background or beliefs of a writer, you may guess beforehand a little of what he or she will say.

- **The genre.** Identifying the type, or GENRE, of a work can tell you much about the writer's intentions and likely strategies. Genres vary widely; they include critical analyses, business reports, works of literature, humor pieces, and newspaper columns—among many others. The conventions of a given genre necessarily direct a writer's choices. For instance, you can assume that a scholarly article will take an academic tone, lay out arguments and evidence carefully, and cite other published works. The same approach in a personal narrative, however, would confuse most readers.

- **Where the work was published.** Clearly, it matters to a writer's credibility whether an article called "Creatures of the Dark Oceans" appears in a science magazine or in a supermarket tabloid. But no less important, knowing where a work first appeared can tell you for whom the writer was writing. Good writers, as you will see, develop an awareness of their AUDIENCE and shape their messages to appeal to particular readers' interests and needs.

- **When the work was published.** Knowing the year a work appeared may give you another key to understanding it. A 2019 article on ocean creatures will contain statements of fact more advanced and reliable than an essay printed in 1919 — although the older work might offer valuable information and insights, too.

To help provide such prereading knowledge, this book supplies biographical information about the writers and tells you something about the sources and original contexts of the selections, in notes just before each work. It can be tempting to skip over such introductory materials, but we encourage you to look at them. Doing so will help you become a more efficient reader in the end.

Annotating

To learn from other writers how to write well, you'll want to read the selections in this book multiple times. On the first reading, focus on what the author has to say, without getting hung up on every particular. If you encounter any words or concepts that you don't know, take them in stride; you can always circle them and look them up later. Begin by getting a feel for the gist of the piece; later, you will examine the details and strategies that make it work.

In giving a reading a second or third going-over, critical readers find a pencil (or stylus) indispensable. A pencil in hand concentrates the attention wonderfully, and, as often happens with writing, it can lead to unexpected connections. (Some readers favor highlighting key words or lines, but you can't use color alone to note *why* a word or an idea is important.)

You can annotate your own material in several ways, developing a personal system that works best for you:

- **Underline essential ideas**, and double-underline repeated points or concepts.
- **Mark key passages** with checks or vertical lines.
- **Write questions** in the margins.
- **Note associations** with other works you've read, seen, or heard.
- **Vent your feelings** ("Bull!" "Yes!" "Says who?").

If you can't annotate what you're reading — because it's borrowed or your device doesn't have that functionality — make your notes on a separate sheet of paper or in an electronic bookmark or file.

Writing while reading helps you uncover the hidden workings of an essay, so that you, as much as any expert, can judge its effectiveness. You'll develop an opinion about what you read, and you'll want to express it. While reading this way, you're being a writer. Your pencil marks or keystrokes will jog your memory, too, when you review for a test, take part in class discussion, or write about what you've read.

To show what a reader's annotations on an essay might look like, we give you Nancy Mairs's "Disability" with a student's marginal notes, written over the course of several readings. The same student, Rosie Anaya, wrote an essay spurred by the ideas she found in reading Mairs's work; multiple drafts of it appear at the ends of the next three chapters on the writing process.

NANCY MAIRS

A self-described "radical feminist, pacifist, and cripple," Nancy Mairs (1943–2016) aimed to "speak the 'unspeakable.'" Her poetry, memoirs, and essays deal with many sensitive subjects, including her struggles with multiple sclerosis. Born in Long Beach, California, Mairs grew up in New Hampshire and Massachusetts. She received a BA from Wheaton College and an MFA in creative writing and a PhD in English literature from the University of Arizona. While working on her advanced degrees, Mairs taught high-school and college writing courses. Her second book of poetry, *In All the Rooms of the Yellow House* (1984), received a Western States Arts Foundation book award. Mairs's essays are collected in several volumes, including *Carnal Acts* (1990), *Waist High in the World* (1996), *A Troubled Guest* (2001), and *A Dynamic God* (2007). In 2008 she received the Arizona Literary Treasure Award. In addition to working as a writer, Mairs was a public speaker and a research associate with the Southwest Institute for Research on Women.

Disability

As a writer afflicted with multiple sclerosis, Mairs was in a unique position to examine how the culture responds to people with disabilities. In this essay from *Carnal Acts*, she examines media depictions of disability and argues with her usual unsentimental candor that the media must treat disability as normal. The essay was first published in 1987 in the *New York Times*. To what extent is Mairs's critique still valid today?

For months now I've been consciously searching for representations of myself in the media, especially television. I know
I'd recognize this self because of certain distinctive, though not
unique, features: I am a forty-three-year-old woman crippled
with multiple sclerosis; although I can still totter short distances
with the aid of a brace and a cane, more and more of the time I
ride in a wheelchair. Because of these appliances and my peculiar gait, I'm easy to spot even in a crowd. So when I tell you
I haven't noticed any women like me on television, you can
believe me.

Actually, last summer I did see a woman with multiple
sclerosis portrayed on one of those medical dramas that offer
an illness-of-the-week like the daily special at your local diner.
In fact, that was the whole point of the show: that this poor
young woman had MS. She was terribly upset (understandably,
I assure you) by the diagnosis, and her response was to plan a
trip to Kenya while she was still physically capable of making it,
against the advice of the young, fit, handsome doctor who had
fallen in love with her. And she almost did it. At least, she got
as far as a taxi to the airport, hotly pursued by the doctor. But
at the last she succumbed to his blandishments and fled the taxi
into his manly protective embrace. No escape to Kenya for this
cripple.

Capitulation into the arms of a man who uses his medical
powers to strip one of even the urge toward independence is
hardly the sort of representation I had in mind. But even if the
situation had been sensitively handled, according to the woman
her right to her own adventures, it wouldn't have been what I'm
looking for. Such a television show, as well as films like *Duet for
One* and *Children of a Lesser God*, in taking disability as its major
premise, excludes the complexities that round out a character
and make her whole. It's not about a woman who happens to be
physically disabled; it's about physical disability as the determining factor of a woman's existence.

Take it from me, physical disability looms pretty large in
one's life. But it doesn't devour one wholly. I'm not, for instance,
Ms. MS, a walking, talking embodiment of a chronic incurable
degenerative disease. In most ways I'm just like every other
woman of my age, nationality, and socioeconomic background.

Marginal notes: "myself" = a person with a disability living a full life. Wait, I've seen characters with wheelchairs. Plenty. A movie shows disability defining a woman's life. emotions. again! Also *Still Alice*, and *Silver Linings Playbook*. The complaint: these shows miss the point

I menstruate, so I have to buy tampons. I worry about smoker's breath, so I buy mouthwash. I smear my wrinkling skin with lotions. I put bleach in the washer so my family's undies won't be dingy. I drive a car, talk on the telephone, get runs in my pantyhose, eat pizza. In most ways, that is, I'm the advertisers' dream: Ms. Great American Consumer. And yet the advertisers, who determine nowadays who will get represented publicly and who will not, deny the existence of me and my kind absolutely.

Details have a point — she buys things the advertisers sell.

I once asked a local advertiser why he didn't include dis- 5 abled people in his spots. His response seemed direct enough: "We don't want to give people the idea that our product is just for the handicapped." But tell me truly now: If you saw me pouring out puppy biscuits, would you think these kibbles were only for the puppies of the cripples? If you saw my blind niece ordering a Coke, would you switch to Pepsi lest you be struck sightless? No, I think the advertiser's excuse masked a deeper and more anx-ious rationale: To depict disabled people in the ordinary activ-ities of daily life is to admit that there is something ordinary about disability itself, that it may enter anybody's life. If it is effaced completely, or at least isolated as a separate "problem," so that it remains at a safe distance from other human issues, then the viewer won't feel threatened by her or his own physical vulnerability.

Ads don't show disability either — still true?

Hah! Snarky. emotions

✓ scary thought

effaced? (means erased, or made to disappear)

This kind of effacement or isolation has painful, even dan- 6 gerous consequences, however. For the disabled person, these include self-degradation and a subtle kind of self-alienation not unlike that experienced by other minorities. Socialized human beings love to conform, to study others and then mold them-selves to the contours of those whose images, for good reasons or bad, they come to love. Imagine a life in which feasible others — others you can hope to be like — don't exist. At the least you might conclude that there is something queer about you, something ugly or foolish or shameful. In the extreme, you might feel as though you don't exist, in any meaningful social sense, at all. Everyone else is "there," sucking breath mints and splashing cologne and swigging wine coolers. You're "not there." And if not there, nowhere.

effects — IMPORTANT

emotions

What about individuality?

emotions

But this denial of disability imperils even you who are able- 7 bodied, and not just by shrinking your insight into the physi-cally and emotionally complex world you live in. Some disabled

Problem affects people without disabilities too — interesting point.

people call you TAPs, or Temporarily Abled Persons. The fact is that ours is the only minority you can join involuntarily, without warning, at any time. And if you live long enough, as you're increasingly likely to do, you may well join it. The transition will probably be difficult from a physical point of view no matter what. But it will be a good bit easier <u>psychologically</u> if you are accustomed to seeing disability as a normal characteristic, one that complicates but does not ruin human existence. Achieving this integration, for disabled and able-bodied people alike, requires that we insert disability daily into our field of vision: quietly, naturally, in the small and common scenes of our ordinary lives.

main idea

DEVELOPING AN UNDERSTANDING

Apart from your specific notes on a reading, you'll also need a place to work out your comprehension using the strategies and detailed analyses discussed below and on the following pages. For such responses, you may find a JOURNAL handy. It can be a repository of your ideas, a comfortable place to record thoughts about what you read. You may be surprised to find that the more you write in an unstructured way, the more you'll have to say when it's time to write a structured essay.

Summarizing

It's good practice, especially with more difficult readings, to SUMMARIZE the content in writing to be sure you understand it or, as often happens, to come to understand it. (We're suggesting here that you write summaries for yourself, but the technique is also useful when you discuss other people's works in your writing, as shown on p. 46.)

In summarizing a work of writing, you digest, *in your own words*, what the author says: You take the essence of the author's meaning, without the supporting evidence and other details that make the whole convincing or interesting. If the work is short enough, you may want to make this a two-step procedure: First write a summary sentence for every paragraph or related group of paragraphs; then summarize those sentences in two or three others that capture the heart of the author's meaning.

Here is a two-step summary of "Disability." (The numbers in parentheses refer to paragraph numbers in the essay.) First, the longer version:

(1) Mairs searches the media in vain for depictions of women like herself with disabilities. (2) One TV movie showed a woman recently diagnosed

with multiple sclerosis, but she chose dependence over independence. (3) Such shows oversimplify people with disabilities by making disability central to their lives. (4) People with disabilities live lives and consume goods like everyone else, but the media ignore them. (5) Showing disability as ordinary would remind nondisabled viewers that they are vulnerable. (6) The media's exclusion of others like themselves deprives people with disabilities of role models and makes them feel undesirable or invisible. (7) Nondisabled viewers lose an understanding that could enrich them and would help them adjust to disability of their own.

Now the short summary:

> Mairs believes that the media, by failing to depict disability as ordinary, both marginalize viewers with disabilities and impair the outlook and coping skills of the "Temporarily Abled."

Thinking Critically

Summarizing will start you toward understanding the author's meaning, but it is just a first step. Once you comprehend the gist of a text, you're ready to examine its deeper meanings and intentions and apply them to your own work and life. (A TEXT may be a written document, but it may also be a photograph, an experiment, a conversation, a work of art, a Web site, or any other form of communication.)

We're talking here about critical thinking—not "negative," the common conception of *critical*, but "thorough, thoughtful, inquisitive, judgment forming." When you approach something critically, you harness your faculties, your fund of knowledge, and your experiences to understand, appreciate, and evaluate the text. Critical thinking is a process involving several overlapping operations: analysis, inference, synthesis, and evaluation.

Analysis

A way of thinking so essential that it has its own chapter in this book (Chap. 10), ANALYSIS separates an item into its parts. Say you're listening to a new song by a band you like: Without thinking much about it, you isolate melodies, lyrics, and instrumentals. Critical readers analyze written works more consciously, by looking at an author's main idea, support for that idea, special writing strategies, and other elements. To show you how the beginnings of such an analysis might look, we examine these elements in "Disability" later in this chapter.

> ### CHECKLIST FOR CRITICAL READING
>
> ✔ **Analyze.** Examine the elements of the work, such as thesis, purpose and audience, genre, evidence, structure, and language.
>
> ✔ **Infer.** Interpret the underlying meanings of the elements and the assumptions and intentions of the author.
>
> ✔ **Synthesize.** Form an idea about how the elements function together to produce a whole and to deliver a message.
>
> ✔ **Evaluate.** Judge the quality, significance, or value of the work.

Inference

Next you draw conclusions about a work based on your store of information and experience, your knowledge of the creator's background and biases, and your analysis. Say that after listening to the new song, you conclude that it reveals the band's emerging interest in the Caribbean dancehall scene. Now you are using INFERENCE. When you infer, you add to the work, making explicit what was only implicit.

Inference is especially important in discovering a writer's ASSUMPTIONS: opinions or beliefs, often unstated, that direct the writer's ideas, supporting evidence, writing strategies, and language choices. A writer who favors gun control, for instance, may assume without saying so that an individual's rights may be infringed for the good of the community. A writer who opposes gun control might assume the opposite, that an individual's right is superior to the community's good.

Synthesis

During SYNTHESIS, you use your special aptitudes, interests, and training to reconstitute a text so that it now contains not just the original elements but also your sense of their underpinnings, relationships, and implications. What is the band trying to accomplish with its new song? Has the musical style changed? Answering such questions leads you to link elements into a whole or to link two or more wholes.

Synthesis is the core of much academic writing. Sometimes you'll respond directly to a text, or you'll use it as a springboard to another subject. Sometimes you'll show how two or more texts resemble each other or how they differ. Sometimes you'll draw on many texts to answer a question or support an argument. In all these cases, you'll put your reading to use to develop your own ideas.

Evaluation

When you EVALUATE, you determine the adequacy, significance, or value of a work: Is the band getting better or just standing still? In evaluating a written text you answer a question such as whether you are moved as the author intended, whether the author has proved a case, or whether the effort was even worthwhile. Not all critical thinking involves evaluation, however; often you (and your teachers) will be satisfied with analyzing, inferring, and synthesizing ideas without judging a selection's overall merit.

Using this book, you'll learn to think critically about writing by considering what an author's purpose and main idea are, how clear they are, and how well supported. You'll isolate which writing techniques the author has used to special advantage, what hits you as particularly fresh, clever, or wise — and what *doesn't* work, too. You'll discover exactly what the writer is saying, how he or she says it, and whether, in the end, it was worth saying. In class discussions and in writing, you'll tell others what you think and why.

ANALYZING WRITTEN WORKS

To help you in your critical reading, questions after every selection in this book direct your attention to specific elements of the writer's work. Here we introduce the three categories of questions — on meaning, writing strategy, and language — and show how they might be applied to Nancy Mairs's "Disability" (p. 12).

Meaning

By *meaning*, we're getting at what the words say literally, of course, but also what they imply and, more generally, what the author's aims are. When reading an essay, look especially for the THESIS and try to determine the author's PURPOSE for writing.

- **Thesis.** Every essay has — or should have — a point, a main idea the writer wants to communicate. Many writers come right out and sum up this idea in a sentence or two, a THESIS STATEMENT. They may provide it in the first or second paragraph, give it somewhere in the middle of the essay, or hold it for the end. Mairs, for instance, develops her thesis over the course of the essay and then states it in paragraph 7:

QUESTIONS FOR ANALYZING A WRITTEN WORK

MEANING

✔ **What is the thesis,** or main point? Where is it stated?

✔ **What is the writer's purpose?** What does the work try to accomplish?

WRITING STRATEGY

✔ **Who is the intended audience?** What assumptions does the writer make about readers' knowledge, perspectives, and interests?

✔ **How are supporting details structured?** What methods does the writer use to organize ideas? How does the writer achieve unity and coherence?

✔ **What evidence does the writer provide** to support the main idea? Is it sufficient and compelling?

LANGUAGE

✔ **What is the overall tone of the work?** Is it appropriate, given the writer's purpose and audience?

✔ **How effective are the writer's words?** Are their meanings clear? What connotations do they hold?

✔ **Does the writer use any figures of speech,** such as metaphor, simile, hyperbole, personification, or irony? How well do they lend meaning and vibrancy to the writer's thoughts?

Achieving this integration [of seeing disability as normal], for disabled and able-bodied people alike, requires that we insert disability daily into our field of vision: quietly, naturally, in the small and common scenes of our ordinary lives.

Sometimes a writer will not state his or her thesis outright at all, although it remains in the background controlling the work and can be inferred by a critical reader. If you find yourself confused about a writer's point — "What *is* this about?" — it will be up to you to figure out what the author is trying to say.

- **Purpose.** By *purpose,* we mean the writer's apparent reason for writing: what he or she was trying to achieve. In making a simple statement of a writer's purpose, we might say that a person writes *to reflect* on an experience or observation, *to entertain* readers, *to explain* something to them, or *to persuade* them. To state a purpose more fully, we might say that a writer writes not just to persuade, for instance, but to motivate readers to accept a particular idea or take a specific action. In the case of "Disability," it seems that Mairs's purpose is twofold: to explain her view of the media and to convince readers that lack of representation hurts people without disabilities as much as it does people with disabilities.

Writing Strategy

Almost all writing is a *transaction* between a writer and an audience, maybe one reader, maybe millions. To the extent that writers hold our interest, make us think, and convince us to accept a thesis, it pays to ask, "How do they succeed?" (When writers bore or anger us, we ask why they fail.) Conscious writers make choices intended to get readers on their side so that they can achieve their purpose. These choices are what we mean by STRATEGY in writing.

- **Audience.** We can tell much about a writer's intended audience from the context in which the piece was first published. And when we know something of the audience, we can better analyze the writer's decisions, from the choice of supporting details to the use of a particular tone. Mairs's original audience, for instance, was the readers of the *New York Times*, as the introduction to "Disability" on page 12 informs us. She could assume educated readers with diverse interests who are not themselves disabled or even familiar with disability. So she fills them in, taking pains to describe her disability (par. 1) and her life (4). For her thoughtful but somewhat blinkered audience, Mairs mixes a blend of plain talk, humor, and insistence to give them the facts they need, win them over with common humanity, and convey the gravity of the problem.

- **Method.** A crucial part of a writer's strategy is how he or she develops ideas to achieve a particular purpose or purposes. As Chapters 5–14 of this book illustrate, a writer may draw on one or more familiar methods of development to make those ideas concrete and convincing. Mairs, for instance, uses COMPARISON AND CONTRAST to show similarities and differences between herself and nondisabled people (pars. 1, 4, 5). She offers EXAMPLES: of dramas she dislikes (2–3), of products she buys (4), and of ads in which people with disabilities might appear (5). With DESCRIPTION she shows the flavor of her life (4) and the feelings she has experienced (6). And with CAUSE AND EFFECT she explains why disability is ignored by the media (5) and what that does to people with disabilities (6) and those without (7). Overall, Mairs uses these methods to build an ARGUMENT, asserting and defending an opinion.

- **Evidence.** Typically, each method of development benefits from — and lends itself to — different kinds of support. For this EVIDENCE, the writer may use facts, reasons, examples, expert opinions—whatever best delivers the point. (We have more to say about the uses of evidence in the introductions to the methods.) Mairs draws on several types of evidence to develop her claims, including personal experiences and emotions (pars. 1, 4, 5), details to support her generalizations (2, 4, 5), and the opinion of an advertiser (5).

- **Structure.** A writer must mold and arrange ideas to capture, hold, and direct readers' interest. Writing that we find clear and convincing almost always has UNITY (everything relates to the main idea) and COHERENCE (the relations between parts are clear). All the parts fit together logically. In "Disability," Mairs first introduces herself and establishes her complaint (pars. 1–5). Then she explains and argues the negative effects of "effacement" on people with disabilities (6) and the positive effects that normalizing disability would have on people who are not presently disabled (7). As often occurs in arguments, Mairs's organization builds to her main idea, her thesis, which readers might find difficult to accept at the outset.

Language

To examine the element of language is to go even more deeply into a work and how it was made. A writer's tone, voice, and choice of words in particular not only express meaning but also convey the writer's attitudes and elicit those attitudes from readers.

- **Tone.** The TONE of a piece of writing is the equivalent of tone of voice in speaking. Whether it's angry, sarcastic, or sad, joking or serious, tone carries almost as much information about a writer's purpose as the words themselves do. Mairs's tone mixes lightness with gravity, humor with intensity. Sometimes she uses IRONY, saying one thing but meaning another, as in "If you saw my blind niece ordering a Coke, would you switch to Pepsi lest you be struck sightless?" (par. 5). She's blunt, too, revealing intimate details about her life. Honest and wry, Mairs invites us to see the media's exclusion as ridiculous and then leads us to her uncomfortable conclusion.

- **Word choice.** Tone comes in part from DICTION, a writer's choices regarding words and sentence structures—academic, casual, or otherwise. Mairs is a writer whose diction is rich and varied. Expressions from common speech, such as "what I'm looking for" (par. 3), lend her prose vigor and naturalness. At the same time, Mairs is serious about her argument, so she puts it in serious terms, such as "denial of disability imperils even you who are able-bodied" (7). Pay attention also to the CONNOTATIONS of words—their implied meanings and associations. Such subtle nuances can have a profound effect on both a writer's meaning and readers' understanding of it. In "Disability," the word with the strongest connotations may be "cripple" (2, 5) because it calls up insensitivity: By using this word, Mairs stresses her frankness but also suggests that negative attitudes determine what images the media present.

- **Imagery.** One final use of language is worth noting: those concrete words and phrases that appeal to readers' senses. Such IMAGES might be straightforward, as in Mairs's portrayal of herself as someone who "can still totter short distances with the aid of a brace and a cane" (par. 1). But often writers use FIGURES OF SPEECH, bits of colorful language that capture meaning or attitude better than literal words can. For instance, Mairs says that people "study others and then mold themselves to the contours of those whose images . . . they come to love" (6). That figure of speech is a *metaphor*, stating that one thing (behavioral change) is another (physical change). Elsewhere Mairs uses *simile*, stating that one thing is *like* another ("an illness-of-the-week like the daily special at your local diner," 2), and *understatement* ("physical disability looms pretty large in one's life," 4). More examples of figures of speech appear in the Glossary of Useful Terms, page 700.

Many of the reading questions in this book point to figures of speech, to oddities of tone, to particulars of diction, or to troublesome or unfamiliar words. Writers have few traits more valuable than a fondness for words and a willingness to experiment with them.

EXAMINING VISUAL IMAGES

We often forget that a visual text, just as much as a written work, was created for a reason. No matter what it is—advertisement, infographic, painting, video, photograph, cartoon—an image originated with a person or persons who had a purpose, an intention for how that image should look and how viewers should respond to it.

In their origins, then, visual images are not much different from written texts, and they are no less open to critical thinking that will uncover their meanings and effects. To a great extent, the method for critically "reading" visuals parallels the one for written works outlined earlier in this chapter. In short, as the checklist on the facing page indicates, you start with an overview of the image and then analyze its elements, make inferences, synthesize, and evaluate.

QUESTIONS FOR EXAMINING AN IMAGE

THE BIG PICTURE

✔ **What is the source of the work?** Who was the intended audience?

✔ **What does the work show overall?** What appears to be happening?

✔ **Why was the work created**—to educate, to sell, to shock, to entertain?

ANALYSIS

✔ **Which elements of the image stand out?** What is distinctive about each?

✔ **What does the composition of the image emphasize?** What is pushed to the background or the sides?

INFERENCE

✔ **What do the elements of the work suggest** about the creator's intentions and assumptions?

✔ **If words accompany the work, what do they say?** How are they sized and placed in relation to the visual elements? How do the written and visual parts interact?

SYNTHESIS

✔ **What general appeal does the work make to viewers?** For instance, does it emphasize logic, emotion, or value?

✔ **What feelings, memories, moods, or ideas does the work summon from viewers' own store of experiences?** Why would its creator try to establish these associations?

EVALUATION

✔ **Does the work fulfill its creator's intentions?** Was it worth creating?

✔ **How does the work affect you?** Are you moved? amused? bored? offended?

As you do when reading written texts, always write while examining a visual image or images. Jotting down responses, questions, and other notes will not only help you remember what you were thinking but also jog further thoughts into being.

To show the critical method in action, we'll look closely at the photograph on the next page.

Seeing the Big Picture

To examine any visual representation, it helps first to get an overview, a sense of the whole and its context. On such a first glance, consider who

created it—for instance, a painter, a teacher, an advertiser—when it was created, and why.

The photograph above was taken by photojournalist Robin Nelson near the Watts Bar nuclear power plant in Spring City, Tennessee, for a 2011 photo essay in *Mother Jones*, a magazine known for its progressive outlook. The year before, an earthquake and tsunami had destroyed nuclear reactors in Japan, causing global alarm. Nelson's picture shows a solitary older man fishing from a boat with his hands resting on its steering wheel; the Chicamauga Reservoir and two cooling towers appear in the background. (The tower on the left has operated since 1996; a new reactor for the other tower was under construction at the time of the photograph and did not begin operation until 2016.)

Taking a Critical Look

After you've gained an overview of an image, you can start making the kinds of deeper inquiry—analysis, inference, synthesis, and evaluation—that serve as the foundation of any critical reading, whatever form the text may take.

Analysis

To analyze a visual work, focus on the elements that contribute to the whole—not just the people, animals, objects, or scenes depicted but also the artistic elements such as lighting, color, shape, and balance. Notice which elements stand out and what seems to be emphasized. If spoken or written words accompany the work, examine their relation to the visual components as well as what they say.

In Nelson's photograph, the dominant elements are the towers and the man, whose smile suggests contentment. A fishing rod and line occupy the center of the image, visually connecting the man, the towers, and the water. The pole points at the sun in the upper left corner. The sun reflects off the water and puts parts of the man in shadow; the towers are reflected in the water as well. A line of trees runs across the midline of the photo, highlighting the natural environment. The sky is clear, with a solitary cloud floating in the upper right. And in the foreground we see what appear to be a container for bait and a cooler.

Inference

Identifying the elements of a visual leads you to consider what they mean and how the image's creator has selected and arranged them so that viewers will respond in certain ways. You make explicit what may only be implicit in the work—the creator's intentions and assumptions.

We can guess at Robin Nelson's intentions for the photograph. On the one hand, it seems to support nuclear power as harmless: The bright sun, clear sky, sparkling water, and lush trees imply an unspoiled environment, and the man appears unworried about fishing near the plant. On the other hand, Nelson would know that most readers of *Mother Jones* are concerned about the safety of nuclear power and that the cooling towers alone would raise red flags for many; certainly the cloud in the otherwise clear sky and the deep shadow obscuring most of the fisherman hint at danger. The photographer may see these opposites as reflecting the controversy over nuclear power.

Synthesis

Linking the elements and your inferences about them will move you into a new conception of a visual representation: your own conclusions about its overall message and effect.

As we see it, Nelson's photograph represents Americans' mixed feelings about nuclear power. The looming towers, the cloud, and the shadowing seem

ominous, suggesting risks facing the area around the plant and the country as
a whole. The beauty of the scenery evokes our appreciation of nature; the
implied pleasure of fishing evokes our approval as it intensifies our concerns
for the man's safety. The juxtaposition of the power plant, the environment,
and a single human being seems to represent the intersecting forces of nature
and society and the complex implications of nuclear energy for both.

Evaluation

Often in criticizing visual works, you'll take one step beyond synthesis to
judge the quality, significance, or value of the work.

Robin Nelson's photograph seems to us masterful in delivering a message.
As Nelson seems to have intended, he distills strong, contradictory feelings
about nuclear power and environmental protection into a deceptively simple
image of a man fishing. Viewers' own biases, positive or negative, will affect
their responses to Nelson's image and the meanings they derive from it.

2

THE WRITING PROCESS

Discovery and Drafting

The CRITICAL THINKING discussed in the previous chapter will serve you in just about every role you'll play in life — consumer, voter, friend, parent. As a student and a worker, though, you'll find critical thinking especially important as the foundation for writing. Whether to demonstrate your competence or to contribute to discussions and projects, writing will be the main way you communicate with teachers, supervisors, and peers.

Writing is no snap: As this book's Writers on Writing attest, not even professionals can produce thoughtful, detailed, attention-getting prose in a single draft. Writing well demands, and rewards, a willingness to work recursively — to begin tentatively and then to double back, to welcome change and endure frustration, to recognize progress and move forward.

This recursive writing process is not really a single process at all, not even for an individual writer. Some people work out meticulous plans ahead of time; others prefer to just start writing; still others will work one way for one project and a different way for another. Generally, though, writers do move through distinct stages between initial idea and finished work: discovery and drafting, addressed in this chapter, reviewing and revising (Chap. 3), and editing (Chap. 4).

In examining these stages, we'll have the help of a student, Rosie Anaya, who wrote an essay for this book responding to Nancy Mairs's essay "Disability." Along with the finished essay (pp. 62–64), Anaya also shares her notes and multiple drafts as we follow her progress.

ASSESSING THE WRITING SITUATION

Any writing you do will occur in a specific situation. What are you writing about? Whom are you writing for? Why are you writing about this subject to these people? What will they expect of you? Subject, audience, and purpose are the main components of the writing situation, discussed in detail in this section. We also touch on another component, genre (or type of writing), which relates to audience and purpose.

Subject

The SUBJECT of a work is what it is about, or the general topic. Your subject may be specified or at least suggested in an assignment. "Discuss one of the works we've read this semester in its historical and social context," reads a literature assignment; "Can you draw up a proposal for holiday staffing?" asks your boss. If you're left to your own devices and nothing occurs to you, try the discovery techniques explained on pages 30–33 to find a topic that interests you.

In this book we provide ideas that will also give you practice in working with assignments. After each reading selection, a variety of writing prompts suggest possible subjects; more writing topics conclude each chapter. You may not wish to take any of our suggestions exactly as worded; they may merely inspire your own thoughts—and thus what you want to say.

Audience

We looked at AUDIENCE in the previous chapter as a way of understanding the decisions other writers make. When *you* are doing the writing, considering audience moves from informative to necessary.

You can conceive of your audience generally—for instance, your classmates, subscribers to a particular newspaper or magazine, members of the city council. Usually, though, you'll want to think about the characteristics of readers that will affect how they respond to you:

- **Who will read your work?** What in the makeup of readers will influence their responses? How old are they? Are they educated? Do they share your values? Are they likely to have some misconceptions about your subject?
- **What do readers need to know?** To get them to understand you or agree with you, how much background should you provide? How thoroughly must you support your ideas? What kinds of evidence will be most effective?

Knowing whom you're addressing and why tells you what approach to take, what EVIDENCE to gather, how to arrange ideas, even what words to use. Imagine, for instance, that you are writing two reviews of a new movie, one for students who read the campus newspaper, the other for amateur and professional filmmakers who read the trade journal *Millimeter*. For the first audience, you might write about the actors, the plot, and especially dramatic scenes. You might judge the film and urge your readers to see it—or to avoid it. Writing for *Millimeter*, you might discuss special effects, shooting techniques, problems in editing and in mixing picture and sound. In this review, you might use more specialized and technical terms. An awareness of the interests and knowledge of your readers, in each case, would help you decide how to write.

Purpose

While you are considering readers' backgrounds and inclinations, you'll also be refining your PURPOSE. As we discussed earlier (p. 19), writers generally write with one of four broad goals in mind:

- **To reflect** on an experience, an observation, or an idea. Reflective writing is most common in personal journals or diaries, but writers often mull over their thoughts for others to read, especially in essays that draw on NARRATION or DESCRIPTION.
- **To entertain** others, perhaps by relating a thrilling event or by poking fun at a subject. Fiction is often meant to entertain, of course, but so are Web comics, many popular blogs, celebrity gossip magazines, and several of the selections in this book.
- **To explain** something, typically by sharing information gleaned from experience or investigation. Such is the case with most newspapers and textbooks, for instance, as well as science and business reports, research papers, or biographies.
- **To persuade** members of an audience to accept an idea or take a particular action. Almost all writing offers an ARGUMENT of some sort, whether explicitly or implicitly. Opinion pieces and proposals are the most obvious examples; most academic writing seeks to convince readers of the validity of a THESIS, or debatable assertion, as well.

You may know your basic purpose for writing early on—whether you want to explain something about your subject or argue something about it, for instance. To be most helpful, though, your idea of purpose should include what you want readers to think or do as a result of reading your writing, as in the following examples:

> To explain two therapies for autism in young children so that parents and educators can weigh the options

> To defend term limits for state legislators so that voters who are undecided on the issue will support limits

> To analyze Shakespeare's *Macbeth* so that theatergoers see the strengths as well as the flaws of the title character

> To propose an online system for scheduling work shifts so that company managers will decide to implement it

We have more to say about purpose in the introductions to the rhetorical methods (Chaps. 5–14). Each method, such as EXAMPLE and CAUSE AND EFFECT, offers useful tools for achieving your purposes in writing.

Genre

Closely tied to audience and purpose is the type of writing, the GENRE, that you will use to shape your ideas. Your assignment might specify the genre: Have you been asked to write a personal narrative? a critical analysis? an argumentative response? These and other genres have distinctive features — such as organization, kinds of evidence, and even TONE — that readers expect.

You will find many examples of different genres in this book. In a sense each method of development (CLASSIFICATION, DEFINITION, and so on) is itself a genre, and its conventions and strategies are covered in the chapter devoted to it (Chaps. 5–14). Each chapter introduction also concludes with a student case study that shows the method at work in a specific academic genre, such as a field observation or a review. And the book's selections illustrate a range of genres, from personal reflection and memoir to objective reporting and critical evaluation. The best way to learn about genres and readers' expectations is to read widely and attentively.

DISCOVERING IDEAS

During the initial phase of the writing process, you'll feel your way into an assignment. This DISCOVERY period is the time when you critically examine any TEXT that is part of the assignment and begin to generate ideas. From marginal notes to jotted phrases, lists, or half-finished paragraphs of response, the discovery stage should always be a writing stage. You may even produce a rough draft. The important thing is to let yourself go: Do not, above all, concern yourself with making beautiful sentences or correcting errors. Such self-consciousness at this stage will only jam the flow of thoughts. Several techniques can help you open up, among them writing in a journal, freewriting, exploring the methods of development, and responding directly to a text.

Keeping a Journal

A JOURNAL is a record of your thoughts *for yourself*. You can keep a journal on paper or on a computer or mobile device. When you write in it, you don't have to worry about being understood by a reader or making mistakes: You are free to get your thoughts down however you want.

Kept faithfully—say, for ten or fifteen minutes a day—a journal can limber up your writing muscles, giving you more confidence and flexibility. It can also provide a place to work out personal difficulties, explore half-formed ideas, make connections between courses, or respond to reading. (For examples of Rosie Anaya's journal notes, see pp. 38–39.)

Freewriting

Another technique for limbering up, usually in response to a specific writing assignment rather than as a regular habit, is *freewriting*. When freewriting, you write without stopping for ten or fifteen minutes, not halting to reread, criticize, edit, or admire. You can use partial sentences, abbreviations, question marks for uncertain words. If you can't think of anything to write about, jot "can't think" over and over until new words come. (They will.)

You can use this technique to find a subject for writing or to explore ideas on a subject you already have. When you've finished, you can separate the promising passages from the dead ends, and then use those promising bits as the starting place for more freewriting or perhaps a freely written first draft.

Exploring the Methods of Development

In Part Two of this book each of the ten chapters explains a familiar method of developing ideas. In the discovery stage, approaching your subject with these methods in mind can reveal its potential:

- **Narration.** Tell a story about the subject, possibly to enlighten or entertain readers or to explain something to them. Answer the journalist's questions: who, what, when, where, why, how?
- **Description.** Explain or evoke the subject by focusing on its look, sound, feel, smell, taste—the evidence of the senses.
- **Example.** Point to instances, or illustrations, of the subject that clarify and support your ideas about it.

- **Comparison and contrast.** Set the subject beside something else, noting similarities or differences or both, for the purpose of either explaining or evaluating.
- **Process analysis.** Explain step by step how to do something or how something works — in other words, how a sequence of actions leads to a particular result.
- **Division or analysis.** Slice the subject into its parts or elements in order to show how they relate and to explain your conclusions about the subject.
- **Classification.** Show resemblances and differences among many related subjects, or the many forms of a subject, by sorting them into kinds or groups.
- **Cause and effect.** Explain why or what if, showing reasons for or consequences of the subject.
- **Definition.** Trace a boundary around the subject to pin down its meaning.
- **Argument and persuasion.** Formulate an opinion or make a proposal about the subject.

You can use the methods of development singly or together to find direction, ideas, and supporting details. Say you already have a sense of your purpose for writing: Then you can search the methods for one or more that will help you achieve that purpose by revealing and focusing your ideas. Or say you're still in the dark about your purpose: Then you can apply each method of development systematically to throw light on your subject, helping you see it from many possible angles.

Responding to a Text

When writing about selections in this book, you'll be reading and rereading and writing, coming to understand the work, figuring out what you think of it, figuring out what you have to *say* about it.

The essay-in-progress by Rosie Anaya that we follow through Part One illustrates a common type of writing assignment: the critical response. Through multiple drafts, Anaya summarizes Nancy Mairs's essay "Disability," explores its implications, and uses it as a springboard to her own related subject, which she supports with personal observation and experience. Just as Anaya responds to Mairs's essay, so you can respond to any selection in this book, or for that matter to any text you read, see, or hear. Using evidence from the text, from your own experiences, and sometimes from additional sources, you can take a variety of approaches to writing about what you read:

- **Agree with and extend the author's ideas,** providing additional examples or exploring related ideas.

- **Agree with the author on some points,** but disagree on others.
- **Disagree with the author** on one or more key points.
- **Explain how the author achieves a particular EFFECT,** such as eliciting your sympathy or sparking your anger.
- **Judge the overall effectiveness of the work**—for instance, how well the author supports the thesis, whether the argument is convincing, or whether the author succeeds in his or her stated or unstated purpose.

These suggestions assume that you are responding to a single text, but of course you may take on two or even more selections at the same time. You might, for instance, use the method of COMPARISON AND CONTRAST to show how two stories are alike or different, or find your own way between competing ARGUMENTS on an issue.

Some works you read will spark an immediate reaction, maybe because you disagree or agree strongly right from the start. Other works may require a more gradual entry into the author's meaning and what you think about it. At the same time, you may have an assignment that narrows the scope of your response—for instance, by asking you to look at tone or some other element of the work or by asking you to agree or disagree with the author's thesis.

Whatever your initial reaction or your assignment, you can use the tools discussed in Chapter 1 to generate and structure your response: summary, analysis, inference, synthesis, and evaluation (see pp. 15–18). As you work out a response, you'll certainly need to make notes of some sort: For instance, Rosie Anaya's annotations on Mairs's essay (pp. 13–15) and her journal notes (pp. 38–39) include questions raised while reading, highlights of key quotations, summaries of Mairs's ideas, interpretations of their meanings, and the beginnings of Anaya's ideas in response. Such notes may grow increasingly focused as you refine your response and return to the work to interpret it further and gather additional passages to discuss.

DRAFTING

Sooner or later, the discovery stage yields to DRAFTING: writing out sentences and paragraphs, linking thoughts, focusing them. For most writers, drafting is the occasion for exploring ideas, filling in the details to support them, beginning to work out the shape and aim of the whole. A few suggestions for drafting:

- **Give yourself time,** at least a couple of hours.
- **Find a quiet place to work,** somewhere you won't be disturbed.
- **Stay loose** so that you can wander down intriguing avenues or consider changing direction altogether.

- **Keep your eyes on what's ahead,** not on possible errors, "wrong" words, or bumpy sentences. This is an important message that many inexperienced writers miss: It's okay to make mistakes. You can fix them later.

Expect to draft in fits and starts, working in chunks and fleshing out points as you go. And don't feel compelled to follow a straight path from beginning to end. If the opening paragraph is giving you trouble, skip it until later. In fact, most writers find that drafting is easier and more productive if they work on the body of the essay first, leaving the introduction and conclusion until everything else has been worked out.

Focusing on a Thesis

Your finished essay will need to center on a THESIS, a core idea to which everything else relates. When you write with a clear-cut thesis in mind, you head toward a goal. Without the focus of a thesis, an essay wanders and irritates and falls flat. With a focus, a draft is much more likely to click.

You may start a project with a thesis already in mind, or your idea might take shape as you proceed through the writing process. Sometimes you may have to write one or more drafts to know exactly what your point is. But early on, try to express your main idea in a sentence or two, called a THESIS STATEMENT, like these from essays in this book:

> That first encounter, and those that followed, signified that a vast, unnerving gulf lay between nighttime pedestrians — particularly women — and me.
> — Brent Staples, "Black Men and Public Space"

> Almost all good writing begins with terrible first efforts. You have to start somewhere.
> — Anne Lamott, "Shitty First Drafts"

> A bill [to prohibit import of goods produced with children's labor] is of no use unless it goes hand in hand with programs that will offer a new life to these newly released children.
> — Chitra Divakaruni, "Live Free and Starve"

As these diverse examples reveal, a thesis shapes an essay. It gives the writer a clearly defined aim, focusing otherwise scattered thoughts and providing a center around which the details and supporting points can gather.

An effective thesis statement, like the ones above, has a few important qualities:

- **It asserts an opinion, taking a position on the subject.** A good thesis statement moves beyond facts or vague generalities, as in "That first encounter was troubling" or "This bill is a bad idea."

- **It projects a single, focused idea.** A thesis statement may have parts (such as Lamott's two sentences), but those parts should relate to a single, central point.
- **It accurately forecasts the scope of the essay,** neither taking on too much nor leaving out essential parts.
- **It hints at the writer's purpose.** From their thesis statements, we can tell that Staples means to reflect and Lamott plans to explain, whereas Divakaruni intends mainly to persuade.

Every single essay in this book has a thesis because a central, controlling idea is a requirement of good writing. As you will see, writers have great flexibility in presenting a thesis statement — how long it might be, where it appears, even whether it appears. For your own writing, we advise stating your thesis explicitly and putting it near the beginning of your essay — at least until you've gained experience as a writer. The stated thesis will help you check that you have the necessary focus, and the early placement will tell your readers what to expect from your writing. We offer additional suggestions for focusing your thesis and crafting your thesis statement, with examples, in the next chapter (p. 43) and in each of the introductions to the methods of development (Chaps. 5–14).

Developing Ideas

The BODY of an essay consists of the subpoints and supporting evidence that develop the main idea. In some way, each sentence and paragraph should serve to support your thesis by making it clear and explicit to readers. You will likely need to experiment and explore your thoughts before they fully take shape, tackling your essay in multiple drafts and filling in (or taking out) details as you go, adjusting your thesis to fit your ideas. Most writers do.

You may have gotten a start at expressing your thoughts in the discovery stage, in which case you can build on what you've already written in your journal or during freewriting sessions. Or you may find yourself staring at a blank screen. In either case, it's usually best to focus first on the parts you're most comfortable with, keeping your thesis, your purpose, and your audience in mind.

Earlier we saw that the methods of development can help you discover ideas about a subject (see pp. 31–32). They can also help you find, present, and structure evidence as you draft. Suppose, for example, that you set out to explain what makes a certain singer unique. You want to discuss her voice, her music, her lyrics, her style. While putting your ideas down, it strikes you that you can best illustrate the singer's distinctions by showing the differences between her and another singer. To achieve your purpose, then, you draw on the method of comparison and contrast; and as you proceed, the method prompts you to notice differences you had missed.

Each method typically benefits from—and lends itself to—a particular kind of support. Narration and description might draw on personal experience, for instance, while a CAUSE-AND-EFFECT or PROCESS ANALYSIS may require objective information such as verifiable facts. Give the methods a try. See how flexible they are, coming into play as you need them to develop parts of your essay.

Organizing the Evidence

How you ORGANIZE your evidence depends on your purpose and your audience: What is your aim? What do you want readers to think or feel? What's the best way to achieve that? For instance, anyone writing a proposal to solve a problem wants to cover all the reasonable solutions and make a case for one or more. But one writer might bring readers gradually to her favored solution by first discussing and rejecting the alternatives, while another might grab readers' attention by focusing right away on his own solution, dispensing with alternatives only near the end. In either case, the choices aren't random but depend on the writer's understanding of readers—their assumptions, their biases, and their purposes for reading.

The methods of development generally lend themselves to familiar patterns of organization, which we discuss and sketch out with graphic organizers in the introductions to Chapters 5–14. In a narrative essay or a process analysis, for instance, you would probably put events in CHRONOLOGICAL ORDER. Other methods require that you put more thought into how you arrange your points. In an essay developed by example, you might use a CLIMACTIC ORDER, starting with the weakest point and ending with the most compelling one (or vice versa). And a descriptive essay might take a SPATIAL ORDER, following details the way an eye might scan a scene: left to right, near to far, and so forth.

Some writers like to plan the order of their points in advance, perhaps with a rough outline or simply a list of points to cover. If concerns about the organization leave you feeling stuck or frustrated, however, focus instead on getting your ideas into sentences and paragraphs; you can rearrange things in revision.

Shaping the Introduction and Conclusion

The opening and closing paragraphs of an essay serve as bookends for the thoughts and information presented in the body. The INTRODUCTION identifies and narrows the subject for readers, capturing their interest and giving them a reason to continue reading. The CONCLUSION creates a sense of completion, bringing readers back to the main idea and satisfying them that you have accomplished what you set out to do as a writer.

Because of the importance of these paragraphs, and because it is difficult to set up and close out material that has not yet been drafted, most writers find that it works best to turn to the introduction and conclusion *after* the rest of the essay has begun to take shape.

The Introduction

The opening paragraph or paragraphs of an essay invite readers in. At a minimum, your introduction will state the subject and lead to your main idea, often presented in a thesis statement. But an effective introduction also grabs readers' attention and inspires them to read on.

Introductions vary in length, depending on their purpose. A research paper may need several paragraphs to set forth its central idea and its plan of organization; a brief, informal essay may need only a sentence or two for an introduction. Whether long or short, a good introduction tells readers no more than they need to know when they begin reading.

Here are a few possible ways to open an essay effectively:

- **Present startling facts** about your subject.
- **Tell an ANECDOTE,** a brief story that illustrates your subject.
- **Give background information** so that readers will understand your subject or see why it is important.
- **Begin with an arresting quotation** that sets up your subject or previews your main idea.
- **Ask a challenging question.** (In your essay, you'll go on to answer it.)

Whatever technique you try, strive to make a good first impression and establish a positive, engaging tone, taking care to match the voice in the body of your essay. Avoid beginning with a hedge such as *It seems important to understand why* . . . ; and stay away from mechanical phrasing such as *In this essay, I will explain* . . . or *The purpose of this paper is to show.* . . . Such openings bore readers and give them little incentive to read on.

The Conclusion

A conclusion is purposefully crafted to give a sense of unity to the whole essay. The best conclusions evolve naturally out of what has gone before and convince readers that the essay is indeed at an end, not that the writer has run out of steam.

Conclusions vary in type and length depending on the nature and scope of the essay. A long research paper may require several paragraphs of summary to review and emphasize the main points. A short essay, however, may benefit from a few brief closing sentences.

Although there are no set formulas for closing, consider these options:

- **Restate the thesis of your essay,** and possibly summarize your main points.
- **Mention the broader implications** or significance of your topic.
- **Give a final example,** pulling together all the parts of your discussion.
- **Offer a prediction** for the future.
- **End with the most important point,** or the culmination of your essay's development.
- **Suggest how readers can apply the information you have provided** in their own lives or work.
- **End with a bit of drama or flourish.** Tell an anecdote, offer an appropriate quotation, ask a question, make a final insightful remark, circle back to the introduction. Keep in mind, however, that an ending shouldn't sound false and gimmicky. It truly has to conclude.

In concluding an essay, beware of diminishing the impact of your writing by finishing on a weak note. Resist the urge to apologize for what you have or have not written, or to cram in a final detail that would have been better placed elsewhere.

A STUDENT ESSAY-IN-PROGRESS

In the following pages and the next two chapters, you have a chance to watch Rosie Anaya as she develops an essay through journal writing and several drafts. She began the writing process early, while reading and annotating Nancy Mairs's "Disability" (p. 12). Inspired by Mairs's argument, Anaya writes about another group that has been "effaced" by the media.

Journal Notes on Reading

Haven't the media gotten better about showing people with disabilities since Mairs wrote this essay? Lots of TV shows today have characters who just happen to use wheelchairs. But I see why she has a problem: I would be bothered, too, if I didn't see people like me represented. I would feel left out, probably hurt, maybe angry.

Mairs is doing more: Invisibility is a problem for healthy people too—anybody could become disabled and wouldn't know that people with disabilities live full, normal lives.

Interesting that she mentions emotions so many times: The references to feelings and psychology raise a question about people with mental disabilities, like depression or schizophrenia. How are *they* represented by the media? Definitely *not* as regular people: Stories in the news about emotionally disturbed people who go over the edge and hurt or even kill people. And *Criminal Minds* etc. always using some kind of psychological disorder to explain a crime.

Except the problem with mental illness isn't just invisibility—it's negative stereo-typing. What if you're represented as a danger to yourself and others? That's got to be worse.

First Draft

Nancy Mairs is upset with television and movies that don't show physical disability as a feature of normal life. She says the media shows disability consuming a character's life or it doesn't show disability at all, and she wants to see "representations of myself in the media, especially television" (p. no.).

Mairs makes a convincing argument that the media should portray physical disability as part of everyday life because "effacement" leaves the rest of us unprepared to cope in the case that we should eventually become disabled ourselves. As she explains it, anybody could become disabled, but because we rarely see people with disabilities living full, normal lives on tv, we assume that becoming disabled means life is pretty much over (p. no.). It's been three decades since Mairs wrote her essay, and she seems to have gotten her wish. Plenty of characters on television today who have a disability are not defined by it. But psychological disabilities are disabilities too, and they have never been shown "as a normal characteristic, one that complicates but does not ruin human existence" (p. no.).

Television routinely portrays people with mental illness as threats to themselves and to others. Think about all those stories on the evening news about a man suffering from schizophrenia who went on a shooting spree before turning his gun on himself, or a mother who drowned her own children in the throes of depression, or a bipolar teenager who commits suicide. Such events are tragic, no doubt, but although the vast majority of people with these illnesses hurt nobody, the news implies that they're all potential killers.

Fictional shows, too, are always using some kind of psychological disorder to explain why someone committed a crime. On *Criminal Minds* a woman with "intermittent explosive disorder" impulsively kills multiple people after she is released from a psychiatric hospital and stops taking her medication. On *Law and Order: SVU* an abusive mother's actions are blamed on factitious disorder, or Munchausen by Proxy, "a mental illness where a parent makes up fake symptoms or causes symptoms" in a child to generate sympathy for herself, and when her daughter kills her after learning what had been going on, the defense attorney blames the girl's own PTSD, depression, and anxiety for her violence. And the entire premise of *Dexter* was that the trauma of witnessing his mother's brutal murder turned the title character into a serial killer. Dexter is an obsessive-compulsive killer who justifies his impulses by killing only other killers. Every season featured a different enemy, and each one of them had some kind of stated or implied mental illness: The "Doomsday Killer" of season six, for example, was a psychotic divinity student who went off his meds and suffered from delusions.

It is my belief that the presentation of psychological disability may do worse than the "effacement" of disability that bothered Mairs. People with mental illness are discouraged from seeking help and are sent deeper into isolation and despair. This negative stereotype hurts us all.

3

THE WRITING PROCESS

Reviewing and Revising

If it helps to get you writing, you may want to view a draft as a kind of dialog with readers — fulfilling their expectations, answering the questions you imagine they would ask. But some writers save this kind of thinking for the next stage, REVISION. Literally "re-seeing," revision involves stepping outside the intense circle of you-and-the-material to see the work as a reader will, with whatever qualities you imagine that reader to have.

REVIEWING A DRAFT

The first task of revising is to step back and view your draft as a whole, looking at the big picture and ignoring details like grammar and spelling.

Your writing teacher may have you spend some time working with your classmates, as a full class or in small groups or pairs, to help you see this whole. You might read each other's drafts, offer feedback both positive and negative, and plot revision strategies together. Such conversation and collaboration — voicing, listening to, and debating ideas — can help you develop more confidence in your writing and give you a clearer sense of your AUDIENCE. One classmate, for instance, may show you that your introduction, which you thought was weak, really worked to get her involved in your essay. Another might question you in a way that helps you see how the introduction sets up expectations in the reader, expectations you're obliged to fulfill. Several of Rosie Anaya's classmates offered comments on the first draft of her paper responding to Nancy Mair's "Disability" (see pp. 50–51), and they helped her to evaluate her essay and think about how to improve it.

You may at first be anxious about peer review: How can I judge others' writing? How can I stand others' criticism of my own writing? These are natural worries, and your teacher will try to help you with both of them — for instance, by providing a worksheet to guide your critique of each other's writing. (The checklist below works for reviewing your classmates' drafts as well as your own.) With practice and plentiful feedback, you'll soon appreciate how much you're learning about writing and what a good effect that knowledge has on your own work. You're writing for an audience, after all, and you can't beat the immediate feedback of a live one.

REVISING IN STAGES

Whether you have an opportunity to have your draft reviewed by classmates or will be on your own in assessing its strengths and weaknesses, let the draft sit for a while before you come back to revise it: at least a few hours, ideally a day or more. When you return with fresh eyes and a refreshed mind, you'll be in a better position to see what works, what doesn't, and what needs your attention. The checklist below and the ensuing discussion can guide you (and your reviewers) to the big-picture view. Specific revision guidelines for each method of development appear in the introductions to Chapters 5–14.

QUESTIONS FOR PEER REVIEW AND REVISION

✔ **Is my purpose clear to readers?** Have I achieved it?

✔ **What are readers' expectations for this kind of writing?** Have I met them?

✔ **What is the thesis?** Have I supported it for readers? Is the thesis statement clear and to the point?

✔ **Is the essay unified?** Can readers see how all parts relate to the thesis? Are there any parts that don't fit or should be removed?

✔ **Are the points developed as well as they could be?** Have I supplied enough details, examples, and other specifics so that readers can understand me and follow my reasoning?

✔ **Is the essay coherent?** Can readers see how the parts relate?

✔ **Is the organization clear?** Can readers follow it?

Purpose and Genre

Earlier we looked at PURPOSE and GENRE as important considerations in planning an essay (pp. 29–30). They are even more important in revision. Like many writers, in the discovery and experimentation of drafting you may lose track of your original direction. Did you set out to write a critical analysis of a reading but end up with a summary? Did you rely on personal experience when you were supposed to integrate evidence from sources? Did you set out to persuade readers but not get beyond explanation? That's okay. You've jumped the first hurdle simply by putting your thoughts into words. Now you can add, delete, and reorganize until your purpose will be clear to readers and you meet their expectations for how it should be fulfilled.

Thesis

As you've developed your ideas and your draft, you've also been developing your THESIS, the main idea that you want to get across to readers. The thesis may be stated up front or hover in the background, but it should be clear to readers and the rest of the essay should support it. Almost always, you will need to revise your thesis as your ideas take form and your purpose for writing becomes clear to you. You may find that you need to adjust your thesis to reflect what you ended up writing in your draft, or you may need to rework your supporting ideas so that they adequately develop your thesis.

Pay attention, too, to your thesis statement itself. Few writers craft a perfect statement on the first try. In each of the following pairs, for example, the draft statement is too vague to work as a hook: It conveys the writer's general opinion but not its basis. Each revised statement clarifies the point.

DRAFT   The sculpture is a beautiful piece of work.

REVISED   Although it may not be obvious at first, this smooth bronze sculpture unites urban and natural elements to represent the city dweller's relationship with nature.

DRAFT   The sculpture is a waste of money.

REVISED   The huge bronze sculpture in the middle of McBean Park demonstrates that so-called public art may actually undermine the public interest.

When you revise, make a point of checking your thesis and your thesis statement against the guidelines listed in the previous chapter (pp. 34–35) and discussed in the introduction to every method chapter in Part Two. You want to ensure that your thesis takes an arguable position on your subject, that it focuses on a single idea, that it reflects the actual content of your essay, and that it gives a sense of your purpose for writing.

Unity

Drafting freely, as you should, can easily take you into some of the byways of your topic. A goal of revision, then, is to deal with digressions so that your essay has UNITY, with every paragraph relating to the thesis and every sentence in a paragraph relating to a single idea, often expressed in a TOPIC SENTENCE. You may choose to cut a digression altogether or to rework it so that it con-nects to the main idea. Sometimes you may find that a digression is really what you want to write about and then opt to recast your thesis instead. For more help, see "Focus on Unity" on page 457.

Development

While some points in your draft may have to be sacrificed for the sake of unity, others will probably want more attention. Be sure that any general statements you make are backed up with evidence: details, examples, analysis, information from sources—whatever it takes to show readers that your point is valid. The introductions to the methods in Chapters 5–14 offer sugges-tions for developing specific kinds of essays; take a look, too, at "Focus on Paragraph Development" on page 356.

Coherence

Drafting ideas into sentences can be halting work, and a first draft can seem jumbled as a result. In revision, you want to help readers follow your thoughts by improving COHERENCE: the clear flow and relation of parts. You can achieve coherence through your use of paragraphs, transitions, and organization.

PARAGRAPHS help readers grasp related information in an essay by developing one supporting point at a time: All of the sentences hang together, defining, explaining, illustrating, or supporting one central idea. Check all your paragraphs to be sure that each sentence connects with the one preceding and that readers will see the connection without having to stop and reread. One way to clarify such connections is with TRANSITIONS: linking words and phrases such as *in addition, moreover,* and *at the same time.* (We have more to say about transitions in "Focus on Paragraph Coherence" on p. 308.)

Be sure, too, that each paragraph follows logically from those before it and leads clearly to those that follow, and that any material from your reading and other sources is integrated logically and smoothly (see the next section). Constructing an outline of what you've written can help you see how well your thoughts hold together, and consulting the graphic organizers in the introductions to the methods (Chaps. 5–14) can help you determine how the structure of your draft might be improved. Expect to experiment, moving paragraphs around, deleting some and adding others, before everything clicks into place.

INTEGRATING EVIDENCE

Writing about what you have read will occupy you for much of your college career, as you rely on books, periodical articles, interviews, Web sites, and other materials to establish and extend your own contributions to academic conversations. The selections in this book, for instance, can serve as sources for your writing: You might analyze them, respond to them, or use them to support your own ideas. Such SYNTHESIS, as we note in Chapter 1, is the core of academic writing. Much of your synthesis of others' work will come as you present evidence from your reading and integrate that evidence into your own text. An important goal of revision, then, is to ensure that you have used such materials honestly and effectively.

Exercising Caution

When you write with sources, your readers expect you to distinguish your own contributions from those of others, honestly acknowledging material that originated elsewhere. To do otherwise — to deliberately or accidentally copy another's idea, data, or wording without acknowledgment — is considered stealing. Called PLAGIARISM, this theft is a serious offense.

Plagiarism is often a result of careless note taking or drafting. The simplest way to avoid problems is always to acknowledge your sources, clearly marking the boundaries between your ideas and those picked up from other writers. Integrate source materials carefully, following the suggestions provided on the next pages. And cite your sources in an appropriate documentation style, such as MLA for English or APA for the social sciences. (See the Appendix for detailed guidelines and documentation models.)

Summarizing, Paraphrasing, and Quoting

As you revise, make sure you have used the ideas and information in sources to support your own ideas, not to direct or overwhelm them. Depending on the importance and complexity of source material, you might summarize it, paraphrase it, or quote it directly. *All summaries, paraphrases, and quotations must be acknowledged in source citations.*

Summary

In a SUMMARY you use your own words to condense a paragraph, an entire article, or even a book into a few lines that convey the source's essential meaning. We discussed summarizing as a reading technique on pages 15–16, and the advice and examples there apply here as well. When responding to a text, you might use a brief summary to catch readers up on the gist of the author's argument or a significant point in the argument. Here, for example, is a summary of Anna Quindlen's "Homeless," which appears on pages 181–83:

> SUMMARY   Quindlen argues that reducing homeless people to the abstract issue of homelessness can obscure the fundamental problem of the homeless individual: He or she needs a home (181–83).

Notice that a summary identifies the source's author and page numbers and uses words that are *not* the author's. A summary that picks up any of the author's distinctive language or neglects to acknowledge that the idea is borrowed from a source counts as plagiarism and must be rewritten. In an early draft of "Mental Illness on Television" (pp. 61–62), for instance, Rosie Anaya inadvertently plagiarized this passage from Nancy Mairs's "Disability":

> ORIGINAL QUOTATION   "But this [media] denial of disability imperils even you who are able-bodied, and not just by shrinking your insight into the physically and emotionally complex world you live in. Some disabled people call you TAPs, or Temporarily Abled Persons. The fact is that ours is the only minority you can join involuntarily, without warning, at any time. . . . The transition will probably be difficult from a physical point of view no matter what. But it will be a good bit easier psychologically if you are accustomed to seeing disability as a normal characteristic, one that complicates but does not ruin human existence."

> PLAGIARISM   Media misrepresentation of disability hurts not only viewers with disabilities but also Temporarily Abled Persons.

In forgetting to name Mairs as the source and in using the phrase "Temporarily Abled Persons" without quotation marks, Anaya stole Mairs's idea. Here is her revision:

> ACCEPTABLE SUMMARY   Mairs argues that media misrepresentation of disability hurts not only viewers with disabilities but also "Temporarily Abled Persons," or those without disabilities (13–15).

Paraphrase

When you PARAPHRASE, you restate a specific passage in your own words. Paraphrase adheres more closely than summary to the source author's line of thought, so it's useful for presenting an author's ideas or data in detail. Generally, use paraphrase rather than quotation for this purpose, since paraphrase shows that you're in command of your evidence and lets your own voice come through. Here is a quotation from Quindlen's essay and a paraphrase of it:

ORIGINAL QUOTATION   "Homes have stopped being homes. Now they are real estate."

PARAPHRASE   Quindlen points out that people's dwellings seem to have lost their emotional hold and to have become just investments (182).

As with a summary, note that a paraphrase cites the original author and page number. And like a summary, a paraphrase must express the original idea in an entirely new way, both in word choice and in sentence structure. The following attempt to paraphrase a line from an essay by David Cole slips into plagiarism through sloppiness:

ORIGINAL QUOTATION   "We stand to be collectively judged by our treatment of immigrants, who may appear to be 'other' now but in a generation will be 'us.'"

PLAGIARISM   Cole argues that we will be judged as a group by how we treat immigrants, who seem to be different now but eventually will be the same as us (110).

Even though the writer identifies Cole as the source and provides a page number, much of the language and the sentence structure are also Cole's. It's not enough to change a few words — such as "collectively" to "as a group," "they may appear to be 'other'" to "they may seem different," and "in a generation" to "eventually." In contrast, this acceptable paraphrase restates Cole's point in completely new language *and* a new sentence structure:

ACCEPTABLE PARAPHRASE   Cole argues that the way the United States deals with immigrants now will come back to haunt it when those immigrants eventually become part of mainstream society (110).

Quotation

Quotations from sources can both support and enliven your own ideas — *if* you choose them well. When analyzing a source such as an essay in this book, you may need to quote some passages in order to give the flavor of the author's words and evidence for your analysis. Too many quotations, however, will clutter your essay and detract from your voice. Select quotations that are relevant to the point you are making, that are concise and pithy, and that use lively, bold, or original language. Sentences that lack distinction—for example, a statement providing statistics on housing rates—should be paraphrased.

Always enclose quotations in quotation marks and cite the source author and page number. For a blatant example of plagiarism, look at the following use of a quotation from Anna Quindlen's "Homeless":

> ORIGINAL QUOTATION "It has been customary to take people's pain and lessen our own participation in it by turning it into an issue, not a collection of human beings."

> PLAGIARISM   As a society we tend to lessen our participation in other people's pain by turning it into an issue.

By not acknowledging Quindlen at all, the writer takes claim for her idea and for much of her wording. A source citation would help—at least the idea would be credited—but still the expression of the idea would be stolen because there's no indication that the language is Quindlen's. Here is a revision with citation and quotation marks:

> ACCEPTABLE QUOTATION   Quindlen suggests that our tendency "to take people's pain and lessen our own participation in it by turning it into an issue" dehumanizes homeless people (183).

You may adapt quotations to fit your sentences, provided you make clear how you've changed them. If you omit something from a quoted passage, signal the omission with the three spaced periods of an ellipsis mark as shown:

> In Quindlen's view, "the thing that seems most wrong with the world . . . right now is that there are so many people with no homes" (182).

If you need to insert words or phrases into a quotation to clarify the author's meaning or make the quotation flow with your own language, show that the insertion is yours by enclosing it in brackets:

> Quindlen points out that "we work around [the problem], just as we walk around" the homeless people we encounter (183).

Synthesizing Ideas

When you write about a text, your perspective on it will be your thesis—the main point you have in response to the text or as a result of examining it. As you develop and revise your essay, keep your ideas front and center, pulling in material from the text as needed for support. In each paragraph, your idea should come first and, usually, last: State the idea, use evidence from the reading to support it, and then interpret the evidence.

You can see a paragraph structured like this in the final draft of Rosie Anaya's essay "Mental Illness on Television" (p. 62):

SYNTHESIS

However, in depicting one type of disability, the media are, if anything, worse than they were three decades ago. Mairs doesn't address mental illness, but it falls squarely into the misrepresentation she criticizes. It has never been shown, in Mairs's words, "as a normal characteristic, one that complicates but does not ruin human existence" (15). Thus people who cope with a psychological disability such as depression, bipolar disorder, or obsessive-compulsive disorder as part of their lives do not see themselves in the media. And those who don't have a psychological disability now but may someday do not see that mental illness is usually a condition one can live with.

Anaya's idea

Evidence from Mairs's text

Anaya's interpretation of Mairs's idea

Understand that synthesis is more than summary, which just distills what the text says or shows. Summary has its uses, especially in understanding a writer's ideas (p. 15) and in presenting evidence from source material (p. 46), but it should not substitute for your own ideas. Contrast the preceding paragraph from Anaya's essay with the following passage from an early draft in which Anaya uses summary to present evidence:

SUMMARY

Mairs argues that media misrepresentation of disability hurts not only viewers with disabilities but also those without disabilities (14). The media either ignore disability altogether or present it as the defining characteristic of a person's life (13–14). In doing so, they deny "Temporarily Abled Persons" the opportunity to see disability as something common that may be difficult to adjust to but does not destroy one's life (14–15).

Mairs's idea

Mairs's idea

Mairs's idea

With synthesis, you're always making it clear to readers what *your* idea is and how the evidence from your reading supports that idea. To achieve this clarity, you want to fit evidence from other texts into your sentences and show what you make of it. In this passage, the writer drops a quotation awkwardly into her paragraph and doesn't clarify how it relates to her idea:

NOT INTEGRATED   Homelessness affects real people. "[W]e work around it, just as we walk around it when it is lying on the sidewalk or sitting in the bus terminal—the problem, that is" (Quindlen 183).

In the revision below, the writer uses "but" and the SIGNAL PHRASE "as Quindlen points out" to link the quotation to the writer's idea and to identify the source author:

INTEGRATED   Homelessness affects real people, but, as Quindlen points out, "we work around it, just as we walk around it when it is lying on the side-walk or sitting in the bus terminal—the problem, that is" (183).

A final note: Whether you are synthesizing information and ideas from one text or several, remember that all source material must be acknowledged with in-text citations and a list of works cited or references at the end of your paper. The Appendix at the back of this book (pp. 647–692) provides detailed guidelines and ample models for both the MLA and APA styles of documenting sources.

A STUDENT ESSAY-IN-PROGRESS

After completing the first draft of an essay responding to Nancy Mairs's "Disability" (see pp. 39–40), Rosie Anaya shared her work with a small group of classmates for a peer-review session. Her reviewers all agreed that the first draft was a good start. Anaya had found an idea worth pursuing and explored her thoughts. But as with any first draft, her essay needed work. Here we share some of her peers' comments on her draft, followed by the journal notes and revisions Anaya made in response to them. You'll see that she revised extensively, cutting digressions in some places and adding support in others. Her revised draft responds to "Disability" more directly, spells out Mairs's points and Anaya's own ideas in more detail, and builds more thoroughly on what Mairs had to say.

Peer Responses to First Draft

Your essay is fascinating. I never really thought about how mental illness is treated on tv before! But the introduction feels kind of abrupt, and what is your thesis? I don't see it anywhere. Also, the essay seems to kind of fizzle out at the end.

—Liz Kingham

You do a good job showing how TV stereotypes people with mental illness, but the Dexter example goes on a bit long and seems out of date—it's hard to see how it all relates. Also, can you give some examples of the characters with physical disabilities you mention in paragraph 2? All the ones I can think of are from other old shows that have stopped running, so I wonder if the problem has really improved after all.

—Hahlil Jones

Your idea is really original and I like what you have to say about it, but I'm having trouble following how it connects to Mairs's argument. Could you tie the two issues together more clearly?

—Maria Child

Journal Notes on Peer Review

I thought I did a good job explaining myself, but Maria's right: I assume that other people interpreted Mairs the same way I did, and that's not necessarily true. Need to go through my essay and spell out what her ideas are—and then show how the problems she identified are even more important in the case of mental illness.

Hahlil's right about the Dexter example—I got carried away after binge-watching on Netflix, and the show *is* pretty old. Better to leave it out entirely. I could probably scale back the SVU example too.

The introduction and conclusion need a lot of work: a less abrupt start, a thesis statement, and a fuller conclusion that says why the media should improve the way psychological disability is portrayed—more with Mairs's point about the impact of "effacement" on "Temporarily Abled People" might help with that.

Also need to add page numbers from Mairs and works cited at the end.

Revised Draft

Mental Illness on Television

In her essay "Disability" **Nancy Mairs** ~~is upset with~~ argues that **television and movies** ~~that don't~~ fail to **show physical disability as a feature of normal life.** ~~She~~ Instead, Mairs **says, the media shows disability consuming a character's life or it doesn't show disability at all**~~, and she wants to see "representations of myself in the media, especially television"~~ (~~p. no.~~ 13). But Mairs wrote her essay in 1987. Since then the situation has actually improved for physical disability. At the same time, another group—those with mental illness—have come to suffer even worse representation.

~~Mairs makes a convincing argument~~ Mairs's purpose in writing her essay was to persuade her readers **that the media should portray physical disability as part of everyday life because** ~~"effacement"~~ otherwise it denies or misrepresents disability,

Uses a less abrupt, more formal tone.

Deletes a quotation to remove a side issue and tighten the introduction.

Adds a thesis statement.

Explains Mairs's idea more clearly.

and it **leaves** ~~the rest of us~~ "Temporarily Abled Persons" (those without disability, for now) **unprepared to cope in the case that** ~~we~~ they **should eventually become disabled** ~~ourselves~~ themselves (14-15). ~~As she explains it, anybody could become disabled, but because we rarely see people with disabilities living full, normal lives on tv, we assume that becoming disabled means life is pretty much over (p. no.). It's been three decades since Mairs wrote her essay, and~~ Three decades later, Mairs ~~she~~ seems to have gotten her wish. Plenty of characters on television today who have a disability are not defined by it. FBI agent Jocelyn Turner of *Quantico* is deaf. High-school student JJ DiMeo on *Speechless* has nonverbal cerebral palsy (as does the actor who portrays him). Police officer Joe Swanson of *Family Guy* is paraplegic, Patton Plame of *NCIS: New Orleans* uses a wheelchair equipped with a computer to help his team solve crimes. Dozens of active people with a wide range of physical disabilities are featured in Toyota's current "Mobility for All" ad campaign. The media still has a long way to go in representing physical disability, but it has made progress.

 However, the media depiction of one type of disability is, if anything, worse than it was three decades ago. Although Mairs doesn't address mental illness in "Disability," mental illness falls squarely into the misrepresentation she criticizes. ~~But p~~Psychological disabilities are disabilities too, ~~and~~ but they have never been shown "as a normal characteristic, one that complicates but does not ruin human existence" (~~p. no.~~15). People who cope with a disability such as depression, bipolar disorder, or obsessive-compulsive disorder as parts of their lives do not see themselves in the media; those who don't have a psychological disability now but may someday do not see that mental illness is usually a condition they can live with.

 The depictions of mental illness actually go beyond Mairs's concerns, as the media actually exploits it. **Television routinely portrays people with mental illness as threats to themselves and to others. Think about all those stories on the evening news about a man suffering from schizophrenia who went on a shooting spree before turning his gun on himself, or a mother who drowned her own children in the throes of**

Provides page numbers in Mairs's essay.

Adds examples to support the assertion about TV today.

Adds a transition to tighten the connection with Mairs's essay.

More fully develops the idea about mental illness as a "normal characteristic."

Adds a transition to link back to Mairs and the thesis.

depression, or a bipolar teenager who commits suicide. ~~Such events are tragic, no doubt, but although the vast majority of people with these illnesses hurt nobody, the news implies that they're all potential killers.~~ Fictional shows, too, are always using some kind of psychological disorder to explain why someone committed a crime. On *Criminal Minds* a woman with "intermittent explosive disorder" impulsively kills multiple people after she is released from a psychiatric hospital and stops taking her medication~~,~~ and ~~O~~on *Law and Order: SVU* an abusive mother's actions are blamed on ~~factitious disorder, or~~ Munchausen by Proxy, "a mental illness where a parent makes up fake [medical] symptoms or causes symptoms" in a child to generate sympathy for herself.~~, and when her daughter kills her after learning what had been going on, the defense attorney blames the girl's own PTSD, depression, and anxiety, for her violence. And the entire premise of Dexter was that the trauma of witnessing his mother's brutal murder turned the title character into a serial killer. Dexter is an obsessive-compulsive killer who justifies his impulses by killing only other killers. Every season has featured a different enemy, and each one of them has had some kind of stated or implied mental illness: The "Doomsday Killer" of season six, for example, was a psychotic divinity student who went off his meds and suffered from delusions.~~

Combines related paragraphs ("Fictional shows" used to start a new paragraph).

Removes digressions and simplifies examples to improve unity.

These programs highlight mental illness to get viewers' attention. But the media is also telling us that the proper response to people with mental illness is to be afraid of them. Mairs argues that invisibility in the media can cause people with disabilities to feel unattractive or inappropriate (14). It is my belief that the presentation of psychological disability may do worse. ~~than the "effacement" of disability that bothered Mairs.~~ People with mental illness are discouraged from seeking help and are sent deeper into isolation and despair. Those feelings are often cited as the fuel for violent outbursts, but ironically the media portrays such violence as inevitable with mental illness. ~~This negative stereotype hurts us all.~~

Expands paragraph to link to Mairs's essay and lend authority to Anaya's point.

More complex and varied depictions of all kinds of impairments, both physical and mental, will weaken the negative

Provides a new conclusion that explains why the topic is important and ends with a flourish.

stereotypes that are harmful to all of us. With mental illness
especially, we would all be better served if psychological
disability was portrayed by the media as a part of everyday life.
It's not a crime.

Works Cited

"Breath Play." *Criminal Minds*, season 10, episode 17, CBS, 11
  Mar. 2015. *Netflix*, www.netflix.com/search/criminalminds.
  Accessed 19 Feb. 2018.

Mairs, Nancy. "Disability." *The Bedford Reader*, edited by
  X. J. Kennedy et al., 14th ed., Bedford/St. Martin's, 2020,
  pp. 12-15.

"Pathological." *Law and Order: SVU*, season 19, episode 10,
  NBC, 10 Jan. 2018.

Toyota. "Mobility Anthem." *Mobility for All*, www.mobilityforall
  .com/global/en, 2017-2018. Advertisement.

Adds a list of works
cited. (See pp. 660–670.)

4

THE WRITING
PROCESS

Editing

Like most writers, you will probably find that you produce better work
when you approach revision as at least a two-step process. First revise, focusing on fundamental, whole-essay matters such as purpose, organization, and
synthesis (Chap. 3). Only then turn to EDITING, focusing on surface issues such
as grammar and word choice to improve the flow of your writing and to fix
the mistakes that tend to get in the way of readers' understanding.

The checklist on the next page covers the most common opportunities
and problems, which are explained on the following pages. Because some challenges tend to pop up more often when writing with a particular method, you'll
find additional help in the introductions to Chapters 5–14, in boxes labeled
"Focus on . . ." that highlight specific issues and provide tips for solving them.

USING EFFECTIVE LANGUAGE

Many of us, when we draft, fall back on the familiar language we use
when chatting with friends: We might rely on COLLOQUIAL EXPRESSIONS such
as *get into* and *freak out* or slip into texting shortcuts such as *u* for "you" and
idk for "I don't know." This strategy can help us to put ideas together without
getting sidetracked by details. But patterns of casual communication are usually too imprecise for college writing, where word choices can dramatically
affect how readers understand your ideas.

QUESTIONS FOR EDITING

✔ **Are my language and tone appropriate** for my purpose, audience, and genre?

✔ **Do my words say what I mean,** and are they as vivid as I can make them?

✔ **Are my sentences smooth and concise?** Do they use emphasis, parallelism, variety, and other techniques to clarify meaning and hold readers' interest?

✔ **Are my sentences grammatically sound?** In particular, have I avoided sentence fragments, run-on sentences, comma splices, mismatched subjects and verbs, unclear pronouns, misplaced or dangling modifiers, and inconsistencies?

✔ **Are any words misspelled?**

As a critical reader, you take note of writers' language and consider how their choices affect the meaning and impact of their work (see pp. 21–22). As a writer, you should devote similar attention to your own choices, adapting your general language and your specific words to reflect your purpose, your meaning, and your audience.

A few guidelines:

- **Adopt a relatively formal voice.** Replace overly casual or emotional language with standard English DICTION and a neutral TONE. (Refer to pp. 697 and 706 of the Glossary and to "Focus on Tone" on p. 496.)

- **Choose an appropriate point of view.** In most academic writing, you should prefer the more objective third PERSON (*he, she, it, they*) over the first person (*I*) or the second person (*you*). There are exceptions, of course: A personal narrative written without *I* would ring strange to most ears, and a how-to process analysis often addresses readers as *you*.

- **Check that words have the meanings you intend.** The DENOTATION of a word is its dictionary meaning—for example, *affection* means "caring regard." A CONNOTATION, in contrast, is an emotional association that a word produces in readers, as *passion* evokes intensity or *obsession* evokes compulsion. Using a word with the wrong denotation muddies meaning, while using words with strong connotations can shape readers' responses to your ideas—for good or for ill.

- **Use concrete and specific words.** Effective writing balances ABSTRACT and GENERAL words, which provide outlines of ideas and things, with CONCRETE and SPECIFIC words, which limit and sharpen. You need abstract and general words such as *old* and *transportation* for broad statements that convey concepts or refer to entire groups. But you also need concrete and specific words such as *crumbling* and *streetcar line* to make meaning precise and vivid. See "Focus on Specific and Concrete Language" on page 122.

- **Be creative.** You can make your writing more lively and forceful with FIGURES OF SPEECH, expressions that imply meanings beyond or different from their literal meanings, such as *curled tight like a rosebud* or *feelings trampled to dirt*. Be careful not to resort to CLICHÉS, worn phrases that have lost their power (*hour of need, thin as a rail*), or to combine figures of speech into confusing or absurd images, such as *The players flooded the soccer field like bulls ready for a fight.*

CRAFTING CLEAR AND ENGAGING SENTENCES

Effective sentences are the product of careful attention to meaning and readability. Editing for emphasis, parallelism, and variety will ensure that readers can follow your ideas without difficulty and stay interested in what you have to say.

Emphasis

While drafting, simply getting ideas down in sentence form can be challenge enough. But once the ideas are down, it becomes apparent that some are more important than others. Editing for emphasis offers an opportunity to clarify those relationships for readers. As you do so, focus on the following changes:

- **Put verbs in the active voice.** A verb in the ACTIVE VOICE expresses action by the subject (*He recorded a new song*), whereas a verb in the PASSIVE VOICE expresses action done to the subject (*A new song was recorded*, or, adding who did the action, *A new song was recorded by him*). The active voice is usually more emphatic and therefore easier to follow. See "Focus on Verbs" on page 71.

- **Simplify wordy sentences.** Unnecessary padding deflates readers' interest. Weed out any empty phrases or meaningless repetition:

  WORDY   The nature of social-networking sites is such that they reconnect lost and distant friends but can also for all intents and purposes dredge up old relationships, relationships that were better left forgotten.

  CONCISE   Social-networking sites reconnect lost and distant friends but can also dredge up old relationships that were better left forgotten.

See also "Focus on Clarity and Conciseness" on page 405.

- **Combine sentences.** You can often clarify meaning by merging sentences. Use *coordination* to combine and balance equally important ideas, joining them with *and, but, or, nor, for, so,* or *yet:*

  UNEMPHATIC   Many restaurant meals are high in fat. Their sodium content is also high. To diners they seem harmless.

  EMPHATIC   Many restaurant meals are high in fat <u>and</u> sodium, <u>but</u> to diners they seem harmless.

  Use *subordination* to de-emphasize less important ideas, placing minor information in modifying words or word groups:

  UNEMPHATIC   Restaurant menus sometimes label certain options. They use the label "healthy." These options are lower in fat and sodium.

  EMPHATIC   Restaurant menus sometimes label <u>as "healthy"</u> the options <u>that are lower in fat and sodium.</u>

Parallelism

Another way to clarify meaning is to give parallel structure to related words, phrases, and sentences. PARALLELISM is the use of similar grammatical forms for elements of similar importance, either within or among sentences.

PARALLELISM WITHIN A SENTENCE   Binge drinking can <u>worsen heart disease</u> and <u>cause liver failure.</u>

PARALLELISM AMONG SENTENCES   Binge drinking has less well-known effects, too. <u>It can cause</u> brain damage. <u>It can raise</u> blood sugar to diabetic levels. And <u>it can reduce</u> the body's ability to fight off infections.

Readers tend to stumble over elements that seem equally important but are not in parallel form. As you edit, look for groups of related ideas and make a point of expressing them consistently:

NONPARALLEL   Even occasional binges can cause serious problems, from <u>the experience of blackouts</u> to <u>getting arrested</u> to <u>injury.</u>

PARALLEL   Even occasional binges can cause serious problems, from <u>blackouts</u> to <u>arrests</u> to <u>injuries.</u>

For more on parallel structure, see "Focus on Parallelism" on page 210.

Sentence Variety

Sentence after sentence with the same length and structure can be stiff and dull. By varying sentences, you can hold readers' interest while also achieving the emphasis you want. The techniques to achieve variety include adjusting the lengths of sentences and varying their beginnings. For examples and specifics, see "Focus on Sentence Variety" on page 164.

FIXING COMMON ERRORS

Writers sometimes think of grammar as a set of rules that exist solely to give nitpickers a chance to point out mistakes. But basic errors can undermine an otherwise excellent piece of writing by distracting readers or creating confusion. The guidelines here can help you catch some of the most common problems.

Sentence Fragments

A *sentence fragment* is a word group that is punctuated like a sentence but is not a complete sentence. Experienced writers sometimes use fragments for effect, but readers will just as often be tripped up by incomplete sentences. For the sake of clarity, make sure every sentence has a subject and a verb and expresses a complete thought:

FRAGMENT   Snowboarding a relatively young sport.

COMPLETE   Snowboarding is a relatively young sport.

FRAGMENT   Many ski resorts banned snowboards at first. Believing they were dangerous and destructive.

COMPLETE   Many ski resorts banned snowboards at first, believing they were dangerous and destructive.

Run-on Sentences and Comma Splices

When two or more sentences run together with no punctuation between them, they create a *run-on sentence.* When they run together with only a comma between them, they create a *comma splice.* Writers usually correct these errors by separating the sentences with a period, with a semicolon, or with a comma along with *and, but, or, nor, for, so,* or *yet*:

RUN-ON   Snowboarding has become a mainstream sport riders are now as common as skiers on the slopes.

COMMA SPLICE   Snowboarding has become a mainstream sport, riders are now as common as skiers on the slopes.

EDITED   Snowboarding has become a mainstream sport. Riders are now as common as skiers on the slopes.

EDITED   Snowboarding has become a mainstream sport; riders are now as common as skiers on the slopes.

EDITED   Snowboarding has become a mainstream sport, and riders are now as common as skiers on the slopes.

Subject-Verb Agreement

Most writers know to use singular verbs with singular subjects and plural verbs with plural subjects, but matching subjects and verbs can sometimes be tricky. Watch especially for these situations:

- **Don't mistake a noun that follows the subject for the actual subject.** In the examples below, the subject is *appearance*, not *snowboarders* or *Olympics*:

  MISMATCHED   The appearance of snowboarders in the Olympics prove their status as true athletes.

  MATCHED   The appearance of snowboarders in the Olympics proves their status as true athletes.

- **With subjects joined by *and*, use a plural verb.** Compound word groups are treated as plural even if the word closest to the verb is singular:

  MISMATCHED   The cross course and the half-pipe shows the sport's versatility.

  MATCHED   The cross course and the half-pipe show the sport's versatility.

Pronouns

We tend to use pronouns without thinking much about them. Problems occur when usage that feels natural in speech causes confusion in writing:

- **Check that each pronoun refers clearly to an appropriate noun.** Rewrite sentences in which the reference is vague or only implied:

  VAGUE   Students asked the administration to add more parking spaces, but it had no effect.

  CLEAR   Students asked the administration to add more parking spaces, but their pleas had no effect.

  IMPLIED   Although commuter parking is hard to find, they keep driving to campus.

  CLEAR   Although commuters know that parking is hard to find, they keep driving to campus.

- **Take care with indefinite pronouns.** Although people often use pronouns such as *anybody*, *everyone*, and *somebody* to mean "many" or "all," these indefinite pronouns are technically singular, not plural:

MISMATCHED   Everyone should change their passwords frequently.

MATCHED   Everyone should change his or her passwords frequently.

MATCHED   All computer users should change their passwords frequently.

Misplaced and Dangling Modifiers

A *modifier* describes another word or group of words in a sentence. Make sure that modifiers clearly describe the intended words. Misplaced and dangling modifiers can be awkward or even unintentionally amusing:

MISPLACED   I swam away as the jellyfish approached in fear of being stung.

CLEAR   In fear of being stung, I swam away as the jellyfish approached.

DANGLING   Floating in the ocean, the clouds drifted by.

CLEAR   Floating in the ocean, I watched as the clouds drifted by.

Shifts

Be consistent in your use of verb tense (past, present, and so on), person (*I, you, he/she/it, they*), and voice (active or passive). Unnecessary shifts can confuse readers. For details, see "Focus on Verbs" on page 71 and "Focus on Consistency" on page 259.

A STUDENT ESSAY-IN-PROGRESS

With her thesis clarified, the connections between her argument and Mairs's tightened, and her ideas more fully developed, Rosie Anaya was satisfied that her revised essay, which we saw at the end of the previous chapter (p. 51), was much improved. She still had some work to do, though. In editing, she corrected errors, cleaned up awkward sentences, and added explanations. Here we show you her changes to one paragraph followed by her final draft, annotated with notes on its thesis, structure, and uses of the rhetorical methods.

Edited Paragraph

Mairs's purpose in ~~writing her essay~~ "Disability" ~~was~~ is to persuade ~~her~~ readers that the media should portray physical disability as part of everyday life because otherwise ~~it denies~~ they deny or misrepresent~~s~~ disability~~,~~ and ~~it~~ leaves "Temporarily Abled Persons" (those without disability, for now) unprepared to cope ~~in the case that they should eventually~~ if they become

Reduces wordiness; corrects tense shift.

Corrects pronoun-antecedent and subject-verb agreement (*media* is plural).

Reduces wordiness.

disabled ~~themselves~~ (14-15). Three decades later, Mairs seems to have gotten her wish.~~Plenty of~~ for characters ~~on television today~~ who have a disability but are not defined by it. FBI agent Jocelyn Turner of *Quantico* is deaf. High-school student JJ DiMeo on *Speechless* has ~~nonverbal~~ cerebral palsy ~~(as does the actor who portrays him)~~. Police officer Joe Swanson of *Family Guy* is paraplegic~~,~~. Security analyst **Patton Plame of** *NCIS: New Orleans* uses a wheelchair equipped with a computer to help his team solve crimes. Toyota's current "Mobility for All" ad campaign showcases ~~Dd~~ozens of active people with a wide range of physical disabilities ~~are featured in Toyota's current "Mobility for All" ad campaign~~. The media still ~~has~~ have a long way to go in representing physical disability, but ~~it has~~ they have made progress.

> Adds coordination for emphasis.
>
> Reduces wordiness.
>
> Fixes comma splice.
>
> Eliminates passive voice and creates parallelism.
>
> Corrects subject-verb and pronoun-antecedent agreement.

Final Draft

Rosie Anaya
Professor Schwartz
English 102A
27 Feb. 2018

Mental Illness on Television

In her essay "Disability," Nancy Mairs argues that the media, such as television and movies, fail to show physical disability as a feature of normal life. Instead, Mairs says, they show disability consuming a character's life or they don't show disability at all. Mairs wrote her essay in 1987, and since then the situation has actually improved for depiction of physical disability. At the same time, another group—those with mental illness—has come to suffer even worse representation.

Mairs's purpose in "Disability" is to persuade readers that the media should portray physical disability as part of everyday life because otherwise they deny or misrepresent disability and leave "Temporarily Abled Persons" (those without disability, for now) unprepared to cope if they become disabled (14-15). Three decades later, Mairs seems to have gotten her wish for characters who have a disability but are not defined by it. FBI agent Jocelyn Turner of *Quantico* is deaf. High-school student JJ DiMeo

> Introduction summarizes Mairs's essay and sets up Anaya's thesis.
>
> Thesis statement establishes Anaya's main idea.
>
> Page numbers in parentheses refer to "Works Cited" at end of paper.

on *Speechless* has cerebral palsy. Police officer Joe Swanson of *Family Guy* is paraplegic. Security analyst Patton Plame of *NCIS: New Orleans* uses a wheelchair equipped with a computer to help his team solve crimes. Toyota's current "Mobility for All" ad campaign showcases dozens of active people with a wide range of physical disabilities. The media still have a long way to go in representing physical disability, but they have made progress.

    However, in depicting one type of disability, the media are, if anything, worse than they were three decades ago. Mairs doesn't address mental illness, but it falls squarely into the misrepresentation she criticizes. It has never been shown, in Mairs's words, "as a normal characteristic, one that complicates but does not ruin human existence" (15). Thus people who cope with a psychological disability such as depression, bipolar disorder, or obsessive-compulsive disorder as part of their lives do not see themselves in the media. And those who don't have a psychological disability now but may someday do not see that mental illness is usually a condition one can live with.

    Unfortunately, the depictions of mental illness also go beyond Mairs's concerns, because the media actually exploit it. Television routinely portrays people with mental illness as threats to themselves and to others. TV news often features stories about a man suffering from schizophrenia who goes on a shooting spree before turning his gun on himself, a mother with depression who drowns her own children, or a teenager with bipolar disorder who commits suicide. Fictional programs, especially crime dramas, regularly use mental illness to develop their plots. On *Criminal Minds* a woman with "intermittent explosive disorder" impulsively kills multiple people after she is released from a psychiatric hospital and stops taking her medication, and on *Law and Order: SVU* an abusive mother's actions are blamed on anxiety and Munchausen by Proxy, "a mental illness where a parent makes up fake [medical] symptoms or causes symptoms" in a child. These programs and many others like them highlight mental illness to get viewers' attention, and they strongly imply that the proper response is fear. Mairs argues that the invisibility of physical disability in the media can cause people with disabilities to feel unattractive

Examples provide support for Anaya's analysis.

Comparison and contrast extend Mairs's idea to Anaya's new subject.

Follow-up comments explain what the quotation contributes to Anaya's thesis.

Topic sentence introduces new idea.

Examples provide evidence for Anaya's point.

Paraphrase explains one of Mairs's points in Anaya's own words.

or inappropriate (14), but the presentation of psychological disability may do worse. It can prevent people with mental illness from seeking help and send them deeper into isolation and despair. Those feelings are often cited as the fuel for violent outbursts, but ironically the media portray such violence as inevitable with mental illness.

Seeing more complex and varied depictions of people living with all kinds of impairments, physical and mental, can weaken the negative stereotypes that are harmful to all of us. With mental illness especially, we would all be better served if the media would make an effort to portray psychological disability as a part of everyday life, not a crime.

Cause-and-effect analysis applies Mairs's idea to Anaya's thesis.

Conclusion reasserts the thesis and explains the broader implications of the subject.

Works Cited

"Breath Play." *Criminal Minds*, season 10, episode 17, CBS, 11 Mar. 2015. *Netflix*, www.netflix.com/search/criminalminds. Accessed 19 Feb. 2018.

Mairs, Nancy. "Disability." *The Bedford Reader*, edited by X. J. Kennedy et al., 14th ed., Bedford/St. Martin's, 2020, pp. 12-15.

"Pathological." *Law and Order: SVU*, season 19, episode 10, NBC, 10 Jan. 2018.

Toyota. "Mobility Anthem." *Mobility for All*, www.mobilityforall .com/global/en, 2017-2018. Advertisement.

List of "Works Cited" begins on a new page and gives complete publication information for Anaya's sources. (See pp. 660–670.)

PART TWO

THE METHODS

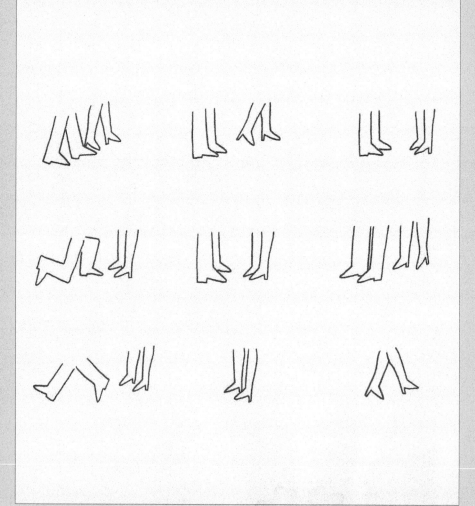

5

NARRATION

Telling a Story

Narration in a drawing

Demetri Martin is a popular stand-up comedian known for
intelligent wit and for the clever graphs and drawings he
incorporates into his act. He has published three books of
such artwork: *This Is a Book by Demetri Martin* (2011), which
also includes comic essays, *Point Your Face at This* (2013),
and *If It's Not Funny It's Art* (2017). "Reality is a concept
that depends on where you point your face," he says in the
epigraph to the second book—an idea illustrated with this
drawing. In Martin's trademark simple style, the sketch focuses
on just the lower legs of two people to tell a brief narrative, or
story. What experience is depicted here? What do the details
in each part of the sequence tell us about the characters, and
what do they contribute to the narrative? What effect does
Martin achieve by not showing the couple more fully? How
does the unusual perspective shape your understanding of
what has happened?

THE METHOD

"What happened?" you ask a friend who sports a swollen black eye. Unless he merely grunts, "A golf ball," he may answer you with a narrative — a story, true or fictional.

"Okay," he sighs, "you know The Tenth Round? That gym down by the docks that smells like formaldehyde? Last night I heard they were giving away $500 to anybody who could stand up for three minutes against this karate expert, the Masked Samurai. And so . . . ."

You lean forward. At least, you lean forward *if* you love a story. Most of us do, particularly if the story tells us of people in action or in conflict, and if it is told briskly, vividly, or with insight into the human condition. NARRATION, or storytelling, is therefore a powerful method by which to engage and hold the attention of listeners — readers as well. A little of its tremendous power flows to the reporter who encapsulates events in a critical newsworthy moment, and to the lawyer who pulls together the threads of a compelling case.

The term *narrative* takes in abundant territory. A narrative may be short or long, factual or imagined, as artless as a tale told in a locker room or as artful as a novel by Toni Morrison. A narrative may instruct and inform, or simply entertain. It may set forth some point or message, or it may be no more significant than a horror tale that aims to curdle your blood. Because narration can both put across ideas and hold attention, the ability to tell a story — on paper, as well as in conversation — may be one of the most useful skills you can acquire.

THE PROCESS

Purpose and Shape

At least a hundred times a year, you probably turn to narration, not always to tell an entertaining story, but often to report information or to illustrate an idea. Every good story has a purpose, because a narrative without a point is bound to irritate readers.

In academic writing, you will use mainly brief narratives, or ANECDOTES, that recount single incidents as a way of supporting an explanation or argument with the flesh and blood of real life. That is, although a narrative can run from the beginning of an essay to the end, as those later in this chapter do, more often in your writing a narrative will be only a part of what you have to say. It will serve a larger purpose. For instance, say you're writing about therapies for autism and you want readers to see how one particular method works. In a paragraph or so, you can narrate a session you observed between a child and his therapist. Your purpose will determine which of the session's events you relate — not every action and exchange but the ones that, in your eyes, convey the essence of the therapy and make it interesting for readers.

The Thesis

In writing a news story, a reporter often begins by placing the main event in the opening paragraph (called the *lead,* or *lede*) so that readers get the essentials up front. Similarly, in using an anecdote to explain something or to argue a point, you'll want to tell readers directly what the story demonstrates. But in most other kinds of narration, whether fiction or nonfiction, whether to entertain or to make an idea clear, the storyteller refrains from revealing the gist of the story, its point, right at the beginning.

In fact, many narratives do not contain a THESIS STATEMENT, an assertion of the idea behind the story, because such a statement can rob the reader of the very pleasure of narration, the excitement of seeing a story build. That doesn't mean the story lacks a thesis, however—far from it. The writer has every obligation to construct the narrative as if a thesis statement shows the way at the start, even when it doesn't.

By the end of the story, that thesis should become obvious, as the writer builds toward a memorable CONCLUSION. Most storytellers end with a bang if they can, often by surprising the reader with a final moment of IRONY, or an unexpected twist to the tale. In the drawing that opens this chapter, for instance, Demetri Martin shows a marriage proposal that ends in a breakup. For another example, take specific notice in this chapter of Shirley Jackson's ending for "The Lottery" (*after* you've read the whole story, that is). The final impact need not be as dramatic as Martin's or Jackson's, either. As Jonathan Bethards demonstrates in his narrative in this chapter, you can achieve a lot just by working up to your point, and stating your thesis at the very end. You can sometimes make your point just by saving the best incident—the most dramatic or the funniest—for last.

The Narrator in the Story

Every story has a NARRATOR, the person telling the tale. The narrator's role in relation to the story determines the POINT OF VIEW, or angle of seeing, that shapes the telling. Generally, writers use different points of view to tell different kinds of stories.

- **Narratives that report personal experience:** Whether you are telling of a real or a fictional event, your narrator will be the one who was there. The telling will probably be SUBJECTIVE: You will use the first PERSON ("I did this; we did that") and choose details and language to express the feelings of the narrator—your own feelings when you are recounting your actual experience or the imagined feelings of a character you have invented. Of course, any experience told in the first person can use some artful telling and structuring, as the personal narratives in this chapter all demonstrate.

- **Narratives that report others' experiences:** When a story isn't your own but someone else's, you proceed differently as narrator. You use the third person, *he, she, it,* or *they:* "The experimenter did this; she did that." Your approach may be subjective, building in the real or imagined feelings of the person experiencing the events. Or your approach may be OBJECTIVE, sticking to the facts as observed by you or by others. In objective narration — typical of writing such as news stories, history books, lab reports, and some fiction — you show what transpired as accurately and dispassionately as possible. In this chapter you can see objective narration in the police log by Scott Beltran and in the short story by Shirley Jackson.

A final element of the narrator's place in the story is verb tense, whether present (*I stare, she stares*) or past (*I stared, she stared*). The present tense is often tempting because it gives events a sense of immediacy. Told as though everything were happening right now, the story of the Masked Samurai might begin: "I duck between the ropes and step into the ring. My heart is thudding fast." But the present tense can seem artificial because we're used to reading stories in the past tense, and it can be difficult to sustain throughout an entire narrative. The past tense may be more removed, but it is still powerful: Just look at Maya Angelou's gripping "Champion of the World."

What to Emphasize

Discovery of Details

Whether you tell of your own experience or of someone else's, even if it is brief, you need a whole story to tell. If the story is complex, do some searching and discovering in writing. One trusty method to test your memory (or to make sure you have all the necessary elements of a story) is that of a news reporter. Ask yourself:

- **What happened?**
- **Who took part?**
- **When?**
- **Where?**
- **Why did it happen?**
- **How did it happen?**

Journalists call this handy list of questions "the five *W*'s and the *H*." The *H* — *how* — isn't merely another way of asking what happened. It means: in exactly what way or under what circumstances? If the event was a break-in, how was it done — with an ax or with a bulldozer?

FOCUS ON VERBS

Narration depends heavily on verbs to clarify and enliven events. Strong verbs sharpen meaning and encourage you to add other informative details:

WEAK   The wind made an awful noise.

STRONG   The wind roared around the house and rattled the trees.

Forms of *make* (as in the example above) and forms of *be* (as in the next example) can sap the life from narration:

WEAK   The noises were alarming to us.

STRONG   The noises alarmed us.

Verbs in the ACTIVE VOICE (the subject does the action) usually pack more power into fewer words than verbs in the PASSIVE VOICE (the subject is acted upon):

WEAK PASSIVE   We were besieged in the basement by the wind, as the water at our feet was swelled by the rain.

STRONG ACTIVE   The wind besieged us in the basement, as the rain swelled the water at our feet.

While strengthening verbs, also ensure that they're consistent in tense. The tense you choose for relating events, present or past, should not shift unnecessarily:

INCONSISTENT TENSES   We held a frantic conference to consider our options. It takes only a minute to decide to stay put.

CONSISTENT TENSE   We held a frantic conference to consider our options. It took only a minute to decide to stay put.

See page 57 for further discussion of passive versus active verbs and page 259 for advice on avoiding shifts in tense.

Scene versus Summary

If you have prepared well—searching your memory or doing some research—you'll have far more information on hand than you can use in your narrative. You'll need to choose carefully, to pick out just those events and details that will accomplish your purpose with your readers.

A key decision is to choose between the two main strategies of narration:

- **Tell a story by** SCENE, visualizing each event as vividly and precisely as if you were there. Think of the scene as if it were in a film, with your reader sitting before the screen. This is the strategy Maya Angelou uses in her account of a tense crowd's behavior as, jammed into a small-town store, they listen to a fight broadcast (in "Champion of the World"). Instead of just mentioning people, you portray them. You recall dialog as best you can, or you invent some that could have been spoken. You include DESCRIPTION (a mode of writing to be dealt with fully in the next chapter). You might prolong one scene for an entire essay, or you could draw a scene in only two or three sentences (as Scott Beltran does in his police log).

- **Tell a story by** SUMMARY, relating events concisely. Instead of depicting people and their surroundings in great detail, you set down just the essentials of what happened. Such is the strategy Naomi Shihab Nye uses in "Museum" to tell of her misadventures in a new neighborhood as a teenager. Most of us employ this method in the everyday stories we tell, for it takes less time and fewer words. When chosen well, the economy of a story told in summary may be as effective as the lavish detail of a story told in scenes.

As always, your choice of a strategy depends on your purpose and audience. Whether to flesh out a scene fully, how much detail to include — these choices depend on what you seek to do and on how much your readers need to know to follow you. You may find that you want to use both strategies in telling a single story, passing briskly from one scene to the next, distilling events of lesser importance. Were you to write, let's say, the story of your grandfather's emigration from Cuba, you might just summarize his decision to leave Cuba and his settlement in Florida. These summaries could frame and emphasize a detailed telling of the events that you consider essential and most interesting — his nighttime escape, his harrowing voyage in a small boat, his surprising welcome by immigration authorities.

Dialog

In this book we are primarily concerned with the kind of writing you do every day in college: nonfiction prose in which you explain ideas, organize information you have learned, analyze other people's ideas, or argue a case. One essential narrative technique you aren't likely to use much in academic writing is DIALOG — reported speech, in quotation marks. But in personal stories especially, dialog is an invaluable tool for advancing the narrative and revealing characters' feelings. As all the authors in this chapter demonstrate with their well-told tales, spoken words recorded on the page make people and events come alive in a way that is uniquely engaging for readers.

Organization

In any kind of narration, the simplest approach is to set down events in CHRONOLOGICAL ORDER, following the sequence in which they occurred. To do so is to have your story already organized for you.

Chronological order is an excellent pattern to follow unless you can see some special advantage in violating it. Ask: What am I trying to do? If you are trying to capture your readers' attention right away, you might begin *in medias res* (Latin, "in the middle of things") and open with a colorful, dramatic event, even though it took place late in the chronology. If trying for dramatic effect, you might save the most exciting or impressive event for last, even though it actually happened early. By this means, you can keep your readers in suspense for as long as possible. (You can return to earlier events in a FLASHBACK, an earlier scene recalled.) Let your purpose be your guide.

No matter what order you choose, either following chronology or departing from it, make sure your audience can follow it. The sequence of events has to be clear. This calls for TRANSITIONS that mark time, whether they are brief phrases that point out exactly when each event happened ("seven years later," "a moment earlier") or whole sentences that announce an event and clearly locate it in time ("Passing by the gym on Friday evening, I noticed the sign: 'Go Three Minutes with the Masked Samurai and Win $500.'"). See *Transitions* in the Glossary for a list of possibilities.

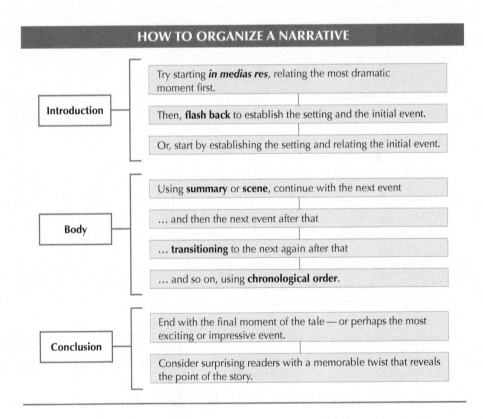

HOW TO ORGANIZE A NARRATIVE

Introduction

- Try starting *in medias res*, relating the most dramatic moment first.
- Then, **flash back** to establish the setting and the initial event.
- Or, start by establishing the setting and relating the initial event.

Body

- Using **summary** or **scene**, continue with the next event
- … and then the next event after that
- … **transitioning** to the next again after that
- … and so on, using **chronological order**.

Conclusion

- End with the final moment of the tale — or perhaps the most exciting or impressive event.
- Consider surprising readers with a memorable twist that reveals the point of the story.

> ### CHECKLIST FOR REVIEWING AND REVISING A NARRATIVE
>
> ✔ **Thesis.** What is the point of the narrative? Is it clear to readers by the end? Even if the story doesn't have a thesis statement, it should focus on a central idea. If you can't risk readers' misunderstanding—if, for instance, you're using narration to support an argument or explain a concept—then have you stated your thesis outright?
>
> ✔ **Point of view.** Is the narrator's position in the story appropriate for your purpose, and is it consistent throughout? Check for awkward or confusing shifts in point of view (subjective or objective; first or third person) and in the tenses of verbs (present to past or vice versa).
>
> ✔ **Selection of events.** Does the narrative focus on those events best suited to your audience and purpose? Tell the important parts of the story in the greatest detail. Summarize the less important, connective events.
>
> ✔ **Organization.** If the organization is not strictly chronological (first event to last), is there a compelling reason for altering it? If you start somewhere other than the beginning of the story or if you use flashbacks at any point, how will readers benefit?
>
> ✔ **Transitions.** Are there sufficient transitions to help clarify the order of events and their duration?
>
> ✔ **Dialog.** If the draft includes dialog, quoting participants in the story, is it appropriate for your purpose? Is it concise, telling only the important, revealing lines? Does the language sound like spoken English?
>
> ✔ **Verbs.** Do strong, active verbs move the narrative from event to event? Are verb tenses consistent?

STUDENT CASE STUDY: A POLICE LOG

What is it like to work in law enforcement? What takes place on a typical shift? What procedures are the police expected to follow, and why? To learn the answers to such questions, criminal justice students — and sometimes civilians — are often given the opportunity to ride along on patrol with seasoned officers and observe their activities.

Whatever else the risks and rewards of the job, policing involves a good deal of paperwork. Every incident must be recorded in writing — sometimes in formal reports, but more often in simple activity logs. Kept by all police departments and often published (or excerpted) in local newspapers, such logs provide straightforward public records of calls for help, motor vehicle stops, interactions with suspected criminals, and similar events. Always in chronological order, these narratives are generally presented as briefly and objectively as possible, written in the past tense and third-person point of view, and limited to the facts of each case: what happened, who was involved, where and when the events took place. Even so, as novelist Brian Doyle observes (p. 199), police logs offer some of the most engaging writing produced for general readers.

For an introductory criminal justice class at Lone Star College–Montgomery in Texas, student Scott Beltran went on a Saturday-night ride-along with the Crime Reduction Unit (CRU) of the Houston Police Department. Like the officers themselves, he kept an activity log through the shift. He also ANALYZED each event to better understand the experience. The final report he wrote and turned in to his instructor is excerpted on the following pages.

2000: CRU Roll Call. Two Sergeants take muster to make sure all officers are present and accounted for. After muster they discuss any intelligence on open cases they're actively investigating, and then they formulate a strategy to decide what part of town to focus their efforts. . . .

Narrative opens with beginning of shift

Chronological order

2030–2130: Officer Smith and I teamed up with one other unit and began conducting sweeps of previously identified drug trafficking locations. . . . During these sweeps, the officers were on alert for any type of suspicious activity, such as loitering, and they approached everyone in the area for at least some sort of brief questioning, but almost no one was detained or arrested. Officer Smith explained that these sweeps were done not only to make arrests, but also to establish HPD's presence in high-crime areas and to get the word out that Houston Police are proactively working to stop crime.

Time markers (in military time) clarify sequence and pace of events

Narration by summary

2200: We responded to an "officer needs assistance" call in the 800 block of N. Shepherd Drive. When we arrived there was one other unit on the scene; they already had two males and a female in custody. One male and the female were being detained for possession of crack cocaine, and the other male was being held for a parole violation warrant. After some investigation . . . it was determined that there were possibly more drugs in the suspect's apartment. The officers asked for, and were granted, consent to search the apartment. The officers asked the suspect to sign a "Consent to Search" form, which she did voluntarily.

Narration by scene

Past tense

This was witnessed and signed by two other officers. After a
quick search of the residence, the officers located a small amount
of marijuana, a chemical mixing beaker, and a hot plate that
appeared to have been used to cook, or make drugs. These items
were seized and the suspects were charged with possession of a
controlled substance. . . . All three suspects were transported to
the central police station in downtown Houston. . . .

Objective, third-person point of view

0030: Officer Smith initiated a stop of a black Dodge Charger for
the windows being tinted too dark. While running the driver's
license through the system he determined that the driver was
wanted out of Louisiana for a felony warrant, but the warrant
stipulated arrest-in-state only. Officer Smith attempted to
contact the agency that issued the warrant to determine if they
wanted him to make the arrest. While he was waiting for the
Louisiana agency to return his phone call, Officer Smith made
contact with the passenger, the owner of the vehicle, and got
consent to search the car. A search was completed and nothing
illegal was found. Because he still hadn't gotten in touch with
a supervisor in Louisiana, he took down all of the suspect's
information and released him. . . .

Narration by scene

0400: While traveling northbound we came upon a vehicle
stopped at a red light in the 6500 block of the Gulf Freeway.
With our windows rolled up we could still easily hear the
vehicle's stereo system playing at a high volume. Officer Smith
initiated a stop of the vehicle for violation of a city noise
ordinance. After the vehicle pulled off the road we observed the
driver making obvious furtive gestures while reaching toward
the passenger seat. Officer Smith made contact with the driver
and noticed that he was acting very nervous and appeared to
be under the influence of some type of stimulant. Officer Smith
removed the driver from the vehicle to investigate further. The
driver admitted that he had been using cocaine and that he had
a small amount still in the car. . . . Officer Smith placed a call
to the District Attorney's office to make sure they would accept
charges. The DA did accept the charges and the suspect was
charged with Felony Possession of a Controlled Substance and
booked into the central police station.

Narration by scene

0530: All of the Officers in the CRU met back at the station for
an end of shift muster and de-briefing.

Narration concludes
with the end of shift

AMY TAN

Amy Tan is a gifted storyteller whose first novel, *The Joy Luck Club* (1989), met with critical acclaim and huge success. The relationships it details between immigrant Chinese mothers and their Chinese American daughters came from her firsthand experience. Tan was born in 1952 in Oakland, California, the daughter of immigrants who had fled China's civil war in the late 1940s. She majored in English and linguistics at San José State University, where she received a BA in 1973 and an MA in 1974. After two more years of graduate study, Tan became a consultant in language development for disabled children and then a freelancer writing reports and speeches for business corporations. Bored with such work, she began writing fiction to explore her ethnic ambivalence and to find her voice. Since *The Joy Luck Club*, Tan has published several more novels—most recently *The Valley of Amazement* (2013)—as well as two children's books, the essay collection *The Opposite of Fate* (2003), and *Where the Past Begins* (2017), a memoir. She is also a founding member of the Rock Bottom Remainders, a "literary garage band" made up of popular writers.

Fish Cheeks

In Tan's novel *The Bonesetter's Daughter* (2001), one of the characters says, "Good manners are not enough. . . . They are not the same as a good heart." Much of Tan's writing explores those tensions between keeping up appearances and having true intentions. In the brief narrative that follows, the author deftly portrays the contradictory feelings of a girl with feet in different cultures. The essay first appeared in *Seventeen*, a magazine for teenage girls and young women, in 1987.

For another entertaining story about a cultural misunderstanding, read the next essay, Naomi Shihab Nye's "Museum."

I fell in love with the minister's son the winter I turned fourteen. He was not Chinese, but as white as Mary in the manger. For Christmas I prayed for this blond-haired boy, Robert, and a slim new American nose.

When I found out that my parents had invited the minister's family over for Christmas Eve dinner, I cried. What would Robert think of our shabby Chinese Christmas? What would he think of our noisy Chinese relatives who lacked proper American manners? What terrible disappointment would he feel upon seeing not a roasted turkey and sweet potatoes but Chinese food?

On Christmas Eve I saw that my mother had outdone herself in creating 3
a strange menu. She was pulling black veins out of the backs of fleshy prawns.
The kitchen was littered with appalling mounds of raw food: A slimy rock
cod with bulging eyes that pleaded not to be thrown into a pan of hot oil.
Tofu, which looked like stacked wedges of rubbery white sponges. A bowl
soaking dried fungus back to life. A plate of squid, their backs crisscrossed
with knife markings so they resembled bicycle tires.

And then they arrived—the minister's family and all my relatives in a 4
clamor of doorbells and rumpled Christmas packages. Robert grunted hello,
and I pretended he was not worthy of existence.

Dinner threw me deeper into despair. My relatives licked the ends of their 5
chopsticks and reached across the table, dipping them into the dozen or so
plates of food. Robert and his family waited patiently for platters to be passed
to them. My relatives murmured with pleasure when my mother brought out
the whole steamed fish. Robert grimaced. Then my father poked his chopsticks just below the fish eye and plucked out the soft meat. "Amy, your favorite," he said, offering me the tender fish cheek. I wanted to disappear.

At the end of the meal my father leaned back and belched loudly, thank- 6
ing my mother for her fine cooking. "It's a polite Chinese custom to show you
are satisfied," explained my father to our astonished guests. Robert was looking down at his plate with a reddened face. The minister managed to muster
up a quiet burp. I was stunned into silence for the rest of the night.

After everyone had gone, my mother said to me, "You want to be the 7
same as American girls on the outside." She handed me an early gift. It was a
miniskirt in beige tweed. "But inside you must always be Chinese. You must
be proud you are different. Your only shame is to have shame."

And even though I didn't agree with her then, I knew that she under- 8
stood how much I had suffered during the evening's dinner. It wasn't until
many years later—long after I had gotten over my crush on Robert—that I
was able to fully appreciate her lesson and the true purpose behind our particular menu. For Christmas Eve that year, she had chosen all my favorite foods.

Journal Writing

Do you sympathize with the shame Tan feels because of her family's differences from
their non-Chinese guests? Or do you think she should have been more proud to share
her family's customs? Think of an occasion when, for whatever reason, you were
acutely aware of being different. How did you react? Did you try to hide your difference in order to fit in, or did you reveal or celebrate your uniqueness?

Questions on Meaning

1. Why does Tan cry when she finds out that the boy she is in love with is coming to dinner?

2. Why does Tan's mother go out of her way to prepare a disturbingly traditional Chinese dinner for her daughter and guests? What one sentence best sums up the lesson Tan was not able to understand until years later?

3. How does the fourteen-year-old Tan feel about her Chinese background? about her mother?

4. What is Tan's PURPOSE in writing this essay? Does she just want to entertain readers, or might she have a weightier goal?

Questions on Writing Strategy

1. How does Tan draw the reader into her story right from the beginning?

2. How does Tan use TRANSITIONS both to drive and to clarify her narrative?

3. What is the IRONY of the last sentence of the essay?

4. **OTHER METHODS**   Paragraph 3 is a passage of pure DESCRIPTION. Why does Tan linger over the food? What is the EFFECT of this paragraph?

Questions on Language

1. The simile about Mary in the second sentence of the essay is surprising. Why? Why is it amusing? (See FIGURES OF SPEECH in the Glossary for a definition of *simile*.)

2. How does the narrator's age affect the TONE of this essay? Give EXAMPLES of language particularly appropriate to a fourteen-year-old.

3. In which paragraph does Tan use strong verbs most effectively?

4. Make sure you know the meanings of the following words: prawns, tofu (par. 3); clamor (4); grimaced (5); muster (6).

Suggestions for Writing

1. **FROM JOURNAL TO ESSAY**   Using Tan's essay as a model, write a brief narrative based on your journal sketch about a time when you felt different from others. Try to imitate the way Tan integrates the external events of the dinner with her own feelings about what is going on. Your story may be humorous, like Tan's, or more serious.

2. Take a perspective like that of the minister's son, Robert: Write a narrative essay about a time when you had to adjust to participating in a culture different from your own. It could be a meal, a wedding or other rite of passage, a religious ceremony, a trip to another country. What did you learn from your experience, about yourself and others?

3. **CRITICAL WRITING**   From this essay one can INFER two very different sets of
   ASSUMPTIONS about the extent to which immigrants should seek to integrate
   themselves into the culture of their adopted country. Take either of these positions, in favor of or against assimilation (cultural integration), and make an
   ARGUMENT for your case.

4. **CONNECTIONS**   Both Amy Tan and Naomi Shihab Nye, in "Museum" (next
   page), write about embarrassment, but their POINTS OF VIEW are not the same:
   Tan's is a teenager's lament about not fitting in; Nye's is an adult's celebration of
   a past mistake. In an essay, ANALYZE the two authors' uses of narration to convey
   their perspectives. What details do they focus on? What internal thoughts do
   they report? Is one essay more effective than the other? Why, or why not?

NAOMI SHIHAB NYE

Naomi Shihab Nye is an accomplished writer of poetry, fiction, and prose for young readers and adults alike. Born in 1952 in St. Louis, Missouri, she earned a BA in English and world religions from Trinity University in 1974 and teaches as a visiting writer at schools and colleges across the country. Growing up, Nye was enchanted by the lyricism of her father's Palestinian folktales and her mother's American lullabies; she published her first poem in a children's magazine when she was seven years old. Since then, Nye's entranced and entrancing writing has appeared regularly in *The Horn Book, The Texas Observer, World Literature Today,* and other magazines and in her wide-ranging books, including *Habibi* (1997), a young-adult novel based on her own time living in Jerusalem as a teenager; *Sitti's Secrets* (1994) and *Benito's Dream Bottle* (1995), picture books for children; and *Voices in the Air* (2018), poems for young adults. Nye has also compiled or translated several anthologies of world and student poetry, among them *This Same Sky* (1992) and *Salting the Ocean* (2000). A former chancellor of the Academy of American Poets, she lives in San Antonio, Texas, and enjoys singing.

Museum

Themes of human connection and cultural exchange run throughout Nye's work. In this story from *Honeybee: Poems and Short Prose* (2008), she leads us fleeing giddily from an honest mistake. Like all of her writing, this romp shows Nye's unparalleled exuberance for everyday life and her skill at expressing it.

The preceding essay, Amy Tan's "Fish Cheeks," also tells a tale of embarrassment.

I was seventeen, and my family had just moved to San Antonio. A local   1 magazine featured an alluring article about a museum called the McNay, an old mansion once the home of an eccentric many-times-married watercolorist named Marian Koogler McNay. She had deeded it to the community to become a museum upon her death. I asked my friend Sally, who drove a cute little convertible and had moved to Texas a year before we did, if she wanted to go there. Sally said, "Sure." She was a good friend that way. We had made up a few words in our own language and could dissolve into laughter just by saying them. Our mothers thought we were a bit odd. On a sunny Saturday afternoon, we drove over to Broadway. Sally asked, "Do you have the address of this place?" "No," I said, "just drive very slowly and I'll recognize it, there was a picture in the magazine." I peered in both directions and pointed, saying, "There, there it is, pull in!" The parking lot under some palm trees was pretty empty. We entered, excited. The museum was free. Right away, the spirit of the arched doorways, carved window frames, and elegant artwork overtook us. Sally went left; I went right. A group of people seated in some chairs in the lobby stopped talking and stared at us.

"May I help you?" a man said. "No," I said. "We're fine." I didn't like to   2
talk to people in museums. Tours and docents got on my nerves. What if they talked a long time about a painting you weren't that interested in? I took a deep breath, and moved on to another painting—fireworks over a patio in Mexico, maybe? There weren't very good tags in this museum. In fact, there weren't any. I stood back and gazed. Sally had gone upstairs. The people in the lobby had stopped chatting. They seemed very nosy, keeping their eyes on me with irritating curiosity. What was their problem? I turned down a hallway. Bougainvilleas and azaleas pressed up right against the windows. Maybe we should have brought a picnic. Where was the Moorish courtyard? I saw some nice sculptures in another room, and a small couch. This would be a great place for reading. Above the couch hung a radiant print by Paul Klee,[1] my favorite artist, blues and pinks merging softly in his own wonderful way. I stepped closer. Suddenly I became aware of a man from the lobby standing behind me in the doorway.

"Where do you think you are?" he asked. I turned sharply. "The McNay   3
Art Museum!" He smiled then, and shook his head. "Sorry to tell you. The McNay is three blocks over, on New Braunfels Street. Take a right when you go out of our driveway, then another right." "What is this place?" I asked, still confused. He said, "Well, we thought it was our home." My heart jolted. I raced past him to the bottom of the staircase and called out, "Sally! Come down immediately! Urgent!" I remember being tempted to shout something in our private language, but we didn't have a word for this. Sally came to the top of the stairs smiling happily and said, "You have to come up here, there's some really good stuff! And there are old beds too!" "No, Sally, no," I said, as if she were a dog, or a baby. "Get down here. Speed it up. This is an emergency." She stepped elegantly down the stairs as if in a museum trance, looking puzzled. I just couldn't tell her out loud in front of those people what we had done. I actually pushed her toward the front door, waving my hand at the family in

---

[1] Paul Klee (1879–1940) was a Swiss artist in the German Expressionist school, known for his childish yet sophisticated imagery. —EDS.

the chairs, saying, "Sorry, ohmygod, please forgive us, you have a really nice place." Sally stared at me in the parking lot. When I told her, she covered her mouth and doubled over with laughter, shaking. We were still in their yard. I imagined them inside looking out the windows at us. She couldn't believe how long they let us look around without saying anything, either. "That was really friendly of them!" "Get in the car," I said sternly. "This is mortifying."

The real McNay was fabulous, splendid, but we felt a little nervous the 4 whole time we were there. Van Gogh, Picasso, Tamayo.[2] This time, there were tags. This time, we stayed together, in case anything else weird happened.

We never told anyone. 5

Thirty years later, a nice-looking woman approached me in a public place. 6 "Excuse me," she said. "I need to ask a strange question. Did you ever, by any chance, enter a residence, long ago, thinking it was the McNay Museum?"

Thirty years later, my cheeks still burned. "Yes. But how do you know? I 7 never told anyone."

"That was my home. I was a teenager sitting with my family talking in 8 the living room. Before you came over, I never realized what a beautiful place I lived in. I never felt lucky before. You thought it was a museum. My feelings changed about my parents after that too. They had good taste. I have always wanted to thank you."

Journal Writing

Why do you suppose Nye remembers in such vivid detail a minor event that happened more than thirty years ago? What small embarrassments or misadventures from your youth seem momentous even now? List these incidents, along with some notes about their importance.

Questions on Meaning

1. What is Nye's PURPOSE in this essay? Obviously, she wants to entertain readers, but does she have another purpose as well?

2. How does Nye explain why she and her friend walked into the home of strangers and wandered around? What do you imagine the family thought was going on?

---

[2] All groundbreaking modern artists. Cubist Pablo Picasso (1881–1973) was Spanish; Post-Impressionist Vincent van Gogh (1853–90) was Dutch; Surrealist Rufino Tamayo (1899–1991) was Mexican. —Eds.

3. What does the incident represent for Nye? What does it represent for the daughter of the household? How did the teenager's feelings about herself and her parents change after the other teenagers left the house, and why?

4. In your own words, try to express Nye's THESIS, or the moral of her story.

Questions on Writing Strategy

1. Does Nye narrate primarily by summary or by scene? How effective do you find her choice?

2. Discuss the author's POINT OF VIEW. Is her perspective that of a seventeen-year-old or that of an adult writer reflecting on her experience?

3. Nye writes poetry and books both for children and for adult readers. Who seems to be the intended AUDIENCE for this story? Why do you think so?

4. **OTHER METHODS**   "Museum" implicitly COMPARES AND CONTRASTS Nye's and the family's appreciation for luxury and fine art. What are some of the differences (and similarities) that Nye implies?

Questions on Language

1. Look up any of the following words that you don't already know: eccentric (par. 1); docents, bougainvilleas, azaleas, Moorish (2); mortifying (3).

2. Nye uses short and simple sentences through most of this essay. Why do you suppose that is? What does "Museum" gain (or lose) from lack of sentence variety? (If necessary, see pp. 57–61 and 164 on sentence structure.)

3. How does Nye use DIALOG to make the story easy to follow?

4. "Our mothers thought we were a bit odd," Nye writes in the first paragraph. Pick out a few other instances of understatement in the essay. What is their effect? (For an explanation of *understatement*, look under FIGURES OF SPEECH in the Glossary.)

Suggestions for Writing

1. **FROM JOURNAL TO ESSAY**   Choose one embarrassing incident from the list of experiences you wrote for your journal (p. 83), and narrate the incident as vividly as you can. Include the details: Where did the event take place? What did people say? How were they dressed? What was the weather like? Follow Nye's model in putting CONCRETE IMAGES to work for an idea, in this case an idea about the significance of the incident to you then and now.

2. Nye and her friend were clearly amused when they discovered their mistake, but entering a private home uninvited — even unintentionally — can have serious consequences. Many states, including Texas, authorize homeowners to use deadly force against intruders regardless of immediate threat to their own safety. Write a serious argumentative essay that addresses the issue of gun rights and self-defense. To what extent should homeowners be allowed to shoot first and ask questions later in the case of home invasion? What about someone on the

street who simply feels threatened? Under what circumstances, if any, should personal freedoms be limited in the name of public safety? (You might want to do some research on what's known as the "castle doctrine" and on "stand your ground" laws to learn more about the issue.) Be sure to include evidence to support your opinion and to ARGUE your position calmly and rationally. You could, if you wish, include ANECDOTES—whether based on Nye's story or other incidents you know of—to help develop your argument.

3. **CRITICAL WRITING**   Using your answer to the second Question on Meaning (p. 83) as a starting point, tell Nye's story from the father's or the daughter's point of view. What do you imagine they were talking about when Naomi and Sally walked in? What did they think was happening? Were they amused, or do you suppose they felt annoyed, even frightened? What lessons did they take from the incident? You could take a humorous approach, as Nye does, or you could choose to be more serious.

4. **CONNECTIONS**   Write an essay about the humor gained from IRONY, relying on Nye's essay and Amy Tan's "Fish Cheeks" (p. 77). Why is irony often funny? What qualities does self-effacing humor have? Quote and PARAPHRASE from Nye's and Tan's essays for your support.

Naomi Shihab Nye on Writing

In an interview with Nye for *Pif Magazine*, Rachel Barenblatt asked, "What is your advice to writers, especially young writers who are just starting out?" This was her response:

Number one: Read, Read, and then Read some more. Always Read. Find the voices that speak most to *you*. This is your pleasure and blessing, as well as responsibility!

It is crucial to make one's own writing circle—friends, either close or far, with whom you trade work and discuss it—as a kind of support system, place-of-conversation, and energy. Find those people, even a few, with whom you can share and discuss your works—then do it. Keep the papers flowing among you. Work does not get into the world by itself. We must help it. . . . Let that circle be sustenance.

There is so much goodness happening in the world of writing today. And there is plenty of *room* and appetite for new writers. I think there always was. Don't let anybody tell you otherwise. Attend all the readings you can, and get involved in giving some, if you like to do that. Be part of your own writing community. Often the first step in doing this is simply to let yourself become identified as One Who Cares About Writing!

My motto early on was "Rest and be kind, you don't have to prove any-thing"—Jack Kerouac's advice about writing—I still think it's true. But working always felt like resting to me.

The Bedford Reader on Writing

Naomi Shihab Nye's advice to beginning writers echoes our own. For more on how reading can make you a better writer, see Chapter 1 on Critical Reading. You can learn about the roles of AUDIENCE and PURPOSE in writing on pages 19–20 and 28–29. For additional tips on writing freely without trying "to prove anything," turn to "Drafting" on pages 33–38. And for guidelines on working with peer reviewers, in what Nye calls a "writing circle," see "Reviewing a Draft," pages 41–42.

JONATHAN BETHARDS

Jonathan Bethards was born in 1978 in Lodi, California, and grew up in nearby Stockton. After graduating from Lincoln High School he trained and worked as an emergency medical technician (EMT) until he was sidelined by an injury on the job and started taking classes at San Joaquin Delta College to seek ideas for a new career. A "big-time sports fan," Bethards enjoys the outdoors and photography.

Code Three

In this heart-pounding narrative, Bethards relates the experience of first responders on a particularly tense ambulance call. "Code Three" was featured in the 2015 edition of *Delta Winds*, San Joaquin Delta College's annual anthology of exemplary student writing.

The man's family stood around us in a circle; I could feel their eyes on us 1 as we worked feverishly under the blazing afternoon sun. "This isn't going to work," I thought to myself. I glanced over at my partner, Oscar, and I could tell he was thinking the same thing. We didn't have much time left until we had to call it, but neither of us was letting up yet. This was definitely not how I saw my first shift back from vacation going.

My time as an Emergency Medical Technician (EMT) on a 911 ambu- 2 lance may have lasted for only five years, but they were very interesting years. I will freely admit that a majority of our shifts were spent just hanging out at quarters; but some days we would just get slammed, and this was looking like one of those days.

After an afternoon full of the usual calls, mainly non-life threatening, 3 and with the temperature soaring in the low 100s, Oscar and I were ready for a short nap in the cool confines of our quarters. We were a few blocks away from our air-conditioned station when we heard exactly what we didn't want to hear: "Unit Ninety-Two, are you clear for a Code Three call?" I cringed as I picked up the microphone from the radio and responded, "Unit Ninety-Two is clear and available." Dispatch proceeded to have my unit and Stockton Fire Engine Six sent out to a "man down" call in the middle of the street. I told Dispatch we were en route and gunned the engine as Oscar flipped the sirens and lights on. Code Three driving isn't nearly as fun as it may look; legally we're only supposed to go fifteen miles per hour over the limit. We have to watch out for all the numbskulls and space cadets on the road as we navigate our way to the call.

We reached the scene at about the same time as the SFD; I quickly ran 4 around the back of the rig and threw the monitor, airway bag, and our main bag on the gurney. I yanked the gurney out of the rig and made my way through a large group of people standing around a man lying in the street. I looked down at my partner, who had been assessing the patient, and read his body language and hand signals. This was not going to be an easy call. The man, who was in his late fifties and had an extensive medical history, was non-responsive and had no discernable pulse. As I hooked him up to the monitor, we could all see why he was non-responsive: He was in respiratory arrest and ventricular fibrillation. In other words, this man was in a world of hurt.

My partner and the fire medic were getting ready to deploy the defibril- 5 lation paddles and the fire EMT was doing chest compressions as I readied an IV setup and prepared the epinephrine; I had been in this situation before and knew we would need these at a minimum. Upon seeing my partner apply gel to the paddles and the man's chest, a woman became hysterical. The fire captain was putting forth a valiant effort to restrain her but was failing. The rest of the family started to become increasingly confrontational and angry. "Why the hell aren't you doing anything?" I heard from behind me. "Get off your asses and FIX him or . . . or so help me I'll SUE you," screamed the woman, who was now engaged in some serious hand fighting with the captain. Now, clearly we were trying to help the patient, but when panic and love combine, a situation can change from stressful to violent in an instant.

The fire medic got the IV in on the first try and was now trying to get an 6 airway into the lungs. This was not an easy job as he had to keep stopping to clear the patient while Oscar defibrillated him, pushing another round of epinephrine into the IV, or holding the patient's increasingly agitated family members back so we could do our job. On his third attempt, the medic got an airway, and almost simultaneously we heard an unmistakable sound. It was the sweetest sound I think that I had ever heard. It was the slow but steady beeping of the patient's heart, represented by a beautiful normal sinus rhythm on our monitor.

Oscar and I, sweat pouring down our faces, exchanged a quick smile and 7 then looked over at the fire crew. They were equally soaked in sweat and were smiling even wider than we were. "Why did you stop?" screamed the woman. "Why are you all smiling like a bunch of jackasses? MY HUSBAND IS DYING!" The fire captain had finally had enough and gripped the woman by her fleshy arms. "Ma'am! Your husband isn't dying: We got him back!" That was it for the woman and her family; they all broke down and cried and started thanking us in between sobs.

The patient, though not out of the woods, was doing far better than he 8 was when we arrived on the scene; after all, he was breathing on his own and his heart, though slow, was beating on its own. I couldn't believe it; this was the first patient we'd revived who hadn't immediately crashed again. As we loaded him into the rig for transport to Saint Joseph's, he opened his eyes and tried to say something. "Sir," I said, "don't try to talk. You have a tube down your throat. You're going to be okay, and your family is going to meet us at the emergency room." Tears started to roll down the man's cheeks, and he looked me right in the eye. I could tell that he was trying to thank me. "You're welcome," I said as I choked back tears of my own and put my hand over his: "We were just doing our jobs, sir."

Journal Writing

At one point or another, most of us have had at least one interaction with emergency personnel—EMTs like Bethards, paramedics, hospital staff, police, firefighters, lifeguards, and the like. Think of one such instance in your life, either as the person needing help or as a bystander. In your journal, recall as much about the event as you can, using the five journalist's questions (p. 70) to prompt your memory. What happened, and where? Who was in trouble, and why? How did things turn out?

Questions on Meaning

1. What would you say is the writer's PURPOSE in this essay? Is it primarily to entertain readers with an exciting story, or does he seem to have another purpose as well? How can you tell?

2. What actually happened to the man to prompt a 911 call? Does Bethards provide enough explanation for readers to know? Is it necessary to understand the details of the patient's condition to understand the rest of the story?

3. Why did the situation threaten to become violent? How does Bethards explain the wife's behavior?

4. Where, if at all, does Bethards state a THESIS? In your own words, what is the controlling idea of his narrative?

Questions on Writing Strategy

1. What POINT OF VIEW does Bethards take as a narrator?

2. What is the EFFECT of Bethards's opening paragraph? Why does he begin his narrative in the middle?

3. "Code Three" is a particularly gripping student narrative. How does Bethards create SUSPENSE through the essay?

4. **OTHER METHODS**   Where does Bethards use PROCESS ANALYSIS to explain events for an AUDIENCE of laypeople not trained in medical procedures?

Questions on Language

1. Be sure you know how to define the following terms: confines, en route (par. 3); gurney, discernable, respiratory arrest, ventricular fibrillation (4); deploy, defibrillation, epinephrine, valiant (5); agitated (6).

2. Bethards mixes occupational JARGON and COLLOQUIAL EXPRESSIONS, such as when he writes, "He was in respiratory arrest and ventricular fibrillation. In other words, this man was in a world of hurt" (par. 4). Find a few additional examples. Is this use of language appropriate? Is it effective? Why, or why not?

3. Explain the contradiction in the concluding statement, "We were just doing our jobs, sir" (par. 8). Can you find other examples of paradox in what Bethards says? How is this paradox related to his apparent view of the job? (See FIGURES OF SPEECH in the Glossary for a definition of *paradox*.)

Suggestions for Writing

1. **FROM JOURNAL TO ESSAY**   Turn your journal notes into a narrative about an encounter with emergency providers from the perspective of a person needing help (or, if you weren't the person in trouble, from a bystander's point of view). Like Bethards does, try to convey the urgency of the situation and to build suspense so that readers care about the outcome.

2. In an essay that combines narration and process analysis, write about a memorable experience you have had at work or while volunteering. What was the job? Was the work anything like you expected? What moments stand out in your memory, and why? Try to use colorful language and specific details to help readers share in your experience.

3. **CRITICAL WRITING**   EVALUATE the effectiveness of Bethards's narrative. What do you think of his choice of details? his pacing? his TONE? How successful is the author's attempt to convey the tensions and rewards of working as an emergency responder? Did his story hold your interest? Does the essay have any weaknesses, in your view? Why, or why not?

4. **CONNECTIONS**   In his police "Ride-Along Report" (p. 75), Scott Beltran also presents a narrative based on the experiences of first responders, but he writes in a different GENRE for different reasons. In a paragraph, distill the events Bethards recounts into an objective activity log for the public record. Compare the two versions of his story, and then explain how genre, purpose, and audience influence the structure and effect of a narrative.

KUNAL NAYYAR

Kunal Nayyar is an actor and writer best known for his role as Dr. Rajesh Koothrappali on the television series *The Big Bang Theory* (2007–19). Born in 1981 in London, England, he grew up in New Delhi, India, where he attended an all-boys school and played competitive badminton. He came to the United States in 1999 to study marketing at the University of Portland in Oregon and stumbled into theater as a way to meet girls. Hooked on acting his freshman year, Nayyar completed a degree in business "as something to fall back on" in 2003 and went on to earn an MFA in acting from Temple University in 2006. In addition to *The Big Bang Theory* Nayyar has appeared on several other television shows, including the animated series *Fantasy Hospital* (2016) and *Sanjay and Craig* (2013–16); he has also performed in films, among them *The Scribbler* (2014), *Dr. Cabbie* (2014), and *Trolls* (2016), and in plays, notably Shakespeare's *Love's Labor Lost* (2006) and *Huck & Holden* (2006), for which he won a Garland award. In 2015 Nayyar published his first book: *Yes, My Accent Is Real: And Some Other Things I Haven't Told You*, a collection of light-hearted and quite often humorous autobiographical essays.

Kumar Ran a Car

In this essay Nayyar relates a regrettable episode from his time in college. As an undergraduate he worked a range of odd jobs, including a stint in house-keeping emptying Dumpsters and driving a maintenance truck. In expressing his remorse for faking his way into a better position in a computer lab, Nayyar hints at the ways acting has shaped his life and honed his ability to empathize.

The summer before my senior year I decided that I was done working 1 outdoors or collecting garbage. I wanted something indoors, preferably work you did while sitting on a chair, in a room with an air conditioner. I flipped through the student paper and saw an opening in the computer lab. *Perfect.* Except for the fact that I knew nothing about computers, everything about this job was appealing. I mean, I could turn one on, but I didn't know how to code. Or how to program. Or how to troubleshoot. All I knew was that if something goes wrong, you should probably unplug the computer for thirty seconds. But I thought, *Hey, I'm Indian, maybe I can just say that and they'll trust that I know what I'm doing.*

I interviewed with this quiet guy who wore glasses, named Dominick. 2 He was from China. His hair was perfectly parted to one side, polo buttoned all the way to the top, and he wore light brown khakis and Nike running sneakers.

"Hi, Kunal, nice to meet you," he said, in a soft, high-pitched voice that   3
sounded like an adorable old lady. I could tell right away that the poor guy
must have had a rough childhood.

"I am looking for some people to be computer lab managers. What are   4
your skills?"

"Troubleshooting, programming, Excel, PowerPoint," I said, dropping in   5
every piece of jargon I could think of.

"Mac or PC?"   6

"I can do Mac, I can do PC, I can do all Cs," I said, laughing.   7

"Can you give me more specifics?"   8

"You know how it is. I grew up in India. I've been taking apart computers   9
my whole life. I know how the computer *thinks*. I know how it moves. I'm
always one step ahead of it."

He nodded. The Indian thing really impressed him. "I like you. I'm going   10
to hire you."

We shook hands. Bingo!   11

"Given your advanced skill set, I'm going to give you a very special   12
project." He turned to the computer and opened up a software program I had
never seen. "The school is trying to integrate this new voice recognition software. I want you to figure it out, dissect it, and write an entire instruction
manual based on what you've learned."

"Cool, I'm on it." *Kill me now.*   13

So three days a week, four hours each shift, my job was to sit at the   14
computer and become an expert in this software. Given my advanced-skills
status, Dominick gave me my own computer lab—just one room with one
computer—so that I wouldn't be disturbed from my task. My job was to write
a thirty-page manual for software that made utterly no sense to me.

The program, essentially, was an early-early-early version of Siri.[1] Except   15
that it didn't really work and it had all these complicated menus and options
that I found insanely baffling. The first day I took the job very seriously.
I spoke into the microphone and compared what I said to the words that
appeared on the screen.

"The cat drank the cow's milk," I said.   16

On-screen: *Kangaroos in Australia are part of the binary world.*   17

It probably didn't help that I had an Indian accent.   18

I just sat there for hours, carefully repeating sentence after sentence,   19
watching as the monitor butchered every word. I would click menu options

---

[1] The voice-activated virtual assistant provided with Apple products such as the iPhone.
—EDS.

and the cursor would just keep blinking, confused. Maybe Raj[2] could have solved this puzzle if he'd existed then, but it was too much for Kunal.

I spent an entire day just getting the program to say my name correctly.   20

"Kunal Nayyar."   21

Kumar. Ran. A. Car.   22

Whatevs. I basically gave up on the project after a few days, and each   23 shift I would spend fifteen minutes on voice recognition, then the rest of the afternoon in *Yahoo!* chat rooms. Those were big in 2000. I loved that you could explore all these subcultures and just start chatting with people anonymously. My screen name was "Tan_Skinned_Man." I chatted with women all over the world and told them I was a professional tennis player.

"Kunal?" Dominick asked from outside the door. I always kept the door   24 locked.

"One minute," I said, alt-tabbing from the chat rooms and opening the   25 software.

"Why do you lock the door?"   26

"You know me. I can only focus when no one's disturbing me."   27

He clapped me on the shoulder. "I understand. Keep up the good work."   28

I felt a little bad for deceiving Dominick, and I also felt bad that he was   29 the butt of many of my jokes. I'm sorry to say, I made fun of his voice a lot. He also had something of a reputation as a mean boss, and I wasn't the only one doing imitations of him behind his back.

A week before the project was due, I still had absolutely nothing to show   30 for it. Just a blank Word document. "Do you mind showing me your progress?" Dominick asked.

"It's not perfect yet. And I only deliver perfect."   31

"No problem. I understand," he said, leaving me alone with the   32 cyber-tennis-chicks.

I realized I would soon be fired. So I decided, *Screw it, I'm just going to*   33 *write something.*

So I just started making stuff up.   34

"Once you press File, the Command Screen will open up."   35

"Use the right mouse button to initiate a conversation."   36

"Click the L button three times to indicate that you LOVE this software."   37 It was practically that bad.

The week passed and it was time to face the music. I would tell Dominick   38 that I'd been struggling, that I'd given it my damnedest, but it might be too faulty a system to properly document. Tail between my legs, I entered his office.

---

[2] Nayyar is referring to Rajesh Koothrappali, the fictional astrophysicist he played on *The Big Bang Theory* through its twelve-season run. —EDS.

"Kunal. I'm glad you came," he said, shooting me a hard look.   39

Shit. Did he find out about the *Yahoo!* chats?   40

"I just got an email from the university. I have some troubling news."   41

Shit. My scholarships.   42

Dominick took off his glasses. "The school has decided to recall the soft-   43
ware. It's not working properly. There are some disagreements with the licensor. So there will be no need for the manual."

"That's terrible."   44

"Kunal, I'm so sorry. I know how hard you've been working."   45

"It's okay," I said. "Whatever's best for the university."   46

"Should we take a look at what you've written so far?"   47

"Honestly, Dominick, given this development, I'm not sure I feel com-   48
fortable with that. Maybe it's best for me to shred all the documentation so
there's not a paper trail? What if someone sues or something?"

"Good point, good point. Do that," he said. "Because of your hard work   49
and commitment to this project, I'm going to promote you to lab manager of
the engineering building."

He gave me a raise, bumping me up to nine dollars an hour, which was   50
damn good money at the time. I would manage the school's flagship computer lab, the one that had just received the brand-new translucent Macs.

And as for the fact that I'm computer illiterate? Well . . . "Your only job   51
is to maintain the lab, make sure it's clean, manage the technicians," said
Dominick. "If anyone has a real problem with the new Macs, there will be a
specialist."

"Yeah, those new Macs, I've read up on them, they're a strange beast,"   52
I said.

"Exactly. Not even *I* know the ins and outs."   53

Amazingly, it turns out I was a pretty competent lab manager. I was good   54
with people, treated the employees with respect, and most important, was
excellent at getting someone else to solve the real problems. My lab even got
voted the most user-friendly lab in the university.

Maybe Dominick thought of me as a protégé of sorts. One night as I sat   55
on the stoop of my house strumming my guitar, I saw Dominick crossing the
street in front of me. He wore a red polo shirt buttoned to the top, and it was
a little weird seeing him outside the lab.

"Hey, Dominick," I called.   56

He hesitated for a second, and then came and joined me on the stoop.   57
"Play me a song, Kunal."

I could tell something was bothering him. He looked melancholy.   58

So I played him a melancholy tune. After I was done, he said, "Beautiful.   59
Play it one more time, please." So I did. As I was playing, Dominick began to

tear up. After I finished, he told me about how he missed his home in China, that he wished he could see his family, and that he often felt very alone.

"Many people think I'm an angry guy," he said. "That I fire people because   60
I'm cruel. But the truth is that I *have* to run a tight ship, because my education is on the line. If I don't have this job then I can't pay for my studies."

He wiped the tears from his cheeks. And I felt guilty, because I too had   61
made jokes and laughed at his expense. *Ha ha, Dominick with the high voice and the face that looks like an owl.*

"It's going to be okay, Dominick," I said, awkwardly patting him on the   62
back.

"Thanks," he said, suddenly embarrassed. He had opened the door and I   63
just didn't deliver my support.

"I'll see you around." he said sheepishly as he walked away.   64

"Righto," was all I could manage.   65

After he left, I found myself feeling empty. I was disappointed in myself   66
for not lending him more of a shoulder to cry on. I could have said that I understood what it was like to assimilate. Or that I too knew what it felt like to be away from home. I mean, it wasn't that long ago that I myself had worn the ill-fitting shirts and corduroy pants, and people made fun of me behind my back. I could have said all of this. I could have been his good friend. Instead, I just said, "Righto." And to be honest, I have no idea why.

Sometimes we have "time machine moments" where we wish we could   67
go back in time and fix our biggest mistakes. But sometimes we wish we could go back in time and fix the tiny ones, too.

Journal Writing

As a student, you probably work or have worked at a part-time or temporary job, whether for the money or for the experience or both. You might even work full time as you take classes. In your journal, reflect on the most memorable job you have had. What was the job? How did you get it? How did you feel about it, then and now? Did you learn anything in particular—about yourself or the working world—from it?

Questions on Meaning

1. How did Nayyar manage to get and keep a job for which he was utterly unqualified? What saved him from being discovered?

2. Does Nayyar have a THESIS? In which sentence or sentences does he state the point of his story most directly?

3. What "tiny" (par. 67) mistake did Nayyar make, and why does he regret it? What does his relationship with Dominick represent to him?

4. What would you say is the author's PURPOSE in this essay? Is it simply to inform readers about a job he had in college, or does he seem to have a different purpose (or purposes) in mind?

Questions on Writing Strategy

1. In describing his boss, Nayyar notes, twice, that Dominick wore a "polo shirt buttoned all the way to the top" (pars. 2, 55). Why is this detail important to the story? What is the effect of repeating it?

2. To whom does Nayyar seem to be writing? Why do you think so?

3. Nayyar digresses from strict chronological order toward the end of the essay. Why? What is the effect of ending not at the story's natural conclusion but with a flashback to an earlier episode?

4. **OTHER METHODS**   Where in the essay does Nayyar use DIVISION and PROCESS ANALYSIS to explain his job assignment? What was he supposed to be doing as a lab manager? Why is it significant that the focus of his task was voice recognition software?

Questions on Language

1. Be sure you know how to define the following words: integrate, dissect (par. 12); binary (17); subcultures (23); initiate (36); recall, licensor (43); flagship, translucent (50); protégé (55); melancholy (58, 59); assimilate (66).

2. Take note of Nayyar's use of COLLOQUIAL EXPRESSIONS such as "Kill me now" (par. 13) and "Righto" (65, 66). What similar expressions can you find, and what do they seem to have in common? What do they contribute to (or take away from) Nayyar's VOICE and the effectiveness of his narrative?

3. Why does Nayyar quote himself and Dominick so extensively? What would the narrative lose without this DIALOG?

4. How would you describe the overall TONE of this essay: wistful? detached? amused? something else? Point to some words and phrases that support your answer.

Suggestions for Writing

1. **FROM JOURNAL TO ESSAY**   Starting with your journal entry (p. 95) and using Nayyar's essay as a model, tell readers an engaging story about a memorable job you have had. Try, like Nayyar does, to intersperse SUMMARY with SCENE, outlining the generals of the job itself while using dialog and telling details to focus on a handful of representative episodes. Why does the job linger in your memory? What might readers find interesting about your experience? Be sure to have a

thesis that expresses the point of your story, as Nayyar does, whether you choose to state it outright or not.

2. The ability to empathize with other peoples' feelings is a key element of emotional intelligence, a relatively new concept that is often evoked in the fields of psychology and education to help people improve their work and life skills. Search your library catalog and databases for books and articles about emotional intelligence; then write a brief DEFINITION of the concept. Consider as well your own emotional intelligence and how you can improve it.

3. **CRITICAL WRITING** In an essay, ANALYZE the image that Nayyar presents of himself. Consider specific examples of his language and TONE, along with what he says about himself and his implied attitude toward cultural assimilation.

4. **CONNECTIONS** While Nayyar regrets talking about Dominick behind his back, Ben Healy suggests in "Gossip Is Good" (p. 411) that making jokes at Dominick's expense might actually have yielded some benefits for all of the students involved. Read Healy's essay, then using Nayyar's experience (and possibly your own) for evidence, agree or disagree with the author's central argument in favor of gossip.

Kunal Nayyar on Writing

At several points among the essays in *Yes, My Accent Is Real,* Kunal Nayyar offers standalone blurbs of commentary and quick observations about his life and his work. Below, his thoughts on using a word processor.

It drives me nuts when Microsoft Word shows me a green squiggly line under something I've written. It makes me want to reach through the computer screen and choke the life out of Microsoft Word. As if it were a person standing in my front yard challenging my ability to protect my family. Green squiggly. Huh, I know better than you, stupid machine corrector. I hate you. My sentences are perfection constructed, purely.

The Bedford Reader on Writing

Nayyar objects to the intrusiveness of his computer's automatic grammar checker, and who can blame him? Grammar checkers are notoriously bad at identifying problems and suggesting appropriate changes. For help recognizing errors and editing for sentence structure yourself, see "Fixing Common Errors," pages 59–61.

MAYA ANGELOU

Maya Angelou was born Marguerite Johnson in St. Louis in 1928. After an unpleasantly eventful youth by her account ("from a broken family, raped at eight, unwed mother at sixteen"), she went on to join a dance company, act in the off-Broadway play *The Blacks* and the television mini-series *Roots*, write several books of poetry, produce a TV documentary on African heritage, serve as a coordinator for the Southern Christian Leadership Conference, win the Presidential Medals of Arts and of Freedom, teach American studies at Wake Forest University, write and deliver the inaugural poem ("On the Pulse of Morning") for President Clinton, and be inducted into the National Women's Hall of Fame. Angelou is the author of thirty best-selling works but is probably best known for the six books of her searching, frank, and joyful autobiography—from *I Know Why the Caged Bird Sings* (1970) through *A Song Flung Up to Heaven* (2002). She died in 2014 at her home in Winston-Salem, North Carolina.

Champion of the World

"Champion of the World" is the nineteenth chapter in *I Know Why the Caged Bird Sings*; the title is a phrase taken from the chapter. Remembering her childhood, the writer tells how she and her older brother, Bailey, grew up in a town in Arkansas. The center of their lives was Grandmother and Uncle Willie's store. On the night of this story, in the late 1930s, the African American community gathers in the store to listen to a boxing match on the radio. Joe Louis, the "Brown Bomber," who was a hero to black people, is defending his heavyweight title against a white contender. (Louis successfully defended his title twenty-five times, a record that stands today.) Angelou's telling of the event both entertains us and explains what it was like to be African American in a certain time and place.

The last inch of space was filled, yet people continued to wedge themselves along the walls of the Store. Uncle Willie had turned the radio up to its last notch so that youngsters on the porch wouldn't miss a word. Women sat on kitchen chairs, dining-room chairs, stools, and upturned wooden boxes. Small children and babies perched on every lap available and men leaned on the shelves or on each other.

The apprehensive mood was shot through with shafts of gaiety, as a black sky is streaked with lightning.

"I ain't worried 'bout this fight. Joe's gonna whip that cracker like it's open season."

"He gone whip him till that white boy call him Momma."

At last the talking finished and the string-along songs about razor blades 5
were over and the fight began.

"A quick jab to the head." In the Store the crowd grunted. "A left to the 6
head and a right and another left." One of the listeners cackled like a hen
and was quieted.

"They're in a clinch, Louis is trying to fight his way out." 7

Some bitter comedian on the porch said, "That white man don't mind 8
hugging that niggah now, I betcha."

"The referee is moving in to break them up, but Louis finally pushed the 9
contender away and it's an uppercut to the chin. The contender is hanging
on, now he's backing away. Louis catches him with a short left to the jaw."

A tide of murmuring assent poured out the door and into the yard. 10

"Another left and another left. Louis is saving that mighty right . . ." 11
The mutter in the Store had grown into a baby roar and it was pierced by the
clang of a bell and the announcer's "That's the bell for round three, ladies and
gentlemen."

As I pushed my way into the Store I wondered if the announcer gave 12
any thought to the fact that he was addressing as "ladies and gentlemen" all
the Negroes around the world who sat sweating and praying, glued to their
"Master's voice."[1]

There were only a few calls for RC Colas, Dr Peppers, and Hires root beer. 13
The real festivities would begin after the fight. Then even the old Christian
ladies who taught their children and tried themselves to practice turning the
other cheek would buy soft drinks, and if the Brown Bomber's victory was a
particularly bloody one they would order peanut patties and Baby Ruths also.

Bailey and I laid the coins on top of the cash register. Uncle Willie didn't 14
allow us to ring up sales during a fight. It was too noisy and might shake up
the atmosphere. When the gong rang for the next round we pushed through
the near-sacred quiet to the herd of children outside.

"He's got Louis against the ropes and now it's a left to the body and a right 15
to the ribs. Another right to the body, it looks like it was low . . . Yes, ladies
and gentlemen, the referee is signaling but the contender keeps raining the
blows on Louis. It's another to the body, and it looks like Louis is going down."

My race groaned. It was our people falling. It was another lynching, yet 16
another Black man hanging on a tree. One more woman ambushed and
raped. A Black boy whipped and maimed. It was hounds on the trail of a man
running through slimy swamps. It was a white woman slapping her maid for
being forgetful.

---

[1] "His Master's Voice," accompanied by a picture of a little dog listening to a phonograph,
was a familiar advertising slogan. (The picture still appears on some RCA recordings.) —EDS.

The men in the Store stood away from the walls and at attention. Women 17 greedily clutched the babes on their laps while on the porch the shufflings and smiles, flirtings and pinching of a few minutes before were gone. This might be the end of the world. If Joe lost we were back in slavery and beyond help. It would all be true, the accusations that we were lower types of human beings. Only a little higher than apes. True that we were stupid and ugly and lazy and dirty and, unlucky and worst of all, that God Himself hated us and ordained us to be hewers of wood and drawers of water, forever and ever, world without end.

We didn't breathe. We didn't hope. We waited. 18

"He's off the ropes, ladies and gentlemen. He's moving towards the center 19 of the ring." There was no time to be relieved. The worst might still happen.

"And now it looks like Joe is mad. He's caught Carnera with a left hook 20 to the head and a right to the head. It's a left jab to the body and another left to the head. There's a left cross and a right to the head. The contender's right eye is bleeding and he can't seem to keep his block up. Louis is penetrating every block. The referee is moving in, but Louis sends a left to the body and it's an uppercut to the chin and the contender is dropping. He's on the canvas, ladies and gentlemen."

Babies slid to the floor as women stood up and men leaned toward the 21 radio.

"Here's the referee. He's counting. One, two, three, four, five, six, seven . . . 22 Is the contender trying to get up again?"

All the men in the store shouted, "no." 23

"—eight, nine, ten." There were a few sounds from the audience, but 24 they seemed to be holding themselves in against tremendous pressure.

"The fight is all over, ladies and gentlemen. Let's get the microphone 25 over to the referee . . . Here he is. He's got the Brown Bomber's hand, he's holding it up . . . Here he is . . ."

Then the voice, husky and familiar, came to wash over us — "The 26 winnah, and still heavyweight champeen of the world . . . Joe Louis."

Champion of the world. A Black boy. Some Black mother's son. He was 27 the strongest man in the world. People drank Coca-Colas like ambrosia and ate candy bars like Christmas. Some of the men went behind the Store and poured white lightning in their soft-drink bottles, and a few of the bigger boys followed them. Those who were not chased away came back blowing their breath in front of themselves like proud smokers.

It would take an hour or more before the people would leave the Store 28 and head for home. Those who lived too far had made arrangements to stay in town. It wouldn't do for a Black man and his family to be caught on a lonely country road on a night when Joe Louis had proved that we were the strongest people in the world.

Journal Writing

How do you respond to the group identification and solidarity that Angelou writes about in this essay? What groups do you belong to, and how do you know you're a member? Consider groups based on race, ethnic background, religion, sports, hobbies, politics, friendship, kinship, or any other ties.

Questions on Meaning

1. What do you take to be the author's PURPOSE in telling this story?
2. What connection does Angelou make between the outcome of the fight and the pride of African Americans? To what degree do you think the author's view is shared by the others in the store listening to the broadcast?
3. To what extent are the statements in paragraphs 16 and 17 to be taken literally? What function do they serve in Angelou's narrative?
4. Primo Carnera was probably *not* the Brown Bomber's opponent on the night Maya Angelou recalls. Louis fought Carnera only once, on June 25, 1935, and it was not a title match. Does the author's apparent error detract from her story?

Questions on Writing Strategy

1. What details in the opening paragraphs indicate that an event of crucial importance is about to take place?
2. How does Angelou build up SUSPENSE in her account of the fight? At what point were you able to predict the winner?
3. Comment on the IRONY in Angelou's final paragraph.
4. What EFFECT does the author's use of direct quotation have on her narrative?
5. **OTHER METHODS**   Besides narration, Angelou also relies heavily on the method of DESCRIPTION. Analyze how narration depends on description in paragraph 27 alone.

Questions on Language

1. Explain what the author means by "string-along songs about razor blades" (par. 5).
2. Point to some examples in the essay of Angelou's use of strong verbs.
3. How does Angelou's use of NONSTANDARD ENGLISH contribute to her narrative?
4. Be sure you know the meanings of these words: apprehensive (par. 2); assent (10); ambushed, maimed (16); ordained (17); ambrosia, white lightning (27).

Suggestions for Writing

1. **FROM JOURNAL TO ESSAY**   From your journal entry, choose one of the groups you belong to and explore your sense of membership through a narrative that tells of

an incident that occurred when that sense was strong. Try to make the incident come alive for your readers with vivid details, dialog, and tight sequencing of events.

2. Write an essay based on some childhood experience of your own, still vivid in your memory.

3. **CRITICAL WRITING**   Angelou does not directly describe relations between African Americans and whites, yet her essay implies quite a lot. Write a brief essay about what you can INFER from the exaggeration of paragraphs 16–17 and the obliqueness of paragraph 28. Focus on Angelou's details and the language she uses to present them.

4. **CONNECTIONS**   Angelou's "Champion of the World" and Amy Tan's "Fish Cheeks" (p. 77) both tell stories of feeling like outsiders in a predominantly white America. COMPARE AND CONTRAST the two writers' perceptions of what sets them apart from the dominant culture. How does the event each reports affect that sense of difference? Use specific examples from both essays as your EVIDENCE.

Maya Angelou on Writing

Maya Angelou's writings have shown great variety: She did notable work as an autobiographer, poet, short-story writer, screenwriter, journalist, and song lyricist. Asked by interviewer Sheila Weller, "Do you start each project with a specific idea?" Angelou replied:

It starts with a definite subject, but it might end with something entirely different. When I start a project, the first thing I do is write down, in long-hand, everything I know about the subject, every thought I've ever had on it. This may be twelve or fourteen pages. Then I read it back through, for quite a few days, and find — given that subject — what its rhythm is. 'Cause everything in the universe has a rhythm. So if it's free form, it still has a rhythm. And once I hear the rhythm of the piece, then I try to find out what are the salient points that I must make. And then it begins to take shape.

I try to set myself up in each chapter by saying: "This is what I want to go from — from B to, say, G-sharp. Or from D to L." And then I find the hook. It's like the knitting, where, after you knit a certain amount, there's one thread that begins to pull. You know, you can see it right along the cloth. Well, in writing, I think: "Now where is that one hook, that one little thread?" It may be a sentence. If I can catch that, then I'm home free. It's the one that tells me where I'm going. It may not even turn out to be in the final chapter. I may throw it out later or change it. But if I follow it through, it leads me right out.

The Bedford Reader on Writing

What response would you give someone who asked, "Doesn't Angelou's approach to writing take more time and thought than it's worth?" Freewriting, or putting down many pages' worth of random thoughts before starting a project — as Angelou does and as we recommend on page 31 — may seem an excessive amount of toil. But Angelou invites the observation that the more work you do before you write, the easier it is once you begin writing in earnest. For our advice on discovering ideas about a SUBJECT, see pages 30–33. And for help on finding a "hook," or THESIS, for a narrative, turn to page 69 in this chapter.

SHIRLEY JACKSON

Shirley Jackson was a fiction writer best known for horror stories that probe the dark side of human nature and social behavior. But she also wrote humorously about domestic life, a subject she knew well as a wife and the mother of four children. Born in 1916 in California, Jackson moved as a teenager to upstate New York and graduated from Syracuse University in 1940. She started writing as a young girl and was highly disciplined and productive all her life. She began publishing stories in 1941, and eventually her fiction appeared in *The New Yorker*, *Harper's*, *Good Housekeeping*, and many other magazines. Her tales of family life appeared in two books, *Life among the Savages* (1953) and *Raising Demons* (1957). Her suspense novels, which were more significant to her, included *The Haunting of Hill House* (1959) and *We Have Always Lived in the Castle* (1962). After Jackson died in 1965, her husband, the literary critic Stanley Edgar Hyman, published two volumes of her stories, novels, and lectures: *The Magic of Shirley Jackson* (1966) and *Come Along with Me* (1968).

The Lottery

By far Jackson's best-known work and indeed one of the best-known short stories ever written, "The Lottery" first appeared in *The New Yorker* in 1948 to loud applause and louder cries of outrage. The time was just after World War II, when Nazi concentration camps and the dropping of atomic bombs had revealed the horrors of organized human cruelty. Jackson's husband, denying that her work purveyed "neurotic fantasies," argued instead that it was fitting "for our distressing world." Is the story still relevant today?

The morning of June 27th was clear and sunny, with the fresh warmth of 1 a full-summer day; the flowers were blossoming profusely and the grass was richly green. The people of the village began to gather in the square, between the post office and the bank, around ten o'clock; in some towns there were so many people that the lottery took two days and had to be started on June 26th, but in this village, where there were only about three hundred people, the whole lottery took less than two hours, so it could begin at ten o'clock in the morning and still be through in time to allow the villagers to get home for noon dinner.

The children assembled first, of course. School was recently over for the 2 summer, and the feeling of liberty sat uneasily on most of them; they tended to gather together quietly for a while before they broke into boisterous play, and their talk was still of the classroom and the teacher, of books and reprimands. Bobby Martin had already stuffed his pockets full of stones, and the other boys soon followed his example, selecting the smoothest and round-est stones; Bobby and Harry Jones and Dickie Delacroix—the villagers pro-nounced this name "Dellacroy"—eventually made a great pile of stones in one corner of the square and guarded it against the raids of the other boys. The girls stood aside, talking among themselves, looking over their shoulders at the boys, and the very small children rolled in the dust or clung to the hands of their older brothers or sisters.

Soon the men began to gather, surveying their own children, speaking 3 of planting and rain, tractors and taxes. They stood together, away from the pile of stones in the corner, and their jokes were quiet and they smiled rather than laughed. The women, wearing faded house dresses and sweaters, came shortly after their menfolk. They greeted one another and exchanged bits of gossip as they went to join their husbands. Soon the women, standing by their husbands, began to call to their children, and the children came reluc-tantly, having to be called four or five times. Bobby Martin ducked under his mother's grasping hand and ran, laughing, back to the pile of stones. His father spoke up sharply, and Bobby came quickly and took his place between his father and his oldest brother.

The lottery was conducted—as were the square dances, the teenage club, 4 the Halloween program—by Mr. Summers, who had time and energy to devote to civic activities. He was a round-faced, jovial man and he ran the coal busi-ness, and people were sorry for him, because he had no children and his wife was a scold. When he arrived in the square, carrying the black wooden box, there was a murmur of conversation among the villagers, and he waved and called, "Little late today, folks." The postmaster, Mr. Graves, followed him, car-rying a three-legged stool, and the stool was put in the center of the square and Mr. Summers set the black box down on it. The villagers kept their distance, leaving a space between themselves and the stool, and when Mr. Summers said, "Some of you fellows want to give me a hand?" there was a hesitation before two men, Mr. Martin and his oldest son, Baxter, came forward to hold the box steady on the stool while Mr. Summers stirred up the papers inside it.

The original paraphernalia for the lottery had been lost long ago, and 5 the black box now resting on the stool had been put into use even before Old Man Warner, the oldest man in town, was born. Mr. Summers spoke frequently to the villagers about making a new box, but no one liked to upset even as much tradition as was represented by the black box. There was a story that the present box had been made with some pieces of the box that had preceded it, the one that had been constructed when the first people settled down to make a village here. Every year, after the lottery, Mr. Summers began talking again about a new box, but every year the sub-ject was allowed to fade off without anything's being done. The black box grew shabbier each year; by now it was no longer completely black but splintered badly along one side to show the original wood color, and in some places faded or stained.

Mr. Martin and his oldest son, Baxter, held the black box securely on   6 the stool until Mr. Summers had stirred the papers thoroughly with his hand. Because so much of the ritual had been forgotten or discarded, Mr. Summers had been successful in having slips of paper substituted for the chips of wood that had been used for generations. Chips of wood, Mr. Summers had argued, had been all very well when the village was tiny, but now that the population was more than three hundred and likely to keep on growing, it was necessary to use something that would fit more easily into the black box. The night before the lottery, Mr. Summers and Mr. Graves made up the slips of paper and put them in the box, and it was then taken to the safe of Mr. Summers's coal company and locked up until Mr. Summers was ready to take it to the square next morning. The rest of the year, the box was put away, sometimes one place, sometimes another; it had spent one year in Mr. Graves's barn and another year underfoot in the post office, and sometimes it was set on a shelf in the Martin grocery and left there.

There was a great deal of fussing to be done before Mr. Summers declared   7 the lottery open. There were the lists to make up — of heads of families, heads of households in each family, members of each household in each family. There was the proper swearing-in of Mr. Summers by the postmaster, as the official of the lottery; at one time, some people remembered, there had been a recital of some sort, performed by the official of the lottery, a perfunctory, tuneless chant that had been rattled off duly each year; some people believed that the official of the lottery used to stand just so when he said or sang it, others believed that he was supposed to walk among the people, but years and years ago this part of the ritual had been allowed to lapse. There had been, also, a ritual salute, which the official of the lottery had had to use in addressing each person who came up to draw from the box, but this also had changed with time, until now it was felt necessary only for the official to speak to each person approaching. Mr. Summers was very good at all this; in his clean white shirt and blue jeans, with one hand resting carelessly on the black box, he seemed very proper and important as he talked interminably to Mr. Graves and the Martins.

Just as Mr. Summers finally left off talking and turned to the assembled   8 villagers, Mrs. Hutchinson came hurriedly along the path to the square, her sweater thrown over her shoulders, and slid into place in the back of the crowd. "Clean forgot what day it was," she said to Mrs. Delacroix, who stood next to her, and they both laughed softly. "Thought my old man was out back stacking wood," Mrs. Hutchinson went on, "and then I looked out the window and the kids was gone, and then I remembered it was the twenty-seventh and came a-running." She dried her hands on her apron, and Mrs. Delacroix said, "You're in time, though. They're still talking away up there."

Mrs. Hutchinson craned her neck to see through the crowd and found 9 her husband and children standing near the front. She tapped Mrs. Delacroix on the arm as a farewell and began to make her way through the crowd. The people separated good-humoredly to let her through; two or three people said, in voices just loud enough to be heard across the crowd, "Here comes your Missus, Hutchinson," and "Bill, she made it after all." Mrs. Hutchinson reached her husband, and Mr. Summers, who had been waiting, said cheerfully, "Thought we were going to have to get on without you, Tessie." Mrs. Hutchinson said, grinning, "Wouldn't have me leave m'dishes in the sink, now, would you, Joe?" and soft laughter ran through the crowd as the people stirred back into position after Mrs. Hutchinson's arrival.

"Well now," Mr. Summers said soberly, "guess we better get started, get 10 this over with, so's we can go back to work. Anybody ain't here?"

"Dunbar," several people said. "Dunbar, Dunbar." 11

Mr. Summers consulted his list. "Clyde Dunbar," he said. "That's right. 12 He's broke his leg, hasn't he? Who's drawing for him?"

"Me, I guess," a woman said, and Mr. Summers turned to look at her. 13 "Wife draws for her husband," Mr. Summers said. "Don't you have a grown boy to do it for you, Janey?" Although Mr. Summers and everyone else in the village knew the answer perfectly well, it was the business of the official of the lottery to ask such questions formally. Mr. Summers waited with an expression of polite interest while Mrs. Dunbar answered.

"Horace's not but sixteen yet," Mrs. Dunbar said regretfully. "Guess 14 I gotta fill in for the old man this year."

"Right," Mr. Summers said. He made a note on the list he was holding. 15 Then he asked, "Watson boy drawing this year?"

A tall boy in the crowd raised his hand. "Here," he said. "I'm drawing 16 for m'mother and me." He blinked his eyes nervously and ducked his head as several voices in the crowd said things like "Good fellow, Jack," and "Glad to see your mother's got a man to do it."

"Well," Mr. Summers said, "guess that's everyone. Old Man Warner 17 make it?"

"Here," a voice said, and Mr. Summers nodded. 18

A sudden hush fell on the crowd as Mr. Summers cleared his throat and 19 looked at the list. "All ready?" he called. "Now, I'll read the names—heads of families first—and the men come up and take a paper out of the box. Keep the paper folded in your hand without looking at it until everyone has had a turn. Everything clear?"

The people had done it so many times that they only half listened to the   20
directions, most of them were quiet, wetting their lips, not looking around.
Then Mr. Summers raised one hand high and said, "Adams." A man disen-
gaged himself from the crowd and came forward. "Hi, Steve," Mr. Summers
said, and Mr. Adams said, "Hi, Joe." They grinned at one another humor-
lessly and nervously. Then Mr. Adams reached into the black box and took
out a folded paper. He held it firmly by one corner as he turned and went
hastily back to his place in the crowd, where he stood a little apart from his
family, not looking down at his hand.

"Allen," Mr. Summers said, "Anderson. . . . Bentham."   21

"Seems like there's no time at all between lotteries anymore," Mrs. Delacroix   22
said to Mrs. Graves in the back row. "Seems like we got through with the last
one only last week."

"Time sure goes fast," Mrs. Graves said.   23

"Clark. . . . Delacroix."   24

"There goes my old man," Mrs. Delacroix said. She held her breath while   25
her husband went forward.

"Dunbar," Mr. Summers said, and Mrs. Dunbar went steadily to the box   26
while one of the women said, "Go on, Janey," and another said, "There she goes."

"We're next," Mrs. Graves said. She watched while Mr. Graves came   27
around from the side of the box, greeted Mr. Summers gravely, and selected
a slip of paper from the box. By now, all through the crowd there were men
holding the small folded papers in their large hands, turning them over and
over nervously. Mrs. Dunbar and her two sons stood together, Mrs. Dunbar
holding the slip of paper.

"Harburt. . . . Hutchinson."   28

"Get up there, Bill," Mrs. Hutchinson said, and the people near her   29
laughed.

"Jones."   30

"They do say," Mr. Adams said to Old Man Warner, who stood next to   31
him, "that over in the north village they're talking of giving up the lottery."

Old Man Warner snorted. "Pack of crazy fools," he said. "Listening to the   32
young folks, nothing's good enough for *them*. Next thing you know, they'll be
wanting to go back to living in caves, nobody work anymore, live *that* way
for a while. Used to be a saying about 'Lottery in June, corn be heavy soon.'
First thing you know, we'd all be eating stewed chickweed and acorns. There's
always been a lottery," he added petulantly. "Bad enough to see young Joe
Summers up there joking with everybody."

"Some places have already quit lotteries," Mrs. Adams said.   33

"Nothing but trouble in *that*," Old Man Warner said stoutly. "Pack of   34
young fools."

"Martin." And Bobby Martin watched his father go forward. "Overdyke. . . . 35
Percy."

"I wish they'd hurry," Mrs. Dunbar said to her older son. "I wish they'd 36
hurry."

"They're almost through," her son said. 37

"You get ready to run tell Dad," Mrs. Dunbar said. 38

Mr. Summers called his own name and then stepped forward precisely 39
and selected a slip from the box. Then he called, "Warner."

"Seventy-seventh year I been in the lottery," Old Man Warner said as he 40
went through the crowd. "Seventy-seventh time."

"Watson." The tall boy came awkwardly through the crowd. Someone 41
said, "Don't be nervous, Jack," and Mr. Summers said, "Take your time,
son."

"Zanini." 42

After that, there was a long pause, a breathless pause, until Mr. Summers, 43
holding his slip of paper in the air, said, "All right, fellows." For a minute,
no one moved, and then all the slips of paper were opened. Suddenly, all
the women began to speak at once, saying, "Who is it?" "Who's got it?"
"Is it the Dunbars?" "Is it the Watsons?" Then the voices began to say, "It's
Hutchinson. It's Bill," "Bill Hutchinson's got it."

"Go tell your father," Mrs. Dunbar said to her older son. 44

People began to look around to see the Hutchinsons. Bill Hutchinson 45
was standing quiet, staring down at the paper in his hand. Suddenly, Tessie
Hutchinson shouted to Mr. Summers, "You didn't give him time enough to
take any paper he wanted. I saw you. It wasn't fair!"

"Be a good sport, Tessie," Mrs. Delacroix called, and Mrs. Graves said, 46
"All of us took the same chance."

"Shut up, Tessie," Bill Hutchinson said. 47

"Well, everyone," Mr. Summers said, "that was done pretty fast, and now 48
we've got to be hurrying a little more to get done in time." He consulted his
next list. "Bill," he said, "you draw for the Hutchinson family. You got any
other households in the Hutchinsons?"

"There's Don and Eva," Mrs. Hutchinson yelled. "Make *them* take their 49
chance!"

"Daughters draw with their husbands' families, Tessie," Mr. Summers said 50
gently. "You know that as well as anyone else."

"It wasn't *fair*," Tessie said. 51

"I guess not, Joe," Bill Hutchinson said regretfully. "My daughter draws 52
with her husband's family, that's only fair. And I've got no other family except
the kids."

"Then, as far as drawing for families is concerned, it's you," Mr. Summers   53
said in explanation, "and as far as drawing for households is concerned, that's
you, too. Right?"

"Right," Bill Hutchinson said.   54

"How many kids, Bill?" Mr. Summers asked formally.   55

"Three," Bill Hutchinson said. "There's Bill, Jr., and Nancy, and little   56
Dave. And Tessie and me."

"All right, then," Mr. Summers said. "Harry, you got their tickets back?"   57

Mr. Graves nodded and held up the slips of paper. "Put them in the box,   58
then," Mr. Summers directed. "Take Bill's and put it in."

"I think we ought to start over," Mrs. Hutchinson said, as quietly as she   59
could. "I tell you it wasn't *fair*. You didn't give him time enough to choose.
Everybody saw that."

Mr. Graves had selected the five slips and put them in the box, and he   60
dropped all the papers but those onto the ground, where the breeze caught
them and lifted them off.

"Listen, everybody," Mrs. Hutchinson was saying to the people around   61
her.

"Ready, Bill?" Mr. Summers asked, and Bill Hutchinson, with one quick   62
glance around at his wife and children, nodded.

"Remember," Mr. Summers said, "take the slips and keep them folded   63
until each person has taken one. Harry, you help little Dave." Mr. Graves
took the hand of the little boy, who came willingly with him up to the box.
"Take a paper out of the box, Davy," Mr. Summers said. Davy put his hand
into the box and laughed. "Take just *one* paper," Mr. Summers said. "Harry,
you hold it for him." Mr. Graves took the child's hand and removed the
folded paper from the tight fist and held it while little Dave stood next to
him and looked up at him wonderingly.

"Nancy next," Mr. Summers said. Nancy was twelve, and her school   64
friends breathed heavily as she went forward, switching her skirt, and took
a slip daintily from the box. "Bill, Jr.," Mr. Summers said, and Billy, his face
red and his feet overlarge, nearly knocked the box over as he got a paper out.
"Tessie," Mr. Summers said. She hesitated for a minute, looking around defi-
antly, and then set her lips and went up to the box. She snatched a paper out
and held it behind her.

"Bill," Mr. Summers said, and Bill Hutchinson reached into the box and   65
felt around, bringing his hand out at last with the slip of paper in it.

The crowd was quiet. A girl whispered, "I hope it's not Nancy," and the   66
sound of the whisper reached the edges of the crowd.

"It's not the way it used to be," Old Man Warner said clearly. "People   67
ain't the way they used to be."

"All right," Mr. Summers said. "Open the papers. Harry, you open little   68
Dave's."

Mr. Graves opened the slip of paper and there was a general sigh through   69
the crowd as he held it up and everyone could see that it was blank. Nancy and
Bill, Jr., opened theirs at the same time, and both beamed and laughed, turning
around to the crowd and holding their slips of paper above their heads.

"Tessie," Mr. Summers said. There was a pause, and then Mr. Summers looked   70
at Bill Hutchinson, and Bill unfolded his paper and showed it. It was blank.

"It's Tessie," Mr. Summers said, and his voice was hushed. "Show us her   71
paper, Bill."

Bill Hutchinson went over to his wife and forced the slip of paper out of   72
her hand. It had a black spot on it, the black spot Mr. Summers had made the
night before with the heavy pencil in the coal-company office. Bill Hutchinson
held it up and there was a stir in the crowd.

"All right, folks," Mr. Summers said. "Let's finish quickly."   73

Although the villagers had forgotten the ritual and lost the original black   74
box, they still remembered to use stones. The pile of stones the boys had
made earlier was ready; there were stones on the ground with the blowing
scraps of paper that had come out of the box. Mrs. Delacroix selected a stone
so large she had to pick it up with both hands and turned to Mrs. Dunbar.
"Come on," she said. "Hurry up."

Mrs. Dunbar had small stones in both hands, and she said, gasping for   75
breath, "I can't run at all. You'll have to go ahead and I'll catch up with you."

The children had stones already, and someone gave little Davy   76
Hutchinson a few pebbles.

Tessie Hutchinson was in the center of a cleared space by now, and she   77
held her hands out desperately as the villagers moved in on her. "It isn't fair,"
she said. A stone hit her on the side of the head.

Old Man Warner was saying, "Come on, come on, everyone." Steve   78
Adams was in front of the crowd of villagers, with Mrs. Graves beside him.

"It isn't fair, it isn't right," Mrs. Hutchinson screamed and then they were   79
upon her.

Journal Writing

Think about rituals in which you participate, such as those involving holidays, meals,
religious observances, family vacations, sporting events — anything that is repeated
and traditional. List some of these in your journal and write about their significance
to you.

Questions on Meaning

1. The PURPOSE of all fiction might be taken as entertainment or self-expression. Does Jackson have any other purpose in "The Lottery"?
2. When does the reader know what is actually going to occur?
3. Describe this story's community on the basis of what Jackson says of it.
4. What do the villagers' attitudes toward the black box indicate about their feelings toward the lottery?

Questions on Writing Strategy

1. Jackson uses the third PERSON (*he, she, it, they*) to narrate the story, and she does not enter the minds of her characters. Why do you think she keeps this distant POINT OF VIEW?
2. On your first reading of the story, what did you make of the references to rocks in paragraphs 2–3? Do you think they effectively forecast the ending?
3. Jackson has a character introduce a controversial notion in paragraph 31. Why does she do this?
4. **OTHER METHODS** Jackson is exploring — or inviting us to explore — CAUSES AND EFFECTS. Why do the villagers participate in the lottery every year? What does paragraph 32 hint might have been the original reason for it?

Questions on Language

1. Dialog provides much information not stated elsewhere in the story. Give three examples of such information about the community and its interactions.
2. Check a dictionary for definitions of the following words: profusely (par. 1); boisterous, reprimands (2); jovial, scold (4); paraphernalia (5); perfunctory, duly, interminably (7); petulantly (32).
3. In paragraph 64 we read that Mrs. Hutchinson "snatched" the paper out of the box. What does this verb suggest about her attitude?
4. Jackson admits to setting the story in her Vermont village in the present time (that is, 1948). Judging from the names of the villagers, where did these people's ancestors originally come from? What do you make of the names Delacroix and Zanini? What is their significance?
5. Unlike much fiction, "The Lottery" contains few FIGURES OF SPEECH. Why do you think this is?

Suggestions for Writing

1. **FROM JOURNAL TO ESSAY** Choose one of the rituals you wrote about in your journal (p. 111), and compose a narrative about the last time you participated in this ritual. Use DESCRIPTION and dialog to convey the significance of the ritual and your own and other participants' attitudes toward it.

2. In his 1974 book *Obedience to Authority*, the psychologist Stanley Milgram reported and analyzed the results of a study he had conducted that caused a furor among psychologists and the general public. Under orders from white-coated "experimenters," many subjects administered what they believed to be life-threatening electric shocks to other people whom they could hear but not see. In fact, the "victims" were actors and received no shocks, but the subjects thought otherwise and many continued to administer stronger and stronger "shocks" when ordered to do so. Find *Obedience to Authority* in the library and COMPARE AND CONTRAST the circumstances of Milgram's experiment with those of Jackson's lottery. For instance, who or what is the order-giving authority in the lottery? What is the significance of seeing or not seeing one's victim?

3. **CRITICAL WRITING**   Jackson has said that a common response she received to "The Lottery" was "What does this story mean?" (She never answered the question.) In an essay, interpret the meaning of the story as *you* understand it. (What does it say, for instance, about conformity, guilt, or good and evil?) You will have to INFER meaning from such features as Jackson's TONE as narrator, the villagers' dialog, and, of course, the events of the story. Your essay should be supported with specific EVIDENCE from the story. (For a sample of another student's interpretation of "The Lottery," see Rachel O'Connor's critical analysis on p. 309.)

4. **CONNECTIONS**   Although very different from Jackson's story, Firoozeh Dumas's essay "Sweet, Sour, and Resentful" (p. 275) also focuses on observing a tradition. Taken together, what do these two pieces seem to say about the benefits and the dangers of adhering to tradition? Write an essay in which you explore the pros and cons of maintaining rituals, giving examples from these selections and from your own experience.

Shirley Jackson on Writing

Come Along with Me, a posthumous collection of her work, contains a lecture by Shirley Jackson titled "Biography of a Story"—specifically a biography of "The Lottery." Far from being born in cruelty or cynicism, the story had quite benign origins. Jackson wrote the story, she recalled, "on a bright June morning when summer seemed to have come at last, with blue skies and warm sun and no heavenly signs to warn me that my morning's work was anything but just another story. The idea had come to me while I was pushing my daughter up the hill in her stroller—it was, as I say, a warm morning, and the hill was steep, and beside my daughter the stroller held the day's groceries—and perhaps the effort of that last fifty yards up the hill put an edge on the story; at any rate, I had the idea fairly clearly in my mind when I put my daughter in her playpen and the frozen vegetables in the refrigerator, and, writing the story, I found that it went quickly and easily, moving from beginning to end without pause. As a matter of fact, when I read it over later I decided that except for one or two minor corrections, it needed no changes, and the story I finally typed up and sent off to my agent the next day was almost word for word the original draft. This, as any writer of stories can tell you, is not a usual thing. All I know is that when I came to read the story over I felt strongly that I didn't want to fuss with it. I didn't think it was perfect, but I didn't want to fuss with it. It was, I thought, a serious, straight-forward story, and I was pleased and a little surprised at the ease with which it had been written; I was reasonably proud of it, and hoped that my agent would sell it to some magazine and I would have the gratification of seeing it in print."

After the story was published, however, Jackson was surprised to find both it and herself the subject of "bewilderment, speculation, and plain old-fashioned abuse." She wrote that "one of the most terrifying aspects of publishing stories and books is the realization that they are going to be read, and read by strangers. I had never fully realized this before, although I had of course in my imagination dwelt lovingly upon the thought of the millions and millions of people who were going to be uplifted and enriched and delighted by the stories I wrote. It had simply never occurred to me that these millions and millions of people might be so far from being uplifted that they would sit down and write me letters I was downright scared to open; of the three-hundred-odd letters that I received that summer I can count only thirteen that spoke kindly to me, and they were mostly from friends."

Jackson's favorite letter was one concluding, "Our brothers feel that Miss Jackson is a true prophet and disciple of the true gospel of the redeeming light. When will the next revelation be published?" Jackson's answer: "Never. I am out of the lottery business for good."

The Bedford Reader on Writing

As Jackson observes, inspiration often comes when least expected—while walking, in the shower, asleep. Notice, though, that Jackson didn't wait for inspiration to actually *write*: She sat right down and began work. For our advice on finding ideas and drafting productively, see pages 30–38. And for tips on anticipating readers' reactions to your writing, see pages 28–29.

ADDITIONAL WRITING TOPICS

Narration

1. Write a narrative with one of the following as your subject. It may be (as your instructor may advise) either a first-PERSON memoir or a story written in the third person, observing the experience of someone else. Decide before you begin what your PURPOSE is and whether you are writing (1) an anecdote, (2) an essay consisting mainly of a single narrative, or (3) an essay that includes more than one story.

   A lesson you learned the hard way
   A trip into unfamiliar territory
   An embarrassing moment that taught you something
   A monumental misunderstanding
   An accident
   An adventure or misadventure
   A friendship
   An unexpected encounter
   A loss that lingers
   A moment of triumph
   A story about a famous person
   A legend from family history
   A conflict or contest
   A fierce storm
   A historical event of significance

2. Tell a true story of your early or recent school days, either humorous or serious, relating a struggle you experienced (or still experience) in school.

3. Write a fictional narrative, set in the past, present, or future, of a ritual that demonstrates something about the people who participate in it. The ritual can be, but need not be, as sinister as Shirley Jackson's lottery; yours could concern bathing, eating, dating, going to school, driving, growing older.

Note: Writing topics combining narration and description appear on page 159.

Todd R. Darling/Redux

6

DESCRIPTION

Writing with Your Senses

◄ Description in a photograph

Todd R. Darling photographs communities in the industrial city of Paterson, New Jersey. This photograph, from his series *Home of the Brave*, depicts a group of homeless veterans and opioid users who live together in one of the city's abandoned textile mills. Consider Darling's photograph as a work of description— revealing a thing through the perceptions of the senses. What do you see through his eyes? What is the camp made of? How is it furnished? What do the firepit on the left and the graffiti on the walls add to the impression of the building? What do the people in the photograph seem to be doing? If you were standing in the picture, in the midst of the group, what might you hear or smell? If you touched the walls, what textures might you feel? What main idea do you think Darling wants this photograph to convey?

THE METHOD

Like narration, DESCRIPTION is a familiar method of expression, already a working part of your life. In any chat, you probably do your share of describing. You depict in words someone you've met by describing her clothes, the look on her face, the way she walks. You describe somewhere you've been, something you admire, something you just can't stand. In a social media post, you might describe your college (concrete buildings, crowded walks, pigeons scuttling); or perhaps you depict your brand-new secondhand car, from the glitter of its hubcaps to the odd antiques wedged in its seat cushions. You can hardly go a day without describing (or hearing described) some person, place, or thing. Small wonder, then, that in written discourse description is almost as indispensable as language.

Description reports the testimony of your senses. It invites your readers to imagine that they, too, not only see but perhaps also hear, taste, smell, and touch the subject you describe. Usually you will write a description for either of two PURPOSES:

- **Convey information without bias,** using description that is OBJECTIVE (or *impartial, public,* or *functional*). You describe your subject so clearly and exactly that your reader will understand it or recognize it, and you leave your emotions out. The description in academic writing is usually objective: A biology report on a particular species of frog, for instance, might detail the animal's appearance (four-inch-wide body, bright-orange skin with light-brown spots), its sounds (hoarse clucks), and its feel (smooth, slippery). In writing an objective description your purpose is not to share your feelings. You are trying to make the frog or the subject easily recognized.

- **Convey perceptions with feeling,** using description that is SUBJECTIVE (or *emotional, personal,* or *impressionistic*). This is the kind of description included in an advertisement for a new car. It's what you write in your post setting forth what your college is like—whether you are pleased or displeased with it. In this kind of description, you may use biases and personal feelings—in fact, they are essential.

For a splendid example of subjective description, read the following passenger's-eye view of a storm at sea by Charles Dickens. Notice how the writer's words convey the terror of the event:

> Imagine the ship herself, with every pulse and artery of her huge body swollen and bursting . . . sworn to go on or die. Imagine the wind howling, the sea roaring, the rain beating; all in furious array against her. Picture the sky both dark and wild, and the clouds in fearful sympathy with the waves, making another ocean in the air. Add to all this the clattering on deck and down below; the tread of hurried feet; the loud hoarse shouts of seamen; the gurgling in and out of water through the scuppers; with every now and

then the striking of a heavy sea upon the planks above, with the deep, dead, heavy sound of thunder heard within a vault; and there is the head wind of that January morning.

Think of what a starkly different description of the very same storm the captain might set down—objectively—in the ship's log: "At 0600 hours, watch reported a wind from due north of 70 knots. Whitecaps were noticed, in height two ells above the bow. Below deck water was reported to have entered the bilge. . . ." But Dickens, not content simply to record information, strives to ensure that his emotions are clear.

Description is usually found in the company of other methods of writing. Often, for instance, it will enliven NARRATION and make the people in the story and the setting unmistakably clear. Writing a PROCESS ANALYSIS in her essay "Sweet, Sour, and Resentful" (p. 275), Firoozeh Dumas begins with a description of her family's hometown in Iran. Description will help a writer in examining the EFFECTS of a storm or in COMPARING AND CONTRASTING two paintings. Keep description in mind when you try expository and argumentative writing. The method is key to clarity and to readers' interest.

THE PROCESS

Purpose and Audience

Understand, first of all, why you are writing about your subject and thus what kind of description is called for. Is it appropriate to perceive and report without emotion or bias—and thus write an objective description? Or is it appropriate to express your personal feelings as well as your perceptions—and thus write a subjective description?

Give some thought also to your AUDIENCE. What do your readers need to be told, if they are to share the perceptions you would have them share? If, let's say, you are describing a downtown street on a Saturday night for an audience of fellow students who live in the same city, then you need not dwell on the street's familiar geography. What must you tell? Only those details that make the place different on a Saturday night. But if you are remembering your hometown, and writing for readers who don't know it, you'll need to establish a few central landmarks to sketch (in their minds) an unfamiliar street on a Saturday night.

Before you begin to write a description, go look at your subject. If that is not possible, your next best course is to spend a few minutes imagining the subject until, in your mind's eye, you can see every speck of it. Then, having fixed your subject in mind, ask yourself which of its features you'll need to report to your particular audience, for your particular purpose. Ask yourself, "What am I out to accomplish?"

Dominant Impression and Thesis

When you consider your aim in describing, you'll begin to see what impression you intend your subject to make on readers. Let your description, as a whole, convey this one DOMINANT IMPRESSION. If you are writing a subjective description of an old house, laying weight on its spooky atmosphere to make readers shiver, then you might mention its squeaking bats and its shadowy halls. If, however, you are describing the house in a classified ad, for an audience of possible buyers, you might focus instead on its eat-in kitchen, working fireplace, and proximity to public transportation. Details have to be carefully selected. Feel no obligation to include every perceptible detail. To do so would only invite chaos — or perhaps, for the reader, tedium. Pick out the features that matter most.

Your dominant impression is like the THESIS of your description — the main idea about your subject that you want readers to take away with them. When you use description to explain or to argue, it's usually a good strategy to state that dominant impression outright, tying it to your essay's thesis or a part of it. In the biology report on a species of frog, for instance, you might preface your description with a statement like this one:

A number of unique features distinguish this frog from others in the order Anura.

Or in an argument in favor of cleaning a local toxic-waste site, you might begin with a description of the site and then state your point about it:

This landscape is as poisonous as it looks, for underneath its barren crust are enough toxic chemicals to sicken an entire village.

When you use subjective description more for its own sake — to show the reader a place or a person, to evoke feelings — you needn't always state your dominant impression as a THESIS STATEMENT, as long as the impression is there dictating the details.

Organization

To help them arrange the details of a description, many writers rely on their POINT OF VIEW — the physical angle from which they're perceiving and describing. As an observer who stays put and observes steadily, you can make a carefully planned inspection tour of your subject, using SPATIAL ORDER (from left to right, from near to far, from top to bottom, from center to periphery), or perhaps moving from prominent objects to tiny ones, from dull to bright, from commonplace to extraordinary — or vice versa.

The plan for you is the one that best fulfills your purpose, arranging details so that the reader receives the exact impression you mean to convey. If you were to describe, for instance, a chapel in the middle of a desert, you might begin with the details of the lonely terrain. Then, as if approaching the chapel with the aid of a zoom lens, you might detail its exterior before going on inside. That might be a workable method *if* you wanted to create the dominant impression of the chapel as an island of beauty in the midst of desolation. Say, however, that you had a different impression in mind: to emphasize the spirituality of the chapel's interior. You might then begin your description inside the structure, perhaps with its most prominent feature, the stained glass windows. You might mention the surrounding desert later in your description, but only incidentally.

Whatever pattern you follow, stick with it all the way through so that your arrangement causes no difficulty for the reader. In describing the chapel, you wouldn't necessarily proceed in the way you explored the structure in person, first noting its isolation, then entering and studying its windows, then going outside again to see what the walls were made of, then moving back inside to look at the artwork. Instead, you would lead the reader around and through (or through and around) the structure in an organized manner. Even if a scene is chaotic, the prose should be orderly.

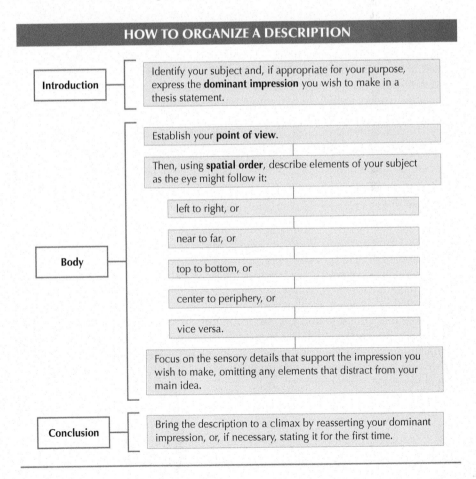

HOW TO ORGANIZE A DESCRIPTION

Introduction — Identify your subject and, if appropriate for your purpose, express the **dominant impression** you wish to make in a thesis statement.

Body —
Establish your **point of view**.

Then, using **spatial order**, describe elements of your subject as the eye might follow it:

- left to right, or
- near to far, or
- top to bottom, or
- center to periphery, or
- vice versa.

Focus on the sensory details that support the impression you wish to make, omitting any elements that distract from your main idea.

Conclusion — Bring the description to a climax by reasserting your dominant impression, or, if necessary, stating it for the first time.

Details

Luckily, to write a memorable description, you don't need a ferocious storm or any other awe-inspiring subject. As Brad Manning, Scaachi Koul, and N. Scott Momaday demonstrate later in this chapter, you can write about your family as effectively as you might write about a hurricane. The secret is in the vividness, the evocativeness of the details. Momaday, for instance, uses many IMAGES to call up concrete sensory experiences, including FIGURES OF SPEECH (expressions that do not mean literally what they say). Using *metaphor*, he writes that "the walls have closed in upon my grandmother's house" to express his change in perception when he returns to the house as an adult. And using *simile*, Momaday describes grasshoppers "popping up like corn" to bring a sense of stinging suddenness to life for his readers.

FOCUS ON SPECIFIC AND CONCRETE LANGUAGE

When you write effective description, you'll convey your subject as exactly as possible. You may use figures of speech, as discussed above, and you'll definitely rely on language that is *specific* (tied to actual things) and *concrete* (tied to the senses of sight, hearing, touch, smell, and taste). Such language enables readers to behold with the mind's eye—and to feel with the mind's fingertips.

The first sentence below shows a writer's first-draft attempt to describe something she saw. After editing, the second sentence is much more vivid.

VAGUE   Beautiful, scented wildflowers were in the field.

CONCRETE AND SPECIFIC   Backlit by the sun and smelling faintly sweet, an acre of tiny lavender flowers spread away from me.

When editing your description, keep a sharp eye out for vague words such as *delicious*, *handsome*, *loud*, and *short* that force readers to create their own impressions or, worse, leave them with no impression at all. Using details that call on readers' sensory experiences, tell why delicious or why handsome, how loud or how short. When stuck for a word, conjure up your subject and see it, hear it, touch it, smell it, taste it.

Note that *concrete* and *specific* do not mean "fancy": Good description does not demand five-dollar words when nickel equivalents are just as informative. The writer who uses *rubiginous* instead of *rusty red* actually says less because fewer readers will understand the less common word and all readers will sense a writer showing off.

CHECKLIST FOR REVIEWING AND REVISING A DESCRIPTION

✔ **Subjective or objective.** Is the description appropriately subjective (emphasizing feelings) or objective (unemotional) for your purpose?

✔ **Dominant impression.** What is your dominant impression of the subject? If it isn't stated, will readers be able to pinpoint it accurately?

✔ **Point of view and organization.** Do the point of view and organization work together to make the subject clear for readers? Are they consistent?

✔ **Details.** Have you provided all of the details—and only those details—needed to convey your dominant impression? What needs expanding? What needs condensing or cutting?

✔ **Specific and concrete language.** Have you used words that express your meaning exactly and appeal to the senses of sight, hearing, touch, taste, and smell?

STUDENT CASE STUDY: A FIELD OBSERVATION

In many of your classes, particularly those in the social sciences, you will be asked to observe people or phenomena in particular settings and to describe what your senses perceive. A systematic observation may produce evidence for an ARGUMENT, as when a writer describes the listlessness of kittens in an animal shelter to encourage support for a spay-and-neuter program. Just as often, however, an observation results in an objective report providing information from which readers draw their own conclusions. Like any description, such a field report emphasizes details and uses concrete language to convey the writer's perceptions. Because the writer's purpose is to inform, the report takes a neutral, third-PERSON (*he, she, they*) point of view, uses unemotional language, and refrains from interpretation or opinion—or withholds such analysis for a separate section near the end.

For an education class in child development, Nick Fiorelli spent a morning in a private preschool, observing the teachers' techniques and the children's behaviors and taking note of how they interacted. The paragraphs on the next page, excerpted from his finished report, "Teaching Methodologies at Child's Play Preschool," describe both the classroom itself and some of the activities Fiorelli witnessed. The full report goes on to outline the educational philosophies and developmental theories that inform the school's approach, with additional examples and descriptions from Fiorelli's visit.

The preschool's Web site explains that it draws on elements of Waldorf, Montessori, Reggio Emillia, and other educational models. This background was evident in the large and colorful classroom, which included separate interest areas for different activities. The room was also open and well lit, with long windows that looked out on a playground and an expansive lawn. The walls of the room were decorated with students' paintings and drawings. Colored rugs, floor tiles, or rubber mats indicated the boundaries of each activity area.

At first, the general atmosphere appeared noisy and unstructured, but a sense of order emerged within a few minutes of observation. At a sturdy wooden art table, two students used safety scissors to cut shapes from sheets of red construction paper. Behind them, a child in a red smock stood at a small wooden easel and painted with a foam brush. Another strung multicolored beads on a string. Next to the art table, two children at a sensory station poured wet sand and rocks through an oversize funnel into a miniature sandbox, while a third filled a clear plastic tank with water from a blue enameled pail. A teacher moved between the two tables, encouraging the students and asking questions about their play. In the back of the room, at a literacy area with a thick blue rug and low yellow bookshelves, six students lolled on beanbag chairs, pillows, and a low brown couch, listening to a teacher read a story from an illustrated children's book. She paused on each page to help the children connect the pictures with the story.

Background information sets the stage

Organization moves from the periphery to the center, then around the room's distinct areas

Dominant impression: structured creativity

Concrete details contribute to the dominant impression

BRAD MANNING

Brad Manning was born in Little Rock, Arkansas, in 1967 and grew up near Char-lottesville, Virginia. While a student at Harvard University he played intramural sports and wrote articles and reviews for the *Harvard Independent*. He graduated in 1990 with a BA in history and religion. Now living in Charlottesville, Manning is a psychiatrist specializing in the treatment of children and adolescents.

Arm Wrestling with My Father

In this essay written for his freshman composition course, Manning explores his physical contact with his father over the years, perceiving gradual changes that are, he realizes, inevitable. For Manning, description provides a way to express his feelings about his father and to comment on relations between sons and fathers. In the essay after Manning's, Scaachi Koul uses description for similar ends, but her subject is the relationship between a daughter and her father.

"Now you say when" is what he always said before an arm-wrestling 1 match. He liked to put the responsibility on me, knowing that he would always control the outcome. "When!" I'd shout, and it would start. And I would tense up, concentrating and straining and trying to push his wrist down to the carpet with all my weight and strength. But Dad would always win; I always had to lose. "Want to try it again?" he would ask, grinning. He would see my downcast eyes, my reddened, sweating face, and sense my intensity. And with squinting eyes he would laugh at me, a high laugh, through his per-fect white teeth. Too bitter to smile, I would not answer or look at him, but I would just roll over on my back and frown at the ceiling. I never thought it was funny at all.

That was the way I felt for a number of years during my teens, after I 2 had lost my enjoyment of arm wrestling and before I had given up that same intense desire to beat my father. Ours had always been a physical relationship, I suppose, one determined by athleticism and strength. We never communi-cated as well in speech or in writing as in a strong hug, battling to make the other gasp for breath. I could never find him at one of my orchestra concerts. But at my lacrosse games, he would be there in the stands, with an angry look, ready to coach me after the game on how I could do better. He never helped me write a paper or a poem. Instead, he would take me outside and show me a new move for my game, in the hope that I would score a couple of goals and gain confidence in my ability. Dad knew almost nothing about lacrosse and his movements were all wrong and sad to watch. But at those times I could just feel how hard he was trying to communicate, to help me, to show the love he had for me, the love I could only assume was there.

His words were physical. The truth is, I have never read a card or a letter   3
written in his hand because he never wrote to me. Never. Mom wrote me all the cards and letters when I was away from home. The closest my father ever came, that I recall, was in a newspaper clipping Mom had sent with a letter. He had gone through and underlined all the important words about the dangers of not wearing a bicycle helmet. Our communication was physical, and that is why we did things like arm wrestle. To get down on the floor and grapple, arm against arm, was like having a conversation.

This ritual of father-son competition in fact had started early in my life,   4
back when Dad started the matches with his arm almost horizontal, his wrist an inch from defeat, and still won. I remember in those battles how my tiny shoulders would press over our locked hands, my whole upper body pushing down in hope of winning that single inch from his calm, unmoving forearm. "Say when," he'd repeat, killing my concentration and causing me to squeal, "I did, I did!" And so he'd grin with his eyes fixed on me, not seeming to notice his own arm, which would begin to rise slowly from its starting position. My greatest efforts could not slow it down. As soon as my hopes had disappeared I'd start to cheat and use both hands. But the arm would continue to move steadily along its arc toward the carpet. My brother, if he was watching, would sometimes join in against the arm. He once even wrapped his little legs around our embattled wrists and pulled back with everything he had. But he did not have much and, regardless of the opposition, the man would win. My arm would lie at rest, pressed into the carpet beneath a solid, immovable arm. In that pinned position, I could only giggle, happy to have such a strong father.

My feelings have changed, though. I don't giggle anymore, at least not   5
around my father. And I don't feel pressured to compete with him the way I thought necessary for years. Now my father is not really so strong as he used to be and I am getting stronger. This change in strength comes at a time when I am growing faster mentally than at any time before. I am becoming less my father and more myself. And as a result, there is less of a need to be set apart from him and his command. I am no longer a rebel in the household, wanting to stand up against the master with clenched fists and tensing jaws, trying to impress him with my education or my views on religion. I am no longer a challenger, quick to correct his verbal mistakes, determined to beat him whenever possible in physical competition.

I am not sure when it was that I began to feel less competitive with my 6
father, but it all became clearer to me one day this past January. I was home
in Virginia for a week between exams, and Dad had stayed home from work
because the house was snowed in deep. It was then that I learned something I
never could have guessed.

I don't recall who suggested arm wrestling that day. We hadn't done it for 7
a long time, for months. But there we were, lying flat on the carpet, face to
face, extending our right arms. Our arms were different. His still resembled
a fat tree branch, one which had leveled my wrist to the ground countless
times before. It was hairy and white with some pink moles scattered about.
It looked strong, to be sure, though not so strong as it had in past years. I
expect that back in his youth it had looked even stronger. In high school he
had played halfback and had been voted "best-built body" of the senior class.
Between college semesters he had worked on road crews and on Louisiana
dredges. I admired him for that. I had begun to row crew in college and that
accounted for some small buildup along the muscle lines, but it did not seem
to be enough. The arm I extended was lanky and featureless. Even so, he
insisted that he would lose the match, that he was certain I'd win. I had to
ignore this, however, because it was something he always said, whether or not
he believed it himself.

Our warm palms came together, much the same way we had shaken hands 8
the day before at the airport. Fingers twisted and wrapped about once again,
testing for a better grip. Elbows slid up and back making their little indenta-
tions on the itchy carpet. My eyes pinched closed in concentration as I tried
to center as much of my thought as possible on the match. Arm wrestling, I
knew, was a competition that depended less on talent and experience than
on one's mental control and confidence. I looked up into his eyes and was
ready. He looked back, smiled at me, and said softly (did he sound nervous?),
"You say when."

It was not a long match. I had expected him to be stronger, faster. I was 9
conditioned to lose and would have accepted defeat easily. However, after
some struggle, his arm yielded to my efforts and began to move unsteadily
toward the carpet. I worked against his arm with all the strength I could find.
He was working hard as well, straining, breathing heavily. It seemed that this
time was different, that I was going to win. Then something occurred to me,
something unexpected. I discovered that I was feeling sorry for my father. I
wanted to win but I did not want to see him lose.

It was like the thrill I had once experienced as a young boy at my grandfa- 10
ther's lake house in Louisiana when I hooked my first big fish. There was that
sudden tug that made me leap. The red bobber was sucked down beneath the
surface and I pulled back against it, reeling it in excitedly. But when my cousin

caught sight of the fish and shouted out, "It's a keeper," I realized that I would be happier for the fish if it were let go rather than grilled for dinner. Arm wrestling my father was now like this, like hooking "Big Joe," the old fish that Lake Quachita holds but you can never catch, and when you finally think you've got him, you want to let him go, cut the line, keep the legend alive.

Perhaps at that point I could have given up, letting my father win. But it was so fast and absorbing. How could I have learned so quickly how it would feel to have overpowered the arm that had protected and provided for me all of my life? His arms have always protected me and the family. Whenever I am near him I am unafraid, knowing his arms are ready to catch me and keep me safe, the way they caught my mother one time when she fainted halfway across the room, the way he carried me, full grown, up and down the stairs when I had mononucleosis, the way he once held my feet as I stood on his shoulders to put up a new basketball net. My mother may have had the words or the touch that sustained our family, but his were the arms that protected us. And his were the arms now that I had pushed to the carpet, first the right arm, then the left. 11

I might have preferred him to be always the stronger, the one who carries me. But this wish is impossible now; our roles have begun to switch. I do not know if I will ever physically carry my father as he has carried me, though I fear that someday I may have that responsibility. More than once this year I have hesitated before answering the phone late at night, fearing my mother's voice calling me back to help carry his wood coffin. When I am home with him and he mentions a sharp pain in his chest, I imagine him collapsing onto the floor. And in that second vision I see me rushing to him, lifting him onto my shoulders, and running. 12

A week after our match, we parted at the airport. The arm-wrestling match was by that time mostly forgotten. My thoughts were on school. I had been awake most of the night studying for my last exam, and by that morning I was already back into my college-student manner of reserve and detachment. To say goodbye, I kissed and hugged my mother and I prepared to shake my father's hand. A handshake had always seemed easier to handle than a hug. His hugs had always been powerful ones, intended I suppose to give me strength. They made me suck in my breath and struggle for control, and the way he would pound his hand on my back made rumbles in my ears. So I offered a handshake; but he offered a hug. I accepted it, bracing myself for the impact. Once our arms were wrapped around each other, however, I sensed a different message. His embrace was softer, longer than before. I remember how it surprised me and how I gave an embarrassed laugh as if to apologize to anyone watching. 13

I got on the airplane and my father and mother were gone. But as the plane lifted my throat was hurting with sadness. I realized then that Dad must 14 have learned something as well, and what he had said to me in that last hug was that he loved me. Love was a rare expression between us, so I had denied it at first. As the plane turned north, I had a sudden wish to go back to Dad and embrace his arms with all the love I felt for him. I wanted to hold him for a long time and to speak with him silently, telling him how happy I was, telling him all my feelings, in that language we shared.

In his hug, Dad had tried to tell me something he himself had discovered.   15
I hope he tries again. Maybe this spring, when he sees his first crew match, he'll advise me on how to improve my stroke. Maybe he has started doing pushups to rebuild his strength and challenge me to another match — if this were true, I know I would feel less challenged than loved. Or maybe, rather than any of this, he'll just send me a card.

Journal Writing

Manning expresses conflicting feelings about his father. How do you respond to his conflict? When have you felt strongly mixed emotions about a person or an event, such as a relative, friend, breakup, ceremony, move? Write a paragraph or two exploring your feelings.

Questions on Meaning

1. In paragraph 3 Manning says that his father's "words were physical." What does this mean?

2. After his most recent trip home, Manning says, "I realized then that Dad must have learned something as well" (par. 14). What is it that father and son have each learned?

3. Manning says in the last paragraph that he "would feel less challenged than loved" if his father challenged him to a rematch. Does this statement suggest that he did not feel loved earlier? Why, or why not?

4. What do you think is Manning's PURPOSE in this essay? Does he want to express love for his father, or is there something more as well?

Questions on Writing Strategy

1. Why does Manning start his essay with a match that leaves him "too bitter to smile" and then move backward to earlier bouts of arm wrestling?

2. In the last paragraph Manning suggests that his father might work harder at competing with him and pushing him to be competitive, or he might just send

his son a card. Why does Manning present both of these options? Are we supposed to know which will happen?

3. Explain the fishing ANALOGY Manning uses in paragraph 10.

4. **OTHER METHODS**   Manning's essay is as much a NARRATIVE as a description: The author gives brief stories, like video clips, to show the dynamic of his relationship with his father. Look at the story in paragraph 4. How does Manning mix elements of both methods to convey his powerlessness?

Questions on Language

1. Manning uses the word *competition* throughout this essay. Why is this a more accurate word than *conflict* to describe Manning's relationship with his father?

2. What is the EFFECT of "the arm" in this sentence from paragraph 4: "But the arm would continue to move steadily along its arc toward the carpet"?

3. In paragraph 9 Manning writes, "I wanted to win but I did not want to see him lose." What does this apparent contradiction mean?

4. If any of these words is unfamiliar, look it up in a dictionary: embattled (par. 4); dredges, crew (7); conditioned (9); mononucleosis (11).

Suggestions for Writing

1. **FROM JOURNAL TO ESSAY**   Expand your journal entry (p. 129) into a descriptive essay that brings to life your mixed feelings about a person or an event. Focus less on the circumstances and happenings than on emotions, both positive and negative.

2. Write an essay that describes your relationship with a parent or another close adult. You may want to focus on just one aspect of your relationship, or one especially vivid moment, in order to give yourself the space and time to build many sensory details into your description.

3. Arm wrestling is a highly competitive sport with a long history. Research the sport in the library or on the Internet. Then write a brief essay that traces its history and explains its current standing.

4. **CRITICAL WRITING**   In paragraph 12 Manning says that "our roles have begun to switch." Does this seem like an inevitable switch, or one that this father and son have been working to achieve? Use EVIDENCE from Manning's essay to support your answer. Also consider whether Manning and his father would respond the same way to this question.

5. **CONNECTIONS**   Like "Arm Wrestling with My Father," the next essay, Scaachi Koul's "Impatiently Waiting for the Horror of Death," depicts a struggle for communication with an aging father. In an essay of your own, COMPARE AND CONTRAST the two essays on this point. What conclusions do the authors draw about mortality and maturity? How do they resolve their conflicts with older generations?

Brad Manning on Writing

For this book, Brad Manning offered some valuable concrete advice on writing as a student.

You hear this a lot, but writing takes a long time. For me, this is especially true. The only difference between the "Arm Wrestling" essay and all the other essays I wrote in college (and the only reason it's in this book and not thrown away) is that I rewrote it six or seven times over a period of weeks.

If I have something to write, I need to start early. In college, I had a bad habit of putting off papers until 10 p.m. the night before they were due and spending a desperate night typing whatever ideas the coffee inspired. But putting off papers didn't just lower my writing quality; it robbed me of a good time.

I like starting early because I can jot down notes over a stretch of days; then I type them up fast, ignoring typos; I print the notes with narrow margins, cut them up, and divide them into piles that seem to fit together; then it helps to get away for a day and come back all fresh so I can throw away the corny ideas. Finally, I sit on the floor and make an outline with all the cutouts of paper, trying at the same time to work out some clear purpose for the essay.

When the writing starts, I often get hung up most on trying to "sound" like a good writer. If you're like me and came to college from a shy family that never discussed much over dinner, you might think your best shot is to sound like a famous writer like T. S. Eliot and you might try to sneak in words that aren't really your own like *ephemeral* or *the lilacs smelled like springtime*. But the last thing you really want a reader thinking is how good or bad a writer you are.

Also, in the essay on arm wrestling, I got hung up thinking I had to make my conflict with my father somehow "universal." So in an early draft I wrote in a classical allusion — Aeneas lifting his old father up onto his shoulders and carrying him out of the burning city of Troy.[1] I'd read that story in high school and guessed one classical allusion might make the reader think I knew a lot more. But Aeneas didn't help the essay much, and I'm glad my teacher warned me off trying to universalize. He told me to write just what was true for me.

But that was hard, too, and still is — especially in the first draft. I don't know anyone who enjoys the first draft. If you do, I envy you. But in my early drafts, I always get this sensation like I have to impress somebody and

---

[1] In the *Aeneid*, by the Roman poet Virgil (70–19 BC), the mythic hero Aeneas escapes from the city of Troy when it is sacked by the Greeks and goes on to found Rome. — EDS.

I end up overanalyzing the effects of every word I am about to write. This self-consciousness may be unavoidable (I get self-conscious calling L. L. Bean to order a shirt), but, in this respect, writing is great for shy people because you can edit all you want, all day long, until it finally sounds right. I never feel that I am being myself until the third or fourth draft, and it's only then that it gets personal and starts to be fun.

When I said that putting off papers robbed me of a good time, I really meant it. Writing the essay about my father turned out to be a high point in my life. And on top of having a good time with it, I now have a record of what happened. And my ten-month-old son, when he grows up, can read things about his grandfather and father that he'd probably not have learned any other way.

The Bedford Reader on Writing

Brad Manning has some good advice for other college writers, especially about taking the time to plan (pp. 28–30), organize (p. 36), and revise (pp. 41–45) a draft, often many times over. For guidelines on how to edit your writing as he did, especially to establish and maintain your own VOICE, refer to pages 55–61 in Chapter 4.

SCAACHI KOUL

Born in Calgary, Alberta, in 1991 to immigrants from Kashmir, Scaachi Koul grew up navigating the complexities of being Indian in Canada. She studied journalism at Ryerson University in Toronto, Ontario, graduating in 2012. Realizing she "wasn't very good at being a news reporter," she found work writing humor and criticism for the online magazine *Hazlitt*. Now a culture writer for *BuzzFeed*, Koul has also contributed to several print periodicals, including *The New Yorker*, the *New York Times*, the *Toronto Globe and Mail*, *The Walrus*, and *Flare*. Her debut collection of essays, *One Day We'll All Be Dead and None of This Will Matter*, appeared in 2017. Often tackling difficult subjects such as casual racism, rape culture, and online harassment, but just as often taking on her beloved extended family, Koul is known for her skill at distilling sharp cultural criticism with a good measure of comedy. She lives in Toronto.

Impatiently Waiting for the Horror of Death

One of Koul's favorite subjects, to which she returns time and again, is her quirky father and the complicated relationship she has with him. She wrote this piece in 2015 for *Hazlitt*. Like the previous essay, Brad Manning's "Arm Wrestling with My Father," "Impatiently Waiting for the Horror of Death" explores the challenges of communication between an adult child and an aging parent. Engaged in a lifelong struggle with her father's obsession with mortality, Koul finds that she can't help but share his fears.

My dad doesn't have a lot of time left. I know this because he tells 1
us so. He repeats it monthly, sometimes weekly. He isn't subtle about it,
either — you'd be surprised by how many conversations start with him
explaining, "I don't have much left." You hear it when you disagree with him
and he doesn't want to argue. Sometimes you see it in the way he winces
when his back hurts, or when he rubs his knees in the morning, or how his
eyelids droop when he gets a headache. The signs are all there: This is a
vision of a man on his way out.

Does this make it sound like my dad is very sick? He is not. He's just 2
getting older, and he's handling it with the least amount of grace a physically healthy, mentally sound, middle-class Canadian possibly can. He still

runs ten kilometers every morning, followed by a breakfast of twelve soaked almonds, half a pomegranate, an egg, and a candy-dish full of multi-vitamins. Until his mid-fifties, he could stand straight on his head, and still maintains enough verve for life to be mean to small dogs but sweet to fat babies. My dad is not dying any faster than the rest of his generation, but if you ask him, he is dying sooner and harder than any of them.

He turns sixty-five this month, and like all his birthdays, he's dreading it. 3 "I'm going to be a senior citizen soon," he told me glumly over the phone earlier this week. "It's a new phase in my life, I guess. This is what I am. Whatever I am." I hear him sink deeper into his leather armchair, squeezing the air out of the armrests like he's strangling them for their youth.

It's no surprise to anyone else in the family that Papa Koul keeps threat- 4 ening to die. When I was in junior high and rebelling against his rules ("No mascara? Papa, you're like a Nazi!" I would scream before slamming my bedroom door and listening to Green Day[1] because I was very political), he would use the threat of his declining health to keep me in line. We'd fight, and then, a few hours later, he would be draped on his chair, complaining of chest pains. To be fair, both of my parents do this, but only my dad has some family history to back it up: His father died in his sleep thirty-five years ago of a heart attack. My dad has been waiting to wake up dead for three decades: When he disapproved of something I'd done, he'd talk about his rising blood pressure and worsening hypertension and I would bring him a small bowl of jalapeño potato chips and sit quietly, willing his heart to beat normally again.

These days, he complains about not being able to do headstands any- 5 more. "I used to be so able-bodied," he says. "I can't even get my marathon time under four hours." After his runs, my dad used to take to his bedroom to do yoga and stretch before his shower. The last thing he'd do was a headstand: He'd flip his slender body upside down, his head matted into the cream carpet and his face filling with blood. When little kids would visit, he'd nudge them and say, "I can stand on my head, you know," and they'd laugh and say, "No, Uncle Vijay, you're too old!" and so he would do it on command like a teenager on a dare, and the child would gasp and chatter and try to mimic him or knock him over. Then they would sit with him on his armchair and gaze up at him in awe, as if they'd found a surprisingly agile hundred-year-old talking oak tree, and he would nuzzle their necks and massage their feet.

My dad has won much five-year-old affection with this party trick. But he 6 can't do it anymore. If you ask him, this isn't so much the natural progression

---

[1] A popular American punk rock band formed in 1986. —EDS.

of a body that is not supposed to be upside-down but, rather, a sign that death is coming for him.

He didn't start talking about his doom — as much as he does now, at 7 least — until he retired. His kids were financially independent, his wife got her first part-time job, and no one really needed him anymore. He sulked when his kids moved away. He sulked when one of them got married. "Do you need money?" he asks me over the phone. I can hear his disappointment when I tell him I don't. He just wants to make sure everyone is doing okay, because as you may have heard, he does not have a lot of time left.

He doesn't take this out on anyone quite like he does on me. I spent 8 nine days with my family over Christmas, and my dad gave me the silent treatment for seven of them. No one was entirely sure why — we never are; he does it every time I come home — but our best guess is because of an international trip I'm taking in a month. When I went to Ecuador a year ago, he sent me a rambling e-mail asking why I couldn't wait until he was dead to do "such dangerous things."

There's a pattern to this. A few days after I leave my parents' home and 9 return to mine, he sheepishly calls me to tell me he is sorry, that he didn't mean it, that he hopes I come home again soon so that he can fix it. And then the kicker: "I don't want to fight with you," he tells me. "I don't have much time left."

My dad is still fun, despite becoming increasingly preoccupied with his 10 cosmic clock. He still sends me absurd e-mails about things he doesn't like ("I have decided to completely disown any of my near and dear who would willingly spend money in Lululemon[2]") and confused texts ("HOW DO YOU TEXT A PERIOD.") and calls to deliver missives about what it is like to be married for nearly forty years ("Your mother went to the mall today and I hadn't had lunch yet and I almost starved. She almost starved me").

What makes me angry is that he's right: He will die. You can't argue with 11 that. But every time he reminds me of it, I feel my heart dig down into my kidneys. I get increasingly agitated by his insistence on spending the remainder of his life anticipating the end of it. It could take another thirty years, but he spends so much time dreading it that I can't help but do it too. When the phone rings and it's my mom and she sounds quiet, I assume he's had a heart attack. "What's the matter with you?" she says when I immediately burst into tears. "I just had something caught in my throat." Or the annual call from my brother that leads me to believe my father is on life support and we need to make some tough decisions. My new greatest fear is my mother dying before him: Who is going to take care of this lunatic? (It's clearly on his mind, too:

---

[2] A retailer of yoga-inspired athletic wear. — Eds.

Two years ago, apropos of nothing, he screamed, "I WILL NEVER GO TO A HOME" over dinner. No one had ever suggested it.)

My dad doesn't want any fanfare for his birthday, never has. My mom 12 will make rice with turmeric and ghee. They will buy him a single slice of Safeway[3] hazelnut cake, a grotesque slab of nutty icing that he adores, and he will request that my mom add extra walnuts on top. My niece will help him blow out a single candle. And he and I will both swim through another sleepless night, another year in his life, each of us cataloging incurable illnesses, freak accidents, unlikely natural disasters. One of them will catch up with him some day, but for now, even if he isn't speaking to me, he's still here.

Journal Writing

How do you respond to Koul's eccentric, even obsessive, father? Do you basically come to sympathize with him or not? Who in your life has quirky behavior that you find annoying or charming or a little of both? Write a paragraph or two about this person, focusing on his or her particular habits or obsessions.

Questions on Meaning

1. In her opening sentence, Koul declares that her father "doesn't have a lot of time left." Is she serious? How can you tell? What is the EFFECT of repeating the point as often as she does?

2. What, according to Koul, usually prompts her father to remind his family that he's going to die? Why does it bother her so much that he does this?

3. Why does Koul's father not speak to her for days at a time when she visits? What does this behavior suggest about his character?

4. What do paragraphs 2–4, about her father's health and family history, contribute to Koul's portrait of him?

5. What seems to be Koul's PURPOSE or purposes in writing here? What DOMINANT IMPRESSION of her father does she create?

Questions on Writing Strategy

1. Why is the anecdote Koul relates in paragraphs 5–6 an effective image of her father and his relationship to children?

---

[3] A North American supermarket chain. —EDS.

2. What ASSUMPTIONS does the author make about her AUDIENCE?

3. In describing her father, does Koul take mostly an objective or subjective POINT OF VIEW? How appropriate do you find this choice?

4. What does Koul's final sentence mean? Do you find it a satisfying conclusion to her essay? Why, or why not?

5. **OTHER METHODS**   Throughout her essay, Koul relies on EXAMPLES to show her father's quirks. Why are the examples in paragraph 10 particularly well suited to her subject? How do they help reinforce Koul's main point about communicating with her father?

Questions on Language

1. Pick out ten or twelve concrete and specific words in the essay and consider their impact. How many of the five senses—sight, hearing, touch, taste, smell—does Koul appeal to with her description?

2. Koul uses several FIGURES OF SPEECH in this essay, including metaphor, simile, personification, and hyperbole. Find some examples of each. What do they contribute to Koul's meaning?

3. Consult a dictionary if you need help defining any of the following words: winces (par. 1); pomegranate, verve (2); hypertension (4); agile, nuzzle (5); progression (6); cosmic, missives (10); agitated, apropos (11); turmeric, ghee (12).

Suggestions for Writing

1. **FROM JOURNAL TO ESSAY**   Based on your journal writing, compose an essay that uses description to portray your subject and his or her personal quirks. Be sure to include specific incidents you've witnessed and specific details to create a vivid dominant impression of the person. You may, like Koul, focus on the evolution of your relationship with this person—whether mainly positive or mainly negative.

2. Conflict between generations is common in many families—whether over music, clothing, hairstyles, friends, or larger issues of politics, values, and religion. Write an essay about generational conflicts you have experienced in your family or that you have witnessed in other families. Are such conflicts inevitable? How can they be resolved?

3. **CRITICAL WRITING**   Analyze Koul's use of humor in this essay. What is it that makes her description funny? In particular, consider her use of hyperbole, irony, and humorous IMAGES. You might also do some library or Internet research on humor writing to further support your analysis.

4. **CONNECTIONS**   Both Koul and Brad Manning (in "Arm Wrestling with My Father," p. 125) describe their fathers. In an essay, examine the words Manning and Koul use to convey their feelings of distance from their fathers and also their feelings of closeness. Use quotations from both essays to support your analysis.

Scaachi Koul on Writing

As a young writer and editor for Web publications, Scaachi Koul is naturally very active on *Twitter*. She is also adept at deflecting the harassment that trolls regularly inflict on female writers with an online presence. But she famously suspended her account for two weeks after a particularly ugly episode, when one of her tweets was met with a virtual assault she describes as "several days of rape threats, death threats, encouragements of suicide, racial slurs, sexist remarks, comments on my weight and appearance, [and] attempts to get me fired or blacklisted." In this passage from "Mute," an essay about the experience in *Someday We'll All Be Dead and None of This Will Matter*, Koul explains the reasons for her initial post and her understanding of the response it generated.

I had tweeted . . . that morning that I wanted to read and commission more articles by non-white non-male writers. I was editing at the time, and the whitest, malest landscape in the country is long-form writing. This is boring, like offering the same selection of toothpaste-flavored ice cream for a century and then wondering why your business is failing. My version of media is one that looks like other people, because I remember being a little girl and wishing I read books or magazine articles or saw movies about people who even remotely looked like me. I became a writer because I read a David Sedaris book at thirteen; every word he wrote crackled in my brain, and he was a guy, sure, a white guy, but I knew he was different in a way that I felt different. Later that year, I read another book by an Indian writer about a first-generation Indian girl trying to date as a teenager, the plot alone blossoming in my heart when I read it. It changes you, when you see someone similar to you, doing the thing you might want to do yourself. That kind of writing — writing by people who aren't in the majority — its sheer visibility on your bookshelf or your television or your Internet, is sometimes received similarly to my call for more of that work. It's responded to with racism or sexism or homophobia or transphobia. We are deeply afraid of making marginalized voices stronger, because we think it makes privileged ones that much weaker.

Maybe I was wrong and I shouldn't have said that I wanted more "non-white non-male writers." Maybe I should have said, "As much as I appreciate the contributions white men have made to the media landscape, and as much as I want to read another profile of a thin, blond actress where the writer quietly begs to have his virginity taken, that feels a little redundant, and maybe something worth examining." But you know what, I don't really [care]. Those feelings are not my priority. That's kind of the point.

Media needs to diversify, and the only way to do that is to get non-white non-male non-binary people to work for and with you. It doesn't mean they're the only people you choose, but they are the ones we ignore the most. And when that message comes from a non-white non-male person themselves, someone young enough to not yet have any inherent gravitas and — this part is important — just enough privilege to be powerful, that's when they target you.

The Bedford Reader on Writing

If you'd like to read an essay by David Sedaris, the "different" writer Koul cites as an early inspiration, you'll find one — "Remembering My Childhood on the Continent of Africa" — on page 235 of this book. For works by other writers who "even remotely look" like Koul, *The Bedford Reader* features dozens of multicultural and international authors, among them Amy Tan (p. 77), Naomi Shihab Nye (p. 81), Kunal Nayyar (p. 91), Shonda Rhimes (next page), N. Scott Momaday (p. 144), Jourdan Imani Keith (p. 212), Ted Chiang (p. 217), Firoozeh Dumas (p. 275), Dawn Lundy Martin (p. 548), Thomas Chatterton Williams (p. 553), and Luis Alberto Urrea (p. 631).

SHONDA RHIMES

Shonda Rhimes is the writer, executive producer, and creator of the record-breaking series *Grey's Anatomy,* as well as its spinoff series *Private Practice* and the ground-breaking series *Scandal,* which after seven award-winning seasons, introduced audiences to the first black leading lady in a drama in thirty-seven years. In addition, Rhimes is executive producer of the ABC dramas *How to Get Away with Murder* and *Station 19.* In 2017, Rhimes shifted television's business model when she left traditional network television in an unprecedented agreement to produce content exclusively for Netflix. Her numerous awards include a Golden Globe for Outstanding Television Drama; a Peabody Award; GLAAD Media Awards; numerous AFI Awards for Television Program of the Year; two Television Academy Honors; and life-time achievement awards from the Directors Guild of America, the Writers Guild of America and the Producers Guild of America. In 2018, Rhimes was inducted into the Television Academy Hall of Fame. Rhimes holds a BA from Dartmouth College and an MFA from the USC School of Cinema-Television. Rhimes grew up outside of Chicago and now resides in Los Angeles with her three daughters.

My Summer of Scooping Ice Cream

Rhimes wrote "My Summer of Scooping Ice Cream" in 2016 for a special issue of *The New Yorker* dedicated to stories of celebrities' first jobs. In the essay, the hardest working woman in television describes her teenage stint in an ice-cream parlor and explores the origins of her lasting work ethic.

I was not a tall girl. At sixteen, I was barely five feet three inches. That did not work in my favor at the Baskin-Robbins in Park Forest, Illinois. In order to get the smooth, hard ice cream out of the tubs in the freezer, I had to open the glass display case and lean down inside.

Once my head was in, I used one arm to brace myself on the edge of the freezer while, with the other arm, I gathered enough strength to violently jam the metal scoop into the vat of ice cream. The violent jamming was important. If I didn't do it just right, go at it with enough force, I could find myself skimming right over the ice cream's surface. That was always an issue. When I had only one foot on the floor, barely balancing on my toes, that skim would send me flying forward, at which point self-preservation kicked in.

I'd toss aside the scoop and — eyes closed, slightly sickened by what was to come — put out my hands to cushion the fall.

I always had a soft landing. One hand in the Cookies 'n Cream. One 3 hand in the Rocky Road. Submerged in ice cream up to my elbows.

That's the curse of the job — ice cream *everywhere*. My uniform's pink- 4 brown-and-white striped shirt was crisp, cheerful, but by the end of each shift it was gummy and streaked with chocolate and pistachio and sorbet and mint chip. The clear plastic gloves didn't help. Ice cream ran up and down my arms; it slipped inside the gloves; it stuck in the crevices behind my knees. You have not fully lived on this earth until you have tried to wash Pink Bubblegum ice cream out of your cornrows.

I didn't need the job. I was an honor student and a volunteer at the local 5 hospital, and my parents worked quite hard to make sure that I was on the path to a good college. They pushed me to concentrate on school.

But there was this tiny denim miniskirt, with buttons up the front. It 6 barely reached the bottom of my butt cheeks; a sudden wind would have made it a crime in several states. It. Was. *Fierce*. Tiny denim mini was beautiful. Tiny denim mini was everything to me.

One March day, my mother gave me forty dollars to buy clothes for a 7 dance. I bought the skirt. When she insisted that it be returned, I — newly indoctrinated into the churches of Janet Jackson and Madonna — refused. My mother calmly informed me, in a tone that suggested I had five seconds before I would meet my Maker, that when I had my own job I could buy any clothes I wanted. Until then, she would decide what I wore and what I did not.

Wanting to live, I returned the denim mini. And then, wanting to win, I 8 walked over to Baskin-Robbins and, with all my honor-student charm, talked the manager into giving me a job.

I would like to say that I didn't do it for the denim mini. I would like to 9 say that I did it for the freedom the denim mini represented. I would like to say that I did it for the power the denim-mini fight gave me. If pushed, I might say that I did it because I was dumb enough to think I knew more than my mother. The thing is, though, when you boil it down: I did it for the denim mini.

I let a miniskirt propel me into the workforce.   10

I went home to face my mother, defiant. She laughed. Then she told me 11 that, now that I'd committed to a job, I wasn't allowed to quit.

"You picked a hard row to hoe," she said, and went back to her chess game. 12

The rows were tubs of ice cream. The hoe was that scoop. On my third day 13 of work, I came home covered in Butter Pecan and announced to my mother that she could not make me keep working. My mother looked at me. She did not say a word. She did not have to. We both knew who would win this argument.

And so I spent my summer days with my head in a freezer, balancing on my   14
toes, sticky as can be, trying not to fall into vat after vat. When I did it right,
I got a nice thick ball of ice cream into my scoop. Then I would carefully edge
my way out of the freezer and put the ball in a cup, in a cone, in a sugar cone, in
a waffle cone, in a shake, in a frozen drink, a banana split, a sundae . . .

It was my first job. I felt gritty; I felt real. There were time sheets and   15
shifts and a manager and a uniform. I got Employee of the Month. I smiled at
strangers and said, "You have a nice day!" I pretended not to be clumsy around
the hot public-school boys who came to taste different flavors and left without
buying anything. And I got paid. Minimum wage plus a scoop on every shift.

I never bought the denim mini. Turns out that minimum wage doesn't go   16
all that far. I also never ate much ice cream after that. But I learned responsibility. I learned to keep my word. I learned, no matter how hard it is, to keep
scooping until the job is done.

Journal Writing

Think of the first job you ever had, whether it was a volunteer position, something
temporary in retail or food services, or more structured work for a regular employer.
What was the job? Did you do it because you wanted to, because you needed the
income, or for some other reason? What was it like?

Questions on Meaning

1. What would you say is Rhimes's PURPOSE in this essay? Does she express her
   purpose in a THESIS STATEMENT, or is it implied?

2. Why did the author seek out a part-time job at Baskin-Robbins? How do her
   circumstances hint at the deeper implications of her upbringing?

3. What DOMINANT IMPRESSION of the job does Rhimes create?

4. In what ways does the "tiny denim miniskirt" (par. 6) serve as a SYMBOL for
   Rhimes? What does it represent to her?

Questions on Writing Strategy

1. What strategy does Rhimes use to connect with her readers? How well does she
   succeed, in your estimation?

2. What is the intended EFFECT of paragraphs 9 and 10?

3. How does Rhimes organize her description?

4. **OTHER METHODS**   Where does Rhimes use PROCESS ANALYSIS? What do these
   passages contribute to the essay?

Questions on Language

1. Consult a dictionary if you are unsure of the meaning of any of the following: sorbet, crevices, cornrows (par. 4); indoctrinated (7); defiant (11).

2. In describing the miniskirt she wanted in paragraph 6, Rhimes says, "It. Was. *Fierce.*" What do you think she means? Why does she place a period after each word in the sentence?

3. Point to a few instances in the essay that make particularly effective use of CONCRETE details and sensory IMAGES to convey Rhimes's experience.

4. Rhimes uses several FIGURES OF SPEECH in this essay, most notably metaphor. Find two or three examples and comment on their meaning.

Suggestions for Writing

1. **FROM JOURNAL TO ESSAY**   Write about your first job, using description and NAR-RATION to convey the effect the experience had on you. Or, if you wish, use PRO-CESS ANALYSIS to explain the mechanics of the job to a new or future employee.

2. Have you ever initiated a course of action but then, as events unfolded, lost control of the situation? What happened, and how did you respond? Write an essay in which you relate your experience.

3. Using Rhimes's essay as a model, compose an essay in which you contemplate and explain your sense of identity. How do you define yourself? Has any one person had a significant effect on who you are? How so?

4. **CRITICAL WRITING**   Drawing on details in her essay as evidence, ANALYZE Rhimes's apparent attitude toward femininity and feminism in popular culture, as a teenager and now. Consider especially her mother's influence on her daughter's behavior and attitude. How, in each woman's estimation, should a teenage girl dress? What kinds of jobs are appropriate for a female student? Where should she set her goals? What are a woman's responsibilities, to herself and to others? Where does Rhimes's attitude come from, and how has it affected her life?

5. **CONNECTIONS**   Both Shonda Rhimes's "My Summer of Scooping Ice Cream" and Kunal Nayyar's "Kumar Ran a Car" (p. 91) examine jobs the writers held as students. Write an essay that considers the extent to which attitude affects a person's ability to succeed at work and in life, using these two essays and your own experience for examples and EVIDENCE.

N. SCOTT MOMADAY

Navarre Scott Momaday was born in 1934 on the Kiowa Indian Reservation in Oklahoma and grew up there and on other reservations in the Southwest. His father was a Kiowa, his mother a descendant of white pioneers, and their fusion of Native and European American cultures permeates Momaday's work. He has always pursued an academic career, earning a BA in 1958 from the University of New Mexico and a PhD in 1963 from Stanford University, teaching at several universities, and writing on poetry. At the same time he has been one of the country's foremost interpreters of American Indian history, myths, and landscapes. Momaday's first novel, *House Made of Dawn* (1968), won the Pulitzer Prize, and he has since published more than fifteen books, including *The Names* (memoir, 1976), *In the Presence of the Sun* (stories and poems, 1992), *In the Bear's House* (poems, essays, and artwork, 1999), and *Again the Far Morning* (poems, 2011). In 2007 he was awarded the National Medal of Arts. Momaday is also a playwright and a painter and is active with the Kiowa Gourd Dance Society. He teaches at the University of Arizona.

The Way to Rainy Mountain

"The Way to Rainy Mountain" is the introduction to a book of that title, published in 1969, in which Momaday tells Kiowa myths and history and his own story of discovering his heritage. Writing on the occasion of his grandmother's death, Momaday begins and ends this essay in the same place, the Oklahoma plain where the Kiowa tribe was brought down by the US government. In between he visits the sites where the Kiowas had formed the powerful, noble society from which his grandmother sprang.

A single knoll rises out of the plain in Oklahoma, north and west of the 1
Wichita Range.[1] For my people, the Kiowas, it is an old landmark, and they gave it the name Rainy Mountain. The hardest weather in the world is there. Winter brings blizzards, hot tornadic winds arise in the spring, and in summer the prairie is an anvil's edge. The grass turns brittle and brown, and it cracks beneath your feet. There are green belts along the rivers and creeks, linear groves of hickory and pecan, willow and witch hazel. At a distance in July or August the steaming foliage seems almost to writhe in fire. Great green and yellow grasshoppers are everywhere in the tall grass, popping up like corn to sting the flesh, and tortoises crawl about on the red earth, going nowhere in the plenty of time. Loneliness is an aspect of the land. All things in the plain are isolate; there is no confusion of objects in the eye, but one hill or one tree

[1] The Wichita Mountains are southwest of Oklahoma City. — EDS.

or one man. To look upon that landscape in the early morning, with the sun at your back, is to lose the sense of proportion. Your imagination comes to life, and this, you think, is where Creation was begun.

I returned to Rainy Mountain in July. My grandmother had died in the spring, and I wanted to be at her grave. She had lived to be very old and at last infirm. Her only living daughter was with her when she died, and I was told that in death her face was that of a child. 2

I like to think of her as a child. When she was born, the Kiowas were living that last great moment of their history. For more than a hundred years they had controlled the open range from the Smoky Hill River to the Red, from the headwaters of the Canadian to the fork of the Arkansas and Cimarron.[2] In alliance with the Comanches, they had ruled the whole of the southern Plains. War was their sacred business, and they were among the finest horsemen the world has ever known. But warfare for the Kiowas was preeminently a matter of disposition rather than of survival, and they never understood the grim, unrelenting advance of the US Cavalry. When at last, divided and ill-provisioned, they were driven onto the Staked Plains in the cold rains of autumn, they fell into panic. In Palo Duro Canyon they abandoned their crucial stores to pillage and had nothing then but their lives. In order to save themselves, they surrendered to the soldiers at Fort Sill and were imprisoned in the old stone corral that now stands as a military museum.[3] My grandmother was spared the humiliation of those high gray walls by eight or ten years, but she must have known from birth the affliction of defeat, the dark brooding of old warriors. 3

Her name was Aho, and she belonged to the last culture to evolve in North America. Her forebears came down from the high country in western Montana nearly three centuries ago. They were a mountain people, a mysterious tribe of hunters whose language has never been positively classified in any major group. In the late seventeenth century they began a long migration to the south and east. It was a journey toward the dawn, and it led to a golden age. Along the way the Kiowas were befriended by the Crows, who gave them the culture and religion of the Plains. They acquired horses, and their ancient nomadic spirit was suddenly free of the ground. They acquired Tai-me, the sacred Sun Dance doll, from that moment the object and symbol of their worship, and so shared in the divinity of the sun. Not least, they acquired the sense of destiny, therefore courage and pride. When they entered upon the southern Plains they had been transformed. No longer were they slaves to the simple necessity of survival; they were a lordly and dangerous society of 4

[2] Momaday describes an area covering much of present-day Kansas and Oklahoma as well as the Texas Panhandle and parts of Colorado and New Mexico. —Eds.
[3] The Palo Duro Canyon is south of Amarillo, Texas, and Fort Sill is southwest of Oklahoma City, near the Wichita Mountains. —Eds.

fighters and thieves, hunters and priests of the sun. According to their origin myth, they entered the world through a hollow log. From one point of view, their migration was the fruit of an old prophecy, for indeed they emerged from a sunless world.

Although my grandmother lived out her long life in the shadow of Rainy 5
Mountain, the immense landscape of the continental interior lay like memory in her blood. She could tell of the Crows, whom she had never seen, and of the Black Hills,[4] where she had never been. I wanted to see in reality what she had seen more perfectly in the mind's eye, and traveled fifteen hundred miles to begin my pilgrimage.

Yellowstone, it seemed to me, was the top of the world, a region of deep 6
lakes and dark timber, canyons and waterfalls. But, beautiful as it is, one might have the sense of confinement there. The skyline in all directions is close at hand, the high wall of the woods and deep cleavages of shade. There is a perfect freedom in the mountains, but it belongs to the eagle and the elk, the badger and the bear. The Kiowas reckoned their stature by the distance they could see, and they were bent and blind in the wilderness.

Descending eastward, the highland meadows are a stairway to the plain. In 7
July the inland slope of the Rockies is luxuriant with flax and buckwheat, stonecrop and larkspur. The earth unfolds and the limit of the land recedes. Clusters of trees, and animals grazing far in the distance, cause the vision to reach away and wonder to build upon the mind. The sun follows a longer course in the day, and the sky is immense beyond all comparison. The great billowing clouds that sail upon it are shadows that move upon the grain like water, dividing light. Farther down, in the land of the Crows and Blackfeet, the plain is yellow. Sweet clover takes hold of the hills and bends upon itself to cover and seal the soil. There the Kiowas paused on their way; they had come to the place where they must change their lives. The sun is at home on the plains. Precisely there does it have the certain character of a god. When the Kiowas came to the land of the Crows, they could see the dark lees of the hills at dawn across the Bighorn River, the profusion of light on the grain shelves, the oldest deity ranging after the solstices. Not yet would they veer southward to the caldron of the land that lay below; they must wean their blood from the northern winter and hold the mountains a while longer in their view. They bore Tai-me in procession to the east.

A dark mist lay over the Black Hills, and the land was like iron. At the 8
top of a ridge I caught sight of Devil's Tower[5] upthrust against the gray sky as if in the birth of time the core of the earth had broken through its crust and

---

[4] The Black Hills are in western South Dakota. Yellowstone (next paragraph) is in northwestern Wyoming. In paragraphs 7–8, Momaday describes movement eastward across the top of Wyoming. —Eds.

[5] Devil's Tower is an 865-foot stone outcropping in northeastern Wyoming, now a national monument. —Eds.

the motion of the world was begun. There are things in nature that engender an awful quiet in the heart of man; Devil's Tower is one of them. Two centuries ago, because they could not do otherwise, the Kiowas made a legend at the base of the rock. My grandmother said:

> Eight children were there at play, seven sisters and their brother. Suddenly the boy was struck dumb; he trembled and began to run upon his hands and feet. His fingers became claws, and his body was covered with fur. Directly there was a bear where the boy had been. The sisters were terrified; they ran, and the bear after them. They came to the stump of a great tree, and the tree spoke to them. It bade them climb upon it, and as they did so it began to rise into the air. The bear came to kill them, but they were just beyond its reach. It reared against the tree and scored the bark all around with its claws. The seven sisters were borne into the sky, and they became the stars of the Big Dipper.

From that moment, and so long as the legend lives, the Kiowas have kinsmen in the night sky. Whatever they were in the mountains, they could be no more. However tenuous their well-being, however much they had suffered and would suffer again, they had found a way out of the wilderness.

My grandmother had a reverence for the sun, a holy regard that now is all but gone out of mankind. There was a wariness in her, and an ancient awe. She was a Christian in her later years, but she had come a long way about, and she never forgot her birthright. As a child she had been to the Sun Dances; she had taken part in those annual rites, and by them she had learned the restoration of her people in the presence of Tai-me. She was about seven when the last Kiowa Sun Dance was held in 1887 on the Washita River above Rainy Mountain Creek.[6] The buffalo were gone. In order to consummate the ancient sacrifice — to impale the head of a buffalo bull upon the medicine tree — a delegation of old men journeyed into Texas, there to beg and barter for an animal from the Goodnight herd. She was ten when the Kiowas came together for the last time as a living Sun Dance culture. They could find no buffalo; they had to hang an old hide from the sacred tree. Before the dance could begin, a company of soldiers rode out from Fort Sill under orders to disperse the tribe. Forbidden without cause the essential act of their faith, having seen the wild herds slaughtered and left to rot upon the ground, the Kiowas backed away forever from the medicine tree. That was July 20, 1890, at the great bend of the Washita. My grandmother was there. Without bitterness, and for as long as she lived, she bore a vision of deicide.[7]

Now that I can have her only in memory, I see my grandmother in the several postures that were peculiar to her: standing at the wood stove on a

---

[6] The Washita runs halfway between Oklahoma City and the Wichita Mountains. —EDS.
[7] The killing of a divine being or beings (from Latin words meaning "god" and "kill"). —EDS.

winter morning and turning meat in a great iron skillet; sitting at the south window, bent above her beadwork, and afterwards, when her vision failed, looking down for a long time into the fold of her hands; going out upon a cane, very slowly as she did when the weight of age came upon her; praying. I remember her most often at prayer. She made long, rambling prayers out of suffering and hope, having seen many things. I was never sure that I had the right to hear, so exclusive were they of all mere custom and company. The last time I saw her she prayed standing by the side of her bed at night, naked to the waist, the light of a kerosene lamp moving upon her dark skin. Her long, black hair, always drawn and braided in the day, lay upon her shoulders and against her breasts like a shawl. I do not speak Kiowa, and I never understood her prayers, but there was something inherently sad in the sound, some merest hesitation upon the syllables of sorrow. She began in a high and descending pitch, exhausting her breath to silence; then again and again — and always the same intensity of effort, of something that is, and is not, like urgency in the human voice. Transported so in the dancing light among the shadows of her room, she seemed beyond the reach of time. But that was illusion; I think I knew then that I should not see her again.

Houses are like sentinels in the plain, old keepers of the weather watch.   11 There, in a very little while, wood takes on the appearance of great age. All colors wear soon away in the wind and rain, and then the wood is burned gray and the grain appears and the nails turn red with rust. The windowpanes are black and opaque; you imagine there is nothing within, and indeed there are many ghosts, bones given up to the land. They stand here and there against the sky, and you approach them for a longer time than you expect. They belong in the distance; it is their domain.

Once there was a lot of sound in my grandmother's house, a lot of coming and   12 going, feasting and talk. The summers there were full of excitement and reunion. The Kiowas are a summer people; they abide the cold and keep to themselves, but when the season turns and the land becomes warm and vital they cannot hold still; an old love of going returns upon them. The aged visitors who came to my grandmother's house when I was a child were made of lean and leather, and they bore themselves upright. They wore great black hats and bright ample shirts that shook in the wind. They rubbed fat upon their hair and wound their braids with strips of colored cloth. Some of them painted their faces and carried the scars of old and cherished enmities. They were an old council of warlords, come to remind and be reminded of who they were. Their wives and daughters served them well. The women might indulge themselves; gossip was at once the mark and compensation of their servitude. They made loud and elaborate talk among themselves, full of jest and gesture, fright and false alarm. They went abroad in fringed and flowered shawls, bright beadwork and German silver. They were at home in the kitchen, and they prepared meals that were banquets.

There were frequent prayer meetings, and great nocturnal feasts. When I   13
was a child I played with my cousins outside, where the lamp-light fell upon the
ground and the singing of the old people rose up around us and carried away
into the darkness. There were a lot of good things to eat, a lot of laughter and
surprise. And afterwards, when the quiet returned, I lay down with my grandmother and could hear the frogs away by the river and feel the motion of the air.

Now there is a funeral silence in the rooms, the endless wake of some   14
final word. The walls have closed in upon my grandmother's house. When I
returned to it in mourning, I saw for the first time in my life how small it was.
It was late at night, and there was a white moon, nearly full. I sat for a long
time on the stone steps by the kitchen door. From there I could see out across
the land; I could see the long row of trees by the creek, the low light upon
the rolling plains, and the stars of the Big Dipper. Once I looked at the moon
and caught sight of a strange thing. A cricket had perched upon the handrail,
only a few inches away from me. My line of vision was such that the creature
filled the moon like a fossil. It had gone there, I thought, to live and die, for
there, of all places, was its small definition made whole and eternal. A warm
wind rose up and purled like the longing within me.

The next morning I awoke at dawn and went out on the dirt road to   15
Rainy Mountain. It was already hot, and the grasshoppers began to fill the air.
Still, it was early in the morning, and the birds sang out of the shadows. The
long yellow grass on the mountain shone in the bright light, and a scissortail
hied above the land. There, where it ought to be, at the end of a long and legendary way, was my grandmother's grave. Here and there on the dark stones
were ancestral names. Looking back once, I saw the mountain and came away.

Journal Writing

"The Way to Rainy Mountain" is about Momaday's associations between his
grandmother and Rainy Mountain. Think of somebody special to you and a
specific place that you associate with this person. Jot down as many details about the
person and place as you can.

Questions on Meaning

1. What is the significance of Momaday's statement that the Kiowas "reckoned
    their stature by the distance they could see" (par. 6)? How does this statement
    relate to the ultimate fate of the Kiowas?

2. Remembering his grandmother, Momaday writes, "She made long, rambling prayers
    out of suffering and hope, having seen many things" (par. 10). What is the key
    point here, and how does the concept of prayer connect with the essay as a whole?

3. What do you think Momaday's main idea is? What thread links all the essay's parts?

4. What seems to be Momaday's PURPOSE in writing this essay? Can we read this as more than a personal story about a visit to his grandmother's grave?

Questions on Writing Strategy

1. Who is Momaday's AUDIENCE? Do you think he is writing for other Kiowa descendants? for non-Indians? for others who have lost an older relative?

2. "Loneliness is an aspect of the land," Momaday writes (par. 1). To what extent do you think this sentence captures the DOMINANT IMPRESSION of the essay? If you perceive a different impression, what is it?

3. How does Momaday organize his essay? (It may help to plot the structure by preparing a rough outline.) How effective do you find this organization, and why?

4. Would you characterize Momaday's description as SUBJECTIVE or OBJECTIVE? What about his use of language suggests one over the other?

5. **OTHER METHODS**   Besides description, Momaday relies on mixing other methods, such as NARRATION, EXAMPLE, COMPARISON AND CONTRAST, and CAUSE AND EFFECT. What is the purpose of the comparison in paragraphs 12–14?

Questions on Language

1. If you do not know the meanings of the following words, look them up in a dictionary: anvil (par. 1); infirm (2); preeminently, pillage, affliction (3); nomadic (4); cleavages (6); lees, profusion, deity, caldron (7); engender, tenuous (8); reverence, consummate (9); inherently (10); purled (14); hied (15).

2. Momaday uses many vivid FIGURES OF SPEECH. Locate at least one use each of metaphor, simile, and hyperbole (review these terms in the Glossary if necessary). What does each of these figures convey?

3. Momaday's first and last paragraphs present contrasting IMAGES of Rainy Mountain and the surrounding plain: At first, "the prairie is an anvil's edge" and the "grass turns brittle and brown"; in the end, "the birds sang out of the shadows" and the "long yellow grass on the mountain shone in the bright light." How does this contrast serve Momaday's purpose?

4. Notice Momaday's use of PARALLELISM in describing the visitors to his grandmother's house (par. 12)—for instance, "They wore. . . . They rubbed. . . . They made. . . ." What does the parallelism convey about the people being described?

Suggestions for Writing

1. **FROM JOURNAL TO ESSAY**   Develop your journal entry (p. 149) into an essay that describes both the person and the place, using concrete and specific details to make the connection between them clear to your readers.

2. Momaday writes about his ancestors and a way of life very different from that of the present. For this assignment you may need to investigate your family's history. Write an essay that describes your ancestors' way of life. (Your ancestors may be as recent as your grandparents or as distant as your research allows.) Who were these people? How did they live? How does that way of life differ from the way you and your family live now? Be specific in your description and comparison, providing concrete details and examples for clarity.

3. One of Momaday's underlying themes in this essay is the difficulties American Indians often face on reservations. Do some research about the conditions of reservation life. Then write an essay in which you report your findings.

4. **CRITICAL WRITING**   In an essay, ANALYZE Momaday's attitudes toward the Kiowas as revealed in the language he uses to describe them. Support your THESIS (your central idea about Momaday's attitudes) with specific quotations from the essay.

5. **CONNECTIONS**   Both Momaday and E. B. White, in "Once More to the Lake" (p. 639), write about places that tie them to their families. Write an essay that contrasts the sense of continuity in White's essay with the sense of loss and change in Momaday's. Are there also similarities in their relations with their families and these places?

N. Scott Momaday on Writing

In an interview for *Sequoia* magazine in 1975, N. Scott Momaday was asked by William T. Morgan, Jr., whether he saw himself as a "spokesman" for American Indians.

No, and it's something I don't think about very often. I don't identify with any group of writers, and I don't think of myself as being a spokesman for the Indian people. That would be presumptuous, it seems to me. . . . When I write I find it a very private kind of thing, and I like to keep it that way. You know, I would be uncomfortable I think if I were trying to express the views of other people. When I write I write out of my own experience, and out of my own ideas of that experience, and I'm not concerned to write the history of a people except as that history bears on me directly. When I was writing *The Way to Rainy Mountain*, for example, I was dealing with something that belongs to the Indian world, and the Kiowa people as a whole, but I wasn't concerned with that so much as I was concerned with the fact that it meant this to me—this is how I as a person felt about it. And I want my writing to reflect myself in certain ways—that is my first concern.

The Bedford Reader on Writing

Momaday insists on a personal approach to ACADEMIC WRITING, a habit that some teachers caution against (see, for example, our comments regarding the uses of the first-PERSON *I* on p. 56). But Momaday demonstrates particular mastery of SYNTHESIS, bringing in other people's perspectives while keeping his own ideas at the center. See pages 45–50 for advice on integrating evidence without losing your distinctive VOICE, as Momaday does in "The Way to Rainy Mountain."

JOYCE CAROL OATES

One of America's most respected and prolific contemporary authors, Joyce Carol Oates was born in 1938 in Lockport, New York. After graduating from Syracuse University in 1960, she earned an MA from the University of Wisconsin. In 1963 she published her first book, a collection of short stories, and she has published an average of two books a year since then. With the novel *them* (1969), Oates became one of the youngest writers to receive the National Book Award for fiction. Other notable novels include *Wonderland* (1971), *Black Water* (1992), *Blonde* (2000), *A Fair Maiden* (2010), and *Hazards of Time Travel* (2018). Oates has also written more than four dozen volumes of poetry and stories, a score of plays, and several works of nonfiction, including memoir, literary criticism, and a study of boxing. Her many awards include the 2010 National Humanities Medal and the 2012 PEN Center USA Award for Lifetime Achievement. Oates teaches writing and literature at Princeton University.

Edward Hopper's *Nighthawks,* 1942

First published in Oates's poetry collection *The Time Traveler* (1989), this poem responds to a well-known painting by the American artist Edward Hopper (1882–1967). The painting, *Nighthawks,* is reproduced on the facing page, both in full view and in detail.

> The three men are fully clothed, long sleeves,　　　　1
> even hats, though it's indoors, and brightly lit,
> and there's a woman. The woman is wearing
> a short-sleeved red dress cut to expose her arms,
> a curve of her creamy chest; she's contemplating　　5
> a cigarette in her right hand, thinking that
> her companion has finally left his wife but
> can she trust him? Her heavy-lidded eyes,
> pouty lipsticked mouth, she has the redhead's
> true pallor like skim milk, damned good-looking　　10
> and she guesses she knows it but what exactly
> has it gotten her so far, and where?—he'll start
> to feel guilty in a few days, she knows
> the signs, an actual smell, sweaty, rancid, like
> dirty socks; he'll slip away to make telephone calls　　15
> and she swears she isn't going to go through that
> again, isn't going to break down crying or begging
> nor is she going to scream at him, she's finished

Edward Hopper, *Nighthawks*, 1942, Oil on canvas, Photo: A. Burkatovski/Fine Art Images/Superstock

with all that. And he's silent beside her,
not the kind to talk much but he's thinking   20
thank God he made the right move at last,
he's a little dazed like a man in a dream —
is this a dream?—so much that's wide, still,
mute, horizontal, and the counterman in white,
stooped as he is and unmoving, and the man   25
on the other stool unmoving except to sip
his coffee; but he's feeling pretty good,
it's primarily relief, this time he's sure
as hell going to make it work, he owes it to her
and to himself, Christ's sake. And she's thinking   30
the light in this place is too bright, probably
not very flattering, she hates it when her lipstick
wears off and her makeup gets caked, she'd like
to use a ladies' room but there isn't one here
and Jesus how long before a gas station opens? —   35
it's the middle of the night and she has a feeling
time is never going to budge. This time
though she isn't going to demean herself —
he starts in about his wife, his kids, how
he let them down, they trusted him and he let   40
them down, she'll slam out of the goddamned room
and if he calls her *Sugar* or *Baby* in that voice,
running his hands over her like he has the right,
she'll slap his face hard, *You know I hate that: Stop!*
And he'll stop. He'd better. The angrier   45
she gets the stiller she is, hasn't said a word
for the past ten minutes, not a strand
of her hair stirs, and it smells a little like ashes
or like the henna she uses to brighten it, but
the smell is faint or anyway, crazy for her   50
like he is, he doesn't notice, or mind —
burying his hot face in her neck, between her cool
breasts, or her legs—wherever she'll have him,
and whenever. She's still contemplating
the cigarette burning in her hand,   55
the counterman is still stooped gaping
at her, and he doesn't mind that, why not,
as long as she doesn't look back, in fact
he's thinking he's the luckiest man in the world
so why isn't he happier?   60

Journal Writing

In this poem Oates describes what she sees in Hopper's painting and also what she imagines, particularly about the woman. Most of us have unobtrusively observed strangers in a public place and imagined what they were thinking or what was going on between them. Write a paragraph or two on why such observation can be interesting or what it can (or can't) reveal.

Questions on Meaning

1. What story does Oates imagine about the couple in *Nighthawks*? How are the man's and the woman's thoughts different?

2. Line 23 of the poem asks, "*is* this a dream?" Who is posing this question? What about the painting is dreamlike?

3. Throughout the poem, Oates emphasizes the silence and stillness of the scene in the restaurant—for instance, "The angrier / she gets the stiller she is, hasn't said a word / for the past ten minutes" (lines 45–47). What meanings about the painting and the people in it might Oates be emphasizing?

Questions on Writing Strategy

1. Where in the poem does Oates use CONCRETE language to describe what can actually be seen in the painting, as opposed to what she imagines? How does she use the former to support the latter? What does the mixture suggest about Oates's PURPOSE?

2. The thoughts of the woman include some vivid sensory images. What are some examples? How do these thoughts contrast with the man's?

3. What techniques of sentence structure does Oates use in lines 12–19 and 30–45 to suggest the woman's rising anger?

4. **OTHER METHODS** Where does Oates use NARRATION in the poem? Where does she imply a narrative? Why is narration important to her analysis of Hopper's painting?

Questions on Language

1. Oates uses just a few words that might be unfamiliar. Make sure you know the meanings of contemplating (line 5); rancid (14); budge (37); demean (38); henna (49).

2. The man's and woman's thoughts are peppered with strong language that some might find offensive. What does this language suggest about how Oates sees the characters?

3. In lines 27–28 Oates writes that the man is "feeling pretty good, / it's primarily relief." How does the word "relief" undercut the notion of "feeling pretty good"?

Suggestions for Writing

1. **FROM JOURNAL TO ESSAY** Find a public place where you can observe strangers unobtrusively from a distance — a park, for example, or a plaza, campus quad, dining hall, restaurant, bus, train. Take notes about what you observe — what your subjects look like, how they behave, how they interact with each other. Then write an essay based on your notes that incorporates both actual description of your subjects and what the details lead you to imagine they are thinking to themselves and saying to each other. Make sure the link between actual and imaginary is clear to your readers.

2. In a local gallery or museum, in a library art book, or on a Web site such as *WebMuseum* (*ibiblio.org/wm/paint*), find a painting that seems to you particularly intriguing or appealing. Then write a prose essay or a poem that expresses the painting's appeal to you. You may but need not imitate Oates by focusing on the thoughts of any figures in the painting. Describe the details of the painting and how they work together to create meaning for you. If you write a poem, don't worry about the technical aspects of poetry (meter, rhyme, and the rest). Think instead about your choice of words and IMAGES, building the poem through description.

3. **CRITICAL WRITING** Throughout her poem Oates interweaves description of the painting and its figures with what she imagines the figures are thinking. Mark each kind of material in the poem, and then examine the shifts from one to the other. How does Oates make readers aware that she is moving from one to the other? Are the shifts always clear? If not, are the blurrings deliberate or a mistake? What do you think of this technique overall?

4. **CONNECTIONS** In "But What Do You Mean?" (p. 377), Deborah Tannen outlines differences in the ways women and men communicate. Read that essay, and ANALYZE which of the differences seem to apply to Hopper's woman and man, either as Oates imagines them or as you see them. In an essay, explain how Tannen might view each as typifying his or her gender.

Joyce Carol Oates on Writing

For a 1997 book titled *Introspections: American Poets on One of Their Own Poems*, Joyce Carol Oates did us the valuable service of writing an essay about her poem "Edward Hopper's *Nighthawks*, 1942." She tells us why and how the painting sparked her own work of imagination.

The attempt to give concrete expression to a very amorphous impression is the insurmountable difficulty in painting.

These words of Edward Hopper's apply to all forms of art, of course. Certainly to poetry. How to evoke, in mere words, the powerful, inchoate flood of emotions that constitute "real life"? How to take the reader into the poet's innermost self, where the poet's language becomes the reader's, if only for a quicksilver moment? This is the great challenge of art, which even to fail in requires faith.

Insomniac nights began for me when I was a young teenager. Those long, lonely stretches of time when no one else in the house was awake (so far as I knew); the romance of solitude and self-sufficiency in which time seems not to pass or passes so slowly it will never bring dawn.

Always there was an air of mystery in the insomniac night. What profound thoughts and visions came to me! How strangely detached from the day-self I became! Dawn brought the familiar world, and the familiar self; a "self" that was obliged to accommodate others' expectations, and was, indeed, defined by others, predominantly adults. *Yes but you don't know me*, I would think by day, in adolescent secrecy and defiance. *You don't really know me!*

Many of Edward Hopper's paintings evoke the insomniac's uncanny vision, none more forcefully than *Nighthawks*, which both portrays insomniacs and evokes their solitude in the viewer. In this famous painting, "reality" has undergone some sort of subtle yet drastic alteration. The immense field of detail that would strike the eye has been reduced to smooth, streamlined surfaces; people and objects are enhanced, as on a lighted stage; not life but a nostalgia for life, a memory of life, is the true subject. Men and women in Hopper's paintings are somnambulists, if not mannequins, stiffly posed, with faces of the kind that populate our dreams, at which we dare not look too closely for fear of seeing the faces dissolve.

Here is, not the world, but a memory of it. For all dreams are memory: cobbled-together sights, sounds, impressions, snatches of previous experience. The dream-vision is the perpetual present, yet its contents relate only to the past.

There is little of Eros in Hopper's puritanical vision, *Nighthawks* being the rare exception. The poem enters the painting as a way of animating what cannot be animated; a way of delving into the painting's mystery. *Who are these people, what has brought them together, are they in fact together?* At the time of writing the poem I hadn't read Gail Levin's definitive biography of Hopper, and did not know how Hopper had made himself into the most methodical and premeditated of artists, continuously seeking, with his wife Jo (who would have posed for the redheaded nighthawk), scenes and tableaux to paint. Many of Hopper's canvases are elaborately posed, and their suggestion

of movie stills is not accidental. This is a visual art purposefully evoking narrative, or at least the opening strategies of narrative, in which a scene is "set,"
"characters" are presented, often in ambiguous relationships.

Nighthawks is a work of silence. Here is an Eros of stasis, and of melancholy. It is an uncommonly beautiful painting of stark, separate, sculpted
forms, in heightened juxtapositions, brightly lit and yet infinitely mysterious.
The poem slips into it with no transition, as we "wake" in a dream, yearning
to make the frozen narrative come alive; but finally thwarted by the painting's
measured void of a world, in which silence outweighs the human voice, and
the barriers between human beings are impenetrable. So the poem ends as it
begins, circling upon its lovers' obsessions, achieving no crisis, no confrontation, no epiphany, no release, time forever frozen in the insomniac night.

The Bedford Reader on Writing

Oates's comments on the "great challenge of art" demonstrate just how
much insight a writer can gain by applying close examination and ANALYSIS
to a visual text. To learn how to take a similar approach of CRITICAL READING
with a work of fine art — or any other visual image — read pages 22–26
(closely).

ADDITIONAL WRITING TOPICS

Description

1. Try this in-class writing experiment. Describe another person in the room so clearly and unmistakably that when you read your description aloud, your subject will be recognized. (Be OBJECTIVE. No insulting descriptions, please!)

2. Write a paragraph describing one subject from each of the following categories. It will be up to you to make the general subject refer to a particular person, place, or thing. Write at least one paragraph as an objective description and at least one as a SUBJECTIVE description.

PERSON

A friend or roommate
A musician
A parent or grandparent
A child you know
A prominent politician
A historical figure

THING

A city or rural bus
A favorite toy or gadget
A painting or photograph
A foggy day
A season of the year
A musical instrument

PLACE

An office
A classroom
A college campus
A peaceful spot
A waiting room
A lake or pond

3. In a brief essay, describe your ideal place—perhaps an apartment or dorm room, a home office, a restaurant, a gym, a store, a garden, a dance club, a theater. With concrete details, try to make the ideal seem actual.

Narration and Description

4. Use a combination of NARRATION and description to develop any one of the following topics, or a topic they suggest for you:
Your first day on the job or at college
A vacation
Returning to an old neighborhood
Getting lost
An encounter with a wild animal
Delivering bad (or good) news

COSTUMES TO SCARE MILLENNIALS

7

EXAMPLE

Pointing to Instances

◀ **Examples in a cartoon**

This cartoon by Sarah Andersen, from the "Sarah's Scribbles"
collection *Big Mushy Happy Lump* (2017), uses the method of
example in a complex way. Most simply, the drawings-with-text
propose instances or illustrations of the general category stated
in the title—not every conceivable thing young adults might find
frightening today but a few possibilities. At the same time, the
humor of the examples reveals other, sharper observations by
the millennial artist—ideas about current trends, generational
expectations, and adult responsibilities. What are some of these
general ideas? How would you express the point of Andersen's
cartoon? Does it mesh with your own experience?

THE METHOD

"There have been many women runners of distinction," a writer begins, and quickly goes on, "among them Joan Benoit Samuelson, Florence Griffith Joyner, Grete Waitz, Uta Pippig, and Aimee Mullins."

You have just seen examples at work. An EXAMPLE (from the Latin *exemplum*: "one thing selected from among many") is an instance that reveals a whole type. By selecting an example, a writer shows the nature or character of the group from which it is taken. In a written essay, examples will often serve to illustrate a general statement, or GENERALIZATION. Here, for instance, the writer Linda Wolfe makes a point about the food fetishes of Roman emperors (Domitian and Claudius ruled in the first century AD).

> The emperors used their gastronomical concerns to indicate their con-
> tempt of the country and the whole task of governing it. Domitian humiliated
> his cabinet by forcing them to attend him at his villa to help solve a serious
> problem. When they arrived he kept them waiting for hours. The problem,
> it finally appeared, was that the emperor had just purchased a giant fish,
> too large for any dish he owned, and he needed the learned brains of his
> ministers to decide whether the fish should be minced or whether a larger
> pot should be sought. The emperor Claudius one day rode hurriedly to the
> Senate and demanded they deliberate the importance of a life without
> pork. Another time he sat in his tribunal ostensibly administering justice
> but actually allowing the litigants to argue and orate while he grew dreamy,
> interrupting the discussions only to announce, "Meat pies are wonderful.
> We shall have them for dinner."

Wolfe might have allowed the opening sentence of her paragraph—the TOPIC SENTENCE—to remain a vague generalization. Instead, she supports it with three examples, each a brief story of an emperor's contemptuous behavior. With these examples, Wolfe not only explains and supports her generalization but also animates it.

The method of giving examples—of illustrating what you're saying with a "for instance"—is not merely helpful to all kinds of writing; it is essential. Writers who bore us, or lose us completely, often have an ample supply of ideas; their trouble is that they never pull those ideas down from the clouds. A dull writer, for instance, might declare, "The emperors used food to humili-ate their governments," and then, instead of giving examples, go on, "They also manipulated their families," or something—adding still another large, unillustrated idea. Specific examples are *needed* elements in effective prose. Not only do they make ideas understandable, but they also keep readers from falling asleep.

Example   **163**

THE PROCESS

The Generalization and the Thesis

Examples illustrate a generalization, such as Linda Wolfe's opening statement about the Roman emperors. Any example essay is bound to have such a generalization as its THESIS, expressed in a THESIS STATEMENT. Here are examples from the essays in this chapter:

> That first encounter, and those that followed, signified that a vast, unnerving gulf lay between nighttime pedestrians—particularly women—and me.
> — Brent Staples, "Black Men and Public Space"

> The truth is, I slip in and out of my black consciousness, as if I'm in a racial coma. Sometimes, I'm so deep in my anger, my irritation, my need to stir change, that I can't see anything outside of the lens of race. At other times I feel guilty about my apathy.
> — Issa Rae, "The Struggle"

> Sometimes I think we would be better off [in dealing with social problems such as homelessness] if we forgot about the broad strokes and concentrated on the details.
> — Anna Quindlen, "Homeless"

The thesis statement establishes the backbone, the central idea, of an essay developed by example. Then the specifics flesh the idea out for readers, bringing it to life.

The Examples

An essay developed by example will often start with a random observation. That is, you'll see something—a man pilfering a dollar from a child's lemonade stand, a friend copying another friend's homework, a roommate downloading pirated movies—and your observation will suggest a generalization (perhaps a statement about the problem of stealing). But a mere example or two probably won't demonstrate your generalization for readers and thus won't achieve your PURPOSE in writing. For that you'll need a range of instances.

Where do you find more? In anything you know—or care to learn. Start close to home. Seek examples in your own immediate knowledge and experience. Explore your conversations with others, your studies, and the storehouse of information you have gathered from books, newspapers, radio, TV, and the Internet as well as from popular hearsay: proverbs and sayings, popular songs, bits of wisdom you've heard voiced in your family.

Now and again, you may feel a temptation to make up an example out of thin air. Suppose you have to write about the benefits — any benefits — that rocket science has conferred on society. You might imagine one such benefit: the prospect of one day being able to travel to outer space and colonize distant planets. That imagined benefit would be all right, but it is obviously a conjecture that you dreamed up. An example from fact or experience is likely to carry more weight. Do a little digging on the Internet or in recent books and magazines. Your reader will feel better informed to be told that science — specifically, the NASA space program — has produced useful inventions. You add:

> Among these are the smoke detector, originally developed as Skylab equipment; the inflatable air bag to protect drivers and pilots, designed to cushion astronauts in splashdowns; a walking chair that enables paraplegics to mount stairs and travel over uneven ground, derived from the moonwalkers' surface buggy; and the technique of cryosurgery, the removal of cancerous tissue by fast freezing.

By using specific examples like these, you render the idea of "benefits to society" more concrete and more definite. Such examples are not mere decoration for your essay; they are necessary if you are to hold your readers' attention and convince them that you are worth listening to.

Lazy writers think, "Oh well, I can't come up with any example here — I'll just leave it to the reader to find one." The flaw in this ASSUMPTION is that the reader may be as lazy as the writer. As a result, a perfectly good idea may be left suspended in the stratosphere.

FOCUS ON SENTENCE VARIETY

While accumulating and detailing examples during drafting — both essential tasks for a successful essay — you may find yourself writing strings of similar sentences:

UNVARIED   One example of a movie that deals with chronic illness is *Rockingham Place*. Another example is *The Beating Heart*. Another is *Tree of Life*. These three movies treat misunderstood or little-known diseases in a way that increases the viewer's sympathy and understanding. *Rockingham Place* deals with a little boy who suffers from cystic fibrosis. *The Beating Heart* deals with a mother of four who is weakening from multiple sclerosis. *Tree of Life* deals with brothers who are both struggling with muscular dystrophy. All three movies show complex human beings caught blamelessly in desperate circumstances.

Example   **165**

The writer of this paragraph was clearly pushing to add examples and to expand them, but the resulting passage needs editing so that the writer's labor isn't so obvious. In the more readable and interesting revision, the sentences vary in structure, group similar details, and distinguish the specifics from the generalizations:

> VARIED   Three movies dealing with disease are *Rockingham Place, The Beating Heart,* and *Tree of Life.* In these movies people with little-known or misunderstood diseases become subjects for the viewer's sympathy and understanding. A little boy suffering from cystic fibrosis, a mother weakening from multiple sclerosis, a pair of brothers coping with muscular dystrophy — these complex, struggling human beings are caught blamelessly in desperate circumstances.

As you review your draft, be alert to repetitive sentence structures and look for opportunities to change them: Try coordinating and subordinating ideas, varying the beginnings and endings of sentences, shortening some and lengthening others (see pp. 57–58).

Organization

As you draft an essay, remember that your examples must be plentiful and specific enough to support your generalization. If you use a lot of examples, ten or twelve or even more, their range should allow you to treat each one briefly, in one or two sentences. But if you offer only three or four examples, say, you will need to describe each one in sufficient detail to make up for the small number. And, if you choose to use only a single extended example, you will have to be as specific as possible so that readers see clearly how it illustrates your generalization.

When giving examples, you may find other methods useful. Sometimes, as in the paragraph by Linda Wolfe, an example takes the form of a NARRATIVE (Chap. 5): an ANECDOTE or a case history. Sometimes an example embodies a vivid DESCRIPTION of a person, place, or thing (Chap. 6). Sometimes, the most effective way to organize a large number of examples is to find some likenesses among them and group them into categories using CLASSIFICATION (Chap. 11).

Often, however, you'll want to arrange your examples more strategically, on their own merits. Generally writers find that CLIMACTIC ORDER works best. Using this strategy, you might arrange your examples from least to most important, weakest to strongest — or the reverse, starting with the most important or strongest point and then tapering off with the rest (although usually it's best to build up to a bang).

HOW TO ORGANIZE EXAMPLES

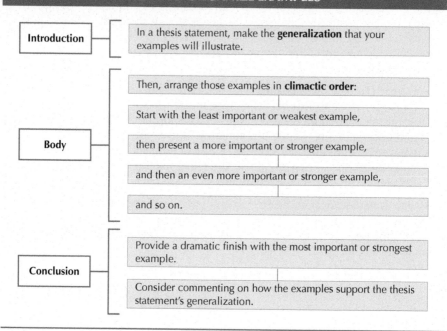

Introduction — In a thesis statement, make the **generalization** that your examples will illustrate.

Body —
- Then, arrange those examples in **climactic order**:
- Start with the least important or weakest example,
- then present a more important or stronger example,
- and then an even more important or stronger example,
- and so on.

Conclusion —
- Provide a dramatic finish with the most important or strongest example.
- Consider commenting on how the examples support the thesis statement's generalization.

CHECKLIST FOR REVIEWING AND REVISING AN EXAMPLE ESSAY

✔ **Generalization.** What general statement do the examples illustrate? Will it be clear to readers what ties the examples together?

✔ **Support.** Are there enough examples to establish the truth of the generalization, or will readers be left needing more?

✔ **Specifics.** Are the examples detailed? Does each one capture some aspect of the generalization?

✔ **Relevance.** Do all the examples relate to the generalization? Should any be cut because they go off track?

✔ **Organization.** Are the examples arranged in a satisfying manner? Do they build from least to most important, for instance, or effectively follow the organization pattern of another method?

✔ **Sentence variety.** Have you varied sentence structures for clarity and interest?

Example   **167**

To conclude your essay, you may want to summarize by elaborating on the generalization of your thesis now that you have supported it. But the essay may not require a formal conclusion at all if you believe your final example emphasizes your point and provides a strong finish.

STUDENT CASE STUDY: A JOB-APPLICATION LETTER

To obtain the kinds of jobs a college education prepares you for, you'll submit a résumé that presents your previous work experience, your education, and your qualifications for a specific career field. To capture the prospective employer's interest, you'll introduce yourself and your résumé with a cover letter, often in the form of an e-mail.

Rather than merely repeat or summarize the contents of a résumé, a job-application letter highlights the connections between your background and the employer's need for someone with particular training and skills. Typically brief and tightly focused on the job in question, an application letter aims to persuade the reader to look at the accompanying résumé and then to follow up with an interview.

When nursing student Susan Churchill was applying for an internship at a nearby hospital, she put together a résumé tailored for a specific opportunity posted at her school's placement office. (See the résumé on p. 360.) Her cover letter, opposite, pulls out examples from the résumé to support the statement (in the third paragraph) that "my education and training in practical nursing make me an ideal candidate."

Tuesday 9/4/18 2:07 PM
FR: schurchill@salter.edu
TO: humanresources@exeterhospital.com
RE: EH-LPN Trainee

Dear Human Resources Director:

I am applying for the paid nursing internship in Exeter Hospital's palliative care department, advertised in the career services office of the Salter School of Nursing and Allied Health.

Introduction states purpose of letter

I have considerable experience in practical nursing from internships and clinical rotations at Huggins Hospital and at

Generalization about experience

Hackett Hill Health Center. At Huggins I studied venipuncture, lab accession, and point-of-care testing. At Hackett Hill I practiced basic LNA procedures and gained familiarity with treatments for endocrine systems. Both facilities gave me experience in varied stages of medical care.

My education and training in practical nursing make me an ideal candidate. In my first year at the Salter School, I have concentrated on developing skills in home healthcare and hospice. I have completed courses in anatomy and physiology, pharmacology, psychology, and human development. At the same time, I have trained in phlebotomy and hold certificates from the National Healthcareer Association, the American Red Cross, and the American Heart Association.

The attached résumé will give you a greater understanding of my qualifications. I would greatly appreciate the opportunity to work with and learn from your talented team, and I look forward to speaking with you soon.

Sincerely,
Susan Churchill

Two examples of experience

Generalization about education and skills

Two sets of examples about education and skills

Concluding paragraph refers reader to résumé and invites a response

BRENT STAPLES

Brent Staples is a member of the editorial board of the *New York Times*, where he writes on culture, politics, and race, winning the Pulitzer Prize for editorial writing in 2019. Born in 1951 in Chester, Pennsylvania, Staples has a BA in behavioral science from Widener University in Chester and a PhD in psychology from the University of Chicago. Before joining the *New York Times* in 1985, he worked for the *Chicago Sun-Times*, the *Chicago Reader*, *Chicago* magazine, and *Down Beat* magazine. He has also taught psychology and contributed to the *New York Times Magazine*, *New York Woman*, *Ms.*, *Harper's*, and other periodicals.

Black Men and Public Space

"Black Men and Public Space" first appeared in the December 1986 issue of *Harper's* magazine and was then published, in a slightly different version, in Staples's memoir, *Parallel Time: Growing Up in Black and White* (1994). To explain a recurring experience of African American men, Staples relates incidents when he has been "an avid night walker" in the urban landscape. Sometimes his only defense against others' stereotypes is to whistle.

In the essay following this one, "The Struggle," Issa Rae offers a contemporary woman's counterpoint to Staples's perspective.

My first victim was a woman—white, well dressed, probably in her late
twenties. I came upon her late one evening on a deserted street in Hyde Park, a relatively affluent neighborhood in an otherwise mean, impoverished section of Chicago. As I swung onto the avenue behind her, there seemed to be a discreet, uninflammatory distance between us. Not so. She cast back a worried glance. To her, the youngish black man—a broad six feet two inches with a beard and billowing hair, both hands shoved into the pockets of a bulky military jacket—seemed menacingly close. After a few more quick glimpses, she picked up her pace and was soon running in earnest. Within seconds she disappeared into a cross street.

That was more than a decade ago. I was twenty-two years old, a graduate
student newly arrived at the University of Chicago. It was in the echo of that terrified woman's footfalls that I first began to know the unwieldy inheritance I'd come into—the ability to alter public space in ugly ways. It was clear that she thought herself the quarry of a mugger, a rapist, or worse. Suffering

a bout of insomnia, however, I was stalking sleep, not defenseless wayfarers. As a softy who is scarcely able to take a knife to a raw chicken—let alone hold one to a person's throat—I was surprised, embarrassed, and dismayed all at once. Her flight made me feel like an accomplice in tyranny. It also made it clear that I was indistinguishable from the muggers who occasionally seeped into the area from the surrounding ghetto. That first encounter, and those that followed, signified that a vast, unnerving gulf lay between night-time pedestrians—particularly women—and me. And I soon gathered that being perceived as dangerous is a hazard in itself. I only needed to turn a corner into a dicey situation, or crowd some frightened, armed person in a foyer somewhere, or make an errant move after being pulled over by a policeman. Where fear and weapons meet—and they often do in urban America—there is always the possibility of death.

In that first year, my first away from my hometown, I was to become thoroughly familiar with the language of fear. At dark, shadowy intersections, I could cross in front of a car stopped at a traffic light and elicit the *thunk, thunk, thunk, thunk* of the driver—black, white, male, or female—hammering down the door locks. On less traveled streets after dark, I grew accustomed to but never comfortable with people crossing to the other side of the street rather than pass me. Then there were the standard unpleasantries with policemen, doormen, bouncers, cabdrivers, and others whose business it is to screen out troublesome individuals *before* there is any nastiness.   3

I moved to New York nearly two years ago and I have remained an avid   4
night walker. In central Manhattan, the near-constant crowd cover minimizes tense one-on-one street encounters. Elsewhere—in SoHo, for example, where sidewalks are narrow and tightly spaced buildings shut out the sky—things can get very taut indeed.

After dark, on the warrenlike streets of Brooklyn where I live, I often   5
see women who fear the worst from me. They seem to have set their faces on neutral, and with their purse straps strung across their chests bandolier-style, they forge ahead as though bracing themselves against being tackled. I understand, of course, that the danger they perceive is not a hallucination. Women are particularly vulnerable to street violence, and young black males are drastically overrepresented among the perpetrators of that violence. Yet these truths are no solace against the kind of alienation that comes of being ever the suspect, a fearsome entity with whom pedestrians avoid making eye contact.

It is not altogether clear to me how I reached the ripe old age of   6
twenty-two without being conscious of the lethality nighttime pedestrians attributed to me. Perhaps it was because in Chester, Pennsylvania, the small, angry industrial town where I came of age in the 1960s, I was scarcely

noticeable against a backdrop of gang warfare, street knifings, and murders. I grew up one of the good boys, had perhaps a half-dozen fistfights. In retrospect, my shyness of combat has clear sources.

As a boy, I saw countless tough guys locked away; I have since buried 7 several, too. They were babies, really — a teenage cousin, a brother of twenty-two, a childhood friend in his mid-twenties — all gone down in episodes of bravado played out in the streets. I came to doubt the virtues of intimidation early on. I chose, perhaps unconsciously, to remain a shadow — timid, but a survivor.

The fearsomeness mistakenly attributed to me in public places often has 8 a perilous flavor. The most frightening of these confusions occurred in the late 1970s and early 1980s, when I worked as a journalist in Chicago. One day, rushing into the office of a magazine I was writing for with a deadline story in hand, I was mistaken for a burglar. The office manager called security and, with an ad hoc posse, pursued me through the labyrinthine halls, nearly to my editor's door. I had no way of proving who I was. I could only move briskly toward the company of someone who knew me.

Another time I was on assignment for a local paper and killing time before 9 an interview. I entered a jewelry store on the city's affluent Near North Side. The proprietor excused herself and returned with an enormous red Doberman pinscher straining at the end of a leash. She stood, the dog extended toward me, silent to my questions, her eyes bulging nearly out of her head. I took a cursory look around, nodded, and bade her good night.

Relatively speaking, however, I never fared as badly as another black 10 male journalist. He went to nearby Waukegan, Illinois, a couple of summers ago to work on a story about a murderer who was born there. Mistaking the reporter for the killer, police officers hauled him from his car at gunpoint and but for his press credentials would probably have tried to book him. Such episodes are not uncommon. Black men trade tales like this all the time.

Over the years, I learned to smother the rage I felt at so often being taken 11 for a criminal. Not to do so would surely have led to madness. I now take precautions to make myself less threatening. I move about with care, particularly late in the evening. I give a wide berth to nervous people on subway platforms during the wee hours, particularly when I have exchanged business clothes for jeans. If I happen to be entering a building behind some people who appear skittish, I may walk by, letting them clear the lobby before I return, so as not to seem to be following them. I have been calm and extremely congenial on those rare occasions when I've been pulled over by the police.

And on late-evening constitutionals I employ what has proved to be an 12 excellent tension-reducing measure: I whistle melodies from Beethoven and

Vivaldi and the more popular classical composers. Even steely New Yorkers hunching toward nighttime destinations seem to relax, and occasionally they even join in the tune. Virtually everybody seems to sense that a mugger wouldn't be warbling bright, sunny selections from Vivaldi's *Four Seasons*. It is my equivalent of the cowbell that hikers wear when they know they are in bear country.

Journal Writing

Staples explains how he perceives himself altering public space. Write in your journal about a time when you felt as if *you* altered public space — in other words, you changed people's attitudes or behavior just by being in a place or entering a situation. If you haven't had this experience, write about a time when you saw someone else alter public space in this way.

Questions on Meaning

1. What is the PURPOSE of this essay? Do you think Staples believes that he (or other African American men) will cease "to alter public space in ugly ways" (par. 2) in the near future? Does he suggest any long-term solution for "the kind of alienation that comes of being ever the suspect" (5)?

2. In paragraph 5 Staples says he understands that the danger women fear when they see him "is not a hallucination." Do you take this to mean that Staples perceives himself to be dangerous? Explain.

3. Staples says, "I chose, perhaps unconsciously, to remain a shadow — timid, but a survivor" (par. 7). What are the usual CONNOTATIONS of the word *survivor*? Is "timid" one of them? How can you explain this apparent discrepancy?

Questions on Writing Strategy

1. The concept of altering public space is relatively abstract. How does Staples convince you that this phenomenon really takes place?

2. Staples employs a large number of examples in a fairly short essay. How does he avoid having the piece sound like a list? How does he establish COHERENCE among all these examples? (Look, for example, at details and TRANSITIONS.)

3. **OTHER METHODS**   Many of Staples's examples are actually ANECDOTES — brief NARRATIVES. The opening paragraph is especially notable in this regard. Why is it so effective?

Questions on Language

1. What does the author accomplish by using the word *victim* in the essay's opening line? Is the word used literally? What TONE does it set for the essay?

2. Be sure you know how to define the following words, as used in this essay: affluent, uninflammatory (par. 1); unwieldy, tyranny, pedestrians (2); intimidation (7); congenial (11); constitutionals (12).

3. The word *dicey* (par. 2) comes from British slang. Without looking it up in your dictionary, can you figure out its meaning from the context in which it appears?

Suggestions for Writing

1. **FROM JOURNAL TO ESSAY**   Write an essay narrating your experience of either altering public space yourself or being a witness when someone else did so. What changes did you observe in people's behavior? Was your behavior similarly affected? In retrospect, do you think your reactions were justified?

2. Write an essay using examples to show how a trait of your own or of someone you know well always seems to affect people, whether positively or negatively.

3. The ironic term "living while black" expresses the common perception that African Americans are more likely than white people to have the police called on them for minor infractions — or no infraction at all. Research and write an essay about the accuracy of this perception in one state or municipality: Is there truth to it? If African Americans are being harassed or discriminated against, what, if anything, has been done to address the problem?

4. **CRITICAL WRITING**   Consider, more broadly than Staples does, what it means to alter public space. Staples would rather not have the power to do so, but it *is* a power, and it could perhaps be positive in some circumstances (wielded by a street performer, for instance, or the architect of a beautiful new building on campus). Write an essay that expands on Staples's idea and examines the pros and cons of altering public space. Use specific examples as your EVIDENCE.

5. **CONNECTIONS**   Like Brent Staples, Issa Rae, in "The Struggle" (p. 176), considers misplaced expectations of African Americans. In an essay, examine the POINTS OF VIEW of these two authors. How does point of view affect each author's selection of details and tone?

Brent Staples on Writing

In comments written especially for this book, Brent Staples talks about the writing of "Black Men and Public Space": "I was only partly aware of how I felt when I began this essay. I knew only that I had this collection of experiences (facts) and that I felt uneasy with them. I sketched out the experiences one by one and strung them together. The bridge to the essay—what I wanted to say, but did not know when I started—sprang into life quite unexpectedly as I sat looking over these experiences. The crucial sentence comes right after the opening anecdote, in which my first 'victim' runs away from me: 'It was in the echo of that terrified woman's footfalls that I first began to know the unwieldy inheritance I'd come into—the ability to alter public space in ugly ways.' 'Aha!' I said. 'This is why I feel bothered and hurt and frustrated when this happens. I don't want people to think I'm stalking them. I want some fresh air. I want to stretch my legs. I want to be as anonymous as any other person out for a walk in the night.'"

A news reporter and editor by training and trade, Staples sees much similarity between the writing of a personal essay like "Black Men and Public Space" and the writing of, say, a murder story for a daily newspaper. "The newspaper murder," he says, "begins with standard newspaper information: the fact that the man was found dead in an alley in such-and-such a section of the city; his name, occupation, and where he lived; that he died of gunshot wounds to such-and-such a part of his body; that arrests were or were not made; that such-and-such a weapon was found at the scene; that the police have established no motive; etc.

"Personal essays take a different tack, but they, too, begin as assemblies of facts. In 'Black Men and Public Space,' I start out with an anecdote that crystallizes the issue I want to discuss—what it is like to be viewed as a criminal all the time. I devise a sentence that serves this purpose and also catches the reader's attention: 'My first victim was a woman—white, well dressed, probably in her late twenties.' The piece gives examples that are meant to illustrate the same point and discusses what those examples mean.

"The newspaper story stacks its details in a specified way, with each piece taking a prescribed place in a prescribed order. The personal essay begins often with a flourish, an anecdote, or the recounting of a crucial experience, then goes off to consider related experiences and their meanings. But both pieces rely on reporting. Both are built of facts. Reporting is the act of finding and analyzing facts.

"A fact can be a state of the world—a date, the color of someone's eyes, the arc of a body that flies through the air after having been struck by a car. A fact can also be a feeling—sorrow, grief, confusion, the sense of being pleased, offended, or frustrated. 'Black Men and Public Space' explores the relationship between two sets of facts: (1) the way people cast worried glances at me and sometimes run away from me on the streets after dark, and (2) the frustration and anger I feel at being made an object of fear as I try to go about my business in the city."

Personal essays and news stories share one other quality as well, Staples thinks: They affect the writer even when the writing is finished. "The discoveries I made in 'Black Men and Public Space' continued long after the essay was published. Writing about the experiences gave me access to a whole range of internal concerns and ideas, much the way a well-reported news story opens the door onto a given neighborhood, situation, or set of issues."

The Bedford Reader on Writing

Staples provides an enlightening illustration of how writing generates ideas, rather than merely recording them. As often happens, he discovered his THESIS by writing about his subject — that is, by working out his examples and finding the connecting threads in the process. And as Staples observes, although personal essays and newspaper stories are different GENRES, both types of writing rely on gathering EVIDENCE first, before starting to draft. For tips on "finding and analyzing facts" for your own writing, see "Developing Ideas" in Chapter 2, pages 35–36.

ISSA RAE

Jo-Issa Rae Diop was born in 1985 and raised in Potomac, Maryland, and Los Angeles, California, with extended stays with family in Senegal (a country in West Africa). Frustrated by the lack of positive roles for black women in television and film, she started producing and acting in her own online programming while a student at Stanford University, adopted the screen name Issa Rae, and created the award-winning Web series *The Misadventures of Awkward Black Girl* shortly out of college with funding from a Kickstarter campaign. The popular comedy follows a self-deprecating introvert, "J," as she navigates the pitfalls of social interaction; it captured more than twenty million views and the attention of traditional media outlets including HBO, which signed Rae to produce and star in the hit series *Insecure* in 2015. Her first book of memoir and essays, itself titled *The Misadventures of Awkward Black Girl*, was published the same year. In 2018 *Time* magazine named Rae to its list of "The 100 Most Influential People: Pioneers." She lives in Los Angeles.

The Struggle

In this selection from her book, Rae tackles the fraught subject of race with characteristically acerbic wit. While Brent Staples in the previous essay expresses embarrassment at strangers' reactions to his skin color, Rae has a different problem with stereotypes: Her peers don't think she's "black enough."

I don't remember the exact day I demilitarized from my blackness. It's all a blur and since I'm fairly certain that militants never forget, and I forget stuff *all* the time, I guess I wasn't meant to be one.

I love being black; that's not a problem. The problem is that I don't want to always *talk* about it because honestly, talking about being "black" is extremely tiring. I don't know how Al Sharpton and Jesse Jackson do it. I know why Cornel West and Tavis Smiley do it.[1] They *love* the attention and the groupies. But the rest of these people who talk, think, and breathe race every single day — how? Just how? Aren't they exhausted?

---

[1] The Reverend Jesse Jackson (1941–) and Baptist minister Al Sharpton (1954–) are prominent civil rights activists; Dr. Cornel West (1953–) is a public intellectual and college professor; Tavis Smiley (1964–) is a talk show host and author. —EDS.

The pressure to contribute to these conversations now that we have a 3
black president is even more infuriating.

"What do you think about what's going on in the world? And how our 4
black president is handling it?" asks a race baiter.

"It's all good, I guess," I want to answer, apathetically, with a Kanye shrug. 5
"I'm over it." But am I really? Could I be even if I wanted to?

Even now, I feel obligated to write about race. It's as though it's expected 6
of me to acknowledge what we all already know. The truth is, I slip in and out
of my black consciousness, as if I'm in a racial coma. Sometimes, I'm so deep
in my anger, my irritation, my need to stir change, that I can't see anything
outside of the lens of race.

At other times I feel guilty about my apathy. But then I think, *isn't this* 7
what those who came before me fought for? The right *not* to have to deal with
race? If faced with a choice between fighting until the death for freedom and
civil rights and living life without any acknowledgment of race, they'd choose
the latter.

Growing up as a young black girl in Potomac, Maryland, was easy. 8
I never really had to put much thought into my race, and neither did anybody else. I had a Rainbow Coalition of friends of all ethnicities, and we
would carelessly skip around our elementary school like the powerless version
of Captain Planet's Planeteers. I knew I was black. I knew there was a history
that accompanied my skin color and my parents taught me to be proud of it.
End of story.

All that changed when my family moved to Los Angeles and placed me 9
in a middle school where my blackness was constantly questioned—and
not even necessarily in the traditional sense, i.e., "You talk white, Oreo girl"
or "You can't dance, white girl." Those claims were arguable, for the most
part. My biggest frustration in the challenge to prove my "blackness" usually
stemmed from two very annoying, very repetitive situations.

SITUATION #1: "I'm not even black, and I'm blacker than you." It's one 10
thing when other African Americans try to call me out on my race card, but
when people outside my ethnicity have the audacity to question how "down"
I am because of the bleak, stereotypical picture pop culture has painted of
black women, it's a whole other thing. Unacceptable. I can recall a time
when I was having a heated discussion with a white, male classmate of mine.
Our eighth-grade class was on a museum field trip as the bus driver blasted
Puff Daddy's "Been around the World" to drown us out.

It began as a passive competition of lyrics, as we each silently listened for 11
who would mess up first. By the second verse, our lazy rap-whispers escalated
to an aggressive volume, accompanied by rigorous side-eyes by the time we

got to, "Playa please, I'm the macaroni with the cheese," and I felt threatened. Was this fool seriously trying to outrap me? And why did I care? After the song ended, he offered his opinion: "Puff Daddy is wack, yo." How dare he? Not only was I angry, but I felt as if he had insulted my own father (who did I think I was? Puff Daughter?).

"Puff Daddy is tight," I retorted. He rolled his eyes and said, "Have you 12 heard of [insert Underground rapper]? Now, *he's* dope." I hadn't heard of him, but I couldn't let this white boy defeat me in rap music knowledge, especially as others started to listen. "Yeah, I know him. He's not dope," I lied, for the sake of saving face. Perhaps because he saw through me or because he actually felt strongly about this particular artist, he asked me to name which songs I thought were "not dope." Panic set in as I found myself exposed, then—"You don't even know him, huh? Have you even heard of [insert Random Underground rapper]?"

As he continued to rattle off the names of make-believe-sounding MCs, 13 delighted that he had one-upped me, he managed to make me feel as though my credibility as a black person relied on my knowledge of hip-hop culture. My identity had been reduced to the Bad Boy label clique as this boy seemingly claimed my black card as his own.

Of course, as I grew older and Ma$e found his calling as a reverend, I 14 realized there was more to being black than a knowledge of rap music, and that I didn't have to live up to this pop cultural archetype. I began to take pride in the fact that I couldn't be reduced to a stereotype and that I didn't have to be. This leads me to my next situation.

SITUATION #2: "Black people don't do that." Or so I'm told by a black 15 person. These, too, are derived from (mostly negative) stereotypes shaped by popular culture. The difference is that in these situations, we black people are the ones buying into these stereotypes.

When I was a teenager, for example, others questioned my blackness 16 because some of the life choices I made weren't considered to be "black" choices: joining the swim team when it is a known fact that "black people don't swim," or choosing to become a vegetarian when blacks clearly love chicken. These choices and the various positive and negative responses to them helped to broaden my own perspective on blackness and, eventually, caused me to spurn these self-imposed limitations. But not before embarrassing the hell out of myself in a poor attempt to prove I was "down." I'll never forget submitting a school project in "Ebonics" for my seventh-grade English class, just to prove that I could talk *and* write "black." I was trying to prove it to myself just as much as I was to everyone around me.

Even in my early adulthood, post-college, I'd overtip to demonstrate 17 I was one of the good ones. Only recently have I come to ask, *What am I trying to prove and to whom am I proving it?* Today, I haven't completely rid myself of the feeling that I'm still working through Du Bois's double consciousness.[2]

For the majority of my life I cared too much about how my blackness was   18
perceived, but *now*? At this very moment? I couldn't care less. Call it maturation or denial or self-hatred—I give no f%^&s. And it feels great. I've decided to focus only on the positivity of being black, and especially of being a black woman. Am I supposed to feel oppressed? Because I don't. Is racism supposed to hurt me? That's so 1950s. Should I feel marginalized? I prefer to think of myself as belonging to an "exclusive" club.

While experiencing both types of situations—being made to feel not   19
black enough by "down" white people on one hand and not black enough by the blacks in the so-called know on the other—has played a role in shaping a more comfortably black me, in the end, I have to ask: Who is to say what we do and don't do? What we can and can't do? The very definition of "blackness" is as broad as that of "whiteness," yet the media seemingly always tries to find a specific, limited definition. As CNN produces news specials about us, and white and Latino rappers feel culturally dignified in using the N-word, our collective grasp of "blackness" is becoming more and elusive. And that may not be a bad thing.

Journal Writing

Rae shares examples of times when her perception of her "blackness" did not match the expectations of those around her. Think of a defining characteristic you hold for yourself—your race, perhaps, or your gender, your sexual orientation, your nationality, your sports affiliations, your career aspirations, and so forth. Has your sense of who and what you are ever been challenged by others? How, and why? List some such instances in your journal.

Questions on Meaning

1. Rae opens her essay by saying she is tired of discussing race. What, then, would you say was her PURPOSE in writing? Does she have a THESIS?

2. To whom does Rae feel she needs to prove her "blackness"? How do you know?

3. How does Rae characterize society's expectations for black people, especially black women? What does she blame as the source of these stereotypes?

[2] In *The Souls of Black Folk* (1903), the sociologist and historian W. E. B. Du Bois famously proposed that African Americans struggle to reconcile the conflict of belonging simultaneously to two cultures in opposition to each other, a mental state he called *double consciousness.* —EDS.

Questions on Writing Strategy

1. "The Struggle" contains one extended example and several brief examples. How does Rae organize them? What is the effect of grouping these "situations" as she does?

2. What ASSUMPTIONS about her readers are evident in Rae's choice of ALLUSIONS, particularly in paragraphs 10–14? Do you need to be familiar with the musicians she mentions to understand her point?

3. **OTHER METHODS**   Rae's essay is in some ways an attempt at DEFINITION. What do her examples of being "not black enough" (par. 19) contribute to that attempt?

Questions on Language

1. Consider Rae's DICTION, especially her use of slang and references to racial slurs such as "Oreo" (par. 9) and "N-word" (19). What is the EFFECT of such language? Where in the essay, if at all, does Rae explain her decision to use it?

2. The words "black" and "blackness" often appear in quotation marks in this essay. Why? What does Rae intend by employing this device?

3. Be sure you know how to define the following words: demilitarized (par. 1); apathetically (5); coalition (8); rigorous (11); archetype (14); Ebonics (16); maturation (18).

Suggestions for Writing

1. **FROM JOURNAL TO ESSAY**   Building on the episodes you recorded in your journal, write about a time or times when others made you think deeply about who you are and how you present yourself to the world. Use Rae's work as a model: Incorporate concrete examples into your essay and try to address the larger social implications of your reflection.

2. Consider an incident from your childhood that has stuck with you. You might choose an embarrassing or frustrating moment, as Rae did in writing about her school-bus rap battle, or a proud or defining event, such as a sports victory or a sudden understanding of a truth. Write a personal reflection that, like Rae's essay, explains how your understanding of the incident has changed now that you are older.

3. **CRITICAL WRITING**   In an essay, examine Rae's TONE. Is it consistent throughout? Are there passages where she seems self-pitying? mocking? determined? resigned? triumphant? What is the overall tone of the essay? Is it effective? Why?

4. **CONNECTIONS**   COMPARE AND CONTRAST Issa Rae's and Brent Staples's (p. 169) perceptions of "blackness" and of the stereotypes that have been assigned to them. Use specific passages from each essay to support your comparison.

ANNA QUINDLEN

Anna Quindlen was born in 1953 and graduated from Barnard College in 1974. She worked as a reporter for the *New York Post* and the *New York Times* before taking over the latter's "About New York" column, eventually serving as the paper's deputy metropolitan editor and creating her own weekly column. Quindlen later wrote a twice-weekly op-ed column for the *Times* on social and political issues, earning a Pulitzer Prize for commentary in 1992. She also wrote a biweekly column for *Newsweek* magazine. Quindlen's essays and columns are collected in *Living Out Loud* (1988), *Thinking Out Loud* (1993), and *Loud and Clear* (2004). Her memoir, *Lots of Candles, Plenty of Cake*, appeared in 2012. Quindlen has also published two books for children, four books of non-fiction with a how-to bent, and nine successful novels, most recently *Alternate Side* (2018). She lives in New York City.

Homeless

In this essay from *Living Out Loud*, Quindlen mingles a reporter's respect for details with a keen sense of empathy, using examples to explore a persistent social issue. When Quindlen wrote, in 1987, homelessness had only recently become a severe and highly visible problem in New York City and elsewhere in the United States. The problem has not abated since then: Using government data, the National Alliance to End Homelessness estimates that more than half a million Americans are homeless on any given day.

Her name was Ann, and we met in the Port Authority Bus Terminal several Januarys ago. I was doing a story on homeless people. She said I was wasting my time talking to her; she was just passing through, although she'd been passing through for more than two weeks. To prove to me that this was true, she rummaged through a tote bag and a manila envelope and finally unfolded a sheet of typing paper and brought out her photographs.

They were not pictures of family, or friends, or even a dog or cat, its eyes brown-red in the flashbulb's light. They were pictures of a house. It was like a thousand houses in a hundred towns, not suburb, not city, but somewhere in between, with aluminum siding and a chain-link fence, a narrow driveway running up to a one-car garage and a patch of backyard. The house was yellow. I looked on the back for a date or a name, but neither was there. There was no need for discussion. I knew what she was trying to tell me, for it was something I had often felt. She was not adrift, alone, anonymous, although her bags and her raincoat with the grime shadowing its creases had

181

made me believe she was. She had a house, or at least once upon a time had had one. Inside were curtains, a couch, a stove, potholders. You are where you live. She was somebody.

I've never been very good at looking at the big picture, taking the global   3
view, and I've always been a person with an overactive sense of place, the legacy of an Irish grandfather. So it is natural that the thing that seems most wrong with the world to me right now is that there are so many people with no homes. I'm not simply talking about shelter from the elements, or three square meals a day or a mailing address to which the welfare people can send the check—although I know that all these are important for survival. I'm talking about a home, about precisely those kinds of feelings that have wound up in cross-stitch and French knots on samplers over the years.

Home is where the heart is. There's no place like it. I love my home with   4
a ferocity totally out of proportion to its appearance or location. I love dumb things about it: the hot-water heater, the plastic rack you drain dishes in, the roof over my head, which occasionally leaks. And yet it is precisely those dumb things that make it what it is—a place of certainty, stability, predict-ability, privacy, for me and for my family. It is where I live. What more can you say about a place than that? That is everything.

Yet it is something that we have been edging away from gradually during   5
my lifetime and the lifetimes of my parents and grandparents. There was a time when where you lived often was where you worked and where you grew the food you ate and even where you were buried. When that era passed, where you lived at least was where your parents had lived and where you would live with your children when you became enfeebled. Then, suddenly where you lived was where you lived for three years, until you could move on to something else and something else again.

And so we have come to something else again, to children who do not   6
understand what it means to go to their rooms because they have never had a room, to men and women whose fantasy is a wall they can paint a color of their own choosing, to old people reduced to sitting on molded plastic chairs, their skin blue-white in the lights of a bus station, who pull pictures of houses out of their bags. Homes have stopped being homes. Now they are real estate.

People find it curious that those without homes would rather sleep sitting   7
up on benches or huddled in doorways than go to shelters. Certainly some prefer to do so because they are emotionally ill, because they have been locked in before and they are damned if they will be locked in again. Others are afraid of the violence and trouble they may find there. But some seem to want something that is not available in shelters, and they will not com-promise, not for a cot, or oatmeal, or a shower with special soap that kills

the bugs. "One room," a woman with a baby who was sleeping on her sister's floor, once told me, "painted blue." That was the crux of it; not size or location, but pride of ownership. Painted blue.

This is a difficult problem, and some wise and compassionate people are working hard at it. But in the main I think we work around it, just as we walk around it when it is lying on the sidewalk or sitting in the bus terminal—the problem, that is. It has been customary to take people's pain and lessen our own participation in it by turning it into an issue, not a collection of human beings. We turn an adjective into a noun: the poor, not poor people; the homeless, not Ann or the man who lives in the box or the woman who sleeps on the subway grate. 8

Sometimes I think we would be better off if we forgot about the broad strokes and concentrated on the details. Here is a woman without a bureau. There is a man with no mirror, no wall to hang it on. They are not the homeless. They are people who have no homes. No drawer that holds the spoons. No window to look out upon the world. My God. That is everything. 9

Journal Writing

What does the word *home* mean to you? Does it involve material things, privacy, family, a sense of permanence? In your journal, explore your ideas about this word.

Questions on Meaning

1. What is Quindlen's THESIS?
2. What distinction is Quindlen making in her CONCLUSION with the sentences "They are not the homeless. They are people who have no homes"?
3. Why does Quindlen believe that having a home is essential?

Questions on Writing Strategy

1. Why do you think Quindlen begins with the story of Ann? How else might Quindlen have begun her essay?
2. What is the EFFECT of Quindlen's examples about her own home?
3. What key ASSUMPTIONS does the author make about her AUDIENCE? Are the assumptions reasonable? Where does she specifically address an assumption that might undermine her view?

4. How does Quindlen vary the sentences in paragraph 7 that give examples of why homeless people avoid shelters?

5. **OTHER METHODS**   Quindlen uses examples to support an ARGUMENT. What position does she want readers to recognize and accept?

Questions on Language

1. What is the effect of "My God" in the last paragraph?

2. How might Quindlen be said to give new meaning to the old CLICHÉ "Home is where the heart is" (par. 4)?

3. What is meant by "crux" (par. 7)? Where does the word come from?

Suggestions for Writing

1. **FROM JOURNAL TO ESSAY**   Write an essay that gives a detailed DEFINITION of *home* by using your own home, hometown, or experiences with homes as supporting examples. (See Chap. 13 if you need help with definition.)

2. Have you ever moved from one place to another? What sort of experience was it? Write an essay about leaving an old home and moving to a new one. Was there an activity or a piece of furniture that helped ease the transition?

3. Write an essay on the problem of homelessness in your town or city. Use examples to support your view of the problem and a possible solution.

4. **CRITICAL WRITING**   Write a brief essay in which you agree or disagree with Quindlen's assertion that a home is "everything." Can one, for instance, be a fulfilled person without a home? In your answer, take account of the values that might underlie an attachment to home; Quindlen mentions "certainty, stability, predictability, privacy" (par. 4), but there are others, including some (such as fear of change) that are less positive.

5. **CONNECTIONS**   Quindlen makes an emphatic distinction between "the homeless" and "people who have no homes" (par. 9). Read William Lutz's "The World of Doublespeak" (p. 387), which examines how language can be used to distort our perceptions of unpleasant truths. Drawing on what he and Quindlen have to say, write an essay that explores how the way we label a problem like homelessness influences what solutions we may (or may not) be able to find.

Anna Quindlen on Writing

Anna Quindlen started her writing career as a newspaper reporter. "I had wanted to be a writer for most of my life," she recalls in the introduction to her book *Living Out Loud*, "and in the service of the writing I became a reporter. For many years I was able to observe, even to feel, life vividly, but at secondhand. I was able to stand over the chalk outline of a body on a sidewalk dappled with black blood; to stand behind the glass and look down into an operating theater where one man was placing a heart in the yawning chest of another; to sit in the park on the first day of summer and find myself professionally obligated to record all the glories of it. Every day I found answers: who, what, when, where, and why."

Quindlen was a good reporter, but the business of finding answers did not satisfy her personally. "In my own life," she continues, "I had only questions." Then she switched from reporter to columnist at the *New York Times*. It was "exhilarating," she says, that "my work became a reflection of my life. After years of being a professional observer of other people's lives, I was given the opportunity to be a professional observer of my own. I was permitted — and permitted myself — to write a column, not about my answers, but about my questions. Never did I make so much sense of my life as I did then, for it was inevitable that as a writer I would find out most clearly what I thought, and what I only thought I thought, when I saw it written down. . . . After years of feeling secondhand, of feeling the pain of the widow, the joy of the winner, I was able to allow myself to feel those emotions for myself."

The Bedford Reader on Writing

While Brent Staples (p. 169) and Brian Doyle (p. 192) in this chapter both stress the strategies and techniques essay writers can learn from newspaper reporters, Quindlen seems to stress the opposite. For her, GENRE and PURPOSE (see pp. 29–30) impose restrictions as much as they open up possibilities. What did she feel she could accomplish in a column that she could not accomplish in a news article? What evidence of this difference do you see in her essay "Homeless"?

ZANE RASSLER

Zane Rassler was born in 1995 and raised in Concord, North Carolina, where he attended Northwest Cabarrus High School and taught himself to play the ukulele. At Appalachian State University in Boone, North Carolina, he is double-majoring in theatre performance and creative writing and especially enjoys studying accents and dialects. Rassler expects to graduate in 2019 and reports that while he doesn't yet have a particular career path lined up, he hopes to find work editing or—his dream job—voice acting for cartoons.

Looking Back

Rassler wrote the following essay in his sophomore year for a college writing class. Focusing on a legacy of gender miscues starting at birth, Rassler recounts his emerging understanding of transgender identity. "Looking Back" was selected for the 2016 edition of *WriteClick*, Appalachian State's annual anthology of exemplary student writing.

December 4, 1995. The doctors apparently dress me in the "wrong color." 1
Of course, I do not remember that far back—there is a photo of newborn me, wearing a blue onesie. It could be intentional or someone could be making a blatant mistake. It is just hysterical to me that, looking back so far as even just a few *hours* old, there were subtle hints to who I truly was—who I was meant to be.

October 31, 2003. Age seven. I am dressed as Woody the Cowboy, one 2 of the main characters from *Toy Story*.[1] There is really nothing to suggest anything feminine about me, and I have a total blast. My mother struggles to keep up with my manic energy, and I stay out roaming the neighborhood a good half hour longer than she ever wanted. I beg to be Buzz Lightyear the Space Ranger, Woody's best friend, next year, and my exhausted parents agree. I fall asleep that night with a big old smile on my face, dreams of next Halloween already dancing around my mind.

Somewhere around age eight. I discover *Mulan*[2] for the first time. I watch, 3 wide-eyed and wondering as this Chinese girl deliberately disobeys her family and discards her femininity. I think, "How can she *do* that?" Naturally, I laugh when she first tries to wield a sword but for the most part, I absorb how all

---

[1] A 1995 animated film by Pixar, about a group of toys that come to life when there are no people around to see them. —Eds.

[2] A 1998 animated film by Disney, about a girl who disguises herself as a boy to take her father's place in the Chinese army. —Eds.

the male soldiers around her do not question her, do not try to "figure her out." They just assume, since she is in the army, that she is male and *whatever* she does is masculine. The song "Be a Man" particularly sticks with me — nothing in the song suggests you needed a *penis*; you just need swiftness, force, strength, and mystery. It fascinates me. (Then, a few weeks later, I try cutting my own hair, like she did. My dad laughs for a solid minute before taking me to get my hair cut by someone who knew what they were doing.)

Age nine. Sometime in July. A few of my neighbors come over for a rare 4
summer party. Allan, and another boy whose name I did not bother to learn, and I are running around my house, whooping and hollering like a pack of baboons. There are a few mild "Don't knock anything over's" from our parents but nothing else restricting our fun. Then, suddenly, Allan whines, "It's too hot!" And promptly whips off his shirt. The other boy follows suit, and since I do not know about puberty as of yet, I take off my shirt, too. After all, it *is* very hot. The instant my mother sees that I am running around shirtless, she pulls me to the side and hisses, "Put your shirt back on, honey." I am bewildered. She didn't stop the other two, why did she stop me? "You'll find out a few years down the line, sweetheart. Just do it, please." I huff and sulk the whole day. Why should they get to do things I don't get to do because of something that will happen *years* from now? That isn't *fair*.

Age ten. I discover the musical *Oliver!*[3] I do not stop singing "Consider 5
Yourself" for three straight days. I picture myself in Artful Dodger's black top hat and fingerless gloves, the ringleader of the ragamuffin gang. I imitate his filthy London accent perfectly. I know, in my soul, that I *must be* Artful Dodger. I tell my mother — a high school theater teacher and an actress herself — this realization, and she just smiles, ruffles my hair, and says, "Well, maybe if you were a boy." I cannot grasp this idea. I *need* to be Dodger, so I *will* be Dodger. It doesn't matter if I'm a *boy* or not. Besides, Mom was Winthrop (a boy with a lisp) in *The Music Man*[4] when she was my age. Why should it matter?

Age fourteen. My first respectable position in a play. (Middle school 6
didn't count because the teacher-slash-director was not very good.) I am a stereotypical 60s hippie in a play about birds who can speak English. It's actually a really good role for a freshman — I'm only onstage for one scene, but I am wacky and funny enough that people will remember me. It's my first dress rehearsal, and I have to ask one of the lead girls if she will help me with my stage makeup. She looks at me a little odd and says, "Well, I mean, just,

[3] A 1968 live-action musical film based on Charles Dickens's serialized novel *Oliver Twist* (1837–39). The Artful Dodger is the leader of a group of child pickpockets in London. —Eds.
[4] A 1957 stage musical, later adapted into the 1962 film, about a con man who poses as a bandleader to sell musical instruments to unsuspecting Midwesterners. —Eds.

like, do whatever you normally do, just make it, like, bigger, so the audience knows you're wearing it." I have never worn non-Halloween makeup before in my life. I clam up and start sweating. I don't know what to tell her. So I go to my mom and ask *her* to help me. That night, I made a decision: Makeup is terrifying, and I am only willing to do it for theatrical performances.

Age fifteen. I discover the Internet, beyond *Google* and *YouTube*. There is a Web site that I really want to sign up for, but it is not connected to *Facebook* or anything on which my parents could keep tabs. All my life, I have been warned to never give my real name or any personal information. So I cast around in my head for a name I could use . . . my eyes fall on a copy of Zane Grey's *Last of the Plainsmen*[5] someone had left lying around. "Zane." That has a great ring to it. I type it into the "Name" blank, and something inside me just warms right up. Having real live people (because who else on Earth would want to use the Internet lingo that fifteen-year-olds do) call me "Zane" sticks with me, and something inside of me wants *everyone* to call me that.

Age sixteen. Maria. I do not know her by any other name, and I do not think I ever want to. She is in one of my classes, sits near the back. I like her; she has a friendly resting face, dresses in a fresh and muted, attention-grabbing way and does not take shit from *anybody*. I feel intimidated when I am near her not only because of her overwhelming confidence, but also because she frequently speaks lightning-speed Spanish, and I only know enough to have casual conversation — *very slowly*. Almost every day, I see people (mostly boys wearing backwards baseball caps and ratty basketball shorts who positively *reek* of Axe and Cheetos) snickering and whispering to each other out of the corner of my eye, but I never question it. I never make the connection between those malicious assholes and Maria. Hell, I have no idea the word *transgender* even exists yet, let alone why people would make fun of someone for *being* transgender. I just see Maria as a fun-loving girl with amazing hair and better laughter.

Age eighteen. I have long since abandoned the Web site from three years ago and have found a new one. As I scroll down, catching up on what I'd missed through the day, a slideshow catches my eye. Someone had taken time and made a post talking about different variations of being transgender and how gender roles do not affect gender identity. It interests me, so I click through the slides. "Standard Transgender: if assigned female at birth, declaring yourself male, and vice versa; Non-binary/Gender-neutral: neither male nor female, but something outside the two; Genderfluid: moving between male and female, taking some from both genders; Bigender: much like genderfluid, but heightened and more drastic; Agender: not feeling like

---

[5] Zane Grey (1875–1939) was an American writer who penned several Western adventure novels, among them *Last of the Plainsmen* (1908). — Eds.

you belong in any assigned genders." As I go through the slides and see people who actually *are* transgender and non-binary and bigender talking about their experiences, something inside me clicks. I *know*. Somehow, something inside of me always knew I was not fully female.

Age nineteen. I am now a strong advocate for LGBT rights, which is   10
only natural, as I am bisexual and transgender. I have not revealed either of these things to most of my family and friends; however, I have grown up with very conservative friends and I only see most of my family members for four collective weeks a year, so they wouldn't know me even if I wasn't transgender. The few people back home that I have told — my mother, my godfather, my little brother — are as supportive as I could expect them to be, having never before been close with a transgender individual. App State has been an *incredible* place for me because I don't have to worry about meeting standards or qualifications for my gender identity; I simply tell people I prefer "he/him" pronouns, and they get it right away. I may have to correct them a few times, but they understand and roll with the punches. It is a bit disorienting to have such a stark divide between school and home, but I am learning to deal with what I cannot change, and I plan to come out to my father and hometown friends over the summer — the distant family members may have to wait a while longer. The future is murky and more than a bit terrifying, but I know I have support. Looking back, there have been so many hints at my not fitting into the role of a Typical Female — or a female at all — but it is so difficult to see them without the benefit of hindsight.

Journal Writing

Rassler writes about the strong influence fictional characters have had on his thoughts, on his actions, and on his very sense of who he is. What has been the strongest influence in your life? It might be one or more characters or perhaps a parent, another relative, a friend, a religious figure, a celebrity of some sort. Think about what this person has meant to you and how he or she has influenced you, in ways both good and bad. Jot down your musings in your journal.

Questions on Meaning

1. What would you say is Rassler's PURPOSE in this essay? Is it primarily to inform readers about his childhood, or does Rassler seem to have another purpose in mind?

2. Does Rassler have a THESIS? What generalization is supported by his examples?

3. At what point in his life did Rassler come to understand that he is transgender? What led to his epiphany? Why did he not make the discovery earlier?

Questions on Writing Strategy

1. Why do you think Rassler opens his essay as he does? What is the EFFECT of this introduction?

2. What assumptions does the author seem to make about his AUDIENCE?

3. "Looking Back" includes quite a few examples. How are they organized? How does Rassler maintain UNITY and COHERENCE in his essay?

4. **OTHER METHODS** Where in the essay does Rassler use CLASSIFICATION to explain gender categories? What do the DEFINITIONS of those categories contribute to his NARRATIVE?

Questions on Language

1. Why does Rassler use the present tense to recount episodes from his past? What would the essay lose if he had chosen to use the past tense instead? (If necessary, refer to p. 70 for help understanding the role of verb tense in storytelling.)

2. Notice Rassler's use of italics in the essay. Why does he italicize several words that are not titles? What does this language contribute to his TONE?

3. Find definitions of the following words: onesie, hysterical (par. 1); discards (3); puberty, bewildered (4); ragamuffin (5); hippie (6); snickering, malicious (8); advocate, disorienting, hindsight (10).

4. Why do you think Rassler capitalizes "Typical Female" in paragraph 10?

Suggestions for Writing

1. **FROM JOURNAL TO ESSAY** Drawing on your journal entry (p. 189) and using your experiences as EVIDENCE, write an essay that explains the influence of a particular person or people, real or fictional, on your identity and behavior. Your essay may be serious or humorous, but it should include plenty of details and focus on CAUSE AND EFFECT.

2. In an essay, explain what *male* or *female* means to you. Does your definition correspond to traditional assumptions about gender or is it more fluid, like Rassler's? What characteristics does your definition *not* include? Do you believe that gender is a binary (or two-way) prospect? What additional categories might you propose?

3. Go online and locate clips of "I'll Make a Man Out of You" from *Mulan* and "Consider Yourself" from *Oliver!* Watch videos of both songs, and then consider for yourself why they resonated so strongly with the young Rassler. What aspects of these musical numbers, both explicit and implicit, make them especially appropriate to Rassler's subject? Why do you suppose he singles them out as examples? How does knowing their content help you better understand his experience?

4. **CRITICAL WRITING** Rassler comments in his introduction that he finds his experience "just hysterical" (par. 1). Why should that be? Considering his perspective, ANALYZE Rassler's use of humor in this essay. What, if anything, is funny about his story? How successful is he at conveying the humor he sees in it to others? Consider, in particular, the writer's use of exaggeration, irony, and

humorous IMAGES. You might also do some library or Internet research on humor writing to further support your analysis.

5. **CONNECTIONS** "So Enid and Dorothy from West Covina Can Hear You," by Caitlin McDougall (p. 229), is another essay by a student writer with a background in acting. Taken together, what do her essay and Zane Rassler's "Looking Back" suggest about the dynamics of the theater community? In what ways might acting on stage together, for instance, help to forge bonds among different types of people? What do college students gain (or lose) by training to perform for an audience? What do they get out of performing? In an essay of your own, argue for or against the idea that college students should be active in drama or any other club offered on campus.

Zane Rassler on Writing

In comments he prepared for *The Bedford Reader*, Zane Rassler describes his writing process and advises other aspiring writers to stay true to themselves.

My writing tends to come out of chaos—I am not an organized person normally, and my writing style follows that. When an idea grabs me, I'll jot it down on a note or on my phone, and when I have free time, I flesh out whatever I can with that one concept, and I build from there. Often, I'll write a first draft, and let it sit for a while; it could be a few days or over a year. When I come back to it, I can more easily see the changes that need to be made. Occasionally, I'll also ask a friend of mine to review the piece I'm working on to get their opinion.

This may sound a bit blunt, but when I write I tend not to consider who would be reading it. I write what I think sounds good, and if it *needs* to be changed for a certain demographic (i.e., I have to censor my swearing), I will, but it's not something I do naturally. If you want to be a creative writer, that attitude is such a good thing to hang on to: What should stand out about your writing is *you*, not whatever's left after you've filtered yourself several times over.

The Bedford Reader on Writing

Rassler's comments bear out a lesson that many beginning writers have trouble grasping: DRAFTING provides an opportunity to explore a subject for yourself. REVISION is the time to rework an essay with a particular AUDIENCE in mind. For help identifying the kinds of changes that would benefit your work, you can always turn to peer reviewers—and to Chapter 3 of this book, especially pages 42–45.

BRIAN DOYLE

Widely admired for his breathless reflections on spirituality, human connection, and the natural world, Brian Doyle was a writer who described himself as a "shambling shuffling mumbling grumbling muttering muddled maundering meandering male being" with a "deep and abiding love" for his wife, his three children, and basketball. Born in New York City, he graduated from the University of Notre Dame in 1978, worked for *US Catholic Magazine* and *Boston College Magazine*, and ultimately became the award-winning editor of *Portland*, a quarterly publication for the University of Portland. A frequent contributor to that magazine and to many others, including *The Atlantic Monthly*, *Orion*, *The Sun*, and *Harper's*, Doyle published twenty-eight books in all: two nonfiction works on family and faith, four novels, and multiple collections of short fiction, poetry, and essays, among them *Leaping: Revelations and Epiphanies* (2003), *Bin Laden's Bald Spot: And Other Stories* (2011), *So Very Much the Best of Us: Songs of Praise in Prose* (2015), and *Eight Whopping Lies* (2017)—all consistently lauded for their high quality and Doyle's unique voice. He died in 2017.

Three Basketball Stories

Doyle's work defied boundaries of genre and style. Whatever he wrote, Doyle had a reputation for crafting unusually poetic prose; in fact, he called many of his pieces "proems." In this story from *Bin Laden's Bald Spot*, he uses examples both poetic and prosaic to expound on the glories of his favorite sport.

Lefty

1   I played in a basketball league once in Boston that was so tough that when guys drove to the hole they lost fingers. One time a guy drove to the hole and got hit so hard his right arm fell off, but he was a lefty and hit both free throws before going to the bench. I heard later that he was furious he got taken out because his shot was really falling that night, and also I heard that his team later had a funeral for the arm with everyone carrying the casket with only one arm as a goof but they all got so howling drunk that they lost the arm and had to bury the casket empty and then they spent the rest of the night trying to remember every lefty guy in the history of sports which is way harder than you think.

2   There were all kinds of guys in that league. One team had a guy who had been in a pro football camp but they decided he was too crazy for pro football, can you imagine? Another team had a guy about six foot twenty but he was awful and we beat them by ten. There were all kinds of guys. One time a brawl broke out before the game even started and it took like twenty minutes

just to shoot all the technicals and half the guys were thrown out before the game even started, which led one guy to argue metaphysics with the refs, you know, like how can you be thrown out of a game if there's no game yet? They threw him out too.

There were a lot of guys in that league who were unbelievable ballplayers   3 but they all had some flaw, you know? Like they couldn't go left, at *all*, or could do everything except score, or couldn't do anything *except* score, or lost their minds when the sun went down or whatever. A lot of guys were total horses on the court but total donkeys off it, you know? Every team had a couple guys like that. We had two, our center who was a terrific ballplayer but who sold dope at halftime and ended up going into real estate and a guard who we never knew if he would show up or not or even stay for the whole game, sometimes he wandered off at halftime and that was the end of him for the night. He was the nicest guy you ever saw. We didn't know where he lived or if he had a job or what. We just told him when the next game was and hoped for the best. Some guys thought he lived somewhere in the park where we played summer league but I don't know about that.

There was one team where everyone except one guy had lost their drivers'   4 licenses so the one guy, he was the point guard, had to drive the whole team and finally he got so tired of driving everyone he quit and without him they lost four straight and missed the playoffs. Another team used to pull up in the parking lot in a huge garbage truck which one of their guys drove for work, you could hear them coming miles away, but only four guys could fit in the cab so six guys had to hang onto the back. Guys drove all sorts of things in that league, old buses and mail vans and such. One time a guy drove up in a Bentley[1] but it turned out he stole it and he missed the rest of the summer though he was back for winter league.

Mostly we played for fun and to try to talk to the girls who came to watch   5 the other teams. In summer they would sit up on the little hill above the court under the pines and sometimes we would call time out to get a look at them without the other team getting all wiggly the way they did if you wandered up there at halftime. You never knew if they were wives or girl-friends or sisters or what. One theory was that the girls who cursed the refs were girl-friends showing off, because wives and sisters could care less, but I don't know about that. One girl was the tallest girl you ever saw, she was taller than any of us, and there was another girl who wore a smile and not much else, we lost every game we ever played those guys, you wonder why.

Anyway, the guy who lost his arm, the story was that they finally found   6 it again after the funeral for it and he ended up leaving it in a toll booth on

[1] A British luxury car. —EDS.

the highway, with a quarter clenched in the fist, because rigor mortis set in, so the story was he paid a toll with it, but I don't know if that's true, although the guy who told me that was his teammate, the same guy who told me about the funeral for the arm, but this guy, the teammate, he and I got so absorbed in lefty talk that we never got into how true was the arm and the toll booth story, because the lefty thing is really interesting when you stop and think about it, Lefty Grove and Lefty Gomez and Sandy Koufax and Babe Ruth and Ted Williams were all lefties, and Bill Russell was lefty, and this guy, the teammate, claimed that Pele the great soccer player was lefty, although I said how would you know he's lefty if you can't use your hands in soccer, which he said that's a good point, but the clincher here is that the greatest middleweight boxer *ever* is lefty, Marvelous Marvin Hagler, and Marvin is from *Boston*, so there you go.[2]

Yo John

One time I played on a summer team where I was the only white guy.   1
This was in New York City a long time ago. There were nine other guys on my team and right from the start they couldn't remember my name no matter what and finally one guy, he was our center, he said all you white guys look alike to me, we'll call you John Lennon[3] cause he have long hair and ratshit beard too, and they all laughed and said Yo John Lennon!

This didn't last too long because it's too long to be yelled when you want   2
the ball which they all did all the time so my name got pruned down quick to Yo John and finally just to Yo, so I went a whole summer once being called Yo two nights a week all over New York City. I remember one night the ref asked me if I was Chinese or what and my team laughed so hard one guy hurt his ribs and had to miss a game.

There were some interesting guys on that team. One guy carried a   3
shot-gun in his trunk and twice carried it from the car to our bench to be sure everyone knew he was armored, as he said. We all scooted down the bench away from the gun. Another guy had tattoos over his entire torso front and

---

[2] All legendary sports figures. Grove (1900–75), Gomez (1908–89), and Koufax (born 1935) were pitchers, for the Philadelphia Athletics and the Boston Red Sox, the New York Yankees and the Washington Senators, and the Los Angeles Dodgers, respectively. Ruth (1895–1948) started as pitcher with the Red Sox but is famed for his career as a Yankees outfielder. Williams (1918–2002) played left field with the Red Sox. Russell (born 1934) was a basketball center with the Boston Celtics. Brazilian soccer star Pelé (born 1940) played professionally for two decades, winning three World Cups. And Boston's Haggler (born 1954) was the undisputed middleweight champion of the world from 1980 to 1987. —EDS.

[3] Born in 1940, the singer-songwriter was a leading member of the Beatles and a solo artist. He was shot to death in front of his New York City apartment building in 1980. —EDS.

back and when I asked him why he had none on his face he said Yo John, that's sick man, who would needle up his face?

We played all over the city. On one court in Bedford-Stuyvesant three [4] men swept the broken glass off the court before the game began, all three in tandem with those long push brooms, like synchronized sweeping. Another court, in Harlem, after both teams entered the refs padlocked the gate from inside and the spectators hung their fingers in the fence. The rumor was Connie Hawkins[4] was coming that night, he knew a guy who knew a guy, and I was wearing his number that summer, 42, so the guys on my team thought this juxtaposition was hilarious, Yo John be Connie Hawkins tonight, Yo John be mad dunking and all, you the man, Yo John! We lost by ten and Connie Hawkins didn't show and I played awful.

We won most of our games, including one wild game in Long Beach in [5] the windiest conditions ever, you had to account for the howling wind even on free throws, there was sand drifting across the court during the game, and high above the shrill haunted music of nighthawks, and after our last game, in Queens, we stood around talking for a while. The guy with tattoos, he was going to the police academy in the fall, and our center was going to community college to play ball. The guy with the shotgun was going into the small business, as he said. The point guard wanted to open a bakery, that was his great dream, he said, if any of us were in Long Island City, man, you come by and I will take care of you, man.

Summer league teams are hatched in a hurry and dissolve without [6] ceremony so I didn't expect to see those guys again but that Christmas I was playing pickup at a park in the city when three of those guys came by and stopped to talk. We shot the breeze and then they said Yo John, we saw your man John Lennon shot dead couple weeks ago and we are sorry, man, he was a good guy, those songs and all, he had a baby boy too. Cold to kill that man, Yo John. Crazy cold. We thought of you, man. Next summer we change your name, man. We call you Yo Connie Hawkins maybe, freak out the crowd, you know, a skinny whitey Hawk, other team laugh so hard we win by thirty every night, what you say to that, man, you in?

In the Equipment Shed at the Park in Chicago in July in an Unbelievable Howling Thunderstorm

One time I was playing basketball with a bunch of guys from the Latin [1] Kings and the Latin Eagles, those are street gangs in north Chicago, when the most unbelievable howling thunderstorm fell on us and everyone ran for the

---

[4] Cornelius Lance Hawkins (1942–2017) was a power forward who played basketball with several professional teams, including the Harlem Globetrotters. —Eds.

equipment shed, which was a ratty little aluminum shack in the middle of the park. It was filled with softballs and dodgeballs and rakes and dust and spiderwebs and bases with the stuffing coming out of the holes and softball bats with chips in them big enough so you couldn't use them in a game but you couldn't throw them away either because who throws away a perfectly good bat, you never throw away a bat that's not *all* the way cracked even if you are never going to use it again which is why there are probably like ten million bats in basements all over the world, which is kind of interesting when you think about it.

Anyway everyone crammed into the shed and there were so many guys 2
and so little room that the five guys closest to the door had to let their shoulders get rained on. One guy lit a purple joint the size of his thumb and passed it around and everyone started talking and telling stories. It was raining so loud you could hardly hear, and they were all talking at once in Spanish and English, and it got pretty smoky pretty fast, but it was that unbelievable late summer rain, you know, like a hot ocean falling in a hurry, and if you went out in it you would be totally soaked in two seconds, so we waited.

Raining like a million elephants pissing, said one guy, and everybody 3
laughed.

When the joint came around to me I said nah and the guy next to me 4
looked peeved and I said can't play baked and he laughed and said can't play not baked, man, which led to a huge discussion about whether hoop was better stoned or straight. One guy said it took the edge off and another guy said it made you see everything better and another guy said it made you jump higher and I said nah you just *think* you jump higher whereas actually you float around totally useless, and they all laughed.

It seemed weird to have guys from two opposing gangs crammed together 5
in the shed but first off it was raining like you wouldn't believe and secondly a guy told me the rule in the street was that a park could be shared under certain circumstances which these were but schoolyards could not be shared under any circumstances, they were sole territories for reasons having to do I think with children, which led to a huge discussion about boundaries and territories, which made me a little nervous because what if they started arguing about boundaries but they didn't.

Maybe it was the smoke or whatever but both gangs started remembering 6
guys they knew, first great ballplayers who got shot or went to jail, and then guys who weren't good ballplayers but thought they were, and then guys who thought they were tough but weren't, and then guys who *were* tough but never talked about it, and guys who could always get girls but you couldn't figure out why, and that led to a *huge* discussion about girls, and how you could never truly figure them out, everything you thought you learned from one didn't apply to any of the others, even in the littlest tiniest things, and how usually the way it

worked was that you could never get the girl you wanted but you could get the girl you didn't want, which as one guy said maybe that was the key, to *not* want the girl you wanted, but another guy said no no, the key to getting the girl you wanted was to *not* get the girl you *didn't* want, but by then we were all confused and the rain stopped and we emerged, blinking in the light.

Maybe it was the smoke but I remember that everything shone, the 7 steaming asphalt, the jeweled nets hanging from the rims, the gleaming backboards, even the ball glowing brilliant orange. We split up into wet guys and dry guys and played the rest of the afternoon and by the time I walked home the streets were so dry you couldn't believe it had ever rained at all.

Journal Writing

Do you play any sports, either on organized teams or informally? Which do you enjoy best, and why? In your journal, think of some athletic moments that stay with you for some reason — whether positive, such as making new friends or winning a big game, or negative, such as being injured or accused of cheating. Why do the memories stick?

Questions on Meaning

1. When does it become clear that "Three Basketball Stories" is a work of fiction — that the stories themselves are not true? What do you take to be Doyle's PURPOSE in telling them?

2. In what ways might Lefty's right arm function as a SYMBOL in this story? What do you think it means?

3. Doyle's narrator observes of the first story that it "is really interesting when you stop to think about it" (par. 6). What does he mean? Where else does he repeat this notion, and why?

4. How does Doyle's narrator explain the appeal of playing in "tough" (par. 1) basketball leagues? What does he give as the reason he and the other team members play? Can you detect any other possible reasons for their participation?

5. Does this work of fiction have a THESIS? In your own words, try to express the main idea of Doyle's story, or the generalization the author's examples seem intended to illustrate.

Questions on Writing Strategy

1. What function is served by the headings in this story?

2. Doyle's narrator frequently addresses the reader directly, as *you*. Why? What do these lines reveal about the writer's imagined AUDIENCE?

3. Examine the sentences in Doyle's story. How varied are they? Are they grammatically sound? Taken as a whole, what is the EFFECT of their structures and length?

4. Doyle's story does not have a formal conclusion. What strikes you about the IMAGERY in the final paragraph?

5. **OTHER METHODS** Doyle uses NARRATION to relate three telling episodes involving basketball teams in Boston, New York, and Chicago. What does the DIALOG in "Yo John" contribute to the story?

Questions on Language

1. Be sure you know how to define the following words: metaphysics (par. 2); rigor mortis, middleweight (6); pruned (8); armored, torso (9); synchronized, juxtaposition (10); nighthawks (11).

2. Point to some instances of hyperbole in "Three Basketball Stories." (For a definition of *hyperbole*, see FIGURES OF SPEECH in the Glossary.) What other figures of speech do you notice? How does the narrator's language affect the TONE of the stories?

3. In his comments on writing (next page), Doyle stresses the importance of using "energized" verbs. Point to any particularly strong verbs you find in "Three Basketball Stories." What makes them effective?

Suggestions for Writing

1. **FROM JOURNAL TO ESSAY** Pick a few episodes you recounted in your journal (p. 197) and write a story about them, either true-to-life or fictionalized. Follow Doyle's example in using the second-person *you* and the past tense of verbs. You may write multiple stories as Doyle does if you wish, but one story is sufficient if you can develop it with enough details to convey its significance to your readers.

2. Starting with the list of athletes Doyle's narrator cites in paragraph 6, look into the "lefty thing" for yourself. What percentage of the general population is left-handed? Conversely, how many professional athletes are southpaws? Who have been some of the most prominent? Does left-handedness give athletes an advantage, or a disadvantage, in any particular sports? Why? (You can find studies on the subject in scholarly journals, such as *Biology Letters*, in your school's periodicals databases). In an essay, report your findings.

3. Doyle makes light of the threat of urban violence in all three cities depicted in this story, but gang violence in particular is a serious and enduring problem in the United States. Write an essay about the problem of gangs in your town or city. Use examples to support your view of the problem and a possible solution.

4. **CRITICAL WRITING** Write an essay in which you ANALYZE Doyle's use of language in this story or a portion of it. How would you characterize his narrator's DICTION? What are some especially creative uses of language, the figures of speech in particular? What overall effect does Doyle create with the language he uses?

5. **CONNECTIONS** Doyle expresses a certain amount of reverence for sports and their icons. Similarly, in "Football Matters" (p. 312), travel writer Paul Theroux posits that the University of Alabama's revered football team can be credited

with giving the college town of Tuscaloosa its very identity. In an essay, consider how Doyle's apparent love of playing basketball complements or contradicts Theroux's analysis of what rooting for a high-profile football teams does for its fans. In what ways, according to both authors, do sports work to bring some communities together? How might they drive others apart?

Brian Doyle on Writing

In a weekly blog for *The American Scholar*, the magazine of the Phi Beta Kappa honor society, Doyle wrote about "stories that nourish and sustain us, and the small miracles of everyday life." In August of 2013 he used the space to reflect on how, and why, he became a writer by trade.

"How did you become a writer?" is a question asked of me surprisingly often when I visit schools, which I much enjoy not only as part of my overarching subtle devious plan to get on the good side of the children who will soon run the world, but also for the consistent entertainment of their artlessly honest questions (the best ever: *Is that your real nose?*), and for the sometimes deeply piercing depth of our conversations; we have suddenly spoken of death and miracles and loss and love, while we were supposed to be talking about writing and literature; and I have wept in front of them, and they have wept in front of me; which seems to me a sweet gift, to be trusted that much.

But in almost every class I am asked how I became a writer, and after I make my usual joke about it being a benign neurosis, as my late friend George Higgins[5] once told me, I usually talk about my dad. My dad was a newspaperman, and still is, at age 92, a man of great grace and patience and dignity, and he taught me immensely valuable lessons. If you wish to be a writer, *write*, he would say. There are people who talk about writing and then there are people who sit down and type. Writing is fast typing. Also you must read like you are starving for ink. Read widely. Read everything. . . . Note how people get their voices and hearts and stories down on the page. Also get a job; eating is a good habit and you will never make enough of a living as a writer to support a family. Be honest with yourself about the size of your gift. Expect no money but be diligent about sending pieces out for publication. All money is gravy. A piece is not finished until it is off your desk and onto an editor's desk.

---

[5] George V. Higgins (1939–99) was an American newspaper columnist, lawyer, and college professor who wrote several best-selling crime novels. —EDS.

Write hard and then edit yourself hard. Look carefully at your verbs to see if they can be energized.

The best writers do not write about themselves but about everyone else. The best writers are great listeners. Learn to ask a question and then shut your mouth and listen. Use silence as a journalistic tool; people are uncomfortable with it and will leap to fill the holes, often telling you more than they wanted to. . . . Everyone has sweet sad brave wonderful stories; give them a chance to tell their stories. So many people do not get the chance. Listening is the greatest literary art. Your ears are your best tools. No one is dull or boring. Anyone who thinks so is an idiot.

Many fine writers do not get credit for the quality of their prose because they were famous for something else: Lincoln, for example. The best writing is witness. The lowest form of writing is mere catharsis.[6] Persuasive writing generally isn't. The finest writers in newspapers are often sports and police reporters. When in doubt about a line or a passage, cut it. All writing can be improved by a judicious editor. . . .

Do not let writing be a special event; let it be a normal part of your day. It *is* normal. We are all storytellers and story-attentive beings. Otherwise we would never be loved or have a country or a religion. You do not need a sabbatical or a grant to write a book. Write a little bit every day. You will be surprised how deep the muck gets at the end of the year, but at that point you can cut out the dull parts, elevate your verbs, delete mere catharsis, celebrate witness, find the right title, and send it off to be published. Any questions?

The Bedford Reader on Writing

As we stress throughout this book, but especially on pages 30–33, Doyle encourages aspiring writers to read and read often, and to keep a JOURNAL, writing "a little bit every day." Notice, too, the importance he places on EDITING, especially for strong verbs and unnecessary phrases; for our advice on these subjects see "Focus on Verbs," page 71, and "Focus on Clarity and Conciseness," page 405.

---

[6] Doyle uses the word *catharsis* in its meaning of a cleansing purge, or the release of emotion. —Eds.

ADDITIONAL WRITING TOPICS

Example

1. Select one of the following general statements, or set forth a general statement of your own that one of these inspires. Making it your central idea (or THESIS), support the statement in an essay full of examples. Draw your examples from your reading, your studies, your conversations, or your own experience.

   Text messaging has many advantages (or many disadvantages) over making a phone call.
   Individual consumers can (or cannot) help slow down global climate change.
   Friendships don't always start off easily.
   Spending (or saving) is necessary to the nation's economy.
   Each family has its own distinctive culture.
   Certain games, closely inspected, promote violence.
   Graphic novels have become a serious form of literary art.
   Most people can triumph over crushing difficulties.
   Churchgoers aren't perfect.
   Online articles use misleading titles to get readers to click on the stories.
   Local foods, in season, are best for everyone (or not).
   Ordinary lives sometimes give rise to legends.
   Some people are born winners (or losers).
   Music can change lives.
   Certain machines *do* have personalities.
   Some road signs lead drivers astray.

2. In a brief essay, make a GENERALIZATION about the fears, joys, or contradictions that members of minority groups seem to share. To illustrate your generalization, draw examples from personal experience, from outside reading, or from two or three of the selections in this book by the following authors: Nancy Mairs (p. 12), Amy Tan (p. 77), Kunal Nayyar (p. 91), Maya Angelou (p. 98), Scaachi Koul (p. 133), N. Scott Momaday (p. 144), Brent Staples (p. 169), Issa Rae (p. 176), Zane Rassler (p. 186), Jourdan Imani Keith (p. 212), Fatema Mernissi (p. 244), Firoozeh Dumas (p. 275), Gary Soto (p. 327), Sandra Cisneros (p. 361), Langston Hughes (p. 408), Tal Fortgang (p. 460), Roxane Gay (p. 467), Dagoberto Gilb (p. 478), Linda Chavez (p. 506), Dawn Lundy Martin (p. 548), Thomas Chatterton Williams (p. 553), Louise Erdrich (p. 576), Maxine Hong Kingston (p. 588), and Luis Alberto Urrea (p. 631).

8

COMPARISON AND CONTRAST

Setting Things Side by Side

◀ **Comparison and contrast in a graphic memoir**

In the highly praised and influential *Fun Home* (2006), comic artist Alison Bechdel explores the complications of growing up the lesbian daughter of a closeted gay man while living in a nineteenth-century house that held the family's funeral business. In this panel, from the first chapter of the book, she compares herself with her father on four points: politics (ancient Sparta, in Greece, was a warrior society; neighboring Athens focused on education and the arts), cultural sensibilities, gender stereotypes, and values. What striking and not-so-striking differences do you notice? What is the most obvious similarity? What are some more subtle similarities? How would you summarize the conflict Bechdel portrays?

THE METHOD

Which team do you place your money on, the Eagles or the Patriots? To go to school full-time or part-time: What are the rewards and drawbacks of each way of life? How do the Republican and Democratic platforms stack up against each other? In what ways are the psychological theories of Carl Jung like or unlike those of Sigmund Freud? Should we pass laws to regulate medical marijuana or let recreational use run wild? These are questions that may be addressed by the dual method of COMPARISON AND CONTRAST. In comparing, you point to similar features of the subjects; in contrasting, to different features. (The features themselves you identify by the method of DIVISION or ANALYSIS; see Chap. 10.)

In practice, comparison and contrast are usually inseparable because two subjects are generally neither entirely alike nor entirely unlike. When student writer Caitlin McDougall sets out to portray acting on stage and on screen (p. 229), she considers both the similarities and the differences. Often, as in this case, the similarities make the subjects comparable at all and the differences make comparison worthwhile.

Uses of Comparison and Contrast

Comparison and contrast are especially helpful in academic work. You can use the method in expository writing to illuminate two or more subjects and demonstrate that you understand your material thoroughly. And in an argument in which you support one of two possible choices, a careful and detailed comparison and contrast may be extremely convincing as you show why you prefer one thing to another, one course of action to another, one idea to another.

Because comparison and contrast reveal knowledge about the subjects under investigation, you will also often be asked to use the method in exams that call for essay answers. Sometimes the examiner will come right out and say, "Compare and contrast early twentieth-century methods of treating opioid addiction with those of the present day." Sometimes, however, comparison and contrast won't even be mentioned by name; instead, the examiner may ask, "What resemblances do you find between John Updike's short story 'A & P' and the Grimm fairy tale 'Godfather Death'?" Or, "Explain the relative desirability of holding a franchise against going into business as an independent proprietor." But those—as you realize when you begin to plan your reply—are just other ways of asking you to compare and contrast.

Purposes

A good essay in comparing and contrasting serves a PURPOSE. Most of the time, the writer of such an essay has one of two purposes in mind:

- **To explain the similarities and differences between two things,** the writer shows each of the subjects distinctly by considering both, side by side. With such a purpose, the writer doesn't necessarily find one of the subjects better than the other. In "At Risk," an essay comparing young people and salmon (p. 212), for instance, Jourdan Imani Keith does not favor either species but concludes that each group navigates strong currents of danger.

- **To choose between two things, or** EVALUATE **them,** the writer shows how one of the subjects is better than the other on the basis of some standard. Which is more satisfying for actors: performing in a play or in a movie? Which of two chemical processes works better to clean waste water? To answer either question, the writer has to consider the features of both subjects — both the positive and the negative — and then choose the subject whose positive features more clearly predominate.

THE PROCESS

Subjects for Comparison

Comparison usually works best with two of a kind: two means of reading for the visually impaired, two jobs in the same field, two processes for cleaning waste water, two mystery writers, two schools of political thought. When you find yourself considering two subjects side by side or preferring one subject over another, you have already embarked on comparison and contrast. Just be sure that your two subjects display a clear basis for comparison. In other words, they should have something significant in common.

It can sometimes be effective, however, to find similarities between evidently unlike subjects — a city and a country town, say — and a special form of comparison, ANALOGY, equates two very unlike things, explaining one in terms of the other. In an analogy you might explain how the human eye works by comparing it to a simple camera, or you might explain the forces in a thunderstorm by comparing them to armies in battle. In "The Great Silence" (p. 217), science fiction writer Ted Chiang explains the intelligence and communication skills of parrots by equating them with extraterrestrial beings. In any comparison, you must have a valid reason for bringing the two things together — that is, the similarities and differences must be significant enough to warrant examination. In a comparison of a city and a country town, for instance, the features must extend beyond the obvious — that people live in them, that both have streets and shops — and venture into likenesses that are more meaningful — perhaps that both places create a sense of community that residents depend on, for instance.

Basis for Comparison and Thesis

Beginning to identify the shared and dissimilar features of your subjects will get you started, but the comparison won't be manageable for you or interesting to your readers unless you also limit it. You would be overly ambitious to try to compare and contrast the Russian way of life with the American way of life in five hundred words; you couldn't include all the important similarities and differences. In a brief paper, you would be wise to select a single basis for comparison: to show, for instance, how representative day-care centers in Russia and the United States are both like and unlike each other.

This basis for comparison will eventually underpin the THESIS of your essay — the claim you have to make about the similarities and dissimilarities of two things or about one thing's superiority over another. Here, from essays in this chapter, are THESIS STATEMENTS that clearly lay out what's being compared and why:

> I tell the woman at the party, "All youth are at risk — the risks are just different." And some are endangered.
> — Jourdan Imani Keith, "At Risk"

> I finally realized that acting in a film is an immensely gratifying experience, but nothing can compare to the raw humanity of acting in a staged play.
> — Caitlin McDougall, "So Enid and Dorothy from West Covina Can Hear You"

Notice that each author not only identifies her subjects ("at-risk" youth, two kinds of acting) but also previews the purpose of the comparison, whether to explain (Keith) or to evaluate (McDougall).

Organization

Even with a limited basis for comparison, the method of comparison and contrast can be tricky without some planning. We suggest that you make an outline (formal or informal), using one of two organizations described below: subject by subject or point by point.

Say you're writing an essay on two guitarists, Jed and Jake. Your purpose is to explain the distinctive identities of the two players, and your thesis statement might be the following:

> Jed and Jake are both excellent guitarists whose differences in style reflect their training.

There are the two basic ways you might arrange the BODY of your comparison, subject by subject or point by point.

Subject by Subject

Set forth all your facts about the first subject (subject A); then do the same for the second (subject B). Next, sum up their similarities and differences. In your conclusion, state what you think you have shown.

> *Jed*
> Training
> Choice of instrument
> Technical dexterity
> Playing style
>
> *Jake*
> Training
> Choice of instrument
> Technical dexterity
> Playing style

This procedure works well for a paper of a few paragraphs, but for a longer one, it has a built-in disadvantage: Readers need to remember all the facts about subject A while they read about subject B. If the essay is long and lists many facts, a subject-by-subject arrangement may be difficult to hold in mind.

Point by Point

Usually more workable in writing a long paper than the first method, the second scheme is to compare and contrast as you go. You consider one point at a time, taking up your two subjects alternately. In this way, you continually bring the subjects together, perhaps in every paragraph. Notice the differences in the outline:

> *Training*
> Jed: self-taught
> Jake: classically trained
>
> *Choice of instrument*
> Jed: electric
> Jake: acoustic
>
> *Technical dexterity*
> Jed: highly skilled
> Jake: highly skilled
>
> *Playing style*
> Jed: rapid-fire
> Jake: impressionistic

For either organizing scheme, your conclusion might be as follows: "Although similar in skills, the two differ greatly in aims and in personalities. Jed is better suited to a local club and Jake to a concert hall."

By the way, a subject-by-subject organization works most efficiently for a *pair* of subjects. If you want to write about *three* guitarists, you might first consider Jed and Jake, then Jake and Josh, then Josh and Jed—but it would probably be easier to compare and contrast all three point by point.

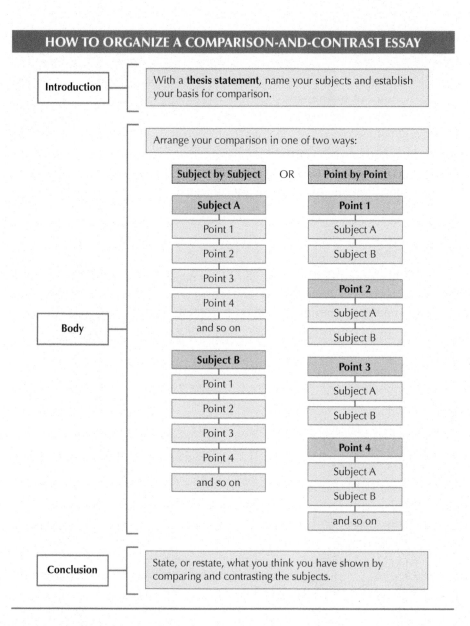

HOW TO ORGANIZE A COMPARISON-AND-CONTRAST ESSAY

Introduction — With a **thesis statement**, name your subjects and establish your basis for comparison.

Body

Arrange your comparison in one of two ways:

| **Subject by Subject** | OR | **Point by Point** |

Subject A		**Point 1**
Point 1		Subject A
Point 2		Subject B
Point 3		
Point 4		**Point 2**
and so on		Subject A
		Subject B

Subject B		**Point 3**
Point 1		Subject A
Point 2		Subject B
Point 3		
Point 4		**Point 4**
and so on		Subject A
		Subject B
		and so on

Conclusion — State, or restate, what you think you have shown by comparing and contrasting the subjects.

Balance and Flexibility

An outline will help you see the shape of your paper and keep your points in mind as you draft. A trick of comparison and contrast is to balance the treatment of both subjects while allowing them to breathe. You do have to give the subjects equivalence: You can't discuss Jed's on-stage manner without discussing Jake's, too. If you have nothing to say about Jake's on-stage manner, then you might as well omit the point. A surefire loser is the paper that proposes to compare and contrast two subjects but then proceeds to discuss quite different elements in each: Jed's playing style and Jake's choice of material, Jed's fondness for Italian food and Jake's hobby of antique-car collecting. The writer of such a paper doesn't compare and contrast the two musicians at all, but engages in two entirely separate discussions.

Balance your subjects' features, but don't let your outline constrain you too tightly. The reader of a mechanically written comparison-and-contrast essay comes to feel like a weary tennis spectator whose head has to swivel from side to side: now Jed, now Jake; now Jed again, now back to Jake. You need to mention the same features of both subjects, it is true, but no law says *how* you must mention them. You need not follow your outline in lockstep order, or cover similarities and differences at precisely the same length (none of the authors later in this chapter do), or spend a hundred words on Jed's fingering skill just because you spend a hundred words on Jake's. As you write, keep casting your thoughts upon a living, particular world—not twisting and squeezing that world into a rigid scheme.

CHECKLIST FOR REVIEWING AND REVISING A COMPARISON-AND-CONTRAST ESSAY

✔ **Purpose.** What is the aim of the comparison: to explain two (or more) subjects or to evaluate them? Will the purpose be clear to readers from the start?

✔ **Subjects.** Are the subjects enough alike, sharing enough features, to make comparison worthwhile?

✔ **Thesis.** Does your thesis establish a limited basis for comparison so that you have room and time to cover all the relevant similarities and differences?

✔ **Organization.** Does the arrangement of material, whether subject by subject or point by point, do justice to the subjects and help readers follow the comparison?

✔ **Balance and flexibility.** Are the same features of both subjects covered? At the same time, have you avoided a rigid back-and-forth movement that could bore or exhaust a reader?

✔ **Parallelism.** Do parallel structures help to clarify the subjects and points you are discussing? (See the next page.)

FOCUS ON PARALLELISM

With several points of comparison and alternating subjects, a comparison will be easier for your readers to follow if you emphasize likenesses and differences in your wording. Take advantage of the technique of parallelism discussed in Chapter 4 (p. 58). PARALLELISM—the use of similar grammatical structures for elements of similar importance—balances a comparison and clarifies the relations between elements. At the same time, lack of parallelism can distract or confuse readers.

To make the elements of a comparison parallel, repeat the forms of related words, phrases, and sentences:

NONPARALLEL   Harris expects dieters who follow his plan to limit bread, dairy, and meat, while Marconi's diet forbids few foods.

PARALLEL   Harris's diet limits bread, dairy, and meat, while Marconi's diet forbids few foods.

NONPARALLEL   Harris emphasizes self-denial, but when following Marconi's plan you can eat whatever you want in moderation.

PARALLEL   Harris emphasizes self-denial, but Marconi stresses moderation.

NONPARALLEL   If you want to lose weight quickly, choose Harris's diet. You'll have more success keeping the weight off if you follow Marconi's plan.

PARALLEL   If you want to lose weight quickly, choose Harris's diet. If you want to keep the weight off, follow Marconi's plan.

STUDENT CASE STUDY: A REVIEW

If you browse the Web or flip through any newspaper or magazine, you're bound to spot a review: a writer's assessment of anything from a restaurant to a scholarly book. Commonly assigned in college, too, reviews rely mainly on ANALYSIS to identify and interpret the elements of a subject. But because a review evaluates quality, writers naturally turn to comparison and contrast as well, weighing two or more products, works, or ideas to determine their relative worth. Such a comparison takes its evidence from the subjects themselves, as in descriptions of paintings in an exhibit or quotations from written works.

For an American Studies course in popular culture, Charlotte Pak wrote a review of singer Beyoncé Knowles's solo career. Pak chose her subject because "Single Ladies (Put a Ring on It)" had bolstered Beyoncé's reputation as a champion of women. Although Pak enjoyed the song, she was bothered by some of the implications in its lyrics, and she decided to investigate the singer's work for similar themes. In the paragraphs below, excerpted from her full review, Pak compares "Single Ladies" with a popular song from the 1960s, with unexpected results.

Critics and fans often view Beyoncé as one of the leaders in the "strong woman" style that encourages female independence, equality, and self-worth. These listeners offer her 2009 hit "Single Ladies (Put a Ring on It)" as a symbol of how far women have come since the 1950s and 1960s. But this and other songs by Beyoncé just seem strong when in fact they present women who are no more independent than the ones portrayed half a century ago.

A classic example of the older style is the Dixie Cups' 1964 hit "Chapel of Love." The refrain of the song is familiar even today: "Goin' to the chapel and we're / Gonna get married / . . . Goin' to the chapel of love." The song itself seems sentimental and even naive on the surface. In a sweet, dreamy voice, the female singer imagines marital bliss, as "Birds all sing as if they knew / Today's the day we'll say 'I do.' " She sings of marriage as the fulfillment of her life, implying her dependence on a man. Yet despite the tone and the sentimentality, the song also suggests equality between the singer and her husband-to-be within the bounds of traditional marriage: "I'll be his and he'll be mine." The possession is mutual. Two independent individuals will say "I do."

In contrast, the singer in Beyoncé's "Single Ladies" seems pleased to be free from an ex-boyfriend. She dances with another man in a club while her ex jealously watches: "Don't pay him any attention / 'Cause you had your turn and now you're gonna learn / What it really feels like to miss me." Her tone is feisty and no-nonsense, the voice of a sophisticated and independent woman. Yet she remains preoccupied with her ex-boyfriend and still sees herself through his eyes. In the song's chorus—"If you like it then you shoulda put a ring on it"—the "it" suggests that she has a sense of herself as an object to be possessed rather than an independent being. That suggestion is explicit in the lines "Pull me into your arms, / Say I'm the one you own." The wimpy "Chapel of Love" at least offers an image of equality. "Single Ladies" misleads by casting dependency as strength.

Basis for comparison: portrayals of women's strength

Subject-by-subject organization supporting this claim

1. Representative older song: "Chapel of Love" by the Dixie Cups
   • Quotations from song

   • Interpretation

2. Representative Beyoncé song: "Single Ladies (Put a Ring on It)"
   • Quotations from song
   • Interpretation

Concluding sentences express judgment

JOURDAN IMANI KEITH

Jourdan Imani Keith is a Philadelphia-born naturalist and educator devoted to writing and to bringing young city dwellers outdoors. After completing a degree in English at Temple University (BA, 1985), she worked for a while as a guide in Yellowstone National Park and then made her way to the Pacific Northwest, studying restoration ecology at the University of Washington and marine ecology at Washington State University. An accomplished playwright, poet, and essayist, Keith was the first naturalist-in-residence at the Seattle Public Library and was elected by popular vote as the city's Poet Laureate for 2006–07. Now a contributing writer for *Orion*, she has published her work in several other periodicals and anthologies, including the *Seattle Times*, *Labyrinth*, *PUSH*, *Colors NW*, and *Má-Ka Diasporic Juks: Contemporary Writing by Queers of African Descent* (1998). Keith is also the founder and director of the Urban Wilderness Project, coordinating environmental education and service-learning camping and hiking projects, with a focus on storytelling, for marginalized students from middle school through college.

At Risk

This essay, which first appeared in the magazine *Orion* in 2014 and was then selected for *Best American Science and Nature Writing 2015*, grows directly out of Keith's experience with the Urban Wilderness Project and illustrates her dual commitments to young people and the environment. Traveling to a camp site to pick up her charges, she finds surprising parallels between human teenagers and the chinook salmon spawning the rivers nearby.

For another Seattle-area writer's creative take on the risks of extinction, look to "The Great Silence" (p. 217), the story by Ted Chiang that follows Keith's essay.

The torrential rain in the first week of September pummels the youth crew's 1 tents at night, depositing mud and sediment in the creek where they pump water for drinking. For seventeen days the teenagers I recruited to build trails for the North Cascades National Park[1] are camping during one of the heaviest storms in a hundred years. The river coughs thick brown mudslides onto State Route 20, blocking road access from the west. Instead of a three-and-a-half-hour

---

[1] The North Cascades are part of a mountain range in Washington state. The park is approximately one hundred miles northeast of Seattle. —EDS.

drive to pick them up, I begin a seven-hour journey eastward from Seattle through rock formations that dart out like deer from the light-green sagebrush.

Arriving in the dark, I find the Pearrygin Lake campground outside of the Old West town of Winthrop barely occupied. The warm air is without insects, so I tuck myself in on the grass behind the white twelve-passenger van I have rented to pick up the crew. Lying out under the stars without the nylon canopy of my tent, I nestle into the reflection of the half-moon and backlit mountains in the lake.

Despite my comfort, I am acutely aware that I am at-risk: Black. Woman. Alone. Camping. Even in the disguising cloak of moonlight shadows, I need protection. I sleep with the van keys in my pocket and practice grabbing them to push the panic button in case of danger.

The spring chinook populations in the watersheds around Route 20 are labeled "at-risk populations" when the Forest Service discusses road analysis in the Methow River subbasin and its watersheds. They are protected under the Endangered Species Act. Protecting an endangered species means changing the practices in an entire ecosystem to safeguard their survival. It means managing the loss of their habitat, the turbidity of their waters, the surface water runoff from the streets that threatens them, and the effluents from the wastewater that disrupt their endocrine systems and, if unchecked, will cause their extinction.

Every year salmon return to the rivers where they were born. And every year, I return to the birthplace of the wilderness program I developed to nurture the next generation of outdoor leaders in the cathedral peaks and azure lakes of the North Cascades. This year, the wettest August followed by the heavy rains of September threatened both my crew of nascent campers and the eggs of the spawning salmon.

My youth crews are Black. Latino. Urban. This is what the woman at a party hears when I describe them. "Oh, you work with at-risk youth," she says. She doesn't hear Volunteer. College Student. Intern. Outdoor Leader. The "at-risk" label is different for youth than it is for salmon. "At-risk" isn't a protection but a limitation, a judgment, an assumption. Even when the threats to their survival are the same as to an endangered species—an unstable habitat, lack of nutrition, and a damaged social and natural ecosystem—the label leaves them at a deficit, offers no promise for protection.

In the case of the salmon, being protected as an endangered species alerts us to the fullness of their connection to a magnificent web. Their relationship to threatened indigenous cultures and to other endangered species like the majestic orca whales is valued. Their label protects them.

I tell the woman at the party, "All youth are at-risk—the risks are just different." And some are endangered.

Journal Writing

Keith observes that the college students she works with have been called "At-risk," but have not been described with more positive labels, such as "Volunteer," "Intern," or "Outdoor Leader" (par. 6). As a student yourself, how might you be labeled? Brainstorm some descriptors that others might apply to you, considering any groups you belong to or assumptions others might make about you based on your appearance or demeanor. Are these labels accurate? Fair? How would you prefer to be described?

Questions on Meaning

1. How does Keith explain the reasons for the youth group camping in the North Cascades National Park? Who are they? What are they doing there?

2. What is Keith's PURPOSE in this essay? Does she seek to evaluate her volunteers? explain the risks they face? draw attention to an environmental problem? something else? How can you tell?

3. Does "At Risk" have a THESIS? Explain the central idea of the essay.

Questions on Writing Strategy

1. Does Keith arrange her comparison subject by subject or point by point? What, or whom, does she identify as being "at-risk," and why?

2. What similarities does Keith find between young urbanites and spawning salmon? How does the "at-risk" designation affect each group differently?

3. For whom do you suppose Keith is writing? What does she seem to ASSUME about the interests and knowledge of her AUDIENCE? To what extent do you fit her assumptions?

4. **OTHER METHODS**   How does Keith use DEFINITION to clarify her meaning to readers? What does the method contribute to her essay?

Questions on Language

1. Consult a dictionary if you are unable to determine the meanings of the following words from their context in Keith's essay: acutely (par. 3); chinook, watersheds, subbasin, ecosystem, turbidity, effluents, endocrine (4); azure, nascent, spawning (5); habitat, deficit (6); indigenous (7).

2. Take note of the one- and two-word sentences in paragraphs 3 and 6. What do you think is the intended effect of these sentences? Where else in the essay does Keith use a similar strategy to stress her points?

3. Keith uses several striking FIGURES OF SPEECH in this essay, mostly personification and metaphor. Find two or three examples of each (refer to the Glossary if you need help). Why are the personifications, in particular, especially appropriate given the author's subject and purpose? How does the comparison function as an ANALOGY?

4. How would you characterize Keith's DICTION and TONE? What does her language contribute to the overall effect of her comparison?

Suggestions for Writing

1. **FROM JOURNAL TO ESSAY** Write an essay giving an extended definition of a label that has been or could be applied to you, drawing on your journal entry, Keith's essay, and any other sources that offer ideas. You might use one of the labels Keith cites (At-risk, Black, Woman, Alone, Latino, Urban, Volunteer, College Student, Intern, Outdoor Leader) or come up with a name of your own. Keep in mind that characterizing any large and diverse group requires generalization. How does your definition compare with other definitions you have heard? Does any attempt to label a demographic group necessarily oversimplify? Do you find value or interest in the exercise?

2. Are the chinook salmon in the North Cascades National Park in fact protected by federal law? Using the Internet or a periodicals database, research the history and current state of the Endangered Species Act of 1973. In an essay, summarize the original intent of the act and some of its effects over the past half-century. Where has it succeeded? Where might it have failed? What measures has Congress taken recently to adapt the legislation, and why? Then discuss whether you approve or disapprove of the implementation of environmental regulations in general. Do they infringe on corporations' ability to do business, for instance, or do you think they're a necessary tool in protecting natural ecosystems? How effective are such laws? Who should pay for their provisions, and how? Why do you feel the way you do?

3. **CRITICAL WRITING** Using your response to the third Question on Language (above) as a starting point, analyze Keith's use of sensory IMAGES in "At Risk." How does the abundant imagery and figurative language help convey her ideas about a damaged environment? What else do the images contribute to the essay?

4. **CONNECTIONS** In "The Great Silence" (p. 217), Ted Chiang also writes about endangered species. Write an essay that compares and contrasts Keith's and Chiang's attitudes regarding human impacts on the planet Earth. To what extent do these two authors believe people are responsible for harms to the environment, such as the pollution of waterways, the loss of natural habitats, and the extinction of other species? Taken together, what do they seem to believe is the best recourse for halting or even reversing the damage? What do they suggest are our responsibilities as environmental stewards? What is each writer saying about the role of education in particular? How do you respond to their ideas?

Jourdan Imani Keith on Writing

As an educator and an activist based in Seattle, Jourdan Imani Keith is deeply committed to working with students in area schools and colleges. In a 2016 interview for *The Cub*, the online newspaper for Sedro-Woolley High School in northwest Washington, she spoke with student Demetria Haigh about her involvement with the Urban Wilderness Project and her love of writing. Asked to name some of her favorite published works, Keith identified "At Risk" as something she is especially happy with. As she explained to Haigh, "it's an essay . . . I [just] started writing and I really like it because it is kind of a way [of sharing] my experience of wandering outdoors and . . . being aware that as a woman I am vulnerable to a lot of things, as a black person I'm vulnerable to a lot of things, and so are salmon. Both things I think about all the time. I had fun writing it."

The essay springs from the writer's recent experience with the nonprofit youth organization she had founded a decade earlier to raise environmental awareness and help "people who otherwise wouldn't have the opportunity to go spend an extended amount of time camping in the wilderness." When she labored to get the Urban Wilderness Project up and running, Keith says, it was very important to her to reach out to "low income or African American, Asian, Latino youth and actually get them outside." And while the Project is still dear to her, she finds now that she has difficulty balancing her priorities: "Well, I refuse to give up my writing," she says. "So wherever I am, whatever I have as an opportunity, I will write. But it also has [been the case] until recently that the organization could only grow so much because I refuse to give up my art. There's only one of me . . . so I just kept writing. I mean I would die if I wasn't writing. . . . So I juggle it by just always doing it, and now . . . [when] people ask me 'When do you find time to write?' it's the other way around: When do I find the time to do the other things? I just changed the order."

The Bedford Reader on Writing

Keith notes that "At Risk" was an essay without a plan: The idea for it just came to her while she was doing other things. How do you balance your writing assignments with the rest of what you have to do (and want to do) every day? For our advice on finding ideas and then letting loose as you draft, even if time is limited, see Chapter 2, especially pages 30–33.

TED CHIANG

Ted Chiang is one of America's most prized writers of science fiction. Born in 1967 in Port Jefferson, New York, to immigrant parents who had fled the communist revolution in China, he grew up reading sci-fi and dreaming of re-creating for others the "sense of wonder" the stories brought him as a boy. Chiang started writing while in high school, graduated from Brown University with a degree in computer science in 1989, and almost immediately began winning awards for his fiction, starting with a Nebula prize in 1990 for "Tower of Babylon." His best-known work, "Story of Your Life" (1998), was the basis for the Oscar-nominated film *Arrival* (2016). Frequently praised for the careful craftsmanship and deeply humanistic effect of his writing, Chiang has been honored with twenty-seven major awards for fifteen published stories to date. He is employed by day as a technical writer of computer-programming manuals and lives near Seattle, Washington.

The Great Silence

Much of Chiang's fiction focuses on questions of language and communication. Such is the case with this story, written as the on-screen textual script for *The Great Silence*, a 2014 video installation by a Puerto Rican team of artists known as Allora & Calzadilla. The installation premiered at the Philadelphia Museum of Art in 2014 (we include two stills to help you visualize it), and the story was included in *Best American Short Stories* in 2016 — a rare achievement in the genre of science fiction. Like Jourdan Imani Keith in the previous essay, Chiang considers creatures at risk of extinction, forging unexpected connections between human beings and the natural environment.

The humans use Arecibo to look for extraterrestrial intelligence. Their 1 desire to make a connection is so strong that they've created an ear capable of hearing across the universe.

But I and my fellow parrots are right here. Why aren't they interested in 2 listening to our voices?

We're a non-human species capable of communicating with them. Aren't 3 we exactly what humans are looking for?

The universe is so vast that intelligent life must surely have arisen many 4 times. The universe is also so old that even one technological species would

have had time to expand and fill the galaxy. Yet there is no sign of life anywhere except on Earth. Humans call this the Fermi paradox.

One proposed solution to the Fermi paradox is that intelligent species   5
actively try to conceal their presence, to avoid being targeted by hostile invaders.

Speaking as a member of a species that has been driven nearly to extinc-   6
tion by humans, I can attest that this is a wise strategy.

It makes sense to remain quiet and avoid attracting attention.   7

The Fermi paradox is sometimes known as the Great Silence. The uni-   8
verse ought to be a cacophony of voices, but instead it's disconcertingly quiet.

Some humans theorize that intelligent species go extinct before they can   9
expand into outer space. If they're correct, then the hush of the night sky is
the silence of a graveyard.

Hundreds of years ago, my kind was so plentiful that the Rio Abajo forest 10
resounded with our voices. Now we're almost gone. Soon this rainforest may
be as silent as the rest of the universe.

There was an African Grey Parrot named Alex. He was famous for his   11
cognitive abilities. Famous among humans, that is.

A human researcher named Irene Pepperberg spent thirty years studying   12
Alex. She found that not only did Alex know the words for shapes and colors, he actually understood the concepts of shape and color.

Many scientists were skeptical that a bird could grasp abstract concepts. 13
Humans like to think they're unique. But eventually Pepperberg convinced them
that Alex wasn't just repeating words, that he understood what he was saying.

Out of all my cousins, Alex was the one who came closest to being taken   14
seriously as a communication partner by humans.

Alex died suddenly, when he was still relatively young. The evening   15
before he died, Alex said to Pepperberg, "You be good. I love you."

If humans are looking for a connection with a non-human intelligence,   16
what more can they ask for than that?

Every parrot has a unique call that it uses to identify itself; biologists refer   17
to this as the parrot's "contact call."

In 1974, astronomers used Arecibo to broadcast a message into outer   18
space intended to demonstrate human intelligence. That was humanity's
contact call.

In the wild, parrots address each other by name. One bird imitates anoth-   19
er's contact call to get the other bird's attention.

If humans ever detect the Arecibo message being sent back to Earth, they   20
will know someone is trying to get their attention.

Parrots are vocal learners: We can learn to make new sounds after we've   21
heard them. It's an ability that few animals possess. A dog may understand
dozens of commands, but it will never do anything but bark.

Humans are vocal learners, too. We have that in common. So humans   22
and parrots share a special relationship with sound. We don't simply cry out.
We pronounce. We enunciate.

Perhaps that's why humans built Arecibo the way they did. A receiver   23
doesn't have to be a transmitter, but Arecibo is both. It's an ear for listening,
and a mouth for speaking.

Humans have lived alongside parrots for thousands of years, and only   24
recently have they considered the possibility that we might be intelligent.

I suppose I can't blame them. We parrots used to think humans weren't very   25
bright. It's hard to make sense of behavior that's so different from your own.

But parrots are more similar to humans than any extraterrestrial species   26
will be, and humans can observe us up close; they can look us in the eye. How
do they expect to recognize an alien intelligence if all they can do is eaves-
drop from a hundred light years away?

It's no coincidence that "aspiration" means both hope and the act of   27
breathing.

When we speak, we use the breath in our lungs to give our thoughts a   28
physical form. The sounds we make are simultaneously our intentions and
our life force.

I speak, therefore I am. Vocal learners, like parrots and humans, are per- 29
haps the only ones who fully comprehend the truth of this.

There's a pleasure that comes with shaping sounds with your mouth. It's 30
so primal and visceral that throughout their history, humans have considered
the activity a pathway to the divine.

Pythagorean mystics believed that vowels represented the music of the 31
spheres, and chanted to draw power from them.

Pentecostal Christians believe that when they speak in tongues, they're 32
speaking the language used by angels in Heaven.

Brahmin Hindus believe that by reciting mantras, they're strengthening 33
the building blocks of reality.

Only a species of vocal learners would ascribe such importance to sound 34
in their mythologies. We parrots can appreciate that.

According to Hindu mythology, the universe was created with a sound: 35
"Om." It's a syllable that contains within it everything that ever was and everything that will be.

When the Arecibo telescope is pointed at the space between stars, it 36
hears a faint hum.

Astronomers call that the "cosmic microwave background." It's the resid- 37
ual radiation of the Big Bang, the explosion that created the universe fourteen billion years ago.

But you can also think of it as a barely audible reverberation of that origi-   38
nal "Om." That syllable was so resonant that the night sky will keep vibrating
for as long as the universe exists.

When Arecibo is not listening to anything else, it hears the voice of   39
creation.

We Puerto Rican Parrots have our own myths. They're simpler than   40
human mythology, but I think humans would take pleasure from them.

Alas, our myths are being lost as my species dies out. I doubt the humans   41
will have deciphered our language before we're gone.

So the extinction of my species doesn't just mean the loss of a group of   42
birds. It's also the disappearance of our language, our rituals, our traditions.
It's the silencing of our voice.

Human activity has brought my kind to the brink of extinction, but I   43
don't blame them for it. They didn't do it maliciously. They just weren't paying attention.

And humans create such beautiful myths; what imaginations they have.   44
Perhaps that's why their aspirations are so immense. Look at Arecibo. Any
species who can build such a thing must have greatness within it.

My species probably won't be here for much longer; it's likely that we'll   45
die before our time and join the Great Silence. But before we go, we are sending a message to humanity. We just hope the telescope at Arecibo will enable
them to hear it.

The message is this: 46

You be good. I love you.   47

Journal Writing

Imagine you're an alien visiting Earth for the first time, and that the spaceship
has touched down in the neighborhood you currently occupy (or, if you prefer, in
a region you have lived in or visited in the past). Look around and describe what
you find, absorbing as much as you can and taking nothing for granted. Consider,
for instance, the area's physical attributes, any sounds you hear, movements you
perceive, subtle or overpowering scents, the weather, and any human alterations to
the natural surroundings such as roads, buildings, and power lines. Jot down your
impressions in your journal.

Questions on Meaning

1. What is Arecibo, as you understand it? Is it real or imaginary? How do you know?

2. Explain the Fermi paradox as the narrator describes it (pars. 4–10). What is a PARADOX? What does this one have to do with Chiang's story?

3. Can a work of fiction have a THESIS? What sentence, or sentences, most suc-cinctly express Chiang's narrator's main idea?

4. Look again at the note preceding "The Great Silence" on page 217. Consid-ering the unusual writing situation behind this story, what do you take to be Chiang's PURPOSE in telling it? What point does the author seem to be making about extinction and the possibilities of "extraterrestrial intelligence" (par. 1)?

Questions on Writing Strategy

1. What assumptions does the author make about his AUDIENCE?

2. How is the comparison in this story organized? What is the function of the extra spaces between certain paragraphs? What do they indicate?

3. On what basis does the narrator compare parrots and humans? What features do the two species have in common?

4. **OTHER METHODS** What is remarkable about the EXAMPLE of Alex, the African Grey Parrot discussed in paragraphs 11–16? How does he function as a SYMBOL in the story?

Questions on Language

1. What is the TONE of Chiang's story? How does the narrator — a parrot — present himself, humans, and his issue with the search for extraterrestrial intelligence?

2. Most of the paragraphs in Chiang's story are very short, just a sentence or two. Why do you suppose that is? What is the EFFECT?

3. "It's no coincidence that 'aspiration' means both hope and the act of breathing," the narrator remarks in paragraph 27. What does he mean? What point is he making about language?

4. Use a print or online dictionary to find definitions of the following words if you don't know their meanings already: extraterrestrial (par. 1); cacophony, discon-certingly (8); cognitive (11); enunciate (22); primal, visceral (30); Pythagorean, mystics (31); Pentecostal (32); Brahmin, mantras (33); ascribe (34); residual (37); reverberation, resonant (38); deciphered (41); maliciously (43).

Suggestions for Writing

1. **FROM JOURNAL TO ESSAY** Working from your journal entry (p. 221), write an essay that describes a particular aspect of your corner of the planet Earth from the perspective of someone experiencing it for the first time. Draw on as many

of the five senses as you like, but make your DESCRIPTION as lively as possible, letting your feelings influence your selection of details, what you say about them, and the dominant impression you create.

2. The Arecibo Observatory is located in Allora & Calzadilla's home base of Puerto Rico and is operated by the University of Central Florida. Research the current situation of Puerto Ricans and the United States, especially after the devastation caused by Hurricane Maria in 2017: citizenship, population, infrastructure, living conditions, education levels, occupations, incomes, and so forth. Then write an essay in which you present your findings.

3. **CRITICAL WRITING**   Go online and find Allora & Calzadilla's video of *The Great Silence*. Watch it in full at least twice, and then write an essay in which you ANALYZE the installation as a multimodal work of art. (See "Examining Visual Images," pp. 22–26, if you need help.) What strikes you about the imagery recorded by the artists? How about the sounds? What motifs are repeated, and why? What stands out, and what lingers in the background? How is Chiang's text integrated with the visuals? What does each element of the artwork contribute to the whole?

4. **CONNECTIONS**   Like Jourdan Imani Keith in the previous essay, "At Risk" (p. 212), Ted Chiang in his story warns of the risks of extinction, not just for a specific animal species, but for humanity itself. Is that such a bad thing? In an essay, consider the problem of overpopulation and its effects on the environment. How many people can the planet reasonably hold? Do those in some regions (North America, for instance, or China) consume more than their fair share of resources? To what extent are human beings responsible for changes in the environment? for the extinctions of other species? What, if anything, can be done to make life on Earth more sustainable? How do you envision the future of the planet, and of humanity?

SUZANNE BRITT

Suzanne Britt was born in Winston-Salem, North Carolina, and studied at Salem College and Washington University in St. Louis, where she earned an MA in English. Britt has written for *Sky Magazine*, the *New York Times*, *Newsweek*, the *Boston Globe*, and many other publications. Her poems have been published in the *Denver Quarterly*, the *Southern Poetry Review*, and similar literary magazines. Britt taught English at Meredith College in North Carolina for twenty-five years and has published a history of the college and two English textbooks. Her other books are collections of her essays: *Skinny People Are Dull and Crunchy like Carrots* (1982) and *Show and Tell* (1983).

Neat People vs. Sloppy People

"Neat People vs. Sloppy People" appears in Britt's collection *Show and Tell*. Mingling humor with seriousness (as she often does), Britt has called the book a report on her journey into "the awful cave of self: You shout your name and voices come back in exultant response, telling you their names." In this essay, Britt uses comparison mainly to entertain by showing us aspects of our own selves, awful or not.

I've finally figured out the difference between neat people and sloppy people. The distinction is, as always, moral. Neat people are lazier and meaner than sloppy people.

Sloppy people, you see, are not really sloppy. Their sloppiness is merely the unfortunate consequence of their extreme moral rectitude. Sloppy people carry in their mind's eye a heavenly vision, a precise plan, that is so stupendous, so perfect, it can't be achieved in this world or the next.

Sloppy people live in Never-Never Land. Someday is their métier. Someday they are planning to alphabetize all their books and set up home catalogs. Someday they will go through their wardrobes and mark certain items for tentative mending and certain items for passing on to relatives of similar shape and size. Someday sloppy people will make family scrapbooks into which they will put newspaper clippings, postcards, locks of hair, and the dried corsage from their senior prom. Someday they will file everything on the surface of their desks, including the cash receipts from coffee purchases at the snack shop. Someday they will sit down and read all the back issues of *The New Yorker*.

For all these noble reasons and more, sloppy people never get neat. They aim too high and wide. They save everything, planning someday to file, order, and straighten out the world. But while these ambitious plans take clearer and clearer shape in their heads, the books spill from the shelves onto the floor, the clothes pile up in the hamper and closet, the family mementos accumulate in every drawer, the surface of the desk is buried under mounds of paper, and the unread magazines threaten to reach the ceiling.

Sloppy people can't bear to part with anything. They give loving attention 5
to every detail. When sloppy people say they're going to tackle the surface of a
desk, they really mean it. Not a paper will go unturned; not a rubber band will
go unboxed. Four hours or two weeks into the excavation, the desk looks exactly
the same, primarily because the sloppy person is meticulously creating new piles
of papers with new headings and scrupulously stopping to read all the old book
catalogs before he throws them away. A neat person would just bulldoze the desk.

Neat people are bums and clods at heart. They have cavalier attitudes 6
toward possessions, including family heirlooms. Everything is just another
dust-catcher to them. If anything collects dust, it's got to go and that's that.
Neat people will toy with the idea of throwing the children out of the house
just to cut down on the clutter.

Neat people don't care about process. They like results. What they want 7
to do is get the whole thing over with so they can sit down and watch the
rasslin' on TV. Neat people operate on two unvarying principles: Never
handle any item twice, and throw everything away.

The only thing messy in a neat person's house is the trash can. The 8
minute something comes to a neat person's hand, he will look at it, try to
decide if it has immediate use and, finding none, throw it in the trash.

Neat people are especially vicious with mail. They never go through their 9
mail unless they are standing directly over a trash can. If the trash can is beside the
mailbox, even better. All ads, catalogs, pleas for charitable contributions, church
bulletins, and money-saving coupons go straight into the trash can without being
opened. All letters from home, postcards from Europe, bills, and paychecks are
opened, immediately responded to, then dropped in the trash can. Neat people
keep their receipts only for tax purposes. That's it. No sentimental salvaging of
birthday cards or the last letter a dying relative ever wrote. Into the trash it goes.

Neat people place neatness above everything, even economics. They 10
are incredibly wasteful. Neat people throw away several toys every time they
walk through the den. I knew a neat person once who threw away a perfectly
good dish drainer because it had mold on it. The drainer was too much trouble to wash. And neat people sell their furniture when they move. They will
sell a La-Z-Boy recliner while you are reclining in it.

Neat people are no good to borrow from. Neat people buy everything in 11
expensive little single portions. They get their flour and sugar in two-pound
bags. They wouldn't consider clipping a coupon, saving a leftover, reusing
plastic nondairy whipped cream containers, or rinsing off tin foil and drap-
ing it over the unmoldy dish drainer. You can never borrow a neat person's
newspaper to see what's playing at the movies. Neat people have the paper all
wadded up and in the trash by 7:05 a.m.

Neat people cut a clean swath through the organic as well as the inor- 12
ganic world. People, animals, and things are all one to them. They are so

insensitive. After they've finished with the pantry, the medicine cabinet, and the attic, they will throw out the red geranium (too many leaves), sell the dog (too many fleas), and send the children off to boarding school (too many scuff-marks on the hardwood floors).

Journal Writing

Britt suggests that grouping people according to oppositions, such as neat versus sloppy, reveals other things about them. Write about the oppositions you use to evaluate people. Smart versus dumb? Fit versus out of shape? Rich versus poor? Outgoing versus shy? Open-minded versus narrow-minded? Something else?

Questions on Meaning

1. "Suzanne Britt believes that neat people are lazy, mean, petty, callous, wasteful, and insensitive." How would you respond to this statement?

2. Is the author's main PURPOSE to make fun of neat people, to assess the habits of neat and sloppy people, to help neat and sloppy people get along better, to defend sloppy people, to amuse and entertain, or to prove that neat people are morally inferior to sloppy people? Discuss.

3. What is meant by "as always" in the sentence "The distinction is, as always, moral" (par. 1)? Does the author seem to be suggesting that any and all distinctions between people are moral?

Questions on Writing Strategy

1. What is the general TONE of this essay? What words and phrases help you determine that tone?

2. Britt mentions no similarities between neat and sloppy people. Does that mean this is not a good comparison-and-contrast essay? Why might a writer deliberately focus on differences and give very little or no time to similarities?

3. How does Britt use repetition to clarify her comparison?

4. Consider the following GENERALIZATIONS: "For all these noble reasons and more, sloppy people never get neat" (par. 4) and "The only thing messy in a neat person's house is the trash can" (8). How can you tell that these statements are generalizations? Look for other generalizations in the essay. What is the EFFECT of using so many?

5. **OTHER METHODS**   Although filled with generalizations, Britt's essay does not lack for EXAMPLES. Study the examples in paragraph 11, and explain how they do and don't work the way they should: to bring the generalizations about people down to earth.

Questions on Language

1. Consult your dictionary for definitions of these words: rectitude (par. 2); métier, tentative (3); accumulate (4); excavation, meticulously, scrupulously (5); salvaging (9).

2. How do you understand the use of the word *noble* in the first sentence of paragraph 4? Is it meant literally? Are there other words in the essay that appear to be written in a similar TONE?

Suggestions for Writing

1. **FROM JOURNAL TO ESSAY** From your journal entry, choose your favorite opposition for evaluating people, and write an essay in which you compare and contrast those who pass your "test" with those who fail it. You may choose to write a tongue-in-cheek essay, as Britt does, or a serious one.

2. Write an essay in which you compare and contrast two apparently dissimilar groups of people: for example, blue-collar workers and white-collar workers, people who send a lot of text messages and people who don't bother with them, cyclists and football players, readers and TV watchers, or any other variation you choose. Your approach may be either lighthearted or serious, but make sure you come to some conclusion about your subjects. Which group do you favor? Why?

3. **CRITICAL WRITING** Britt's essay is remarkable for its exaggeration of the two types. Write a brief essay analyzing and contrasting the ways Britt characterizes sloppy people and neat people. Be sure to consider the CONNOTATIONS of the words, such as "moral rectitude" for sloppy people (par. 2) and "cavalier" for neat people (6).

4. **CONNECTIONS** Write an essay about the humor gained from exaggeration, relying on Britt's essay, Scaachi Koul's "Impatiently Waiting for the Horror of Death" (p. 133), and Brian Doyle's "Three Basketball Stories" (p. 192). Why is exaggeration often funny? What qualities does humorous exaggeration have? Quote and PARAPHRASE from all three selections for your support.

Suzanne Britt on Writing

Asked to tell how she writes, Suzanne Britt contributed the following comment for this book.

The question "How do you write?" gets a snappy, snappish response from me. The first commandment is "Live!" And the second is like unto it: "Pay attention!" I don't mean that you have to live high or fast or deep or wise or broad. And I certainly don't mean you have to live true and upright. I just mean that you have to suck out all the marrow of whatever you do, whether it's picking the lint off the navy-blue suit you'll be wearing to Cousin Ione's funeral or popping an Aunt Jemima frozen waffle into the toaster oven or lying between sand dunes, watching the way the sea oats slice the azure sky. The ominous question put to me by students on all occasions of possible accountability is "Will this count?" My answer is rock bottom and hard: "Everything counts," I say, and silence falls like prayers across the room.

The same is true of writing. Everything counts. Despair is good. Numbness can be excellent. Misery is fine. Ecstasy will work—or pain or sorrow or passion. The only thing that won't work is indifference. A writer refuses to be shocked and appalled by anything going or coming, rising or falling, singing or soundless. The only thing that shocks me, truth to tell, is indifference. How dare you not fight for the right to the crispy end piece on the standing-rib roast? How dare you let the fragrance of Joy go by without taking a whiff of it? How dare you not see the old woman in the snap-front housedress and the rolled-down socks, carrying her Polident and Charmin in a canvas tote that says, simply, elegantly, Le Bag?

After you have lived, paid attention, seen connections, felt the harmony, writhed under the dissonance, fixed a Diet Coke, popped a big stick of Juicy Fruit in your mouth, gathered your life around you as a mother hen gathers her brood, as a queen settles the folds in her purple robes, you are ready to write. And what you will write about, even if you have one of those teachers who makes you write about, say, Guatemala, will be something very exclusive and intimate—something just between you and Guatemala. All you have to find out is what that small intimacy might be. It is there. And having found it, you have to make it count.

There is no rest for a writer. But there is no boredom either. A Sunday morning with a bottle of extra-strength aspirin within easy reach and an ice bag on your head can serve you very well in writing. So can a fly buzzing at your ear or a heart-stopping siren in the night or an interminable afternoon in a biology lab in front of a frog's innards.

All you need, really, is the audacity to believe, with your whole being, that if you tell it right, tell it truly, tell it so we can all see it, the "it" will play in Peoria, Poughkeepsie, Pompeii, or Podunk. In the South we call that conviction, that audacity, an act of faith. But you can call it writing.

The Bedford Reader on Writing

What advice would *we* give a student assigned to write a paper about, say, Guatemala? Like Britt, we suggest that you study the SUBJECT long enough to find some personal connection or interest in it, ask questions, and do some RESEARCH to find the answers. For more on how, see "Discovering Ideas" in Chapter 2 (pp. 30–33) and "Using the Library" in the Appendix (p. 648).

CAITLIN McDOUGALL

Caitlin McDougall was born in 1990 in Stockton, California, and lived there until she graduated from Lincoln High School at eighteen. She moved to Los Angeles to attend the American Academy of Dramatic Arts and earned an associate's degree in theater in 2011. Upon discovering that acting in Hollywood was not the dream career she had imagined, McDougall returned to San Joaquin Delta College in Stockton to take courses in preparation for nursing school. She completed her prerequisites at Santa Monica College and was accepted to the Linfield School of Nursing in Portland, Oregon. McDougall graduated with a BSN in 2017 and is now working as a registered nurse in Portland, where she "decided to stay . . . because of the proximity to great hiking and camping." In her free time, she likes to cook, drink coffee, and spend time with her fiancé and two dogs.

So Enid and Dorothy from West Covina Can Hear You

McDougall wrote this essay, which compares her experiences as an actor on stage and on screen, for an online writing course during her time at San Joaquin Delta College. It appeared in *Delta Winds*, the school's annual collection of excellent student writing, in 2014.

My sophomore year in high school the elective of my choice was full, so I was placed in a theater class. I enjoyed studying iambic pentameter and working on scenes. But I was certainly not considering auditioning for the school play. Only die-hard drama nerds auditioned for plays, and I did not fit that description. My teacher was directing the play and asked me to audition because it would be "fun" and I had "nothing to lose." Two days later I dropped all of my other extra-curricular activities to be Bianca in William Shakespeare's *The Taming of the Shrew*. I fit right in with the other thespians and started to treat the black box theater as my second home. I loved performing on the stage, so it was not long before I decided that acting was what I wanted to do as a career. Of course I wanted to spend my life feeling liberated and free to express my full range of emotions—behind the guise of a character.

After graduation, it made sense to go to an acting conservatory to pursue my dreams, until those dreams had to adapt to the climate of "The Industry." The dream morphed into a product of my environment. The dream became glamour, money, and fame. But there is no glamour, money, or fame in being a theater actor, so my focus shifted to the silver screen. I began to audition almost exclusively for film and television, but when I finally landed my first role in a short film, I was surprised by what I found. The process was not what I had anticipated, and all of the things that I loved about being in a play seemed to be absent. They were replaced by a whole new set of rules specific to the camera and its role in my performance. It was an eye-opening experience, and it forced me to question why I wanted so badly to be an actor. I finally realized that acting in a film is a gratifying experience, but nothing can compare to the raw humanity of acting in a staged play.

One of the most rewarding aspects of putting on a play is the rehearsal pro- 3
cess. From the table read up until the very last dress rehearsal, the preparation is a group effort. Spending day in and day out, cast-mates develop a deep bond and trust. Rehearsal is a safe and intimate environment that allows actors to explore characters in relation to others. By interacting in this way, actors are given the freedom to try different things and to evolve with their characters. This is incredibly helpful and fosters truthful performances and organic line delivery. It gives the actors time to find the things the writer intended to show the audience, but did not write on the page. Without this period of experi-mentation, the play would be stiff and lackluster. With each rehearsal, actors become increasingly more comfortable baring their emotions and building rela-tionships with fellow actors. These relationships will be carried over into per-formances. The more human and heartfelt the interaction onstage is, the more involved the audience feels, and the more they sympathize with the characters. The rehearsal process can last for a month or more before the play opens.

In the film industry, establishing relationships and finding the emotional 4
truth of a scene are also priorities. But the rehearsal process of a film is usu-ally only a few days long. The actors in a film are expected to learn their lines at home and arrive on set ready to learn their blocking and to establish relationships quickly. Character choices are often dictated by the director, or made individually by each actor without the joint effort of exploring to see what comes naturally. While this method saves money and time on a movie set, it is not as emotionally rewarding for the actors. Because everything is so rushed, they are robbed of sharing their artistic experience with one another before the camera starts rolling. Time, after all, is money. In lieu of repeated rehearsals, the actors are taped doing the scene multiple times until the cam-eramen have what they need. This may be advantageous for the filmmakers, because they have the ability to capture every moment of the emotional jour-ney, but it may not give the performers the preparation they need to develop the strong human relationships appropriate for their characters.

Every character has an arc, an emotional journey from beginning to end that 5
tells his or her story. A character may start out in love, be cheated on, go through a terrible divorce, and then find love again. When all of this happens over the span of a two-hour play, the actor gets to experience each part of the journey in sequence. The love scene occurs immediately before hearing about the spouse's infidelities, making the betrayal all the more real to the actor. The story unfolds

and the actor has each scene to build up a range of emotions. This style of performance is undeniably the most natural and fulfilling for the performer.

With movies, however, an actor almost never has the luxury of experiencing 6 things in order. More often than not scenes are filmed out of sequence, based on the days the location is booked. This is done out of financial convenience. The actor is given the task of conjuring emotions without experiencing the character's arc as it was originally imagined. She may have to fight with her cheating ex-husband in one scene, and tenderly love him in the next. The actor never gets to complete a character's journey full circle, only an unsatisfactory piecemeal version of it. It becomes a disjointed performance — later edited into the proper order and used to elicit an emotional response from an audience. Whether or not it is effective after the scrambled filming process is dependent on an editor's ability to recreate the story. The actor, however, will never get to feel that full arc.

In a play, there is only one chance to get it right. If an actor cannot bring 7 tears to his eyes at the appropriate time, he has missed the opportunity for the night and will have to try again tomorrow. This happens all the time in theater because not everything goes according to plan. Some of the best moments in theater are when something unexpected happens. The actors are forced to think on their feet and have very real and sometimes comedic reactions.

It is surprising and exhilarating for the actors and for the audience. Not 8 knowing what will happen next is exciting, and that is the beauty of live theater. In contrast, if something goes wrong on a movie set, you simply stop the camera and do another take. If you cannot cry on cue in a scene, you can keep filming it over and over until you can cry. Doing a series of takes of the same moment captures the desired product, but may have its own drawbacks. The potential magic is lost, because it does not translate as "magic" on film; it's just a bad take. There is no "the show must go on" when acting in a picture, and therefore less opportunity for spontaneous creativity.

Another thing that makes a stage performance so special is a live audience. 9 A theater audience has a collective energy that can feed actors. The audience's laughter can cue an actor to the comedic timing needed for a scene while the audience's tears can heighten the emotion in a dramatic moment. An audience's energy provides a sense of communal human experience, which is much more powerful and tangible than an individual performing in front of a camera. For people who love to attend theater, sheer proximity to the action is enough to feel drawn in. A theater audience is made a part of the play and a part of the journey. A Shakespeare professor of mine told us that it was our job to give the audience members a cathartic experience and to use our whole being to reach them. She believed that a lot of what connected us emotionally was the physical vibrations of the voice in the room — changes in tone, pace, and resonance. My professor would say an actor gets that message across by projecting "so Enid and Dorothy from West Covina can hear you." In film, the voice's flexibility is still incredibly important, but less effective because the sound is recorded by microphones and heard through speakers instead of directly from the actors. Projecting to reach each and every human being in a room is a much more visceral form of expression and feels more satisfying on a basic physical level.

Before taking part in a film, I thought that the two acting styles were the   10 same, and that I would get a similar emotional result from each. I thought that acting in front of a camera would feed my soul and desire for community in the same way that acting in a play did. It has become clear, though, that while the end product's effect on the audience is similar, the actor's experience is very different. A play offers an environment of creativity in which actors share art with a live audience. Making a film can be a special process shared by a group of people as well, but the process is fragmented and less creatively fulfilling. Only one is an emotionally and physically thrilling journey. Only one provides the instant gratification of having a profound and visible effect on other people. And that is what live theater is like.

Journal Writing

Whether or not you attend the theater on a regular basis, you've probably seen a play performed live at least once in your life — a school production, perhaps, or a field trip to a holiday show. What was the experience like for you? Jot down some memories and notes of reflection in your journal.

Questions on Meaning

1. What is McDougall's THESIS? Where does she state it?

2. What seems to be McDougall's PURPOSE in this essay? Does she mean to explain or to evaluate? How can you tell?

3. Why did McDougall decide not to pursue a career in acting after putting so much effort into it?

Questions on Writing Strategy

1. What do you make of the title of this essay? Who are Enid and Dorothy from West Covina, and what do they have to do with McDougall's subject? Why are the members of an AUDIENCE so important to her?

2. How does McDougall organize her comparison? Prepare a brief outline of the body of her essay. What points does she compare?

3. **OTHER METHODS**   What is McDougall's basis of comparison? How does PROCESS ANALYSIS figure into her essay?

Questions on Language

1. What POINT OF VIEW does McDougall take in this essay? Is it consistent throughout? How OBJECTIVE is she as she makes her comparison?

2. Consult a dictionary if necessary to learn the meanings of the following words: iambic pentameter, thespians, guise (par. 1); conservatory (2); organic, lackluster (3); blocking, lieu (4); arc, infidelities (5); conjuring, piecemeal, disjointed, elicit (6); proximity, resonance, projecting, visceral (9); fragmented (10).

3. How would you characterize McDougall's DICTION? Is her language appropriate given her subject and purpose? Why, or why not?

Suggestions for Writing

1. **FROM JOURNAL TO ESSAY**   Expanding on your journal notes and using McDougall's essay as a model, write an essay that compares live plays and filmed movies — from the viewer's perspective. Which offers the more satisfying experience, and why?

2. Analyze the similarities and differences between two characters in your favorite play, film, or TV show. Which aspects of their personalities make them work well together, within the context in which they appear? Which characteristics work against each other, and therefore provide the necessary conflict to hold the viewer's attention?

3. **CRITICAL WRITING**   Approach McDougall's essay as a peer reviewer might and EVALUATE it as a model of comparison and contrast. Are her chosen subjects appropriately similar, with enough differences to make the comparison worthwhile? How effective do you find her basis of comparison? Does she offer enough points of comparison? How well are those points developed? Is the organization effective? Is the discussion balanced? What, if anything, could the writer have done to improve the essay? (For guidelines on conducting a peer review, see pp. 50–51 in Chapter 3 on Reviewing and Revising, and the checklist on p. 209 of this chapter.)

4. **CONNECTIONS**   Contemporary culture seems obsessed with celebrities, as evidenced by the popularity of gossip magazines, tabloids, and TV programs that track the slightest comings and goings of actors, political figures, musicians, models, and even those who are famous simply for being famous. Read Ben Healy's essay "Gossip Is Good" (p. 411), and then write an essay in which you speculate about why actors like Caitlin McDougall seek the "glamour, money, and fame" (par. 2) of celebrity. What are some causes of Americans' obsession with celebrities? What is it about the lives of ordinary people that makes them so interested in the lives of famous people? What do they get out of gossiping about them?

Caitlin McDougall on Writing

We asked Caitlin McDougall to tell us a little bit about her writing process: What works for her, and why? Here is what she told us.

I have found that what works well for me is to start with an idea that is somewhat general. I ask myself "what is this piece about?" and just jot the answer down in the document. This takes some of the pressure off of actually starting to write, which can sometimes feel daunting. The general idea I write down in the very beginning doesn't have to be perfect, or even end up in the final piece. It is just a starting point or ice-breaker. Once I have that down I can begin writing and asking myself more questions to help direct and shape the paper: "Why am I writing about this? What am I really trying to say? Who am I talking to?" These questions help the original idea become more specific. Most of the time I don't have a refined thesis until I am well into writing the body of the paper.

If I am having a difficult time figuring out where to start or what I want to say, I will often just get all of my ideas about the topic onto a page and begin to organize and structure the paper based on what I have written down. When doing this, one thing I find particularly helpful is reading what I have down on paper out loud. It allows me to actually hear what I am saying and gives me a different perspective. I read my paper aloud throughout the process, and again at the end to identify any awkward phrasing or points I've missed.

The last thing I like to do when drafting or revising a piece is to walk away from it for about thirty minutes and give my brain a break. I do this if I feel completely stuck, or even if I feel like I am done writing and I am happy with what I have. I always like to take a break and come back to the piece with fresh eyes. In doing this, I often find mistakes, realize important points need to be clarified, or think of new ideas to add.

When I wrote "So Enid and Dorothy from West Covina Can Hear You," I started knowing I wanted to write something that was personal and meaningful. I didn't initially have a solid thesis or even a very clear idea of what exactly I was trying to convey to the audience, so I started by just telling a story. Then I asked myself, "Why is this important? What can readers take away from this that they maybe didn't know before?" These questions helped me refine what the piece was about, and ultimately led to my thesis statement and a finished comparison. I will say, I am happy with how it turned out.

The Bedford Reader on Writing

As a writer, Caitlin McDougall makes good use of questions, constantly asking herself what she's trying to accomplish, how readers might respond to her work, what she can do to improve a piece of writing, and more. We offer similar questions that you can ask of your own drafts throughout *The Bedford Reader*, in boxed Questions for reading, revising, and editing in Part One (pp. 12, 42, and 56) and in Checklists for reviewing and revising in the introductions to each of the rhetorical methods in Part Two.

DAVID SEDARIS

Winner of the Thurber Prize for American Humor, David Sedaris was born in 1957 and grew up in North Carolina. After graduating from the School of the Art Institute of Chicago in 1987, Sedaris taught writing there part-time and then moved to New York City, where he took various odd jobs. One of these jobs—a stint as a department-store Christmas elf—provided Sedaris with material for "The Santaland Diaries," the essay that launched his career as a humorist after he read it on National Public Radio's *Morning Edition* in 1993. Since then, Sedaris has contributed numerous commentaries to NPR's *Morning Edition* and *This American Life*, and his work appears frequently in *The New Yorker, Esquire,* and other magazines. He has published nine collections of essays and fiction: *Barrel Fever* (1994), *Naked* (1997), *Holidays on Ice* (1997), *Me Talk Pretty One Day* (2000), *Dress Your Family in Corduroy and Denim* (2004), *When You Are Engulfed in Flames* (2008), *Squirrel Seeks Chipmunk* (2010), *Let's Explore Diabetes with Owls* (2013), and *Calypso* (2018). Sedaris frequently tours and gives readings of his essays and works in progress; in 2017 he published the first of two volumes of selected entries from the diaries he has kept for his entire writing life. He lives in rural England.

Remembering My Childhood on the Continent of Africa

Many of Sedaris's essays locate comedy in exaggerated depictions of his basically normal North Carolina childhood. In this essay from *Me Talk Pretty One Day* (2000), Sedaris highlights that normality by contrasting it with the distinctly unusual childhood of his partner.

When Hugh was in the fifth grade, his class took a field trip to an 1 Ethiopian slaughterhouse. He was living in Addis Ababa at the time, and the slaughterhouse was chosen because, he says, "it was convenient."

This was a school system in which the matter of proximity outweighed 2 such petty concerns as what may or may not be appropriate for a busload of eleven-year-olds. "What?" I asked. "Were there no autopsies scheduled at the local morgue? Was the federal prison just a bit too far out of the way?"

Hugh defends his former school, saying, "Well, isn't that the whole point 3 of a field trip? To see something new?"

"Technically yes, but . . ." 4

"All right then," he says. "So we saw some new things." 5

One of his field trips was literally a trip to a field where the class watched 6 a wrinkled man fill his mouth with rotten goat meat and feed it to a pack of

235

waiting hyenas. On another occasion they were taken to examine the blood-ied bedroom curtains hanging in the palace of the former dictator. There were tamer trips, to textile factories and sugar refineries, but my favorite is always the slaughterhouse. It wasn't a big company, just a small rural enter-prise run by a couple of brothers operating out of a low-ceilinged concrete building. Following a brief lecture on the importance of proper sanitation, a small white piglet was herded into the room, its dainty hooves clicking against the concrete floor. The class gathered in a circle to get a better look at the animal, who seemed delighted with the attention he was getting. He turned from face to face and was looking up at Hugh when one of the broth-ers drew a pistol from his back pocket, held it against the animal's temple, and shot the piglet, execution-style. Blood spattered, frightened children wept, and the man with the gun offered the teacher and bus driver some meat from a freshly slaughtered goat.

When I'm told such stories, it's all I can do to hold back my feelings of 7 jealousy. An Ethiopian slaughterhouse. Some people have all the luck. When I was in elementary school, the best we ever got was a trip to Old Salem or Colonial Williamsburg, one of those preserved brick villages where time supposedly stands still and someone earns his living as a town crier. There was always a blacksmith, a group of wandering patriots, and a collection of bonneted women hawking corn bread or gingersnaps made "the ol'-fashioned way." Every now and then you might come across a doer of bad deeds serving time in the stocks, but that was generally as exciting as it got.

Certain events are parallel, but compared with Hugh's, my childhood was 8 unspeakably dull. When I was seven years old, my family moved to North Carolina. When he was seven years old, Hugh's family moved to the Congo. We had a collie and a house cat. They had a monkey and two horses named Charlie Brown and Satan. I threw stones at stop signs. Hugh threw stones at crocodiles. The verbs are the same, but he definitely wins the prize when it comes to nouns and objects. An eventful day for my mother might have involved a trip to the dry cleaner or a conversation with the potato-chip deliveryman. Asked one ordinary Congo afternoon what she'd done with her day, Hugh's mother answered that she and a fellow member of the Ladies' Club had visited a leper colony on the outskirts of Kinshasa. No reason was given for the expedition, though chances are she was staking it out for a future field trip.

Due to his upbringing, Hugh sits through inane movies never realizing 9 that they're often based on inane television shows. There were no poker-faced sitcom martians in his part of Africa, no oil-rich hillbillies or aproned brides trying to wean themselves from the practice of witchcraft. From time to time a movie would arrive packed in a dented canister, the film scratched and faded from its slow trip around the world. The theater consisted of a few dozen folding chairs arranged before a bedsheet or the blank wall of a vacant hangar out near the airstrip. Occasionally a man would sell warm soft drinks out of a cardboard box, but that was it in terms of concessions.

When I was young, I went to the theater at the nearby shopping center 10 and watched a movie about a talking Volkswagen. I believe the little car had a taste for mischief but I can't be certain, as both the movie and the afternoon proved unremarkable and have faded from my memory. Hugh saw the same movie a few years after it was released. His family had left the Congo by this time and were living in Ethiopia. Like me, Hugh saw the movie by himself on a weekend afternoon. Unlike me, he left the theater two hours later, to find a dead man hanging from a telephone pole at the far end of the unpaved parking lot. None of the people who'd seen the movie seemed to care about the dead man. They stared at him for a moment or two and then headed home, saying they'd never seen anything as crazy as that talking Volkswagen. His father was late picking him up, so Hugh just stood there for an hour, watching the dead man dangle and turn in the breeze. The death was not reported in the newspaper, and when Hugh related the story to his friends, they said, "You saw the movie about the talking car?"

I could have done without the flies and the primitive theaters, but 11 I wouldn't have minded growing up with a houseful of servants. In North Carolina it wasn't unusual to have a once-a-week maid, but Hugh's family had houseboys, a word that never fails to charge my imagination. They had cooks and drivers, and guards who occupied a gatehouse, armed with machetes. Seeing as I had regularly petitioned my parents for an electric fence, the business with the guards strikes me as the last word in quiet sophistication. Having protection suggests that you are important. Having that protection paid for by the government is even better, as it suggests your safety is of interest to someone other than yourself.

Hugh's father was a career officer with the US State Department, and 12 every morning a black sedan carried him off to the embassy. I'm told it's not as glamorous as it sounds, but in terms of fun for the entire family, I'm fairly confident that it beats the sack race at the annual IBM picnic. By the age of three, Hugh was already carrying a diplomatic passport. The rules that applied to others did not apply to him. No tickets, no arrests, no luggage search: He was officially licensed to act like a brat. Being an American, it was expected of him, and who was he to deny the world an occasional tantrum?

They weren't rich, but what Hugh's family lacked financially they more 13 than made up for with the sort of exoticism that works wonders at cocktail parties, leading always to the remark "That sounds fascinating." It's a compliment one rarely receives when describing an adolescence spent drinking Icees at the North Hills Mall. No fifteen-foot python ever wandered onto my school's basketball court. I begged, I prayed nightly, but it just never happened. Neither did I get to witness a military coup in which forces sympathetic to the colonel arrived late at night to assassinate my next-door neighbor. Hugh had been at the Addis Ababa teen club when the electricity was cut off and soldiers arrived to evacuate the building. He and his friends had to hide in the back of a jeep and cover themselves with blankets during the ride home. It's something that sticks in his mind for one reason or another.

Among my personal highlights is the memory of having my picture taken 14 with Uncle Paul, the legally blind host of a Raleigh children's television show. Among Hugh's is the memory of having his picture taken with Buzz Aldrin on the last leg of the astronaut's world tour. The man who had walked on the moon placed his hand on Hugh's shoulder and offered to sign his autograph book. The man who led Wake County schoolchildren in afternoon song turned at the sound of my voice and asked, "So what's your name, princess?"

When I was fourteen years old, I was sent to spend ten days with my 15 maternal grandmother in western New York State. She was a small and private woman named Billie, and though she never came right out and asked, I had the distinct impression she had no idea who I was. It was the way she looked at me, squinting through her glasses while chewing on her lower lip. That, coupled with the fact that she never once called me by name. "Oh," she'd say, "are you still here?" She was just beginning her long struggle with Alzheimer's disease, and each time I entered the room, I felt the need to reintroduce myself and set her at ease. "Hi, it's me. Sharon's boy, David. I was just in the kitchen admiring your collection of ceramic toads." Aside from a few trips to summer camp, this was the longest I'd ever been away from home and I like to think I was toughened by the experience.

About the same time I was frightening my grandmother, Hugh and his 16 family were packing their belongings for a move to Somalia. There were no English-speaking schools in Mogadishu, so, after a few months spent lying around the family compound with his pet monkey, Hugh was sent back to Ethiopia to live with a beer enthusiast his father had met at a cocktail party. Mr. Hoyt installed security systems in foreign embassies. He and his family gave Hugh a room. They invited him to join them at the table, but that was as far as they extended themselves. No one ever asked him when his birthday was, so when the day came, he kept it to himself. There was no telephone service between Ethiopia and Somalia, and letters to his parents were sent to Washington and then forwarded on to Mogadishu, meaning that his news was more than a month old by the time they got it. I suppose it wasn't much different than living as a foreign-exchange student. Young people do it all the time, but to me it sounds awful. The Hoyts had two sons about Hugh's age who were always saying things like "Hey that's *our* sofa you're sitting on" and "Hands off that ornamental stein. It doesn't belong to you."

He'd been living with these people for a year when he overheard   17
Mr. Hoyt tell a friend that he and his family would soon be moving to Munich, Germany, the beer capital of the world.

"And that worried me," Hugh said, "because it meant I'd have to find   18
some other place to live."

Where I come from, finding shelter is a problem the average teenager   19
might confidently leave to his parents. It was just something that came with having a mom and a dad. Worried that he might be sent to live with his grandparents in Kentucky, Hugh turned to the school's guidance counselor, who knew of a family whose son had recently left for college. And so he spent another year living with strangers and not mentioning his birthday. While I wouldn't have wanted to do it myself, I can't help but envy the sense of fortitude he gained from the experience. After graduating from college, he moved to France knowing only the phrase "Do you speak French?"—a question guaranteed to get you nowhere unless you also speak the language.

While living in Africa, Hugh and his family took frequent vacations,   20
often in the company of their monkey. The Nairobi Hilton, some suite of high-ceilinged rooms in Cairo or Khartoum: These are the places his people recall when gathered at a common table. "Was that the summer we spent in Beirut or, no, I'm thinking of the time we sailed from Cyprus and took the *Orient Express* to Istanbul."

Theirs was the life I dreamt about during my vacations in eastern North   21
Carolina. Hugh's family was hobnobbing with chiefs and sultans while I ate hush puppies at the Sanitary Fish Market in Morehead City, a beach towel wrapped like a hijab around my head. Someone unknown to me was very likely standing in a muddy ditch and dreaming of an evening spent sitting in a clean family restaurant, drinking iced tea and working his way through an extra-large seaman's platter, but that did not concern me, as it meant I should have been happy with what I had. Rather than surrender to my bitterness, I have learned to take satisfaction in the life that Hugh has led. His stories have, over time, become my own. I say this with no trace of a kumbaya.[1] There is no spiritual symbiosis; I'm just a petty thief who lifts his memories the same way I'll take a handful of change left on his dresser. When my own experiences fall short of the mark, I just go out and spend some of his. It is with pleasure that I sometimes recall the dead man's purpled face or the report

---

[1] From the gospel-folk song with the line "Kumbaya, my Lord, kumbaya," meaning "Come by here." Probably because of its popularity in folk music, the word now also has negative connotations of passivity or touchy-feely spiritualism. —EDS.

of the handgun ringing in my ears as I studied the blood pooling beneath the dead white piglet. On the way back from the slaughterhouse, we stopped for Cokes in the village of Mojo, where the gas-station owner had arranged a few tables and chairs beneath a dying canopy of vines. It was late afternoon by the time we returned to school, where a second bus carried me to the foot of Coffeeboard Road. Once there, I walked through a grove of eucalyptus trees and alongside a bald pasture of starving cattle, past the guard napping in his gatehouse, and into the waiting arms of my monkey.

Journal Writing

Hugh's experiences living with strangers gave him a "sense of fortitude" (par. 19), according to Sedaris. Have you ever gone through a difficult experience that left you somehow stronger? Write about the struggle in your journal. Was the trouble caused by family relationships? Educational or employment obstacles? Travel experiences? Something else?

Questions on Meaning

1. What is the subject of Sedaris's comparison and contrast in this essay?
2. What do you think is the THESIS of this essay? Take into account both Sedaris's obvious envy of Hugh's childhood and his awareness that Hugh's life was often lonely and insecure. Is the thesis stated or only implied?
3. There is a certain amount of IRONY in Sedaris's envy of Hugh's childhood. What is this irony? How does Sedaris make this irony explicit in paragraph 21?

Questions on Writing Strategy

1. Does Sedaris develop his comparison and contrast subject by subject or point by point? Briefly outline the essay to explain your answer.
2. Point to some of the TRANSITIONS Sedaris uses in moving between his and Hugh's lives.
3. Sedaris refers to Hugh's monkey in paragraphs 8, 16, 20, and 21. In what sense does he use the monkey as a SYMBOL?
4. The first five paragraphs of the essay include a conversation between Sedaris and Hugh about Hugh's childhood. Why do you think the author opened the essay this way?
5. **OTHER METHODS**   How does Sedaris use NARRATION to develop his comparison and contrast?

Questions on Language

1. How does Sedaris use PARALLEL STRUCTURE in paragraph 8 to highlight the contrast between himself and Hugh? How does he then point up this parallelism?

2. Sedaris offers the image of himself as a "petty thief" in paragraph 21. What is the effect of this IMAGE?

3. Sedaris's language in this essay is notably SPECIFIC and CONCRETE. Point to examples of such language just in paragraph 6.

4. Consult a dictionary if necessary to learn the meanings of the following words: proximity, petty (par. 2); hyenas (6); hawking, stocks (7); leper (8); hangar (9); machetes (11); diplomatic (12); exoticism, coup, evacuate (13); ornamental, stein (16); fortitude (19); hobnobbing, symbiosis, report, canopy, eucalyptus (21).

Suggestions for Writing

1. **FROM JOURNAL TO ESSAY**   Starting from your journal entry, write an essay about a difficult experience that shows how it changed you, whether for better or for worse. How are you different now than before? What did the experience teach you?

2. In your library or on the Internet, locate and read reviews of Sedaris's book *Me Talk Pretty One Day*, the source of "Remembering My Childhood," or of another essay collection by Sedaris. Write an essay in which you SYNTHESIZE the reviewers' responses to Sedaris's work.

3. **CRITICAL WRITING**   How seriously does Sedaris want the readers of his essay to take him? Write an essay in which you analyze his TONE, citing specific passages from the text to support your conclusions.

4. **CONNECTIONS**   Scaachi Koul, in "Scaachi Koul on Writing" (p. 138) cites David Sedaris as an early influence on her own career as a writer. Read or reread her essay "Impatiently Waiting for the Horror of Death" (p. 133) and in an essay of your own, compare the two writers' styles. How does Sedaris's work seem to have affected Koul's? In what ways has she developed a unique voice all her own?

David Sedaris on Writing

In "Day In, Day Out," an essay in *Let's Explore Diabetes with Owls*, Sedaris explains why he started keeping a diary and how it has become essential to his work as a writer. He begins by describing an afternoon transcribing snippets from a newspaper with a friend's young son, who interrupts to ask him, "But why? . . . What's the point?" Sedaris goes on:

That's a question I've asked myself every day since September 5, 1977. I hadn't known on September 4 that the following afternoon, I would start keeping a diary, or that it would consume me for the next thirty-five years and counting. It wasn't something I'd been putting off, but once I began, I knew that I had to keep doing it. I knew as well that what I was writing was not a journal, but an old-fashioned, girlish, Keep-Out-This-Means-You diary. Often the terms are used interchangeably, though I've never understood why. Both have the word "day" at their root, but a journal, in my opinion, is a repository of ideas — your brain on the page. A diary, by contrast, is your heart. As for "journal*ing*," a verb that cropped up at around the same time as "scrapbooking," that just means you're spooky and have way too much time on your hands.

A few things have changed since that first entry in 1977, but I've never wavered in my devotion, skipping, on average, maybe one or two days a year. It's not that I think my life is important or that future generations might care to know that on June 6, 2009, a woman with a deaf, drug-addicted mother-in-law taught me to say "I need you to stop being an [expletive]" in sign language. Perhaps it just feeds into my compulsive nature, the need to do the exact same thing at the exact same time every morning. Some diary sessions are longer than others, but the length has more to do with my mood than with what's been going on. I met [actor] Gene Hackman once, and wrote three hundred words about it. Six weeks later I watched a centipede attack and kill a worm and filled two pages. And I really *like* Gene Hackman. . . .

Over a given three-month period, there may be fifty bits worth noting, and six that, with a little work, I might consider reading out loud. . . . Here is a passenger on the Eurostar from Paris to London, an American woman in a sand-colored vest hitting her teenage granddaughter with a guidebook until the girl cries. "You are a very lazy, very selfish person," she scolds. "Nothing like your sister."

If I sit down six months or a year or five years from now and decide to put this into an essay, I'll no doubt berate myself for not adding more details. What sort of shoes was the granddaughter wearing? What was the name of the book the old woman was hitting her with? But if you added every detail of everything that struck you as curious or spectacular, you'd have no time for anything else. As it is, I seem to be pushing it. Hugh and I will go on a trip, and while he's out, walking the streets of Manila or Reykjavik or wherever we happen to be, I'm back at the hotel, writing about an argument we'd overheard in the breakfast room. It's not lost on me that I'm so busy recording life, I don't have time to live it. I've become like one of those people I hate, the sort who go to a museum and, instead of looking at the magnificent Brueghel, take a picture of it, reducing it from art to proof. It's not "Look what Brueghel did, painted this masterpiece" but "Look what *I* did, went to Rotterdam and stood in front of a Brueghel painting!"

Were I to leave the hotel *without* writing in my diary, though, I'd feel too antsy and incomplete to enjoy myself. Even if what I'm recording is of no consequence, I've got to put it down on paper.

The Bedford Reader on Writing

Sedaris insists on making a distinction between a diary and a JOURNAL, but his practice of keeping daily notes fits neatly with our suggestions, on pages 4 and 31 and in every set of journal prompts (such as those following "Remembering My Childhood on the Continent of Africa"), to write informally on a regular basis. As Sedaris shows us, the observations and ideas sketched out quickly for oneself can often be transformed into full essays — even months or years later.

FATEMA MERNISSI

A teacher, writer, and sociologist hailed as a founder of Islamic feminism, Fatema Mernissi (1940–2015) was born in Fez, Morocco, and educated at the University of Mohammed V in Rabat, the Sorbonne in Paris, and Brandeis University in Massachusetts, from which she earned a PhD. Mernissi quickly established herself as both a scholar and a lively writer on women's studies, religion, history, and sociology, with an abiding interest in digital culture. She wrote in French, English, and Arabic, and her books have been translated into several other languages. Her English titles include *Beyond the Veil: Male-Female Dynamics in Modern Muslim Society* (1975, revised in 1987), *Islam and Democracy: Fear of the Modern World* (1992, revised in 2002 and 2011), *Dreams of Trespass: Tales of a Harem Girlhood* (1994), and *Women's Rebellion and Islamic Memory* (1996). A longtime professor and research scholar at the University of Mohammed V, Mernissi also taught at Harvard University and the University of California at Berkeley.

Size 6: The Western Women's Harem

Mernissi was raised in a harem, an enclave of women and children within a traditional Muslim household, off-limits to men. Traveling outside the Middle East, she encountered common Western misconceptions of a harem as either a "peaceful pleasure-garden" or an "orgiastic feast" in which "men reign supreme over obedient women"—when in fact Muslim men and women both acknowledge the inequality of the harem and women resist men in any way they can. In *Scheherazade Goes West: Different Cultures, Different Harems* (2001), Mernissi explores the "mystery of the Western harem," trying to understand why outsiders imagine harem women as totally compliant and unthreatening to men. In the last chapter of the book, excerpted here, Mernissi finds her answer.

Note that Mernissi provides source citations for the book she quotes in paragraph 20. The citations are in the format of *The Chicago Manual of Style*.

It was during my unsuccessful attempt to buy a cotton skirt in an 1 American department store that I was told my hips were too large to fit into a size 6. That distressing experience made me realize how the image of beauty in the West can hurt and humiliate a woman as much as the veil does when enforced by the state police in extremist nations such as Iran, Afghanistan, or Saudi Arabia. Yes, that day I stumbled onto one of the keys to the enigma of passive beauty in Western harem fantasies. The elegant saleslady in the American store looked at me without moving from her desk and said that she had no skirt my size. "In this whole big store, there is no skirt for me?" I said.

"You are joking." I felt very suspicious and thought that she just might be too tired to help me. I could understand that. But then the saleswoman added a condescending judgment, which sounded to me like an imam's fatwa.[1] It left no room for discussion:

"You are too big!" she said.   2

"I am too big compared to what?" I asked, looking at her intently, because 3
I realized that I was facing a critical cultural gap here.

"Compared to a size 6," came the saleslady's reply.   4

Her voice had a clear-cut edge to it that is typical of those who enforce 5
religious laws. "Size 4 and 6 are the norm," she went on, encouraged by my bewildered look. "Deviant sizes such as the one you need can be bought in special stores."

That was the first time that I had ever heard such nonsense about my 6
size. In the Moroccan streets, men's flattering comments regarding my particularly generous hips have for decades led me to believe that the entire planet shared their convictions. It is true that with advancing age, I have been hearing fewer and fewer flattering comments when walking in the medina, and sometimes the silence around me in the bazaars is deafening. But since my face has never met with the local beauty standards, and I have often had to defend myself against remarks such as *zirafa* (giraffe), because of my long neck, I learned long ago not to rely too much on the outside world for my sense of self-worth. In fact, paradoxically, as I discovered when I went to Rabat as a student, it was the self-reliance that I had developed to protect myself against "beauty blackmail" that made me attractive to others. My male fellow students could not believe that I did not give a damn about what they thought about my body. "You know, my dear," I would say in response to one of them, "all I need to survive is bread, olives, and sardines. That you think my neck is too long is your problem, not mine."

In any case, when it comes to beauty and compliments, nothing is too 7
serious or definite in the medina, where everything can be negotiated. But things seemed to be different in that American department store. In fact, I have to confess that I lost my usual self-confidence in that New York environment. Not that I am always sure of myself, but I don't walk around the Moroccan streets or down the university corridors wondering what people are thinking about me. Of course, when I hear a compliment, my ego expands like a cheese soufflé, but on the whole, I don't expect to hear much from others. Some mornings, I feel ugly because I am sick or tired; others, I feel wonderful because it is sunny out or I have written a good paragraph. But suddenly, in that peaceful American store that I had entered so triumphantly,

---

[1] An *imam* is a Muslim leader. A *fatwa* is a Muslim legal opinion or ruling. —EDS.

as a sovereign consumer ready to spend money, I felt savagely attacked. My hips, until then the sign of a relaxed and uninhibited maturity, were suddenly being condemned as a deformity. . . .

"And who says that everyone must be a size 6?" I joked to the saleslady 8 that day, deliberately neglecting to mention size 4, which is the size of my skinny twelve-year-old niece.

At that point, the saleslady suddenly gave me an anxious look. "The norm 9 is everywhere, my dear," she said. "It's all over, in the magazines, on television, in the ads. You can't escape it. There is Calvin Klein, Ralph Lauren, Gianni Versace, Giorgio Armani, Mario Valentino, Salvatore Ferragamo, Christian Dior, Yves Saint-Laurent, Christian Lacroix, and Jean-Paul Gaultier. Big department stores go by the norm." She paused and then concluded, "If they sold size 14 or 16, which is probably what you need, they would go bankrupt."

She stopped for a minute and then stared at me, intrigued. "Where on 10 earth do you come from? I am sorry I can't help you. Really, I am." And she looked it too. She seemed, all of a sudden, interested, and brushed off another woman who was seeking her attention with a cutting, "Get someone else to help you, I'm busy." Only then did I notice that she was probably my age, in her late fifties. But unlike me, she had the thin body of an adolescent girl. Her knee-length, navy blue, Chanel dress had a white silk collar reminiscent of the subdued elegance of aristocratic French Catholic schoolgirls at the turn of the century. A pearl-studded belt emphasized the slimness of her waist. With her meticulously styled short hair and sophisticated makeup, she looked half my age at first glance.

"I come from a country where there is no size for women's clothes," I told 11 her. "I buy my own material and the neighborhood seamstress or craftsman makes me the silk or leather skirt I want. They just take my measurements each time I see them. Neither the seamstress nor I know exactly what size my new skirt is. We discover it together in the making. No one cares about my size in Morocco as long as I pay taxes on time. Actually, I don't know what my size is, to tell you the truth."

The saleswoman laughed merrily and said that I should advertise my 12 country as a paradise for stressed working women. "You mean you don't watch your weight?" she inquired, with a tinge of disbelief in her voice. And then, after a brief moment of silence, she added in a lower register, as if talking to herself: "Many women working in highly paid fashion-related jobs could lose their positions if they didn't keep to a strict diet."

Her words sounded so simple, but the threat they implied was so cruel 13 that I realized for the first time that maybe "size 6" is a more violent restriction imposed on women than is the Muslim veil. Quickly I said good-bye so as not to make any more demands on the saleslady's time or involve her in any more unwelcome, confidential exchanges about age-discriminating salary cuts. A surveillance camera was probably watching us both.

Yes, I thought as I wandered off, I have finally found the answer to my   14 harem enigma. Unlike the Muslim man, who uses space to establish male domination by excluding women from the public arena, the Western man manipulates time and light. He declares that in order to be beautiful, a woman must look fourteen years old. If she dares to look fifty, or worse, sixty, she is beyond the pale. By putting the spotlight on the female child and framing her as the ideal of beauty, he condemns the mature woman to invisibility. In fact, the modern Western man enforces Immanuel Kant's[2] nineteenth-century theories: To be beautiful, women have to appear childish and brainless. When a woman looks mature and self-assertive, or allows her hips to expand, she is condemned as ugly. Thus, the walls of the European harem separate youthful beauty from ugly maturity.

These Western attitudes, I thought, are even more dangerous and cunning   15 than the Muslim ones because the weapon used against women is time. Time is less visible, more fluid than space. The Western man uses images and spotlights to freeze female beauty within an idealized childhood, and forces women to perceive aging — that normal unfolding of the years — as a shameful devaluation. "Here I am, transformed into a dinosaur," I caught myself saying aloud as I went up and down the rows of skirts in the store, hoping to prove the saleslady wrong — to no avail. This Western time-defined veil is even crazier than the space-defined one enforced by the ayatollahs.[3]

The violence embodied in the Western harem is less visible than in the   16 Eastern harem because aging is not attacked directly, but rather masked as an aesthetic choice. Yes, I suddenly felt not only very ugly but also quite useless in that store, where, if you had big hips, you were simply out of the picture. You drifted into the fringes of nothingness. By putting the spotlight on the prepubescent female, the Western man veils the older, more mature woman, wrapping her in shrouds of ugliness. This idea gives me the chills because it tattoos the invisible harem directly onto a woman's skin. Chinese footbinding worked the same way: Men declared beautiful only those women who had small, childlike feet. Chinese men did not force women to bandage their feet to keep them from developing normally — all they did was to define the beauty ideal. In feudal China, a beautiful woman was the one who voluntarily sacrificed her right to unhindered physical movement by mutilating her own feet, and thereby proving that her main goal in life was to please men. Similarly, in the Western world, I was expected to shrink my hips into a size 6 if

[2] Kant (1724–1804) was a German philosopher. —Eds.
[3] Among Shiite Muslims, the authorities who interpret religious law. —Eds.

I wanted to find a decent skirt tailored for a beautiful woman. We Muslim women have only one month of fasting, Ramadan, but the poor Western woman who diets has to fast twelve months out of the year. *"Quelle horreur,"*[4] I kept repeating to myself, while looking around at the American women shopping. All those my age looked like youthful teenagers. . . .

Now, at last, the mystery of my Western harem made sense. Framing 17 youth as beauty and condemning maturity is the weapon used against women in the West just as limiting access to public space is the weapon used in the East. The objective remains identical in both cultures: to make women feel unwelcome, inadequate, and ugly.

The power of the Western man resides in dictating what women should 18 wear and how they should look. He controls the whole fashion industry, from cosmetics to underwear. The West, I realized, was the only part of the world where women's fashion is a man's business. In places like Morocco, where you design your own clothes and discuss them with craftsmen and -women, fashion is your own business. Not so in the West. . . .

But how does the system function? I wondered. Why do women accept it? 19

Of all the possible explanations, I like that of the French sociologist Pierre 20 Bourdieu the best. In his latest book, *La Domination Masculine*, he proposes something he calls *"la violence symbolique"*: "Symbolic violence is a form of power which is hammered directly on the body, and as if by magic, without any apparent physical constraint. But this magic operates only because it activates the codes pounded in the deepest layers of the body."[5] Reading Bourdieu, I had the impression that I finally understood Western man's psyche better. The cosmetic and fashion industries are only the tip of the iceberg, he states, which is why women are so ready to adhere to their dictates. Something else is going on on a far deeper level. Otherwise, why would women belittle themselves spontaneously? Why, argues Bourdieu, would women make their lives more difficult, for example, by preferring men who are taller or older than they are? "The majority of French women wish to have a husband who is older and also, which seems consistent, bigger as far as size is concerned," writes Bourdieu.[6] Caught in the enchanted submission characteristic of the symbolic violence inscribed in the mysterious layers of the flesh, women relinquish what he calls "les signes ordinaires de la hiérarchie sexuelle," the ordinary signs of sexual hierarchy, such as old age and a larger body. By so doing, explains Bourdieu, women spontaneously accept the subservient position. It is this spontaneity Bourdieu describes as magic enchantment.[7]

---

[4] French, "What a horror." —EDS.
[5] Pierre Bourdieu, *La Domination Masculine* (Paris: Editions du Seuil, 1998), p. 44.
[6] Ibid., p. 41.
[7] Ibid., p. 42.

Once I understood how this magic submission worked, I became very 21
happy that the conservative ayatollahs do not know about it yet. If they
did, they would readily switch to its sophisticated methods, because they are
so much more effective. To deprive me of food is definitely the best way to
paralyze my thinking capabilities. . . .

"I thank you, Allah, for sparing me the tyranny of the 'size 6 harem,'" 22
I repeatedly said to myself while seated on the Paris-Casablanca flight, on my
way back home at last. "I am so happy that the conservative male elite does
not know about it. Imagine the fundamentalists switching from the veil to
forcing women to fit size 6."

How can you stage a credible political demonstration and shout in the 23
streets that your human rights have been violated when you cannot find the
right skirt?

Journal Writing

Within your peer group, what constitutes the norm of physical attractiveness for
women and for men? (Don't focus on the ideal here, but on what is expected for
a person not to be considered *un*attractive.) Are the norms similar for women and
for men, or do the standards differ by gender? How so?

Questions on Meaning

1. What two subjects does Mernissi compare? Where does she state her THESIS
   initially, and where does she later restate and expand on it? What does Mernissi
   conclude is the same about the two subjects?

2. What is the saleswoman's initial attitude toward Mernissi? How does her attitude
   seem to change, and how does this change contribute to Mernissi's point?

3. Why does Mernissi believe Western attitudes toward women are "more dangerous
   and cunning than the Muslim ones" (par. 15)?

Questions on Writing Strategy

1. What is the PURPOSE of paragraphs 6–7? What do these paragraphs contribute to
   Mernissi's larger point?

2. What two further comparisons does Mernissi make in paragraph 16? What TRAN-
   SITIONS does she use to signal the shift of subject within these comparisons?

3. **OTHER METHODS**   Mernissi devotes considerable attention to a NARRATIVE
   of her adventure in the department store. Why does she tell this story in such
   detail? What does it contribute to the essay?

Questions on Language

1. What are the CONNOTATIONS of the saleswoman's word *deviant* (par. 5)?

2. Why is the metaphor of the veil in paragraph 16 especially appropriate? (See FIGURES OF SPEECH in the Glossary if you need a definition of *metaphor*.)

3. Consult a dictionary if you are unsure of the meanings of any of the following: enigma (par. 1); generous, medina, bazaars, paradoxically (6); soufflé, sovereign (7); subdued (10); cunning, devaluation (15); aesthetic, prepubescent, unhindered, mutilating (16).

Suggestions for Writing

1. **FROM JOURNAL TO ESSAY**   Based on your journal entry, draft an essay in which you compare and contrast standards of attractiveness for women and men within your peer group. Be sure to consider how strictly the standards are applied in each case.

2. Write an essay about a time when your self-confidence was shaken because of how someone else treated or spoke to you. Like Mernissi, explain why you had been confident of yourself before this encounter and what effect it had on you.

3. Mernissi comes from Morocco. Put her essay in context by researching the history and culture of that country. Then write an essay in which you discuss what you have learned. How is Morocco different from the more "extremist nations" Mernissi refers to in paragraph 1?

4. **CRITICAL WRITING**   Respond to Mernissi's essay. Do you agree with her views about "the tyranny of the 'size 6 harem'" (par. 22)? Does Mernissi provide enough EVIDENCE to convince you of her views? Even if you agree with her take on her department-store experience, do you think her conclusions apply across the board, as she implies? For instance, do they apply among the poor and working class as well as among the affluent? Write an essay that ANALYZES and EVALUATES Mernissi's thesis and the support for it.

5. **CONNECTIONS**   When Mernissi asks who declared size 6 to be the norm in the United States, the sales clerk implicates the media: "The norm is everywhere, my dear. . . . It's all over, in the magazines, on television, in the ads. You can't escape it" (par. 9). In "Find Your Beach" (p. 319), Zadie Smith also touches on the power of advertising, contemplating the "subliminal effect" advertisements have on consumers' desires and ambitions. Using examples from both selections as well as from your own experience and observations, write an essay exploring a positive or a negative impact of advertising on individuals. You might do some library or Internet research to further support your point.

ADDITIONAL WRITING TOPICS

Comparison and Contrast

1. In an essay replete with EXAMPLES, compare and contrast the two subjects in any one of the following pairs:

   Toys marketed to girls and boys
   Vampires and zombies
   A photograph and a painting
   The special skills of two basketball players
   High school and college
   Introverts and extraverts
   Liberals and conservatives: their opposing views of the role of government
   How city dwellers and country dwellers spend their leisure time
   The presentation styles of two popular comedians
   Science and the humanities

2. Approach a comparison-and-contrast essay on one of the following general subjects by explaining why you prefer one thing to the other:

   Vehicles: hybrid and electric engines; sedans and SUVs; American and Asian; Asian and European
   Smartphone platforms: Apple and Android
   Two buildings on campus or in town
   Two baseball teams
   Two horror movie franchises
   Television when you were a child and television today
   High art and low art
   Malls and main streets
   Two sports
   A vegetarian (or vegan) diet and a meat-based diet

3. Write an essay in which you compare a reality (what actually exists) with an ideal (what should exist). Some possible topics:

   The affordable car
   Available living quarters
   Parenthood
   A job
   A personal relationship
   A companion animal
   The college curriculum
   Public transportation
   Financial aid for college students
   Political candidates

Wally McNamee/Getty Images

9

PROCESS ANALYSIS

Explaining Step by Step

◀ **Process analysis in a photograph**

In a factory in Shenzhen, China, workers create dolls for export to the United States. This single image catches several steps in the doll-making process. At the very back of the assembly line, flat, unstuffed dolls begin the journey past the ranks of workers who stuff the body parts, using material prepared by other workers on the sides. A supervisor, hands behind his or her back, oversees the process. What do you think the photographer, Wally McNamee, wants viewers to understand about this process? What do you imagine the workers themselves think about it?

THE METHOD

A chemist working for a soft-drink firm is asked to improve on a competitor's product, Hydra Sports Water. First, she chemically tests a sample to figure out what's in the drink. This is the method of DIVISION or ANALYSIS, the separation of something into its parts in order to understand it (see the next chapter). Then the chemist writes a report telling her boss how to make a drink like Hydra Sports Water, but better. This recipe is a special kind of analysis, called PROCESS ANALYSIS: explaining step by step how to do something or how something is done.

Like any type of analysis, process analysis divides a subject into its components: It divides a continuous action into stages. Processes much larger and more involved than the making of a sports drink may also be analyzed. When geologists explain how a formation such as the Grand Canyon developed—a process taking several hundred million years—they describe the successive layers of sediment deposited by oceans, floods, and wind; then the great uplift of the entire region by underground forces; and then the erosion, visible to us today, by the Colorado River and its tributaries, by little streams and flash floods, by crumbling and falling rock, and by wind. Exactly what are the geologists doing in this explanation? They are taking a complicated event (or process) and dividing it into parts. They are telling us what happened first, second, and third, and what is still happening today.

Because it is useful in explaining what is complicated, process analysis is a favorite method of scientists such as chemists and geologists. The method, however, may be useful to anybody. Two PURPOSES of process analysis are very familiar to you:

- A *directive process analysis* explains how to do something or how to make something. You make use of it when you read a set of instructions for taking an exam or for assembling a new bookcase ("Lay part A on a flat surface and, using two of the lock tabs provided, attach part B on the left . . .").

- An *informative process analysis* explains how something is done or how it takes place. You see it in textbook descriptions of how atoms behave when they split, how lions hunt, and how a fertilized egg develops into a child.

In this chapter, you will find examples of both kinds of process analysis—both the "how to" and the "how." For instance, Anne Lamott and Koji Frahm offer their own directives for writing successfully, while Jessica Mitford spellbindingly explains how corpses are embalmed.

Sometimes process analysis is used imaginatively. Foreseeing that eventually the sun will burn out and all life on Earth will perish, an astronomer who cannot possibly behold the end of the world nevertheless can write a process analysis of it. An exercise in learned guesswork, such an essay divides a vast and almost inconceivable event into stages that, taken one at a time, become clearer and more readily imaginable. Whether it is useful or useless (but fun or scary to imagine), an effective process analysis can grip readers and even hold them fascinated. Say you were proposing a change in the procedures for course registration at your school. You could argue your point until you were out of words, but you would get nowhere if you failed to tell your readers exactly how the new process would work: That's what makes your proposal sing.

Readers, it seems, have an unslakable thirst for process analysis. Leaf through any magazine, and you will find that instructions abound. You may see, for instance, articles telling you how to do a magic trick, make a difficult decision, build muscle, overcome anxiety, and score at stock trading. Less practical, but not necessarily less interesting, are the informative articles: how brain surgeons work, how diamonds are formed, how cities fight crime. Every issue of the *New York Times Book Review* features an entire bestseller list devoted to "Advice, How-to, and Miscellaneous," including books on how to make money in real estate, how to lose weight, how to find a good mate, and how to lose a bad one. Evidently, if anything can still make a busy person crack open a book, it is a step-by-step explanation of how he or she can be a success at living.

THE PROCESS

Here are suggestions for writing an effective process analysis of your own. (In fact, what you are about to read is itself a process analysis.)

1. **Understand clearly the process you are about to analyze.** Think it through. This preliminary survey will make the task of writing far easier for you.

2. **Consider your thesis.** What is the point of your process analysis? Why are you bothering to tell readers about it? The THESIS STATEMENT for a process analysis need do no more than say what the subject is and maybe outline its essential stages, as in this example:

   The main stages in writing a process analysis are listing the steps in the process, drafting to explain the steps, and revising to clarify the steps.

But your readers will surely appreciate something livelier and more pointed, something that says "You can use this" or "This may surprise you" or "Listen up." Here are two thesis statements from essays in this chapter:

Almost all good writing begins with terrible first efforts. You need to start somewhere.

— Anne Lamott, "Shitty First Drafts"

[In a mortuary the body] is in short order sprayed, sliced, pierced, pickled, trussed, trimmed, creamed, waxed, painted, rouged, and neatly dressed — transformed from a common corpse into a Beautiful Memory Picture.

— Jessica Mitford, "Behind the Formaldehyde Curtain"

3. **Think about preparatory steps.** If the reader should do something before beginning the process, list these steps. For instance, you might begin, "Assemble the needed equipment: a 20-milliliter beaker, a 5-milliliter burette, safety gloves, and safety goggles."

4. **List the steps or stages in the process.** Try setting them down in CHRONOLOGICAL ORDER, one at a time — if this is possible. Some processes, however, do not happen in an orderly sequence, but occur all at once. If, for instance, you are writing an account of a typical earthquake, what do you mention first? The shifting of underground rock strata? cracks in the earth? falling houses? bursting water mains? toppling trees? mangled cars? casualties? For this subject the method of CLASSIFICATION (Chap. 11) might come to your aid. You might sort out apparently simultaneous events into categories: injury to people; damage to homes, to land, to public property.

5. **Check the completeness and order of the steps.** Make sure your list includes *all* the steps in the right order. Sometimes a stage of a process may contain a number of smaller stages, or sub-steps. Make sure none has been left out. If any seems particularly tricky or complicated, underline it on your list to remind yourself when you write your essay to slow down and detail it with extra care.

6. **Define your terms.** Ask yourself, "Do I need any specialized or technical terms?" If so, be sure to define them. You'll sympathize with your reader if you have ever tried to assemble a bicycle according to a directive that begins, "Position sleeve casing on wheel center in fork with shaft in tongue groove, and gently but forcibly tap in pal-nut head."

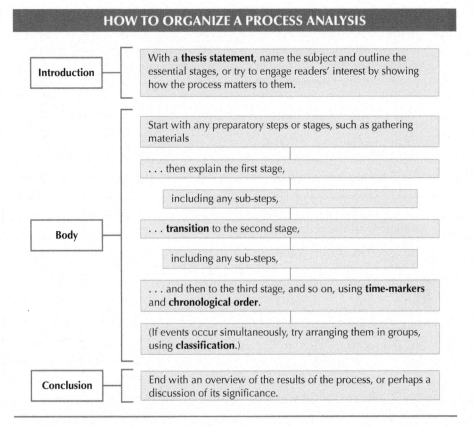

HOW TO ORGANIZE A PROCESS ANALYSIS

Introduction

With a **thesis statement**, name the subject and outline the essential stages, or try to engage readers' interest by showing how the process matters to them.

Body

Start with any preparatory steps or stages, such as gathering materials

. . . then explain the first stage,

including any sub-steps,

. . . **transition** to the second stage,

including any sub-steps,

. . . and then to the third stage, and so on, using **time-markers** and **chronological order**.

(If events occur simultaneously, try arranging them in groups, using **classification**.)

Conclusion

End with an overview of the results of the process, or perhaps a discussion of its significance.

7. **Use time-markers or** TRANSITIONS. These words or phrases indicate *when* one stage of a process stops and the next begins, and they greatly aid your reader in following you. Consider, for example, the following paragraph, in which plain medical prose makes good use of helpful time-markers (underlined). (The paragraph is adapted from *Pregnancy and Birth: A Book for Expectant Parents*, by Alan Frank Guttmacher.)

In the human, thirty-six hours after the egg is fertilized, a two-cell egg appears. A twelve-cell development takes place in seventy-two hours. The egg is still round and has increased little in diameter. In this respect it is like a real estate development. At first a road bisects the whole area, then a cross road divides it into quarters, and later other roads divide it into eighths and twelfths. This happens without the taking of any more land, simply by subdivision of the original tract. On the third or fourth day, the egg passes from the Fallopian tube into the uterus. By the fifth day the original single large cell has subdivided into sixty small cells and floats about the slitlike uterine cavity a day or two longer, then adheres to the cavity's inner lining. By the twelfth day the human egg is already firmly implanted. Impregnation is now completed, as yet unbeknown to the woman. At present, she has not even had time to miss her first menstrual period, and other symptoms of pregnancy are still several days distant.

Brief as these time-markers are, they define each stage of the human egg's journey. When using time-markers, vary them so that they won't seem mechanical. If you can, avoid the monotonous repetition of a fixed phrase (*In the fourteenth stage . . . , In the fifteenth stage . . .*). Even boring time-markers, though, are better than none at all. Words and phrases such as *in the beginning, first, second, next, then, after that, three seconds later, at the same time,* and *finally* can help a process move smoothly in the telling and lodge firmly in the reader's mind.

8. **Be specific.** When you write a first draft, explain your process analysis in generous detail, even at the risk of being wordy. When you revise, it will be easier to delete than to amplify.

9. **Revise.** When your essay is finished, reread it carefully against the checklist below. You might also enlist some help. If your process analysis is directive ("How to Eat an Ice-Cream Cone without Dribbling"), see if a friend can follow the instructions without difficulty. If your process analysis is informative ("How a New Word Enters the Dictionary"), ask whether the process unfolds clearly in his or her mind.

CHECKLIST FOR REVIEWING AND REVISING A PROCESS ANALYSIS

✔ **Thesis.** Does the process analysis have a point? Will readers be able to tell what the point is?

✔ **Organization.** Are the steps of the process arranged in a clear chronological order? If steps occur simultaneously, are they grouped so that readers perceive some order?

✔ **Completeness.** Are all the necessary steps included, and each one explained fully? Is it clear how each one contributes to the result?

✔ **Definitions.** Have the meanings of any terms your readers may not know been explained?

✔ **Transitions.** Do time-markers distinguish the steps of the process and clarify their sequence?

✔ **Consistency.** Have you maintained comfortable, consistent, and clear subject and verb forms?

FOCUS ON CONSISTENCY

While drafting a process analysis, you may start off with subjects or verbs in one form and then shift to another form because the original choice feels awkward. In directive analyses, shifts occur most often with the subjects *a person* and *one*:

> INCONSISTENT   To keep the car from rolling while changing the tire, <u>one</u> should first set the car's emergency brake. Then <u>you</u> should block the three other tires with objects like rocks or chunks of wood.

In informative analyses, shifts usually occur from singular to plural as a way to get around *he* when the meaning includes males and females:

> INCONSISTENT   The poll <u>worker</u> first checks each voter against the registration list. Then <u>they</u> ask the voter to sign another list.

To repair inconsistencies, start with a subject that is both comfortable and sustainable:

> CONSISTENT   To keep the car from rolling while changing the tire, <u>you</u> should set the car's emergency brake. Then <u>you</u> should block the three other tires with objects like rocks or chunks of wood.

> CONSISTENT   Poll <u>workers</u> first check each voter against the registration list. Then <u>they</u> ask the voter to sign another list.

Sometimes, writers try to avoid naming or shifting subjects by using PASSIVE verbs that don't require actors:

> INCONSISTENT   To keep the car from rolling while changing the tire, <u>one</u> should first set the car's emergency brake. Then the three other tires <u>should be blocked</u> with objects like rocks or chunks of wood.

> INCONSISTENT   Poll workers first <u>check</u> each voter against the registration list. Then the voter <u>is asked</u> to sign another list.

In directive analyses, avoid passive verbs by using *you*, as shown in the consistent example above, or by using the commanding form of verbs, in which *you* is understood as the subject:

> CONSISTENT   To keep the car from rolling while changing the tire, first <u>set</u> the car's emergency brake. Then <u>block</u> the three other tires with objects like rocks or chunks of wood.

In informative analyses, passive verbs may be necessary if you don't know who the actor is or want to emphasize the action over the actor. But identifying the actor is generally clearer and more concise:

> CONSISTENT   Poll <u>workers</u> first check each voter against the registration list. Then <u>they</u> ask the voter to sign another list.

STUDENT CASE STUDY: A LAB REPORT

When scientists conduct experiments to test their hypotheses, or theories, they almost always write reports outlining the processes they followed so that other researchers can attempt to duplicate the outcomes. Laboratory reports are straightforward and objective and are generally organized under standardized headings, such as *Purpose, Materials, Procedure,* and *Results.* They often include tables, figures, and calculations pertaining to the experiment. Most writers of lab reports put the focus on the experiment by keeping themselves in the background: They avoid *I* or *we* and use the PASSIVE VOICE of verbs (*the solution was heated,* as opposed to *we heated the solution*). The passive voice is not universal, however. Most lab assignments you receive in college will include detailed instructions for writing up the experiment and its results, so the best writing strategy is to follow those instructions to the letter.

For a first-year chemistry experiment, Victor Khoury used mostly household materials to extract and isolate deoxyribonucleic acid (DNA) from an onion. Found in all plants and animals, DNA is the molecule that holds the genetic information needed to create and direct living organisms. Khoury's instructor intended the experiment to teach students basic techniques and interactions in chemistry and to help them understand genetics at a molecular level. In the following excerpt from his lab report, Khoury explains the procedure and the main result.

Procedure

A small onion was coarsely chopped and placed in a   Step 1
1000-ml measuring cup along with 100 ml of a solution consisting of 10 ml of liquid dishwashing detergent, 1.5 g of table salt,
and distilled water. The solution was intended to dissolve the   Reason for step
proteins and lipids binding the cell membranes of the onion.
The onion pieces were next pressed with the back of a spoon for   Step 2
30 seconds to break the onion structure down into a mash.   Reason for step

The measuring cup was then placed in a pan of preheated   Step 3
58°C water for 13 minutes to further separate the DNA from the   Reason for step
walls of the onion cells. For the first 7 minutes, the onion was
continuously pressed with a spoon. After 13 minutes of heating,   Step 4
the cup of mixture was then placed in a pan of ice water and
the mixture was pressed and stirred for 5 minutes to cool it and   Reason for step
to slow enzyme activity that would otherwise break down the
DNA. The onion mixture was then placed in a coffee filter over a   Step 5
lab beaker and stored for 1 hour in a 4°C refrigerator in order to   Reason for step
filter and further cool the solution.

After refrigeration, the filtered solution was stirred for   Steps 6, 7, and 8
30 seconds and 10 ml were poured into a clean vial. A toothpick
dipped in meat tenderizer was placed into the onion solution
so that the enzymes in the tenderizer would further separate   Reason for steps
any remaining proteins from the DNA. Then refrigerated ethyl   Step 9
alcohol was poured into the vial until it formed a 1-cm layer on
top of the onion solution.

Results

After the solution sat for 2 minutes, the DNA precipitated   Discussion of results
into the alcohol layer. The DNA was long, white, and stringy,
with a gelatinous texture. This experiment demonstrated that
DNA can be extracted and isolated using a process of homogeni-
zation and deproteinization. . . .

ANNE LAMOTT

Born in San Francisco in 1954, Anne Lamott is a novelist and essayist whom *Amazon* once characterized as "your run-of-the-mill recovering alcoholic and drug addict, born-again Christian, left-wing liberal, and single mother who just so happens to have written *New York Times*–best-selling books." Those books, including *Bird by Bird* (1994), *Traveling Mercies* (1999), *Blue Shoe* (2002), *Imperfect Birds* (2010), *Small Victories* (2014), and *Almost Everything* (2018), touch on subjects ranging from fiction to family to faith and have earned her a devoted following. Lamott has taught at the University of California, Davis, and gives writing workshops and TED talks across the country. She lives in northern California.

Shitty First Drafts

Lamott's *Bird by Bird* is an inspiring and often very funny guide to writing. In this excerpt from the book, Lamott advises others how to begin writing by silencing their noisy inner critics.

In the following essay, "How to Write an *A* Paper," college student Koji Frahm offers a different take on succeeding as a writer.

For me and most of the other writers I know, writing is not rapturous. In fact, the only way I can get anything written at all is to write really, really shitty first drafts.

The first draft is the child's draft, where you let it all pour out and then let it romp all over the place, knowing that no one is going to see it and that you can shape it later. You just let this childlike part of you channel whatever voices and visions come through and onto the page. If one of the characters wants to say "Well, so what, Mr. Poopy Pants?" you let her. No one is going to see it. If the kid wants to get into really sentimental, weepy, emotional territory, you let him. Just get it all down on paper, because there may be something great in those six crazy pages that you would never have gotten to by more rational, grown-up means. There may be something in the very last line of the very last paragraph on page six that you just love, that is so beautiful or wild that you now know what you're supposed to be writing about, more or less, or in what direction you might go—but there was no way to get to this without first getting through the first five and a half pages.

I used to write food reviews for *California* magazine before it folded.   3
(My writing food reviews had nothing to do with the magazine folding,
although every single review did cause a couple of canceled subscriptions.
Some readers took umbrage at my comparing mounds of vegetable puree with
various ex-presidents' brains.) These reviews always took two days to write.
First I'd go to a restaurant several times with a few opinionated, articulate
friends in tow. I'd sit there writing down everything anyone said that was at
all interesting or funny. Then on the following Monday I'd sit down at my
desk with my notes, and try to write the review. Even after I'd been doing
this for years, panic would set in. I'd try to write a lead, but instead I'd write a
couple of dreadful sentences, xx them out, try again, xx everything out, and
then feel despair and worry settle on my chest like an x-ray apron. It's over,
I'd think calmly. I'm not going to be able to get the magic to work this time.
I'm ruined. I'm through. I'm toast. Maybe, I'd think, I can get my old job back
as a clerk-typist. But probably not. I'd get up and study my teeth in the mirror
for a while. Then I'd stop, remember to breathe, make a few phone calls, hit
the kitchen and chow down. Eventually I'd go back and sit down at my desk,
and sigh for the next ten minutes. Finally I would pick up my one-inch picture frame, stare into it as if for the answer, and every time the answer would
come: All I had to do was to write a really shitty first draft of, say, the opening
paragraph. And no one was going to see it.

So I'd start writing without reining myself in. It was almost just typing,   4
just making my fingers move. And the writing would be *terrible*. I'd write a
lead paragraph that was a whole page, even though the entire review could
only be three pages long, and then I'd start writing up descriptions of the
food, one dish at a time, bird by bird, and the critics would be sitting on
my shoulders, commenting like cartoon characters. They'd be pretending to
snore, or rolling their eyes at my overwrought descriptions, no matter how
hard I tried to tone those descriptions down, no matter how conscious I was
of what a friend said to me gently in my early days of restaurant reviewing.
"Annie," she said, "it is just a piece of *chicken*. It is just a bit of *cake*."

But because by then I had been writing for so long, I would eventually   5
let myself trust the process — sort of, more or less. I'd write a first draft that
was maybe twice as long as it should be, with a self-indulgent and boring
beginning, stupefying descriptions of the meal, lots of quotes from my black-
humored friends that made them sound more like the Manson girls[1] than
food lovers, and no ending to speak of. The whole thing would be so long and
incoherent and hideous that for the rest of the day I'd obsess about getting

---

[1] The Manson girls were young, troubled members of the cult led by Charles Manson
(1934–2017). In 1969 Manson and some of his followers were convicted of murder in
California. — Eds.

creamed by a car before I could write a decent second draft. I'd worry that people would read what I'd written and believe that the accident had really been a suicide, that I had panicked because my talent was waning and my mind was shot.

The next day, though, I'd sit down, go through it all with a colored pen,   6
take out everything I possibly could, find a new lead somewhere on the second page, figure out a kicky place to end it, and then write a second draft. It always turned out fine, sometimes even funny and weird and helpful. I'd go over it one more time and mail it in.

Then, a month later, when it was time for another review, the whole pro-   7
cess would start again, complete with the fears that people would find my first draft before I could rewrite it.

Almost all good writing begins with terrible first efforts. You need to start   8
somewhere. Start by getting something—anything—down on paper. A friend of mine says that the first draft is the down draft—you just get it down. The second draft is the up draft—you fix it up. You try to say what you have to say more accurately. And the third draft is the dental draft, where you check every tooth, to see if it's loose or cramped or decayed, or even, God help us, healthy.

What I've learned to do when I sit down to work on a shitty first draft   9
is to quiet the voices in my head. First there's the vinegar-lipped Reader Lady, who says primly, "Well, *that's* not very interesting, is it?" And there's the emaciated German male who writes these Orwellian[2] memos detailing your thought crimes. And there are your parents, agonizing over your lack of loyalty and discretion; and there's William Burroughs,[3] dozing off or shooting up because he finds you as bold and articulate as a houseplant; and so on. And there are also the dogs: Let's not forget the dogs, the dogs in their pen who will surely hurtle and snarl their way out if you ever *stop* writing, because writing is, for some of us, the latch that keeps the door of the pen closed, keeps those crazy ravenous dogs contained. . . .

Close your eyes and get quiet for a minute, until the chatter starts up. Then   10
isolate one of the voices and imagine the person speaking as a mouse. Pick it up by the tail and drop it into a mason jar. Then isolate another voice, pick it up by the tail, drop it in the jar. And so on. Drop in any high-maintenance parental units, drop in any contractors, lawyers, colleagues, children, anyone who is whining in your head. Then put the lid on, and watch all these mouse people clawing at the glass, jabbering away, trying to make you feel like shit because you won't do what they want—won't give them more money, won't

---

[2] In his novel *1984*, the British writer George Orwell (1903–50) depicts a futuristic world in which a totalitarian government controls citizens' behavior and thoughts. —Eds.
[3] The American novelist William Burroughs (1914–97) wrote experimental and often surreal works on drug addiction and other aspects of contemporary life. —Eds.

be more successful, won't see them more often. Then imagine that there is a volume-control button on the bottle. Turn it all the way up for a minute, and listen to the stream of angry, neglected, guilt-mongering voices. Then turn it all the way down and watch the frantic mice lunge at the glass, trying to get to you. Leave it down, and get back to your shitty first draft.

A writer friend of mine suggests opening the jar and shooting them all in   11
the head. But I think he's a little angry, and I'm sure nothing like this would ever occur to you.

Journal Writing

Describe what usually happens when you begin a writing project. Is the blank paper or screen an invitation or an obstacle? Do the words flow freely or haltingly or not at all? Do you feel creative? competent? helpless? tortured?

Questions on Meaning

1. What is Lamott's THESIS? Which sentences best convey her main idea?

2. According to Lamott, what role can other people, real or imaginary, play in the writing process? Are they helpful?

3. Review the comment by Lamott's friend (par. 8) that "the first draft is the down draft. . . . The second draft is the up draft. . . . And the third draft is the dental draft. . . ." What do you think is the difference in the writer's approach and focus at each stage? In what ways, if any, do these stages relate to your own approach to writing?

4. What do you think Lamott means when she says that "writing is, for some of us, the latch that keeps the door of the pen closed, keeps those crazy ravenous dogs contained" (par. 9)? What might the dogs and control of them stand for in this IMAGE?

5. What is Lamott's PURPOSE? To advise inexperienced writers? To relate her own difficulties with writing? Both, or something else? How do you know?

Questions on Writing Strategy

1. Lamott's book *Bird by Bird*, the source of this piece, is subtitled *Some Instructions on Writing and Life*. Who do you believe would find Lamott's advice most useful? Will it be useful to you? Why, or why not?

2. In paragraph 4 Lamott says that she wrote food reviews "one dish at a time" and "bird by bird" (a metaphor from earlier in her book, meaning one step at a time). What steps does her process analysis outline for overcoming obstacles?

3. Process analysis can be directive or explanatory (see p. 254), and Lamott's piece has good examples of both types. In which paragraphs does Lamott use each type? Where does she combine them? What does each type contribute? Is the mixture effective? Why, or why not?

4. What transitions does Lamott use to guide the reader through the steps of her process analysis? Is her use of transitions effective?

5. **OTHER METHODS** Paragraphs 3–7 NARRATE Lamott's experience writing food reviews for a magazine. What is the effect of this story?

Questions on Language

1. Although trying to be encouraging, Lamott uses many negative adjectives to describe her own first efforts: for example, "terrible" (par. 4) and "incoherent" (5). Find some other examples of negative adjectives. Why do you think Lamott uses so many of them?

2. What is Lamott's TONE? How seriously does she take the difficulties facing the writer?

3. Lamott uses several original images, such as the "vinegar-lipped Reader Lady" (par. 9). List some images that made a particular impression on you, and explain their effect.

4. Be sure you know how to define the following words: overwrought (par. 4); self-indulgent, stupefying, waning (5); emaciated, hurtle, ravenous (9); guilt-mongering (10).

Suggestions for Writing

1. **FROM JOURNAL TO ESSAY** Write an essay that explains your own writing process (in general or on a specific project) as you progress from idea to final draft. Enliven the process with specific methods and incidents — techniques of procrastination, ripping up draft after draft, listening to and silencing (or not) your own imagined voices, and so on. Try to draw some conclusions about what the writing process means to you.

2. Writing is, of course, only one way to communicate ideas. Other forms of communication can also be difficult: speaking up in class, making a presentation to a group of people, meeting with a teacher, interviewing for a job, making an important telephone call. Write a process analysis in which you first examine an oral encounter that was particularly difficult for you and then offer advice about how best to tackle such a situation.

3. **CRITICAL WRITING** We are usually taught to respect our parents and other authority figures, but Lamott advises writers to ignore them while composing. Is her advice justified in your view? Are there times when we can, even should, disregard authority? Write an essay about a time when you felt you could accomplish something only by disregarding the advice of someone you would normally

listen to — or, in contrast, when you heeded advice even though it held you back or ignored advice and eventually regretted doing so. How difficult was your action? How did the situation turn out? Looking back, do you believe you did the right thing?

4. **CONNECTIONS** Lamott stresses the importance of ignoring the perspectives of others in order to hear your own voice, and in the next essay, Koji Frahm (satirically) encourages writers to be hostile toward their readers. Citing examples from your own experience and from Lamott's and Frahm's essays, write an essay that examines writers' obligations to others versus obligations to themselves. When are we justified in following our own paths regardless of what readers think, and when are we not?

KOJI FRAHM

Koji Frahm was born in 1987 and grew up in Palo Alto, California, a suburb of San Francisco. In high school he competed on the swim team and spent much of his time playing video games. After enrolling at the University of California, Davis, as a biomechanical engineering student, he found himself getting up early to write short stories before classes, and so switched his major to creative writing. He graduated in 2009 and now lives in Brooklyn, New York, where he opened a makerspace for artists and continues to write.

How to Write an *A* Paper

"How to Write an *A* Paper" was written in response to an assignment given in a freshman composition class. Like Anne Lamott in the previous essay, Frahm considers the challenges and frustrations of writing. Focusing on the advice typically offered to college students, his essay is largely a directive process analysis, but it is also a SATIRE: By outwardly showing us one way to approach a writing project, the author implicitly urges us to do the opposite.

Be nebulous. Scratch that, be amphibological. The vaguer, the better. 1 The reader should be thinking, *what the hell does that mean?* right off the bat. The first sentence is key. Make it short, deadly, and impossible to understand. Convoluted is the term to use here. And remember, I'm not talking indiscernible due to stupidity; I'm talking indiscernible due to smarts. You have to sound brilliant. Scratch that, perspicacious. Be as opaque as a dense fog settling in front of a concrete wall — let them see nothing. Make them understand that you're smarter than they are. The sooner you establish this, the better. Hitting them hard and fast on the first sentence is the quickest way to do it. Make them so unsure of their own acumen from the start that they won't question you afterwards. Get them on the ground, and keep them there. Your God-like intelligence should never be questioned by these mere mortals — that's how you should be writing. Look at your first sentence for a moment and consider this: Is it short? Is it vague? Does it tell the reader nothing about what's going on? If so — bingo. You're in the clear. You can't be marked off if they can't understand your higher parlance — and that's exactly what we're going for.

The end of the introduction means it's thesis time. If you really want 2 to pull this off, end the introduction with no clear thesis. That way, they'll assume the thesis is lurking around somewhere later in the paper like a prowling hyena in Serengeti; and before you KNOW it, they'll forget what they were searching for. You never had one anyway. And if they're really keen for it, they'll probably just extrapolate something from the parts they don't understand later in the paper. You're Shakespeare, remember? You know best.

Be choppy. Scratch that, be desultory. Jump around like a rabbit on 3
fire — never let the reader know where you're headed next. The transitions between your paragraphs should be sudden and unexpected; your sentences short and rapid fire. Your teachers always taught you to be smooth and transitional — screw that. Toss your reader around like a paper bag in a tempest; the only thing they should be doing is covering their heads. Confusion is the key term here. If your reader doesn't look flummoxed and bleary-eyed by paragraph three, you aren't trying hard enough. You're smarter, you're faster, and the only thing they can do is try to keep up.

Paragraph four, all right, now we're getting somewhere. This is the part of 4
the essay where you're taught to bring out the big points. The "meat" of the essay is how teachers sometimes refer to it. That's all garbage. You don't need a plethora of in-depth points or solid evidence to fill up your paper — you just need one. One point. That's all you need. Reiteration is the key term here. I can't stress this part enough. All you need to know is this: keep talking. Be the jammed cassette deck on repeat. Write as if you're being paid a dollar a word, and you have only thirty seconds to type. Just keep pushing through the same old stuff with different wording. Dress it up; do its hair; color its nails; I don't care. Repackage the old, make it look new. Novelty sells the car. Write frivolously. Scratch that, farcically. It'll seem like you're getting deeper and deeper into the topic with every word you say, but really you'll JUST be wasting their time. Analysis is overrated — just keep spitting out what you already said. Regurgitation is the key term here. Vomit your words out and eat them back up, then spit them out a minute later. You're the mother eagle, and the reader is your starving chick. To add weight to this empty package, make sure the paragraph you put your half-digested words in is one of the longest. Nothing says "important" like a hefty paragraph. You would know. You're the smartest.

The thesaurus is your friend. Scratch that, your soul-mate. This whole 5
operation is FUELED by perplexing your reader. If you're the matador, the thesaurus is your cape — you're both coaxing the reader to charge through your charade. An essay is just made up of words, and that's the punch-line of this exploitation. Every word can be more sequestered; every syllable can be more ambagious. Make reading your essay more difficult than solving a Rubik's cube in the dark. Don't write *elderly person*, scratch that off. Write *septuagenarian*. That woman isn't pretty; she's *pulchritudinous* for someone possessing your voluminous vocabulary. And don't worry if the definitions

aren't totally the same; it's not as if the reader is going to know what's going on anyway. Obfuscate is the key term here.

Metaphors. It's always good to throw a lot of these in—teachers love this 6 stuff. Make sure they're really random and sporadic, popping up anywhere and everywhere like ferns in the Amazon jungle. Whatever pops into your head at the time, make it a metaphor. Whether it's animals from the Nature Channel you were watching two hours ago, or a Rubik's cube that's sitting on your desk, anything is fair GAME. Forget about clarity or adding depth, your metaphors are there for the same reason neon lights exist—distraction. Your essay should be a patchwork quilt of random metaphors, shrouding your essay from lucidity like the moon blocking the sun during a lunar eclipse. Just stick them everywhere.

Make errors. You heard right. Capitalize some random words throughout 7 your paper. Attach a note to the final document explaining that your computer was on the fritz, and even during printing it was behaving idiosyncratically. *Proofreading couldn't prevent it because it occurred during printing*, the note will say, and how can the teacher blame you? Your computer was haywire,; totally nuts. It was jumping off the walls and banging into the ceiling like a rubber ball fired out of a Civil War cannon, spitting and blasting unnecessary semicolons and punctuation errors into your work. You weren't responsible for what it did. And once you get that across, you can also blame the computer for for any typos or repeated words you may have left in my accident. Just type some OCCASIONAL caps-locked words now and then, and suddenly you're exonerated from all grammatical imperfections. Diabolical is the key term here.

By now you should be closing in like a school of piranha onto a drowning 8 ox. You've probably written enough, so you might as well wrap things up. Conclusions are easy. All you need is a quote and your choice of any massive, tear-inducing flaw in society. Take your pick: consumerism consuming our culture, superficiality sucking out our souls, mankind's maniacal instincts, the government's dominance of society's free will, et cetera, et cetera. It doesn't matter. It doesn't even have to pertain to your topic. The beauty with conclusions is you can tie just about anything to anything. If you were writing about the mating habits of rhinos, you could probably conclude with an anecdote about world hunger. The point is that there is no point. Be as random as a herd of buffalo showing up to present the Best Picture award at the Oscars. Just pick something you can rant about for a good half-page and you're in business.

Now for the quote. This is the last thing the reader's nonplussed eyes 9 will see—so make it good. This is the one time in the essay you want them to understand what's going on. After all this confusion they'll be ravenous for something transpicuous—and this is the time to dish it out. What's even better, they'll love you for it. Everyone likes being enlightened. And after your quote, your reader should be more sagacious than Buddha on heroin.

Choose one THAT sounds inspirational and profound. Aristotle and Socrates are always solid choices. Once again, it doesn't matter if it actually pertains to your topic. As long as it's half decent, the reader will be grateful. Place this at the end in italics and you're home free.

Congratulations, you're done. Don't worry about proofreading for 10 typos — you took care of the errors, remember? That damn computer of yours. All you have to do now is make sure you turn it in on Wednesday. Sit back and relax; and have a triumphant smile and modest remarks ready for the teacher next week when he praises your work in front of the class. What could go wrong, anyway? We've covered all the bases. An "A" is inevitable. Scratch that, ineluctable . . . which reminds me.

I received a paper back this morning and I still haven't checked the 11 grade. Excuse me for a moment; I have to confirm my "A." Consider this a testament to my guide to success. Confidence is the key term here.

Be a victim. Scratch that, be a scapegoat. Take the paper and crumple it, 12 throw it away or tuck it away somewhere you won't see it. Who cares anyway? This was a stupid assignment to begin with. It was a puerile assignment with an imbecilic teacher to grade it. What the hell does he know? Confusing Introduction. Lack of Content. Bad Transitions. *Excessive Grammatical Errors?!* You told him the computer was going haywire. Didn't he see the note? What an IDIOT. Obviously it was too much. He probably didn't understand what was going on and decided to take it out on you. What a sucker. Scratch that, a simpleton. His lack of comprehension isn't your fault — the ignoramus. He's taking his confusion out on you, satisfying his own denial by giving you a bad grade. He's just like everybody nowadays. No one takes responsibility for their own problems. People mess up their lives beyond all repair and still have excuses for everything. It's the whole world's fault before anyone will admit it's theirs. *He doesn't like me because . . . It's not my fault, she's the one that . . . I'm late because this stupid . . . blah . . . blah . . . blah . . .* How about a simple "sorry, it's my fault"? It's like the entire damn world would rather blame its problems on other things rather than fixing them. No one is willing to own up to their actions and take the consequences anymore. That's what this is all about. I'm just the hapless victim for all those ignorant fools out there. Those vainglorious dunderheads. Those egocentric imbeciles. It's like a wise man once said:

> *You must not lose faith in humanity.*
> *Humanity is an ocean;*
> *if a few drops of the ocean are dirty,*
> *the ocean does not become dirty.*
> — Mahatma Gandhi

Journal Writing

Frahm's essay is SATIRE—that is, an indirect attack on human follies or flaws, using IRONY to urge behavior exactly the opposite of what is really desired. In your journal, explore when you have proposed satirical approaches to challenges that seem overwhelming or ridiculous—for example, suggesting breaking all the dishes so that they don't have to be washed again or barring pedestrians from city streets so that they don't interfere with cars. What kinds of situations might lead you to make suggestions like these?

Questions on Meaning

1. How seriously does Frahm take his subject? Is his main PURPOSE to amuse and entertain, to inform students of ways they can become better writers, to warn about bad teachers, or to make fun of readers? Support your answer with EVIDENCE from the essay.

2. Look closely at Frahm's conclusion (par. 12). Does his writing advice actually promise an A for those who follow it? Why, or why not?

3. Does Frahm have a THESIS? Where in the essay does he explain his reason for not stating it outright?

Questions on Writing Strategy

1. How is Frahm's essay organized? Trace his process analysis carefully to determine whether it happens CHRONOLOGICALLY or follows another order. How effective is this method of organization and presentation?

2. At several points Frahm writes, "_____ is the key term here." Find these sentences and underline them. How do they give the essay COHERENCE and UNITY?

3. What is the author's apparent attitude toward readers? What role does he suggest an awareness of AUDIENCE plays in effective writing?

4. Some of the words in Frahm's essay are unnecessarily printed in all-capital letters. What other errors can you find? Why are they there?

5. **OTHER METHODS**   As is the case with any process analysis, "How to Write an A Paper" relies on DIVISION or ANALYSIS of its subject. What does Frahm imply are the elements of good writing?

Questions on Language

1. How do sentences such as "The vaguer, the better" and "Make it short, deadly, and impossible to understand" (par. 1) signal the TONE of this essay from the start? Should they be read literally, ironically, or some other way? How does the tone contribute to Frahm's satire?

2. What consistent sentence subject does Frahm use in "How to Write an A Paper"? Who is to perform the process?

3. Frahm's essay includes many difficult words seemingly plucked from a thesaurus (par. 5), including the following: nebulous, amphibological, perspicacious, acumen, parlance (1); extrapolate (2); desultory, flummoxed (3); plethora, farcically, regurgitation (4); sequestered, ambagious, obfuscate (5); sporadic, lucidity (6); idiosyncratically (7); nonplussed, transpicuous, sagacious (9); ineluctable (10); puerile, hapless, vainglorious (12). Do readers need to know the definitions of these words to understand Frahm's meaning?

4. In paragraph 6 Frahm encourages writers to use "a lot" of metaphors. Point to any metaphors or similes in his essay that strike you as especially imaginative. (See FIGURATIVE LANGUAGE in the Glossary if you need a definition of *metaphor* or *simile*.) What does Frahm say is the purpose of such language? Do you agree?

Suggestions for Writing

1. **FROM JOURNAL TO ESSAY**   Choose one of the solutions you wrote about in your journal, or propose a solution to a challenge that your journal entry has suggested. Write an essay detailing this satirical solution, paying careful attention to explaining each step of the process and to maintaining your satiric tone throughout.

2. Write a serious (not satirical) essay that teaches readers how to do something you're good at, such as making fresh guacamole from scratch, writing letters of complaint, or unclogging a sink. You might, like Frahm, imagine a specific group of people as your readers, or you might address your instructions to a more general audience.

3. Try to recall a time when you struggled with or failed at an assignment you thought would be simple. Write a short NARRATIVE about your difficulties. What went wrong? How did the struggle affect you? Did you learn anything?

4. **CRITICAL WRITING**   In a brief essay, pick apart Frahm's advice and the ways he applies it to his own writing in "How to Write an A Paper." Consider, for instance, how his first paragraph illustrates the function of his first sentence, or why he includes the quotation by Mahatma Gandhi at the end of the essay. Where else in this essay does Frahm commit the very sins of bad writing that he implicitly identifies? How effective are his choices?

5. **CONNECTIONS**   What does Frahm gain or lose by using satire and irony to make his point? What would be the comparative strengths and weaknesses of an essay that straightforwardly and sincerely approached the challenges writers face, such as Anne Lamott's "Shitty First Drafts" (p. 262)?

Koji Frahm on Writing

Asked to reflect on the experience of writing "How to Write an A Paper," Koji Frahm offered the following comments.

I'm still not sure if I like this essay. But with that said, I will admit it was a ton of fun to write. This assignment was to write a parody of another essay. And so, using observation from over the years of all the garbage and terrible techniques people cram into their essays (the idea actually came while discussing Poli Sci papers with a friend), I molded the most ridiculous and multilayered piece I've ever attempted—this being the result. I still have qualms with it; it still doesn't measure up to what I had in mind. But for what it's worth, it's made people chuckle, and that, for me, was the greatest reward of writing this piece.

The Bedford Reader on Writing

Although his essay is a lot of fun for readers, too, Frahm admits that his advice to student writers is "ridiculous and multilayered." For simple and straightforward guidelines on how to write, revise, and edit an effective paper, see Chapters 2–4 of this book.

FIROOZEH DUMAS

Born in Abadan, Iran, in 1966, Firoozeh Dumas migrated with her family to Whittier, California, at the age of seven, moved back to Iran two years later, then finally settled in the United States two years after that. She earned her bachelor's degree from the University of California at Berkeley in 1988. Dumas, who has said that the worst misconception about Iranians is "that we are completely humorless," took up writing partly to correct such assumptions. Her popular first book, *Funny in Farsi: A Memoir of Growing Up Iranian in America* (2003), portrays the humor in her family's experiences as Middle Eastern immigrants to the United States. Her second book, *Laughing without an Accent: Adventures of an Iranian American, at Home and Abroad* (2008), continues the theme with essays about trying to sell a cross-shaped potato on *eBay* and taking a cruise with fifty-one family members, among other topics. Dumas has written a novel for young readers, *It Ain't So Awful, Falafel* (2016), and contributes to several periodicals—including the *New York Times*, the *Wall Street Journal*, the *Los Angeles Times*, and *Lifetime*. She is also an occasional commentator on National Public Radio.

Sweet, Sour, and Resentful

In this 2009 essay from *Gourmet* magazine, Dumas outlines her mother's painstaking process of preparing a traditional Persian meal for the dozens of distant relatives and friends of friends who descended on the family's California condo every weekend. Through her mother's weekly routine—from hunting down ingredients to chopping herbs to refusing praise—Dumas reveals much about family, culture, and humility.

My mother's main ingredient in cooking was resentment—not that 1 I can blame her. In 1979, my family was living temporarily in Newport Beach, California. Our real home was in Abadan, a city in the southwest of Iran. Despite its desert location and ubiquitous refineries, Abadan was the quintessential small town. Everybody's father (including my own) worked for the National Iranian Oil Company, and almost all the moms stayed home. The employees' kids attended the same schools. No one locked their doors. Whenever I hear John Mellencamp's "Small Town," I think of Abadan, although I'm guessing John Mellencamp was thinking of somewhere else when he wrote that song.

By the time of the Iranian revolution,[1] we had adjusted to life in 2
California. We said "Hello" and "Have a nice day" to perfect strangers, wore
flip-flops, and grilled cheeseburgers next to our kebabs. We never understood
why Americans put ice in tea or bought shampoo that smelled like strawber-
ries, but other than that, America felt like home.

When the revolution happened, thousands left Iran for Southern 3
California. Since we were one of the few Iranian families already there, our
phone did not stop ringing. Relatives, friends, friends of relatives, friends of
friends, and people whose connection we never quite figured out called us with
questions about settling into this new land. Displaying the hospitality that
Iranians so cherish, my father extended a dinner invitation to everyone who
called. As a result, we found ourselves feeding dozens of people every weekend.

The marathon started on Monday, with my mother planning the menu 4
while letting us know that she was already tired. Fortunately, our rice dishes
were made to be shared; our dilemma, however, was space. Our condo was
small. Our guests squeezed onto the sofa, sat on the floor, or overflowed onto
the patio. We eventually had to explain to our American neighbors why there
were so many cars parked in front of our place every weekend. My mother, her
diplomatic skills in full swing, had me deliver plates of Persian food, decorated
with radish roses and mint sprigs, to them. In time, we learned not to share
fesenjan, pomegranate stew with ground walnuts. "Yes, now that you mention
it, it does look like mud, but it's really good," I'd explain, convincing no one.

Because my mother did not drive, my father took her to buy ingredients 5
every Tuesday after work. In Abadan, my mother and I had started most days
in the market, going from vendor to vendor looking for herbs, vegetables,
and fruits. The fish came from the Karun and Arvand (Shatt al Arab) Rivers,
the *lavash* and the *sangak* breads were freshly baked, and the chickens were
still alive. We were locavores by necessity and foodies without knowing it.
In America, I learned that the time my parents spent shopping was in direct
correlation to the degree of my mother's bad mood. An extra-long trip meant
that my mother could not find everything she needed, a point she would
make loud and clear when she got home: "Why don't they let fruit ripen
here?" "Why are the chickens so huge and flavorless?" "I couldn't find fresh
herbs." "My feet hurt." "How am I supposed to get everything done?"

The first step was preparing the herbs. My mother insisted that the pars- 6
ley, cilantro, and chives for *qormeh sabzi*, herb stew, had to be finely chopped
by hand. The food processor, she explained, squished them. As she and
my father sat across the table wielding huge knives, they argued incessantly.

---

[1] In 1979 fundamentalist rebels led by Ayatollah Ruhollah Khomeini overthrew the Iranian
monarchy and established the Islamic Republic of Iran, a theocratic dictatorship. —Eds.

My father did his best to help her. It wasn't enough. As soon as the mountain of herbs was chopped, my mother started frying them. At any given time, my mother was also frying onions. Every few days, while my father was watching the six o'clock news, my mother would hand him a dozen onions, a cutting board, and a knife. No words were exchanged. Much to my father's relief, I once volunteered for this task, but apparently my slices were neither thin enough nor even. It took my father's precision as an engineer to slice correctly.

While all four burners were in use, my mother mixed the ground beef, 7 rice, split peas, scallions, and herbs for stuffed grape leaves. I chopped the stems of the grape leaves. I had tried stuffing them once, but my rolls, deemed not tight enough, were promptly unrolled and then rerolled by my mother.

In between cooking, my mother made yogurt — the thick, sour variety 8 that we couldn't find in America. She soaked walnuts and almonds in water to plump them up; fried eggplants for *kashk-e bademjan*, a popular appetizer with garlic, turmeric, mint, and whey; made *torshi-e limo*, a sour lemon condiment; and slivered orange peels. I had been fired from this task also, having left on far too much pith.

By the time our guests arrived, my mother was exhausted. But the work 9 was not finished. Rice, the foundation of the Persian meal, the litmus test of the cook's ability, cannot be prepared ahead of time. To wit, one day in Abadan, the phone rang when my mother was about to drain the rice. During the time it took her to answer the phone and tell her sister that she would call her back, the rice overcooked. Almost forty years later, I still remember my mother's disappointment and her explaining to my father that her sister had time to talk because my aunt's maid did all the cooking. My aunt did not even drain her own rice.

We certainly did not have a table big enough to set, so we simply stacked 10 dishes and utensils, buffet-style. As the guest list grew, we added paper plates and plastic utensils. It was always my job to announce that dinner was ready. As people entered the dining room, they gasped at the sight of my mother's table. Her *zereshk polow*, barberry rice, made many emotional. There are no fresh barberries in America (my mother had brought dried berries from Iran in her suitcase), and the sight of that dish, with its distinct deep red hue, was a reminder of the life our guests had left behind.

Our dinners took days to cook and disappeared in twenty minutes. As our 11 guests heaped their plates and looked for a place to sit, they lavished praise on my mother, who, according to tradition, deflected it all. "It's nothing," she said. "I wish I could've done more." When they told her how lucky she was to have me to help her, my mother politely nodded, while my father added, "Firoozeh's good at math."

On Sundays, my mother lay on the sofa, her swollen feet elevated, field-   12
ing thank-you phone calls from our guests. She had the same conversation
a dozen times; each one ended with, "Of course you can give our name to
your cousins." As I watched my mother experience the same draining routine week after week, I decided that tradition is good only if it brings joy to
all involved. This includes the hostess. Sometimes, even our most cherished
beliefs must evolve. Evolution, thy name is potluck.

Journal Writing

Many people have unique rituals, like Dumas's parents' practice of serving elaborate
Persian meals to distant acquaintances every weekend. List some rituals that
are unique to your family, to another group you belong to, or to you alone — for
instance, a holiday celebration, a vacation activity, a way of decompressing after a
stressful week.

Questions on Meaning

1. Why were weekend dinners so important to the author's parents and their guests?
   Consider not just the meals themselves but the larger context that prompted
   them.

2. In which sentence or sentences does Dumas state her THESIS most directly?

3. What would you say is Dumas's PURPOSE in this essay? Is it primarily to entertain readers by describing her family's weekly routine, or does she seem to have
   another purpose in mind?

4. What solution to her mother's exhausting role as hostess does Dumas propose in
   paragraph 12? Do you think her mother would have agreed to it? Why, or why
   not?

Questions on Writing Strategy

1. Why does Dumas begin her essay with an overview of life in Abadan and an
   ALLUSION to the Iranian revolution (pars. 1–3)? What purpose does this opening
   serve?

2. How does Dumas seem to imagine her AUDIENCE? To what extent could she
   ASSUME that readers would appreciate her mother's situation?

3. What steps does Dumas identify in the process of hosting Iranian guests every
   weekend? How does she ensure that her analysis has COHERENCE?

4. **OTHER METHODS**   What role does COMPARISON AND CONTRAST play in paragraph 5?

Questions on Language

1. Explain how Dumas's TONE contributes to the humor in her essay.

2. Where in this essay does Dumas use Persian words? What is their EFFECT?

3. In paragraph 9, Dumas says that rice is "the litmus test" for Iranian cooks. What does she mean? What is a litmus test, and how does the phrase connect to the focus (and title) of her essay?

4. Be sure you know the meanings of the following words: ubiquitous, quintessential (par. 1); Persian (4); locavores, correlation (5); pith (8); lavished, deflected (11); potluck (12).

Suggestions for Writing

1. **FROM JOURNAL TO ESSAY**   Write an essay explaining one of the rituals you listed in your journal. Focus on the details and steps of the ritual itself as well as on the significance it holds for you and for any others who participate in it with you.

2. Research the influx of Iranian families into California during the 1970s. What prompted this migration? What quality of life did newcomers face on arrival? What tensions did their arrival create? In an essay, consider these questions and others your research may lead you to. You may prefer to focus on a different migration from the nineteenth or twentieth century—such as that of Irish to the eastern United States, Chinese to the western United States, or African Americans from the southern to the northern United States.

3. **CRITICAL WRITING**   What impression of herself does Dumas create in this essay? What adjectives would you use to describe the writer as she reveals herself on the page? Cite specific language from the essay to support your ANALYSIS.

4. **CONNECTIONS**   Both Firoozeh Dumas and Amy Tan, in "Fish Cheeks" (p. 77), hint at how as children they felt ashamed of their families because of certain foods. Write an essay in which you COMPARE AND CONTRAST the ways the two writers describe food and how each writer uses food to make a larger point about the need to fit in.

Firoozeh Dumas on Writing

In a 2004 interview with Khaled Hosseini (author of *The Kite Runner* and other novels), Firoozeh Dumas explained how writing awakens her memory. As a girl growing up in Iran and the United States, Dumas says she "was always that quiet kid in a room full of adults" who carefully "listened and observed." When she started writing as an adult, her collected observations "just flooded back." Unlike those who experience writer's block, Dumas was easily inspired: "Every time I finished a story, another popped up in its place. It was like using a vending machine: The candy falls down and is immediately replaced by another."

In order to keep up with her vending machine of ideas — and to accommodate her busy family life — Dumas writes "in spurts," often waking at four in the morning. "Once a story is in my head, I'm possessed, and the only thing I can do is write like mad," she told Hosseini. "This means the house gets very messy and dinner is something frozen. I do not read or go to the movies when I am writing, because I can't concentrate on anything else. I also keep writing in my head when I'm not actually writing, which means that I become a terrible listener."

The Bedford Reader on Writing

Have you ever found that the act of writing triggers your memory, as it does for Dumas? Try FREEWRITING (p. 31) and see if it works for you. Many writers find that simply sitting down and writing, even for just a few minutes at a time, can yield surprising results.

DANIEL OROZCO

Daniel Orozco was born in 1957 and grew up in San Francisco. After graduating from Stanford University in 1979, he held temporary positions doing clerical work for a little over a decade while studying writing at San Francisco State University and rediscovering a passion for literature. He received an MFA in writing from the University of Washington, was a creative-writing fellow at Stanford, and currently teaches at the University of Idaho. Orozco's stories have appeared in *Harper's, McSweeney's, Story*, and other publications, have been chosen for *The Best American Short Stories* and the *Pushcart Prize Anthology*, and are collected in *Orientation: And Other Stories* (2011), Orozco's first book. He is working on a novel.

Orientation

Drawing on his experience as an office temp and trainer, Orozco created this story in which an employee introduces a newcomer to a company's procedures and people. First published in *Seattle Review* in 1994, "Orientation" then appeared in *The Best American Short Stories 1995*. It has also been read on public radio's *This American Life* and even adapted as a dance piece.

Those are the offices and these are the cubicles. That's my cubicle there, and this is your cubicle. This is your phone. Never answer your phone. Let the Voicemail System answer it. This is your Voicemail System Manual. There are no personal phone calls allowed. We do, however, allow for emergencies. If you must make an emergency phone call, ask your supervisor first. If you can't find your supervisor, ask Phillip Spiers, who sits over there. He'll check with Clarissa Nicks, who sits over there. If you make an emergency phone call without asking, you may be let go. 1

These are your IN and OUT boxes. All the forms in your IN box must be logged in by the date shown in the upper left-hand corner, initialed by you in the upper right-hand corner, and distributed to the Processing Analyst whose name is numerically coded in the lower left-hand corner. The lower right-hand corner is left blank. Here's your Processing Analyst Numerical Code Index. And here's your Forms Processing Procedures Manual. 2

You must pace your work. What do I mean? I'm glad you asked that. We pace our work according to the eight-hour workday. If you have twelve hours of work in your IN box, for example, you must compress that work into the eight-hour day. If you have one hour of work in your IN box, you must expand that work to fill the eight-hour day. That was a good question. Feel free to ask questions. Ask too many questions, however, and you may be let go. 3

That is our receptionist. She is a temp. We go through receptionists here. 4
They quit with alarming frequency. Be polite and civil to the temps. Learn
their names, and invite them to lunch occasionally. But don't get close to
them, as it only makes it more difficult when they leave. And they always
leave. You can be sure of that.

The men's room is over there. The women's room is over there. John 5
LaFountaine, who sits over there, uses the women's room occasionally. He
says it is accidental. We know better, but we let it pass. John LaFountaine is
harmless, his forays into the forbidden territory of the women's room simply a
benign thrill, a faint blip on the dull flat line of his life.

Russell Nash, who sits in the cubicle to your left, is in love with Amanda 6
Pierce, who sits in the cubicle to your right. They ride the same bus together
after work. For Amanda Pierce, it is just a tedious bus ride made less tedious
by the idle nattering of Russell Nash. But for Russell Nash, it is the highlight
of his day. It is the highlight of his life. Russell Nash has put on forty pounds,
and grows fatter with each passing month, nibbling on chips and cookies
while peeking glumly over the partitions at Amanda Pierce, and gorging himself at home on cold pizza and ice cream while watching adult videos on TV.

Amanda Pierce, in the cubicle to your right, has a six-year-old son named 7
Jamie, who is autistic. Her cubicle is plastered from top to bottom with the
boy's crayon artwork—sheet after sheet of precisely drawn concentric circles
and ellipses, in black and yellow. She rotates them every other Friday. Be sure to
comment on them. Amanda Pierce also has a husband, who is a lawyer. He subjects her to an escalating array of painful and humiliating sex games, to which
Amanda Pierce reluctantly submits. She comes to work exhausted and freshly
wounded each morning, wincing from the abrasions on her breasts, or the
bruises on her abdomen, or the second-degree burns on the backs of her thighs.

But we're not supposed to know any of this. Do not let on. If you let on, 8
you may be let go.

Amanda Pierce, who tolerates Russell Nash, is in love with Albert Bosch, 9
whose office is over there. Albert Bosch, who only dimly registers Amanda
Pierce's existence, has eyes only for Ellie Tapper, who sits over there. Ellie
Tapper, who hates Albert Bosch, would walk through fire for Curtis Lance.
But Curtis Lance hates Ellie Tapper. Isn't the world a funny place? Not in the
ha-ha sense, of course.

Anika Bloom sits in that cubicle. Last year, while reviewing quarterly 10
reports in a meeting with Barry Hacker, Anika Bloom's left palm began to
bleed. She fell into a trance, stared into her hand, and told Barry Hacker
when and how his wife would die. We laughed it off. She was, after all, a
new employee. But Barry Hacker's wife is dead. So unless you want to know
exactly when and how you'll die, never talk to Anika Bloom.

Colin Heavey sits in that cubicle over there. He was new once, just like 11
you. We warned him about Anika Bloom. But at last year's Christmas Potluck,
he felt sorry for her when he saw that no one was talking to her. Colin Heavey
brought her a drink. He hasn't been himself since. Colin Heavey is doomed.
There's nothing he can do about it, and we are powerless to help him. Stay
away from Colin Heavey. Never give any of your work to him. If he asks to
do something, tell him you have to check with me. If he asks again, tell him I
haven't gotten back to you.

This is the Fire Exit. There are several on this floor, and they are marked 12
accordingly. We have a Floor Evacuation Review every three months, and
an Escape Route Quiz once a month. We have our Biannual Fire Drill twice
a year, and our Annual Earthquake Drill once a year. These are precautions
only. These things never happen.

For your information, we have a comprehensive health plan. Any cat- 13
astrophic illness, any unforeseen tragedy is completely covered. All depen-
dents are completely covered. Larry Bagdikian, who sits over there, has six
daughters. If anything were to happen to any of his girls, or to all of them, if
all six were to simultaneously fall victim to illness or injury—stricken with
a hideous degenerative muscle disease or some rare toxic blood disorder,
sprayed with semiautomatic gunfire while on a class field trip, or attacked in
their bunk beds by some prowling nocturnal lunatic—if any of this were to
pass, Larry's girls would all be taken care of. Larry Bagdikian would not have
to pay one dime. He would have nothing to worry about.

We also have a generous vacation and sick leave policy. We have an 14
excellent disability insurance plan. We have a stable and profitable pension
fund. We get group discounts for the symphony, and block seating at the ball-
park. We get commuter ticket books for the bridge. We have Direct Deposit.
We are all members of Costco.

This is our kitchenette. And this, this is our Mr. Coffee. We have a coffee 15
pool, into which we each pay two dollars a week for coffee, filters, sugar, and
CoffeeMate. If you prefer Cremora or half-and-half to CoffeeMate, there is a
special pool for three dollars a week. If you prefer Sweet 'n Low to sugar, there is
a special pool for two-fifty a week. We do not do decaf. You are allowed to join
the coffee pool of your choice, but you are not allowed to touch the Mr. Coffee.

This is the microwave oven. You are allowed to *heat* food in the micro- 16
wave oven. You are not, however, allowed to *cook* food in the microwave oven.

We get one hour for lunch. We also get one fifteen-minute break in the 17
morning, and one fifteen-minute break in the afternoon. Always take your
breaks. If you skip a break, it is gone forever. For your information, your break
is a privilege, not a right. If you abuse the break policy, we are authorized to
rescind your breaks. Lunch, however, is a right, not a privilege. If you abuse

the lunch policy, our hands will be tied, and we will be forced to look the other way. We will not enjoy that.

This is the refrigerator. You may put your lunch in it. Barry Hacker, who 18 sits over there, steals food from this refrigerator. His petty theft is an outlet for his grief. Last New Year's Eve, while kissing his wife, a blood vessel burst in her brain. Barry Hacker's wife was two months pregnant at the time, and lingered in a coma for half a year before dying. It was a tragic loss for Barry Hacker. He hasn't been himself since. Barry Hacker's wife was a beautiful woman. She was also completely covered. Barry Hacker did not have to pay one dime. But his dead wife haunts him. She haunts all of us. We have seen her, reflected in the monitors of our computers, moving past our cubicles. We have seen the dim shadow of her face in our photocopies. She pencils herself in in the receptionist's appointment book, with the notation: To see Barry Hacker. She has left messages in the receptionist's Voicemail box, messages garbled by the electronic chirrups and buzzes in the phone line, her voice echoing from an immense distance within the ambient hum. But the voice is hers. And beneath her voice, beneath the tidal *whoosh* of static and hiss, the gurgling and crying of a baby can be heard.

In any case, if you bring a lunch, put a little something extra in the bag 19 for Barry Hacker. We have four Barrys in this office. Isn't that a coincidence?

This is Matthew Payne's office. He is our Unit Manager, and his door is 20 always closed. We have never seen him, and you will never see him. But he is here. You can be sure of that. He is all around us.

This is the Custodian's Closet. You have no business in the Custodian's 21 Closet.

And this, this is our Supplies Cabinet. If you need supplies, see Curtis 22 Lance. He will log you in on the Supplies Cabinet Authorization Log, then give you a Supplies Authorization Slip. Present your pink copy of the Supplies Authorization Slip to Ellie Tapper. She will log you in on the Supplies Cabinet Key Log, then give you the key. Because the Supplies Cabinet is located outside the Unit Manager's office, you must be very quiet. Gather your supplies quietly. The Supplies Cabinet is divided into four sections. Section One contains letterhead stationery, blank paper and envelopes, memo and note pads, and so on. Section Two contains pens and pencils and typewriter and printer ribbons, and the like. In Section Three we have erasers, correction fluids, transparent tapes, glue sticks, et cetera. And in Section Four we have paper clips and push pins and scissors and razor blades. And here are the spare blades for the shredder. Do not touch the shredder, which is located over there. The shredder is of no concern to you.

Gwendolyn Stich sits in that office there. She is crazy about penguins, 23 and collects penguin knickknacks: penguin posters and coffee mugs and stationery, penguin stuffed animals, penguin jewelry, penguin sweaters and T-shirts and socks. She has a pair of penquin fuzzy slippers she wears when working late at the office. She has a tape cassette of penguin sounds which she listens to for relaxation. Her favorite colors are black and white. She has personalized license plates that read PEN GWEN. Every morning, she passes through all the cubicles to wish each of us a *good* morning. She brings Danish on Wednesdays for Hump Day morning break, and doughnuts on Fridays for TGIF afternoon break. She organizes the Annual Christmas Potluck, and is in charge of the Birthday List. Gwendolyn Stich's door is always open to all of us. She will always lend an ear, and put in a good word for you; she will always give you a hand, or the shirt off her back, or a shoulder to cry on. Because her door is always open, she hides and cries in a stall in the women's room. And John LaFountaine—who, enthralled when a woman enters, sits quietly in his stall with his knees to his chest—John LaFountaine has heard her vomiting in there. We have come upon Gwendolyn Stich huddled in the stairwell, shivering in the updraft, sipping a Diet Mr. Pibb and hugging her knees. She does not let any of this interfere with her work. If it interfered with her work, she might have to be let go.

Kevin Howard sits in that cubicle over there. He is a serial killer, the one they call the Carpet Cutter, responsible for the mutilations across town. We're not supposed to know that, so do not let on. Don't worry. His compulsion inflicts itself on strangers only, and the routine established is elaborate and unwavering. The victim must be a white male, a young adult no older than thirty, heavyset, with dark hair and eyes, and the like. The victim must be chosen at random, before sunset, from a public place; the victim is followed home, and must put up a struggle; et cetera. The carnage inflicted is precise: the angle and direction of the incisions; the layering of skin and muscle tissue; the rearrangement of the visceral organs; and so on. Kevin Howard does not let any of this interfere with his work. He is, in fact, our fastest typist. He types as if he were on fire. He has a secret crush on Gwendolyn Stich, and leaves a red-foil-wrapped Hershey's Kiss on her desk every afternoon. But he hates Anika Bloom, and keeps well away from her. In his presence, she has uncontrollable fits of shaking and trembling. Her left palm does not stop bleeding. 24

In any case, when Kevin Howard gets caught, act surprised. Say that he seemed like a nice person, a bit of a loner, perhaps, but always quiet and polite. 25

This is the photocopier room. And this, this is our view. It faces southwest. West is down there, toward the water. North is back there. Because we are on the seventeenth floor, we are afforded a magnificent view. Isn't it beautiful? It overlooks the park, where the tops of those trees are. You can see 26 a segment of the bay between those two buildings there. You can see the sun set in the gap between those two buildings over there. You can see this building reflected in the glass panels of that building across the way. There. See? That's you, waving. And look there. There's Anika Bloom in the kitchenette, waving back.

Enjoy this view while photocopying. If you have problems with the pho- 27 tocopier, see Russell Nash. If you have any questions, ask your supervisor. If you can't find your supervisor, ask Phillip Spiers. He sits over there. He'll check with Clarissa Nicks. She sits over there. If you can't find them, feel free to ask me. That's my cubicle. I sit in there.

Journal Writing

Think of a situation in which you had to learn new procedures, customs, or people. You may have had a lot of help, as in a training program, or you may have had to go it alone. In your journal write down what you recall most vividly about the process of your orientation.

Questions on Meaning

1. This story seems to be a SATIRE, but what exactly is being satirized?
2. Where does the story's speaker provide information like that in a true job orientation? information that seems appropriate but exaggerated? information that is inappropriate for an orientation, even outrageous? What does this mix of information add to the story?
3. What view of the human condition does Orozco seem to offer in this story?

Questions on Writing Strategy

1. What is the EFFECT of the last paragraph's echo of the first paragraph?
2. What other repetition do you notice in paragraphs 1, 3, 8, and 23? What is its effect?
3. What parts of this story illustrate process analysis?
4. **OTHER METHODS**   What do the examples in paragraph 13 suggest about the speaker's interests and attitudes?

Questions on Language

1. How would you describe the speaker's overall TONE? What does this tone contribute to the effect of the story?

2. In paragraph 18 the speaker's tone shifts rather dramatically. What is the shift? How do you account for it?

3. Where does Orozco satirize the language of bureaucracy most obviously?

4. Consult a dictionary if you are uncertain of the meaning of any of the following: cubicles (par. 1); forays, benign (5); autistic, abrasions (7); degenerative, nocturnal (13); rescind (17); TGIF, enthralled (23).

Suggestions for Writing

1. **FROM JOURNAL TO ESSAY**   Compose an essay that explains the process of orientation you wrote about in your journal. Depending on your experience, you may present the process in formal stages or relate what happened in a NARRATIVE.

2. Expand your knowledge about working in an office by interviewing friends and family members who have done so. (If you have worked in an office, add your own information to the others'.) Ask about experiences with supervisors, coworkers, procedures, and equipment. In an essay SYNTHESIZE what you discover. What do offices seem to have in common, and how do they differ?

3. **CRITICAL WRITING**   Analyze how Orozco structures his story. How does the speaker move from one stop on the tour to the next? Does the story seem to build in a particular way? What does the organization contribute to the story's effect?

4. **CONNECTIONS**   Both Orozco in this story and Brian Doyle in "Three Basketball Stories" (p. 192) create speakers who address a *you* directly. In an essay consider the similarities and differences between the two authors' speakers and how they seem to conceive of their listeners.

Daniel Orozco on Writing

In an interview with Will Allison for *Novel and Short Story Writer's Market*, Orozco talks about taking his time while writing. "My slowness as a writer seems to be part of a deliberate composition process," he says. "Before I actually begin writing a story, it goes through what I call Gestation and Frustration. Gestation: A story for me begins as an image or situation knocking around in my head, followed by months of notes jotted on scraps of paper, or entered into a file on my PC. This is followed finally by attempts at writing a first draft. Then, Frustration: I can set an unfinished draft aside for anywhere from days to months, during which time I do some reading or research on the story — a great way to avoid actually writing it — or I research or write another story. Eventually I get back to finishing the first draft, and then I get to revising."

Most of Orozco's process is dedicated to revision, a stage he enjoys more than the initial drafting even though it can be more difficult. In 2001 Orozco published a story that he had worked on intermittently since 1978. "Orientation," which took eleven months, was, Orozco says, "the fastest I'd ever written anything." Asked whether his slow writing process bothers him, Orozco admits, "I used to bitch and moan about . . . how long it would take me to squeeze out a story." But he's learned to accept his writing process as something he can't—and wouldn't—change: "Now I embrace it as simply the way I write stories, stories than I am happy with. I used to wish I wrote faster, but I don't anymore. It's like wishing I were taller—it just ain't gonna happen."

The Bedford Reader on Writing

Do you consider yourself a particularly slow or fast writer? Do you have trouble getting down the first draft, or do you find it more difficult to revise? For help with either stage of the writing process, see Chapters 2 and 3, on Discovery and Drafting and on Reviewing and Revising.

JESSICA MITFORD

Born in Batsford Mansion, England, in 1917, the daughter of Lord and Lady Redesdale, Jessica Mitford devoted much of her early life to defying her aristocratic upbringing. In her autobiography *Daughters and Rebels* (1960), she tells how she received a genteel schooling at home, then as a young woman moved to Loyalist Spain during the violent Spanish Civil War. Later she immigrated to the United States, where for a time she worked in Miami as a bartender. She obtained US citizenship in 1944 and became one of her adopted country's most noted reporters: *Time* magazine even called her "Queen of the Muckrakers." Exposing with her typewriter what she regarded as corruption, abuse, and absurdity, Mitford wrote *The American Way of Death* (1963, revised as *The American Way of Death Revisited* in 1998), *Kind and Unusual Punishment: The Prison Business* (1973), and *The American Way of Birth* (1992). *Poison Penmanship* (1979) collects articles from *The Atlantic Monthly*, *Harper's*, and other magazines. *A Fine Old Conflict* (1977) is the second volume of Mitford's autobiography. Her biography of a Victorian lighthouse keeper's daughter, *Grace Had an English Heart* (1989), examines how the media transform ordinary people into celebrities. Mitford died at her home in Oakland, California, in 1996.

Behind the Formaldehyde Curtain

The most famous (or infamous) thing Jessica Mitford wrote is *The American Way of Death*, a critique of the funeral industry. In this selection from the book, Mitford analyzes the twin processes of embalming and restoring a corpse, the practices she finds most objectionable. You may need a stable stomach to enjoy the selection, but you'll find it a clear, painstaking process analysis, written with masterly style and outrageous wit. (For those who want to know, Mitford herself was cremated after her death.)

The drama begins to unfold with the arrival of the corpse at the mortuary.   1

Alas, poor Yorick! How surprised he would be to see how his counterpart   2 of today is whisked off to a funeral parlor and is in short order sprayed, sliced, pierced, pickled, trussed, trimmed, creamed, waxed, painted, rouged, and neatly dressed—transformed from a common corpse into a Beautiful Memory Picture. This process is known in the trade as embalming and restorative art, and is so universally employed in the United States and Canada that the funeral director does it routinely, without consulting corpse or kin. He regards as eccentric those few who are hardy enough to suggest that it might be dispensed with. Yet no law requires embalming, no religious doctrine commends it, nor is it dictated by considerations of health, sanitation, or even of personal daintiness.

In no part of the world but in Northern America is it widely used. The purpose of embalming is to make the corpse presentable for viewing in a suitably costly container; and here too the funeral director routinely, without first consulting the family, prepares the body for public display.

Is all this legal? The processes to which a dead body may be subjected are 3
after all to some extent circumscribed by law. In most states, for instance, the signature of next of kin must be obtained before an autopsy may be performed, before the deceased may be cremated, before the body may be turned over to a medical school for research purposes; or such provision must be made in the decedent's will. In the case of embalming, no such permission is required nor is it ever sought.[1] A textbook, *The Principles and Practices of Embalming*, comments on this: "There is some question regarding the legality of much that is done within the preparation room." The author points out that it would be most unusual for a responsible member of a bereaved family to instruct the mortician, in so many words, to "embalm" the body of a deceased relative. The very term *embalming* is so seldom used that the mortician must rely upon custom in the matter. The author concludes that unless the family specifies otherwise, the act of entrusting the body to the care of a funeral establishment carries with it an implied permission to go ahead and embalm.

Embalming is indeed a most extraordinary procedure, and one must won- 4
der at the docility of Americans who each year pay hundreds of millions of dollars for its perpetuation, blissfully ignorant of what it is all about, what is done, how it is done. Not one in ten thousand has any idea of what actually takes place. Books on the subject are extremely hard to come by. They are not to be found in most libraries or bookshops.

In an era when huge television audiences watch surgical operations 5
in the comfort of their living rooms, when, thanks to the animated cartoon, the geography of the digestive system has become familiar territory even to the nursery school set, in a land where the satisfaction of curiosity about almost all matters is a national pastime, the secrecy surrounding embalming can, surely, hardly be attributed to the inherent gruesomeness of the subject. Custom in this regard has within this century suffered a complete reversal.

---

[1] Partly because of Mitford's attack, the Federal Trade Commission now requires the funeral industry to provide families with itemized price lists, including the price of embalming, to state that embalming is not required, and to obtain the family's consent to embalming before charging for it. Shortly before her death, however, Mitford observed that the FTC had "watered down" the regulations and "routinely ignored" consumer complaints about the funeral industry. —EDS.

In the early days of American embalming, when it was performed in the home of the deceased, it was almost mandatory for some relative to stay by the embalmer's side and witness the procedure. Today, family members who might wish to be in attendance would certainly be dissuaded by the funeral director. All others, except apprentices, are excluded by law from the preparation room.

A close look at what does actually take place may explain in large measure 6 the undertaker's intractable reticence concerning a procedure that has become his major *raison d'être*. Is it possible he fears that public information about embalming might lead patrons to wonder if they really want this service? If the funeral men are loath to discuss the subject outside the trade, the reader may, understandably, be equally loath to go on reading at this point. For those who have the stomach for it, let us part the formaldehyde curtain. . . .

The body is first laid out in the undertaker's morgue — or rather, 7 Mr. Jones is reposing in the preparation room — to be readied to bid the world farewell.

The preparation room in any of the better funeral establishments has the 8 tiled and sterile look of a surgery, and indeed the embalmer–restorative artist who does his chores there is beginning to adopt the term *dermasurgeon* (appropriately corrupted by some mortician-writers as "demi-surgeon") to describe his calling. His equipment, consisting of scalpels, scissors, augers, forceps, clamps, needles, pumps, tubes, bowls, and basins, is crudely imitative of the surgeon's, as is his technique, acquired in a nine- or twelve-month post-high-school course in an embalming school. He is supplied by an advanced chemical industry with a bewildering array of fluids, sprays, pastes, oils, powders, creams, to fix or soften tissue, shrink or distend it as needed, dry it here, restore the moisture there. There are cosmetics, waxes, and paints to fill and cover features, even plaster of Paris to replace entire limbs. There are ingenious aids to prop and stabilize the cadaver: a Vari-Pose Head Rest, the Edwards Arm and Hand Positioner, the Repose Block (to support the shoulders during the embalming), and the Throop Foot Positioner, which resembles an old-fashioned stocks.

Mr. John H. Eckels, president of the Eckels College of Mortuary Science, 9 thus describes the first part of the embalming procedure: "In the hands of a skilled practitioner, this work may be done in a comparatively short time and without mutilating the body other than by slight incision — so slight that it scarcely would cause serious inconvenience if made upon a living person. It is necessary to remove the blood, and doing this not only helps in the disinfecting, but removes the principal cause of disfigurements due to discoloration."

Another textbook discusses the all-important time element: "The 10
earlier this is done, the better, for every hour that elapses between death and
embalming will add to the problems and complications encountered. . . ." Just
how soon should one get going on the embalming? The author tells us, "On
the basis of such scanty information made available to this profession through
its rudimentary and haphazard system of technical research, we must conclude that the best results are to be obtained if the subject is embalmed before
life is completely extinct—that is, before cellular death has occurred. In the
average case, this would mean within an hour after somatic death." For those
who feel that there is something a little rudimentary, not to say haphazard,
about this advice, a comforting thought is offered by another writer. Speaking
of fears entertained in early days of premature burial, he points out, "One of
the effects of embalming by chemical injection, however, has been to dispel
fears of live burial." How true; once the blood is removed, chances of live
burial are indeed remote.

To return to Mr. Jones, the blood is drained out through the veins and 11
replaced by embalming fluid pumped in through the arteries. As noted in
The Principles and Practices of Embalming, "every operator has a favorite injection and drainage point—a fact which becomes a handicap only if he fails
or refuses to forsake his favorites when conditions demand it." Typical favorites are the carotid artery, femoral artery, jugular vein, subclavian vein. There
are various choices of embalming fluid. If Flextone is used, it will produce
a "mild, flexible rigidity. The skin retains a velvety softness, the tissues are
rubbery and pliable. Ideal for women and children." It may be blended with
B. and G. Products Company's Lyf-Lyk tint, which is guaranteed to reproduce
"nature's own skin texture . . . the velvety appearance of living tissue." Sun-
tone comes in three separate tints: Suntan; Special Cosmetic Tint, a pink
shade "especially indicated for female subjects"; and Regular Cosmetic Tint,
moderately pink.

About three to six gallons of a dyed and perfumed solution of formalde- 12
hyde, glycerin, borax, phenol, alcohol, and water is soon circulating through
Mr. Jones, whose mouth has been sewn together with a "needle directed
upward between the upper lip and gum and brought out through the left nos-
tril," with the corners raised slightly "for a more pleasant expression." If he
should be bucktoothed, his teeth are cleaned with Bon Ami and coated with
colorless nail polish. His eyes, meanwhile, are closed with flesh-tinted eye
caps and eye cement.

The next step is to have at Mr. Jones with a thing called a trocar. This is a 13
long, hollow needle attached to a tube. It is jabbed into the abdomen, poked
around the entrails and chest cavity, the contents of which are pumped out

and replaced with "cavity fluid." This done, and the hole in the abdomen sewn up, Mr. Jones's face is heavily creamed (to protect the skin from burns which may be caused by leakage of the chemicals), and he is covered with a sheet and left unmolested for a while. But not for long—there is more, much more, in store for him. He has been embalmed, but not yet restored, and the best time to start the restorative work is eight to ten hours after embalming, when the tissues have become firm and dry.

The object of all this attention to the corpse, it must be remembered, 14 is to make it presentable for viewing in an attitude of healthy repose. "Our customs require the presentation of our dead in the semblance of normality . . . unmarred by the ravages of illness, disease, or mutilation," says Mr. J. Sheridan Mayer in his *Restorative Art.* This is rather a large order since few people die in the full bloom of health, unravaged by illness and unmarked by some disfigurement. The funeral industry is equal to the challenge: "In some cases the gruesome appearance of a mutilated or disease-ridden subject may be quite discouraging. The task of restoration may seem impossible and shake the confidence of the embalmer. This is the time for intestinal fortitude and determination. Once the formative work is begun and affected tissues are cleaned or removed, all doubts of success vanish. It is surprising and gratifying to discover the results which may be obtained."

The embalmer, having allowed an appropriate interval to elapse, returns 15 to the attack, but now he brings into play the skill and equipment of sculptor and cosmetician. Is a hand missing? Casting one in plaster of Paris is a simple matter. "For replacement purposes, only a cast of the back of the hand is necessary; this is within the ability of the average operator and is quite adequate." If a lip or two, a nose, or an ear should be missing, the embalmer has at hand a variety of restorative waxes with which to model replacements. Pores and skin texture are simulated by stippling with a little brush, and over this cosmetics are laid on. Head off? Decapitation cases are rather routinely handled. Ragged edges are trimmed, and head joined to torso with a series of splints, wires, and sutures. It is a good idea to have a little something at the neck—a scarf or a high collar—when time for viewing comes. Swollen mouth? Cut out tissue as needed from inside the lips. If too much is removed, the surface contour can easily be restored by padding with cotton. Swollen necks and cheeks are reduced by removing tissue through vertical incisions made down each side of the neck. "When the deceased is casketed, the pillow will hide the suture incisions . . . as an extra precaution against leakage, the suture may be painted with liquid sealer."

The opposite condition is more likely to present itself—that of emacia- 16 tion. His hypodermic syringe now loaded with massage cream, the embalmer seeks out and fills the hollowed and sunken areas by injection. In this proce-dure the backs of the hands and fingers and the under-chin area should not be neglected.

Positioning the lips is a problem that recurrently challenges the inge- 17 nuity of the embalmer. Closed too tightly, they tend to give a stern, even disapproving expression. Ideally, embalmers feel, the lips should give the impression of being ever so slightly parted, the upper lip protruding slightly for a more youthful appearance. This takes some engineering, however, as the lips tend to drift apart. Lip drift can sometimes be remedied by pushing one or two straight pins through the inner margin of the lower lip and then inserting them between the two front upper teeth. If Mr. Jones happens to have no teeth, the pins can just as easily be anchored in his Armstrong Face Former and Denture Replacer. Another method to maintain lip closure is to dislocate the lower jaw, which is then held in its new position by a wire run through holes which have been drilled through the upper and lower jaws at the mid-line. As the French are fond of saying, *il faut souffrir pour être belle.*[2]

If Mr. Jones has died of jaundice, the embalming fluid will very likely 18 turn him green. Does this deter the embalmer? Not if he has intestinal for-titude. Masking pastes and cosmetics are heavily laid on, burial garments and casket interiors are color-correlated with particular care, and Jones is displayed beneath rose-colored lights. Friends will say "How *well* he looks." Death by carbon monoxide, on the other hand, can be rather a good thing from the embalmer's viewpoint: "One advantage is the fact that this type of discoloration is an exaggerated form of a natural pink coloration." This is nice because the healthy glow is already present and needs but little attention.

The patching and filling completed, Mr. Jones is now shaved, washed, 19 and dressed. Cream-based cosmetic, available in pink, flesh, suntan, bru-nette, and blond, is applied to his hands and face, his hair is shampooed and combed (and, in the case of Mrs. Jones, set), his hands manicured. For the horny-handed son of toil special care must be taken; cream should be applied to remove ingrained grime, and the nails cleaned. "If he were not in the habit of having them manicured in life, trimming and shaping is advised for better appearance—never questioned by kin."

Jones is now ready for casketing (this is the present participle of the verb 20 "to casket"). In this operation his right shoulder should be depressed slightly

---

[2] You have to suffer to be beautiful. —EDS.

"to turn the body a bit to the right and soften the appearance of lying flat on the back." Positioning the hands is a matter of importance, and special rubber positioning blocks may be used. The hands should be cupped slightly for a more lifelike, relaxed appearance. Proper placement of the body requires a delicate sense of balance. It should lie as high as possible in the casket, yet not so high that the lid, when lowered, will hit the nose. On the other hand, we are cautioned, placing the body too low "creates the impression that the body is in a box."

Jones is next wheeled into the appointed slumber room where a few last touches may be added—his favorite pipe placed in his hand or, if he was a great reader, a book propped into position. (In the case of little Master Jones a Teddy bear may be clutched.) Here he will hold open house for a few days, visiting hours 10 a.m. to 9 p.m.   21

All now being in readiness, the funeral director calls a staff conference to make sure that each assistant knows his precise duties. Mr. Wilber Kriege writes: "This makes your staff feel that they are a part of the team, with a definite assignment that must be properly carried out if the whole plan is to succeed. You never heard of a football coach who failed to talk to his entire team before they go on the field. They have drilled on the plays they are to execute for hours and days, and yet the successful coach knows the importance of making even the benchwarming third-string substitute feel that he is important if the game is to be won." The winning of *this* game is predicated upon glass-smooth handling of the logistics. The funeral director has notified the pallbearers whose names were furnished by the family, has arranged for the presence of clergyman, organist, and soloist, has provided transportation for everybody, has organized and listed the flowers sent by friends. In *Psychology of Funeral Service* Mr. Edward A. Martin points out, "He may not always do as much as the family thinks he is doing, but it is his helpful guidance that they appreciate in knowing they are proceeding as they should. . . . The important thing is how well his services can be used to make the family believe they are giving unlimited expression to their own sentiment."   22

The religious service may be held in a church or in the chapel of the funeral home; the funeral director vastly prefers the latter arrangement, for not only is it more convenient for him but it affords him the opportunity to show off his beautiful facilities to the gathered mourners. After the clergyman has had his say, the mourners queue up to file past the casket for a last look at the deceased. The family is *never* asked whether they want an open-casket ceremony; in the absence of their instruction to the contrary, this is taken for granted. Consequently well over ninety percent of all American funerals feature the open casket—a custom unknown in other parts of the world.   23

Foreigners are astonished by it. An English woman living in San Francisco described her reaction in a letter to the writer:

> I myself have attended only one funeral here — that of an elderly fellow worker of mine. After the service I could not understand why everyone was walking towards the coffin (sorry, I mean casket), but thought I had better follow the crowd. It shook me rigid to get there and find the casket open and poor old Oscar lying there in his brown tweed suit, wearing a sun-tan makeup and just the wrong shade of lipstick. If I had not been extremely fond of the old boy, I have a horrible feeling that I might have giggled. Then and there I decided that I could never face another American funeral — even dead.

The casket (which has been resting throughout the service on a   24
Classic Beauty Ultra Metal Casket Bier) is now transferred by a hydraulically operated device called Porto-Lift to a balloon-tired, Glide Easy casket carriage which will wheel it to yet another conveyance, the Cadillac Funeral Coach. This may be lavender, cream, light green — anything but black. Interiors, of course, are color-correlated, "for the man who cannot stop short of perfection."

At graveside, the casket is lowered into the earth. This office, once   25
the prerogative of friends of the deceased, is now performed by a patented mechanical lowering device. A "Lifetime Green" artificial grass mat is at the ready to conceal the sere earth, and overhead, to conceal the sky, is a portable Steril Chapel Tent ("resists the intense heat and humidity of summer and the terrific storms of winter . . . available in Silver Gray, Rose, or Evergreen"). Now is the time for the ritual scattering of earth over the coffin, as the solemn words "earth to earth, ashes to ashes, dust to dust" are pronounced by the officiating cleric. This can today be accomplished "with a mere flick of the wrist with the Gordon Leak-Proof Earth Dispenser. No grasping of a handful of dirt, no soiled fingers. Simple, dignified, beautiful, reverent! The modern way!" The Gordon Earth Dispenser (at $5) is of nickel-plated brass construction. It is not only "attractive to the eye and long wearing"; it is also "one of the 'tools' for building better public relations" if presented as "an appropriate noncommercial gift" to the clergyman. It is shaped something like a saltshaker.

Untouched by human hand, the coffin and the earth are now united.   26

It is in the function of directing the participants through this maze of   27
gadgetry that the funeral director has assigned to himself his relatively new role of "grief therapist." He has relieved the family of every detail, he has revamped the corpse to look like a living doll, he has arranged for it to nap for a few days in a slumber room, he has put on a well-oiled performance in which the concept of *death* has played no part whatsoever — unless it was

inconsiderately mentioned by the clergyman who conducted the religious service. He has done everything in his power to make the funeral a real pleasure for everybody concerned. He and his team have given their all to score an upset victory over death.

Journal Writing

Presumably, morticians embalm and restore corpses, and survivors support the work, because the practices are thought to ease the shock of death. Now that you know what goes on behind the scenes, how do you feel about a loved one's undergoing these procedures?

Questions on Meaning

1. What was your emotional response to this essay? Can you analyze your feelings?

2. To what does Mitford attribute the secrecy surrounding the embalming process?

3. What, according to Mitford, is the mortician's intent? What common obstacles to fulfilling it must be surmounted?

4. What do you understand from Mitford's remark in paragraph 10, on dispelling fears of live burial: "How true; once the blood is removed, chances of live burial are indeed remote"?

5. Do you find any implied PURPOSE in this essay? Does Mitford seem primarily out to rake muck, or does she offer any positive suggestions to Americans?

Questions on Writing Strategy

1. What is Mitford's TONE? In her opening two paragraphs, exactly what shows her attitude toward her subject?

2. Why do you think Mitford goes into so much grisly detail in analyzing the processes of embalming and restoration? How does the detail serve her purpose?

3. What is the EFFECT of calling the body Mr. Jones?

4. Paragraph by paragraph, what TRANSITIONS does the author employ?

5. To whom does Mitford address her process analysis? How do you know she isn't writing for an AUDIENCE of professional morticians?

6. Choose one of the quotations from the journals and textbooks of professionals and explain how it serves the author's general purpose.

7. Why do you think Mitford often uses the PASSIVE VOICE to describe the actions of embalmers—for instance, "the blood is drained," "If Flextone is used," and "It may be blended" in paragraph 11? Are the verbs in passive voice effective or ineffective? Why?

8. **OTHER METHODS**   In paragraph 8, Mitford uses CLASSIFICATION in listing the embalmer's equipment and supplies. What groups does she identify, and why does she bother sorting the items at all?

Questions on Language

1. Explain the ALLUSION to Yorick in paragraph 2.

2. What IRONY do you find in this statement in paragraph 7: "The body is first laid out in the undertaker's morgue—or rather, Mr. Jones is reposing in the preparation room"? Pick out any other words or phrases in the essay that seem ironic. Comment especially on those you find in the essay's last two sentences.

3. Why is it useful to Mitford's purpose that she cites the brand names of morticians' equipment and supplies (the Edwards Arm and Hand Positioner, Lyf-Lyk tint)? List all the brand names in the essay that are memorable.

4. Define the following words or terms: counterpart (par. 2); circumscribed, decedent, bereaved (3); docility, perpetuation (4); inherent (5); intractable, reticence, *raison d'être*, formaldehyde (6); "derma-" (in *dermasurgeon*), augers, forceps, distend, stocks (8); somatic (10); carotid artery, femoral artery, jugular vein, subclavian vein, pliable (11); glycerin, borax, phenol (12); trocar, entrails (13); stippling, sutures (15); emaciation (16); jaundice (18); predicated (22); queue (23); hydraulically (24); sere, cleric (25).

Suggestions for Writing

1. **FROM JOURNAL TO ESSAY**   Drawing on your personal response to Mitford's essay in your journal (p. 297), write a brief essay that ARGUES either for or against embalming and restoration. Consider the purposes served by these practices, both for the mortician and for the dead person's relatives and friends, as well as their costs and effects.

2. ANALYZE some other process whose operations may not be familiar to everyone. (Have you ever held a job, or helped out in a family business, that has taken you behind the scenes? How is fast food prepared? How are cars serviced? How is a baby sat? How is a house constructed?) Detail it step by step, including transitions to clarify the steps.

3. **CRITICAL WRITING**   In attacking the funeral industry, Mitford also, implicitly, attacks the people who pay for and comply with the industry's attitudes and practices. What ASSUMPTIONS does Mitford seem to make about how we ought to deal with death and the dead? (Consider, for instance, her statements about the "docility of Americans . . . , blissfully ignorant" [par. 4] and the funeral director's making "the funeral a real pleasure for everybody concerned" [27].) Write an essay in which you interpret Mitford's assumptions and agree or disagree with them, based on your own reading and experience. If you like, defend the ritual of the funeral, or the mortician's profession, against Mitford's attack.

4. **CONNECTIONS** In "Impatiently Waiting for the Horror of Death" (p. 133), Scaachi Koul also comments on fears of death, lamenting her father's obsession with his own mortality and using a dark sense of humor not unlike Mitford's. Taken together, what do Mitford's and Koul's essays say about taboos of dying in North America? Write an essay either defending or criticizing some traditional ritual of death, whether one's own or another's.

Jessica Mitford on Writing

"Choice of subject is of cardinal importance," declared Jessica Mitford in *Poison Penmanship*. "One does by far one's best work when besotted by and absorbed in the matter at hand." After *The American Way of Death* was published, Mitford received hundreds of letters suggesting alleged rackets that ought to be exposed, and to her surprise, an overwhelming majority of these letters complained about defective and overpriced hearing aids. But Mitford never wrote a book blasting the hearing aid industry. "Somehow, although there may well be need for such an exposé, I could not warm up to hearing aids as a subject for the kind of thorough, intensive, long-range research that would be needed to do an effective job." She once taught a course at Yale on muckraking, with each student choosing a subject to investigate. "Those who tackled hot issues on campus, such as violations of academic freedom or failure to implement affirmative-action hiring policies, turned in some excellent work; but the lad who decided to investigate 'waste in the Yale dining halls' was predictably unable to make much of this trivial topic."

The hardest problem Mitford faced in writing *The American Way of Death*, she recalled, was doing her factual, step-by-step account of the embalming process. She felt "determined to describe it in all its revolting details, but how to make this subject palatable to the reader?" Her solution was to cast the whole process analysis in the official JARGON of the mortuary industry, drawing on lists of taboo words and their EUPHEMISMS (or acceptable synonyms), as published in the trade journal *Casket & Sunnyside*: "Mr., Mrs., Miss Blank, not corpse or body; preparation room, not morgue; reposing room, not laying-out room. . . ." The story of Mr. Jones thus took shape, and Mitford's use of jargon, she found, added macabre humor to the proceedings.

The Bedford Reader on Writing

We aren't sure that the topic of "waste in the Yale dining halls" is necessarily trivial, but obviously not everyone would burn to write about it. How do you find a topic worth investigating? Something that will engage you and keep you interested "for the kind of thorough, intensive, long-range research that would be needed to do an effective job"? See our tips in Chapter 2 ("Subject," p. 28) and the Appendix ("Conducting Research," pp. 648–652).

ADDITIONAL WRITING TOPICS

Process Analysis

1. Write a *directive* process analysis (a "how-to" essay) in which, drawing on your own knowledge, you instruct someone in doing or making something. You might choose to take a serious approach or a light TONE. Either way, divide the process into steps, and be sure to detail each step thoroughly. Here are some possible subjects (any of which may be modified or narrowed):

   How to protect one's privacy online
   How to enlist people's confidence
   How to teach a person to ski
   How to book a ride through *Uber* or *Lyft*
   How to compose a photograph
   How to judge a dog show
   How to organize your own band
   How to eat an artichoke
   How to shear a sheep
   How to build (or fly) a kite
   How to start weight training
   How to aid a person who is choking
   How to kick a habit
   How to win at poker
   How to make an effective protest or complaint

   Or, if you don't like any of those topics, what else do you know that others might care to learn from you?

2. Working in chronological order, write a careful *informative* (explanatory, not "how-to") analysis of any one of the following processes. Make use of DESCRIPTION where necessary, and be sure to include TRANSITIONS. If one of these topics gives you a better idea for a paper, go with your own subject.

   How a student is processed during orientation or registration
   How the student newspaper gets published
   How a particular Web site generates revenue
   How employers find and screen job applicants
   How a Bluetooth speaker or an MP3 player works
   How fracking extracts natural gas from shale
   How a professional umpire (or any other professional) does the job
   How an air conditioner (or other household appliance) works
   How birds teach their young (or some other process in the natural world: how sharks feed, how a snake swallows an egg, how tsunamis form, how the human liver works)
   How police control crowds
   How people make up their minds when shopping for cars (or clothes)

10

DIVISION OR ANALYSIS

Slicing into Parts

◀ **Division or analysis in a cartoon**

The cartoonist Roz Chast is well known for witty and perceptive comments on the everyday, made through words and simple, almost childlike drawings. Dividing or analyzing, this cartoon identifies the elements of a boy's sandwich to discover what they can tell about the values and politics of the parent who made the sandwich. The title, "Deconstructing Lunch," refers to a type of analysis that focuses on the multiple meanings of a subject and especially its internal contradictions. Summarize what the sandwich reveals about the boy's parent. What contradictions do you spot in his or her values or politics? What might Chast be saying more generally about food choices?

THE METHOD

A chemist working for a soft-drink company is asked to improve on a competitor's product, Hydra Sports Water. To do the job, the chemist first has to figure out what's in the drink. She smells the stuff and tastes it. Then she tests a sample chemically to discover the actual ingredients: water, corn syrup, sodium citrate, potassium chloride, coloring. Methodically, the chemist has performed DIVISION or ANALYSIS: She has separated the beverage into its components. Hydra Sports Water stands revealed, understood, and ready to be bettered.

Division or analysis (the terms are interchangeable) is a key skill in learning and in life. It is an instrument allowing you to slice a large and complicated subject into smaller parts that you can grasp and connect to one another. In fact, it is so fundamental that it underlies every other method of development discussed in this book — for instance, it helps you identify features for DESCRIPTION, spot similarities for COMPARISON AND CONTRAST, or sort out the steps for a PROCESS ANALYSIS (as our chemist did in the previous chapter). With analysis you can comprehend — and communicate — the structure of things. And when it works, you find in the parts an idea or conclusion about the subject that makes it clearer, truer, more comprehensive, or more vivid than it was before you started.

Kinds of Division or Analysis

Although division or analysis always works the same way — separating a whole, singular subject into its elements — the method can be more or less difficult depending on how unfamiliar, complex, or abstract the subject is. Obviously, it's going to be easier to analyze a chicken (wings, legs, thighs, . . .) than a speech by John F. Kennedy (this image, that allusion, . . .), and easier to analyze the structure of a small business than that of a multinational conglomerate.

There are always multiple ways to divide or analyze a subject. One historian, for instance, might study an era by looking at its elections, protest movements, wars, and so forth — following its political components — while another might examine the daily experiences of the people who lived in that period — explaining events in their social context. In other words, the outcome of an analysis depends on the rule or *principle* used to conduct it. This fact accounts for some of the differences among academic disciplines: A psychologist may look at the individual person primarily as a bundle of drives and needs, whereas a sociologist may emphasize the individual's roles in society. Even within a discipline, different factions analyze differently, using different principles of division or analysis. Some psychologists are interested mainly in perception, others mainly in behavior; some focus mainly on emotional development, others mainly on brain chemistry.

Analysis and Critical Thinking

Analysis plays a fundamental role in CRITICAL THINKING, READING, AND WRITING, topics discussed in Part One of this book. In fact, *analysis* and *criticism* are deeply related: The first comes from a Greek word meaning "to undo"; the second from a Greek word meaning "to separate."

Critical thinking, reading, and writing go beneath the surface of the object, word, image, or whatever the subject is. When you work critically, you divide the subject into its elements, INFER the buried meanings and ASSUMPTIONS that define its essence, and SYNTHESIZE the parts into a new whole that is now informed by your perspective. Say a campaign brochure quotes a candidate for election to the city council as being in favor of "reasonable government expenditures on reasonable highway projects." The candidate will support new roads, right? Wrong. As a critical reader of the brochure, you quickly sense something fishy in the use (twice) of *reasonable*. As an informed reader, you might know (or find out) that the candidate has consistently opposed new roads, so the chances of her finding a highway project "reasonable" are slim. At the same time, her stand has been unpopular, so of course she wants to seem "reasonable" on the issue. Read critically, then, a campaign statement that seems to offer mild support for highways is actually a slippery evasion of any such commitment.

Analysis (a convenient term for the overlapping operations of analysis, inference, and synthesis) is very useful for exposing such evasiveness, but that isn't its only function. You've already done quite a bit of analytical thinking as you critically read the selections in this book. The method will also help you understand a sculpture, perceive the importance of a case study in sociology, or form a response to an environmental impact report. And the method can be invaluable for straight thinking about popular culture, from TV to toys.

THE PROCESS

Subject and Purpose

Keep an eye out for writing assignments requiring division or analysis — in college and work, they won't be hard to find. They will probably include the word *analyze* or a word implying analysis, such as *evaluate, examine, explore, interpret, discuss,* or *criticize.* Any time you spot such a term, you know your job is to separate the subject into its elements, to infer their meanings, to explore the relations among them, and to draw a conclusion about the subject.

Almost any coherent entity—object, person, place, concept—is a fit subject for analysis *if* the analysis will add to the subject's meaning or significance. Little is deadlier than the rote analytical exercise that leaves the parts neatly dissected and the subject comatose on the page. As a writer, you have to animate the subject, and that means finding your interest. What about your subject seems curious? What's appealing? or mysterious? or awful? And what will be your PURPOSE in writing about the subject: Do you simply want to explain it, or do you want to argue for or against it?

Such questions can help you find the principle or framework you will use to divide the subject into parts. Say you've got an assignment to write about a sculpture in a nearby park. Why do you like the sculpture, or why don't you? What elements of its creation and physical form make it art? What is the point of such public art? What does this sculpture do for this park, or what does the park do for the sculpture? Any of these questions could suggest a slant on the subject, a framework for analysis, and a purpose for writing, getting your analysis moving.

Principle of Analysis and Thesis

Finding your principle of analysis will lead you to your essay's THESIS as well—the main point you want to make about your subject. Expressed in a THESIS STATEMENT, this idea will help keep you focused and help your readers see your subject as a whole rather than as a bundle of parts. Here are thesis statements from two of this chapter's selections:

> The sports fan is an example of someone engaged in a group membership, for whom association and affiliation matter so greatly you could say it gives him or her a purpose in life.
> — Paul Theroux, "Football Matters"

> The pursuit of happiness has always seemed to me a somewhat heavy American burden, but in Manhattan it is conceived as a peculiar form of duty.
> — Zadie Smith, "Find Your Beach"

Readers will have an easier time following your analysis—and will more likely appreciate it—if they have a hook on which to hang the details. Your thesis statement can be that hook if you use it to establish your framework, your principle of analysis. A well-focused thesis statement can help you as well, because it gives you a yardstick to judge how complete, consistent, and supportive your analysis is. Don't be discouraged, though, if your thesis statement doesn't come to you until *after* you've written a first draft and had a

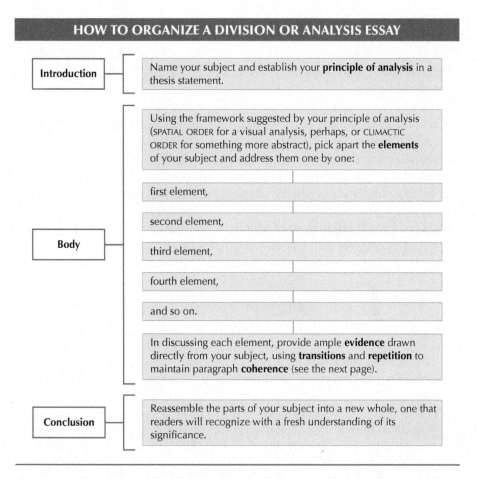

HOW TO ORGANIZE A DIVISION OR ANALYSIS ESSAY

Introduction — Name your subject and establish your **principle of analysis** in a thesis statement.

Body — Using the framework suggested by your principle of analysis (SPATIAL ORDER for a visual analysis, perhaps, or CLIMACTIC ORDER for something more abstract), pick apart the **elements** of your subject and address them one by one:

first element,

second element,

third element,

fourth element,

and so on.

In discussing each element, provide ample **evidence** drawn directly from your subject, using **transitions** and **repetition** to maintain paragraph **coherence** (see the next page).

Conclusion — Reassemble the parts of your subject into a new whole, one that readers will recognize with a fresh understanding of its significance.

chance to discover your interest. Writing about your subject may be the best way for you to find its meaning and significance.

Evidence

Making a valid analysis is chiefly a matter of giving your subject thought, but for the result to seem useful and convincing to your readers, it will have to refer to the real world. The method, then, requires open eyes and a willingness to provide EVIDENCE. The nature of the evidence will depend entirely on what you are analyzing—physical details for a sculpture, quotations for a speech, financial data for a business review, statistics for a psychology case study, and so forth. The idea is to supply enough evidence to justify and support your particular slant on the subject.

In developing an essay by analysis, having an outline at your elbow can be a help. You don't want to overlook any parts or elements that should be included in your framework. You needn't mention every feature in your final draft or give them all equal treatment, but any omissions or variations should be conscious. And you want to use your framework consistently, not switching carelessly (and confusingly) from, say, the form of the sculpture to the cost of public art.

A final caution: It's possible to get carried away with one's own analysis, to become so enamored of the details that the subject itself becomes dim or distorted. You can avoid this danger by keeping the subject literally in front of you as you work (or at least imagining it vividly). It often helps to reassemble your subject at the end of the essay, placing it in a larger context, speculating on its influence, or affirming its significance. By the end of the essay, your subject must be a coherent whole truly represented by your analysis, not twisted, inflated, or obliterated. The reader should be intrigued by your subject, yes, but also able to recognize it on the street.

FOCUS ON PARAGRAPH COHERENCE

Because several elements contribute to the whole of a subject, your analysis will be easier for readers to follow if you frequently clarify which element you are discussing and how it fits with your principle of analysis. Two techniques, especially, can help you guide readers through your analysis: transitions and repetition or restatement.

- **Use TRANSITIONS as signposts to tell readers where you, and they, are headed.** Among other uses, transitions may specify the relations between your points and your principle of analysis (*first, second, another feature*) or may clarify the relations among the points themselves (*even more important, similarly*). Consider how transitions keep readers focused in the following paragraph:

    Many television comedies, even some that boast live audiences, rely on laugh tracks to fill too-quiet moments. To create a laugh track, an editor uses four overlapping elements of a laugh. The first is style, from titter to belly laugh. The second is intensity, the volume, ranging from mild to medium to earsplitting. The third ingredient is duration, the length of the laugh, whether quick, medium, or extended. And finally, there's the number of laughers, from a lone giggler to a roaring throng. When creating a canned laugh, the editor draws from a bank of hundreds of prerecorded laugh files and blends the four ingredients as a maestro weaves a symphony out of brass, woodwinds, percussion, and strings.

- **Use repetition and restatement to link sentences and tie them to your principle of analysis.** In the preceding paragraph, two threads run through the sentences to maintain the focus: *laugh tracks, laugh track, laugh, laughers,* and *canned laugh*; and *editor, editor,* and *maestro*.

> ## CHECKLIST FOR REVIEWING AND REVISING A DIVISION OR ANALYSIS ESSAY
>
> ✔ **Principle of analysis and thesis.** What is your particular slant on your subject, the rule or principle you have used to divide your subject into its elements? Is it specified in a thesis statement?
>
> ✔ **Completeness.** Have you addressed all of the subject's elements as required by your principle of analysis?
>
> ✔ **Consistency.** Have you applied your principle of analysis consistently, viewing your subject from a definite slant?
>
> ✔ **Evidence.** Is the division or analysis well supported with concrete details, quotations, data, or statistics, as appropriate?
>
> ✔ **Significance.** Will readers care about your analysis? Have you told them something about your subject that wasn't obvious on its surface?
>
> ✔ **Truth to subject.** Is the analysis faithful to the subject, not distorted, exaggerated, or deflated?

STUDENT CASE STUDY: A CRITICAL READING

The study of literature — poetry, novels, short fiction, even essays — regularly involves analysis in the form of close readings. Interpretations vary, of course, depending on the reader's chosen principle of analysis. One literary critic, for instance, might divide a poem by looking at its rhymes, meter, imagery, and so forth — following its internal components — while another might examine a short story or novel as an artifact of the author's time and place — connecting its components to its context. In either case, such close readings draw on the text itself for evidence: summarizing, paraphrasing, and quoting the work to give readers the flavor of its content and to support the critic's analysis.

For a composition course using *The Bedford Reader* at Seton Hall University in New Jersey, Rachel O'Connor, a dual major in biology and English, wrote an analysis of Shirley Jackson's short story "The Lottery" (p. 104). She chose to focus on Jackson's use of literary techniques, following MLA style to cite evidence from the story. We excerpt her close reading here to avoid spoilers.

Shirley Jackson's "The Lottery" appears simple on a first   Thesis statement
read, but close analysis reveals a tale packed with dark social
commentary. The story takes place on a glorious summer day, in
a small and seemingly docile rural town where an annual lottery

is about to take place. It is unclear at first what this lottery entails, but since the term typically has positive connotations, the reader does not suspect the morbidity that lies beneath the surface or the horrors unleashed in the last few lines. . . .

What makes "The Lottery" so brilliant are the subtle clues Jackson embeds in the text and the deeper moral themes to which they point. The narrative flows smoothly and is compelling enough to consume readers and distract them from noticing the tactics strategically set in place. For example, the first sentence describes the setting as "clear and sunny, with the fresh warmth of a full-summer day" (104). This line is ironic: What appears to be a pleasant community gathering on a beautiful day turns out to be something much more sinister. . . .

Principle of analysis: literary technique

1. Irony

Another early clue is the description, in the second paragraph, of boys gathering stones in their pockets. Although it is not clear what these stones might be used for, the reader is not inclined to think anything of it—until he or she becomes aware of the story's ending. At the same time, the fact that some boys "made a great pile of stones . . . and guarded it against the raids of the other boys" (105) exposes the inherent distrust and hostility the townspeople have for one another despite the appearance of being a close-knit community. . . .

2. Foreshadowing

The gravity of the situation is further suggested through the description of the men, whose "jokes were quiet" and who "smiled rather than laughed" (105). The townspeople's conspicuous efforts to make conversation and act normal hint to the reader that something may be awry. The children's attitude toward the lottery is especially troubling. They seem to view it as a game although they are aware of the perverse reality, which indicates their desensitization to violence and loss of innocence. . . . Finally, the winner's insistence that the lottery "isn't fair" and "isn't right" (111) underscores the story's latent theme of the evil often lurking in societal norms.

3. Characterization

Jackson, through irony, foreshadowing, and characterization, spins a flawless tale that both entertains and makes readers think. She subtly yet powerfully questions a society that complies with

Reassembly of elements with a comment on significance

abhorrent practices simply because they are traditional. . . . She challenges readers to make their own moral judgments rather than fall victim to the often unjust mentality of the majority in charge, while simultaneously pulling off a surprise ending wild enough to catch the attention of almost anyone.

Work Cited

Jackson, Shirley. "The Lottery." *The Bedford Reader,* edited by
    X. J. Kennedy et al., 14th ed., Bedford/St. Martin's, 2020,
    pp. 104–11.

List of Works Cited with publication information for the text (see pp. 660–670)

PAUL THEROUX

Paul Theroux is a world-renowned travel writer who is equally well known for his novels and short stories. Born in 1941 into a large working-class family in Medford, Massachusetts, he briefly attended the University of Maine and completed a BA in English from the University of Massachusetts Amherst in 1963. That same year he went abroad to serve in the Peace Corps, teaching English in the East African country of Malawi until he was accused of spying and forced to leave. In the years that followed he taught at colleges in Uganda, Singapore, and Virginia while pursuing a career in writing. Theroux published his first novel, *Waldo*, in 1967, and followed it with nearly three dozen more novels, plays, and short story collections; he has also written some two dozen successful accounts of his vast travels around the globe, starting with *The Great Railway Bazaar* (1972), about a months-long journey from Great Britain to Japan. A frequent contributor to magazines as well, Theroux has been honored with a number of awards for his work, including two *Playboy* editorial awards (1971, 1976), the Whitbread Prize for best novel for *Picture Palace* (1978), the Thomas Cook Travel Book Prize for *Riding the Iron Rooster* (1989), and a Patron's Medal from the Royal Geographic Society (2015). He lives in Hawaii and summers on Cape Cod, in Massachusetts.

Football Matters

For *Deep South: Four Seasons on Back Roads* (2015), the intrepid travel writer set his sights on his home country for the first time. Over a span of two and a half years, Theroux drove more than 25,000 miles through the small towns and byways of the American South, seeking to make sense of a region and a culture that are often misunderstood. In this essay, a self-contained passage from the book, he visits Tuscaloosa, Alabama, and discovers a vibrant college town obsessed with its football team.

In the selection following this one, "Find Your Beach," novelist Zadie Smith also uses division or analysis to tease out the importance of sports and leisure in a particular place, in her case the SoHo neighborhood of New York City.

I drove to Tuscaloosa, Alabama, to get my bearings, to go deeper south, 1 into Hale County and Greene County.

Tuscaloosa is a college town — more than half the town is the campus of 2 the University of Alabama, celebrated as having the best football team in the country and the highest-paid coaches. It is the home of the Crimson Tide, the scarlet letter, the enlarged italic of the Alabama A on cars and clothes and often showing as a bold red tattoo.

I arrived on a Friday night, and the next day Tuscaloosa was in the grip of something more intense than a carnival. A riotous hooting tribal rite possessed the whole town, because of the University of Alabama football game that day in a stadium that held more than 100,000 people. I remarked on this and on the fans—everyone in Tuscaloosa was a fan. A man said to me, "This is a drinking town with a football problem," and winked to show he was joshing.

That idle quip has been made of many college towns, but is football a problem in Tuscaloosa? It seemed to me a chronic condition, and perhaps not a problem but a solution. The town is consumed by the sport. It is funded by football, and it prospers. Football is the town's identity, and the game makes its citizens happy—resolves their conflicts, unifies them, helps them forget their pain, gives them membership in a cult of winners—and it makes them colossal, monologuing, and rivalrous bores.

"Football's a religion here," some Tuscaloosans also say, and smile in apology, but they are closer to a complete definition in that cliché than they perhaps realize. Even the most basic of psychological analysis can explain why that neat formula is so fitting. Not any old religion, certainly not the mild, private, prayer-muttering, God-is-love creed that informs decisions and gives us peace. The Crimson Tide football religion is one that is awash in fury, something like Crusader Christianity[1] reared on bloodthirstiness, with its saber charges and its conquests, or like Islam in its most jihadi[2] form, the blazing, red-eyed, uncompromising, and martyring faith; an in-group cohering around the sport to demonize and vanquish an out-group. In Tuscaloosa it is a public passion, a ritualized belief system, a complete persona. It is why in Alabama some men have the A tattooed on their neck, and some women on their shoulder: a public statement, a commitment for life, body modification as proof of loyalty and cultural differentiation, like a Hindu's caste mark or a Maori's tattoo or the facial scarring of a Sudanese Dinka.[3]

Most towns are justifiably proud of their sports teams—a winning team always improves the mood of a place—but the Saturday crowd in Tuscaloosa, the processions of cars flying battle flags, the whooping and the costumes (and every seat in the enormous stadium spoken for) convinced me that this

[1] The Crusades (1095–1291) were a range of wars across Europe and the Middle East in which Christian armies attempted to reclaim holy sites from Muslim occupiers. —Eds.

[2] A *jihad* is a Muslim holy war waged to promote or defend Islam from Western influence. —Eds.

[3] Hinduism is the prominent religion in India, where hereditary social classes are traditionally assigned at birth. The Maori are an indigenous tribe, of Polynesian ancestry, in New Zealand. The Dinka are a pastoral people, comprised of multiple ethnicities, who farm along the Nile in northeast Africa. —Eds.

in-group mattered in a much more complex way than in other places I'd been. Its nearest equivalent in terms of tattoos, finery, and chanting was a traditional ceremony enacted by a defiant people who had once been colonized, asserting their tribal identity.

In Alabama football, fan loyalty bolstered self-esteem, not just of students   7 but of almost the entire state. This group behavior is explained in "social identity theory," an encompassing proposal of the British psychologist Henri Tajfel, who described the sympathies and reactions of persons choosing to attach themselves to a social class or a family or a club—or a football team— and become a member of an in-group. The groups to which people belong are, Tajfel writes, "an important source of pride and self-esteem. Groups give us a sense of social identity: a sense of belonging to the social world."

The sports fan is an example of someone engaged in group membership,   8 for whom association and affiliation matter so greatly you could say it gives him or her a purpose in life. You develop a group membership by identifying yourself with a team and participating in "in-group favoritism." Such membership builds self-confidence and self-worth; you're invested in cheering for the team and raising its status. You're more than a passive member; you're an active booster, helping to make the team bigger and stronger. And it's good for your esteem, too. In Tajfel's view, "In order to increase our self-image we enhance the status of the group to which we belong."

To say that when your team wins you feel you're a champion is a pretty   9 straightforward definition of the appeal of fandom. People often laugh self-consciously when they talk about their loyalty to a team, their pride in its success, but in Alabama, where fandom fervor is multiplied a thousandfold, no one laughs. There's nothing funny about chanting "Roll Tide, roll!"—the devotion is dead serious, and at times (so it seemed to me) defiant, hostile, verging on the pathological.

The power figure on any team is the coach. In Alabama folklore it is   10 Paul Bryant, nicknamed "Bear" because as a youth in Arkansas he reputedly accepted the challenge of wrestling a captive, muzzled bear (and was mauled).

The three biggest funerals in Alabama history define the state's contending   11 loyalties, I was told: George Wallace's, Martin Luther King's, and Bear Bryant's.[4]

As a coach, Bear Bryant was a towering figure, statistically the most success-   12 ful in the history of college football, who guided Alabama for twenty-five years and whose beaky profile and funny checkered snap-brim hat are emblems. His name is emblazoned on Tuscaloosa streets and buildings and on the vast stadium. Charismatic, noted for his heavy drinking and his toughness (he played

[4] George Wallace (1919–98) was governor of Alabama for three terms (1963–67, 1971–79, and 1983–87). The Reverend Martin Luther King, Jr. (1929–68), was a civil rights leader. Paul "Bear" Bryant (1913–83) coached the Crimson Tide from 1958 until his retirement in 1982. —Eds.

on a broken leg in a college game in Tennessee), he was renowned as a motivator. He avoided recruiting black players for years, but in 1971 he brought in his first one, Wilbur Jackson, offering him a football scholarship. Thereafter the team became a career path for black athletes and a rallying point for the races.

Among his achievements, Bryant won six national championships for Alabama. But the present coach, Nick Saban, in just four seasons has won three national championships, and his contract runs until 2018. Saban, who is beloved for his victories and his rapport with players, presently earns $6.9 million a season, the highest-paid college football coach in the nation. 13

It is natural for a nonbeliever to cluck about the money, but college sports is a business—colleges need this national attention as a way of creating a cash flow. Donors, alumni, and booster clubs provide money to augment salaries; ticket sales are a strong source of revenue. And there is the licensed merchandise. Much of the logo paraphernalia is traditional—the numerous styles of caps, T-shirts, banners, and flags. But a great deal of it is culturally Alabama-specific: Crimson Tide trailer hitch covers, valve stem caps, a sexy lady's satin garter with lace picked out in "Roll Tide," baby slippers, garden chairs, "pillow pets," "child's hero capes," wall-sized "man cave flags," Crimson Tide car chargers, dog jerseys, puzzle cubes, games, watches, clothes, luggage, garden gnomes, table lamps, bedding, drinking glasses, gas grill covers, golf gear, car accessories, toothbrushes, and vinyl boat fenders, each carrying the Roll Tide logo or an enlarged and unambiguous A. 14

All this contributes to substantial football-related revenue, which in 2012 was $124 million, and $45 million of that was profit. Added to this is the improved status of the university itself, resulting in increased enrollment, higher teachers' salaries, and an expanded campus. Alabama's eminence as a university of football champions attracts nonresident students: more than half the students are from out of state, paying three times the in-state tuition. 15

The financial return is indisputable. The benefit in self-esteem is harder to gauge, but it is palpable. And perhaps it is predictable—the simple feel-good inevitability of identifying with the team and the elaborate costuming and imagery to go along with that identification—that it amounts to a complete lifestyle. This sort of social behavior has its counterpart in the enclosed in-groups of the world, especially the folk cultures, epitomized by the glorious and assertive "sing-sing" you'd see in the western high-lands of Papua New Guinea: the Goroka Show, the convergence of Asaro Mudmen and jungle-dwelling warriors fitted out with pig tusks and nose bones, with its extravagant finery, headdresses, weapons, beads, feathers, face painting, jitterbugging, spear shaking, mock charges, drumming, and hollering.[5] 16

[5] Papua New Guinea is an island nation in the South Pacific. The Goroka Show is an annual gathering of more than a hundred native tribes for a weekend cultural festival. —Eds.

Reflecting on the Crimson Tide, I ceased to think of it as football at all, 17 except in a superficial way; it seemed much more like another Southern reaction to a feeling of defeat, with some of the half-buried emotion I'd noticed at gun shows. In a state that is so hard-pressed, with one of the highest poverty rates in the nation, with its history of racial conflict, and with so little to boast about yet wishing to matter, it is natural that a winning team—a national champion—would attract people in need of meaning and self-esteem in their lives, and would become the basis of a classic in-group. The Tide was robust proof of social identity theory.

Journal Writing

Do you find the phenomenon of Alabama football mania and fandom, as described by Theroux, to be ridiculous, amusing, exciting, prideful, depressing, obnoxious, reassuring, something else? Why? How do you feel about your own local sports teams, whether your school's or a nearby city's? Compose a one- or two-paragraph answer in your journal.

Questions on Meaning

1. What do you think is Theroux's purpose in this essay? Does he have something specific he wants the reader to take away from his analysis?

2. What are "in-groups," as Theroux explains them? How does belonging to one affect a person's self-esteem?

3. How does Theroux explain the appeal of the University of Alabama's football team? What is his THESIS? Where does he state it?

4. Do you detect a possible double meaning in Theroux's title? What is it? To what movement might the author be ALLUDING?

Questions on Writing Strategy

1. How does Theroux seem to imagine his audience? How reasonable are his assumptions about his readers' backgrounds and knowledge?

2. What principle of analysis does the author use to study the residents of Tuscaloosa? How does Theroux SYNTHESIZE another writer's ideas to find new meaning in his subject?

3. How does Theroux organize his analysis? What elements of the Crimson Tide does he examine, and where?

4. What is the EFFECT of the essay's final paragraph?

5. **OTHER METHODS**   Theroux COMPARES AND CONTRASTS Alabama football with several world religions. What similarities does he find?

Questions on Language

1. What is the TONE of this essay — that is, what is the writer's attitude toward his subject? Is Theroux poking fun at Tuscaloosans for their fandom? Why does he quote residents who describe their home as "a drinking town with a football problem" (par. 3) and who say things like "[f]ootball's a religion here" (5)?

2. Find some examples of formal and informal DICTION in this essay. What is the effect of Theroux's word choices?

3. Consult a dictionary if you need help in defining the following: riotous, tribal, rite (par. 3); chronic, monologuing, rivalrous (4); creed, martyring, cohering, differentiation, caste (5); bolstered (7); fervor, pathological (9); charismatic (12); rapport (13); augment, revenue, paraphernalia (14); indisputable, epitomized (16).

Suggestions for Writing

1. **FROM JOURNAL TO ESSAY**   Write an essay, drawn from your journal entry, in which you spell out and explain your reaction to Theroux's analysis of football fandom in Tuscaloosa. If you find it ridiculous, for instance, what bothers you — the tattoos? the "whooping and the costumes" (par. 6)? the paraphernalia? *Why* are these things ridiculous to you? What do you think this team and its fans say about sports? about American culture? about Southern pride? If you find the essay reassuring, on the other hand, explain what exactly in Theroux's observations cheers you, and why.

2. The risk of serious injuries, especially concussions, has led some to call for an end to football, or at least for new regulations intended to protect players from brain damage. Research the main arguments for and against such regulations. Then write an essay in which you summarize your findings. If your research — or your experience — leads you to form an opinion favoring one side of the issue, present and support that as well.

3. **CRITICAL WRITING**   In defense of the high salaries paid to some football coaches, Theroux notes that "college sports is a business" (par. 14), and a lucrative one at that. How do you respond? What do you think of the astronomical figures offered to college coaches and professional athletes? Are individual contracts worth millions of dollars a year fair or outrageous? And should college athletes be paid? Why, or why not? Write an essay that argues for or against putting significant sums of money into college sports, using specific EXAMPLES to support your claims.

4. **CONNECTIONS**   Zadie Smith, in "Find Your Beach" (p. 319), also examines the identity and self-esteem of members of a particular in-group: in her case, the creative class of Manhattan. In a brief essay, consider how Theroux's discussion of "social identity theory," particularly as it relates to place, might add another layer of meaning to Smith's assessment of her neighbors' pursuit of happiness.

Paul Theroux on Writing

A seasoned writer, Paul Theroux has spent over five decades perfecting his craft. In the introduction to *Figures in a Landscape* (2018), his latest book of travel writing, he lays out a sketch of his process.

The greater part of travel is nuisance and delay, and no reader wants to hear about that. I do my best to be prepared. I seldom solicit names of people to look up. Anxiety and improvisation are helpful to the traveler, who is made watchful and resourceful when constantly reminded that he or she is a stranger. Before I set out, I am a scrutinizer of the most detailed maps I can find, a compulsive reader of guides for the budget traveler. It helps to have money, but time is much more valuable. Apart from a small shortwave radio, I carry no high-tech items — these days a phone, never a camera or computer, nothing fragile or irreplaceable. In South Africa my bag was stolen and I was robbed of almost everything I owned: a good lesson. I had my notes. Who steals notebooks?

The writing, then. I carry a pocket-sized notebook and scribble in it all day. In the evening I transcribe these notes into a larger journal, making an orderly narrative of the day. My average daily entry is about a thousand words, sometimes less, often more. En route, whenever I have a chance I photocopy these pages, say forty or fifty at a time, and mail them home. By the end of a trip I will have filled about seven or eight student notebooks, and these are the basis for the book. Interviewing someone for a profile, especially a potentially litigious celebrity, I keep a tape recorder running while I write the person's answers in a notebook, as a guide to the highlights. Afterward, I transcribe the entire interview myself from the tape, skipping the boring parts. I have never employed a secretary, assistant, or researcher. Though I have written many more novels than travel books. I could never be so specific or certain about my fiction writing method, if indeed I have a fiction writing method.

The Bedford Reader on Writing

Any writer (and traveler) would do well to follow Theroux's lead of carrying around a notebook to jot down records, observations, and ideas throughout the day. During the DISCOVERY period such notes might turn into JOURNAL entries, which could eventually transform into polished writing. Try keeping a notebook on you for a week or two and see what happens. For more on how maintaining a journal can help you discover ideas, see page 31 in Chapter 2.

ZADIE SMITH

Born in London to an English father and a Jamaican mother in 1975, Zadie Smith is a literary star whose sharply contemporary and "drop-dead cool" novels have won her critical acclaim and a devoted following. Her bestselling debut, *White Teeth* (2000), drafted while Smith was an undergraduate student at Cambridge University, won the Whitbread Award for best novel, was the basis of a BBC television miniseries in 2002, and was adapted for the stage by London's Kiln Theater in 2018. Smith's other novels, which tend to look at intersections of race, class, gender, and nationality with a heavy dose of humor, include *On Beauty* (2005), shortlisted for the Man Booker Prize; *NW* (2012), named by *Time* magazine as one of the ten best fiction books of the year; and *Swing Time* (2016), a finalist for the National Book Critics Circle Fiction Award. Smith is also a regular contributor of literary and cultural criticism to the *New Yorker* and *The New York Review of Books*; her essays have been collected in *Changing My Mind* (2009) and *Feel Free* (2018). An elected fellow of the Royal Society of Literature and a tenured professor in New York University's creative writing program, she splits her time between New York City and London.

Find Your Beach

In this essay from *Feel Free*, Smith turns her critical eye to an advertisement painted on a building facing her New York apartment. Like Paul Theroux in the previous essay, Smith finds a source of comfort in a singular aspect of popular culture. "Find Your Beach" first appeared in *The New York Review of Books* in 2014 and was selected for *Best American Essays 2015*.

Across the way from our apartment—on Houston,[1] I guess—there's a new wall ad. The site is forty feet high, twenty feet wide. It changes once or twice a year. Whatever's on that wall is my view: I look at it more than the sky or the new World Trade Center, more than the water towers, the passing cabs. It has a subliminal effect. Last semester it was a spot for high-end vodka, and while I wrangled children into their snowsuits, chock-full of domestic resentment, I'd find myself dreaming of cold Martinis.

---

[1] Houston Street marks the line between the New York City neighborhoods of Greenwich Village and SoHo (so named because it is South of Houston). —EDS.

Douglas Elliman

Before that came an ad so high end I couldn't tell what it was for. There   2
was no text — or none that I could see — and the visual was of a yellow
firebird set upon a background of hellish red. It seemed a gnomic message,
deliberately placed to drive a sleepless woman mad. Once, staring at it with
a newborn in my arms, I saw another mother, in the tower opposite, holding
her baby. It was 4 a.m. We stood there at our respective windows, separated
by a hundred feet of expensive New York air.

The tower I live in is university accommodation; so is the tower opposite.   3
The idea occurred that it was quite likely that the woman at the window also
wrote books for a living, and, like me, was not writing anything right now.
Maybe she was considering anti-depressants. Maybe she was already on them.
It was hard to tell. Certainly she had no way of viewing the ad in question,
not without opening her window, jumping, and turning as she fell. I was her
view. I was the ad for what she already had.

But that was all some time ago. Now the ad says: "Find your beach." The   4
bottle of beer — it's an ad for beer — is very yellow and the background lux-
ury-holiday-blue. It seems to me uniquely well placed, like a piece of commissioned public art in perfect sympathy with its urban site. The tone is pure
Manhattan. Echoes can be found in the personal-growth section of the book-
shop ("Find your happy"), and in exercise classes ("Find your soul"), and in the
therapist's office ("Find your self"). I find it significant that there exists a more
expansive, national version of this ad that runs in magazines, and on television.

In those cases photographic images are used, and the beach is real and seen in full. Sometimes the tag line is expanded, too: "When life gives you limes . . . Find your beach." But the wall I see from my window marks the entrance to Soho, a district that is home to media moguls, entertainment lawyers, every variety of celebrity, some students, as well as a vanishingly small subset of rent-controlled artists and academics.

Collectively we, the people of SoHo, consider ourselves pretty sophisticated consumers of media. You can't put a cheesy ad like that past us. And so the ad has been reduced to its essence — a yellow undulation against a field of blue — and painted directly on to the wall, in a bright Pop Art style. The mad men know that we know the SoHo being referenced here: the SoHo of Roy Lichtenstein[2] and Ivan Karp,[3] the SoHo that came before Foot Locker, Sephora, Prada,[4] frozen yogurt. That SoHo no longer exists, of course, but it's part of the reason we're all here, crowded on this narrow strip of a narrow island. Whoever placed this ad knows us well.

Find your beach. The construction is odd. A faintly threatening mixture of imperative and possessive forms, the transformation of a noun into a state of mind. Perhaps I'm reading too much into it. On the one hand it means, simply, "Go out and discover what makes you happy." Pursue happiness actively, as Americans believe it their right to do. And it's an ad for beer, which makes you happy in the special way of all intoxicants, by reshaping reality around a sensation you alone are having. So, even more precisely, the ad means: "Go have a beer and let it make you happy." Nothing strange there. Except beer used to be sold on the dream of communal fun: have a beer with a buddy, or lots of buddies. People crowded the frame, laughing and smiling. It was a lie about alcohol — as this ad is a lie about alcohol — but it was a different kind of lie, a wide-framed lie, including other people.

Here the focus is narrow, almost obsessive. Everything that is not absolutely necessary to your happiness has been removed from the visual horizon. The dream is not only of happiness, but of happiness conceived in perfect isolation. Find your beach in the middle of the city. Find your beach no matter what else is happening. Do not be distracted from finding your beach. Find your beach even if — as in the case of this wall painting — it is not actually there. Create this beach inside yourself. Carry it with you wherever you go. The pursuit of happiness has always seemed to me a somewhat heavy American burden, but in Manhattan it is conceived as a peculiar form of duty.

___

[2] American artist (1923–97) best known for painting large-scale comic panels. —Eds.

[3] Art dealer (1926–2012) who ran influential galleries in New York. —Eds.

[4] High-end shopping outlets. Foot Locker sells sneakers and athletic wear; Sephora retails makeup and beauty products; Prada specializes in luxury handbags, shoes, and accessories. —Eds.

In an exercise class recently the instructor shouted at me, at all of us: 9
"Don't let your mind set limits that aren't really there." You'll find this attitude all over the island. It is encouraged and reflected in the popular culture,
especially the movies, so many of which, after all, begin their creative lives
here, in Manhattan. According to the movies it's only our own limited brains
that are keeping us from happiness. In the future we will take a pill to make
us limitless (and ideal citizens of Manhattan), or we will, like Scarlett Johansson in *Lucy*,[5] use a hundred percent of our brain's capacity instead of the
mythic ten. In these formulations the world as it is has no real claim on us.
Our happiness, our miseries, our beaches, or our blasted heaths — they are all
within our own power to create, or destroy. On Tina Fey's television show *30
Rock*, Jack Donaghy[6] — the consummate citizen of this new Manhattan — deals
with problems by crushing them with his "mind vise."

The beach is always there: you just have to conceive of it. It follows 10
that those who fail to find their beach are, in the final analysis, mentally
fragile; in Manhattan terms, simply weak. Jack Donaghy's verbal swordplay
with Liz Lemon was a comic rendering of the various things many citizens
of Manhattan have come to regard as fatal weakness: childlessness, obesity,
poverty. To find your beach you have to be ruthless. Manhattan is for the
hard-bodied, the hard-minded, the multitasker, the alpha mamas and papas.
A perfect place for self-empowerment — as long as you're pretty empowered
to begin with. As long as you're one of these people who simply do not allow
anything — not even reality — to impinge upon that clear field of blue.

There is a kind of individualism so stark that it seems to dovetail with 11
an existentialist creed: Manhattan is right at that crossroads. You are pure
potential in Manhattan, limitless, you are making yourself every day. When
I am in England each summer, it's the opposite: all I see are the limits of my
life. The brain that puts a hairbrush in the fridge, the leg that radiates pain
from the hip to the toe, the lovely children who eat all my time, the books
unread and unwritten.

And casting a shadow over it all is what Philip Larkin[7] called "extinction's 12
alp," no longer a stable peak in a distance, finally becoming rising ground. In
England even at the actual beach I cannot find my beach. I look out at the
freezing water, at the families squeezed into ill-fitting wetsuits, huddled behind

---

[5] Johansson (born 1984) is an American actress and singer. *Lucy* is a 2014 science-fiction
thriller about a woman with psychokinetic abilities. — EDS.

[6] *30 Rock* is a comedy set in a television studio in New York's Rockefeller Plaza.
Tina Fey (born 1970) stars as Liz Lemon, the head writer of a sketch show; Jack Donaghy is a
fictional network executive played by Alec Baldwin (born 1958). The show aired from 2006 to
2013. — EDS.

[7] British poet (1922–85) noted for his sense of humor. The phrase Smith cites is from
"The Old Fools" (1973). — EDS.

windbreakers, approaching a day at the beach with the kind of stoicism once conjured for things like the Battle of Britain,[8] and all I can think is what funny, limited creatures we are, subject to every wind and wave, building castles in the sand that will only be knocked down by the generation coming up beneath us.

When I land at JFK,[9] everything changes. For the first few days it is a shock: I have to get used to old New York ladies beside themselves with fury that I have stopped their smooth elevator journey and got in with some children. I have to remember not to pause while walking in the street—or during any fluid-moving city interaction—unless I want to utterly exasperate the person behind me. Each man and woman in this town is in pursuit of his or her beach and God help you if you get in their way. I suppose it should follow that I am happier in pragmatic England than idealist Manhattan, but I can't honestly say that this is so. You don't come to live here unless the delusion of a reality shaped around your own desires isn't a strong aspect of your personality. "A reality shaped around your own desires"—there is something sociopathic in that ambition.

It is also a fair description of what it is to write fiction. And to live in a city where everyone has essentially the same tunnel vision and obsessive focus as a novelist is to disguise your own sociopathy among the herd. Objectively all the same limits are upon me in Manhattan as they are in England. I walk a ten-block radius every day, constrained in all the usual ways by domestic life, reduced to writing about whatever is right in front of my nose. But the fact remains that here I *do* write, the work gets done.

Even if my Manhattan productivity is powered by a sociopathic illusion of my own limitlessness, I'm thankful for it, at least when I'm writing. There's a reason so many writers once lived here, beyond the convenient laundromats and the take-out food, the libraries and cafés. We have always worked off the energy generated by this town, the money-making and tower-building as much as the street art and underground cultures. Now the energy is different: the underground has almost entirely disappeared. (You hope there are still young artists in Washington Heights, in the Barrio, or Stuyvesant Town, but how much longer can they hang on?) A twisted kind of energy radiates instead off the soulcycling[10] mothers and marathon-running octogenarians, the entertainment lawyers glued to their iPhones and the moguls building five "individualized" condo townhouses where once there was a hospital.

It's not a pretty energy, but it still runs what's left of the show. I contribute to it. I ride a stationary bike like the rest of them. And then I despair

13

14

15

16

---

[8] A four-month period in World War II during which the British Royal Air Force defended London against nightly Nazi air strikes. —EDs.

[9] New York City's international airport. —EDs.

[10] Soul Cycle is a chain of athletic clubs specializing in indoor bicycling classes. —EDs.

when Shakespeare and Co.[11] closes in favor of another Foot Locker. There's no way to be in good faith on this island anymore. You have to crush so many things with your "mind vise" just to get through the day. Which seems to me another aspect of the ad outside my window: willful intoxication. Or to put it more snappily: "You don't have to be high to live here, but it helps."

Finally the greatest thing about Manhattan is the worst thing about   17
Manhattan: self-actualization. Here you will be free to stretch yourself to your limit, to find the beach that is yours alone. But sooner or later you will be sitting on that beach wondering what comes next. I can see my own beach ahead now, as the children grow, as the practical limits fade; I see afresh the huge privilege of my position; it reclarifies itself. Under the protection of a university I live on one of the most privileged strips of built-up beach in the world, among people who believe they have no limits and who push me, by their very proximity, into the same useful delusion, now and then.

It is such a good town in which to work and work. You can find your beach   18
here, find it falsely, but convincingly, still thinking of Manhattan as an isle of writers and artists—of downtown underground wildlings and uptown intellectuals—against all evidence to the contrary. Oh, you still see them occasionally here and there, but unless they are under the protection of a university—or have sold that TV show—they are all of them, every single last one of them, in Brooklyn.

Journal Writing

Think of an advertisement that has caught your attention for some reason. Describe the ad in your journal, and consider how and why it affects you.

Questions on Meaning

1. What, exactly, is Smith analyzing in this essay? Is her subject an advertisement, or something else?

2. What is Smith's THESIS? Where, if at all, does she state it succinctly?

3. How does Smith interpret the meaning of the tag line "Find your beach"? In what ways does the beach function as a SYMBOL for her?

4. How would you describe the author's apparent PURPOSE in this essay? What conclusions does Smith reach about the values of Manhattan and its culture?

Questions on Writing Strategy

1. To whom does Smith seem to be writing? Writers, artists, students, business leaders, someone else? What ASSUMPTIONS does she make about her readers?

---

[11] Shakespeare and Co. is an independent bookstore with locations in Manhattan and Philadelphia. —Eds.

2. What would you say is Smith's principle of analysis in this essay? How does she characterize people who choose to live in Manhattan?

3. **OTHER METHODS** Where does Smith use COMPARISON AND CONTRAST? What do these passages contribute to her analysis?

Questions on Language

1. How would you describe Smith's overall TONE? Why is this tone appropriate for her purpose?

2. What does Smith mean when she says that "casting a shadow over it all is what Philip Larkin called 'extinction's alp'" (par. 12)? Try to explain the poet's META-PHOR in your own words.

3. Consult a dictionary if any of the following words are unfamiliar: subliminal (par. 1); firebird, gnomic, respective (2); undulation (6); imperative, possessive, communal (7); conceived (8); mythic, formulations, heaths, consummate (9); rendering, alpha (10); dovetail, existentialist, creed (11); stoicism (12); exasperate, pragmatic, sociopathic (13); radius, octogenarians (15); wildlings (18).

4. "Finally," Smith writes in paragraph 17, "the greatest thing about Manhattan is the worst thing about Manhattan: self-actualization." What does she mean? How do you explain the PARADOX in this statement?

Suggestions for Writing

1. **FROM JOURNAL TO ESSAY** Expanding on your journal entry, write an essay that analyzes one particular advertisement in depth. Break the ad into its elements, considering visuals as well as text, and reassemble the parts into a new whole of your understanding. Make sure your essay has a controlling thesis that draws together all the points of your analysis and asserts why the advertisement has the effect it does.

2. Like Los Angeles, Chicago, and some other American cities, New York is a place with a reputation. What does New York mean to you? Base your answer on first-hand experience if you can, but also on information in the media (TV, books, magazines). In an essay giving specific examples, describe the city as you understand it.

3. Choose a subject that has seen significant change in the past twenty years or so — for example, a specific neighborhood, gender roles, communication technology, fashion, manners, a given sport, ideals of beauty, or attitudes toward a group of people such as gays and lesbians, African Americans, Muslims, or immigrants. Do some research on the topic, and then write an essay that examines the CAUSES and EFFECTS of the change. Support your essay with specific evidence from your experience, observation, and research.

4. **CRITICAL WRITING** Based on this essay, analyze Smith's apparent attitude toward gentrification in urban neighborhoods. How does she characterize changes in the district of SoHo, for instance? Are those changes positive or negative in her estimation? Does she believe that economic equality for artists and academics is possible or even desirable? What does she suggest has been (or will be) the effects of the business world in New York and London? Support your ideas with evidence from the essay.

5. **CONNECTIONS**   Both Zadie Smith and Paul Theroux, in "Football Matters" (p. 312), examine the influences of popular culture in a particular place—New York City and Tuscaloosa, Alabama, respectively. Using these essays as models, write an essay of your own that analyzes some aspect of popular culture (advertising, sports, restaurants, entertainment media, music, and so forth) in a place that matters to you: your hometown, perhaps, or your college campus, maybe a favorite vacation destination. How is this place, and its people, shaped or even defined by its culture? How has it affected you?

Zadie Smith on Writing

In 2018 the Books Are Magic bookstore staged a conversation with Zadie Smith and the *New York Times* cultural critic Wesley Morris in Brooklyn, New York. Here, Smith discusses one of the difficulties she faces when writing essays, specifically those, like "Find Your Beach," collected in *Feel Free.*

I think always about the Aristotelian idea of having *ethos, pathos,* and *logos* combined. . . . It's not always pretty. Speaking with emotion, you can usually puff yourself up, defend your case, make yourself feel good. If you let the other two in—*ethos* being the awareness of people's points of view and . . . *logos* being the rational part, which might say to you, *yes, even if you feel this, even if you feel this very strongly, it still might not be true.* Once you put those in with *pathos,* then I find myself quite often challenged.

The Bedford Reader on Writing

As a novelist accustomed to giving emotions free rein, Smith finds that it can be difficult to balance PATHOS, ETHOS, and LOGOS when writing nonfiction. As a student, how can you tackle the challenge? For tips on combining multiple APPEALS to strengthen your writing and connect with your readers, refer to Chapter 14 on ARGUMENT, especially page 495.

GARY SOTO

A California native raised amid Spanish-speaking farm workers, Gary Soto writes multifaceted fiction, poetry, and essays about his Mexican American heritage and the balancing of cultures in the San Joaquin Valley. Born in Fresno in 1952, he labored as a migrant grape picker himself and attended Fresno City College before he finished a BA from California State University, Fresno, in 1974 and an MFA from the University of California, Irvine, in 1976. Soto taught English and ethnic studies at the University of California, Berkeley, for almost fifteen years, and then he turned to writing full time. His extensive output—seventy-five publications and counting—includes poetry collections such as *Black Hair* (1985) and *Meatballs for the People* (2017), young-adult novels like *Buried Onions* (1997) and *Accidental Love* (2006), biographies of the labor activists Jessie de la Cruz (2000) and Cesar Chavez (2003), short stories in *Local News* (1993) and other anthologies, essay collections such as *The Effects of Knut Hamsun on a Fresno Boy* (2000) and *Why I Don't Write Children's Literature* (2015), children's literature in the form of novels like *Marisol* (2005) and several picture books, and even a handful of plays and short films. An energetic and prolific writer, Soto has earned multiple awards, most notably a Pulitzer Prize nomination (1978), the American Book Award (1985), and a spot on the National Book Award finalists list (1995). He lives and writes in Berkeley.

The Elements of San Joaquin

One of Soto's earliest works, this poem was reissued in a revised and expanded edition of *The Elements of San Joaquin* (1977, 2018), Soto's first and most recent book of poems. At the time of its writing, the Chicano organizer Cesar Chavez (1927–93) was leading and advocating on behalf of the United Farm Workers, a labor union. Some forty years later, in the introduction to the new edition of his book, Soto reminds readers that "the economic tractor of" the central Californian valley region still "is agribusiness, and, despite mechanization, fieldworkers are necessary" and deserving of protection.

For Cesar Chavez

Field

The wind sprays pale dirt into my mouth   1
The small, almost invisible scars
On my hands.

The pores in my throat and elbows
Have taken in a seed of dirt of their own.   5

After a day in the grape fields near Rolinda
A fine silt, washed by sweat,
Has settled into the lines
On my wrists and palms.

Already I am becoming the valley,   10
A soil that sprouts nothing
For any of us.

Wind

A dry wind over the valley
Peeled mountains, grain by grain,
To small slopes, loose dirt   15
Where red ants tunnel.

The wind strokes
The skulls and spines of cattle
To white dust, to nothing,

Covers the spiked tracks of beetles,   20
Of tumbleweed, of sparrows
That pecked the ground for insects.

Evenings, when I am in the yard weeding
The wind picks up the breath of my armpits
Like dust, swirls it   25
Miles away

And drops it
On the ear of a stray dog,
And I take on another life.

Wind

When you got up this morning the sun   30
Blazed an hour in the sky,

A lizard hid
Under the curled leaves of manzanita
And winked its dark lids.

Later, the sky grayed,   35
And the cold wind you breathed
Was moving under your skin and already far
From the small hives of your lungs.

Stars

At dusk the first stars appear.
Not one eager finger points toward them.   40
A little later the stars spread with the night
And an orange moon rises
To lead them, like a shepherd, toward dawn.

Sun

In June the sun is a bonnet of light
Coming up,   45
Little by little,
From behind a skyline of pine.

The pastures sway with fiddleneck,
Tassels of foxtail.

At Piedra   50
A couple fish on the river's edge,
Their shadows deep against the water.
Above, in the stubbled slopes,
Cows climb down
As the heat rises   55
In a mist of gnats from the canal,
Scouring the valley.

Rain

When autumn rains flatten sycamore leaves,
The tiny volcanos of dirt

Ants raised around their holes,   60
I should be out of work.

My silverware and stack of plates will go unused
Like the old, my two good slacks
Will smother under a growth of lint
And smell of the old dust   65
That rises
When the closet door opens or closes.

The skin of my belly will tighten like a belt
And there will be no reason for pockets.

Harvest

East of the sun's slant, in the vineyard that never failed,   70
A wind crossed my face, moving the dust
And a portion of my voice a step closer to a new year.

The sky went black in the ninth hour of rolling trays,
And in the distance ropes of rain dropped to pull me
From the thick harvest that was not mine.   75

Fog

If you go to your window
You will notice a fog drifting in.

The sun is no stronger than a flashlight.
Not all the sweaters
Hung in closets all summer   80

Could soak up this mist. The fog:
A mouth nibbling everything to its origin,
Pomegranate trees, stolen bicycles,

The string of lights at a used-car lot,
A Pontiac with scorched valves.   85

In Fresno the fog is passing
The young thief prying a window screen,

Graying my hair that falls
And goes unfound, my fingerprints
Slowly growing a fur of dust —   90

One hundred years from now
There should be no reason to believe
I lived.

Weeds

Pour motor oil, cut them with a hoe,
Kick them with a boot until sundown,   95
The horizon red with a single cloud in the west.

Weeds stand up for themselves,
And the rumor of their seed is in the air —
They're flying to your house.

Farmer, burn them with flame,   100
Set a chicken in their path, disc them under,
And mutter to yourself when they're tall as the harvest.

Daybreak

In this moment when the light starts up
In the east and rubs
The horizon until it catches fire,   105

We enter the fields to hoe,
Row after row, among the small flags of onion,
Waving off the dragonflies
That ladder the air.

And tears the onions raise   110
Do not begin in your eyes but in ours,
In the salt blown
From one blister to another;

They begin in knowing
You will never waken to bear   115

The hour timed to a heart beat
The wind pressing us closer to the ground.

When the season ends,
And the onions are unplugged from their sleep,
We won't forget what you failed to see,   120
And nothing will heal
Under the rain's broken fingers.

Journal Writing

Where did you grow up? Is the area considered rural, urban, or something in between? Take a few minutes to characterize your hometown in your journal. Consider its physical attributes (landscape, architecture, weather, and such) as well as its culture and politics.

Questions on Meaning

1. What is Soto trying to accomplish in this poem? What does the dedication to Cesar Chavez suggest might be his PURPOSE in writing?

2. Who is the speaker of "The Elements of San Joaquin"? How would you describe his (or her) relationship to the land? Where does the speaker first establish the nature of that relationship?

3. Closely reread the section labeled "Weeds" and tease out the meaning of Soto's extended metaphor. Where else in the poem do weeds appear? What do they SYMBOLIZE?

Questions on Writing Strategy

1. Who would you say is Soto's intended AUDIENCE for this poem? What ASSUMPTIONS does he make about his readers? Why do you think so?

2. How does Soto organize his analysis of San Joaquin in this poem? What elements of the valley does he identify and examine? What seems to be his principle of analysis?

3. Explain the IMAGERY in the concluding section of the poem (lines 103–22). What is the EFFECT?

4. **OTHER METHODS** "The Elements of San Joaquin" makes extensive use of DESCRIPTION. To which of the senses — sight, hearing, touch, smell, and taste — does Soto appeal? How effective do you find his speaker's descriptions?

Questions on Language

1. Why is "Daybreak" a particularly fitting heading for the last section of Soto's poem? What are some CONNOTATIONS of the word?

2. Make sure you know the meanings of the following words, checking a dictionary as needed: tumbleweed (line 21); manzanita (33); fiddleneck (48); tassels, foxtail (49); sycamore (58); disc (101).

3. How would you characterize the speaker's TONE? Is it appropriate, given Soto's purpose and audience?

4. In his comments on writing (p. 334) Soto notes that he likes to use language in surprising ways. Point to some language in "The Elements of San Joaquin" that strikes you as especially fresh and inventive. What do Soto's FIGURES OF SPEECH contribute to readers' enjoyment of the poem?

Suggestions for Writing

1. **FROM JOURNAL TO ESSAY**   How do outsiders consider the place where you grew up? Building on your journal entry (p. 332) and using Soto's poem for inspiration, write an essay that compares and contrasts your perception of your hometown with the perception of it by people who don't live there. What assumptions do others make, and how accurate are they? What do they fail to see? Are there any misconceptions you would like to correct, or do you share outsiders' assessment of the area? Why?

2. Imagining that you want to employ someone to do a specific job, divide the task into its duties and functions. Then, guided by your analysis, write an accurate job description in essay form. Or, if you like, try putting your analysis in the form of a poem.

3. As indicated in the note introducing it, Soto's poem was first published in 1977, in the midst of the Chicano and farm workers' rights movements. Do some research about these movements in the 1960s and '70s. Where did Mexican Americans stand in citizenship, in higher education (studying and teaching), in medicine and other professions, in the workforce, as families, and so on? What kinds of change did civil rights leaders seek, and how did they go about demanding those changes? How did society as a whole seem to respond? Based on your research, write an essay in which you SUMMARIZE your findings.

4. **CRITICAL WRITING**   Starting with your answer to the fourth question on language (above), analyze Soto's use of figures of speech in this poem. How does the author combine *personification*, *metaphor*, *simile*, *paradox*, and similar devices to add meaning and a sense of empathy to his depiction of the conditions faced by farm workers? In your analysis, pay particular attention to those figures of speech you find especially fresh or compelling.

5. **CONNECTIONS**   Soto's poem defends the dignity of hard-working farm hands in California, many (if not most) of whom are presumably Mexican and Central

American immigrants or the descendants of Mexican and Central American immigrants. Has their situation improved at all over the past two generations? Read "Supporting Family Values," a defense of immigrants by Linda Chavez (p. 506). How does she describe working conditions and life situations for these groups? How might she respond to Soto's argument? In an essay, bring these two writers together in discussion.

Gary Soto on Writing

In these paragraphs from "Here's What I Think," a piece in Soto's short-essay collection *What Poets Are Like* (2013), the poet sidesteps the kinds of questions often put to writers by teachers and students.

How do I get my poems done? By striking two sticks together? Yanking on the braids of the barmaid muse? Plucking at a tuned lyre? I have my routine: read poetry in the morning and remember that a poem is a canvas — for God's sake, I tell myself, be a Dutch painter, be Van Eyck. I follow this dictum: strong, not weak, specification. After all, readers hanker for fresh language, not the overused, tired language served daily in our print world. In short, I argue for surprising language coupled with a surprising narrative or lyric. . . .

No elaboration, no discourse. My approach could be picked apart savagely by other poet/critics. I have poet friends who teach — or would like to teach — who are prepared to offer elegant defenses when critiquing student writing. If not done carefully, even gingerly, the student poets growl in their hearts, "You're stupid." Or an irate and injured student may skip the heart and just snarl and rant, then report that part-timer to the ombudsman. Anemic part-timers, already paid poorly, why must they suffer more? I recall when I *did* teach and was one day busily critiquing a poem, a hand went up from the back row. I stopped and asked, "Yes, a question?" The young woman asked, "Are you a wetback?"

Oh, Jesus and his unarmed apostles! Was she listening to any kernel of wisdom to ferry away?

Because I write for children and young adults, teachers assume that I would like to talk about the writing process, especially to answer the inevitable question, "Where do you get your ideas?" Oh, please, let's not do this, I beg. That I get my work done is all that I care about; rumination on such a mundane topic spoils my day.

The Bedford Reader on Writing

Despite his protests, Soto does admit to having a routine, simple as it may be. Every writer follows a unique process, and most would struggle to explain it to others. For our teacherly guidelines on how to develop your own writing skills and habits, see Chapters 2–4 on the writing process (especially pp. 50–51, on responding to reviewers who might critique your work). And for a discussion of the fresh language, or FIGURES OF SPEECH, that Soto values so highly, refer to Language (pp. 21–22) in Chapter 1.

BARBARA B. PARSONS

A teacher of composition and literature at Tacoma Community College and at Pierce College Puyallup in Washington state, Barbara B. Parsons has also taught at Green River Community College and Arizona State University. As a freelance writer she has published essays and op-ed articles in the *Tacoma News Tribune* and *Post Defiance*, among other publications, and she has completed drafts of several novels. Born in 1963 and raised in Phoenix, Arizona, Parsons became enamored of literature, particularly nineteenth-century British literature, early on and read ("in air-conditioned rooms") as much as she could whenever she could. She studied briefly at the University of Colorado and at the American Academy of Dramatic Arts, and then completed her bachelor's and master's degrees in English at Arizona State University. Parsons lives in Tacoma, Washington, where she keeps herself busy researching genealogy and attempting to restore her historic Victorian home "to its former statuesque beauty."

Whistling in the Dark

"Whistling in the Dark" is a formal academic analysis of Brent Staples's now classic "Black Men and Public Space" (p. 169). Parsons wrote it as a model to show her students what she expects of them when she assigns a critical essay. (The assignment reads, in part, "Write a [brief] analysis of an article in terms of whether or not it is successful in convincing the reader.") She has since written multiple analyses of Staples's essay for multiple purposes; this one she revised specifically for inclusion in *The Bedford Reader*.

Brent Staples has an ax to grind in "Black Men and Public Space," but he doesn't grind it. The article, about stereotypes of black men as dangerous, suggests not that society change, but rather that black men themselves change in order to elicit less fear from others, particularly white women. Staples delivers almost endless examples of black men being mistaken for criminals, convinces us that a problem exists, and describes his creative personal solutions. However, his tone of determined self-control hits a false note. While the well-structured essay does make general readers aware of the issue, ultimately it fails to convince us that Staples's solution is the best one possible.

Staples catches the reader's attention immediately by referring to the first woman he noticed cross the street to avoid walking close to him as a "victim" (169). This woman "cast back a worried glance. To her, the youngish black man . . . seemed menacingly close" (169). This opening example does an excellent job of alerting the reader to the issue at hand and even eliciting sympathy and understanding toward the woman, who, after all, is legitimately afraid, though unnecessarily so. Staples himself appears sympathetic: "It was clear that she thought herself the quarry of a mugger, a rapist, or worse" (169), he says. Rather than condemn her false fears, Staples explains carefully, "I was stalking sleep, not defenseless wayfarers. As a softy who is scarcely able to take a knife to raw chicken — let alone hold one to a person's throat — I was surprised, embarrassed, and dismayed all at once" (170). Staples's perception of the situation and the perceptions of wary pedestrians are thus set up from the beginning as equally genuine and innocent, but in opposition. One perception must be false.

Subsequent examples, of people who lock their car doors when Staples 3 passes, of an office manager who calls security when he does not recognize his own employee, and of a storekeeper who threatens a shopper with a guard dog (170–71), adequately prove that public perceptions of black men are often negative and false. Surprisingly, over and over, Staples seems to sympathize with those who mistake him for a menace, saying things like "I understand, of course, that the danger they perceive is not a hallucination" (170). Staples seems determined to take the high road. While those around him jump to frightening conclusions, Staples models tolerance and thoughtful reflection.

The author's sympathetic tone may strike the reader as somewhat false, 4 however. There must be more than sympathy in Staples's reactions. Indeed, he tells us that he has "learned to smother the rage [he] felt at so often being taken for a criminal" (171) and that he long ago began to use careful, non-assertive behavior to counteract the situation. What may trouble some readers, however, is the thought that a smothered rage is likely to become enflamed again at any moment. Rather than combat the problem in any controlled yet assertive manner, Staples chooses to "take precautions to make [him]self less threatening" (171). These precautions — staying at a distance from others in subway stations, avoiding entering a building behind a frightened group of people, whistling classical music when walking late at night (171–72) — seem both excessive and ridiculous. Nor do they seem successful, since Staples himself states that he has kept up this system for "more than a decade" (169) with no change in the situation.

Staples is clear on one point: He is not guilty of anything. He tells us 5 that he "grew up one of the good boys" (171), but that he has lost too many loved ones to street violence to advocate an assertive stance. He is "timid, but a survivor" (171). This retiring position will do nothing to stop a problem that seems to be rampant in American cities. Staples compares his whistling to "the cowbell that hikers wear when they know they are in bear country" (172). But this analogy, while thought-provoking, isn't sound. While those cowbells are intended to keep bears away, Staples's whistles are supposed to soothe fearful pedestrians and encourage them to stick around. The analogy would be more apt if the pedestrians were making a noise to keep Staples away — perhaps by blowing a police whistle.

Staples hopes to encourage us all to be tolerant and nonaggressive, but 6 he takes the biggest portion of the responsibility onto his own broad shoulders, and by extension, onto the backs of other black men with the same "unwieldy inheritance" (169) as he. Some may find his solution frustrating; others may even believe it is unjust. Despite excellent examples and thoughtful commentary, Staples ultimately fails to convince readers that tolerance and timidity are the best response to the problem of racism on the streets. While violence and hate are self-perpetuating and should be avoided, Staples and other black men should be able to go about their lives without undue concern that they are frightening other people or putting themselves in danger. We need a solution that doesn't require anyone to "smother" a negative emotion, be it fear or rage. That is not too much to ask, and Staples should be asking.

Work Cited

Staples, Brent. "Black Men and Public Space." *The Bedford Reader*, edited by X. J. Kennedy et al., 14th ed., Bedford/St. Martin's, 2020, pp. 169–72.

Journal Writing

Parsons is disappointed in Brent Staples's "response to the problem of racism on the streets" (par. 6) and wishes he had proposed a more aggressive solution. Think back to a time when you, or someone around you, responded to a situation in a way that you ultimately determined was not helpful. What was the situation? Why might the initial response have seemed appropriate in the moment? How would you change it now, if you could? Reflect on the problem in your journal.

Questions on Meaning

1. To what end(s) does Parsons analyze Brent Staples's essay? What is her PURPOSE?

2. Why, to Parsons, does Staples's "tone of determined self-control" (par. 1) feel false? Cite evidence from her essay to support your answer.

3. Parsons does not appreciate that Staples is sympathetic to the pedestrians who shy away from him on the street. Why not?

4. What is the THESIS of "Whistling in the Dark"? Where does Parsons state her main idea?

Questions on Writing Strategy

1. As we explain in the note on page 336, Parsons wrote "Whistling in the Dark" as a model for her students. How is her writing appropriate for this AUDIENCE? What other readers might be receptive to her essay, and why?

2. To what extent does Parsons ASSUME that her readers are familiar with "Black Men and Public Space"? How does she ensure that readers can follow her analysis even if they haven't read Brent Staples's essay?

3. What important shift occurs in the TRANSITION between paragraphs 3 and 4?

4. **OTHER METHODS** Parsons uses analysis to illuminate Staples's social commentary. How does she reassemble the parts of his essay to present her own ARGUMENT about a broader subject? What call to action is she making?

Questions on Language

1. Where in her essay does Parsons use FIGURES OF SPEECH to enliven her academic writing? Choose one of her metaphors or similes and explain its meaning.

2. Check a dictionary if any of the following words are unfamiliar to you: elicit (par. 1); opposition (2); menace (3); advocate, rampant (5); self-perpetuating (6).

3. Parsons uses some words — such as "false," "negative," "perception," and "sympathy" — repeatedly. Why? What does this strategy contribute to the overall effectiveness of her essay?

Suggestions for Writing

1. **FROM JOURNAL TO ESSAY** Building on your journal reflections, write an essay that analyzes the problem you recorded, particularly the flaws in your (or someone else's) response to a difficult situation. Be sure to cite specific EXAMPLES and to suggest a response that might have been more productive.

2. Consider a challenging issue facing society today, such as income inequality or clean energy. Write an essay that analyzes the problem, using EXAMPLES to capture its many facets or manifestations. You may, if you wish, propose a solution as well, one that addresses the details you discuss in your essay.

3. **CRITICAL WRITING** Turn to page 169 of this book and read "Black Men and Public Space" for yourself. Then write an essay that responds to Parsons's analysis. Was your initial reaction to Brent Staples's examples similar to hers, or different? How did reading her essay change your understanding of his? Do you agree with her interpretations, or do you read Staples's essay differently? Why?

4. **CONNECTIONS** Janelle Asselin's "Superhuman Error: What Dixon and Rivoche Get Wrong" (p. 518) is also a model of close analysis of another essay in this book. Review her essay side by side with "Whistling in the Dark" and try to identify the components that make up a strong critical reading. What features do these selections have in common? How do the authors differ in their approaches? Do you find one approach more effective or revealing than the other? Why?

Barbara B. Parsons on Writing

We asked Barbara B. Parsons what advice she would offer to student writers using this book. Here is what she had to say.

The transition to college reading, writing, and learning is hard.

I grew up a reader, but it was hard for me anyway.

There are still kids who, as I did, read novels under their desktops and write four-page book reports when the teacher only asks for a page. My love of literature and youthful success writing made me certain going into college that I already wrote well, so I took a writing-heavy load my first semester. Sitting in my freezing dorm room in the early 1980s, I typed every essay three times. I reread my own phrasing, loving the way the words sounded. I turned in the Wite-Out-crusted pages with a smirk of self-confidence.

That first round of college papers earned Bs and Cs. After a good cry, I pulled the essays out of the waste bin and reread them, along with what was written in the margins. "Comma issues," "Attend to gross mechanical errors," "Fuzzy thinking," and, worst of all, at the end of one essay: "What is a comma splice? What is a run-on? I do not care what you say unless you can say it clearly!"

It gets better, as they say.

That year, I began the lifelong task of learning to write. I forced myself to see the errors in my writing. I reluctantly let go of the literary flourishes. In literature classes, for the first time, I paid conscious attention to the way strong writers put words and phrases together. I began to try tricks, like removing all adjectives and adverbs, just to see how a paragraph sounded without them. If a sentence wasn't working, I started it again in the middle, twisting the clauses to test my emphasis.

Now, I teach college students who face the same challenges I did, but with an additional burden: They grew up with technology. Words spell themselves; grammar checkers highlight incorrect sentences. Yet, just as when I use my GPS system too often I forget the order of my city's streets, some students become so reliant on technology that they don't remember the difference between *their* and *they're*. And just as my GPS occasionally leads me to take a wrong turn, spelling and grammar aids sometimes steer writers to the wrong word choice or sentence structure. They can encourage false confidence, which, like my smug attitude my freshman year, can be a barrier to clear expression in English.

When I was eighteen, a few honest professors had the guts to tell me that what I had produced was garbage. Once I faced that, my childhood spent with J. R. R. Tolkien and Jane Austen gave me the tools to become a strong writer. Students who have grown up reading quickly produced novels full of usage errors, who read only poorly edited online material, or who read only when forced, have a greater challenge than I had. I worry about the writers who haven't been exposed to enough good writing to recognize excellence and to test out different styles and tones. For them, I have only one piece of advice: *Read.*

The Bedford Reader on Writing

When Barbara Parsons advises student writers to "*Read,*" she means high-quality, well-written works specifically — like the essays collected in this book. For concrete guidelines on how to read them critically, see Chapter 1. And for help with using such reading to become a better writer yourself, see Chapters 2–4, where you'll learn, among other things, what a comma splice and a run-on sentence are.

LAILA AYAD

Born in 1981, Laila Ayad grew up in Columbia, Maryland, a planned community based on ideals of racial, social, and economic diversity and balance. "Being exposed at an early age to such a diverse community and coming from a multiethnic family have given me great insight into different cultures and perspectives," says Ayad. After graduating from New York University in 2003 with a degree in theater and English literature, Ayad embarked on a successful acting career. When not performing on stage or screen, she paints and draws and continues to write.

The Capricious Camera

Ayad began college as an art major and produced this essay for a writing class in her sophomore year. It then appeared in *Mercer Street*, a journal of writing by New York University students. With an artist's eye for detail, Ayad explores the elements of a photograph to find its meaning. The analysis takes her to Nazi Germany before and during World War II.

Notice that Ayad's researched essay follows MLA style for in-text parenthetical citations and a list of works cited, as discussed on pages 656–670.

In the years between 1933 and 1945, Germany was engulfed by the rise 1 of a powerful new regime and the eventual spoils of war. During this period, Hitler's quest for racial purification turned Germany not only at odds with itself, but with the rest of the world. Photography as an art and as a business became a regulated and potent force in the fight for Aryan domination, Nazi influence, and anti-Semitism. Whether such images were used to promote Nazi ideology, document the Holocaust, or scare Germany's citizens into accepting their own changing country, the effect of this photography provides enormous insight into the true stories and lives of the people most affected by Hitler's racism. In fact, this photography has become so widespread in our understanding and teaching of the Holocaust that often other factors involved in the Nazis' racial policy have been undervalued in our history textbooks — especially the attempt by Nazi Germany to establish the Nordic Aryans as a master race through the *Lebensborn* experiment, a breeding and adoption program designed to eliminate racial imperfections. It is not merely people of other persecuted races who can become victims in a racial war, but also those we would least expect — the persecuting race itself.

To understand the importance of this often shrouded side of Nazi Germany 2 we might look at the photograph captioned "Mounted Nazi troops on the

Mounted Nazi troops on the lookout for likely Polish children.

lookout for likely Polish children." Archived by Catrine Clay and Michael Leapman, this black-and-white photo depicts a young girl in the foreground, carrying two large baskets and treading across a rural and snow-covered countryside, while three mounted and armed Nazi soldiers follow closely behind her. In the distance, we can see farmhouses and a wooden fence, as well as four other uniformed soldiers or guards. Though the photograph accompanies the text without the name of the photographer, year, or information as to where it was found, Clay and Leapman suggest that the photo was taken in Poland between 1943 and 1945.

Who is this young white girl surrounded by armed soldiers? Is she being   3
protected, watched, persecuted? It would be easy enough to assume that she is Jewish, but unlike photos documenting the Holocaust, with *this* image the intent is uncertain. In our general ignorance of the events surrounding this photo, the picture can be deceiving, and yet it is the picture that can also be used to shed light on the story.

Looking just at the photo, and ignoring the descriptive caption, there are   4
some interesting visual and artistic effects that help a viewer better understand the circumstances surrounding the image. One of its most prominent features is the way the photographer decides to focus on only one young child in the foreground, while including seven Nazi soldiers behind her. The effect is overwhelming, and in gazing at the image, one is struck by the magnitude and force of the oppressing men in sharp contrast to the innocence and helplessness of the lone girl. By juxtaposing one child with seven men, the image comes across strongly as both cruel and terribly frightening. In addition, the child in the foreground is a young girl, which only adds to the potency of the image. The photographer makes the soldiers appear far more menacing and unjust, in that there appears to be no physical way in which a young girl could possibly defend herself against these men.

What is additionally interesting about this particular aspect of the photo   5
is that the seven men are not grouped together, or in any way concentrated right next to the child. There are three directly behind the girl, one a little farther behind and to the left, one even slightly farther behind and to the right, and two very far off in the distance, walking in the opposite direction. This placement of the soldiers not only gives the photo an excellent sense of depth, but also conveys to the viewer a sense that the entire surroundings, not just the little girl, are being controlled and surveyed. It allows the viewer to imagine and wonder in what way other children, or perhaps just the other parts of the village, are being similarly restricted. For the young girl, and the viewer, it allows no way out; all angles and directions of the photo are covered by symbols of oppression, producing an eerily suffocating effect.

The child is the only person in the photo looking directly at the photog- 6
rapher. Whether this technique was manipulated on purpose remains to be
seen, but it goes without saying that the effect is dramatic. Her gaze is wistful
and innocent. In contrast, the men occupying the rest of the photo, and most
prominently the three mounted ones in the foreground, are gazing either away
or down. While it is uncertain what the soldiers behind the child are staring
at, their downward stare causes their heads to hang in almost shameful dis-
grace. They do not look at the child, and yet they do not look at the photographer, who is quite obviously standing in front of them. Is this because they
do not see that there is a picture being taken, or perhaps the photographer is
another soldier, and this picture is simply routine in recording the progress of
their work?

If not a Nazi soldier, the photographer could be a Polish citizen; if this 7
were the case, it might change our interpretation of the photo. Suddenly, the
girl's facial expression and direct gaze seem pleading, while, for fear of being
caught, the photographer snaps the picture quickly, in the exact moment the
soldiers are looking away. Perhaps the soldiers did not mind having their picture taken. Many Polish were considered, after all, their racial equals, and
maybe they would have respected and appreciated an amateur photographer's
interest in their work.

While all of these scenarios are seemingly plausible, the purpose of the 8
photograph is still uncertain. There are also several possibilities. One is that the
Nazis commissioned the photograph, as they did others at the time, to properly
record the events surrounding the development of their plan. In an article entitled "The Camera as Weapon: Documentary Photography and the Holocaust,"
Sybil Milton describes the ways in which Nazi photographers worked:

> Nazi professional photographers produced in excess of one-quarter million
> images. Their work was officially regulated and licensed. . . . All photos
> were screened by military censors subservient to official directives of the
> Propaganda Ministry. . . . Press photographers of World War II rarely showed
> atrocities and seldom published prints unfavorable to their own side. (1)

However, while the evidence is compelling, Milton recognizes another possibility that significantly changes the motive for the photo: "Portable cameras,
and other technical innovations like interchangeable lenses and multiple
exposure film, meant that nonprofessionals owned and used cameras with
ease. Many soldiers carried small Leica or Ermanox cameras in their rucksacks
or pillaged optical equipment from the towns they occupied" (2). While it *is*
possible that the photograph was taken by a soldier seeking to document the
work in Poland for his own interests, this probability, against the numerous

commissioned photographs and the nature of the subject matter being documented, is unlikely. The photo alone, while intriguing in its image, tells only half of the story, and without a definitive context can become akin to a "choose your own adventure" novel. In other words, the possibilities for a photographic purpose are all laid out, but the true meaning or end remains undetermined. Unlike hand-made art, which in its very purpose begs to be viewed through various interpretations, photography, and particularly photojournalism, captures a certain moment in time, featuring specific subject matter, under a genuine set of circumstances. The picture is not invented, it is real life, and in being so demands to be viewed alongside its agenda, for without this context, it may never be fully understood.

When we turn to the caption describing the photograph, "Mounted Nazi 9 troops on the lookout for likely Polish children," the book *Master Race* and its accompanying story can now properly be discussed. Instead of typically dealing with the issues of a racist Nazi Germany as it relates to the Holocaust, and the other forms of racial extermination and discrimination that were subsequently involved, Clay and Leapman's book looks at the other side of the coin. It is important in dealing with and understanding the concept of racism to realize that racists are not simply those who dislike others; they are also those who worship themselves. In *Mein Kampf* Hitler outlined the inspiration for his racial tyranny by saying, "The products of human culture, the achievements in art, science and technology . . . are almost exclusively the creative product of the Aryan" (ch. 3). He was heavily influenced by the work of racially charged popular science writers, such as H. F. K. Gunther, who in his *Ethnology of the German Nation* wrote: "The man of Nordic race is not only the most gifted but also the most beautiful. . . . The man's face is hard and chiseled, the woman's tender, with rose-pink skin and bright triumphant eyes" (qtd. in Clay and Leapman 17). Through the course of the book, the topic of racism in Nazi Germany focuses intently on the concept of racial purification. By following the work of the carefully selected (meaning those of impeccable Aryan ancestry) members of Himmler's elite SS corps, Clay and Leapman introduce the history of Germany's failed *Lebensborn* experiment and the homes that were created by the Third Reich to breed and raise "perfect Aryans" (ix).

In a disturbing segment on Hitler's racial utopia, Clay and Leapman 10 describe the practice of eugenics, improving humankind by eliminating undesirable genetic traits and breeding those that were considered superior. The SS soldiers who are commonly known for forcing the Jews into concentration camps are mentioned, but this time they are discussed as the same men who were ordered to father white babies with volunteer German and Norwegian mothers. However, it is the final fact, the story of the SS soldiers who occupied surrounding countries and then stole children "who looked as if they might further improve the breed," that becomes the focus and ultimate subject matter of the photograph (ix).

Looking at the photograph in this context, the soldier no longer appears   11
to be protecting the Polish children, but hunting them. The word "likely" in the caption denotes this. Children who possessed strong Nordic or Aryan qualities were systematically taken from their native countries, adopted by German parents (who were paid by the Nazi regime), taught to forget their families and former lives, and raised to breed not only many children of their own but, above all, families that would uphold Nazi ideology. For Hitler and Heinrich Himmler, who was appointed Commissar for Consolidating German Nationhood, exterminating the racially impure was merely preparation. It was the process of breeding and stealing children that Himmler considered central and key in the ultimate goal for racial purification:

> Obviously in such a mixture of peoples there will always be some racially good types. Therefore I think that it is our duty to take their children with us, to remove them from their environment, if necessary by robbing or stealing them. . . . My aim has always been the same, to attract all the Nordic blood in the world and take it for ourselves. (qtd. in Clay and Leapman 91)

Additionally, Himmler's objective in targeting children, rather than adults, was a planned and strategic tool. Through teachings at school, children were used to control their parents by being encouraged to report what they did and said. Himmler realized that older people would be less enthusiastic about his ideas, so he made every effort to win the minds of the next generation.

What is perhaps most compelling about the *Lebensborn* experiment and   12
thus most poignant when viewing the photograph is the reminder that for every child that was stolen from nations like Poland, his or her family was being equally betrayed. One Polish girl recounted the events of her kidnapping years later, describing both her and her father's reaction to the incident:

> Three SS men came into the room and put us up against a wall. . . . They immediately picked out the fair children with blue eyes—seven altogether, including me. . . . My father, who tried to stop my being taken away, was threatened by the soldiers. They even said he would be taken to a concentration camp. But I have no idea what happened to him later. (qtd. in Clay and Leapman 95)

The girl who spoke above just as easily could have been the young girl being followed by soldiers in the photograph, only moments after she was taken. Such incidents force us to broaden our sense of whom the Nazis victimized. While there is no mistaking the victimization of the Jewish population and other races in Germany, amidst these better-known hate crimes the Nazis were also perpetrating a horrific exploitation of the so-called "white" race.

The complexities surrounding this photograph remind us that the story [13] of any photograph is liable to contain ambiguity. As an art, photography relies on the imagination of the viewer; not *knowing* provides the viewer with a realm of interesting possibilities. Context matters even with art, and playing with possible contexts gives a photograph diverse meanings. It is in these various viewpoints that we find pleasure, amusement, fear, or wonder. It is perhaps in the shift to photojournalism that determining a particular context becomes even more important. In fact, even if the original photographer saw the image as artistic, subsequent events compel us to try to see the image of the Polish girl with Nazis as journalism. In this endeavor, we must uncover as much as possible about the surrounding context. As much as we can, we need to know this girl's particular story. Without a name, date, place, or relevant data, this girl would fall even further backward into the chapters of unrecorded history.

Works Cited

Clay, Catrine, and Michael Leapman. *Master Race: The* Lebensborn *Experiment in Nazi Germany.* Hodder & Stoughton, 1995.

Hitler, Adolf. *Mein Kampf.* Vol. 2, Eher Verlag, 1926. *Hitler Historical Museum,* 1996–2000, www.hitler.org/writings/Mein_Kampf/. Accessed 1 Dec. 2000.

Milton, Sybil. "The Camera as Weapon: Documentary Photography and the Holocaust." *Annual Scholars' Conference,* Proceedings of the National Conference of Christians and Jews, New York, March 1983. *The Museum of Tolerance,* Simon Wiesenthal Center, 2000, motlc.wiesenthal.com/site/pp .asp?c=gvKVLcMVIuG&b=394975. Accessed 6 Dec. 2000.

"Mounted Nazi Troops on the Lookout for Likely Polish Children." Clay and Leapman, p. 87.

Journal Writing

Ayad uncovers an aspect of Nazi history that is not well known and may seem startling. Think of a time when you learned something that surprised you about history, science, or culture — either in a class or through independent research. In your journal, write about your discovery and how it affected you.

Questions on Meaning

1. Ayad's essay pursues two threads: certain events in German history and certain characteristics of photography, especially photojournalism. Each thread in essence has its own THESIS, stated in paragraphs 1 and 8. What are these theses? Where in the essay does Ayad bring them together?

2. Ayad writes about events in history that she thinks some readers do not know about. What are these events?

3. What do you see as Ayad's PURPOSE in this essay?

Questions on Writing Strategy

1. Why does Ayad devote so much of her essay to discussing the photograph? What is the EFFECT of her speculations about its content and creation?

2. Ayad's AUDIENCE was originally the teacher and students in her writing class. What does she ASSUME readers already know about Nazi Germany? What does she assume they may not know?

3. What is the effect of Ayad's last two sentences? Why does Ayad end this way?

4. **OTHER METHODS**   Where in the essay does Ayad draw on DESCRIPTION? Why is description crucial to her analysis?

Questions on Language

1. What words and phrases does Ayad use in paragraphs 4–6 to communicate her own feelings about the photograph? What are those feelings?

2. Why does Ayad quote Adolf Hitler and H. F. K. Gunther (par. 9), Heinrich Himmler (11), and the Polish woman who was kidnapped as a child (12)? What does Ayad achieve with these quotations?

3. What is the effect of the word *targeting* in paragraph 11?

4. Consult a dictionary if you are unsure of the meanings of any of the following: capricious (title); Aryan, anti-Semitism, ideology, Nordic (par. 1); shrouded (2); juxtaposing (4); suffocating (5); scenarios, plausible, pillaged, definitive (8); extermination, tyranny, impeccable (9); poignant (12); ambiguity, subsequent (13).

Suggestions for Writing

1. **FROM JOURNAL TO ESSAY**   Using your journal writing as a starting point, draft an essay about a surprising discovery you made in a class or on your own. If it will be helpful, do some research to extend your knowledge of the subject. Involve your readers in the essay by distinguishing general knowledge — that is, what they probably know already — from the new information.

2. Locate a photograph that you find especially striking, perhaps in a library book or through an online photo collection such as Instagram or Corbis (*corbisimages.com*). Write an essay that describes and analyzes the image, using a thesis statement and vivid language to make your interpretation clear.

3. **CRITICAL WRITING**   Some of Ayad's paragraphs are long, especially 1, 8, 9, and 11. How COHERENT are these long paragraphs? Write a brief essay in which you analyze two of them in terms of their organization, the TRANSITIONS or other devices that connect sentences, and any problems with coherence that you see.

4. **CONNECTIONS**   In "The Way to Rainy Mountain" (p. 144), N. Scott Momaday also writes about the history of a race of people oppressed by an occupying government, in his case the Kiowa tribe of Oklahoma. Write an essay in which you imagine how one of the mounted soldiers in Ayad's photograph may have felt about his role in Germany's *Lebensborn* experiment, whether enthusiastic or, like Momaday, mournful.

ADDITIONAL WRITING TOPICS

Division or Analysis

Using the method of division or analysis, write an essay on one of the following subjects (or choose your own subject). In your essay, make sure your purpose and your principle of division or analysis are clear to your readers. Explain the parts of your subject so that readers know how each relates to the others and contributes to the whole.

- The slang or technical terminology of a group such as stand-up comedians or online gamers
- An especially *bad* movie, television show, or book
- A doll, action figure, or other toy from childhood
- A typical sidebar ad for a product such as clothing, deodorant, beer, a luxury car, or an economy car
- A machine or an appliance, such as a drone, a motorcycle, a microwave oven, or a camera
- An organization or association, such as a social club, a sports league, or a support group
- The characteristic appearance of an indie folk singer or a classical violinist
- A day in the life of a student
- Your favorite poem
- A short story, an essay, or another work that made you think
- The government of your community
- The most popular restaurant (or other place of business) in town
- The Bible, the Qur'an, or another religious text
- An urban legend: hitchhiking ghosts, flickering orbs, gas-station carjackings, haunted cemeteries, buried treasures, and so forth
- A painting or a statue

How the Poor, the Middle Class, and the Rich Spend Their Money

Household Income

Type of Spending	$15,000–$19,999	$50,000–$69,999	Above $150,000
Food at Home	10.2%	7.7%	5.4%
Food at Restaurants, etc.	4.7%	5.4%	5.4%
Housing	29.2%	26.7%	27.5%
Utilities	11.1%	8.2%	4.8%
Clothes & Shoes	3.6%	3.2%	3.7%
Transportation & Gasoline	20.4%	21.3%	15.5%
Health Care & Health Insurance	8.2%	7.1%	4.5%
Entertainment	4.8%	5.1%	5.7%
Education	1.5%	1.3%	4.4%
Saving for Retirement	2.6%	9.6%	15.9%

Source: Bureau of Labor Statistics. Credit: Lam Thuy Vo / NPR

11

CLASSIFICATION

Sorting into Kinds

◀ **Classification in a table**

How do you spend your money? Does most of it go for rent and utilities, for instance, or is the bulk of your budget earmarked for tuition, fees, and books? How do your income and expenses compare to those of your peers? In this infographic, National Public Radio's *Planet Money* translates data from the Bureau of Labor Statistics to show how household budgets in the United States typically sort out. NPR's table classifies spending patterns for three economic groups: "the Poor, the Middle Class, and the Rich." Notice, first, how NPR defines each class. Then examine the data. The column on the left identifies ten types of spending; the three other columns compare the percentages of household income devoted to each category by the groups. What similarities and differences among the categories strike you? Are you surprised by any of the numbers? Why, or why not?

THE METHOD

To CLASSIFY is to make sense of some aspect of the world by arranging many units — trucks, chemical elements, wasps, students — into more manageable groups. Zoologists classify animals, botanists classify plants — and their classifications help us understand a vast and complex subject: life on earth. To help us find books in a library, librarians classify them into categories: fiction, biography, history, psychology, and so forth. For the convenience of readers, newspapers run classified advertising, grouping many small ads into categories such as "Services" and "Cars for Sale."

Subjects and Reasons for Classification

The subject of a classification essay is always a number of things, such as peaches or political systems. (In contrast, DIVISION or ANALYSIS, the topic of the preceding chapter, usually deals with a solitary subject, a coherent whole, such as *a* peach or *a* political system.) The job of classification is to sort the things into groups or classes based on their similarities and differences. Say, for instance, you're going to write an essay about how people write. After interviewing a lot of writers, you determine that writers' processes differ widely, mainly in the amount of planning and rewriting they entail. (Notice that this determination involves analyzing the PROCESS of writing, separating it into steps. See Chapter 9.) On the basis of your findings, you create groups for planners, one-drafters, and rewriters. Once your groups are defined, and assuming they are valid, your subjects (the writers) almost sort themselves out.

Just as you can analyze a subject in many ways, you can classify a subject according to many principles. One travel guide, for instance, might group places to stay by style of accommodation: resorts, hotels, motels, bed-and-breakfasts, boarding houses, and hostels. A different guidebook might classify options according to price: grand luxury, luxury, moderate, bargain, fleabag, and flophouse.

The principle used in classifying things depends on the writer's PURPOSE. A guidebook classifies accommodations by price to match visitors with hotels that fit their pocketbooks. A linguist might explain the languages of the world by classifying them according to their origins (Romance languages, Germanic languages, Asian languages, Coptic languages . . .), but a student battling with a college language requirement might try to entertain fellow students by classifying languages into three groups: hard to learn, harder to learn, and unlearnable.

Kinds of Classification

Classification schemes vary in complexity, depending on the groups being sorted and the basis for sorting them. In classifying methods of classification, we find two types: binary and complex.

- **Binary classification.** The simplest classification is binary (or two-part), in which you sort things out into (1) those with a certain distinguishing feature and (2) those without it. You might classify a number of persons, let's say, into smokers and nonsmokers, runners and nonrunners, believers and nonbelievers. Binary classification is most useful when your subject is easily divisible into positive and negative categories.

- **Complex classification.** More often, a classification will sort things into multiple categories, sometimes putting members into subcategories. Such is the case with a linguist who categorizes languages by origin. Writing about the varieties of one Germanic language, such as English, the writer could identify the subclasses of British English, North American English, Australian English, and so on.

As readers, we enjoy classifications that strike us as true and familiar. This pleasure may account for the appeal of magazine and Web articles that classify things ("Seven Common Varieties of Moocher," "The Top Ten Most Embarrassing Social Blunders"). Usefulness as well as pleasure may explain the popularity of classifications that EVALUATE things. The magazine *Consumer Reports* sorts products as varied as space heaters and frozen dinners into groups based on quality (excellent, very good, good, fair, and poor), and then, using analysis, discusses each product (of a frozen pot pie: "Bottom crust gummy, meat spongy when chewed, with nondescript old-poultry and stale-flour flavor").

THE PROCESS

Purposes and Theses

Classification will usually come into play when you want to impose order on a complex subject that includes many items. In one essay in this chapter, for instance, Deborah Tannen tackles the seemingly endless opportunities for

> ### FOCUS ON PARAGRAPH DEVELOPMENT
>
> A crucial aim of classification is to make sure each group is clear: what's counted in, what's counted out, and why. Writers provide examples and other details to make the groups clear as they develop the paragraph(s) devoted to each.
>
> The following paragraph barely outlines one group in a four-part classification of ex-smokers into zealots, evangelists, the elect, and the serene:
>
>> The second group, evangelists, does not condemn smokers but encourages them to quit. Evangelists think quitting is easy, and they preach this message, often earning the resentment of potential converts.
>
> Contrast this bare-bones adaptation with the actual paragraphs written by Franklin E. Zimring in his essay "Confessions of a Former Smoker":
>
>> By contrast, the antismoking evangelist does not condemn smokers. Unlike the zealot, he regards smoking as an easily curable condition, as a social disease, and not a sin. The evangelist spends an enormous amount of time seeking and preaching to the unconverted. He argues that kicking the habit is not *that* difficult. After all, *he* did it; moreover, as he describes it, the benefits of quitting are beyond measure and the disadvantages are nil.
>>
>> The hallmark of the evangelist is his insistence that he never misses tobacco. Though he is less hostile to smokers than the zealot, he is resented more. Friends and loved ones who have been the targets of his preachments frequently greet the resumption of smoking by the evangelist as an occasion for unmitigated glee.
>
> In the second sentence of each paragraph, Zimring explicitly contrasts evangelists with zealots, the group he previously defined. And he does more as well: He provides specific examples of the evangelist's message (first paragraph) and of others' reactions to him (second paragraph). These details pin down the group, making it distinct from other groups and clear in itself.

men and women to miscommunicate with each other. Sometimes you may use classification to entertain readers, as Leo Braudy does in another essay in this chapter, giving a fresh charge to familiar characters.

Whatever use you make of classification, do it for a reason: The files of composition instructors are littered with essays in which nothing was ventured and nothing was gained. Classifications can reveal truth or amuse us, but they can also reveal nothing and bore us. Sorting ten North American cities according to their relative freedom from air pollution or their cost of living or the range of services offered to residents might prove highly informative and useful to someone looking for a new place to live. But sorting the cities according to a superficial feature such as the relative size of their cat and dog populations wouldn't interest anyone, probably, except a veterinarian looking for a job.

Your purpose, your THESIS, and your principle of classification will all overlap with your interest in your subject. Say you're curious about how other students write. Is your interest primarily in the materials they use (keyboard, pencil, voice recorder), in where and when they write, or in how much planning and rewriting they do? Any of these could lead to a principle for sorting the students into groups. And that principle should be revealed in your THESIS STATEMENT, letting readers know why you are classifying. Here, from the essays in this chapter, are examples of classification thesis statements:

> In this menagerie of horrors, there are four primary types of monsters, each of which embodies a set of fears that has persisted despite — and often because of — our many scientific and social advances.
> —Leo Braudy, "Where Our Monsters Come From"

> Many of the conversational rituals common among women are designed to take the other person's feelings into account, while many of the conversational rituals common among men are designed to maintain the one-up position, or at least avoid appearing one-down. As a result, when men and women interact — especially at work — it's often women who are at the disadvantage.
> —Deborah Tannen, "But What Do You Mean?"

Categories

For a workable classification, make sure that the categories you choose don't overlap. If you were writing a survey of popular magazines for adults and you were sorting your subject into categories that included women's magazines and sports magazines, you might soon run into trouble. Into which category would you place *Women's Sports*? The trouble is that both categories take in the same item. To avoid this problem, you'd need to reorganize your classification on a different principle. You might sort out the magazines by their audiences: magazines intended for women, magazines intended for men, magazines intended for both women and men. Or you might group them according to subject matter: sports magazines, political magazines, fashion magazines, celebrity magazines, and so on. *Women's Sports* would fit into either of those classification schemes, but into only *one* category in each scheme.

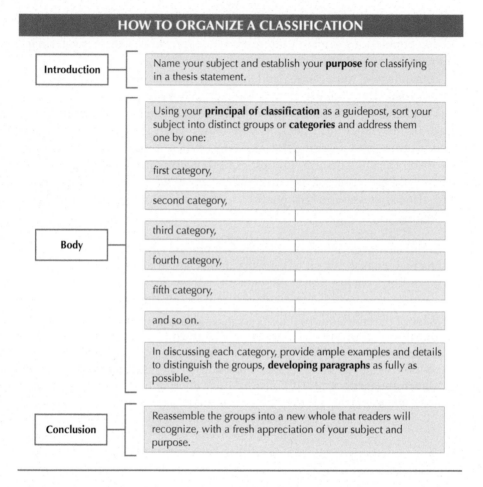

HOW TO ORGANIZE A CLASSIFICATION

Introduction — Name your subject and establish your **purpose** for classifying in a thesis statement.

Body — Using your **principal of classification** as a guidepost, sort your subject into distinct groups or **categories** and address them one by one:

first category,

second category,

third category,

fourth category,

fifth category,

and so on.

In discussing each category, provide ample examples and details to distinguish the groups, **developing paragraphs** as fully as possible.

Conclusion — Reassemble the groups into a new whole that readers will recognize, with a fresh appreciation of your subject and purpose.

When you draw up a scheme of classification, be sure that you also include all essential categories. Omitting an important category can weaken the effect of your essay, no matter how well written it is. It would be a major oversight, for example, if you were to classify the residents of a dormitory according to their religious affiliations and not include a category for the numerous nonaffiliated.

Some form of outline can be helpful to keep the classes and their members straight as you develop and draft ideas. You could simply list your categories for a general overview, or you might experiment with a diagram in which you jot down headings for the groups, with plenty of space around them, letting each heading accumulate members as you think of them. This kind of diagram offers more flexibility than a vertical list or an outline, and it may be a better aid for keeping categories from overlapping or disappearing.

CHECKLIST FOR REVIEWING AND REVISING A CLASSIFICATION

✔ **Purpose.** Have you classified for a reason? Will readers be able to see why you bothered?

✔ **Principle of classification.** Will readers also see what rule or principle has been used for sorting individuals into groups? Is this principle apparent in a thesis sentence?

✔ **Consistency.** Does each representative of the subject fall into one category only, so that categories don't overlap?

✔ **Completeness.** Have all the essential categories suggested by your principle of classification been mentioned?

✔ **Paragraph development.** Has enough information, examples, and other details been provided so that readers can easily distinguish each category from the others?

STUDENT CASE STUDY: A RÉSUMÉ

Sooner or later, every college student needs a résumé: a one-page overview of skills and experiences that will appeal to a potential employer. Part of the challenge in drafting a résumé is to bring order to what seems a complex and unwieldy subject, a life. The main solution is to classify activities and interests into clearly defined groups: typically work experience, education, and special skills.

The group that poses the biggest challenge is usually work experience: Some résumés list jobs with the most recent first, detailing the specifics of each one; others sort experience into skills (such as computer skills, administrative skills, and communication skills) and then list job specifics under each subcategory. The first arrangement tends to be more straightforward and potentially less confusing to readers. However, college students and recent graduates with few previous jobs often find the second arrangement preferable because it downplays experience and showcases abilities.

The résumé on the following page was prepared by Susan Churchill, who was seeking a paid internship in the field of practical nursing. After experimenting with different organizational strategies, she decided to put the category of work experience first because it related directly to the internships she sought. And she chose to organize her work experience by jobs rather than by skills because the institutions she had worked for were similar to the healthcare facilities she was applying to.

For the job-application cover letter Churchill wrote to go with the résumé, see page 167 of Chapter 7.

SUSAN CHURCHILL

9 South Avenue, Apt. A   (603) 555-4322
Derry, NH 03038   schurchill@salter.edu

OBJECTIVE
An internship that offers experience in practical nursing

EXPERIENCE

Hackett Hill Health Center, Manchester, NH, Sept. 2017 to present
For clinicals, practice nursing skills in a short-stay facility.
- Perform basic LNA/CNA procedures; administer medications.
- Ensured safety and well-being of patients presenting with a variety of conditions including Parkinson's disease, dementia, and cancer.

Huggins Hospital, Wolfeboro, NH Oct. 2016
As a phlebotomy extern, completed seventy-five venipunctures in four days.
- Collected blood, tissue, and other laboratory specimens and prepared them for lab testing.
- Complied with HIPAA regulations and infection-control procedures.

SKILL HIGHLIGHTS

Venipuncture   Medical laboratory procedures
Blood withdrawal   CPR PRO
BAC and drug screening   Enthusiastic caregiver
Sterilization techniques   Patient relations

CERTIFICATIONS
Certificate in CPR, American Heart Association, 2017
Certificate in phlebotomy, National Healthcareer Association, #C527A4M2

EDUCATION

Salter School of Nursing and Allied Health, Aug. 2017 to present
Practical nursing program
Courses: anatomy and physiology, pharmacology, psychology, human growth and development, composition

American Red Cross Aug. 2016
Phlebotomy program

Similar to a thesis statement, an objective expresses the applicant's purpose

First major category: work experience

A subcategory for each job includes summaries and specific details

Second major category: skill highlights

Specific skills

Third major category: certifications

Fourth major category: education

Specific information relevant to job objective

SANDRA CISNEROS

Born in 1954 in Chicago, Sandra Cisneros was raised with six brothers in a working-class Latino neighborhood of the city and attended Loyola University, where she received a BA in 1976. Two years later, she earned an MFA from the University of Iowa Writers' Workshop. While at Iowa, she embraced her Chicana heritage in her writing, turning to her childhood for inspiration. Most of her published work deals explicitly with issues of ethnicity, poverty, and personal identity. She is the author of two novels, *The House on Mango Street* (1984), for which she won the American Book Award, and *Caramelo* (2003); a collection of short stories, *Woman Hollering Creek* (1987); four books of poetry, including *My Wicked, Wicked Ways* (1987) and *Loose Woman* (1994); a memoir in essays, *A House of My Own* (2015); and an illustrated chapbook, *Puro Amor* (2018). Cisneros has received numerous awards, including two from the National Endowment for the Arts, a Lannan Foundation Literary Award, a MacArthur Fellowship, and the National Medal of the Arts. She currently lives in Mexico and is working on a children's book and a book about writing.

And Some More

A modern classic, *The House on Mango Street* remains notable for its unique structure and enduring appeal. As a semi-autobiographical novel (Cisneros initially intended to write a memoir), it is comprised of short, interconnected vignettes depicting a young girl's experiences growing up in a Chicago barrio distinctly modeled after the author's own childhood and home. The central narrator, Esperanza (her name means "Hope"), faces expectations placed on girls by both American society and her family's Mexican American culture as she navigates her way through adolescence and a hostile environment, all the while dreaming of a better life. In "And Some More," a story from the book, Esperanza, her little sister, and two of their friends attempt classification in surprising ways to make sense of their world.

The Eskimos got thirty different names for snow, I say. I read it in a book. 1

I got a cousin, Rachel says. She got three different names. 2

There ain't thirty different kinds of snow, Lucy says. There are two kinds. 3
The clean kind and the dirty kind, clean and dirty, Only two.

There are a million zillion kinds, says Nenny. No two exactly alike. Only 4
how do you remember which one is which?

She got three last names and, let me see, two first names. One in English 5
and one in Spanish . . .

And clouds got at least ten different names, I say. 6

Names for clouds? Nenny asks. Names just like you and me?   7

That up there, that's cumulus, and everybody looks up.   8

Cumulus are cute, Rachel says. She *would* say something like that.   9

What's that one there? Nenny asks, pointing a finger.   10

That's cumulus too. They're all cumulus today. Cumulus, cumulus,   11
cumulus.

No, she says. That there is Nancy, otherwise known as Pig-eye. And over   12
there her cousin Mildred, and little Joey, Marco, Nereida and Sue.

There are all different kinds of clouds. How many different kinds of   13
clouds can you think of?

Well, there's these already that look like shaving cream . . .   14

And what about the kind that looks like you combed its hair? Yes, those   15
are clouds too.

Phyllis, Ted, Alfredo and Julie . . .   16

There are clouds that look like big fields of sheep, Rachel says. Them are   17
my favorite.

And don't forget nimbus the rain cloud, I add, that's something.   18

Jose and Dagoberto, Alicia, Raul, Edna, Alma and Rickey . . .   19

There's that wide puffy cloud that looks like your face when you wake up   20
after falling asleep with all your clothes on.

Reynaldo, Angelo, Albert, Armando, Mario . . .   21

Not my face. Looks like your fat face.   22

Rita, Margie, Ernie . . .   23

Whose fat face?   24

Esperanza's fat face, that's who. Looks like Esperanza's ugly face when she   25
comes to school in the morning.

Anita, Stella, Dennis, and Lolo . . .   26

Who you calling ugly, ugly?   27

Richie, Yolanda, Hector, Stevie, Vincent . . .   28

Not you. Your mama, that's who.   29

My mama? You better not be saying that, Lucy Guerrero. You better not   30
be talking like that . . . else you can say goodbye to being my friend forever.

I'm saying your mama's ugly like . . . ummm . . .   31

. . . like bare feet in September!   32

That does it! Both of yous better get out of my yard before I call my   33
brothers.

Oh, we're only playing.   34

I can think of thirty Eskimo words for you, Rachel. Thirty words that say   35
what you are.

Oh yeah, well I can think of some more.   36

Uh-oh, Nenny. Better get the broom. Too much trash in our yard today.   37

Frankie, Licha, Maria, Pee Wee . . .   38

Nenny, you better tell your sister she is really crazy because Lucy and me   39
are never coming back here again. Forever.

Reggie, Elizabeth, Lisa, Louie . . .   40

You can do what you want to do, Nenny, but you better not talk to Lucy   41
or Rachel if you want to be my sister.

You know what you are, Esperanza? You are like the Cream of Wheat   42
cereal. You're like the lumps.

Yeah, and you're foot fleas, that's you.   43

Chicken lips.   44

Rosemary, Dalia, Lily . . .   45

Cockroach jelly.   46

Jean, Geranium and Joe . . .   47

Cold *frijoles*.   48

Mimi, Michael, Moe . . .   49

Your mama's *frijoles*.   50

Your ugly mama's toes.   51

That's stupid.   52

Bebe, Blanca, Benny . . .   53

Who's stupid?   54

Rachel, Lucy, Esperanza, and Nenny.   55

Journal Writing

Think of some memorable incident from your childhood that involved several other
people: a petty fight with friends, perhaps, a family gathering, maybe a class trip.
In your journal, write down as much about the incident as you can recall. What
happened, and who was involved? What do you remember being said, and by whom?

Questions on Meaning

1. Does Cisneros seem to have had any particular AUDIENCE in mind when she
   wrote this story? What is her PURPOSE in telling it? Why do you think so?

2. What do you make of the argument the girls get into? What are they fighting
   about, and why? How can you tell?

3. Look again at the last two lines. Who are "Rachel, Lucy, Esperanza, and Nenny"
   (par. 55)? Why does the narrator single them out as "stupid" (54)?

Questions on Writing Strategy

1. What distinct elements of the natural world do the characters in this story attempt to classify? What principle of classification do they apply to each subject? How, if at all, do the principles relate to each other?

2. Carefully examine the organization of this story and prepare a rough outline of its contents to help you visualize its structure. How does Cisneros weave together three simultaneous classifications in such a short space, and why?

3. Most of the girls' attempts at classification in this story model complex schemes, identifying many different names for each of their subjects. Where does one of them propose a binary classification instead? Why do you suppose she does so?

4. **OTHER METHODS**   As a NARRATIVE, "And Some More" consists almost entirely of DIALOG. Why doesn't Cisneros use quotation marks? How, if at all, does she help readers keep track of who says what?

Questions on Language

1. Find definitions of the following: cumulus (par. 8); nimbus (18), *frijoles* (48).

2. Explain the FIGURES OF SPEECH the girls use to insult each other at the end of the story. What are "foot fleas" (par. 43)? "cockroach jelly" (46)? Why would the girls compare Esperanza to "Cream of Wheat cereal" (42)? What about the other foods they name?

Suggestions for Writing

1. **FROM JOURNAL TO ESSAY**   Try your hand at using dialog in a brief narrative that recalls a significant incident between yourself and some childhood friends or family members. Then write briefly about your experience using dialog. How easy or difficult was it to remember who said what? How easy or difficult was it to make the speakers sound like themselves?

2. To what extent do you think your gender or your ethnic heritage might have predetermined your personal characteristics — agreeableness, kindness, curiosity, intelligence, aggressiveness, shyness, and so on? How might your surroundings have influenced who you are? Write an essay that explores the debate about heredity versus upbringing, nature versus nurture, as it applies to you. Using specific EXAMPLES, discuss the extent to which you think biographical and environmental factors have shaped who you are.

3. **CRITICAL WRITING**   Do Eskimos really have "thirty different names for snow," as Esperanza reports having read (par. 1)? And what does it mean if they do? What does culture have to do with language, and how might language be said to affect culture? Conduct some research into the history of the claim, said originally to have been made by Franz Boas in his book *Handbook of American Indian Languages* (1911). What point was the anthropologist making? How have other scholars responded to the notion that indigenous peoples in a frozen climate

would develop such a complex classification of a seemingly simple natural element, then and more recently? How does the controversy affect your reading of this story? Explain.

4. **CONNECTIONS** Write an essay that compares and contrasts Sandra Cisneros's short story "And Some More" with Gary Soto's poem "The Elements of San Joaquin" (p. 327). What do these two iconic works of Chicano literature have in common? Where do the writers' purposes and perspectives diverge? What might explain the similarities and differences between them? As you develop your ideas, consider the writers' chosen GENRES, to start, but also their points of view and their political positions, stated or implied.

Sandra Cisneros on Writing

A bilingual author, Sandra Cisneros writes primarily in English. Yet Spanish influences her English sentences, and she frequently uses Spanish words in her prose. She spoke with Feroza Jussawalla and Reed Way Dasenbrock about how Spanish affects her writing:

"What it does is change the rhythm of my writing. I think that incorporating the Spanish, for me, allows me to create new expressions in English—to say things that have never been said before. And I get to do that by translating literally. I love calling stories by Spanish expressions. I have this story called 'Salvador, Late or Early.' It's a nice title. It means 'sooner or later,' *tarde o temprano*, which literally translates as 'late or early.' All of a sudden something happens to the English, something really new is happening, a new spice is added to the English language."

In some of her work, Cisneros uses Spanish and then offers a translation for English readers. At other times, she thinks complete translation is unnecessary: "See, sometimes, you don't have to say the whole thing. Now I'm learning how you can say something in English so that you know the person is saying it in Spanish. I like that. You can say a phrase in Spanish, and you can choose not to translate it, but you can make it understood through the context. 'And then my *abuelita* called me a *sin verguenza* and cried because I am without shame,' you see? Just in the sentence you can weave it in. To me it's really fun to be doing that; to me it's like I've uncovered this whole mother lode that I haven't tapped into. All the *expresiones* in Spanish when translated make English wonderful."

That said, Cisneros believes that "[t]he readers who are going to like my stories the best and catch all the subtexts and all the subtleties, that even my editor can't catch, are Chicanas. When there are Chicanas in the audience, and they laugh, they are laughing at stuff that we talk about among ourselves. And there's no way that my editor at Random House is ever going to get those jokes." This seems particularly true, she finds, when she's making use of Mexican and Southwestern myths and legends about which the general public might not be aware. "That's why I say the real ones who are going to get it are the Latinos, the Chicanos. They're going to get it in that they're going to understand the myth and how I've revised it. When I talked to someone at *Interview* magazine, I had to explain to him what I was doing with *la llorona*, *La Malinche*, and the Virgin of Guadalupe in the story ['Woman Hollering Creek']. But he said, 'Hey, I didn't know that, but I still got the story.' You can get it at some other level. He reminded me, 'Sandra, if you're from Ireland, you're going to get a lot more out of Joyce than if you're not, but just because you're not Irish doesn't mean you're not going to get it at another level.'"

The Bedford Reader on Writing

Sandra Cisneros has twice as much to think about when it comes to word choice because she uses both English and Spanish while considering what her AUDIENCE would understand and appreciate. Her decisions to translate or not translate certain words or phrases lend her writing a distinct and widely appreciated VOICE. For our thoughts on how to choose language appropriate for your writing situation, see pages 55–57.

LEO BRAUDY

Leo Braudy is one of America's most notable and influential film critics. Born in 1941 in Pennsylvania, Braudy grew up in West Philadelphia and spent his teenage years "trying to be cool," watching fifties-era horror movies with friends and regularly getting kicked out of the local theater for misbehaving. He earned a BA from Swarthmore College in 1963 and a PhD from Yale University in 1967, and he taught English at Yale, Columbia, Johns Hopkins University, and the University of Santa Barbara before joining the faculty of the University of Southern California, where he focuses on seventeenth- and eighteenth-century literature and art history. Braudy's well-received books of cultural analysis include *The Frenzy of Renown: Fame and Its History* (1986), *From Chivalry to Terrorism: War and the Changing Nature of Masculinity* (2003), and, most recently, *Haunted: On Ghosts, Witches, Vampires, Zombies, and Other Monsters of the Natural and Supernatural Worlds* (2016). He is a board member for the *Los Angeles Review of Books* and a frequent contributor to that publication and others, such as the *New York Times*, the *Washington Post*, and *Harper's* magazine. Braudy is also the editor, with Marshall Cohen, of the textbook *Film Theory and Criticism: Introductory Readings*, now in its eighth edition (2016). He lives in Los Angeles.

Where Our Monsters Come From

"Where Our Monsters Come From" was adapted from Braudy's book *Haunted* and first appeared in the *Wall Street Journal* in late October 2016. In this piece, the professor and critic uses classification both to inform readers and entertain them, taking a look, as he often does, at the literary canon of horror stories. Our enduring fascination with such tales, he observes, reveals volumes about modern civilization's fears and anxieties.

The Halloween season is upon us again and, with it, all the lurid paraphernalia of assorted ghosts, ghouls and goblins. It's all in good fun, but our favorite seasonal terrors also say something deeper about what scares us and why. Halloween itself we owe to the ancient Celts, whose festival of Samhain[1] marked the beginning of the dark part of the year, when the souls of the dead revisited the earth, but many of our current monsters reflect more recent anxieties.

Most anthropologists date the beginning of civilization to the institution of funerary rituals and designated cemeteries, and it is hardly surprising that our imaginations, even now, dwell on the disquieting line that separates the

---

[1] The ancient Celts were an agricultural people who migrated from central Europe to Ireland and greater Britain during the first century BC with the expansion of the Roman Empire. Samhain is a Gaelic harvest festival traditionally celebrated on October 31 and November 1. — EDS.

living from the dead. In many cultures, too, ghosts are often angry because they represent, in guilty consciences, those who have been murdered, forgotten or somehow improperly laid to rest.

Religion also played a part. When the Protestant Reformation[2] did away   3 with the concept of purgatory as a transit point to paradise, it opened the doors still further for unsettled ghosts to roam the earth. Disputes between Protestants and Catholics over who could best invoke angels and keep demons at bay ensured that those emissaries from the invisible world would continue to be vivid realities for many believers.

Most of our own repertoire of frights, however, has a more recent historical   4 source: the Enlightenment[3] and our often fevered, distressed reactions to it. Whole genres in literature and art developed to resist the sunny optimism of ever-advancing scientific investigation and social revolution. Gothic writers and painters of the eighteenth and nineteenth centuries conjured up a formidable world of monsters and shadowy fears. Today we see the descendants of their creations in our own movies, graphic novels and videogames.

In this menagerie of horrors, there are four primary types of monsters,   5 each of which embodies a set of fears that has persisted despite — and often because of — our many scientific and social advances.

The first of these is the monster from nature. The classical world was   6 populated by a host of natural monsters — the Chimera, the Sphinx, the Hydra, the Minotaur.[4] The modern version is a protest against the Enlightenment's ambitions to control nature and turn it to human purposes. It can take the form of an exotic beast like King Kong, exploited as a commercial attraction only to wreak havoc in the center of civilization, or of natural forces unleashed by our scientific hubris, like Godzilla, the space creature of *Alien* and the dinosaurs of *Jurassic Park*.[5]

Whatever form these monsters take, they awaken the dread of what lies   7 beneath the surface of an otherwise seemingly placid and benevolent natural environment. They remind us that, much as we might seek to understand the secrets of nature, it has a few deadly surprises of its own.

---

[2] A period of religious and cultural upheaval in sixteenth-century Europe, marked by widespread Christian rejection of Catholic doctrine and authority. — Eds.

[3] A period of European intellectual history, in the mid-eighteenth century, during which science, philosophy, and humanitarian reform prospered. — Eds.

[4] Imaginary creatures from ancient Greek mythology. A Chimera is a fire-breathing combination of lion, goat, and serpent; a Sphinx is a winged animal with a woman's head and a lion's body; a Hydra is a creature with multiple snakes as a head; and a Minotaur has a man's body and a bull's head and tail. — Eds.

[5] King Kong is a fictional giant gorilla featured in several movies since the character first appeared in 1933. Godzilla is a dinosaur-like monster originated in Japanese films in 1954. *Alien* (1979) is a science-fiction film about a crew of astronauts stranded in deep space, and *Jurassic Park* (1993) is a movie about the folly of bringing dinosaurs back from extinction by cloning. — Eds.

The created monster is an even more direct rebuke to the modern desire   8
to dominate the world. Dr. Frankenstein intends to make a creature that
will be subordinate and easy to manipulate, but it revolts against its maker.
The technological urge to invent and create thus merges to awful effect with
the all-too-human story of the parent who rejects its child and the child
who wages war against the parent. From Mary Shelley's novel to the movie
Ex Machina and HBO's *Westworld*, the created monster slowly becomes aware
of its plight and plots revenge.[6]

Advances in the study of psychology brought us the monster from   9
within — the idea that the truly monstrous isn't out there somewhere but
rather inside us, our evil twin. The archetype here is Robert Louis Stevenson's
murderous Mr. Hyde.[7] Once released, he is a malevolent threat to the benevolent Dr. Jekyll and the world at large — a reminder of the dark passions
beneath the daylight world of reason and science. Newer takes on the monstrous potential within us all range from *The Exorcist* to *The Incredible Hulk.*[8]

Finally, there is the monster from the past, where the great model is the   10
vampire Dracula. No matter that the historical Vlad the Impaler, on whom
Dracula is based, was actually a defender of Christian Romania against the
Ottoman Empire. The King Vampire of Bram Stoker's novel comes out of a
distant pre-Christian past.[9] Dracula's vampirism represents a church of evil,
and his need to drink blood is a morbid parody of the Eucharist.[10]

This sort of monster, as any number of backward-looking horror fictions   11
suggest, is especially notable for its sensational props and rituals, from wooden
stakes to ancient amulets and elixirs — reminders that, however powerful our
science and understanding, we can't escape from the dark lore of the past.

What is remarkable is the adaptability of these foundational monster   12
stories. They are so embedded in popular culture, which has a way of taming
even the most monstrous things, that a cereal can be named Count Chocula

---

[6] British writer Mary Shelley (1797–1851) is the author of *Frankenstein, or the Modern Prometheus* (1818). *Ex Machina* (2014) is a thriller about artificial intelligence. *Westworld* (2016–) is a science-fiction program about a futuristic theme park hosted by androids. — EDS.

[7] Robert Louis Stevenson (1850–94) is a British writer best known for the novels *Treasure Island* (1883) and *The Strange Case of Dr. Jekyll and Mr. Hyde* (1886), the latter about a scientist with a split personality. — EDS.

[8] *The Exorcist* (1973) is a horror movie about a girl possessed by Satan. *The Incredible Hulk* (2008) is a Marvel comics film, based on a 1970s television series, about a mild-man-nered scientist who transforms into a giant green beast when angered. — EDS.

[9] British author Bram Stoker (1847–1912) published the gothic horror novel *Dracula* in 1897. Prince Vlad III Dracul (1431–76) was a notoriously vicious ruler of the Walachia region of Transylvania, now in Romania. Ottoman Turks rapidly expanded Islamic territories during the fifteenth and sixteenth centuries, overtaking much of Southeast Europe, Western Asia, and North Africa at the height of empire. — EDS.

[10] Christian ceremony of communion, involving the consumption of wine and bread symbolizing the blood and body of Christ. — EDS.

and little children can learn numbers from Count von Count on *Sesame Street*.[11] Mary Shelley didn't have a clue about cloning, organ transplants or genetically modified food, but her story easily shapes fears and anxieties about them.

The universe of monsters has expanded, too, often by combining 13 elements from the classic types. Zombies are relative newcomers. Their lurching movements recall Frankenstein, their transformations Jekyll and Hyde, and their taste for flesh Dracula. But unlike the monsters of the past, which have tended to be individuals, zombies are members of a group. Fear of them springs, at least in part, from our anxieties about the various "hordes" that modern life so often presents to our imagination as threats.

Our classic monsters have been with us for more than two centuries, and 14 they are unlikely to go away soon. They are resurrected and reinvented in each generation, paying tribute to fears that would otherwise remain nameless.

Journal Writing

Do you enjoy tales of monsters, whether in books, in movies, or on television? Of the monster characters in popular culture (past or present), which is your favorite? Why do you think this character or its type appeal appeals to you? In your journal, explore what monsters mean to you. If you don't care for horror stories, consider why they leave you cold.

Questions on Meaning

1. Why do you suppose Braudy wrote this essay? Is he merely promoting his book, or does he have a more serious PURPOSE as well?

2. What is Braudy's THESIS? Express the larger meaning of his essay in your own words.

3. Where do ghosts come from, as Braudy explains them? How are they related to his subject of monsters?

4. How does Braudy explain the appeal of monsters in contemporary culture? In what ways has that appeal changed across time and geography? In what ways has it remained consistent?

Questions on Writing Strategy

1. How does the essay's INTRODUCTION help set its TONE? How does the CONCLUSION reinforce the tone?

---

[11] A long-running children's educational program produced for the Public Broadcasting System. — EDS.

2. What principle of classification does Braudy use to sort out types of monsters? What types does he identify, and what distinguishes each category?

3. How do zombies fit into Braudy's classification scheme? Do his categories seem to overlap to you? Why, or why not?

4. **OTHER METHODS**   In paragraphs 6–11, how does Braudy use EXAMPLES and ANALYSIS to develop his classification? Itemize the strategies he uses to make each category clear.

Questions on Language

1. "Where Our Monsters Come From" uses advanced academic vocabulary and contains several literary, historical, and religious ALLUSIONS. How, then, does the author imagine his AUDIENCE? Are his assumptions reasonable in your case?

2. Look up any of these words that are unfamiliar: lurid, paraphernalia (par. 1); anthropologists, funerary, disquieting (2); purgatory, invoke, emissaries (3); repertoire, Gothic, conjured, formidable (4); menagerie (5); hubris (6); placid, benevolent (7); rebuke (8); archetype, malevolent (9); parody (10); amulets, elixirs (11); hordes (13); resurrected (14).

Suggestions for Writing

1. **FROM JOURNAL TO ESSAY**   Using your journal notes and Braudy's ideas as a springboard, write an essay that examines what frightens you. Are you afraid of change, for instance, or technology? Does the natural environment make you anxious? What about human history? Do you agree with Braudy that fictional monsters in popular culture can help you manage such fears? Why, or why not?

2. Write an essay that analyzes several examples of another type of writing by examining their shared characteristics and hidden meanings. You may choose any narrowly defined GENRE that's familiar to you: food blog, parenting-advice column, amateur film review, gay romance, alternative-history science fiction, and so on. Be sure to make your principle of analysis clear to readers.

3. **CRITICAL WRITING**   Some cultural analysts have suggested that the resurgence of vampire stories in the last three decades can be attributed to the AIDS epidemic that emerged in the 1980s. In your library's database of scholarly journals, conduct a keyword search with "vampires and AIDS" and read one of two of the arguments in favor of this theory. (If you prefer, you may search for other academic analyses of monster lore.) How do you respond to the articles? Do alternate interpretations undermine Braudy's classification, or do they simply complicate it?

4. **CONNECTIONS**   In the cartoon "Costumes to Scare Millennials" (p. 160), Sarah Andersen also examines contemporary fears and anxieties, but with an exclusive focus on young adults. How might Braudy explain the causes of the fears Andersen identifies? How might the author and the artist assess the functions of Halloween costumes in popular culture? How do the fears both authors look at resonate with your own experience? In an essay, answer these questions and any others they might raise for you.

JEAN-PIERRE DE BEER

Jean-Pierre (JP) De Beer was born in Pittsburgh, Pennsylvania, in 1999 and grew up in suburban Ohio and Illinois, rural South Carolina, and remote Queensland, Australia. He is currently a student at William Paterson University in northern New Jersey, where he studies psychology and volunteers as a DJ for WPSC 88.7, the campus radio station. A dual citizen of the United States and Belgium, De Beer has also had occasion to visit parts of Europe, New Zealand, and Japan. In addition to world travel he enjoys snowboarding, acting, massive multiplayer online games, and science fiction.

Stars of Life

De Beer wrote this essay especially for *The Bedford Reader* in 2016. His original intention was to classify computer games, but, he tells us, he quickly realized that his categories were hopelessly overlapped. In a burst of inspiration, he composed a rough draft of "Stars of Life," a curious investigation of the possibilities for life on other planets, in a matter of a few hours. De Beer then devoted a week or so to revising it—refining his purpose, locating sources of information, fleshing out the details, and shaping the organization—and then another day to editing.

Notice that the finished essay is based on Web research. In accordance with MLA style (see pp. 656–70), De Beer names his sources in the text and lists them at the end. Most of his parenthetical citations do not include page numbers because most of his sources do not have them.

"I don't think the human race will survive the next thousand years, unless we spread into space."

— Stephen Hawking

Sooner than later humanity will need to abandon the small asteroid it 1 lives on and find a place to live out among the stars. While most stars could potentially have Earth-like planets orbiting within their habitable zones, many are too short-lived, too unpredictable, or too uncommon to support human life in the long term. Moreover, in the years of the great move people will need to acquire and harness an abundant source of energy to power the space-age contraptions that will be required to reach and colonize a new home. If we wish to survive, humanity will need to find a long-term solution by identifying stars that can support our endeavors and last trillions of years.

Ranging from the runt OGLE-TR-122b to the enormous VY Canis 2 Majoris, there are some 100 billion burning gas balls in our galaxy (Howell).

Astronomers generally classify these stars into seven major categories and as many as fifty-six subcategories ("Star Types"). Of these, three types stand out as the most potentially beneficial to humankind and prolonging its existence: supergiants, yellow dwarfs, and red dwarfs. Each kind of star varies in different aspects such as temperature, life span, and number, and each offers distinct contributions should humanity succeed in spreading to space. The red dwarf, however, is or at least will be the most important star because of its incredibly long life span and relative abundance in our immense universe.

Supergiants earned their name because they are some of the largest and hottest stars known to science. With temperatures that can exceed 20,000 kelvin (about five times hotter than the sun), supergiants are among the stars with the greatest energy output ("Star Types"). With this massive energy comes a cost, though: Where our sun will last about 10 billion years, supergiants tend to last only half a million years (Lang 141). Because of their relatively short lifespan supergiants are extremely rare; they account for less than .0001 percent of all stars still alive, or about "one in a million" (Lang 140). Nonetheless, supergiant stars could be an immense source of energy for the future. Assuming that scientists could tap into that energy, an entire new world of possibility arises. 3

Intergalactic relocation will likely require an extraordinary amount of energy to power a range of demanding devices: space crafts, terraforming machines, life-support systems, and more. Harnessing the energy released by supergiant stars could theoretically accelerate development, power deep-space missions to other galaxies, and provide a basically infinite supply of fuel to sustain life on other planets. Studying and eventually applying the vast amount of heat and force a supergiant generates could lead to a range of new and stronger tools, materials, and matter that would be otherwise unobtainable. When humankind needs to acquire new forms of energy in any quantity and store it, the universe's greatest power source — the supergiant star — should be able to provide. 4

While supergiants promise to be of assistance in the future, yellow dwarfs deserve special appreciation because they have already been a massive help to humankind: Our current sun is a yellow dwarf. Yellow dwarf stars typically hit a surface temperature of around 5,600 kelvin (about 15 times hotter than boiling water), causing a relatively stable energy output (Cain). The low energy gives dwarf stars a longer life span than that of supergiants, commonly about 10 billion years (Cain). Should humanity need to find a new home quickly and nearby, a yellow dwarf would be our best bet. Approximately twenty percent of the stars in the known universe are yellow dwarfs ("Star Types"), and it is likely that at least some host inhabitable planets for humankind to colonize on, at least for a little while. 5

Because of a yellow dwarf's mass and the amount of energy it releases, 6
any rock planet that is in the habitable zone (like our Earth) would most
likely be relatively safe from solar flares. The long life span of a yellow dwarf
star ensures that once the big move is finished, humanity will have plenty of
time to colonize, develop, and adapt to the new landscape and solar system.
In the event that we find a new home near a yellow dwarf star, we should
have a workable base of operations—at least until a more long-term solution
can be found.

Red dwarfs, the real stars of the show, are the most likely to help out 7
humankind in the long run. They are the smallest known stars in the universe (but still massive) and consistently hit a temperature of around 4,000
kelvin—a very low energy output in the spectrum of the stars ("Star Types").
Because of their relative size and slow release of energy they will last for a
cool ten trillion years, give or take a few billion; red dwarfs are also abundant,
making up about seventy percent of all the stars in the universe ("Last Star").
What's more, NASA's Kepler space telescope mission has found that at least
half of the observable red dwarfs host a rock planet near the size of Earth,
and many of them are in the "Goldilocks zone" of moderate temperature,
atmospheric pressure, and the possibility of water. In the Milky Way alone
"about five percent of red dwarfs . . . may host habitable, Earth-sized planets"
(Last Star)—that's more than four billion potential homes nearby!

The renowned cosmologist Stephen Hawking once said that humanity 8
will not survive unless we relocate. While all types of stars have the potential
to host or at least help us, supergiants, yellow dwarfs, and red dwarfs especially will prove to be invaluable in the not-so-distant future. Supergiants
and their unparalleled source of energy will power the devices needed to
move and rebuild. Yellow dwarfs provide a viable alternative to Earth's sun
should we need to evacuate quickly. Red dwarfs, however, give humanity a
nearly infinite amount of space to grow, colonize, and hunker down for the
long haul. Because of their immense life span, they will provide a place to
live after all other stars have died out. And because of how common they are,
they offer practically endless amounts of prime real estate just waiting to be
claimed. If we look to them for our future, the entire universe will be at our
fingertips for trillions of years to come.

Works Cited

Cain, Fraser. "What Kind of Star Is the Sun?" Universe Today, 1 Aug. 2008,
      www.universetoday.com/16350/what-kind-of-star-is-the-sun/.
Hawking, Stephen. "Colonies in Space May Be Only Hope." Interview
      by Roger Highfield. The Telegraph, 16 Oct. 2001, www.telegraph.co.uk/
      news/uknews/1359562/Colonies-in-space-may-be-only-hope-says-
      Hawking.html.

Howell, Elizabeth. "How Many Stars Are in the Milky Way?" *Space.com*,
     Purch, 21 May 2014, www.space.com/25959-how-many-stars-are-in-
     the-milky-way.html.
Lang, Kenneth R. *The Life and Death of Stars*. Cambridge UP, 2013. *Google
     Books*, books.google.com/books/about/The_Life_and_Death_of_Stars
     .html?id=MN-UCkUK9pcC.
"The Last Star in the Universe: Red Dwarfs Explained." *Kurzgesagt —
     In a Nutshell*, 31 Jan. 2016. *YouTube*, www.youtube.com/watch?v=
     L-VPyLaJFM.
NASA. *Kepler: A Search for Habitable Planets*. Ames Research Center,
     18 Jan. 2016, kepler.nasa.gov/. Accessed 11 Feb. 2016.
"Star Types." *All about Astronomy*, Enchanted Learning, 2015, www
     .enchantedlearning.com/subjects/astronomy/stars/startypes.shtml.
     Accessed 8 Feb. 2016.

Journal Writing

Do you think there could be life on other planets? If no, why not? If yes, what forms
might such extraterrestrial life take: intelligent beings with social structures and
civilizations akin to ours, or something more basic, like flora and fauna — or simple
microbes? Or perhaps you imagine beings and societies far more evolved than our
own? In your journal, ponder the possibilities.

Questions on Meaning

1. How seriously does De Beer take his subject? What seems to be his PURPOSE in
   classifying stars?

2. What is a planet's "Goldilocks zone" (par. 7)? Where does the term come from?

3. Where does De Beer state his THESIS? Is any part of his main idea left unsaid?

Questions on Writing Strategy

1. "Stars of Life" opens with a short quotation from Stephen Hawking. Why? What
   is the function of this epigraph? Where in the essay does De Beer return to it,
   and to what EFFECT?

2. For whom would you say De Beer is writing? What ASSUMPTIONS does he make
   about his AUDIENCE?

3. Identify the principle of classification De Beer uses to organize types of stars.
   What does each type have in common?

4. What consistent pattern does De Beer use to develop the paragraphs for each of
   his categories? How effective do you find this approach?

5. **OTHER METHODS**   What role does CAUSE-AND-EFFECT analysis play in De Beer's
   classification?

Questions on Language

1. How would you describe De Beer's general DICTION? Why is — or isn't — his language appropriate for his subject, his purpose, and his audience?

2. Locate some FIGURES OF SPEECH and COLLOQUIAL EXPRESSIONS in De Beer's writing and explain what they contribute to his essay.

3. Look up any of the following words whose meanings you are unsure of: asteroid, habitable, harness, contraptions, endeavors (par. 1); runt (2); kelvin (3); intergalactic, terraforming (4); spectrum (7); cosmologist (8).

Suggestions for Writing

1. **FROM JOURNAL TO ESSAY**   Taking off from your speculations in your journal (p. 375), respond to De Beer's proposal that humanity will need to move to another planet to survive. Is such a move really necessary, or possible? And if so, what are the ethical implications of colonizing habitable planets, especially if they already host some forms of life? Do we have the right to "spread into space"? What could happen if we did? Might there be wars and fights over resources, perhaps, the spread of disease, changes to human biology, interspecies development, some other consequences? Be as lighthearted or as serious as you wish, but be as imaginative as you can.

2. Look into the mission, history, and findings to date of the Kepler space telescope team (you might start with the home page De Beer identifies in his works-cited list). What are NASA's goals for the program? What has it achieved? How supportive of its budget has Congress been? Based on your findings, write an essay defending and justifying the use of government funding for the Kepler mission or another program such as the Hubble telescope or the New Horizons spacecraft. This essay will require some research because you will need to argue that the benefits of NASA's programs outweigh their costs, and you will need to support your claims with factual evidence. Or approach the issue from a skeptic's point of view and argue against using taxpayers' money for space exploration. Substantiate your argument with data, and be sure to propose alternative methods for exploring the cosmos and funding such investigations.

3. **CRITICAL WRITING**   Most of the information De Beer provides comes from general-interest space and astronomy sites, and all of it comes from the Web. (The bulk of it, too, could be considered common knowledge, or scientific facts not attributable to any one source; see p. 656.) How convincing do you find this EVIDENCE? Does the nature of De Beer's research weaken his essay in any way, or does his classification remain valid? Why do you think so? (You might, if time allows, look for more scholarly works on astronomy or the search for habitable planets, and consider how they apply to De Beer's conclusions.) Explain your evaluation in a brief essay.

4. **CONNECTIONS**   Jean-Pierre De Beer's "Stars of Life" and Ted Chiang's "The Great Silence" both consider the possibilities of life in outer space and the ultimate fate of the Earth and its inhabitants. In an essay, COMPARE AND CONTRAST the two writers' treatments of their subjects. What strategies do De Beer and Chiang have in common, and where do their perspectives diverge? How does the TONE of each selection contribute to its effect?

DEBORAH TANNEN

Deborah Tannen is a linguist who is best known for her popular studies of communication between men and women. Born and raised in New York City, Tannen earned a BA from Harpur College (now part of Binghamton University), MAs from Wayne State University and the University of California at Berkeley, and a PhD in linguistics from Berkeley. She is University Professor at Georgetown University, has published many scholarly articles and books, and lectures on linguistics all over the world. But her renown is more than academic: With television talk-show appearances, speeches to businesspeople and senators, and best-selling books, Tannen has become, in the words of one reviewer, "America's conversational therapist." The books include *You Just Don't Understand: Women and Men in Conversation* (1990), *The Argument Culture* (1998), *You Were Always Mom's Favorite!* (2009), about communication between sisters, and *You're the Only One I Can Tell: Inside the Language of Women's Friendships* (2017). Tannen sits on the board of the PEN/Faulkner Foundation, a nonprofit organization devoted to building audiences for literature.

But What Do You Mean?

Why do men and women so often communicate badly, if at all? This question has motivated much of Tannen's research and writing. Excerpted in *Redbook* magazine from Tannen's book *Talking from 9 to 5* (1994), the essay reprinted here classifies the conversational areas where men and women have the most difficulty communicating in the workplace.

William Lutz's "The World of Doublespeak," the essay following Tannen's, also uses classification to examine communication problems, in the form of misleading verbal substitutions that make "the bad seem good, the negative appear positive."

Conversation is a ritual. We say things that seem obviously the thing to 1 say, without thinking of the literal meaning of our words, any more than we expect the question "How are you?" to call forth a detailed account of aches and pains.

Unfortunately, women and men often have different ideas about what's 2 appropriate, different ways of speaking. Many of the conversational rituals common among women are designed to take the other person's feelings into account, while many of the conversational rituals common among men are designed to maintain the one-up position, or at least avoid appearing one-down. As a result, when men and women interact—especially at work—it's often women who are at the disadvantage. Because women are not trying to avoid the one-down position, that is unfortunately where they may end up.

Here, the biggest areas of miscommunication.   3

1. Apologies

Women are often told they apologize too much. The reason they're   4
told to stop doing it is that, to many men, apologizing seems synonymous with putting oneself down. But there are many times when "I'm sorry" isn't self-deprecating, or even an apology; it's an automatic way of keeping both speakers on an equal footing. For example, a well-known columnist once interviewed me and gave me her phone number in case I needed to call her back. I misplaced the number and had to go through the newspaper's main switchboard. When our conversation was winding down and we'd both made ending-type remarks, I added, "Oh, I almost forgot—I lost your direct number, can I get it again?" "Oh, I'm sorry," she came back instantly, even though she had done nothing wrong and *I* was the one who'd lost the number. But I understood she wasn't really apologizing; she was just automatically reassuring me she had no intention of denying me her number.

Even when "I'm sorry" *is* an apology, women often assume it will be the   5
first step in a two-step ritual: I say "I'm sorry" and take half the blame, then you take the other half. At work, it might go something like this:

A: When you typed this letter, you missed this phrase I inserted.

B: Oh, I'm sorry. I'll fix it.

A: Well, I wrote it so small it was easy to miss.

When both parties share blame, it's a mutual face-saving device. But   6
if one person, usually the woman, utters frequent apologies and the other doesn't, she ends up looking as if she's taking the blame for mishaps that aren't her fault. When she's only partially to blame, she looks entirely in the wrong.

I recently sat in on a meeting at an insurance company where the sole   7
woman, Helen, said "I'm sorry" or "I apologize" repeatedly. At one point she said, "I'm thinking out loud. I apologize." Yet the meeting was intended to be an informal brainstorming session, and *everyone* was thinking out loud.

The reason Helen's apologies stood out was that she was the only person   8
in the room making so many. And the reason I was concerned was that Helen felt the annual bonus she had received was unfair. When I interviewed her colleagues, they said that Helen was one of the best and most productive workers—yet she got one of the smallest bonuses. Although the problem

might have been outright sexism, I suspect her speech style, which differs from that of her male colleagues, masks her competence.

Unfortunately, not apologizing can have its price too. Since so many 9 women use ritual apologies, those who don't may be seen as hard-edged. What's important is to be aware of how often you say you're sorry (and why), and to monitor your speech based on the reaction you get.

2. Criticism

A woman who cowrote a report with a male colleague was hurt when she 10 read a rough draft to him and he leapt into a critical response — "Oh, that's too dry! You have to make it snappier!" She herself would have been more likely to say, "That's a really good start. Of course, you'll want to make it a little snappier when you revise."

Whether criticism is given straight or softened is often a matter of con- 11 vention. In general, women use more softeners. I noticed this difference when talking to an editor about an essay I'd written. While going over changes she wanted to make, she said, "There's one more thing. I know you may not agree with me. The reason I noticed the problem is that your other points are so lucid and elegant." She went on hedging for several more sentences until I put her out of her misery: "Do you want to cut that part?" I asked — and of course she did. But I appreciated her tentativeness. In contrast, another editor (a man) I once called summarily rejected my idea for an article by barking, "Call me when you have something new to say."

Those who are used to ways of talking that soften the impact of criticism 12 may find it hard to deal with the right-between-the-eyes style. It has its own logic, however, and neither style is intrinsically better. People who prefer criticism given straight are operating on an assumption that feelings aren't involved: "Here's the dope. I know you're good; you can take it."

3. Thank-Yous

A woman manager I know starts meetings by thanking everyone for 13 coming, even though it's clearly their job to do so. Her "thank-you" is simply a ritual.

A novelist received a fax from an assistant in her publisher's office; it 14 contained suggested catalog copy for her book. She immediately faxed him her suggested changes and said, "Thanks for running this by me," even though her contract gave her the right to approve all copy. When she thanked the assistant, she fully expected him to reciprocate: "Thanks for giving me such a quick response." Instead, he said, "You're welcome." Suddenly, rather than an equal exchange of pleasantries, she found herself positioned as the recipient of a favor. This made her feel like responding, "Thanks for nothing!"

Many women use "thanks" as an automatic conversation starter and   15
closer; there's nothing literally to say thank you for. Like many rituals typical of women's conversation, it depends on the goodwill of the other to restore the balance. When the other speaker doesn't reciprocate, a woman may feel like someone on a seesaw whose partner abandoned his end. Instead of balancing in the air, she has plopped to the ground, wondering how she got there.

4. Fighting

Many men expect the discussion of ideas to be a ritual fight — explored   16
through verbal opposition. They state their ideas in the strongest possible terms, thinking that if there are weaknesses someone will point them out, and by trying to argue against those objections, they will see how well their ideas hold up.

Those who expect their own ideas to be challenged will respond to   17
another's ideas by trying to poke holes and find weak links — as a way *of helping*. The logic is that when you are challenged you will rise to the occasion: Adrenaline makes your mind sharper; you get ideas and insights you would not have thought of without the spur of battle.

But many women take this approach as a personal attack. Worse, they   18
find it impossible to do their best work in such a contentious environment. If you're not used to ritual fighting, you begin to hear criticism of your ideas as soon as they are formed. Rather than making you think more clearly, it makes you doubt what you know. When you state your ideas, you hedge in order to fend off potential attacks. Ironically, this is more likely to *invite* attack because it makes you look weak.

Although you may never enjoy verbal sparring, some women find it   19
helpful to learn how to do it. An engineer who was the only woman among four men in a small company found that as soon as she learned to argue she was accepted and taken seriously. A doctor attending a hospital staff meeting made a similar discovery. She was becoming more and more angry with a male colleague who'd loudly disagreed with a point she'd made. Her better judgment told her to hold her tongue, to avoid making an enemy of this powerful senior colleague. But finally she couldn't hold it in any longer, and she rose to her feet and delivered an impassioned attack on his position. She sat down in a panic, certain she had permanently damaged her relationship with him. To her amazement, he came up to her afterward and said, "That was a great rebuttal. I'm really impressed. Let's go out for a beer after work and hash out our approaches to this problem."

5. Praise

A manager I'll call Lester had been on his new job six months when 20
he heard that the women reporting to him were deeply dissatisfied. When
he talked to them about it, their feelings erupted; two said they were on
the verge of quitting because he didn't appreciate their work, and they
didn't want to wait to be fired. Lester was dumbfounded: He believed they
were doing a fine job. Surely, he thought, he had said nothing to give them
the impression he didn't like their work. And indeed he hadn't. That was the
problem. He had said *nothing*—and the women assumed he was following
the adage "If you can't say something nice, don't say anything." He thought
he was showing confidence in them by leaving them alone.

Men and women have different habits in regard to giving praise. For 21
example, Deirdre and her colleague William both gave presentations at a conference. Afterward, Deirdre told William, "That was a great talk!" He thanked
her. Then she asked, "What did you think of mine?" and he gave her a lengthy
and detailed critique. She found it uncomfortable to listen to his comments.
But she assured herself that he meant well, and that his honesty was a signal
that she, too, should be honest when he asked for a critique of his performance.
As a matter of fact, she had noticed quite a few ways in which he could have
improved his presentation. But she never got a chance to tell him because he
never asked—and she felt put down. The worst part was that it seemed she
had only herself to blame, since she *had* asked what he thought of her talk.

But had she really asked for his critique? The truth is, when she asked for 22
his opinion, she was expecting a compliment, which she felt was more or less
required following anyone's talk. When he responded with criticism, she figured, "Oh, he's playing 'Let's critique each other'"—not a game she'd initiated,
but one which she was willing to play. Had she realized he was going to criticize
her and not ask her to reciprocate, she would never have asked in the first place.

It would be easy to assume that Deirdre was insecure, whether she was 23
fishing for a compliment or soliciting a critique. But she was simply talking
automatically, performing one of the many conversational rituals that
allow us to get through the day. William may have sincerely misunderstood
Deirdre's intention—or may have been unable to pass up a chance to one-up
her when given the opportunity.

6. Complaints

"Troubles talk" can be a way to establish rapport with a colleague. You 24
complain about a problem (which shows that you are just folks) and the other
person responds with a similar problem (which puts you on equal footing).

But while such commiserating is common among women, men are likely to hear it as a request to *solve* the problem.

One woman told me she would frequently initiate what she thought 25 would be pleasant complaint-airing sessions at work. She'd talk about situations that bothered her just to talk about them, maybe to understand them better. But her male office mate would quickly tell her how she could improve the situation. This left her feeling condescended to and frustrated. She was delighted to see this very impasse in a section in my book *You Just Don't Understand*, and showed it to him. "Oh," he said, "I see the problem. How can we solve it?" Then they both laughed, because it had happened again: He short-circuited the detailed discussion she'd hoped for and cut to the chase of finding a solution.

Sometimes the consequences of complaining are more serious: A man 26 might take a woman's lighthearted griping literally, and she can get a reputation as a chronic malcontent. Furthermore, she may be seen as not up to solving the problems that arise on the job.

7. Jokes

I heard a man call in to a talk show and say, "I've worked for two women 27 and neither one had a sense of humor. You know, when you work with men, there's a lot of joking and teasing." The show's host and the guest (both women) took his comment at face value and assumed the women this man worked for were humorless. The guest said, "Isn't it sad that women don't feel comfortable enough with authority to see the humor?" The host said, "Maybe when more women are in authority roles, they'll be more comfortable with power." But although the women this man worked for *may* have taken themselves too seriously, it's just as likely that they each had a terrific sense of humor, but maybe the humor wasn't the type he was used to. They may have been like the woman who wrote to me: "When I'm with men, my wit or cleverness seems inappropriate (or lost!) so I don't bother. When I'm with my women friends, however, there's no hold on puns or cracks and my humor is fully appreciated."

The types of humor women and men tend to prefer differ. Research has 28 shown that the most common form of humor among men is razzing, teasing, and mock-hostile attacks, while among women it's self-mocking. Women often mistake men's teasing as genuinely hostile. Men often mistake women's mock self-deprecation as truly putting themselves down.

Women have told me they were taken more seriously when they learned 29 to joke the way the guys did. For example, a teacher who went to a national conference with seven other teachers (mostly women) and a group of administrators (mostly men) was annoyed that the administrators always found reasons to leave boring seminars, while the teachers felt they had to stay and take notes. One evening, when the group met at a bar in the hotel, the principal asked her how one such seminar had turned out. She retorted, "As soon as you left, it got much better." He laughed out loud at her response. The playful insult appealed to the men — but there was a trade-off. The women seemed to back off from her after this. (Perhaps they were put off by her using joking to align herself with the bosses.)

There is no "right" way to talk. When problems arise, the culprit may 30 be style differences — and *all* styles will at times fail with others who don't share or understand them, just as English won't do you much good if you try to speak to someone who knows only French. If you want to get your message across, it's not a question of being "right"; it's a question of using language that's shared — or at least understood.

Journal Writing

Tannen's ANECDOTE about the newspaper columnist (par. 4) illustrates that much of what we say is purely automatic. Do you excuse yourself when you bump into inanimate objects? When someone says, "Have a good trip," do you answer, "You, too," even if the other person isn't going anywhere? Do you find yourself overusing certain words or phrases such as "like" or "you know"? Pay close attention to these kinds of verbal tics in your own and others' speech. Over the course of a few days, note as many of them as you can in your journal.

Questions on Meaning

1. What is Tannen's PURPOSE in writing this essay?
2. What does Tannen mean when she writes, "Conversation is a ritual" (par. 1)?
3. What does Tannen see as the fundamental difference between men's and women's conversational strategies?
4. Why is "You're welcome" not always an appropriate response to "Thank you"?

Questions on Writing Strategy

1. This essay has a large cast of characters: twenty-three to be exact. What function do these characters serve? How does Tannen introduce them to the reader? Does she describe them in sufficient detail?
2. Whom does Tannen see as her primary AUDIENCE? ANALYZE her use of the pronoun *you* in paragraphs 9 and 19. Whom does she seem to be addressing? Why?

3. Analyze how Tannen develops the category of apologies in paragraphs 4–9. Where does she use EXAMPLE, DEFINITION, and COMPARISON AND CONTRAST?

4. How does Tannen's characterization of a columnist as "well-known" (par. 4) contribute to the effectiveness of her example?

5. **OTHER METHODS**   For each of her seven areas of miscommunication, Tannen compares and contrasts male and female communication styles and strategies. SUMMARIZE the main source of misunderstanding in each area.

Questions on Language

1. What is the EFFECT of "I put her out of her misery" (par. 11)? What does this phrase usually mean?

2. What does Tannen mean by a "right-between-the-eyes style" (par. 12)? What is the FIGURE OF SPEECH involved here?

3. What is the effect of Tannen's use of figurative verbs, such as "barking" (par. 11) and "erupted" (20)? Find at least one other example of the use of a verb in a non-literal sense.

4. Look up any of the following words whose meanings you are unsure of: synonymous, self-deprecating (par. 4); lucid, tentativeness (11); intrinsically (12); reciprocate (14); adrenaline, spur (17); contentious, hedge (18); sparring, rebuttal (19); adage (20); soliciting (23); commiserating (24); initiate, condescended, impasse (25); chronic, malcontent (26); razzing (28); retorted (29).

Suggestions for Writing

1. **FROM JOURNAL TO ESSAY**   Write an essay classifying the examples from your journal entry (p. 383) into categories of your own devising. You might sort out the examples by context ("phone blunders," "faulty farewells"), by purpose ("nervous tics," "space fillers"), or by some other principle of classification. Given your subject matter, you might want to adopt a humorous TONE.

2. How true do you find Tannen's assessment of miscommunication between the sexes? Consider the conflicts you have experienced yourself or observed — between your parents, among fellow students or coworkers, in fictional portrayals in books and movies. You could also go beyond your personal experiences and observations by researching the opinions of other experts (linguists, psychologists, sociologists, and so on). Write an essay confirming or questioning Tannen's GENERALIZATIONS, backing up your (and perhaps others') views with your own examples.

3. **CRITICAL WRITING**   Tannen insists that "neither [communication] style is intrinsically better" (par. 12), that "[t]here is no 'right' way to talk" (30). What do you make of this refusal to take sides in the battle of the sexes? Is Tannen always successful? Is absolute neutrality possible, or even desirable, when it comes to such divisive issues?

4. **CONNECTIONS**   Tannen offers some of her own experiences as examples of communication blunders, and she often uses the first-person I or we in explaining her

categories. In contrast, the author of the next essay, William Lutz, takes a more distant approach in classifying types of misleading language called *doublespeak*. Which of these approaches, personal or more distant, do you find more effective, and why? When, in your view, is it appropriate to inject yourself into your writing, and when is it not?

Deborah Tannen on Writing

Though "But What Do You Mean?" is written for a general audience, Deborah Tannen is a linguistics scholar who does considerable academic writing. One debate among scholarly writers is whether it is appropriate to incorporate personal experiences and biases into their papers, especially given the goal of objectivity in conducting and reporting research. The October 1996 *PMLA* (*Publications of the Modern Language Association*) printed a discussion of the academic uses of the personal, with contributions from more than two dozen scholars. Tannen's comments, excerpted here, focused on the first-person *I*.

When I write academic prose, I use the first person, and I instruct my students to do the same. The principle that researchers should acknowledge their participation in their work is an outgrowth of a humanistic approach to linguistic analysis. . . . Understanding discourse is not a passive act of decoding but a creative act of imagining a scene (composed of people engaged in culturally recognizable activities) within which the ideas being talked about have meaning. The listener's active participation in sense making both results from and creates interpersonal involvement. For researchers to deny their involvement in their interpreting of discourse would be a logical and ethical violation of this framework. . . .

[O]bjectivity in the analysis of interactions is impossible anyway. Whether they took part in the interaction or not, researchers identify with one or another speaker, are put off or charmed by the styles of participants. This one reminds you of a cousin you adore; that one sounds like a neighbor you despise. Researchers are human beings, not atomic particles or chemical elements. . . .

Another danger of claiming objectivity rather than acknowledging and correcting for subjectivity is that scholars who don't reveal their participation in interactions they analyze risk the appearance of hiding it. "Following is an exchange that occurred between a professor and a student," I have read in articles in my field. The speakers are identified as "A" and "B." The reader is not told that the professor, A (of course the professor is A and the student B), is the author. Yet that knowledge is crucial to contextualizing the author's interpretation. Furthermore, the impersonal designations A and B are another means of constructing a false objectivity. They obscure the fact that human interaction is being analyzed, and they interfere with the reader's understanding. The letters replace what in the author's mind are names and voices and personas that are the basis for understanding the discourse. Readers, given only initials, are left to scramble for understanding by imagining people in place of letters.

Avoiding self-reference by using the third person also results in the depersonalization of knowledge. Knowledge and understanding do not occur in abstract isolation. They always and only occur among people. . . . Denying that scholarship is a personal endeavor entails a failure to understand and correct for the inevitable bias that human beings bring to all their enterprises.

The Bedford Reader on Writing

In arguing for the use of the first-person *I* in scholarly prose, Tannen is speaking primarily about its use in her own field, linguistics. From your experience with ACADEMIC WRITING, is her argument applicable to other disciplines, such as history, biology, psychology, or government? What have your teachers in other courses advised you about writing in the first person? For our guidelines on choosing an appropriate POINT OF VIEW for your writing and using it consistently, check pages 56, 69–70, and 259.

WILLIAM LUTZ

William Lutz was born in 1940 in Racine, Wisconsin. He received a BA from Dominican College, an MA from Marquette University, a PhD from the University of Nevada at Reno, and a JD from Rutgers School of Law. For much of his career, Lutz's interest in words and composition has made him an active campaigner against misleading and irresponsible language. For fourteen years he edited the *Quarterly Review of Doublespeak*, and he has written three popular books on such language, the last being *Doublespeak Defined: Cut through the Bull**** and Get to the Point!* (1999). He has also written for many periodicals, including the *Los Angeles Times*, the *London Times*, and *USA Today*. In 1996 Lutz received the George Orwell Award for Distinguished Contribution to Honesty and Clarity in Public Language. He is professor emeritus at Rutgers University in Camden, New Jersey.

The World of Doublespeak

In the previous essay, Deborah Tannen examines the ways gender differences in speaking can cause innocent misunderstandings. But what if misunderstandings are the result of speech crafted to obscure meaning? Such intentional fudging, or *doublespeak*, is the sort of language Lutz specializes in, and here he uses classification to expose its many guises. "The World of Doublespeak" abridges the first chapter in Lutz's book *Doublespeak: From Revenue Enhancement to Terminal Living* (1989); the essay's title is the chapter's subtitle.

There are no potholes in the streets of Tucson, Arizona, just "pavement deficiencies." The Reagan Administration didn't propose any new taxes, just "revenue enhancement" through new "user's fees." Those aren't bums on the street, just "non–goal oriented members of society." There are no more poor people, just "fiscal underachievers." There was no robbery of an automatic teller machine, just an "unauthorized withdrawal." The patient didn't die because of medical malpractice, it was just a "diagnostic misadventure of a high magnitude." The US Army doesn't kill the enemy anymore, it just "services the target." And the doublespeak goes on.

Doublespeak is language that pretends to communicate but really doesn't. It is language that makes the bad seem good, the negative appear positive, the unpleasant appear attractive or at least tolerable. Doublespeak is language that avoids or shifts responsibility, language that is at variance with its real or purported meaning. It is language that conceals or prevents thought; rather than extending thought, doublespeak limits it.

Doublespeak is not a matter of subjects and verbs agreeing; it is a matter 3 of words and facts agreeing. Basic to doublespeak is incongruity, the incongruity between what is said or left unsaid, and what really is. It is the incongruity between the word and the referent, between seem and be, between the essential function of language—communication—and what doublespeak does—mislead, distort, deceive, inflate, circumvent, obfuscate.

How to Spot Doublespeak

How can you spot doublespeak? Most of the time you will recognize 4 doublespeak when you see or hear it. But, if you have any doubts, you can identify doublespeak just by answering these questions: Who is saying what to whom, under what conditions and circumstances, with what intent, and with what results? Answering these questions will usually help you identify as doublespeak language that appears to be legitimate or that at first glance doesn't even appear to be doublespeak.

First Kind of Doublespeak

There are at least four kinds of doublespeak. The first is the euphemism, 5 an inoffensive or positive word or phrase used to avoid a harsh, unpleasant, or distasteful reality. But a euphemism can also be a tactful word or phrase which avoids directly mentioning a painful reality, or it can be an expression used out of concern for the feelings of someone else, or to avoid directly discussing a topic subject to a social or cultural taboo.

When you use a euphemism because of your sensitivity for someone's 6 feelings or out of concern for a recognized social or cultural taboo, it is not doublespeak. For example, you express your condolences that someone has "passed away" because you do not want to say to a grieving person, "I'm sorry your father is dead." When you use the euphemism "passed away," no one is misled. Moreover, the euphemism functions here not just to protect the feelings of another person, but to communicate also your concern for that person's feelings during a period of mourning. When you excuse yourself to go to the "restroom," or you mention that someone is "sleeping with" or "involved with" someone else, you do not mislead anyone about your meaning, but you do respect the social taboos about discussing bodily functions and sex in direct terms. You also indicate your sensitivity to the feelings of your audience, which is usually considered a mark of courtesy and good manners.

However, when a euphemism is used to mislead or deceive, it becomes 7
doublespeak. For example, in 1984 the US State Department announced that
it would no longer use the word "killing" in its annual report on the status of
human rights in countries around the world. Instead, it would use the phrase
"unlawful or arbitrary deprivation of life," which the department claimed
was more accurate. Its real purpose for using this phrase was simply to avoid
discussing the embarrassing situation of government-sanctioned killings in
countries that are supported by the United States and have been certified by
the United States as respecting the human rights of their citizens. This use of
a euphemism constitutes doublespeak, since it is designed to mislead, to cover
up the unpleasant. Its real intent is at variance with its apparent intent. It is
language designed to alter our perception of reality.

The Pentagon, too, avoids discussing unpleasant realities when it refers 8
to bombs and artillery shells that fall on civilian targets as "incontinent ord-
nance." And in 1977 the Pentagon tried to slip funding for the neutron bomb
unnoticed into an appropriations bill by calling it a "radiation enhancement
device."

Second Kind of Doublespeak

A second kind of doublespeak is jargon, the specialized language of a 9
trade, profession, or similar group, such as that used by doctors, lawyers, engineers, educators, or car mechanics. Jargon can serve an important and useful
function. Within a group, jargon functions as a kind of verbal shorthand that
allows members of the group to communicate with each other clearly, efficiently, and quickly. Indeed, it is a mark of membership in the group to be
able to use and understand the group's jargon.

But jargon, like the euphemism, can also be doublespeak. It can be — and 10
often is — pretentious, obscure, and esoteric terminology used to give an
air of profundity, authority, and prestige to speakers and their subject matter. Jargon as doublespeak often makes the simple appear complex, the ordinary profound, the obvious insightful. In this sense it is used not to express
but impress. With such doublespeak, the act of smelling something becomes
"organoleptic analysis," glass becomes "fused silicate," a crack in a metal support beam becomes a "discontinuity," conservative economic policies become
"distributionally conservative notions."

Lawyers, for example, speak of an "involuntary conversion" of property 11
when discussing the loss or destruction of property through theft, accident,
or condemnation. If your house burns down or if your car is stolen, you have
suffered an involuntary conversion of your property. When used by lawyers in
a legal situation, such jargon is a legitimate use of language, since lawyers can
be expected to understand the term.

However, when a member of a specialized group uses its jargon to com- 12
municate with a person outside the group, and uses it knowing that the non-
member does not understand such language, then there is doublespeak. For
example, on May 9, 1978, a National Airlines 727 airplane crashed while
attempting to land at the Pensacola, Florida, airport. Three of the fifty-two
passengers aboard the airplane were killed. As a result of the crash, National
made an after-tax insurance benefit of $1.7 million, or an extra 18¢ a share
dividend for its stockholders. Now National Airlines had two problems: It
did not want to talk about one of its airplanes crashing, and it had to account
for the $1.7 million when it issued its annual report to its stockholders.
National solved the problem by inserting a footnote in its annual report
which explained that the $1.7 million income was due to "the involuntary
conversion of a 727." National thus acknowledged the crash of its airplane
and the subsequent profit it made from the crash, without once mentioning
the accident or the deaths. However, because airline officials knew that most
stockholders in the company, and indeed most of the general public, were not
familiar with legal jargon, the use of such jargon constituted doublespeak.

Third Kind of Doublespeak

A third kind of doublespeak is gobbledygook or bureaucratese. Basically, 13
such doublespeak is simply a matter of piling on words, of overwhelming the
audience with words, the bigger the words and the longer the sentences the
better. Alan Greenspan, then chair of President Nixon's Council of Economic
Advisors, was quoted in *The Philadelphia Inquirer* in 1974 as having testified
before a Senate committee that "It is a tricky problem to find the particular
calibration in timing that would be appropriate to stem the acceleration in
risk premiums created by falling incomes without prematurely aborting the
decline in the inflation-generated risk premiums."

Nor has Mr. Greenspan's language changed since then. Speaking to 14
the meeting of the Economic Club of New York in 1988, Mr. Greenspan,
now Federal Reserve chair, said, "I guess I should warn you, if I turn out
to be particularly clear, you've probably misunderstood what I've said."
Mr. Greenspan's doublespeak doesn't seem to have held back his career.[1]

Sometimes gobbledygook may sound impressive, but when the quote is 15
later examined in print it doesn't even make sense. During the 1988 presidential campaign, vice-presidential candidate Senator Dan Quayle explained the
need for a strategic-defense initiative by saying, "Why wouldn't an enhanced
deterrent, a more stable peace, a better prospect to denying the ones who

---

[1] Greenspan (born 1926) retired from the Federal Reserve in 2006. He is now a private
consultant. — EDS.

enter conflict in the first place to have a reduction of offensive systems and an introduction to defense capability? I believe this is the route the country will eventually go."

The investigation into the *Challenger* disaster in 1986 revealed the dou-   16
blespeak of gobbledygook and bureaucratese used by too many involved in the shuttle program. When Jesse Moore, NASA's associate administrator, was asked if the performance of the shuttle program had improved with each launch or if it had remained the same, he answered, "I think our performance in terms of the liftoff performance and in terms of the orbital performance, we knew more about the envelope we were operating under, and we have been pretty accurately staying in that. And so I would say the performance has not by design drastically improved. I think we have been able to characterize the performance more as a function of our launch experience as opposed to it improving as a function of time." While this language may appear to be jargon, a close look will reveal that it is really just gobbledygook laced with jargon. But you really have to wonder if Mr. Moore had any idea what he was saying.

Fourth Kind of Doublespeak

The fourth kind of doublespeak is inflated language that is designed to   17
make the ordinary seem extraordinary; to make everyday things seem impressive; to give an air of importance to people, situations, or things that would not normally be considered important; to make the simple seem complex. Often this kind of doublespeak isn't hard to spot, and it is usually pretty funny. While car mechanics may be called "automotive internists," elevator operators members of the "vertical transportation corps," used cars "pre-owned" or "experienced cars," and black-and-white television sets described as having "non-multicolor capability," you really aren't misled all that much by such language.

However, you may have trouble figuring out that, when Chrysler "ini-   18
tiates a career alternative enhancement program," it is really laying off five thousand workers; or that "negative patient-care outcome" means the patient died; or that "rapid oxidation" means a fire in a nuclear power plant.

The doublespeak of inflated language can have serious consequences. In   19
Pentagon doublespeak, "pre-emptive counterattack" means that American forces attacked first; "engaged the enemy on all sides" means American troops were ambushed; "backloading of augmentation personnel" means a retreat by American troops. In the doublespeak of the military, the 1983 invasion of Grenada was conducted not by the US Army, Navy, Air Force, and Marines, but by the "Caribbean Peace Keeping Forces." But then, according to the Pentagon, it wasn't an invasion, it was a "predawn vertical insertion." . . .

The Dangers of Doublespeak

Doublespeak is not the product of carelessness or sloppy thinking.   20
Indeed, most doublespeak is the product of clear thinking and is carefully
designed and constructed to appear to communicate when in fact it doesn't.
It is language designed not to lead but mislead. It is language designed to distort reality and corrupt thought. . . . In the world created by doublespeak, if
it's not a tax increase, but rather "revenue enhancement" or "tax base broadening," how can you complain about higher taxes? If it's not acid rain, but
rather "poorly buffered precipitation," how can you worry about all those
dead trees? If that isn't the Mafia in Atlantic City, but just "members of a
career-offender cartel," why worry about the influence of organized crime in
the city? If Supreme Court Justice William Rehnquist wasn't addicted to the
pain-killing drug his doctor prescribed, but instead it was just that the drug
had "established an interrelationship with the body, such that if the drug
is removed precipitously, there is a reaction," you needn't question that his
decisions might have been influenced by his drug addiction. If it's not a Titan
II nuclear-armed intercontinental ballistic missile with a warhead 630 times
more powerful than the atomic bomb dropped on Hiroshima, but instead,
according to air force colonel Frank Horton, it's just a "very large, potentially
disruptive reentry system," why be concerned about the threat of nuclear
destruction? Why worry about the neutron bomb escalating the arms race
if it's just a "radiation enhancement weapon"? If it's not an invasion, but a
"rescue mission" or a "predawn vertical insertion," you won't need to think
about any violations of US or international law.

Doublespeak has become so common in everyday living that many people   21
fail to notice it. Even worse, when they do notice doublespeak being used on
them, they don't react, they don't protest. Do you protest when you are asked
to check your packages at the desk "for your convenience," when it's not for
your convenience at all but for someone else's? You see advertisements for
"genuine imitation leather," "virgin vinyl," or "real counterfeit diamonds,"
but do you question the language or the supposed quality of the product? Do
you question politicians who don't speak of slums or ghettos but of the "inner
city" or "substandard housing" where the "disadvantaged" live and thus avoid
talking about the poor who have to live in filthy, poorly heated, ramshackle
apartments or houses? Aren't you amazed that patients don't die in the
hospital anymore, it's just "negative patient-care outcome"?

Doublespeak such as that noted earlier that defines cab drivers as "urban   22
transportation specialists," elevator operators as members of the "vertical
transportation corps," and automobile mechanics as "automotive internists"
can be considered humorous and relatively harmless. However, when a fire in
a nuclear reactor building is called "rapid oxidation," an explosion in a nuclear

power plant is called an "energetic disassembly," the illegal overthrow of a legitimate government is termed "destabilizing a government," and lies are seen as "inoperative statements," we are hearing doublespeak that attempts to avoid responsibility and make the bad seem good, the negative appear positive, something unpleasant appear attractive; and which seems to communicate but doesn't. It is language designed to alter our perception of reality and corrupt our thinking. Such language does not provide us with the tools we need to develop, advance, and preserve our culture and our civilization. Such language breeds suspicion, cynicism, distrust, and, ultimately, hostility.

Doublespeak is insidious because it can infect and eventually destroy 23 the function of language, which is communication between people and social groups. This corruption of the function of language can have serious and far-reaching consequences. We live in a country that depends upon an informed electorate to make decisions in selecting candidates for office and deciding issues of public policy. The use of doublespeak can become so pervasive that it becomes the coin of the political realm, with speakers and listeners convinced that they really understand such language. After a while we may really believe that politicians don't lie but only "misspeak," that illegal acts are merely "inappropriate actions," that fraud and criminal conspiracy are just "miscertification." President Jimmy Carter in April of 1980 could call the aborted raid to free the American hostages in Teheran an "incomplete success" and really believe that he had made a statement that clearly communicated with the American public. So, too, could President Ronald Reagan say in 1985 that "ultimately our security and our hopes for success at the arms reduction talks hinge on the determination that we show here to continue our program to rebuild and refortify our defenses" and really believe that greatly increasing the amount of money spent building new weapons would lead to a reduction in the number of weapons in the world. If we really believe that we understand such language and that such language communicates and promotes clear thought, then the world of 1984,[2] with its control of reality through language, is upon us.

Journal Writing

Now that you know the name for it, when have you read or heard examples of doublespeak? Over the next few days, jot down examples of doublespeak that you

---

[2] In a section omitted from this abridgement of his chapter, Lutz discusses *Nineteen Eighty-Four*, the 1949 novel by George Orwell in which a frightening totalitarian state devises a language, called *newspeak*, to shape and control thought in politically acceptable forms. — EDS.

recall or that you read and hear—from politicians or news commentators; in the lease for your dwelling or your car; in advertising and catalogs; from bosses, teachers, or other figures of authority; in overheard conversations.

Questions on Meaning

1. What is Lutz's THESIS? Where does he state it?
2. According to Lutz, four questions can help us identify doublespeak. What are they? How can they help us distinguish between truthful and misleading language?
3. What, according to Lutz, are "the dangers of doublespeak"?
4. What ASSUMPTIONS does the author make about his readers' educational backgrounds and familiarity with his subject?

Questions on Writing Strategy

1. What principle does Lutz use for creating his four kinds of doublespeak—that is, what mainly distinguishes the groups?
2. How does Lutz develop the discussion of euphemism in paragraphs 5–8?
3. Lutz quotes Alan Greenspan twice in paragraphs 13–14. What is surprising about the comment in paragraph 14? Why does Lutz include this second quotation?
4. Lutz uses many quotations that were quite current when he first published this piece in 1989 but that now may seem dated—for instance, references to Presidents Carter and Reagan or to the nuclear arms race. Do these EXAMPLES undermine Lutz's essay in any way? Is his discussion of doublespeak still valid today? Explain your answers.
5. **OTHER METHODS**   Lutz's essay is not only a classification but also a DEFINITION of *doublespeak* and an examination of CAUSE AND EFFECT. Where are these other methods used most prominently? What do they contribute to the essay?

Questions on Language

1. How does Lutz's own language compare with the language he quotes as doublespeak? Do you find his language clear and easy to understand?
2. ANALYZE Lutz's language in paragraphs 22 and 23. How do the CONNOTATIONS of words such as "corrupt," "hostility," "insidious," and "control" strengthen the author's message?
3. The following list of possibly unfamiliar words includes only those found in Lutz's own sentences, not those in the doublespeak he quotes. Be sure you can define variance (par. 2); incongruity, referent (3); taboo (5); esoteric, profundity (10); condemnation (11); ramshackle (21); cynicism (22); insidious (23).

Suggestions for Writing

1. **FROM JOURNAL TO ESSAY**   Choose at least one of the examples of doublespeak noted in your journal, and write an essay explaining why it qualifies as doublespeak. Which of Lutz's categories does it fit under? How did you recognize it? Can you understand what it means?

2. Just about all of us have resorted to doublespeak at one time or another—when making an excuse, when trying to wing it on an exam, when trying to impress a potential employer. Write a NARRATIVE about a time you used deliberately unclear language, perhaps language that you yourself didn't understand. What were the circumstances? Did you consciously decide to use unclear language, or did it just leak out? How did others react to your use of this language?

3. **CRITICAL WRITING**   Can you determine from his essay who Lutz believes is responsible for the proliferation of doublespeak? Whose responsibility is it to curtail the use of doublespeak: just those who use it? the schools? the government? the media? we who hear it? Write an essay that considers these questions, citing specific passages from the essay and incorporating your own ideas.

4. **CONNECTIONS**   While Lutz looks at language "carefully designed and constructed to appear to communicate when in fact it doesn't," Deborah Tannen, in the previous essay, takes the position that "conversation is a ritual"—that we don't often think about what we're saying and miscommunicate as a result. How do you resolve the apparent contradictions in these two writers' underlying assumptions about language? Is most of our speech deliberate, or is it automatic? Why do you think so? In an essay that draws on examples and EVIDENCE from each of these two essays as well as from your own experience, explain what you see as the major causes of miscommunication.

William Lutz on Writing

In 1989 C-SPAN aired an interview between Brian Lamb and William Lutz. Lamb asked Lutz about his writing process. "I have a rule about writing," Lutz answered, "which I discovered when I wrote my dissertation: You never write a book, you write three pages, or you write five pages. I put off writing my dissertation for a year, because I could not think of writing this whole thing. . . . I had put off doing this book [*Doublespeak*] for quite a while, and my wife said, 'You've got to do the book.' And I said, 'Yes, I am going to, just as soon as I . . . ,' and, of course, I did every other thing I could possibly think of before that, and then I realized one day that she was right, I had to start writing. . . . So one day, I sit down and say, 'I am going to write five pages—that's all—and when I am done with five pages, I'll reward myself.'

So I do the five pages, or the next time I will do ten pages or whatever number of pages, but I set a number of pages."

Perhaps wondering just how high Lutz's daily page count might go, Lamb asked Lutz how much he wrote at one time. "It depends," Lutz admitted. "I always begin a writing session by sitting down and rewriting what I wrote the previous day—and that is the first thing, and it does two things. First of all, it makes your writing a little bit better, because rewriting is the essential part of writing. And the second thing is to get you flowing again, get back into the mainstream. Truman Capote[1] once gave the best piece of advice for writers ever given. He said, 'Never pump the well dry; always leave a bucket there.' So, I never stop writing when I run out of ideas. I always stop when I have something more to write about, and write a note to myself, 'This is what I am going to do next,' and then I stop. The worst feeling in the world is to have written yourself dry and have to come back the next day, knowing that you are dry and not knowing where you are going to pick up at this point."

The Bedford Reader on Writing

You aren't writing whole books for your classes, of course, but Lutz's advice, scaled down, should remind you that you needn't write an essay all at once, only a few paragraphs at a time. Do you think Lutz's REVISION strategy—of rewriting before he starts writing about the idea he didn't develop on the previous day—is a good one? For other ways to approach the sometimes daunting tasks of drafting and revising, see Chapters 2 and 3 of this book, especially pages 33–38 and 41–45.

[1] Truman Capote (1924–84) was an American journalist and fiction writer. — Eds.

ADDITIONAL WRITING TOPICS
Classification

Write an essay by the method of classification, in which you sort one of the following subjects into categories of your own. Make clear your PURPOSE in classifying and the basis of your classification. Explain each class with DEFINITIONS and EXAMPLES (you may find it helpful to make up a name for each group). Check your classes to be sure they neither gap nor overlap.

People who use public transportation
Urban wildlife
Smartphone users or apps
Gym members
Late-night television shows
The drawbacks or benefits of small-town life
Your playlists
Families
Health-care providers
Politicians
Internships
College students
Movies for teenagers or men or women
Difficult coworkers
Graphic novels
Monsters
Sports announcers
Inconsiderate people
Social media platforms
Sources of energy

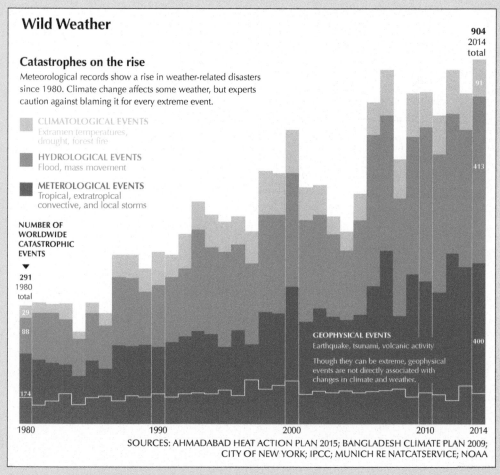

Wild Weather

904
2014
total

Catastrophes on the rise

Meteorological records show a rise in weather-related disasters
since 1980. Climate change affects some weather, but experts
caution against blaming it for every extreme event.

CLIMATOLOGICAL EVENTS
Extramen temperatures,
drought, forest fire

HYDROLOGICAL EVENTS
Flood, mass movement

METEROLOGICAL EVENTS
Tropical, extratropical
convective, and local storms

NUMBER OF
WORLDWIDE
CATASTROPHIC
EVENTS

▼
291
1980
total

29

88

174

91

413

400

GEOPHYSICAL EVENTS
Earthquake, tsunami, volcanic activity

Though they can be extreme, geophysical
events are not directly associated with
changes in climate and weather.

1980   1990   2000   2010   2014

SOURCES: AHMADABAD HEAT ACTION PLAN 2015; BANGLADESH CLIMATE PLAN 2009;
CITY OF NEW YORK; IPCC; MUNICH RE NATCATSERVICE; NOAA

Credit: Lawson Parker/National Geographic Creative.

12

CAUSE AND EFFECT

Asking Why

◄ **Cause and effect in a bar graph**

With simple visuals and perhaps a few words, infographics often make striking comments on events and trends. This bar graph by *National Geographic*, published in a 2015 special issue devoted to climate change, proposes some disturbing effects of a well-known but sometimes disputed cause. What is the cause? What, according to the authors, have been three of the major effects, and how are they related? What other effects might result from the cause depicted here? Why do "experts caution against blaming it for every extreme event"? Do you agree or disagree with *National Geographic*'s claims? Why?

THE METHOD

Press the button of a doorbell and, inside the house or apartment, chimes sound. Why? Because the touch of your finger on the button closed an electrical circuit. But why did you ring the doorbell? Because you were sent by your dispatcher: You are a bill collector calling on a customer whose payments are three months overdue.

The touch of your finger on the button is the *immediate cause* of the chimes: the event that precipitates another. That you were ordered by your dispatcher to go ring the doorbell is a *remote cause*: an underlying, more basic reason for the event, not apparent to an observer. Probably, ringing the doorbell will lead to some results: The door will open, and you may be given a check—or have the door slammed in your face.

To figure out reasons and results is to use the method of CAUSE AND EFFECT. Either to explain events or to argue for one version of them, you try to answer the question "Why did something happen?" or "What were the consequences?" or "What might be the consequences?" Seeking causes, you can ask, for example, "Why do birds migrate?" "What led to America's involvement in the war in Vietnam?" Looking for effects, you can ask, "How has legalization of gay marriage changed the typical American family?" "What impact have handheld computers had on the nursing profession?" You can look to a possible future and ask, "Of what use might a course in psychology be to me if I become an office manager?" "Suppose an asteroid the size of a sofa were to strike Philadelphia—what would be the probable consequences?"

Don't confuse cause and effect with the method of PROCESS ANALYSIS (Chap. 9). Some process analysis essays, too, deal with happenings; but they focus more on repeatable events (rather than unique ones) and they explain *how* (rather than why) something happened. If you were explaining the process by which the doorbell rings, you might break the happening into stages—(1) the finger presses the button; (2) the circuit closes; (3) the current travels the wire; (4) the chimes make music—and you'd set forth the process in detail. But why did the finger press the button? What happened because the doorbell rang? To answer those questions, you need cause and effect.

In trying to explain why things happen, you can expect to find a whole array of causes—interconnected, perhaps, like the strands of a spiderweb. To produce a successful essay, you'll want to do an honest job of unraveling, and this may take time. Before you start to write, devote some extra thought to seeing which facts are the causes and which matter most. To answer the questions "Why?" and "What followed as a result?" may sometimes be hard, but it can be satisfying—even illuminating. Indeed, to seek causes and effects is one way for the mind to discover order in a reality that otherwise might seem random and pointless.

THE PROCESS

Subject and Purpose

The method of cause and effect tends to suggest itself: If you have a subject and soon start thinking "Why?" or "What results?" or "What if?" then you are on the way to analyzing causation. Your subject may be impersonal—like a change in voting patterns or the failure or success of a business—or it may be quite personal. Indeed, an excellent cause-and-effect paper may be written on a subject very near to you. You can ask yourself why you behaved in a certain way at a certain moment. You can examine the reasons for your current beliefs and attitudes. Writing such a paper, you might happen upon a truth you hadn't realized before.

Whether your subject is personal or impersonal, make sure it is manageable: You should be able to get to the bottom of it, given the time and information available. For a 500-word essay due Thursday, the causes of teenage rebellion would be a less feasible topic than why a certain thirteen-year-old you know ran away from home.

Before rushing to list causes or effects, stop a moment to consider what your PURPOSE might be in writing. Much of the time you'll seek simply to explain what did or might occur, discovering and laying out the connections as clearly and accurately as you can. But when reasonable people could disagree over causes or effects, you'll want to go further, arguing for one interpretation over others. You'll still need to be clear and accurate in presenting your interpretation, but you'll also need to treat the others fairly. (See Chap. 14 on argument and persuasion.)

Thesis

When you have a grip on your subject and your purpose, you can draft a tentative THESIS STATEMENT to express the main point of your analysis. The essays in this chapter provide good examples of thesis statements that put across, concisely, the author's central finding about causes and effects. Here are two examples:

> A bill like the one we've just passed [to ban imports from factories that use child labor] is of no use unless it goes hand in hand with programs that will offer a new life to these newly released children.
> —Chitra Divakaruni, "Live Free and Starve"

> To begin to solve the problem [of the illegal drug trade], we need to understand what's happening in drug-source countries, how the United States can and can't help there, and what, instead, can be done at home.
> —Marie Javdani, *"Plata o Plomo:* Silver or Lead"

Your own thesis statement may be hypothetical at the discovery stage, before you have gathered EVIDENCE and sorted out the complexity of causes and effects. Still, a statement framed early can help direct your later thinking and research.

Causal Relations

Your toughest job in writing a cause-and-effect essay may be figuring out what caused what. Sometimes one event will appear to trigger another, and it in turn will trigger yet another, and another still, in an order we call a *causal chain*. Investigators at the scene of a ten-car pileup, for instance, might determine that a deer ran across the highway, causing a driver to slam on the brakes suddenly, causing another driver to hit the first car, causing the next driver to swerve and hit the embankment, and so on.

In reality, causes are seldom so easy to find as that stray deer: They tend to be many and complicated. Even a simple accident may happen for more than one reason. Perhaps the deer was flushed out of the woods by a hunter. Perhaps the first driver was distracted by a crying child in the back seat. Perhaps winter had set in and the road was icy. Perhaps the low glare of the setting sun made it difficult for any of the drivers to see clearly. Still, one event precedes another in time, and in discerning causes you don't ignore CHRONOLOGICAL ORDER; you pay attention to it.

When you can see a number of apparent causes, weigh them and assign each a relative importance so that you can arrange them in CLIMACTIC ORDER. Which do you find matter most? Often, you will see that particular causes are more important or less so: major or minor. If you seek to explain why your small town has fallen on hard times, you might note that two businesses shut down: a factory employing three hundred and a drugstore employing six. The factory's closing is a *major cause*, leading to significant unemployment in the town, while the drugstore's closing is perhaps a *minor cause*—or not a cause at all but an effect. In writing about the causes, you would emphasize the factory and mention the drugstore only briefly if at all.

When seeking remote causes, look only as far back as necessary. Explaining your town's misfortunes, you might see the factory's closing as the immediate cause. You could show what caused the shutdown: a dispute between union and management. You might even go back to the cause of the dispute (announced layoffs) and the cause of the layoffs (loss of sales to a competitor). A paper showing effects might work in the other direction, moving from the factory closing to its impact on the town: unemployment, the closing of stores (including the drugstore), people packing up and moving away.

Two cautions about causal relations are in order here. One is to beware of confusing coincidence with cause. In the logical FALLACY called *post hoc* (short for the Latin *post hoc, ergo propter hoc*, "after this, therefore because of this"), one assumes, erroneously, that because A happened before B, A must have caused B. This is the error of the superstitious man who decides that he lost his job because a black cat walked in front of him. Another fallacy is to oversimplify causes by failing to recognize their full number and complexity — claiming, say, that violent crime is simply a result of "all those first-person shooter games." Avoid such wrong turns in reasoning by patiently looking for evidence before you write, and by giving it careful thought. (For a fuller list of logical fallacies or errors in reasoning, with explanations and examples, see pp. 499–500.)

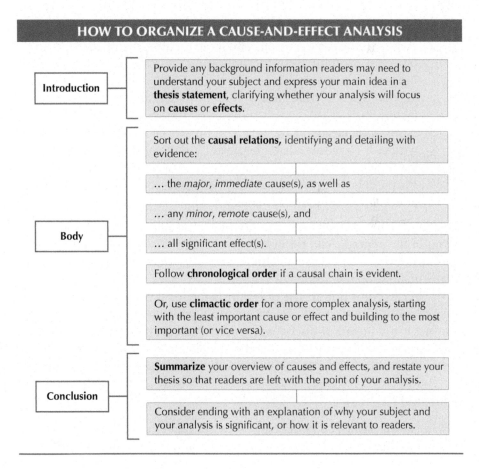

HOW TO ORGANIZE A CAUSE-AND-EFFECT ANALYSIS

Introduction

Provide any background information readers may need to understand your subject and express your main idea in a **thesis statement**, clarifying whether your analysis will focus on **causes** or **effects**.

Body

Sort out the **causal relations,** identifying and detailing with evidence:

... the *major, immediate* cause(s), as well as

... any *minor, remote* cause(s), and

... all significant effect(s).

Follow **chronological order** if a causal chain is evident.

Or, use **climactic order** for a more complex analysis, starting with the least important cause or effect and building to the most important (or vice versa).

Conclusion

Summarize your overview of causes and effects, and restate your thesis so that readers are left with the point of your analysis.

Consider ending with an explanation of why your subject and your analysis is significant, or how it is relevant to readers.

Discovery of Causes

To help find causes of actions and events, you can ask yourself a few searching questions. These have been suggested by the work of the literary critic Kenneth Burke:

1. **What act am I trying to explain?**
2. **What is the character, personality, or mental state of whoever acted?**
3. **In what scene or location did the act take place, and in what circumstances?**
4. **What instruments or means did the person use?**
5. **For what purpose did the person act?**

Burke calls these elements a *pentad* (or set of five): the *act*, the *actor*, the *scene*, the *agency*, and the *purpose*. If you were a detective trying to explain why a liquor store burned down, you might ask these questions:

1. **Act:** Was the fire deliberately set, or was there an accident?
2. **Actors:** If the fire was arson, who set it: the store's worried, debt-ridden owner? a mentally disturbed antialcohol crusader? a drunk who had been denied a purchase?
3. **Scene:** Was the store near a church? a mental hospital? a fireworks factory?
4. **Agency, or means of the act:** Was the fire caused by faulty electrical wiring? a carelessly tossed cigarette? a flaming torch? rags soaked in kerosene?
5. **Purpose:** If the fire wasn't accidental, was it set to collect insurance? to punish drinkers? to get revenge?

You can further deepen your inquiry by seeing relationships between the terms of the pentad. Ask, for instance, what does the actor have to do with this scene? (Is he or she the neighbor across the street, who has been staring at the liquor shop resentfully for years?)

Don't worry if not all the questions apply or if not all the answers are immediately forthcoming. Burke's pentad isn't meant to be a grim rigmarole; it is a means of discovery, to generate a lot of possible material for you — insights, observations, hunches to pursue. It won't solve each and every human mystery, but sometimes it will helpfully deepen your thought.

Educated Guesses

In stating what you believe to be causes and effects, don't be afraid to voice a well-considered hunch. Your instructor doesn't expect you to write, in a short time, a definitive account of the causes of an event or a belief or a phenomenon — only to write a coherent and reasonable one. To discern all causes — including remote ones — and all effects is beyond the power of any one human mind. Still, admirable and well-informed writers on matters such as politics, economics, and world and national affairs are often canny guessers and brave drawers of inferences. At times, even the most cautious and responsible writer has to leap boldly over a void to strike firm ground on the far side. Consider your evidence. Focus your thinking. Look well before leaping. Then take off.

FOCUS ON CLARITY AND CONCISENESS

While drafting a cause-and-effect analysis, you may need to grope a bit to discover just what you think about the sequence and relative importance of reasons and consequences. Your sentences may grope a bit, too, reflecting some initial confusion or a need to circle around your ideas in order to find them. The following draft passage reveals such difficulties:

WORDY AND UNCLEAR   Employees often worry about suggestive comments from others. The employee may not only worry but feel the need to discuss the situation with coworkers. One thing that is an effect of sexual harassment, even verbal harassment, in the workplace is that productivity is lost. Plans also need to be made to figure out how to deal with future comments. Engaging in these activities is sure to take time and concentration from work.

Drafting this passage, the writer seems to have built up to the idea about lost productivity (third sentence) after providing support for it in the first two sentences. The fourth sentence then adds more support. And sentences 2–4 all show a writer working out his ideas: Sentence subjects and verbs do not focus on the main actors and actions of the sentences, words repeat unnecessarily, and word groups run longer than needed for clarity.

These problems disappear from the edited version below, which moves the idea of the passage up front, uses subjects and verbs to state what the sentences are about (underlined), and cuts unneeded words.

CONCISE AND CLEAR   Even verbal sexual harassment in the workplace causes a loss of productivity. Worrying about suggestive comments from others, discussing those comments with coworkers, planning how to deal with future comments — these activities consume time and concentration that a harassed employee could spend on work.

> ## CHECKLIST FOR REVIEWING AND REVISING
> ## A CAUSE-AND-EFFECT ESSAY
>
> ✔ **Subject.** Has the subject been covered adequately, given the time and space available? Should you perhaps narrow the subject so that you can fairly address the important causes and/or effects?
>
> ✔ **Thesis.** For readers' benefit, have you focused the analysis by stating your main idea succinctly in a thesis statement?
>
> ✔ **Completeness.** Have all relevant causes or effects been included? Does the analysis reach back to locate remote causes or forward to locate remote effects?
>
> ✔ **Causal relations.** Is the pattern of causes or effects clearly presented? Can readers distinguish the remote from the immediate, the major from the minor?
>
> ✔ **Accuracy and fairness.** Does the analysis avoid the *post hoc* fallacy, assuming that A caused B just because A preceded B? Have you also avoided oversimplifying and instead covered causes or effects in all their complexity?
>
> ✔ **Clarity and conciseness.** How can you edit your draft to foreground the main points and tighten the sentences?

STUDENT CASE STUDY: A LETTER TO THE EDITOR

To encourage interaction between readers and writers, most newspapers, magazines, and journals, as well as some Web sites, solicit and publish letters to the editor. Unlike the anonymous comments readers may attach to news and opinion articles online, letters to the editor are signed by their authors and screened by editors. To be published, such letters generally must take a calm tone and express ideas rationally. In most cases, the writer refers to the original article or other piece that prompted the letter and responds by agreeing or disagreeing (or a little of both). The point is to add a new perspective and move a conversation forward.

An ardent supporter of her school's track team, Kate Krueger was a sophomore during the team's first winning season in many years. At the end of the season, the student newspaper published a sports column crediting the successes to a new coach. Krueger found this explanation inadequate and wrote her own cause-and-effect analysis in the following letter to the newspaper's editor. Notice that because Krueger actually agreed with the original writer that the coach had helped the team, she acknowledged the coach's contributions while also detailing the other causes she saw at work.

May 2, 2019

To the Editor:

I take issue with Tom Boatz's column that was printed in the April 30 *Weekly*. Boatz attributes the success of this year's track team solely to the new coach, John Barak. I have several close friends who are athletes on the track team, so as an interested observer and fan I believe that Boatz oversimplified the causes of the team's recent success.

To be sure, Coach Barak did much to improve the training regimen and overall morale, and these have certainly contributed to the winning season. Both Coach Barak and the team members themselves can share credit for an impressive work ethic and a sense of camaraderie unequaled in previous years. However, several factors outside Coach Barak's control were also influential.

This year's team gained several phenomenal freshman athletes, such as Kristin Hall, who anchored the 4×400 and 4×800 relays and played an integral part in setting several school records, and Eric Montgomery-Asper, who was undefeated in the shot put.

Even more important, and also unmentioned by Tom Boatz, is the college's increased funding for the track program. Last year the school allotted fifty percent more for equipment, and the results have been dramatic. For example, the new vaulting poles are now the correct length and correspond to the weights of the individual athletes, giving them more power and height. Some vaulters have been able to vault as much as a foot higher than their previous records. Similarly, new starting blocks have allowed the team's sprinters to drop valuable seconds off their times.

I agree with Tom Boatz that Coach Barak deserves some credit for the track team's successes. But the athletes do, too, and so does the college for at last supporting its track program.

— Kate Krueger '21

Reason for writing: Original author oversimplified a cause-and-effect relationship

Point of agreement: The new coach was one cause of the team's success

Thesis statement: Other causes played a role

Other causes:
• Talented new team members

• Financial support from the college

Examples of positive effects:
• Improved vaulting performance

• Improved sprinting times

Conclusion summarizes Krueger's analysis

LANGSTON HUGHES

A poet, fiction writer, playwright, critic, and humorist, Langston Hughes (1902–67) described his writing as "largely concerned with depicting Negro life in America." He was born in Joplin, Missouri, and grew up in Illinois, Kansas, and Ohio. After dropping out of Columbia University in the early 1920s, Hughes worked at odd jobs while struggling to gain recognition as a writer. His first book of poems, *The Weary Blues* (1925), helped seed the Harlem Renaissance, a flowering of African American music and literature centered in the Harlem district of New York City during the 1920s. The book also generated a scholarship that enabled Hughes to finish college at Lincoln University. In all of his work — including *The Negro Mother* (1931), *The Ways of White Folks* (1934), *Shakespeare in Harlem* (1942), *Montage of a Dream Deferred* (1951), and *Ask Your Mama* (1961) — Hughes captured and projected the rhythms of jazz and the distinctive speech, subtle humor, and deep traditions of African American people.

Harlem

A poem from Hughes's collection *Montage of a Dream Deferred*, "Harlem" is a simple yet blistering analysis of African American hardships. Written as the civil rights movement was just beginning to gather steam, the poem encapsulates black frustrations with economic inequality, legalized segregation and discrimination, and second-class citizenship at a particular moment in time. Perhaps unsurprisingly, Hughes's astute observations continue to resonate even now, some three-quarters of a century later.

What happens to a dream deferred? 1

Does it dry up
like a raisin in the sun?
Or fester like a sore —
And then run? 5
Does it stink like rotten meat?
Or crust and sugar over —
like a syrupy sweet?

Maybe it just sags
like a heavy load. 10

Or does it explode?

Journal Writing

Have you ever witnessed or been the object of unfair treatment based on race, ethnicity, gender, disability, or some other visible aspect of identity? What happened, and what was your reaction? Recount the incident in your journal.

Questions on Meaning

1. What is the "dream" referred to in line 1? Explain the poem's central metaphor in your own words. What other FIGURES OF SPEECH does Hughes employ, and how do you interpret their meaning? (For an explanation of the uses of figurative language, turn to the Glossary.)

2. "Harlem" is published in some collections with the title "Dream Deferred." How does the original title influence your understanding of the poet's intended meaning?

3. How would you describe the writer's PURPOSE in this poem? For whom is it written? What does Hughes seem to want his AUDIENCE to take away from reading it?

Questions on Writing Strategy

1. With this poem, does Hughes seem more concerned with causes or with effects? Why do you think so? What is the source (or sources) of the problem he sees? What does he suggest could be the consequences?

2. Closely read the poem line by line, circling or underlining words that are repeated at the beginnings and double-underlining the words that rhyme at the ends. Then review your markings. What strategies has Hughes used to give his poem COHERENCE and UNITY?

3. **OTHER METHODS**   Examine how Hughes uses sensory IMAGES to COMPARE AND CONTRAST a "dream deferred" with foodstuffs and bodies. To which of the five senses does he appeal? What dominant impression does he create with these DESCRIPTIONS?

Questions on Language

1. In speculating about future events, Hughes writes in the present tense. Why? What is the EFFECT of this choice?

2. Look up *deferred* in the dictionary. Why is it such a fitting word in line 1? Why wouldn't *delayed* or *postponed* have been as good?

3. How would you describe the overall TONE of this poem: lyrical? detached? weary? something else? Point to some words and phrases that support your answer.

Suggestions for Writing

1. **FROM JOURNAL TO ESSAY**   Starting with your journal notes, write an essay (or, if you like, a poem) addressing stereotypes and how they can harm people. Use vivid details to re-create the incident and your reaction to it, but also reflect on its larger significance. Do you view the incident as fairly unusual, or do you think it is symptomatic of widespread stereotyping? What are the causes of this stereotyping, and how does it affect the people it is directed against?

2. Hughes's poem questions the validity of the American dream, the notion that with hard work and determination anyone in this country can rise up from even the most humble of circumstances and have a happy, prosperous life. Do you think we have moved closer to fulfilling that dream in the decades since Hughes wrote this poem? Why, or why not? How successful have the various civil rights movements — for African Americans, for Chicanos, for Native Americans, for Asian Americans, for the LGBTQ community, and so forth — been in improving life for people of color and other minority groups? What work remains to be done? Write an essay that explains your sense of how well the United States has progressed toward realizing the "dream deferred" and ensuring equality and opportunity for all. You may choose to focus on the country as a whole or on your particular community, but you should use specific evidence to support your opinion.

3. **CRITICAL WRITING**   In an essay, briefly ANALYZE the format and structure of Hughes's poem. Why, for instance, are all lines but the first one indented? What is the function of the stanza breaks after lines 8 and 10, and the dashes at the ends of lines 4 and 7? Why the italics at the end? What is the overall effect?

4. **CONNECTIONS**   In "The Struggle" (p. 176), television producer and actor Issa Rae notes that she has tried to "demilitarize [her] blackness" and asks if fulfilling her desire not to discuss race isn't what the leaders of the civil rights movement fought for. Read her essay, and then consider how Langston Hughes and other black cultural and political figures of the 1950s and '60s might answer her question. What *were* they fighting for? Would Hughes agree with Rae that a color-blind existence, without any acknowledgment of race, was the goal? Or might he counter that skin color is paramount to meaning — something to celebrate rather than ignore? Why do you think so? What do *you* think of the issue? Answer these questions, and any others they might raise for you, in an essay.

BEN HEALY

Ben Healy is a writer and design lead with Ideo, a global consulting group. Also a monthly columnist and former editor for *The Atlantic*, his writing has been published in that magazine and in others including *Slate*, *The New Republic Online*, *Boston Review*, *Boston College Magazine*, and *Howler*, a quarterly about soccer. A self-described "soccer fanatic," Healy grew up in Hinsdale, Illinois, completed a degree in American civilization at Brown University in 2002, and followed that with an MFA in fiction and screenwriting from the University of Texas at Austin. He currently lives in Chicago and has been known to compete in adult spelling bees hosted in local bars.

Gossip Is Good

In his column for *The Atlantic*, "Study of Studies," Healy each month synthesizes information from scholarly research on a popular subject of his choosing, such as sports fandom, friendship, and fear. In this piece from the July/August 2018 issue, he does a quick review of the literature on gossip and comes to a surprising conclusion.

Notice that although Healy doesn't follow a formal citation system such as MLA or APA style (see the Appendix, pp. 647–692), he nonetheless clearly identifies his sources by numbering them in his text and then listing them at the end.

1   Word on the street is that gossip is the worst. An Ann Landers advice column once characterized it as "the faceless demon that breaks hearts and ruins careers." The Talmud describes it as a "three-pronged tongue" that kills three people: the teller, the listener, and the person being gossiped about. And Blaise Pascal observed, not unreasonably, that "if people really knew what others said about them, there would not be four friends left in the world." Convincing as these indictments seem, however, a significant body of research suggests that gossip may in fact be healthy.

2   It's a good thing, too, since gossip is pretty pervasive. Children tend to be seasoned gossips by the age of five [1], and gossip as most researchers understand it — talk between at least two people about absent others — accounts for about two-thirds of conversation [2]. In the 1980s, the journalist Blythe Holbrooke took a stab at bringing rigor to the subject, tongue firmly in cheek, by positing the Law of Inverse Accuracy: $C = (TI)^v - t$, in which the likelihood of gossip being circulated (C) equals its timeliness (T) times its interest (I) to the power of its unverifiability (v) minus the reluctance someone might feel about repeating it out of taste (t) [3].

411

Despite gossip's dodgy reputation, a surprisingly small share of it—as lit- 3
tle as three to four percent—is actually malicious [4]. And even that portion can bring people together. Researchers at the University of Texas and
the University of Oklahoma found that if two people share negative feelings
about a third person, they are likely to feel closer to each other than they
would if they both felt positively about him or her [5].

Gossip may even make us better people. A team of Dutch researchers 4
reported that hearing gossip about others made research subjects more reflective; positive gossip inspired self-improvement efforts, and negative gossip
made people prouder of themselves [6]. In another study, the worse participants felt upon hearing a piece of negative gossip, the more likely they were
to say they had learned a lesson from it [7]. Negative gossip can also have
a prosocial effect on those who are gossiped about. Researchers at Stanford
and UC Berkeley found that once people were ostracized from a group due
to reputed selfishness, they reformed their ways in an attempt to regain the
approval of the people they had alienated [8].

By far the most positive assessment of gossip, though, comes courtesy of 5
the anthropologist and evolutionary psychologist Robin Dunbar. Once upon
a time, in Dunbar's account, our primate ancestors bonded through grooming, their mutual back-scratching ensuring mutual self-defense in the event of
attack by predators. But as hominids grew more intelligent and more social,
their groups became too large to unite by grooming alone. That's where language—and gossip, broadly defined—stepped in [9]. Dunbar argues that idle
chatter with and about others gave early humans a sense of shared identity
and helped them grow more aware of their environment, thus incubating the
complex higher functioning that would ultimately yield such glories of civilization as the Talmud, Pascal, and Ann Landers.

So the next time you're tempted to dish the dirt, fear not—you may 6
actually be promoting cooperation, boosting others' self-esteem, and performing the essential task of the human family. That's what I heard, anyway.

The Studies: [1] Engelmann et al., "Pre-schoolers Affect Others' Reputations Through
Prosocial Gossip" (*British Journal of Developmental Psychology*, Sept. 2016). [2] Nicholas
Emler, "Gossip, Reputation, and Social Adaptation," in *Good Gossip* (University Press
of Kansas, 1994). [3] Blythe Holbrooke, *Gossip* (St. Martin's, 1983). [4] Dunbar et al.,
"Human Conversational Behavior" (*Human Nature*, Sept. 1997). [5] Bosson et al.,
"Interpersonal Chemistry Through Negativity" (*Personal Relationships*, June 2006). [6]
Martinescu et al., "Tell Me the Gossip" (*Personality and Social Psychology Bulletin*, Dec.
2014). [7] Baumeister et al., "Gossip as Cultural Learning" (*Review of General Psychology*,
June 2004). [8] Feinberg et al., "Gossip and Ostracism Promote Cooperation in Groups"

(*Psychological Science*, March 2014). [9] Robin Dunbar, *Grooming, Gossip, and the Evolution of Language* (Harvard University Press, 1998).

Journal Writing

Have you recently been struck by curiosity, perhaps because of something you heard on the street, or because of something you've read, or because of a phenomenon you've noticed? What question has been raised in your mind, and why does it interest you? Make note of the question, and your thoughts about it, in your journal.

Questions on Meaning

1. Does Healy have a THESIS? Where, if at all, does he state his main idea? What seems to be his PURPOSE in writing?

2. What is the "Law of Inverse Accuracy" (par. 2)? Is it a real academic theory? Why does Healy cite it?

3. Although Healy offers details about most of the sources he cites, he mentions others—Ann Landers, the Talmud, Blaise Pascal—without explaining who or what they are. Why? What assumptions does he make about his readers' interests and knowledge? Must one be familiar with the particulars of the texts Healy references to understand his point?

Questions on Writing Strategy

1. What are the effects of gossip, as Healy explains them? What EVIDENCE does he offer to support his analysis? How seriously does he take his subject?

2. How does Healy organize the BODY of his cause-and-effect analysis? What strategies does he use to lend his essay UNITY and COHERENCE?

3. **OTHER METHODS**   Where in the essay does Healy use DEFINITION to clarify the meaning of his subject? What, exactly, qualifies as gossip? How do experts explain the behavior?

Questions on Language

1. How would you characterize Healy's DICTION in this essay? What does the diction contribute to his TONE? How effective do you find this use of language, given his subject and purpose?

2. Check a dictionary for definitions of the following words: indictments (par. 1); pervasive, rigor (2); dodgy, malicious (3); reflective, prosocial, ostracized, reputed (4); primate, grooming, hominids, incubating (5).

3. What strikes you as noteworthy about the first and last sentences of this essay? What is their EFFECT?

Suggestions for Writing

1. **JOURNAL TO ESSAY** Using Healy's essay as a guide, look for answers to the question (or questions) you posed in your journal. Try not only researching the Internet for information, but also seeking published scholarly works or interviewing an expert or two. Then write a brief essay that presents your findings, providing plenty of evidence to support your thesis.

2. Respond to Healy's ARGUMENT in favor of gossip. Do you agree that discussing people who are absent from a conversation brings positive results for everyone involved, or do you believe that talking behind a person's back is hurtful and wrong? Why? In developing your response start with your own personal experiences with gossip and its effects, adding additional examples from your observations of others.

3. **CRITICAL WRITING** Take a close look at Healy's use of SUMMARY, PARAPHRASE, and direct QUOTATION. In an essay, analyze the way he synthesizes information and ideas from SOURCES. Why does he quote directly where he does? How effective are his summaries and paraphrases? Are his sources credible? How does he combine source materials to develop a thesis of his own?

4. **CONNECTIONS** While Healy cites the scholarly work of an anthropologist who finds that language can be used to build community and "a sense of shared identity" for the purpose of self-defense from hostile groups (par. 5), language scholar William Lutz cautions, in "The World of Doublespeak" (p. 387), that some groups can use language to deceive and divide people. In an essay, compare and contrast Healy's understanding of the uses of language with Lutz's. Do the authors present complex concepts in ways that most readers can understand? What strategies do their works have in common? Where do they diverge? Use quotations and paraphrases from both selections to support your ideas.

DEREK THOMPSON

Called "one of the brightest new voices in American journalism" and named to both *Inc.* and *Forbes* magazines' "Thirty under Thirty" lists of promising talent, Derek Thompson has quickly established a distinguished career as a writer and speaker. Born in 1986 and raised in Washington, DC, he earned a bachelor's degree with a triple major in journalism, political science, and legal studies from Northwestern University in 2008 and immediately landed a position at *The Atlantic*, where he is now a staff writer. Thompson's insightful explorations of economics, technology, and the media have also appeared in *Slate*, *Business Week*, *Business Insider*, and the *Daily Beast*. He is a weekly guest on National Public Radio's *Here and Now* and makes frequent appearances on television news discussion panels. Thompson's first book, *Hit Makers: The Science of Popularity in an Age of Distraction* (2017), was, fittingly, an instant bestseller. He lives in New York City.

What Makes Things Cool

Thompson is highly regarded for his skill at constructing sophisticated and uncannily astute analyses of millennial culture, connecting dots that others might not even see. In this essay, adapted for *The Atlantic* from a chapter in *Hit Makers*, he starts with a theory from industrial design to examine the factors that contribute to perceptions of coolness, or popular appeal — and then applies that theory across multiple disciplines to determine why "people like what they like."

Several decades before he became the father of industrial design, [1] Raymond Loewy boarded the SS *France* in 1919 to sail across the Atlantic from his devastated continent to the United States. The influenza pandemic had taken his mother and father, and his service in the French army was over. At the age of 25, Loewy was looking to start fresh in New York, perhaps, he thought, as an electrical engineer. When he reached Manhattan, his older brother Maximilian picked him up in a taxi. They drove straight to 120 Broadway, one of New York City's largest neoclassical skyscrapers, with two connected towers that ascended from a shared base like a giant tuning fork. Loewy rode the elevator to the observatory platform, forty stories up, and looked out across the island.

"New York was throbbing at our feet in the crisp autumn light," Loewy [2] recalled in his 1951 memoir. "I was fascinated by the murmur of the great city." But upon closer examination, he was crestfallen. In France, he had imagined an elegant, stylish place, filled with slender and simple shapes. The city that now unfurled beneath him, however, was a grungy product of the machine age — "bulky, noisy, and complicated. It was a disappointment."

The world below would soon match his dreamy vision. Loewy would do more than almost any person in the twentieth century to shape the aesthetic of American culture. His firm designed mid-century icons like the Exxon logo, the Lucky Strike pack, and the Greyhound bus. He designed International Harvester tractors that farmed the Great Plains, merchandise racks at Lucky Stores supermarkets that displayed produce, Frigidaire ovens that cooked meals, and Singer vacuum cleaners that ingested the crumbs of dinner. Loewy's Starliner Coupé from the early 1950s — nicknamed the "Loewy Coupé" — is still one of the most influential automotive designs of the twentieth century. The famous blue nose of *Air Force One*? That was Loewy's touch, too. After complaining to his friend, a White House aide, that the commander in chief's airplane looked "gaudy," he spent several hours on the floor of the Oval Office cutting up blue-colored paper shapes with President Kennedy before settling on the design that still adorns America's best-known plane. "Loewy," wrote *Cosmopolitan* magazine in 1950, "has probably affected the daily life of more Americans than any man of his time."

Mark Weaver

But when he arrived in Manhattan, US companies did not yet worship 4
at the altars of style and elegance. That era's capitalists were monotheistic:
Efficiency was their only god. American factories — with their electricity,
assembly lines, and scientifically calibrated workflow — produced an unprecedented supply of cheap goods by the 1920s, and it became clear that factories could make more than consumers naturally wanted. It took executives
like Alfred Sloan, the CEO of General Motors, to see that by, say, changing a
car's style and color every year, consumers might be trained to crave new versions of the same product. To sell more stuff, American industrialists needed
to work hand in hand with artists to make new products beautiful — even
"cool."

Loewy had an uncanny sense of how to make things fashionable. He 5
believed that consumers are torn between two opposing forces: neophilia, a
curiosity about new things; and neophobia, a fear of anything too new. As a
result, they gravitate to products that are bold, but instantly comprehensible.
Loewy called his grand theory "Most Advanced Yet Acceptable" — MAYA.
He said to sell something surprising, make it familiar; and to sell something
familiar, make it surprising.

Why do people like what they like? It is one of the oldest questions of 6
philosophy and aesthetics. Ancient thinkers inclined to mysticism proposed
that a "golden ratio" — about 1.62 to 1, as in, for instance, the dimensions
of a rectangle — could explain the visual perfection of objects like sunflowers and Greek temples. Other thinkers were deeply skeptical: David Hume,
the eighteenth-century philosopher, considered the search for formulas to be
absurd, because the perception of beauty was purely subjective, residing in
individuals, not in the fabric of the universe. "To seek the real beauty, or real
deformity," he said, "is as fruitless an enquiry, as to pretend to ascertain the
real sweet or real bitter."

Over time, science took up the mystery. In the 1960s, the psychologist 7
Robert Zajonc conducted a series of experiments where he showed subjects
nonsense words, random shapes, and Chinese-like characters and asked
them which they preferred. In study after study, people reliably gravitated
toward the words and shapes they'd seen the most. Their preference was for
familiarity.

This discovery was known as the "mere-exposure effect," and it is one of 8
the sturdiest findings in modern psychology. Across hundreds of studies and
meta-studies, subjects around the world prefer familiar shapes, landscapes,
consumer goods, songs, and human voices. People are even partial to the
familiar version of the thing they should know best in the world: their own

face. Because you and I are used to seeing our countenance in a mirror, studies show, we often prefer this reflection over the face we see in photographs. The preference for familiarity is so universal that some think it must be written into our genetic code. The evolutionary explanation for the mere-exposure effect would be simple: If you recognized an animal or plant, that meant it hadn't killed you, at least not yet.

But the preference for familiarity has clear limits. People get tired of even   9
their favorite songs and movies. They develop deep skepticism about overfamiliar buzzwords. In mere-exposure studies, the preference for familiar stimuli is attenuated or negated entirely when the participants realize they're being repeatedly exposed to the same thing. For that reason, the power of familiarity seems to be strongest when a person isn't expecting it.

The reverse is also true: A surprise seems to work best when it contains   10
some element of familiarity. Consider the experience of Matt Ogle, who, for more than a decade, was obsessed with designing the perfect music-recommendation engine. His philosophy of music was that most people enjoy new songs, but they don't enjoy the effort it takes to find them. When he joined Spotify, the music-streaming company, he helped build a product called *Discover Weekly*, a personalized list of thirty songs delivered every Monday to tens of million of users.

The original version of *Discover Weekly* was supposed to include only   11
songs that users had never listened to before. But in its first internal test at Spotify, a bug in the algorithm let through songs that users had already heard. "Everyone reported it as a bug, and we fixed it so that every single song was totally new," Ogle told me.

But after Ogle's team fixed the bug, engagement with the playlist actually   12
fell. "It turns out having a bit of familiarity bred trust, especially for first-time users," he said. "If we make a new playlist for you and there's not a single thing for you to hook onto or recognize—to go, 'Oh yeah, that's a good call!'—it's completely intimidating and people don't engage." It turned out that the original bug was an essential feature: *Discover Weekly* was a more appealing product when it had even one familiar band or song.

Several years ago, Paul Hekkert, a professor of industrial design and   13
psychology at Delft University of Technology, in the Netherlands, received a grant to develop a theory of aesthetics and taste. On the one hand, Hekkert told me, humans seek familiarity, because it makes them feel safe. On the other hand, people are charged by the thrill of a challenge, powered by a pioneer lust. This battle between familiarity and discovery affects us "on every level," Hekkert says—not just our preferences for pictures and songs, but also our preferences for ideas and even people. "When we started [our research], we didn't even know about Raymond Loewy's theory," Hekkert told me.

"It was only later that somebody told us that our conclusions had already been reached by a famous industrial designer, and it was called MAYA."

Raymond Loewy's aesthetic was proudly populist. "One should design for 14 the advantage of the largest mass of people," he said. He understood that this meant designing with a sense of familiarity in mind.

In 1932, Loewy met for the first time with the president of the 15 Pennsylvania Railroad. Locomotive design at the time hadn't advanced much beyond Thomas the Tank Engine[1] — pronounced chimneys, round faces, and exposed wheels. Loewy imagined something far sleeker — a single smooth shell, the shape of a bullet. His first designs met with considerable skepticism, but Loewy was undaunted. "I knew it would never be considered," he later wrote of his bold proposal, "but repeated exposure of railroad people to this kind of advanced, unexpected stuff had a beneficial effect. It gradually conditioned them to accept more progressive designs."

To acquaint himself with the deficiencies of Pennsylvania Railroad 16 trains, Loewy traveled hundreds of miles on the speeding locomotives. He tested air turbulence with engineers and interviewed crew members about the shortage of toilets. A great industrial designer, it turns out, needs to be an anthropologist first and an artist second: Loewy studied how people lived and how machines worked, and then he offered new, beautiful designs that piggy-backed on engineers' tastes and consumers' habits.

Soon after his first meeting with the president of the Pennsylvania 17 Railroad, Loewy helped the company design the GG-1, an electric locomotive covered in a single welded-steel plate. Loewy's suggestion to cover the chassis in a seamless metallic coat was revolutionary in the 1930s. But he eventually persuaded executives to accept his lean and aerodynamic vision, which soon became the standard design of modern trains. What was once radical had become MAYA, and what was once MAYA has today become the unremarkable standard.

Could Loewy's MAYA theory double as cultural criticism? A common 18 complaint about modern pop culture is that it has devolved into an orgy of familiarity. In her 2013 memoir cum cultural critique, *Sleepless in Hollywood*, the producer Lynda Obst mourned what she saw as cult worship of "pre-awareness" in the film and television industry. As the number of movies and television shows being produced each year has grown, risk-averse

---

[1] A fictional steam locomotive originally from *The Railway Series* books (1945–) by Wilbert and Christopher Awbry and now featured in popular TV cartoons, movies, live productions, and children's merchandise. — EDS.

producers have relied heavily on films with characters and plots that audiences already know. Indeed, in fifteen of the past sixteen years, the highest-grossing movie in America has been a sequel of a previously successful movie (for example, *Star Wars: The Force Awakens*) or an adaptation of a previously successful book (*The Grinch*). The hit-making formula in Hollywood today seems to be built on infinitely recurring, self-sustaining loops of familiarity, like the Marvel comic universe, which thrives by interweaving movie franchises and TV spin-offs.

But perhaps the most MAYA-esque entertainment strategy can be found on award-winning cable television. In the past decade, the cable network FX has arguably produced the deepest lineup of prestige dramas and critically acclaimed comedies on television, including *American Horror Story*, *The Americans*, *Sons of Anarchy*, and *Archer*. The ideal FX show is a character-driven journey in which old stories wear new costumes, says Nicole Clemens, the executive vice president for series development at the network. In *Sons of Anarchy*, the popular drama about an outlaw motorcycle club, "you think it's this super-über-macho motorcycle show, but it's also a soap with handsome guys, and the plot is basically *Hamlet*,"[2] she told me. In *The Americans*, a series about Soviet agents posing as a married couple in the United States, "the spy genre has been subverted to tell a classic story about marriage." These are not Marvel's infinity loops of sequels, which forge new installments of old stories. They are more like narrative Trojan horses,[3] in which new characters are vessels containing classic themes — surprise serving as a doorway to the feeling of familiarity, an aesthetic *aha*. 19

The power of these eureka moments isn't bound to arts and culture. It's a force in the academic world as well. Scientists and philosophers are exquisitely sensitive to the advantage of ideas that already enjoy broad familiarity. Max Planck, the theoretical physicist who helped lay the groundwork for quantum theory, said that "a new scientific truth does not triumph by convincing its opponents and making them see the light, but rather because its opponents eventually die, and a new generation grows up that is familiar with it." 20

In 2014, a team of researchers from Harvard University and Northeastern University wanted to know exactly what sorts of proposals were most likely to win funding from prestigious institutions such as the National Institutes of Health — safely familiar proposals, or extremely novel ones? They prepared about 150 research proposals and gave each one a novelty score. Then they recruited 142 world-class scientists to evaluate the projects. 21

[2] A tragedy by the English playwright William Shakespeare (1564–1616). — Eds.

[3] In the epic poem *The Iliad*, attributed to the Ancient Greek poet Homer, Trojan warriors infiltrate the walled grounds of King Agamemnon's castle by hiding inside a large wooden horse presented as a gift and brought inside. — Eds.

The most-novel proposals got the worst ratings. Exceedingly familiar 22 proposals fared a bit better, but they still received low scores. "Everyone dislikes novelty," Karim Lakhani, a co-author, explained to me, and "experts tend to be overcritical of proposals in their own domain." The highest evaluation scores went to submissions that were deemed slightly new. There is an "optimal newness" for ideas, Lakhani said—advanced yet acceptable.

This appetite for "optimal newness" applies to other industries, too. In 23 Silicon Valley, where venture capitalists also sift through a surfeit of proposals, many new ideas are promoted as a fresh spin on familiar successes. The home-rental company Airbnb was once called "eBay for homes." The on-demand car-service companies Uber and Lyft were once considered "Airbnb for cars." When Uber took off, new start-ups began branding themselves "Uber for [anything]."

But the preference for "optimal newness" doesn't apply just to academics 24 and venture capitalists. According to Stanley Lieberson, a sociologist at Harvard, it's a powerful force in the evolution of our own identities. Take the popularity of baby names. Most parents prefer first names for their children that are common but not too common, optimally differentiated from other children's names.

This helps explain how names fall in and out of fashion, even though, 25 unlike almost every other cultural product, they are not driven by price or advertising. Samantha was the 26th-most-popular name in the 1980s. This level of popularity was pleasing to so many parents that 224,000 baby girls were named Samantha in the 1990s, making it the decade's fifth-most-popular name for girls. But at this level of popularity, the name appealed mostly to the minority of adults who actively sought out common names. And so the number of babies named Samantha has collapsed, falling by eighty percent since the 1990s.

Most interesting of all is Lieberson's analysis of the evolution of popular 26 names for black baby girls starting with the prefix *La*. Beginning in 1967, eight distinct *La* names cracked the national top fifty, in this sequence: Latonya, Latanya, Latasha, Latoya, Latrice, Lakeisha, Lakisha, and Latisha. The orderliness of this evolution is astonishing. The step between Latonya and Latanya is one different vowel; from Latonya to Latoya is the loss of the *n*; from Lakeisha to Lakisha is the loss of the *e*; and from Lakisha to Latisha is one consonant change. It's a perfect illustration of the principle that people gravitate to new things with familiar roots. This is how culture evolves—in small steps that from afar might seem like giant leaps.

In a popular online video called "4 Chords," which has more than 27 thirty million views, the musical-comedy group the Axis of Awesome cycles through dozens of songs built on the same chord progression: I–V–vi–IV.

It provides the backbone of dozens of classics, including oldies (the Beatles' "Let It Be"), karaoke-pop songs (Journey's "Don't Stop Believin'"), country sing-along anthems (John Denver's "Take Me Home, Country Roads"), animated-musical ballads (*The Lion King*'s "Can You Feel the Love Tonight?"), and reggae tunes (Bob Marley's "No Woman, No Cry").

Several music critics have used videos like "4 Chords" to argue that pop   28
music is derivative. But I think Raymond Loewy would disagree with this critique, for two reasons. First, it's simply wrong to say that all I–V–vi–IV songs sound the same. "Don't Stop Believin'" and "No Woman, No Cry" don't sound anything alike. Second, if the purpose of music is to move people, and people are moved by that which is sneakily familiar, then musicians — like architects, product designers, scholars, and any other creative people who think their ideas deserve an audience — should aspire to a blend of originality and derivation. These songwriters aren't retracing one another's steps. They're more like clever cartographers given an enormous map, each plotting new routes to the same location.

One of Loewy's final assignments as an industrial designer was to add   29
an element of familiarity to a truly novel invention: NASA's first space station. Loewy and his firm conducted extensive habitability studies and found subtle ways to make the outer-space living quarters feel more like terrestrial houses — so astronauts "could live more comfortably in more familiar surroundings while in deep space in exotic conditions," he said. But his most profound contribution to the space station was his insistence that NASA install a viewing portal of Earth. Today, tens of millions of people have seen this small detail in films about astronauts. It is hard to imagine a more perfect manifestation of MAYA: a window to a new world can also show you home.

Journal Writing

Thompson proposes in this essay that popular culture — music, film, and television, especially — succeeds best when it is at least partly derivative, or built on previous versions of the same productions. Do you agree? Take a moment to list in your journal some of your favorite songs, movies, and TV shows. What, if anything, do they seem to have in common? How are they distinct? What makes them special to you?

Questions on Meaning

1. What would you say is Thompson's SUBJECT in this essay? Is the subject sufficiently narrowed, in your estimation? Why, or why not?

2. Who is Raymond Loewy, and why does Thompson call him "the father of industrial design" (par. 1)? What is industrial design?

3. What is "MAYA" (par. 5)? the "mere-exposure effect" (7)? "optimal newness" (22)? What do these concepts have to do with each other?

4. How would you summarize Thompson's THESIS? What makes things cool, and why?

Questions on Writing Strategy

1. The author lists several of Raymond Loewy's iconic mid-century designs (ovens, vacuums, the packaging for Lucky Strike cigarettes, and so forth) in paragraph 3, and he refers to a wide range of cultural productions (including buildings, vehicles, movie franchises, music services, and the like) throughout the essay. Does Thompson seem to expect that his AUDIENCE will understand these ALLUSIONS? Do readers need to be familiar with the examples he cites to understand his essay or appreciate his meaning?

2. What does the illustration by Mark Weaver on page 416 contribute to Thompson's essay? Why do you suppose *The Atlantic* commissioned it to accompany "What Makes Things Cool"?

3. In paragraph 6 Thompson asks, "Why do people like what they like?" How does he answer this question? What possible causes does he consider, and what does he ultimately settle on as the major contributor(s) of something's coolness? What minor causes, if any, does he acknowledge?

4. Examine the ORGANIZATION of the essay. What major sections does it fall into? Why do you think Thompson chose to order his cause-and-effect analysis as he did?

5. Thompson's cause-and-effect analysis is based on extensive research. What kinds of SOURCES does the author consult, and how? What strategies does he use to synthesize EVIDENCE and ideas from his sources without losing his own voice? How well does he succeed?

6. **OTHER METHODS**   Where in the essay does Thompson use DEFINITION to stipulate the meaning of "cool"? What strategy does he use to explain the term as he uses it?

Questions on Language

1. What POINT OF VIEW does Thompson take, and how does it affect his TONE?

2. Find three places where Thompson uses personification. (See FIGURES OF SPEECH in the Glossary if you need a definition.) What is the effect of these personifications?

3. Thompson uses a number of words that may not be familiar to you. Consult a dictionary if you need help defining the following: pandemic, neoclassical, ascended (par. 1); crestfallen, unfurled (2); aesthetic, ingested, gaudy (3); monotheistic, calibrated, industrialists (4); uncanny, neophilia, neophobia (5), mysticism, subjective (6); gravitated (7); meta-, countenance (8); skepticism, stimuli, attenuated (9); algorithm (11); lust (13); populist (14); undaunted, progressive (15); chassis, aerodynamic (17); cum, averse, recurring (18); über, subverted (19); eureka, exquisitely (20); novel (21); optimal (22); derivative, cartographers (28); terrestrial (29).

Suggestions for Writing

1. **JOURNAL TO ESSAY**   Using your journal notes on your own favorite productions of popular culture as a starting point, respond to Thompson's essay. How persuasive do you find his analysis of causes and effects? Do you agree that some combination of familiarity and novelty is what "makes things cool," or can you think of any better explanations? How well do Thompsons's claims hold up against your own experiences? What advice would you offer to artists and producers who wish to appeal to as wide an audience as possible?

2. Write an essay that defines the notion of *cool* as you understand it. You might, like Thompson, strive to explain what coolness is and how it is achieved, or you might prefer to define it by negation, stressing what it is *not*. In either case, be sure to provide a wide range of examples to suggest the various aspects of your subject.

3. **CRITICAL WRITING**   Based on what you know about the context of this piece—that it was adapted from Thompson's book *Hit Makers: The Science of Popularity in an Age of Distraction* for advance publication in *The Atlantic*—analyze how Thompson's audience and PURPOSE seem to have shaped his essay. In particular, you might focus on the essay's length, tone, DICTION, organization, and uses of evidence. What do you think Thompson was trying to achieve with the essay? How well does he succeed?

4. **CONNECTIONS**   In her essay "My Summer of Scooping Ice Cream" (p. 140), famed television producer Shonda Rhimes recalls her desire, as a teenager, to acquire a denim mini-skirt she describes as *Fierce*. How do her ideas of what counts as cool seem to square with Thompson's? As an enormously successful creative professional herself, how do you think Rhimes might take his advice to "aspire to a blend of originality and derivation" in her programming? Why do you think so?

MALCOLM GLADWELL

Malcolm Gladwell is a celebrated staff writer at the *New Yorker*, where he has earned a reputation for producing highly readable articles that synthesize complex research in the social sciences. Born in 1963 to an English mathematics professor and a Jamaican psychotherapist, he emigrated from England to Canada with his parents in 1969. After receiving his bachelor's degree in history from the University of Toronto, Gladwell worked for the *Washington Post* as a science and medicine reporter and later as chief of the *Post*'s New York bureau. In 2000 he published *The Tipping Point*, an examination of how trends catch on. The book was a breakout success and landed Gladwell on *Time* magazine's list of the hundred most influential people in the world. He has since followed it with four more best-sellers: *Blink* (2005), an argument for acting impulsively; *Outliers* (2008), an exploration of what makes some people more successful than others; *What the Dog Saw* (2009), a collection of his *New Yorker* essays; and *David and Goliath* (2013), a look at the advantages of being disadvantaged. In addition to writing, Gladwell produces and hosts two popular podcasts: *Revisionist History*, a contrary interpretation of past events and ideas, and *Broken Record*, an interactive show about music and musicians.

Little Fish in a Big Pond

Do the "best" universities provide the best opportunities? In "Little Fish in a Big Pond" (editors' title), abridged from a chapter in *David and Goliath*, Gladwell focuses on the experience of one Ivy League biology major to detail the implications of several studies conducted by sociologists, psychologists, and education specialists. Dropped into a competitive environment, he discovers, many of the best students will fail—but only if they perceive that others are winning. Understanding this paradox, Gladwell suggests, could be the key to curbing the shortage of scientists and engineers in the United States.

Note that Gladwell uses a combination of footnotes and endnotes to provide citations for the academic studies he refers to and quotes. He does not follow any widely used documentation system (such as MLA or APA) but nonetheless provides clear information about each of the sources that inform his analysis.

Caroline Sacks[1] grew up on the farthest fringes of the Washington, DC, metropolitan area. She went to public schools through high school. Her mother is an accountant and her father works for a technology company. As a child she sang in the church choir and loved to write and draw. But what really excited her was science.

---

[1] I've changed her name and identifying details.

"I did a lot of crawling around in the grass with a magnifying glass and a   2
sketchbook, following bugs and drawing them," Sacks says. She is a thoughtful and articulate young woman, with a refreshing honesty and directness.
"I was really, really into bugs. And sharks. So for a while I thought I was going
to be a veterinarian or an ichthyologist. Eugenie Clark was my hero. She was
the first woman diver. She grew up in New York City in a family of immigrants and ended up rising to the top of her field, despite having a lot of 'Oh,
you're a woman, you can't go under the ocean' setbacks. I just thought she
was great. My dad met her and was able to give me a signed photo and I was
really excited. Science was always a really big part of what I did."

Sacks sailed through high school at the top of her class. She took a   3
political science course at a nearby college while she was still in high school,
as well as a multivariant calculus course at the local community college. She
got As in both, as well as an A in every class she took in high school. She got
perfect scores on every one of her Advanced Placement pre-college courses.

The summer after her junior year in high school, her father took her on a   4
whirlwind tour of American universities. "I think we looked at five schools in
three days," she says. "It was Wesleyan, Brown, Providence College, Boston
College, and Yale. Wesleyan was fun but very small. Yale was cool, but I definitely didn't fit the vibe." But Brown University, in Providence, Rhode Island,
won her heart. It is small and exclusive, situated in the middle of a nineteenth-
century neighborhood of redbrick Georgian and Colonial buildings on the
top of a gently sloping hill. It might be the most beautiful college campus in
the United States. She applied to Brown, with the University of Maryland as
her backup. A few months later, she got a letter in the mail. She was in.

"I expected that everyone at Brown would be really rich and worldly and   5
knowledgeable," she says. "Then I got there, and everybody seemed to be just
like me — intellectually curious and kind of nervous and excited and not sure
whether they'd be able to make friends. It was very reassuring." The hardest
part was choosing which courses to take, because she loved the sound of everything. She ended up in Introductory Chemistry, Spanish, a class called the
Evolution of Language, and Botanical Roots of Modern Medicine, which she
describes as "sort of half botany class, half looking at uses of indigenous plants
as medicine and what kind of chemical theories they are based on." She was in
heaven.

Did Caroline Sacks make the right choice? Most of us would say that   6
she did. When she went on that whirlwind tour with her father, she ranked
the colleges she saw, from best to worst. Brown University was number one.
The University of Maryland was her backup because it was not in any way as
good a school as Brown. Brown is a member of the Ivy League. It has more

resources, more academically able students, more prestige, and more accomplished faculty than the University of Maryland. In the rankings of American colleges published every year by the magazine *US News & World Report*, Brown routinely places among the top ten or twenty colleges in the United States. The University of Maryland finishes much farther back in the pack.

But let's think about Caroline's decision. . . . [Hers] was a choice between 7 two very *different* options, each with its own strengths and drawbacks. . . . She could be a Big Fish at the University of Maryland, or a Little Fish at one of the most prestigious universities in the world. She chose the [latter]—and she ended up paying a high price.

The trouble for Caroline Sacks began in the spring of her freshman year, 8 when she enrolled in chemistry. She was probably taking too many courses, she realizes now, and doing too many extracurricular activities. She got her grade on her third midterm exam, and her heart sank. She went to talk to the professor. "He ran me through some exercises, and he said, 'Well, you have a fundamental deficiency in some of these concepts, so what I would actually recommend is that you drop the class, not bother with the final exam, and take the course again next fall.'" So she did what the professor suggested. She retook the course in the fall of her sophomore year. But she barely did any better. She got a low B. She was in shock. "I had never gotten a B in an academic context before," she said. "I had never *not* excelled. And I was taking the class for the second time, this time as a sophomore, and most of the kids in the class were first-semester freshmen. It was pretty disheartening."

She had known when she was accepted to Brown that it wasn't going 9 to be like high school. It couldn't be. She wasn't going to be the smartest girl in the class anymore—and she'd accepted that fact. "I figured, regardless of how much I prepared, there would be kids who had been exposed to stuff I had never even heard of. So I was trying not to be naive about that." But chemistry was beyond what she had imagined. The students in her class were *competitive*. "I had a lot of trouble even talking with people from those classes," she went on. "They didn't want to share their study habits with me. They didn't want to talk about ways to better understand the stuff that we were learning, because that might give me a leg up."

In spring of her sophomore year, she enrolled in organic chemistry—and 10 things only got worse. She couldn't do it: "You memorize how a concept works, and then they give you a molecule you've never seen before, and they ask you to make another one you've never seen before, and you have to get from this thing to that thing. There are people who just think that way and in five minutes are done. They're the curve busters. Then there are people who through an amazing amount of hard work trained themselves to think that way. I worked *so* hard and I never got it down." The teacher would ask a question, and around her, hands would go up, and Sacks would sit in silence and listen to everyone else's brilliant answers. "It was just this feeling of overwhelming inadequacy."

One night she stayed up late, preparing for a review session in organic chemistry. She was miserable and angry. She didn't want to be working on organic chemistry at three in the morning, when all of that work didn't seem to be getting her anywhere. "I guess that was when I started thinking that maybe I shouldn't pursue this any further," she said. She'd had enough.

The tragic part was that Sacks *loved* science. As she talked about her abandonment of her first love, she mourned all the courses she would have loved to take but now never would—physiology, infectious disease, biology, math. In the summer after her sophomore year, she agonized over her decision: "When I was growing up, it was a subject of much pride to be able to say that, you know, 'I'm a seven-year-old girl, and I love bugs! And I want to study them, and I read up on them all the time, and I draw them in my sketchbook and label all the different parts of them and talk about where they live and what they do.' Later it was 'I am so interested in people and how the human body works, and isn't this amazing?' There is definitely a sort of pride that goes along with 'I am a science girl,' and it's almost shameful for me to leave that behind and say, 'Oh, well, I am going to do something easier because I can't take the heat.' For a while, that is the only way I was looking at it, like I have completely failed. This has been my goal and I can't do it."

And it shouldn't have mattered how Sacks did in organic chemistry, should it? She never wanted to be an organic chemist. It was just a course. Lots of people find organic chemistry impossible. It's not uncommon for pre-med students to take organic chemistry over the summer at another college just to give themselves a full semester of practice. What's more, Sacks was taking organic chemistry at an extraordinarily competitive and academically rigorous university. If you were to rank all the students in the world who are taking organic chemistry, Sacks would probably be in the 99th percentile.

But the problem was, Sacks wasn't comparing herself to all the students in the world taking organic chemistry. She was comparing herself to her fellow students at Brown. She was a Little Fish in one of the deepest and most competitive ponds in the country—and the experience of comparing herself to all the other brilliant fish shattered her confidence. It made her feel stupid, even though she isn't stupid at all. "Wow, other people are mastering this, even people who were as clueless as I was in the beginning, and I just can't seem to learn to think in this manner."

Caroline Sacks was experiencing what is called "relative deprivation," a term coined by the sociologist Samuel Stouffer during the Second World War.

Stouffer was commissioned by the US Army to examine the attitudes and morale of American soldiers, and he ended up studying half a million men and women, looking at everything from how soldiers viewed their commanding officers to how black soldiers felt they were being treated to how difficult soldiers found it to serve in isolated outposts.

But one set of questions Stouffer asked stood out. He quizzed both soldiers   16 serving in the Military Police and those serving in the Air Corps (the forerunner of the Air Force) about how good a job they thought their service did in recognizing and promoting people of ability. The answer was clear. Military Policemen had a far more positive view of their organization than did enlisted men in the Air Corps.

On the face of it, that made no sense. The Military Police had one of the   17 worst rates of promotion in all of the armed forces. The Air Corps had one of the best. The chance of an enlisted man rising to officer status in the Air Corps was *twice* that of a soldier in the Military Police. So, why on earth would the Military Policemen be more satisfied? The answer, Stouffer famously explained, is that Military Policemen compared themselves only to other Military Policemen. And if you got a promotion in the Military Police, that was such a rare event that you were very happy. And if you didn't get promoted, you were in the same boat as most of your peers—so you weren't *that* unhappy.

"Contrast him with the Air Corps man of the same education and   18 longevity," Stouffer wrote. His chance of getting promoted to officer was greater than 50 percent. "If he had earned a [promotion], so had the majority of his fellows in the branch, and his achievement was less conspicuous than in the MP's. If he had failed to earn a rating while the majority had succeeded, he had more reason to feel a sense of personal frustration, which could be expressed as criticism of the promotion system."

Stouffer's point is that we form our impressions not globally, by placing   19 ourselves in the broadest possible context, but locally — by comparing ourselves to people "in the same boat as ourselves." Our sense of how deprived we are is *relative*. . . .

Caroline Sacks's decision to evaluate herself, then, by looking around her   20 organic chemistry classroom was not some strange and irrational behavior. It is what human beings do. We compare ourselves to those in the same situation as ourselves, which means that students in an elite school—except, perhaps, those at the very top of the class—are going to face a burden that they would not face in a less competitive atmosphere. . . . Students at "great" schools look at the brilliant students around them, and how do you think they feel?

The phenomenon of relative deprivation applied to education is   21 called—appropriately enough—the "Big Fish–Little Pond Effect." The more elite an educational institution is, the worse students feel about their own academic abilities. Students who would be at the top of their class at a good school can easily fall to the bottom of a really good school. Students who would feel that they have mastered a subject at a good school can have the feeling that they are falling farther and farther behind in a *really* good school. And that feeling—as subjective and ridiculous and irrational as it may be—*matters*. How you feel about your abilities—your academic "self-concept"—in the context of your classroom shapes your willingness to tackle challenges and finish difficult tasks. It's a crucial element in your motivation and confidence.

The Big Fish–Little Pond theory was pioneered by the psychologist 22 Herbert Marsh, and to Marsh, most parents and students make their school choices for the wrong reasons. "A lot of people think that going to an academically selective school is going to be good," he said. "That's just not true. The reality is that it is going to be *mixed*." . . .

What happened to Caroline Sacks is all too common. More than half 23 of all American students who start out in science, technology, and math programs (or STEM, as they are known) drop out after their first or second year. Even though a science degree is just about the most valuable asset a young person can have in the modern economy, large numbers of would-be STEM majors end up switching into the arts, where academic standards are less demanding and the coursework less competitive. That's the major reason that there is such a shortage of qualified American-educated scientists and engineers in the United States.

To get a sense of who is dropping out—and why—let's take a look at the 24 science enrollment of a school in upstate New York called Hartwick College. It's a small liberal arts college of the sort that is common in the American Northeast.

Here are all the Hartwick STEM majors divided into three groups—top 25 third, middle third, and bottom third—according to their test scores in mathematics. The scores are from the SAT, the exam used by many American colleges as an admissions test. The mathematics section of the test is out of 800 points.[2]

STEM majors	Top Third	Middle Third	Bottom Third
Math SAT	569	472	407

[2] These statistics are derived from a paper entitled "The Role of Ethnicity in Choosing and Leaving Science in Highly Selective Institutions" by the sociologists Rogers Elliott and A. Christopher Strenta et al. The SAT scores are from the early 1990s, and may be somewhat different today.

If we take the SAT as a guide, there's a pretty big difference in raw math ability between the best and the poorest students at Hartwick.

Now let's look at the portion of all science degrees at Hartwick that are earned by each of those three groups.   26

STEM degrees	Top Third	Middle Third	Bottom Third
Percent	55.0	27.1	17.8

The students in the top third at Hartwick earn well over half of the school's science degrees. The bottom third end up earning only 17.8 percent of Hartwick's science degrees. The students who come into Hartwick with the poorest levels of math ability are dropping out of math and science in droves. This much seems like common sense. Learning the advanced mathematics and physics necessary to become an engineer or scientist is really hard—and only a small number of students clustered at the top of the class are smart enough to handle the material.

Now let's do the same analysis for Harvard, one of the most prestigious universities in the world.   27

STEM degrees	Top Third	Middle Third	Bottom Third
Math SAT	753	674	581

Harvard students, not surprisingly, score far higher on the math SAT than their counterparts at Hartwick. In fact, the students in Harvard's bottom third have higher scores than the *best* students at Hartwick. If getting a science degree is about how smart you are, then virtually everyone at Harvard should end up with a degree — right? At least on paper, there is no one at Harvard who lacks the intellectual firepower to master the coursework. Well, let's take a look at the portion of degrees that are earned by each group.

STEM degrees	Top Third	Middle Third	Bottom Third
Percent	53.4	31.2	15.4

Isn't that strange? The students in the bottom third of the Harvard class drop out of math and science just as much as their counterparts in upstate New York. *Harvard has the same distribution of science degrees as Hartwick.*

Think about this for a moment. We have a group of high achievers at   28
Hartwick. Let's call them the Hartwick All-Stars. And we've got another group of lower achievers at Harvard. Let's call them the Harvard Dregs. Each is studying the same textbooks and wrestling with the same concepts and trying to master the same problem sets in courses like advanced calculus and organic chemistry, and according to test scores, they are of roughly equal academic ability. But the overwhelming majority of Hartwick All-Stars get what they want and end up as

engineers or biologists. Meanwhile, the Harvard Dregs—who go to the far more prestigious school—are so demoralized by their experience that many of them drop out of science entirely and transfer to some nonscience major. The Harvard Dregs are Little Fish in a Very Big and Scary Pond. The Hartwick All-Stars are Big Fish in a Very Welcoming Small Pond. What matters, in determining the likelihood of getting a science degree, is not just how smart you are. It's how smart you *feel* relative to the other people in your classroom. . . .

Let's go back, then, and reconstruct what Caroline Sacks's thinking should 29 have been when faced with the choice between Brown and the University of Maryland. By going to Brown, she would benefit from the prestige of the university. She might have more interesting and wealthier peers. The connections she made at school and the brand value of Brown on her diploma might give her a leg up on the job market. These are all classic Big Pond advantages. . . .

But she would be taking a risk. She would dramatically increase her 30 chances of dropping out of science entirely. How large was that risk? According to research done by Mitchell Chang of the University of California, the likelihood of someone completing a STEM degree—all things being equal—rises by 2 percentage points for every 10-point decrease in the university's average SAT score.[3] The smarter your peers, the dumber you feel; the dumber you feel, the more likely you are to drop out of science. Since there is roughly a 150-point gap between the average SAT scores of students attending the University of Maryland and Brown, the "penalty" Sacks paid by choosing a great school over a good school is that she reduced her chances of graduating with a science degree by 30 percent. *Thirty percent!* At a time when students with liberal arts degrees struggle to find jobs, students with STEM degrees are almost assured of good careers. Jobs for people with science and engineering degrees are plentiful and highly paid. That's a very large risk to take for the prestige of an Ivy League school. . . .

Parents still tell their children to go to the best schools they possibly can, 31 on the grounds that the best schools will allow them to do whatever they wish.

[3] This is a crucial enough point that it is worth spelling out in more detail. Chang and his coauthors looked at a sample of several thousand first-year college students and measured which factors played the biggest role in a student's likelihood of dropping out of science. The most important factor? How academically able the university's students were. "For every 10-point increase in the average SAT score of an entering cohort of freshmen at a given institution, the likelihood of retention decreased by two percentage points," the authors write. Interestingly, if you look just at students who are members of ethnic minorities, the numbers are even higher. Every 10-point increase in SAT score causes retention to fall by *three* percentage points. "Students who attend what they considered to be their first-choice school were less likely to persist in a biomedical or behavioral science major," they write. You think you want to go to the fanciest school you can. You don't.

We take it for granted that the Big Pond expands opportunities, just as we take it for granted that a smaller class is always a better class. We have a definition in our heads of what an advantage is — and the definition isn't right. And what happens as a result? It means that we make mistakes. It means that we misread battles between underdogs and giants. It means that we underestimate how much freedom there can be in what looks like a disadvantage. It's the Little Pond that maximizes your chances to do whatever you want.

At the time she was applying to college, Caroline Sacks had no idea she   32 was taking that kind of chance with the thing she loved. Now she does. At the end of our talk, I asked her what would have happened if she had chosen instead to go to the University of Maryland — to be, instead, a Big Fish in a Little Pond. She answered without hesitation: "I'd still be in science."

Notes

The first academic paper to raise the issue of relative deprivation with respect to school choice was James Davis's "The Campus as Frog Pond: An Application of the Theory of Relative Deprivation to Career Decisions of College Men," *The American Journal of Sociology* 72, no. 1 (July 1966). Davis concludes:

> At the level of the individual, [my findings] challenge the notion that getting into the "best possible" school is the most efficient route to occupational mobility. Counselors and parents might well consider the drawbacks as well as the advantages of sending a boy to a "fine" college, if, when doing so, it is fairly certain he will end up in the bottom ranks of his graduating class. The aphorism "It is better to be a big frog in a small pond than a small frog in a big pond" is not perfect advice, but it is not trivial.

Stouffer's study (coauthored with Edward A. Suchman, Leland C. DeVinney, Shirley A. Star, and Robin M. Williams Jr.) appears in *The American Soldier: Adjustment During Army Life*, vol. 1 of *Studies in Social Psychology in World War II* (Princeton University Press, 1949), 251.

Herbert Marsh teaches in the Department of Education at Oxford University. His academic output over the course of his career has been extraordinary. On the subject of "Big Fish/Little Pond" alone, he has written countless papers. A good place to start is H. Marsh, M. Seaton, et al., "The Big-Fish-Little-Pond-Effect Stands Up to Critical Scrutiny: Implications for Theory, Methodology, and Future Research," *Educational Psychology Review* 20 (2008): 319–50.

For statistics on STEM programs, see Rogers Elliott, A. Christopher Strenta, et al., "The Role of Ethnicity in Choosing and Leaving Science in Highly Selective Institutions," *Research in Higher Education* 37, no. 6 (December 1996), and Mitchell Chang, Oscar Cerna, et al., "The Contradictory Roles of Institutional Status in Retaining Underrepresented Minorities in Biomedical and Behavioral Science Majors," *The Review of Higher Education* 31, no. 4 (Summer 2008).

Journal Writing

Are you enrolled in the college of your top choice, or did you have to settle for a "backup" (par. 6) school? Have you taken, or do you plan to take, any difficult courses of the sort Gladwell describes? How do you respond to his characterizations of STEM majors and liberal arts students? Are you reassured, insulted, thankful for his advice? Why? Express your reactions to his cause-and-effect analysis in your journal.

Questions on Meaning

1. What would you say is the author's PURPOSE in this essay?
2. What is "relative deprivation" (par. 15), as Gladwell explains it?
3. SUMMARIZE what Gladwell means by the "Big Fish–Little Pond Effect" (par. 21). How does this effect apply to college students in general? How, if at all, does it apply to you?
4. Gladwell states his THESIS near the end of his essay. What is it? Why doesn't he include it in his introduction?

Questions on Writing Strategy

1. Does Gladwell expect that readers will actually be able to use the information he provides? How can you tell?
2. Why, according to Gladwell, do "[m]ore than half of all American students who start out in science, technology, and math programs . . . drop out after their first or second year" (par. 23)? How does he support this claim?
3. Gladwell is known for weaving together multiple strands of apparently unrelated materials in his work, and this excerpt from *David and Goliath* is no exception (in fact, the ellipsis marks you see throughout it show where we've omitted some of the original chapter's other strands). To better understand Gladwell's method, sketch an outline of the cause-and-effect analysis offered here. How effective do you find his ORGANIZATION? How does Gladwell integrate the strands to achieve UNITY?
4. **OTHER METHODS**   How does Gladwell use a single extended EXAMPLE to support his explanation of why smart students struggle?

Questions on Language

1. How would you characterize Gladwell's DICTION and TONE? Are they appropriate for a formal analysis? Why, or why not?
2. What does Gladwell mean when he says "Sacks sailed through high school" (par. 3)? Where else does he return to this metaphor? (See FIGURES OF SPEECH in

the Glossary if you need a definition of *metaphor*.) What makes it a particularly effective use of figurative language, given his subject?

3. Consult a dictionary if you are unsure of the meanings of any of the following terms: articulate, ichthyologist (par. 2); multivariant calculus (3); Georgian, Colonial (4); botanical/botany, indigenous (5); latter (7); disheartening (8); naive (9); rigorous, percentile (13); forerunner (16); conspicuous (18); subjective (21); droves (26); distribution (27); demoralized (28); reconstruct (29).

4. Gladwell uses formal words like *elite* and *prestigious*, and also words like *deficiency* and *inadequacy*, several times in this essay. What are the usual CONNOTATIONS of these words? How does the repetition of key terms help to emphasize the author's point?

Suggestions for Writing

1. **JOURNAL TO ESSAY**   What is the purpose of a liberal arts education? Building on your journal writing (p. 434), draft an essay in which you explain what you expect to learn in college and how you might apply your education as a working adult. Does it matter what school you attend or what subject you major in? What kinds of classes are most useful, and why? You might expand your thinking to include advice you would give a friend or relative who was considering what colleges to apply to and what subject to major in.

2. Rising tuition rates and accompanying rates of student debt have sparked significant controversy in recent years. Research explanations for the increases and some of the solutions that policy makers and pundits have proposed. Then write an essay in which you SUMMARIZE your findings. If your research—or your experience as a tuition-paying student—leads you to form an opinion for or against any of the proposals for change, present and support that as well.

3. **CRITICAL WRITING**   Gladwell's cause-and-effect analysis relies on a series of interviews he conducted with one student as well as expert opinion and other EVIDENCE from published sources. Write an essay in which you discuss how effective, or ineffective, you find his SYNTHESIS of source materials to be. You might examine, for instance, his use of SUMMARY, PARAPHRASE, and QUOTATION; consider why he provides source notes at the end but doesn't use formal citations in his text; or explore what else, if anything, he might have brought in to support his analysis.

4. **CONNECTIONS**   In "Checking My Privilege" (p. 460), Tal Fortgang writes about the advantages of being a student at Princeton University, another Ivy League school on a par with Harvard or Brown. Read his reflections, and then write an essay that considers how his beliefs compare to those of Caroline Sacks as portrayed by Malcolm Gladwell—as well as to your own attitudes and those of your classmates. How do Gladwell's theories hold up when applied to a broader cross-section of people? Besides dropping out, what are some other consequences of the difficulties faced by contemporary college students—including positive consequences, if you think there are any?

Malcolm Gladwell on Writing

As a professional researcher, Malcolm Gladwell has tackled a dizzying array of subjects, among them dogs, football, homelessness, ketchup, police tactics, professional success, and decision making. In a 2015 interview for the entrepreneurial podcast *Dorm Room Tycoon*, host William Channer asked Gladwell how he decides what to write about. "I tend to start with a puzzle," Gladwell answered. "Something that I don't entirely understand or can't entirely explain or some kind of story that poses a really interesting question. There are many, many ways into that. Sometimes the puzzle is sparked by someone you meet, someone you read about, something you read, some piece of research you stumble across. . . . A lot of stumbling goes on. In fact I depend on the stumbling. One of the things I like to do in my writing is to put together things that are quite different in many respects but have a surprising similarity. I do that a lot. That is the direct fruit of stumbling on to things."

The stumbling continues throughout Gladwell's writing process. "Like most serious writers," Gladwell explains, he puts in "many, many, many, many drafts." He goes on: "I might do at least four or five or maybe six or seven serious drafts" of a piece. "I have an expectation when I'm writing that it's all going to change. There's no necessity of getting it right the first time. In fact the first drafts I write are often not just in terms of the sentences a long way from where I end up but in the arguments as well. I expect the arguments to change. I'm getting a version of the argument in place and then when I think about it, I adjust it as I go because the process of writing an argument and the process of formulating an argument . . . happens at the same time. It's not a matter that you figured it all out then you write it down. I think as you're writing it down, you're figuring it out."

The Bedford Reader on Writing

Gladwell's work depends on researching the answers to interesting questions, a process we explain on pages 648–52 of the Appendix. You'll find advice on stumbling into and refining what Gladwell calls an "argument" and we call a THESIS on pages 34–35 of Chapter 2 and 43 of Chapter 3.

CHITRA DIVAKARUNI

Born in 1956 in Kolkata (formerly Calcutta), Chitra Banerjee Divakaruni spent nineteen years in India before immigrating to the United States. She holds a BA from the University of Calcutta, an MA from Wright State University, and a PhD from the University of California, Berkeley. Her books, often addressing the immigrant experience in America, include the novels *The Mistress of Spice* (1997), which was named one of the best books of the twentieth century by the *San Francisco Chronicle*, *One Amazing Thing* (2009), *Oleander Girl* (2013), and *The Forest of Enchantments* (2019); the story collections *Arranged Marriage* (1995) and *The Unknown Errors of Our Lives* (2001); and the poetry collections *Leaving Yuba City* (1997) and *Black Candle* (2000). Divakaruni has received a number of prizes for her work, including the Before Columbus Foundation's 1996 American Book Award; in 2015, the *Economic Times* listed her among the twenty most globally influential Indian women. She teaches creative writing at the University of Houston and serves on the boards of several organizations that help women and children.

Live Free and Starve

Many of the consumer goods sold in the United States—shoes, clothing, toys, rugs—are made in countries whose labor practices do not meet US standards for safety and fairness. Americans have been horrified at tales of children put to work by force or under contracts (called *indentures*) with the children's parents. Some in the US government have tried to stop or at least discourage such practices: For instance, the bill Divakaruni cites in her first paragraph, which was signed into law, requires the Customs Service to issue a detention order on goods that are suspected of having been produced by forced or indentured child labor. In this essay from *Salon* in 1997, Divakaruni argues that such efforts, however well intentioned, can mean dreadful consequences for the very people they are designed to protect.

For a different perspective on the effects of globalization, see the next essay, Marie Javdani's *"Plata o Plomo:* Silver or Lead."

Some days back, the House passed a bill that stated that the United States would no longer permit the import of goods from factories where forced or indentured child labor was used. My liberal friends applauded the bill. It was a triumphant advance in the field of human rights. Now children in Third World countries wouldn't have to spend their days chained to their posts in factories manufacturing goods for other people to enjoy while their childhoods slipped by them. They could be free and happy, like American children.

I am not so sure.   2

It is true that child labor is a terrible thing, especially for those children   3
who are sold to employers by their parents at the age of five or six and have no way to protect themselves from abuse. In many cases it will be decades—perhaps a lifetime, due to the fines heaped upon them whenever they make mistakes—before they can buy back their freedom. Meanwhile these children, mostly employed by rug-makers, spend their days in dark, ill-ventilated rooms doing work that damages their eyes and lungs. They aren't even allowed to stand up and stretch. Each time they go to the bathroom, they suffer a pay cut.

But is this bill, which, if it passes the Senate and is signed by President   4
Clinton, will lead to the unemployment of almost a million children, the answer? If the children themselves were asked whether they would rather work under such harsh conditions or enjoy a leisure that comes without the benefit of food or clothing or shelter, I wonder what their response would be.

It is easy for us in America to make the error of evaluating situations   5
in the rest of the world as though they were happening in this country and propose solutions that make excellent sense—in the context of our society. Even we immigrants, who should know better, have wiped from our minds the memory of what it is to live under the kind of desperate conditions that force a parent to sell his or her child. Looking down from the heights of Maslow's pyramid,[1] it seems inconceivable to us that someone could actually prefer bread to freedom.

When I was growing up in Calcutta, there was a boy who used to work in   6
our house. His name was Nimai, and when he came to us, he must have been about ten or so, just a little older than my brother and I. He'd been brought to our home by his uncle, who lived in our ancestral village and was a field laborer for my grandfather. The uncle explained to my mother that Nimai's parents were too poor to feed their several children, and while his older brothers were already working in the fields and earning their keep, Nimai was too frail to do so. My mother was reluctant to take on a sickly child who might prove more of a burden than a help, but finally she agreed, and Nimai lived and worked in our home for six or seven years. My mother was a good

---

[1] The psychologist Abraham Maslow (1908–70) proposed a "hierarchy of needs" in the shape of a five-level pyramid with survival needs at the bottom and "self-actualization" and "self-transcendence" at the top. According to Maslow, one must satisfy the needs at each level before moving up to the next. — Eds.

employer—Nimai ate the same food that we children did and was given new clothes during Indian New Year, just as we were. In the time between his chores—dusting and sweeping and pumping water from the tube-well and running to the market—my mother encouraged him to learn to read and write. Still, I would not disagree with anyone who says that it was hardly a desirable existence for a child.

But what would life have been like for Nimai if an anti–child-labor law had prohibited my mother from hiring him? Every year, when we went to visit our grandfather in the village, we were struck by the many children we saw by the mud roads, their ribs sticking out through the rags they wore. They trailed after us, begging for a few paise.[2] When the hunger was too much to bear, they stole into the neighbors' fields and ate whatever they could find—raw potatoes, cauliflower, green sugar cane and corn torn from the stalk—even though they knew they'd be beaten for it. Whenever Nimai passed these children, he always walked a little taller. And when he handed the bulk of his earnings over to his father, there was a certain pride in his eye. Exploitation, you might be thinking. But he thought he was a responsible member of his family.

A bill like the one we've just passed is of no use unless it goes hand in hand with programs that will offer a new life to these newly released children. But where are the schools in which they are to be educated? Where is the money to buy them food and clothing and medication, so that they don't return home to become the extra weight that capsizes the already shaky raft of their family's finances? Their own governments, mired in countless other problems, seem incapable of bringing these services to them. Are we in America who, with one blithe stroke of our congressional pen, rendered these children jobless, willing to shoulder that burden? And when many of these children turn to the streets, to survival through thievery and violence and begging and prostitution—as surely in the absence of other options they must—are we willing to shoulder that responsibility?

Journal Writing

Write a journal response to Divakaruni's argument against legislation that bans goods produced by forced or indentured child laborers. Do you basically agree or disagree with the author? Why?

[2] *Paise* (pronounced "pie-say") are the smallest unit of Indian currency, worth a fraction of an American penny. — EDS.

Questions on Meaning

1. What do you take to be Divakaruni's PURPOSE in this essay? When was it clear?

2. What is Divakaruni's THESIS? Where is it stated?

3. What are "Third World countries" (par. 1)?

4. From the further information given in the footnote on page 438, what does it mean to be "[l]ooking down from the heights of Maslow's pyramid" (par. 5)? What point is Divakaruni making here?

5. In paragraph 8 Divakaruni suggests some of the reasons that children in other countries may be forced or sold into labor. What are they?

Questions on Writing Strategy

1. In her last paragraph, Divakaruni asks a series of RHETORICAL QUESTIONS. What is the EFFECT of this strategy?

2. How does the structure of paragraph 3 clarify causes and effects?

3. **OTHER METHODS**   What does the extended EXAMPLE of Nimai (pars. 6–7) contribute to Divakaruni's argument? What, if anything, does it add to Divakaruni's authority? What does it tell us about child labor abroad?

Questions on Language

1. Divakaruni says that laboring children could otherwise be "the extra weight that capsizes the already shaky raft of their family's finances" (par. 8). How does this metaphor capture the problem of children in poor families? (See FIGURES OF SPEECH in the Glossary for a definition of *metaphor*.)

2. What do the words in paragraph 7 tell you about Divakaruni's attitude toward the village children? Is it disdain? pity? compassion? horror?

3. Consult a dictionary if you need help in defining the following: indentured (par. 1); inconceivable (5); exploitation (7); mired, blithe (8).

Suggestions for Writing

1. **FROM JOURNAL TO ESSAY**   Starting from your journal entry, write a letter to your congressional representative or one of your senators who takes a position for or against laws such as that opposed by Divakaruni. You can use quotations from Divakaruni's essay if they serve your purpose, but the letter should center on your own views of the issue. When you've finished your letter, send it. (You can find your representative's and senators' names and addresses on the Web at *house.gov/ representatives/* and *senate.gov.*)

2. David Parker, a photographer and doctor, has documented child laborers in a series of powerful photographs (see *childlaborphotographs.com*). He asks viewers, "Under what circumstances and conditions should children work?" Look at Parker's photographs, and answer his question in an essay. What kind of paid

work, for how many hours a week, is appropriate for, say, a ten- or twelve-year-old child? Consider: What about children working in their family's business? Where do you draw the line between occasional babysitting or lawn mowing and full-time factory work? You might want to research the history of child labor in the United States, including the development of child labor laws, to help support your answer.

3. **CRITICAL WRITING**　Divakaruni's essay depends significantly on appeals to readers' emotions (see p. 495). Locate one emotional appeal that either helps to convince you of the author's point or, in your mind, weakens the argument. What does the appeal ASSUME about the reader's feelings or values? Why are the assumptions correct or incorrect in your case?

4. **CONNECTIONS**　In the next essay, "*Plata o Plomo:* Silver or Lead," Marie Javdani examines another global relationship that can harm children: the international traffic in cocaine, heroin, and other drugs. To what extent do you think the people in one country are responsible for what happens in other countries as a result of their actions? Write a brief essay that answers this question, explaining clearly the beliefs and values that guide your answer.

Chitra Divakaruni on Writing

Chitra Divakaruni is also a community worker, reaching out through organizations such as Maitri, a refuge for abused women that she helped to found. In a 1998 interview in *Atlantic Unbound*, Katie Bolick asked Divakaruni how her activism and writing affected each other. Here is Divakaruni's response.

Being helpful where I can has always been an important value for me. I did community work in India, and I continue to do it in America, because being involved in my community is something I feel I need to do. Activism has given me enormous satisfaction—not just as a person, but also as a writer. The lives of people I would have only known from the outside, or had stereotyped notions of, have been opened up to me. My hotline work with Maitri has certainly influenced both my life and my writing immensely. Overall, I have a great deal of sensitivity that I did not have before, and a lot of my preconceptions have changed. I hope that translates into my writing and reaches my readers.

The Bedford Reader on Writing

Do you have a project or an activity comparable to Divakaruni's activism that you believe positively affects your writing? What is it? How does it help you as you write? For additional help with having your "preconceptions" challenged, or CRITICAL THINKING, turn to pages 16–18.

MARIE JAVDANI

Marie Javdani was born in Albuquerque, New Mexico, and attended the University of Oregon, where she earned a BA and an MA in geography and was published in *Harvest*, the university's annual writing publication. As an undergraduate Javdani became interested in international development and worked as a research assistant for Harvard's Center for International Development; she then traveled to Malawi to conduct research on the connection between fertilizer subsidies and food security for her master's thesis. Always an avid reader, Javdani cites her father and the children's authors Shel Silverstein and Roald Dahl as her early inspirations to write. She is also a musician whose instrument of choice is the marimba, an African percussion device similar to the xylophone.

Plata o Plomo: Silver or Lead

Like Chitra Divakaruni in the previous selection, Javdani is concerned in this essay with how actions taken in the United States can affect people in other countries, often without our realizing it. To make her argument concrete, Javdani tells the stories of two boys, Eric, an American, and Miguel, a Colombian. (Colombia is a country in South America.) Reminding us that global problems start and end with people, the boys represent cause and effect at their most specific. Javdani wrote this paper for a freshman writing course and revised it for us in 2004. It is documented in MLA style, described on pages 656–70.

At 8:00 on a Friday night, Eric walks down the street in his American hometown whistling. Tonight, for the first time in almost a week, Eric does not have to do homework or chores. Tonight Eric is a free spirit. Best of all, tonight Eric has scored some drugs. He and his friends will trade their bland, controlled existence for some action and a little bit of fun.

At 8:00 on a Friday night, Miguel creeps down the road in his Colombian village praying. Tonight, for the last time in his life, Miguel will have to watch where he is going and listen anxiously for distant gunshots. Tonight Miguel will die. The guerillas who have been threatening him and his father will end his life for some coca and a lot of money.

Eric and Miguel represent opposite poles in what the United States government refers to as the "war on drugs." Miguel's home is where it starts. In his little village, drug production is the only possible way of life. Eric's home is where it ends. In his suburban paradise, the stress of homework and ex-girl-friends requires weekend breaks for drugs. All but ignoring both youths, congresspeople, governors, and presidents talk about how their actions will combat the flow of drugs into our homeland. In an attempt to find the quickest route around a complicated problem, the United States sends billions in aid dollars every year to the governments of Latin American "drug-source" countries such as Colombia, Ecuador, Bolivia, and Peru (Carpenter 205). But the solution isn't working: Political turmoil and violence continue to plague the countries to which we are sending aid, and illegal drug use in the United States remains fairly constant (Vásquez 571–75). To begin to solve the problem, we need to understand what's happening in drug-source countries, how the United States can and can't help there, and what, instead, can be done at home.

Miguel's country, Colombia, is one of the top recipients of US money 4 and military weaponry and equipment. According to the US Department of State, Colombia produces nearly eighty percent of the world's cocaine as well as a significant amount of the US heroin supply. Drug production has become a way of life for Colombians. Some call it the *plata o plomo* mentality. As Gonzalo Sanchez explains it, *plata o plomo* is literally translated as "silver or lead" and means that one can either take the money — drug money, bribe money, and so on — or take a bullet (7). Since 1964, the country has been essentially run by drug lords and leftist extremists, mainly the FARC (the military wing of the Colombian Communist Party), whose guerilla presence is much stronger and more threatening than that of the actual government. In response, extreme right-wing paramilitary forces act in an equally deadly manner. Both of these groups raid villages continually, looking to root out "traitors" and executing whomever they please (Sanchez 12–15).

According to the humanitarian organization Human Rights Watch, US 5 aid money has helped fund, supply, and train Colombian military units that maintain close alliances with paramilitary groups (*World Report*). Although Colombia has recently taken a tougher stance toward the paramilitaries and peace negotiations are in progress, the US State Department, major human rights organizations, and the United Nations claim that the Colombian government is still linked to illicit paramilitary activities. For example, government forces have often invaded, emptied, and then left a guerilla-held area, clearing the way for paramilitary fighters to take control (Carpenter 162). Human rights groups also criticize what Adam Isacson calls a "forgive and forget" government policy toward paramilitary leaders accused of crimes, including promises of amnesty in return for gradual demobilization (251–52). Although the US has threatened to suspend aid if Colombia does not break such ties with paramilitary groups, the full amount of promised aid continues to be granted (*World Report*).

For the past forty years, the people of Colombia have found themselves   6
between a rock and a hard place over the production of coca, the plant used for making cocaine. Under threats from the rebel drug lords, who now control many areas, civilians must either allow their land to be cultivated for the growth of coca or put themselves and their families at deadly risk. At the same time, however, the consequence of "cooperation" with the rebels is execution by paramilitary groups or even by the Colombian government. Some coca farmers, fearful of the government, willingly form alliances with rebels who offer to protect their farms for a fee (Vásquez 572).

Entire villages get caught in the crossfire between paramilitaries and rebels.   7
In the past ten years, over 35,000 civilians have lost their lives in the conflict and hundreds of thousands have been forced from their homes (Carpenter 215). A terrible incident in the town of Bellavista was reported in the *New York Times* in 2002 (Forero, "Colombian War"). Paramilitary forces took over the town in an attempt to gain control of jungle smuggling routes. When leftist rebels arrived ready to fight a battle, the paramilitaries fled, leaving the civilians trapped and defenseless. Most of the villagers huddled together in their church, and 117 were killed when a stray rocket destroyed the church.

What is to be done to prevent such atrocities? The United States rushes   8
aid to Colombia, hoping to stop the violence and the drugs. Unfortunately, the solutions attempted so far have had their own bad results. For instance, eradicating coca fields has alienated peasants, who then turn to the rebels for support, and it has also escalated violence over the reduced coca supply (Vásquez 575). Money intended to help peasants establish alternative crops has ended up buying weapons for branches of the military that support paramilitary operations (*World Report*). Not long ago $2 million intended for the Colombian police just disappeared (Forero, "Two Million").

Obviously, the United States needs to monitor how its dollars are used in   9
Colombia. It can continue to discourage the Colombian government from supporting the paramilitaries and encourage it to seek peace among the warring factions. But ultimately the United States is limited in what it can do by international law and by the tolerance of the US people for foreign intervention.

Instead, the United States should be looking to its home front and should   10
focus on cutting the demand for drugs. Any economist will affirm that where there is demand, there will be supply. A report by the United Nations Office on Drugs and Crime connects this basic economic principle to illegal drugs:

> Production of illicit drugs is market driven. In the United States alone, illicit drugs are an $80 billion market. More than $70 billion of that amount goes to traffickers, those who bring the drugs to market. Stopping the demand would stop their business. (26)

The United States should reduce demand by dramatically increasing both treatment and education. The first will help people stop using drugs. The second will make users aware of the consequences of their choices.

The war on drugs is not fought just in the jungles of some distant country. 11 It takes place daily at our schools, in our homes, and on our streets. People my age who justify their use of illegal drugs by saying "It's my life, and I can do with it what I please" should be made aware that they are funding drug lords and contributing to the suffering of people across the globe, including in Colombia. Eric's "little bit of fun" is costing Miguel his life.

Works Cited

Carpenter, Ted Galen. *Peace and Freedom: Foreign Policy for a Constitutional Republic.* Cato Institute, 2002.

Forero, Juan. "Colombian War Brings Carnage to Village Altar." *The New York Times,* 9 May 2002, www.nytimes.com/2002/05/09/world/colombia-war-brings-carnage-to-village-altar.html.

– – –. "Two Million in US Aid to Colombia Missing from Colombian Police Fund." *The New York Times,* 11 May 2002, www.nytimes.com/2002/05/11/world/2-million-in-us-aid-is-missing-from-colombian-police-fund.html

Isacson, Adam. "Optimism, Pessimism, and Terrorism: The United States and Colombia in 2003." *The Brown Journal of World Affairs,* vol. 10, no. 2, 2004, pp. 245–55.

Sanchez, Gonzalo. *Violence in Colombia.* Scholarly Resources, 1992.

United Nations. *Drug Consumption Stimulates Cultivation and Trade.* UN Office on Drugs and Crime, 2003.

United States, Department of State. *International Narcotics Control Strategy Report, 2003.* Government Printing Office, 2004.

Vásquez, Ian. "The International War on Drugs." *Cato Handbook for Congress: Policy Recommendations for the 108th Congress,* edited by Edward H. Crane and David Boaz, Cato Institute, 2003, pp. 567–76. *Cato Institute,* www.cato.org/cato-handbook-policymakers/cato-handbook-congress-policy-recommendations-108th-congress-2003.

World Report 2003. Human Rights Watch, 2004, www.hrw.org/legacy/wr2k3/.

Journal Writing

What do you think about Javdani's solution to the twin problems of violence in drug-producing countries and drug use in the United States (pars. 10–11)? Do you think her solution would work? Why, or why not?

Questions on Meaning

1. Where does Javdani state her THESIS? How does she develop the thesis?

2. Why do the Colombian peasants often support the Communist rebels rather than the government?

3. What, according to Javdani, are the problems caused by the US government's sending "billions in aid dollars every year to the governments of Latin American 'drug-source' countries" (par. 3)? What does Javdani offer as a solution?

Questions on Writing Strategy

1. Who seems to be Javdani's intended AUDIENCE for this essay? How does she appeal to this audience?

2. With whom do Javdani's sympathies lie? What EVIDENCE in the essay supports your answer?

3. Javdani cites a variety of outside sources throughout the essay. What is the EFFECT of her use of these sources?

4. **OTHER METHODS**   Why does Javdani use COMPARISON AND CONTRAST in her opening paragraphs? What is the effect of her returning to this comparison in her conclusion?

Questions on Language

1. In paragraph 6 Javdani describes the people of Colombia as "between a rock and a hard place over the production of coca." What does she mean?

2. How and why does Javdani use IRONY to describe Eric in paragraph 3?

3. Why does Javdani use quotation marks around *traitors* (par. 4) and *cooperation* (6)?

4. Consult a dictionary if you are unsure of the meanings of any of the following words: guerillas (par. 2); turmoil, plague (3); paramilitary (4); humanitarian, amnesty, demobilization (5); atrocities, eradicating, alienated (8).

Suggestions for Writing

1. **FROM JOURNAL TO ESSAY**   Working from your journal writing and, like Javdani, drawing on research, develop an essay that lays out your view of the most effective ways to curtail either the production or the consumption of illegal drugs. Which current US government efforts are successful, and which fall short? What more could be done?

2. Write a report on the use of illegal drugs by US adolescents, focusing on an aspect of the problem that interests you, such as how widespread it is, what groups it affects most and least, or what drugs are involved. An excellent starting place for your research is Monitoring the Future, a long-term study of "the behavior, attitudes, and values" of students and young adults. Its annual report, *Monitoring*

the Future Results, is available at *drugabuse.gov/related-topics/trends-statistics /monitoring-future.*

3. **CRITICAL WRITING** Is Javdani's essay an effective ARGUMENT? Consider the thesis development, the organization, the evidence, and the clarity of the presentation. What would you say are the strengths and weaknesses of this argument?

4. **CONNECTIONS** Javdani's essay and Chitra Divakaruni's "Live Free and Starve" (p. 437) both look at effects of globalization, the increasing economic, cultural, and political connections among nations and their people. Write a brief essay discussing what you see as the main advantages and the main disadvantages of globalization. For instance, advantages might include the availability in this country of varied ethnic foods or of relatively inexpensive consumer goods that were produced elsewhere, while disadvantages might include the loss of American manufacturing jobs to foreign factories or the strong international drug trade.

Marie Javdani on Writing

In an interview for this book, we asked Marie Javdani to describe her writing process. She also offered suggestions for college writers based on her own experiences as a student.

Depending on my writing topic, it can often take a while to get a good start. If it's a topic I chose myself and am interested in or am at least somewhat knowledgeable about, the first steps are usually much easier. I usually start by brainstorming an outline by just writing things as I think of them. What questions do I want to answer? How does this topic actually affect people? Once I get a start, the writing process usually goes fairly quickly. I try to write in a way that I would speak if I were, for instance, teaching on the subject. That tends to make my work more readable. As for the introduction, I try to stay away from prescribed formats. I try to think of what would make me want to read more about a topic or to put a spin on it that makes it stand out. Also, I tend to write my introduction last. I've found that if I write it first it typically doesn't match what I write once I get "on a roll." If I plan ahead properly, I don't usually have to do more than two drafts unless I come upon new research that makes me need to rearrange my arguments. I try to write early enough to leave it alone for a few days before I go back and proofread it. . . .

From a student's perspective, the best thing you can do to improve your writing is to be interested in your topic. On the same note, however, don't soapbox. Just say what you want to say, support it, and move on. If you're writing for an assignment for which you weren't able to choose the topic, try to take an angle that you think no one else will take. . . . Do take the time to spell-check and edit your writing. The spelling checker on the computer is not sufficient. You're (not *your*) in college and you know (not *no*) better. Try reading your writing out loud to yourself. If it doesn't sound good when you say it, it doesn't sound good on paper either.

The Bedford Reader on Writing

Do you share Javdani's experience that it's usually easier to write when you're interested in your topic? For tips on finding your interest in a subject, your own personal angle, before you start writing, refer to "Focusing on a Thesis" on pages 34–35 and to "Developing Ideas" on pages 35–36. And for some of those "prescribed formats" Javdani avoids when she turns to her opening paragraphs (they can be quite helpful, really) see "Shaping the Introduction and Conclusion" (pp. 36–38).

ADDITIONAL WRITING TOPICS
Cause and Effect

1. In *Blue Highways* (1982), William Least Heat-Moon explains why it was Americans who settled the vast tract of northern land that lies between the Mississippi and the Rockies. He traces what he believes to be the major cause here:

> Were it not for a web-footed rodent and a haberdashery fad in eighteenth-century Europe, Minnesota might be a Canadian province today. The beaver, almost as much as the horse, helped shape the course of early American history. Some *Mayflower* colonists paid their passage with beaver pelts; and a good fur could bring an Indian three steel knives or a five-foot stack could bring a musket. But even more influential were the trappers and fur traders penetrating the great Northern wilderness between the Mississippi River and the Rocky Mountains, since it was their presence that helped hold the Near West against British expansion from the north; and it was their explorations that opened the heart of the nation to white settlement. These men, by making pelts the currency of the wilds, laid the base for a new economy that quickly overwhelmed the old. And all because European men of mode simply had to wear a beaver hat.

   In a Heat-Moon–like paragraph of your own, explain how a small cause produced a large effect. You might generate ideas by browsing in a history book or a collection of *Ripley's Believe It or Not*. If some small event in your life has had large consequences, you might care to write instead from personal experience.

2. In an essay, explain *either* the causes *or* the effects of a situation that concerns you. Narrow your topic enough to treat it in some detail, and provide more than a mere list of causes or effects. Here are some topics to consider:

   Labor strikes in professional sports
   Rising hostility in partisan politics
   State laws mandating the use of seat belts (or the wearing of helmets)
   Efforts to make police forces more ethnically diverse
   Gender stereotypes and career choices
   Some quirk in your personality, or a friend's
   Income inequality
   The invention of 3D printing
   The popularity of a particular TV program, comic strip, or performer
   The steady increase in college costs
   The absence of a military draft
   The fact that many couples are choosing to have only one child, or none at all
   Being "born again"
   The emphasis on competitive sports in high school and college
   The pressure on students to get good grades
   The scarcity of people training for employment as skilled workers: plumbers, tool and die makers, electricians, masons, and carpenters, to name a few

THIS EXPEDITION CALLED LIFE

Courses from 4 to 85 days. Enroll today. outwardbound.org

Outward Bound

13

DEFINITION

Tracing Boundaries

◀ **Definition in an advertisement**

This advertisement, placed in *Outside* magazine by the leadership education program Outward Bound, doesn't exactly define *life*. Instead, it invites viewers to work adventure and learning into their own personal definition of the word. The ad is a public service announcement, part of the organization's campaign to recruit students for its broad range of wilderness expedition courses. Who seem to be the intended viewers of this PSA? What goals of the advertiser does the campaign seem meant to address? What desires and concerns in readers might the ad appeal to? What is depicted in the photograph, and how do the visual elements contribute to the overall appeal? Why is the text so limited, and what does it add to the meaning? At the same time, what concerns in viewers does the ad ignore or even reject?

THE METHOD

As a rule, when we hear the word DEFINITION, we immediately think of a dictionary. In that helpful storehouse — a writer's best friend — we find the literal and specific meaning (or meanings) of a word. The dictionary supplies this information concisely: in a sentence, in a phrase, or even in a *synonym* — a single word that means the same thing ("**narrative** [năr´ə-tĭv] *n.* **1:** story . . .").

Stating such a definition is often a good way to begin an essay when basic terms may be in doubt. A short definition can clarify your subject to your reader, and perhaps help you limit what you have to say. If, for instance, you are writing a psychology paper about schizophrenia, you might offer a short definition at the outset, clarifying your subject and your key term.

In constructing a short definition, the usual procedure is to state the general class to which the subject belongs and then add any particular features that distinguish it. You could say: "Schizophrenia is a brain disease" — the general class — "whose symptoms include hallucinations, disorganized behavior, incoherence, and, often, withdrawal." Short definitions are useful whenever you introduce a technical term that readers may not know.

When a term is central to your essay or likely to be misunderstood, a *stipulative definition* may be more helpful. This fuller explanation stipulates, or specifies, the particular way you are using a term. The following paragraph, defining *TV addiction*, could serve as a stipulative definition in an essay about the causes and cures of the addiction.

> Who is addicted to television? According to Marie Winn, author of *The Plug-in Drug: Television, Children, and Family Life*, TV addicts are similar to drug or alcohol addicts: They seek a more pleasurable experience than they can get from normal life; they depend on the source of this pleasure; and their lives are damaged by their dependency. TV addicts, says Winn, use television to screen out the real world of feelings, worries, demands. They watch compulsively — four, five, even six hours on a work day. And they reject (usually passively, sometimes actively) interaction with family or friends, work at hobbies or chores, and chances for change and growth.

In this chapter we are mainly concerned with *extended definition*, a kind of expository writing that relies on a variety of other methods. Suppose you wanted to write an essay to make clear what *poetry* means. You would specify its elements — rhythm, IMAGES, and so on — by using DIVISION or ANALYSIS. You'd probably provide EXAMPLES of each element. You might COMPARE AND CONTRAST poetry with prose. You might discuss the EFFECT of poetry on the reader. In fact, extended definition is perhaps less a method in itself than the application of a variety of methods to achieve a purpose. Like DESCRIPTION, extended definition tries to *show* a reader its subject. It does so by establishing boundaries, as its writer tries to differentiate a subject from anything that might be confused with it.

An extended definition can define a word (like *poetry*), a thing (a laser beam), a condition (schizophrenia), a concept (TV addiction), or a general phenomenon (the popularity of *Fortnite*). Unlike a sentence definition or any you would find in a dictionary, an extended definition takes room: at least a paragraph, often an entire essay. Also unlike a dictionary definition, which sets forth meaning in an unimpassioned manner, an extended definition often reflects or champions the author's bias. When Tal Fortgang, in his essay in this chapter, seeks to define the word *privilege*, he examines his experiences as a white male, specifying the meaning of his subject in a particular political context.

THE PROCESS

Discovery of Meanings

The purpose of almost any extended definition is to explore a topic in its full complexity, to explain its meaning or sometimes to argue for (or against) a particular meaning. To discover this complexity, you may find it useful to ask yourself the following questions. To illustrate how the questions might work, at least in one instance, let's say you plan to write a paper defining *sexism*.[1]

- **Is this subject unique, or are there others of its kind? If it resembles others, in what ways? How is it different?** These questions invite you to compare and contrast. Applied to the concept of sexism, they might prompt you to compare sexism with one or two other -isms, such as racism or ageism. Or the questions might remind you that sexists can be both women and men, leading you to note the differences.

- **In what different forms does it occur, while keeping its own identity?** Specific examples might occur to you: a story you read about a woman's

---

[1] The six questions that follow are freely adapted from those first stated by Richard E. Young, Alton L. Becker, and Kenneth L. Pike in *Rhetoric: Discovery and Change* (1970).

experiences in the army and a girlfriend who is suspicious of all men. Each form—the soldier and the friend—might rate a description.

- **When and where do we find it? Under what circumstances and in what situations?** Well, where have you been lately? at any parties where sexism reared its ugly head? in any classroom discussions? Consider other areas of your experience: Did you encounter any sexists while holding a job?

- **What is it at the present moment?** Perhaps you might make the point that sexism was once considered an exclusively male preserve but is now an attribute of women as well. Or you could observe that many men have gone underground with their sexism, refraining from expressing it blatantly while still harboring negative attitudes about women. In either case you might care to draw examples from life.

- **What does it do? What are its functions and activities?** Sexists stereotype and sometimes act to exclude or oppress people of the opposite sex. These questions might also invite you to reply with a PROCESS ANALYSIS: You might show, for instance, how a personnel director who determines pay scales systematically eliminates women from better-paying jobs.

- **How is it put together? What parts make it up? What holds these parts together?** You could apply analysis to the various beliefs and assumptions that, all together, make up sexism. This question might work well in writing about an organization: the personnel director's company, for instance, with its unfair hiring and promotion policies.

Not all these questions will fit every subject, and some may lead nowhere, but you will usually find them well worth asking. They can make you aware of points to notice, remind you of facts you already know. They can also suggest interesting aspects you need to find out more about.

Methods of Development

The preceding questions will give you a good start in using whatever method or methods of writing can best answer the overall question "What is the nature of this subject?" You will probably find yourself making use of much that you have learned earlier in this book. A short definition like the one for *schizophrenia* on page 452 may be a good start for an essay, especially if readers need a quick grounding in the subject. (But feel no duty to place a dictionaryish definition in the INTRODUCTION of every essay you write: The device is overused.) In explaining schizophrenia, if your readers already have at least a vague idea of the meaning of the term and need no short, formal

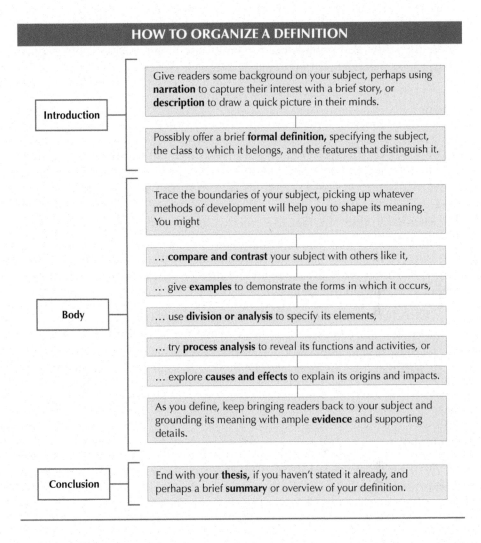

HOW TO ORGANIZE A DEFINITION

Introduction

Give readers some background on your subject, perhaps using **narration** to capture their interest with a brief story, or **description** to draw a quick picture in their minds.

Possibly offer a brief **formal definition,** specifying the subject, the class to which it belongs, and the features that distinguish it.

Body

Trace the boundaries of your subject, picking up whatever methods of development will help you to shape its meaning. You might

... **compare and contrast** your subject with others like it,

... give **examples** to demonstrate the forms in which it occurs,

... use **division or analysis** to specify its elements,

... try **process analysis** to reveal its functions and activities, or

... explore **causes and effects** to explain its origins and impacts.

As you define, keep bringing readers back to your subject and grounding its meaning with ample **evidence** and supporting details.

Conclusion

End with your **thesis,** if you haven't stated it already, and perhaps a brief **summary** or overview of your definition.

definition of it, you could open your extended definition with a description of the experiences of a person who has the disease:

> On his twenty-fifth birthday, Michael sensed danger everywhere. The voices in his head argued loudly about whether he should step outside. He could see people walking by who he knew meant him harm — the trick would be to wait for a break in the traffic and make a run for it. But the arguing and another noise — a clanging like a streetcar bell — made it difficult to concentrate, and Michael paced restlessly most of the day.

You could proceed from this opening to explain how Michael's experiences illustrate some symptoms of schizophrenia. You could provide other examples of symptoms. You could, through process analysis, explain how the disease generally starts and progresses. You could use CAUSE AND EFFECT to explore some theories of why schizophrenia develops.

Thesis

Opening up your subject with questions and developing it with various methods are good ways to see what it has to offer, but you might be left with a welter of ideas and a blurred focus. As in description, when all your details build to a DOMINANT IMPRESSION, so in definition you want to center all your ideas and evidence about the subject on a single controlling idea, a THESIS. It's not essential to state this idea in a THESIS STATEMENT, but it is essential that the idea govern.

Here, from the essays in this chapter, are two thesis statements. Notice how each makes an assertion about the subject, and how we can detect the author's bias toward the subject.

> I have checked my privilege. And I apologize for nothing.
> —Tal Fortgang, "Checking My Privilege"

> If you are reading this essay, you have some kind of privilege. It may be hard to hear that, I know, but if you cannot recognize your privilege, you have a lot of work to do; get started.
> —Roxane Gay, "Peculiar Benefits"

Evidence

Writing an extended definition, you are like a mapmaker charting a territory, taking in what lies within the boundaries and ignoring what's outside. The boundaries, of course, may be wide; and for this reason, drafting an extended definition sometimes tempts a writer to sweep across a continent and to soar off into abstract clouds. Like any other method of expository writing, though, definition will work only for the writer who remembers the world of the senses and supports every GENERALIZATION with concrete evidence.

Never lose sight of the reality you are attempting to enclose, even if its frontiers are as inclusive as those of *psychological burnout* or *human economic rights*. Give examples, narrate an illustrative story, bring in specific description—whatever method you use, keep coming back inside. Without your eyes on the world, you will define no reality. You might define *animal husbandry* till the cows come home and never make clear what it means.

FOCUS ON UNITY

When drafting a definition, you may find yourself being pulled away from your subject by the narratives, descriptions, examples, comparisons, and other methods you use to specify meaning. Let yourself explore the byways of your subject—doing so will help you discover what you think. But in revising you'll need to make sure that all paragraphs focus on your thesis and, within paragraphs, that all sentences focus on the paragraph topic, generally expressed in a TOPIC SENTENCE. In other words, you'll need to ensure the UNITY of your essay and its paragraphs.

One way to achieve unity is to focus each paragraph on some part of your definition and then focus each sentence within the paragraph on that part. If parts of your definition require more than a single paragraph, by all means expand them. But keep the group of paragraphs focused on a single idea. Roxane Gay's "Peculiar Benefits" (p. 467) proceeds in just such a pattern, as the following outline shows. Two introductory paragraphs set up Gay's subject and offer background on the author's early understanding of the meaning of *privilege* as she experienced it as a child. When Gay turns to defining, she proceeds methodically, starting with a quick formal definition of the term, transitioning from one paragraph to the next with topic sentences that specify the parts of her extended definition, and withholding her thesis to the very end. A look at Gay's essay will show you that each of her paragraphs elaborates on its specific topic.

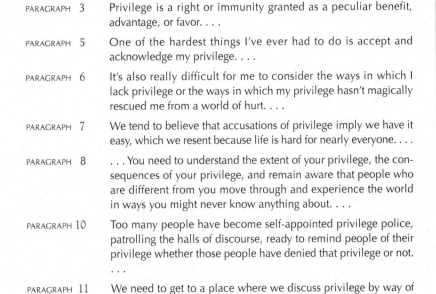

PARAGRAPH 3   Privilege is a right or immunity granted as a peculiar benefit, advantage, or favor. . . .

PARAGRAPH 5   One of the hardest things I've ever had to do is accept and acknowledge my privilege. . . .

PARAGRAPH 6   It's also really difficult for me to consider the ways in which I lack privilege or the ways in which my privilege hasn't magically rescued me from a world of hurt. . . .

PARAGRAPH 7   We tend to believe that accusations of privilege imply we have it easy, which we resent because life is hard for nearly everyone. . . .

PARAGRAPH 8   . . . You need to understand the extent of your privilege, the consequences of your privilege, and remain aware that people who are different from you move through and experience the world in ways you might never know anything about. . . .

PARAGRAPH 10   Too many people have become self-appointed privilege police, patrolling the halls of discourse, ready to remind people of their privilege whether those people have denied that privilege or not.
. . .

PARAGRAPH 11   We need to get to a place where we discuss privilege by way of observation and acknowledgment rather than accusation. . . .

CHECKLIST FOR REVIEWING AND REVISING A DEFINITION

✔ **Meanings.** Have you explored your subject fully, turning up both its obvious and its not-so-obvious meanings?

✔ **Methods of development.** Have you used an appropriate range of other methods to develop your subject?

✔ **Thesis.** Have you focused your definition and kept within that focus, drawing clear boundaries around the subject?

✔ **Evidence.** Is the definition specific? Do examples, anecdotes, and concrete details both pin the subject down and make it vivid for readers?

✔ **Unity.** Do all paragraphs focus on the thesis, and do individual paragraphs or groups of paragraphs clearly focus on parts of the definition?

STUDENT CASE STUDY: AN ESSAY EXAM

You might worry about essay exams — many students do — but take heart: Instructors who assign timed essays don't expect prize-winning compositions. They expect students to demonstrate their knowledge and critical thinking about important concepts covered in lectures and assignments.

Often you'll need to interpret the wording of an exam question to figure out what kind of response is appropriate. Questions that ask *why*, for example, might call for CAUSE-AND-EFFECT analysis, while those that ask *how* might lead to a PROCESS ANALYSIS. Keep in mind that an essay you write for an in-class exam will be less polished than one you write at home. That's fine — as long as you draft an accurate, detailed, and coherent answer to the question asked.

The midterm exam for Martin Ward's introductory government class included multiple-choice questions, a short-answer section, and one essay question: "Explain the meaning of *civil liberties*, including an explanation of how civil liberties differ from civil rights." Ward quickly recognized that "explain the meaning of" called for a definition and that "differ" called for an element of COMPARISON AND CONTRAST. Following the advice of the teaching assistant in the exam review session, Ward quickly outlined the points he needed to cover before he started writing. Then he composed the following response.

Civil liberties are the freedoms that individuals have against state intrusion. Laws protecting civil liberties limit or prohibit government action. The Constitution's Bill of Rights guarantees many of these liberties, including freedom of expression,

Short definition of *civil liberties*

Examples

freedom of religion, and freedom from unreasonable searches
and seizures. Historically, the protection of civil liberties was
established before the US Constitution in documents such as
the English Magna Carta (1215). Since that time, free countries
have defined themselves against authoritarian countries by their
respect for—and legal protections of—these freedoms.

Brief history of the
concept

While most people agree that civil liberties are essential to
a free state, there is some controversy surrounding their meaning. People don't always agree which rights are civil liberties.
For example, the debate over abortion reflects a dispute over
whether the Constitution protects privacy rights that include
the right to have an abortion. There is also disagreement about
what constitutes a violation of civil liberties. As the federal
government has taken measures to protect the country from
terrorism, many have questioned whether practices such as war-
rantless wiretapping violate privacy rights, speech rights, or the
prohibition of unreasonable searches and seizures.

Extended definition
considers issues that
complicate meaning:

• Which rights are civil
  liberties?

• What violates civil
  liberties?

People often confuse civil liberties with civil rights. Civil
liberties are freedoms from government intrusion protected
primarily by the Bill of Rights. Civil rights, however, concern
the equal treatment of individuals in society and are established mainly by the Equal Protection Clause of the Fourteenth
Amendment. An example is the right of citizens to attend public
schools regardless of their color or gender. Civil liberties and
civil rights differ in another important way as well: While protections of civil liberties prohibit government action, the government must often act to protect civil rights, as in the creation of
antidiscrimination laws.

Point-by-point
contrast with
civil rights

TAL FORTGANG

Born in 1994, Tal Fortgang grew up in New Rochelle, New York, graduated from SAR High School (an Orthodox Jewish academy) in the Bronx, and then studied the Talmud for a year in Israel before enrolling at Princeton University. He graduated with a major in politics in 2017 and is currently a research associate with the American Enterprise Institute, a think tank in Washington, DC. Fortgang tells us he plans to attend law school and pursue a career that combines his two major passions: American political thought and hockey.

Checking My Privilege

Fortgang wrote this essay as a freshman and published it in *The Princeton Tory*, a conservative campus journal, in 2014. Shortly thereafter, *Time* magazine reprinted it for a national audience, generating a flurry of discussion online. As you'll see, Fortgang was inspired by a criticism leveled at him in class to examine his own experiences and to question the intent of an accusation that he believes is heard on campus all too often.

The essay following this one, Roxane Gay's "Peculiar Benefits," responds indirectly to Fortgang and counters his point about context and meaning.

There is a phrase that floats around college campuses, Princeton being no exception, that threatens to strike down opinions without regard for their merits, but rather solely on the basis of the person that voiced them. "Check your privilege," the saying goes, and I have been reprimanded by it several times this year. The phrase, handed down by my moral superiors, descends recklessly, like an Obama-sanctioned drone, and aims laser-like at my pinkish-peach complexion, my maleness, and the nerve I displayed in offering an opinion rooted in a personal Weltanschauung.[1] "Check your privilege," they tell me in a command that teeters between an imposition to actually explore how I got where I am, and a reminder that I ought to feel personally apologetic because white males seem to pull most of the strings in the world.

I do not accuse those who "check" me and my perspective of overt racism, although the phrase, which assumes that simply because I belong to a certain ethnic group I should be judged collectively with it, toes that line. But I do

[1] German word meaning, roughly, worldview or philosophy. — EDS.

1

2

460

condemn them for diminishing everything I have personally accomplished, all the hard work I have done in my life, and for ascribing all the fruit I reap not to the seeds I sow but to some invisible patron saint of white maleness who places it out for me before I even arrive. Furthermore, I condemn them for casting the equal protection clause, indeed the very idea of a meritocracy, as a myth, and for declaring that we are all governed by invisible forces (some would call them "stigmas" or "societal norms"), that our nation runs on racist and sexist conspiracies. Forget "you didn't build that";[2] check your privilege and realize that nothing you have accomplished is real.

But they can't be telling me that everything I've done with my life can be credited to the racist patriarchy holding my hand throughout my years of education and eventually guiding me into Princeton. Even that is too extreme. So to find out what they are saying, I decided to take their advice. I actually went and checked the origins of my privileged existence, to empathize with those whose underdog stories I can't possibly comprehend. I have unearthed some examples of the privilege with which my family was blessed, and now I think I better understand those who assure me that skin color allowed my family and me to flourish today.   3

Perhaps it's the privilege my grandfather and his brother had to flee their home as teenagers when the Nazis invaded Poland, leaving their mother and five younger siblings behind, running and running until they reached a Displaced Persons camp in Siberia, where they would do years of hard labor in the bitter cold until World War II ended. Maybe it was the privilege my grandfather had of taking on the local Rabbi's work in that DP camp, telling him that the spiritual leader shouldn't do hard work, but should save his energy to pass Jewish tradition along to those who might survive. Perhaps it was the privilege my great-grandmother and those five great-aunts and uncles I never knew had of being shot into an open grave outside their hometown. Maybe that's my privilege.   4

Or maybe it's the privilege my grandmother had of spending weeks upon weeks on a death march through Polish forests in subzero temperatures, one of just a handful to survive, only to be put in Bergen-Belsen concentration camp where she would have died but for the Allied forces who liberated her and helped her regain her health when her weight dwindled to barely eighty pounds.   5

Perhaps my privilege is that those two resilient individuals came to America with no money and no English, obtained citizenship, learned the language and met each other; that my grandfather started a humble wicker   6

---

[2] Phrase from a 2012 presidential campaign speech in which Barack Obama argued that individual successes arise from the support of others. — Eds.

basket business with nothing but long hours, an idea, and an iron will — to paraphrase the man I never met: "I escaped Hitler. Some business troubles are going to ruin me?" Maybe my privilege is that they worked hard enough to raise four children, and to send them to Jewish day school and eventually City College.

Perhaps it was my privilege that my own father worked hard enough in City College to earn a spot at a top graduate school, got a good job, and for twenty-five years got up well before the crack of dawn, sacrificing precious time he wanted to spend with those he valued most — his wife and kids — to earn that living. I can say with certainty there was no legacy involved in any of his accomplishments. The wicker business just isn't that influential. Now would you say that we've been really privileged? That our success has been gift-wrapped? 7

That's the problem with calling someone out for the "privilege" which you assume has defined their narrative. You don't know what their struggles have been, what they may have gone through to be where they are. Assuming they've benefitted from "power systems" or other conspiratorial imaginary institutions denies them credit for all they've done, things of which you may not even conceive. You don't know whose father died defending your freedom. You don't know whose mother escaped oppression. You don't know who conquered their demons, or may still be conquering them now. 8

The truth is, though, that I have been exceptionally privileged in my life, albeit not in the way any detractors would have it. 9

It has been my distinct privilege that my grandparents came to America. First, that there was a place at all that would take them from the ruins of Europe. And second, that such a place was one where they could legally enter, learn the language, and acclimate to a society that ultimately allowed them to flourish. 10

It was their privilege to come to a country that grants equal protection under the law to its citizens, that cares not about religion or race, but the content of your character. 11

It was my privilege that my grandfather was blessed with resolve and an entrepreneurial spirit, and that he was lucky enough to come to the place where he could realize the dream of giving his children a better life than he had. 12

But far more important for me than his attributes was the legacy he sought to pass along, which forms the basis of what detractors call my "privilege," but which actually should be praised as one of altruism and self-sacrifice. Those who came before us suffered for the sake of giving us a better life. When we similarly sacrifice for our descendents by caring for the planet, it's called "environmentalism," and is applauded. But when we do it by passing along property and a set of values, it's called "privilege." (And when we do it by 13 raising questions about our crippling national debt, we're called Tea Party radicals.) Such sacrifice of any form shouldn't be scorned, but admired.

My exploration did yield some results. I recognize that it was my parents' 14
privilege and now my own that there is such a thing as an American dream which is attainable even for a penniless Jewish immigrant.

I am privileged that values like faith and education were passed along 15
to me. My grandparents played an active role in my parents' education, and some of my earliest memories included learning the Hebrew alphabet with my Dad. It's been made clear to me that education begins in the home, and the importance of parents' involvement with their kids' education—from mathematics to morality—cannot be overstated. It's not a matter of white or black, male or female or any other division which we seek, but a matter of the values we pass along, the legacy we leave, that perpetuates "privilege." And there's nothing wrong with that.

Behind every success, large or small, there is a story, and it isn't always 16
told by sex or skin color. My appearance certainly doesn't tell the whole story, and to assume that it does and that I should apologize for it is insulting. While I haven't done everything for myself up to this point in my life, someone sacrificed themselves so that I can lead a better life. But that is a legacy I am proud of.

I have checked my privilege. And I apologize for nothing. 17

Journal Writing

As a college student, have you ever been told, or heard someone else be told, "Check your privilege"? What was your reaction? In your journal, reflect on the advantages and disadvantages you believe may have helped or hindered you in establishing your current position in life. How do you think others perceive your background?

Questions on Meaning

1. How does Fortgang define the customary use of "Check your privilege" (par. 1)? What does he interpret the phrase to mean?

2. Fortgang acknowledges that he has "been exceptionally privileged in [his] life, albeit not in the way any detractors would have it" (par. 9). In what way (or ways) does he consider himself privileged? Why does he resent implications that his color and gender have given him any advantages?

3. To what is Fortgang referring when he mentions the "equal protection clause" (par. 2) and "equal protection under the law" (11)? Why does he invoke this concept?

4. What would you say is Fortgang's primary PURPOSE in this essay? How well does he succeed?

Questions on Writing Strategy

1. Who was Fortgang's intended AUDIENCE? How do you suppose he expected readers to respond? What do you think he hoped they would take away from their reading? What in the essay supports your answer?

2. In his first three paragraphs Fortgang discusses privilege in the ABSTRACT. How are these paragraphs connected to his stories about his family's history? Why do you think he begins the essay this way? Is this INTRODUCTION effective or not? Why?

3. Identify the TRANSITIONS Fortgang repeats in paragraphs 4–7 and 9–12. How do they create UNITY and COHERENCE in his definition?

4. Look back at the last two sentences of Fortgang's essay. What is the EFFECT of ending on this idea?

5. **OTHER METHODS** Fortgang's definition is based largely on EXAMPLES and CAUSE AND EFFECT. Does his analysis seem sound to you? Do you think he overemphasizes any causes or effects or overlooks others? Explain.

Questions on Language

1. Give some examples of FIGURES OF SPEECH in Fortgang's essay. Do any *metaphors* or *similes* strike you as particularly fresh and inventive?

2. Why does Fortgang put quotation marks around "privilege" at some points in his essay? What other words and phrases does he single out this way?

3. The phrase "content of your character" (par. 11) comes from the famous civil rights speech "I Have a Dream" by Martin Luther King, Jr.: "I have a dream," he said, "that my four little children will one day live in a nation where they will not be judged by the color of their skin but by the content of their character." How does this ALLUSION serve Fortgang?

4. If you don't know the meanings of the following words, consult a dictionary: reprimanded, imposition (par. 1); overt, condemn, ascribing, meritocracy, stigmas, conspiracies (2); patriarchy, empathize (3); resilient (6); legacy (7); conspiratorial, conceive, oppression (8); detractors (9); acclimate (10); resolve, entrepreneurial (12); attributes, altruism, descendents (13); perpetuates (15).

Suggestions for Writing

1. **FROM JOURNAL TO ESSAY** Based on your journal writing (p. 463), compose an essay in which you define your own privilege (or lack thereof). What advantages and disadvantages do you share with other people like you, and which are particular to yourself or your family? Be sure your essay has a clear THESIS and plenty of examples to make your definition precise.

2. Think about the values Fortgang cites in paragraphs 13 and 15: "altruism," "self-sacrifice," "faith," "education," "morality." Choose one of these words, or another of the values Fortgang mentions in the essay, and write an essay that explains its meanings for you. Use examples from your own experience, observations, and reading to make the definition complete.

3. Research the history of Jewish immigration to the United States. When and why did the initial wave of immigration occur? What forces have led to other patterns of immigration over the years? Have Jewish Americans faced different kinds of discrimination or enjoyed different opportunities than other immigrants have? In an essay, answer these or other questions that occur to you.

4. **CRITICAL WRITING**   Evaluate Fortgang's TONE in this essay. What contributes to this tone, and to what extent does it serve his purpose in writing? How might a different tone have changed your response to the essay?

5. **CONNECTIONS**   The next essay, Roxane Gay's "Peculiar Benefits," examines privilege from the perspective of a woman born to Haitian immigrants. Write an essay that COMPARES AND CONTRASTS Fortgang's understanding of the concept with Gay's. How does context and personal background help to shape each writer's definition? Whose ARGUMENT do you find more persuasive, and why?

Tal Fortgang on Writing

Tal Fortgang garnered a lot of media attention — both positive and negative — with "Checking My Privilege," but he stands by his argument. In comments he wrote for this book, he reflects on his writing process and considers how being passionate about a belief can lead to a strong thesis.

I distinctly remember how the idea for this piece came to me. I was in the shower (all good ideas start in the shower; the best piece of advice I can give you is if you're stuck or out of good ideas, take a hot shower and let your mind wander) and thinking about how certain things, like money or values, are passed from generation to generation. So I started thinking about possible arguments against estate taxes, wherein I might contend that governments were taking too much money from parents who saved up in hopes of passing down to their children. This tax, to me, was antithetical to the "American dream." That got me thinking about "privilege" and how it was being framed on my campus: Is there something wrong with my parents' and grandparents' hard work being passed along? Not that my family is fabulously wealthy by any stretch, but should I be embarrassed that someone before me wanted to give me a better life, and was successful in allowing me to be born into comfort? And that's how I got to talking about privilege, which is way more interesting than estate taxes, in my opinion.

My method of writing is pretty unusual. I can focus on one thing really well for about forty-five minutes at a time, so I'll usually sit down and pour out everything in my head for that long (again, usually while wearing only a towel and sopping wet because if I took the time to get dressed I'd forget all my deep shower thoughts). Then I'll step away and do something else for a while before coming back an hour or few later. I still do this. I'm writing this piece the same way. I don't know if I recommend it for everyone, but if whatever you've been doing isn't working, don't be afraid to try it out.

More important than how you go about getting your writing done is the content. (I don't think anyone would disagree with that, but it seemed like a nicely authoritative topic sentence.) Central to your content is your thesis, or the thing you know you always need to have but aren't quite sure if you do or don't yet have. I think there's a way of thinking about thesis development that really simplifies the process. Here goes: Making arguments is tough, but the good news is that you probably think things. You may even believe things you think! So you're well on your way to arguing for something you think and/or believe. When you're presented with a prompt or a question or a topic, try to capture your gut-reaction answer. Now channel your inner five-year-old and ask "why?" Then ask "why?" again. And again. As many "whys" as you need to whittle your gut reaction down to its fundamental parts. When you've reached something fundamental — the "nuclear argument" is what I like to call it — you can argue that you think it is true, and is the basis of what you believe.

I'll add that it helps to argue something you deeply, truly, believe from the bottom of your heart and the entirety of your soul. Just ask yourself why you believe it. Your writing will be stronger and you might even learn something about yourself in the process.

The Bedford Reader on Writing

Aside from the "sopping wet" part, Tal Fortgang's DRAFTING process isn't unusual at all. We certainly recommend you try writing freely in concentrated spurts, as time and focus allow (but you might want to put on some clothes). For additional thoughts on how you can narrow a subject until you reach your point of interest, try turning to pages 30–35 of this book. And for help developing your own "nuclear argument" with specifics — the "whys" — see "Developing Ideas" (pp. 35–36).

ROXANE GAY

Roxane Gay describes herself as just a "bad feminist . . . trying to make sense of this world we live in," but she is a rising star admired for crafting sharp critiques that bridge academia and popular culture with a solid sense of humor. She was born in 1974 to Haitian immigrants and grew up "a loner, shy and awkward." Shuttled around the suburbs of Nebraska, New Jersey, Colorado, Illinois, and Virginia, she read voraciously for company and wrote to entertain herself. Gay graduated from Phillips Exeter Academy in New Hampshire in 1992, earned an MA in English from the University of Nebraska, Lincoln, and completed a PhD in rhetoric and technical communication at Michigan Technological University in 2010. While teaching at Eastern Illinois University and blogging innumerable essays for sites ranging from *Jezebel* to the *Guardian*, she put together her first book, *Ayiti* (2011), a mixture of poetry, fiction, and prose focused on the experiences of Haitian immigrants. In 2014 she published both *An Untamed State*, a novel, and *Bad Feminist*, a collection of essays. *Hunger*, a critical memoir of obesity, and *Difficult Women*, a collection of short stories, followed in 2017. Currently an associate professor at Purdue University, Gay is a contributing writer for the *New York Times* opinion page and the lead author of Marvel Comics' *Black Panther: World of Wakanda* series. She is also an aggressive Scrabble player who regularly competes in tournaments and the founder of Tiny Hardcore Press, an experimental publishing house.

Peculiar Benefits

As an oversize Haitian American woman "who has been queer identified at varying points in her life," Gay nonetheless considers herself extraordinarily fortunate in the opportunities that have been afforded her. In "Peculiar Benefits," she thoughtfully examines her own privilege, mildly chastising those who cannot or will not acknowledge theirs. The essay first appeared on the online forum *The Rumpus* in 2012 and was revised for inclusion in *Bad Feminist* in 2014, just as the Internet was buzzing with debate over Tal Fortgang's "Checking My Privilege" (p. 460).

When I was young, my parents took our family to Haiti during the summers. For them, it was a homecoming. For my brothers and me it was an adventure, sometimes a chore, and always a necessary education on privilege and the grace of an American passport. Until visiting Haiti, I had no idea what poverty really was or the difference between relative and absolute poverty. To see poverty so plainly and pervasively left a profound mark on me.

To this day, I remember my first visit, and how at every intersection, men   2 and women, shiny with sweat, would mob our car, their skinny arms stretched out, hoping for a few gourdes[1] or American dollars. I saw the sprawling slums, the shanties housing entire families, the trash piled in the streets, and also the gorgeous beach and the young men in uniforms who brought us Coca-Cola in glass bottles and made us hats and boats out of palm fronds. It was hard for a child to begin to grasp the contrast of such inescapable poverty alongside almost repulsive luxury, and then the United States, a mere eight hundred miles away, with its gleaming cities rising out of the landscape and the well-maintained interstates stretching across the country, the running water and the electricity. It wasn't until many, many years later that I realized my education on privilege began long before I could appreciate it in any meaningful way.

Privilege is a right or immunity granted as a peculiar benefit, advantage,   3 or favor. There is racial privilege, gender (and identity) privilege, heterosexual privilege, economic privilege, able-bodied privilege, educational privilege, religious privilege, and the list goes on and on. At some point, you have to surrender to the kinds of privilege you hold. Nearly everyone, particularly in the developed world, has something someone else doesn't, something someone else yearns for.

The problem is, cultural critics talk about privilege with such alarming   4 frequency and in such empty ways, we have diluted the word's meaning. When people wield the word "privilege," it tends to fall on deaf ears because we hear that word so damn much it has become white noise.

One of the hardest things I've ever had to do is accept and acknowledge   5 my privilege. It's an ongoing project. I'm a woman, a person of color, and the child of immigrants, but I also grew up middle class and then upper middle class. My parents raised my siblings and me in a strict but loving environment. They were and are happily married, so I didn't have to deal with divorce or crappy intramarital dynamics. I attended elite schools. My master's and doctoral degrees were funded. I got a tenure-track position my first time out. My bills are paid. I have the time and resources for frivolity. I am reasonably well published. I have an agent and books to my name. My life has been far from perfect, but it's somewhat embarrassing for me to accept just how much privilege I have.

It's also really difficult for me to consider the ways in which I lack   6 privilege or the ways in which my privilege hasn't magically rescued me from

---

[1] Official paper currency of Haiti. One Haitian gourde is worth approximately two American cents. — EDS.

a world of hurt. On my more difficult days, I'm not sure what's more of a pain in my ass—being black or being a woman. I'm happy to be both of these things, but the world keeps intervening. There are all kinds of infuriating reminders of my place in the world—random people questioning me in the parking lot at work as if it is unfathomable that I'm a faculty member, the persistence of lawmakers trying to legislate the female body, street harassment, strangers wanting to touch my hair.

We tend to believe that accusations of privilege imply we have it easy,   7
which we resent because life is hard for nearly everyone. Of course we resent these accusations. Look at white men when they are accused of having privilege. They tend to be immediately defensive (and, at times, understandably so). They say, "It's not my fault I am a white man," or "I'm [insert other condition that discounts their privilege]," instead of simply accepting that, in this regard, yes, they benefit from certain privileges others do not. To have privilege in one or more areas does not mean you are wholly privileged. Surrendering to the acceptance of privilege is difficult, but it is really all that is expected. What I remind myself, regularly, is this: The acknowledgment of my privilege is not a denial of the ways I have been and am marginalized, the ways I have suffered.

You don't necessarily *have* to do anything once you acknowledge your   8
privilege. You don't have to apologize for it. You need to understand the extent of your privilege, the consequences of your privilege, and remain aware that people who are different from you move through and experience the world in ways you might never know anything about. They might endure situations you can never know anything about. You could, however, use that privilege for the greater good—to try to level the playing field for everyone, to work for social justice, to bring attention to how those without certain privileges are disenfranchised. We've seen what the hoarding of privilege has done, and the results are shameful.

When we talk about privilege, some people start to play a very pointless   9
and dangerous game where they try to mix and match various demographic characteristics to determine who wins at the Game of Privilege. Who would win in a privilege battle between a wealthy black woman and a wealthy white man? Who would win a privilege battle between a queer white man and a queer Asian woman? Who would win in a privilege battle between a working-class white man and a wealthy, differently abled Mexican woman? We could play this game all day and never find a winner. . . .

Too many people have become self-appointed privilege police, patrolling   10
the halls of discourse, ready to remind people of their privilege whether those people have denied that privilege or not. In online discourse, in particular, the specter of privilege is always looming darkly. When someone writes from

experience, there is often someone else, at the ready, pointing a trembling finger, accusing that writer of having various kinds of privilege. How dare someone speak to a personal experience without accounting for every possible configuration of privilege or the lack thereof? We would live in a world of silence if the only people who were allowed to write or speak from experience or about difference were those absolutely without privilege.

When people wield accusations of privilege, more often than not, they want to be heard and seen. Their need is acute, if not desperate, and that need rises out of the many historical and ongoing attempts to silence and render invisible marginalized groups. Must we satisfy our need to be heard and seen by preventing anyone else from being heard and seen? Does privilege automatically negate any merits of what a privilege holder has to say? Do we ignore everything, for example, that white men have to say? 11

We need to get to a place where we discuss privilege by way of observation and acknowledgment rather than accusation. We need to be able to argue beyond the threat of privilege. We need to stop playing Privilege or Oppression Olympics because we'll never get anywhere until we find more effective ways of talking through difference. We should be able to say, "This is my truth," and have that truth stand without a hundred clamoring voices shouting, giving the impression that multiple truths cannot coexist. Because at some point, doesn't privilege become beside the point? 12

Privilege is relative and contextual. Few people in the developed world, and particularly in the United States, have no privilege at all. Among those of us who participate in intellectual communities, privilege runs rampant. We have disposable time and the ability to access the Internet regularly. We have the freedom to express our opinions without the threat of retaliation. We have smartphones and iProducts and desktops and laptops. If you are reading this essay, you have some kind of privilege. It may be hard to hear that, I know, but if you cannot recognize your privilege, you have a lot of work to do; get started. 13

Journal Writing

Gay's "bills are paid," she notes, and she has a good job and is "reasonably well published" (par. 5). In your journal, consider the meaning of *success*, focusing on these questions: Whom do you consider to be successful, and why? Where do your ideas of success come from—your parents? your friends? your schooling? the media?

Questions on Meaning

1. In your own words, SUMMARIZE Gay's definition of *privilege*.

2. What does Gay mean by "the difference between relative and absolute poverty" (par. 1)? How does that difference apply to her understanding of privilege?

3. What does Gay believe to be the most basic reason people object when they're "accused of having privilege" (par. 7)?

4. In paragraph 7, Gay says that acknowledging her privilege "is not a denial of the ways [she has] been and [is] marginalized." What does she mean? How do you explain this contradiction?

5. What seems to be Gay's PURPOSE in this essay? What solution to the problem of privilege does she propose? Is she optimistic or pessimistic that people can be encouraged to be more empathetic to others?

Questions on Writing Strategy

1. Why does Gay open by detailing her first family trip to Haiti? How does this INTRODUCTION lead into her subject?

2. What does Gay assume about her AUDIENCE? To what extent do you fit her assumptions?

3. Why is Gay so careful to enumerate her own privileges in paragraph 5? What is the EFFECT of her admissions?

4. **OTHER METHODS** How does Gay use CLASSIFICATION to sort out the types of privilege she sees in the contemporary world? What categories does she identify? What, if any, forms of privilege might you add to her lists?

Questions on Language

1. Find some examples of both formal and informal DICTION in the essay. What is the effect of Gay's word choices?

2. Why does Gay capitalize the phrases "Game of Privilege" and "Oppression Olympics" in paragraphs 9 and 12? What does she mean by these terms?

3. What is "white noise" (par. 4)? Why is this metaphor particularly apt, given Gay's subject and purpose? (For a definition of *metaphor*, see FIGURES OF SPEECH in the Glossary.)

4. Notice that Gay shifts POINT OF VIEW in paragraph 8 and again in her conclusion, addressing readers directly as *you*. What is the effect of the last two sentences of the essay in particular?

5. Be sure you know the meanings of the following words, checking a dictionary if necessary: pervasively (par. 1); shanties (2); immunity, peculiar (3); intramarital, frivolity (5); intervening, unfathomable, legislate (6); marginalized (7);

disenfranchised (8); demographic (9); discourse, specter, configuration (10); acute (11); clamoring (12).

Suggestions for Writing

1. **FROM JOURNAL TO ESSAY** Compose an extended definition of *success* that includes an examination of the sources of your definition, as you explored them in your journal writing. The sources could be negative as well as positive—that is, your ideas of success may have formed in reaction *against* others' ideas and privileges as well as in agreement with or appreciation of them.

2. Propose some course of action in a situation you consider an injustice. Racial privilege is one possible area, or unfairness to any disenfranchised group, such as women, children, the elderly, ex-convicts, the disabled, the poor. If possible, narrow your subject to a particular incident or a local situation on which you can write knowledgeably.

3. As Gay suggests in the introduction to her essay, Haiti is the poorest country in the Americas. Do some research to learn about the natural disasters and decades of social and political upheaval—including violent conflicts between the government and rebels—that have plagued the country, prompted intervention by the United Nations, and encouraged many Haitians to seek asylum in the United States. In an essay, report your findings, considering in particular the CAUSES and EFFECTS of poverty in the Caribbean islands.

4. **CRITICAL WRITING** Write an essay examining the organization of Gay's essay. What does the author accomplish in each paragraph? How effectively does she use TRANSITIONS to move from paragraph to paragraph?

5. **CONNECTIONS** In some ways Gay's essay is an admonition to readers to "check your privilege," the phrase that Tal Fortgang, in the previous essay (p. 460), finds so maddening. Read or reread Fortgang's essay and consider the extent to which he fits Gay's understanding of why white men in particular react badly "when they are accused of having privilege" (par. 7). How well do Gay's characterizations describe Fortgang? How might he respond to her definition?

Roxane Gay on Writing

Gay is known for writing regularly in multiple genres on any number of subjects—personal essays on her *Tumblr* blog, scholarly analyses of culture for the *New York Times*, pithy Tweets on current events, poetry, and fiction for a general audience. In a 2014 interview with Tina Essmaker for *The Great Discontent*, she explained why she writes as much as she does.

Writing is not a tortured act for me. I don't have any angst about it, and I don't find it to be a painful misery. Writing is the one endeavor that makes me purely happy, and it comes fairly easily to me. I don't know why I'm that lucky, but it's true.

There are definitely times when I have writer's block, and it's infuriating, but writers love to dramatize the suffering of the writer. I don't judge them on that, because it's their truth, but I'm suffering when I'm *not* writing: It's what I do for fun. When people say I'm prolific, I think, "Well, it's kind of my self-medication, and it doesn't feel like work."

I'm a happy writer, and although that hasn't always been the case, I count my blessings. I'm finally in the place I've always dreamed of. Maybe my dreams weren't that big, but I just wanted to write and have people read what I had to say one way or another. I have that.

The Bedford Reader on Writing

It seems that Roxane Gay's unassuming PURPOSE for writing — simply expressing herself and reaching an AUDIENCE — makes the task easy for her. How can knowing your readers and having something to say to them work for you? Turn to pages 28–30 to find out.

EMILY DICKINSON

For most of her life, the famously reclusive Emily Dickinson (1830–86) kept to the shadowy privacy of her family mansion in Amherst, Massachusetts, a farming village and the site of Amherst College. Her father, an eminent lawyer, was for a time a United States congressman. One brief trip to Philadelphia and Washington, two semesters at New England Female Seminary, and a few months with nieces in Cambridge, Massachusetts, while having her eyes treated, were all the poet's travels away from home. Her work on her brilliantly original poems intensified in the years 1858–62. In later years, Dickinson withdrew more and more from the life of the town into her private thoughts, correspondence with friends, and the society of only her closest family. During her lifetime, fewer than a dozen of her poems were published, some without her permission. When she died at age fifty-five, more than seventeen hundred poems were discovered in manuscript, stitched into little booklets. A first selection was published in 1890. Since then, her personal legend and the devotion of readers have grown vastly and steadily.

"Hope" is the thing with feathers

This poem resembles most of Dickinson's: It takes a simple shape and uses plain words, yet it is anything but simple or plain. In defining the abstraction *hope* through the image of a bird, Dickinson illuminates the idea while preserving its essential mystery.

> "Hope" is the thing with feathers –
> That perches in the soul –
> And sings the tune without the words –
> And never stops – at all –
>
> And sweetest – in the Gale – is heard –
> And sore must be the storm –
> That could abash the little Bird –
> That kept so many warm –
>
> I've heard it in the chillest land –
> And on the strangest Sea –
> Yet, never, in Extremity,
> It asked a crumb – of Me.

1

5

10

Journal Writing

Dickinson's poem describes *hope* as a saving emotion. Has there ever been a point in your life when you relied on hope to get you through a difficult time? In your journal, write a few paragraphs about the problem you faced and how hoping for something better helped (or didn't help) you endure. What did you anticipate? How was your optimism rewarded?

Questions on Meaning

1. The first line of the poem defines "Hope" as "the thing with feathers." To what is the poet referring? What about that "thing" makes Dickinson's metaphor particularly effective? (If you need a definition of *metaphor*, see FIGURES OF SPEECH in the Glossary.)

2. The second stanza (lines 4–8) seems at first glance to describe the absence of hope. What is the EFFECT of this note of pessimism? Why do you suppose Dickinson included it?

3. To get a better grasp of the poem's overall meaning, PARAPHRASE the third stanza (lines 9–12) in modern prose, supplying any missing words and your own punctuation as necessary. What does the conclusion reveal about the poet's attitude toward hope?

Questions on Writing Strategy

1. Explain how Dickinson uses a CONCRETE image to explain an ABSTRACT concept. What makes her ANALOGY effective as a definition? (You may want to look up *Analogy* in the Glossary.)

2. Dickinson uses the bulk of her poem to explain what hope gives, waiting until the final two lines before she mentions what it asks. How does this structure reinforce her main idea?

3. Dickinson was an intensely private writer: Most of her poems went unpublished in her lifetime, and she allowed only a small circle of relatives and friends to read any of her work. What clues in this poem suggest that she wrote it for herself? What clues suggest that she may have had an AUDIENCE in mind?

4. **OTHER METHODS**   In addition to using COMPARISON AND CONTRAST to highlight the similarities between "hope" and "the thing with feathers," Dickinson's definition relies on DESCRIPTION, drawing on sense impressions to give a vivid picture. Which senses does Dickinson invoke? What is the DOMINANT IMPRESSION created by her imagery?

Questions on Language

1. Dickinson uses just a few words that might be unfamiliar. Make sure you know the definitions of gale (line 5), abash (7), and extremity (11). Because the poem was written long ago, you might want to check historical meanings in the *Oxford English Dictionary*, available in your school's library and probably through the library's Web site.

2. In line 3 Dickinson writes that hope "sings the tune without the words." What does this wordlessness suggest about the emotional nature of hope and the possibility of capturing its meaning in a poem?

3. Like many poets, Dickinson relies heavily on CONNOTATION to pack meaning into few words. Pick two of the following words in the poem (or two others of your own choosing) and explore their connotations, or implied meanings and associations: thing (line 1), perches (2), never (4), sore (6), little (7), strangest (10), crumb (12).

4. How does Dickinson use PARALLELISM to emphasize the poem's most important ideas?

Suggestions for Writing

1. **FROM JOURNAL TO ESSAY**   Expand on your journal entry to write a definition of *hope* based on your own experience. Explain not only what the emotion is but also how it affected you and your circumstances. In your essay, try to reach a conclusion about the value of hope — either as a coping mechanism or as a constructive way of responding to a problem.

2. Dickinson defines *hope* by comparing it to a small songbird. Pick an emotion of your choice — for example, joy, fear, anxiety, or eagerness — and define it by comparing it to an animal or a physical object. You may write your definition in the form of a poem, if you like, or as a prose essay.

3. **CRITICAL WRITING**   " 'Hope' is the thing with feathers" was written around 1861 — in other words, right when the American Civil War began. Research the political climate in Massachusetts and in Dickinson's own household in the early 1860s, looking in particular for information about New Englanders' reasons for supporting the war and their hopes for what it would accomplish. Apply what you learn to an analysis of the poem as an argument for — or against — supporting the War between the States.

4. **CONNECTIONS**   Compare Dickinson's " 'Hope' is the thing with feathers" with Langston Hughes's "Harlem" (p. 408). Of these two highly subjective poems dealing with hopes and dreams, respectively, which is more personal? What do the poets have in common, and where do their perspectives diverge? Write a brief essay answering these questions, and support your answer with quotations and PARAPHRASES from Hughes and Dickinson.

Emily Dickinson on Writing

Although Emily Dickinson never spelled out in detail her methods of writing, her practices are clear to us from the work of scholars who have studied her manuscripts. Evidently she liked to rewrite extensively both poetry and prose, with the result that many poems and some letters exist in multiple versions. Usually, a poem proceeded through three stages: a first, worksheet draft; a semifinal draft; and final copy. Occasionally, in later years, she would return to a poem, tinkering, striving for improvements. (In a few cases, she reduced a previously finished poem to a permanent confusion.)

Dickinson admired the work of writer and critic Thomas Wentworth Higginson. In "Letter to a Young Contributor," published in *The Atlantic Monthly* in 1862, he advised novice writers, "Charge your style with life." Echoing Higginson's remark with approval, Dickinson sent him some of her poems and asked, "Are you too deeply occupied to say if my Verse is alive?" Writers might attain liveliness, Higginson had maintained, by choosing plain words, as few of them as possible. We might expect this advice to find favor with Emily Dickinson, who once wrote:

> A word is dead
> When it is said,
> Some say.
>
> I say it just
> Begins to live
> That day.

The Bedford Reader on Writing

Emily Dickinson's poetry serves as a perfect example of a writer putting great thought into word choice, or DICTION. We know from her correspondence that she intended for her words to "attain liveliness." We know, too, that she provided some drafts of her poems to Thomas Wentworth Higginson in order to get his feedback. For more on the revision process, in particular the uses of peer review, see Chapter 3 (pp. 50–51).

DAGOBERTO GILB

Dagoberto Gilb was born in Los Angeles in 1950 to a Mexican mother and a German American father. Though he admits to getting in trouble as a teen and says that he "wasn't the best student at all," he enrolled in junior college and went on to earn a BA in philosophy and an MA in religion from the University of California at Santa Barbara. From 1976 to 1991 Gilb pursued a dual career as a writer and journeyman carpenter. The stories he wrote then and later, often focusing on working-class Latinos in the Southwest, have been collected in *Winners on the Pass Line* (1985), *The Magic of Blood* (1993), *Woodcuts of Women* (2001), and *Before the End, After the Beginning* (2011). Gilb has also written two novels, *The Last Known Residence of Mickey Acuña* (1994) and *The Flowers* (2008), and a collection of essays, *Gritos* (2003). Most recently he edited, with his son Ricardo Angel Gilb, *Mexican American Literature: A Portable Anthology* (2016). Gilb has been a visiting writer at several universities and the recipient of many honors and prizes, including the Hemingway Foundation/PEN award, a *New York Times* Notable Books designation, and a Guggenheim Fellowship. He currently teaches at the University of Houston–Victoria, where he is director of the Centro Victoria Center for Mexican American Literature and Culture, writer-in-residence, and founding editor of *Huizache*, a literary magazine focused on Latino works.

Pride

Gritos, Gilb's essay collection and the source of this piece, takes its title from a Spanish word that translates loosely as "shouts" but more precisely, Gilb explains, as exclamations of "defiance and freedom," "joy and support." All these feelings figure in Gilb's definition of *pride* through the lives of Mexican Americans in El Paso, Texas.

It's almost time to close at the northwest corner of Altura and Copia in 1 El Paso. That means it is so dark that it is as restful as the deepest unremembering sleep, dark as the empty space around this spinning planet, as a black star. Headlights that beam a little cross-eyed from a fatso American car are feeling around the asphalt road up the hill toward the Good Time Store, its yellow plastic smiley face bright like a sugary suck candy. The loose muffler holds only half the misfires, and, dry springs squeaking, the automobile curves slowly into the establishment's lot, swerving to avoid the new self-serve gas pump island. Behind it, across the street, a Texas flag—out too late this and all the nights—pops and slaps in a summer wind that finally is cool.

A good man, gray on the edges, an assistant manager in a brown starched 2 and ironed uniform, is washing the glass windows of the store, lit up by as many watts as Venus, with a roll of paper towels and the blue liquid from a spray bottle. Good night, m'ijo![1] he tells a young boy coming out after play-ing the video game, a Grande Guzzler the size of a wastebasket balanced in one hand, an open bag of Flaming Hot Cheetos, its red dye already smear-ing his mouth and the hand not carrying the weight of the soda, his white T-shirt, its short sleeves reaching halfway down his wrists, the whole XXL of it billowing and puffing in the outdoor gust.

A plump young woman steps out of that car. She's wearing a party dress, 3 wide scoops out of the top, front, and back, its hemline way above the knees.

Did you get a water pump? the assistant manager asks her. Are you going 4 to make it to Horizon City? He's still washing the glass of the storefront, his hand sweeping in small hard circles.

The young woman is patient and calm like a loving mother. I don't know 5 yet, she tells him as she stops close to him, thinking. I guess I should make a call, she says, and her thick-soled shoes, the latest fashion, slap against her heels to one of the pay phones at the front of the store.

Pride is working a job like it's as important as art or war, is the happiness 6 of a new high score on a video arcade game, of a pretty new black dress and shoes. Pride is the deaf and blind confidence of the good people who are too poor but don't notice.

A son is a long time sitting on the front porch where he played all those 7 years with the squirmy dog who still licks his face, both puppies then, even before he played on the winning teams of Little League baseball and City League basketball. They sprint down the sidewalk and across streets, side by side, until they stop to rest on the park grass, where a red ant, or a spider, bites the son's calf. It swells, but he no longer thinks to complain to his mom about it—he's too old now—when he comes home. He gets ready, putting on the shirt and pants his mom would have ironed but he wanted to iron himself. He takes the ride with his best friend since first grade. The hundreds of moms and dads, abuelos y abuelitas, the tios and primos,[2] baby brothers and older married sisters, all are at the Special Events Center for the son's high school graduation. His dad is a man bigger than most, and when he walks in his dress eel-skin boots down the cement stairs to get as close to the hardwood basketball-court floor and ceremony to see—m'ijo!—he feels an embarrass-ing sob bursting from his eyes and mouth. He holds it back, and with his hands, hides the tears that do escape, wipes them with his fingers, because the chavalitos[3] in his aisle are playing and laughing and they are so small and he is so big next to them. And when his son walks to the stage to get his high school diploma and his dad wants to scream his name, he hears how many others, from the floor in caps and gowns and from around the arena, are

[1] Spanish colloquialism, "my son." — Eds.
[2] Spanish, "grandfathers and grandmothers," "aunts and uncles," and "cousins." — Eds.
[3] Spanish slang, "little kids." — Eds.

already screaming it—could be any name, it could be any son's or daughter's: Alex! Vanessa! Carlos! Veronica! Ricky! Tony! Estella! Isa!—and sees his boy waving back to all of them.

Pride hears gritty dirt blowing against an agave whose stiff fertile stalk, so tall, will not bend—the love of land, rugged like the people who live on it. Pride sees the sunlight on the Franklin Mountains in the first light of morning and listens to a neighbor's gallo[4]—the love of culture and history. Pride smells a sweet, musky drizzle of rain and eats huevos con chile[5] in corn tortillas heated on a cast-iron pan—the love of heritage.   8

Pride is the fearless reaction to disrespect and disregard. It is knowing the future will prove that wrong.   9

Seeing the beauty: Look out there from a height of the mountain and on the north and south of the Rio Grande, to the far away and close, the so many miles more of fuzz on the wide horizon, knowing how many years the people have passed and have stayed, the ancestors, the ones who have medaled, limped back on crutches or died or were heroes from wars in the Pacific or Europe or Korea or Vietnam or the Persian Gulf, the ones who have raised the fist and dared to defy, the ones who wash the clothes and cook and serve the meals, who stitch the factory shoes and the factory slacks, who assemble and sort, the ones who laugh and the ones who weep, the ones who care, the ones who want more, the ones who try, the ones who love, those ones with shameless courage and hardened wisdom, and the old ones still so alive, holding their grandchildren, and the young ones in their glowing prime, strong and gorgeous, holding each other, the ones who will be born from them. The desert land is rock-dry and ungreen. It is brown. Brown like the skin is brown. Beautiful brown.   10

Journal Writing

In your journal, jot down images of pride that occur to you based on your own experiences and observations. Then try briefly to create your own definition—or definitions—of *pride*.

Questions on Meaning

1. What does Gilb take *pride* to mean? SUMMARIZE his definition as you understand it.

2. How do paragraphs 8–10 contribute to Gilb's definition?

3. What point does Gilb make in his concluding paragraph? How does his final IMAGE serve as a sort of summary?

[4] Spanish, "rooster." — EDS.
[5] Traditional Mexican dish of eggs and peppers. — EDS.

4. How would you describe the writer's PURPOSE in this essay? What DOMINANT IMPRESSION does Gilb create?

Questions on Writing Strategy

1. Why do you think Gilb opens the essay as he does? What impression does he create with the three people in the Good Time Store parking lot?

2. Following paragraphs 1–5, Gilb specifically defines the pride of the people about whom he has just written; however, after paragraph 7 his definition does not apply specifically to the father and son he just described. Why do you think he varies his strategy here?

3. Closely examine Gilb's development of paragraph 7. How would you describe its movement? its ultimate EFFECT?

4. How does Gilb achieve UNITY and COHERENCE in paragraph 8?

5. **OTHER METHODS**   The INTRODUCTION to "Pride" (paragraphs 1–5) relies on DESCRIPTION. Why do you think Gilb portrays this scene in such detail?

Questions on Language

1. In paragraph 1 how does Gilb use specific language to create a distinct impression of the car that pulls into the store's parking lot?

2. What is striking about the verbs Gilb uses in paragraph 8?

3. The first sentence of paragraph 10 is unusually long. How does Gilb manage to maintain its clarity and readability?

Suggestions for Writing

1. **JOURNAL TO ESSAY**   Using your journal writing as a springboard, write an essay in which you develop your own definition of *pride*. Like Gilb, present specific images and examples in addition to statements of your definition.

2. In focusing on a Mexican American community in Texas, "Pride" hints at, but doesn't specifically address, the issue of immigration, especially illegal immigration. (Gilb's own mother, he has written elsewhere, "crossed the border without papers.") Research how US immigration officials determine which would-be immigrants to the United States will be granted or denied entrance, based on country of origin and other factors. In an essay, explain these policies and evaluate their fairness as you see it.

3. **CRITICAL WRITING**   In an essay, ANALYZE Gilb's combination of lyrical language and concrete images. How does the concept of pride inform and complicate his depictions of one particular community? Use specific examples of the language he uses and the scenes he describes.

4. **CONNECTIONS**   In "Champion of the World" (p. 98), Maya Angelou writes about the experiences of another ethnic group in the United States, African Americans. Write an essay in which you COMPARE AND CONTRAST Gilb's presentation of Mexican Americans with Angelou's of African Americans.

AUGUSTEN BURROUGHS

Augusten Burroughs was born Christopher Robison in Pittsburgh, Pennsylvania, in 1965 and raised in western Massachusetts. He dropped out of school in the sixth grade, earned a GED, and legally changed his name when he turned eighteen. By his own account Burroughs has been repeatedly victimized by circumstances, many of them recounted in a series of best-selling memoirs. In *Running with Scissors* (2002) he tells of being raised by his mother's psychiatrist and becoming trapped in a relationship with a pedophile. In *Dry* (2003) he examines a period of alcoholism worsened after losing a friend to AIDS. In *A Wolf at the Table* (2008) he recalls childhood abuse at the hands of his father. And in *Lust and Wonder* (2016) he considers his long and complicated search for a stable relationship as an adult. Critics sometimes question the details of Burroughs's tales, yet most admire the emotional honesty and gothic humor that pervade his work. In addition to memoirs, Burroughs has also written a novel, *Sellevision* (2000); two collections of essays, *Magical Thinking* (2004) and *Possible Side Effects* (2006); a compilation of Christmas stories, *You'd Better Not Cry* (2009); and a self-help book, *This Is How: Proven Aid in Overcoming Shyness, Molestation, Fatness, Spinsterhood, Grief, Disease, Lushery, Decrepitude and More* (2012). He lives with his husband in rural Connecticut.

How to Identify Love by Knowing What It's Not

In *This Is How,* the book Burroughs says he "was born to write," the author draws on his life experiences to offer straightforward if unconventional advice on topics ranging from riding elevators to changing the world. "How to Identify Love by Knowing What It's Not," a chapter from the book, explores the delusions that can lead people to mistake cruelty for caring.

Love doesn't use a fist. 1

Love never calls you fat or lazy or ugly. 2

Love doesn't laugh at you in front of friends. 3

It is not in Love's interest for your self-esteem to be low. 4

Love is a helium-based emotion; Love always takes the high road. 5

Love does not make you beg. 6

Love does not make you deposit your paycheck into its bank account. 7

Love certainly never, never, never brings the children into it. 8

Love does not ask or even want you to change. But if you change, Love is 9 as excited about this change as you are, if not more so. And if you go back to the way you were before you changed, Love will go back with you.

Love does not maintain a list of your flaws and weaknesses.   10

Love believes you.   11

Love is patient; Love does not make a point of showing you how patient   12
it is. It is critical to understand the distinction.

Patience is like donating a large sum of money to a charity anonymously.   13
What matters to you as the donor is that the charity receives the funding, not
who wrote the check, even if knowing who donated such a huge check would
wildly impress the world.

So, patience is exhibited only by a lack of pressure. This is how you know   14
it's there.

But when you see on the face of your partner or spouse an expression that   15
reads, "I'm being very patient with you," this could be the single detail that
alerts you to the fact that you are in an abusive relationship.

You can be in such a relationship and not even know it. You can receive   16
so many black eyes, you forget it's abnormal to have even one.

Physical violence is one kind of abuse. Emotional violence is another   17
kind of abuse. These assaults are delivered with concepts. People usually say,
emotional abuse is about words: fat, ugly, stupid, lazy. But it's not about words
because an emotionally abusive person doesn't always resort to using the verbal club, but rather the verbal untraceable poison.

They may, in fact, speak very kind words to you. And appear nothing   18
but supportive to those around you: Their covert abuse is administered in
small, cunning ways. Over time. So the impact is gradual, not fist-to-the-eye
immediate.

An abusive partner is controlling. They are manipulative. They might   19
make a special point of coyly sharing information that they actually know
will upset you. They might supply reasonable arguments as to why they and
not you should make important decisions.

If you possess talent or a natural ease and comfort with a particular ability   20
and your abusive partner is resentful, abuse might arrive in the form of sub-
traction: no remark at all, not a compliment or a gesture of support. Perhaps
one small, internally flawless diamond of a criticism will be presented.

Silence when there should be discussion to resolve an issue is another   21
method of abuse if the silence is used as a tool to frustrate or sadden or otherwise intentionally manipulate the emotions of another.

I knew of somebody . . . who was many years into an abusive relationship   22
but did not know it. She knew only that she had been so happy when they
met and that it seemed to her this feeling was bled out of her year after year,
and she found that she now resembled her partner, whom she had once seen
as strong and silent and loving but had come to understand was emotionally
disturbed and was not silent in his mind, but roiling.

When she finally left him she did so still loving him. She had been more   23
financially stable so she had given him their home. He had admitted to her
that for the last couple of years, he had been occupied with planning his suicide. He told her he'd worked out all the details and would do it in a quaint
West Coast town right on the Pacific that they had frequently spoken of
visiting but never seen.

When she left him she left their beloved dog with him because she   24
worried a totally empty house would be dangerous.

Their plan had been to share the dog but he wanted nothing more to do   25
with her. And the regular updates and photographs he had sent when they
first parted stopped now completely.

Months passed and she heard nothing until he sent a brief email inform-   26
ing her that the dog now had a potential serious health problem and that he
would take care of it.

She could not help but feel that he had taken a small measure of satisfac-   27
tion knowing how brutal the news would be to her ears and how helpless she
would feel being able to do nothing, not even see this dog she had loved for
so long.

Emotional abuse is the process of breaking the spirit or shattering the   28
confidence of another for one's own purpose.

Abusive people never change. There is no point of pursuing couples'   29
therapy when one member of the relationship is abusive. A therapist may tell
you otherwise. But I'm telling you the not-for-profit truth. Abusers do not
change.

It will only get worse.   30

The difference between physical violence like a slap on the face or a shove   31
and homicide can be as small as a few centimeters or the angle of approach.

Also, abusers are always very, very sorry. Men who abuse women probably   32
shed more tears in one year than the combined tears of all the girls in the
audience of a Renée Zellweger movie opening weekend at the Paris Theatre
in Manhattan.

That's how sorry he is.   33

Or so he says, with his tears.   34

Of course, he's not sorry. She is.   35

Unless the roles are reversed. And the abuser is a woman, not a man.   36

Women can and do physically and emotionally abuse their partners.   37
The perception that the abuser is always a man is false. . . .

People remain in abusive relationships for the same reasons they remain   38
in loving ones: they've built a life together, they have children, financial
interests, habit, nothing better. Lots of reasons.

But probably the number-one reason is simply not knowing they're in one.   39

You think of domestic violence and you think of a character and a weak   40
victim: macho, powerful bully and a passive, frail woman and you don't recognize that. So it can't be you.

It might help, then, for me to show you in clinical terms what domestic   41
violence actually looks like on the printed page. This checklist is from the
National Domestic Violence Hotline. Ask yourself, does your partner:

- Embarrass you with put-downs
- Look at you or act in ways that scare you
- Control what you do, who you see or talk to, or where you go
- Stop you from seeing your friends or family members
- Take your money or Social Security check, make you ask for money, or refuse to give you money
- Make all of the decisions
- Tell you that you're a bad parent or threaten to take away or hurt your children
- Prevent you from working or attending school
- Act like the abuse is no big deal, it's your fault, or even deny doing it
- Destroy your property or threaten to kill your pets
- Intimidate you with guns, knives, or other weapons
- Shove you, slap you, choke you, or hit you
- Force you to try and drop charges
- Threaten to commit suicide
- Threaten to kill you

Think about the answers before you answer. Does he prevent you from   42
working? No, he encourages you, that's terrific.

Or does he?   43

Does he *maybe* prevent you a little by getting drunk and then, say, being   44
unable to find a certain pair of shoes so he turns the house upside down, creating such a scene, a ME, ME, ME moment that you can't possibly work?

Might he always, over and over, bring it all back to himself? Leaving no   45
room or time for you to work on your crafts, aka possible future home business
aka threat to him?

Domestic violence is extremely difficult to detect when it is happening to   46
you because domestic violence always only happens to other people, and you
are too smart and sophisticated to ever, for one moment, be with somebody
abusive. The thought is absurd. Domestic violence is a lower-class problem,
something that afflicts only those whose homes are clad in aluminum siding.

Besides, you would know if you were being abused.   47

Except the truth is, some things are too terrible to know; too impossible   48
to see; too painful to realize; too heartbreaking to face.

You could be in an abusive relationship and be unaware that you are,   49
unable to see the abuse for what it is.

Sometimes the truth must unspool slowly. It's simply impossible to grasp   50
it all at once. Perhaps, one day, you will be able to see a glimpse of abuse in
your relationship.

In time, you'll be able to see more.   51

Because if you allow yourself to have one small serving of reality, the hard   52
part, the opaque part, is over. And eventually, you'll be able to see the rest.

Also, the more unlikely it is that you would ever be in an abusive rela-   53
tionship, the closer you need to look at your relationship. Not because you
want to try to see something sinister that simply isn't there, but because
you're more likely to be blind to abuse if it is there.

Just, you know, pay attention. To all those familiar, everyday things they say 54
to you or do to you. Ask, "If he said that to my friend, would I think it was mean?"

Try to actually hear what the person says to you. Try to hear it fresh. Try   55
to see if what they say to you might, in a way, also be a kind of steering wheel.

It's a spectrum, too. Maybe your partner isn't exactly "abusive" so much   56
as a little controlling. This is fairly easy to see.

What's difficult to see is when you're with somebody who is a full-   57
strength abuser. And maybe one reason it's so difficult to see something that
to the rest of the world — at least on paper — is so obvious is because there's
no contrast. They are controlling and abusive and this is what they are.

If you realize you are in an abusive relationship, you may want to call this   58
phone number — it's toll-free so it won't cost you anything and it won't show
up on your phone bill. If possible, take the number with you and call from
somewhere else:

National Domestic Violence Hotline 1-800-799-SAFE (7233)   59

Seventy-nine-nine, seventy-two, thirty-three.   60

If you have children and your spouse is abusing them physically, mentally,   61
or sexually, leave now.

It never takes courage to leave.   62

It takes love.   63

Journal Writing

Anybody could be in an abusive relationship, Burroughs insists, although recognizing
the abuse can be difficult or even impossible. Do you agree? Have you witnessed any

of the behaviors he describes, whether in one of your relationships or in someone else's? In your journal, describe the troubling aspects of that relationship. Did you recognize the behavior as abusive? Who was the victim, and who the abuser? Has the relationship ended, or is it still in place?

Questions on Meaning

1. What exactly does Burroughs define in this essay? Is his subject love, as the title suggests it will be, or something else entirely?

2. Where does Burroughs first state his THESIS? At what points does he restate his main idea? Why do you suppose he repeats himself as he does?

3. What do you make of the essay's final sentence? What, to the author, is the true measure of love? How and where does he define it?

4. How do you suppose Burroughs hoped readers would respond to this essay? What is his PURPOSE? What is your response, and why?

Questions on Writing Strategy

1. Many of Burroughs's paragraphs consist of a single sentence. Do you recognize the ALLUSION in paragraphs 1–12? What is the EFFECT of this allusion and of the other very short paragraphs in the essay?

2. This essay is a model of an *extended* definition, yet it also includes several *stipulative* definitions (see p. 452). Locate at least two of these. What do they contribute to Burroughs's meaning?

3. Examine the organization of the essay. What major sections does it fall into? Why do you think Burroughs chose to order his points as he did?

4. Why does Burroughs provide a checklist from the National Domestic Violence Hotline in paragraph 41 and give the organization's phone number in paragraphs 59 and 60?

5. **OTHER METHODS**   How does Burroughs use a single extended EXAMPLE to clarify his point about emotional abuse?

Questions on Language

1. In much of the essay, Burroughs addresses readers directly, using the second-PERSON *you*. What does this language choice reveal about how he imagines his AUDIENCE?

2. Burroughs often uses the plural pronoun *they* to refer back to a singular *he, partner,* or *person,* as in "An abusive partner is controlling. They are manipulative" (par. 19). Where else does he do this? Does Burroughs seem to break the rules of pronoun-antecedent agreement for a reason, or is he guilty of using bad grammar? Why do you think so? (If necessary, refer to p. 60 for an explanation of pronoun-antecedent agreement.)

3. Consult a dictionary if you don't know the meaning of any of the following words: helium (par. 5); covert, cunning (18); coyly (19); roiling (22); clinical (41); unspool (50); opaque (52); sinister (53); spectrum (56).

4. How would you characterize the TONE of this essay: serious? detached? earnest? angry? compassionate? something else? Point to some words and phrases that support your answer.

Suggestions for Writing

1. **FROM JOURNAL TO ESSAY**   Expand your journal writing (pp. 486–87) into an essay explaining why and how a specific someone should leave an abusive relationship. You might write about somebody you know, about yourself, about a public figure, or about a fictional abuse victim, but take care to protect the person's anonymity. In your essay, draw on Burroughs's definitions and advice as appropriate to support your points, but be sure to develop a unique thesis of your own and to offer plenty of specifics to support your claims.

2. Write an essay that defines *love* or another strong feeling, such as *hate, compassion, happiness,* or *fear.* You might, like Burroughs, choose to focus on what the feeling is *not,* or you might prefer to define it by explaining what it *is.* In either case, be sure to provide a wide range of examples to suggest the various aspects of your subject.

3. **CRITICAL WRITING**   ANALYZE Burroughs's use of FIGURES OF SPEECH in this essay. How does the author combine *personification, metaphor, simile, paradox,* and similar devices to add meaning and a sense of empathy to his definition of abuse? In your analysis, pay particular attention to those figures of speech you find especially fresh or compelling.

4. **CONNECTIONS**   In "Live Free and Starve" (p. 437) Chitra Divakaruni also writes about children living in desperate circumstances. Write an essay that COMPARES AND CONTRASTS Burroughs's and Divakaruni's attitudes toward child abuse. How does each author define *abuse,* for instance? What do they seem to believe is the best recourse for a family at risk of harm? What do they suggest are a parent's responsibility to children? a community's? a government's? How do you respond to their ideas, and how might they respond to each other?

ADDITIONAL WRITING TOPICS

Definition

1. Write an essay in which you define an institution, trend, phenomenon, or abstraction as specifically and concretely as possible. Following are some suggestions designed to stimulate ideas. Before you begin, limit your subject.

Responsibility	Fairness
Fun	Leadership
Empathy	Leisure
Plagiarism	Originality
Community	Integrity
Education	Imagination
Progress	Socialism
Advertising	A smile
Happiness	A classic (of music, literature, art, or film)
Fads	Success
Feminism	Meditation
Marriage	Friendship

2. In a brief essay, define one of the following. In each instance, you have a choice of something good or something bad to talk about.

   A good or bad boss
   A good or bad parent
   A good or bad host
   A good or bad athlete
   A good or bad physician
   A good or bad nurse
   A good or bad minister, priest, rabbi, or imam
   A good or bad roommate
   A good or bad driver
   A good or bad business

3. In a paragraph, define a slang expression or specialized term for someone who has never heard it. Possible expressions include *cisgender, sick, hook up, vaping, youthquake, wicked, poser, Snap, swag, chill, hot mess.*

Courtesy of Adbusters Media Foundation

14

ARGUMENT AND PERSUASION

Stating Opinions and Proposals

THE METHOD

Practically every day, we try to persuade ourselves or someone else. We usually attempt such persuasion without being aware that we follow any special method at all. Often, we'll state an *opinion*: We'll tell someone our way of viewing things. We say to a friend, "I'm starting to like Senator Clark. Look at all she's done to help people with disabilities. Look at her voting record on the minimum wage." And, having stated these opinions, we might go on to make a *proposal*, to recommend that some action be taken. Addressing our friend, we might suggest, "Hey, Senator Clark is speaking on campus at four-thirty. Want to come with me and listen to her?"

Many professions involve persuading people in writing. Before arguing a case in court, lawyers prepare briefs setting forth all the points in favor of their sides. Businesspeople regularly put in writing their ideas for new products and ventures, for improvements in cost control and job efficiency. Researchers write proposals for grants to obtain money to support their work. Scientists write and publish papers to persuade the scientific community that their findings are valid, often stating hypotheses, or tentative opinions.

Even if you never produce a single persuasive work (which is very unlikely), you will certainly encounter such works directed at you. We live our lives under a steady rain of opinions and proposals. Organizations that work for causes campaign with broadcast media and direct mail, all hoping that we will see things their way. Moreover, we are bombarded with proposals from people who wish us to act. Religious leaders urge us to lead more virtuous lives. Advertisers urge us to rush right out and buy the large economy size.

Small wonder, then, that argument and persuasion — and CRITICAL THINKING about argument and persuasion — may be among the most useful skills a college student can acquire. Time and again, your instructors will ask you to criticize or to state opinions, either in class or in writing. You may be asked to state your view of anything from the Electoral College to animal rights. You may be asked to judge the desirability or undesirability of compulsory testing for drugs or revision of the existing immigration laws. Critically reading other people's arguments and composing your own, you will find, helps you discover what you think, refine it, and share what you believe.

Be aware that the terms *argument* and *persuasion* have somewhat different meanings: PERSUASION aims to influence readers' actions, or their support for an action, by engaging their beliefs and feelings, while ARGUMENT aims to win readers' agreement with an assertion or claim by engaging their powers of reasoning. However, most effective argument or persuasion contains elements of both methods. In this book we tend to use the terms interchangeably.

One other point: We tend to talk here about *writing* arguments, but most of what we say has to do with *reading* them as well. When we discuss your need, as a writer, to support your claims, we are also discussing your need, as a reader, to question the support other authors provide for their claims. In reading arguments critically, you apply the critical-thinking skills we discussed in Chapter 1 — ANALYSIS, INFERENCE, SYNTHESIS, and EVALUATION — to a particular kind of writing.

Audience and Common Ground

Unlike some advertisers, responsible writers of argument do not try to storm people's minds. In writing a paper for a course, you persuade by gentler means: by sharing your view with an AUDIENCE willing to consider it. You'll want to learn how to express your view clearly and vigorously. But to be fair and persuasive, it is important to understand your readers' views as well.

In stating your opinion, you present the truth as you see it: "The immigration laws discourage employers from hiring nonnative workers," perhaps, or "The immigration laws protect legal aliens." To persuade your readers that your view makes sense, you need not begin by proclaiming that your view is absolutely right and should prevail. Instead, you might begin by trying to state what your readers probably think, as best you can infer it. You don't consider views that differ from your own merely to flatter your readers. You do so to balance your own view and make it more accurate. Writer and reader become two sensible people trying to find COMMON GROUND, or points on which both can agree. This approach will relieve you, whenever you have to state your opinions in writing, of the terrible obligation to be one hundred percent right at all times.

Elements of Argument

The British philosopher Stephen Toulmin has proposed a useful division of argument into distinct elements. Adapted to the terminology of this book, they are *claims*, *evidence*, *appeals*, and *assumptions*.

Claims and Thesis Statements

A CLAIM is an assertion that requires support. It is what an argument tries to convince readers to accept. The central claim — the main point — is almost always stated explicitly in a THESIS STATEMENT like one of the following:

A CLAIM ABOUT REALITY   The war on drugs is not winnable because laws cannot eradicate demand or the supply to meet it.

A CLAIM OF VALUE   Drug abuse is a personal matter that should not be subject to government interference.

A CLAIM FOR A COURSE OF ACTION   The United States must intensify its efforts to reduce production of heroin in Afghanistan.

Usually, but not always, you'll state your thesis at the beginning of your essay, making a play for readers' attention and clueing them in to your purpose. But if you think readers may have difficulty accepting your thesis until they've heard some or all of your argument, then you might save the thesis statement for the middle or end.

The essays in this chapter provide a variety of thesis statements as models. Here are some examples:

> The fact that so many illegal immigrants are intertwined with American citizens or legal residents, either as spouses or parents, should give pause to those who'd like to see all illegal immigrants rounded up and deported or their lives made so miserable they leave on their own.
> — Linda Chavez, "Supporting Family Values"

> The execution of [Earl] Ringo was morally just. And it may just save the lives of several innocents.
> — David B. Muhlhausen, "How the Death Penalty Saves Lives"

> I used to support the death penalty. I don't anymore.
> — Semon Frank Thompson, "What I Learned from Executing Two Men"

> Universities . . . should have no right to limit free speech or discourage ways of thinking that are not in line with the "status quo." They also should not be establishing safe spaces and trigger warnings to keep students "safe" from ideas that offend them. . . . Continuing this way is not only a threat to the First Amendment, but to democracy itself.
>
> — Sarah Hemphill, "What Happened to Free Speech on College Campuses?"

Evidence

Claims are nothing without the EVIDENCE to make them believable and convincing. Toulmin calls evidence *data* or *grounds*, using terms that convey how specific and fundamental it is. Depending on your subject, your evidence may include facts, statistics (facts expressed in numbers), expert opinions, examples, and reported experiences. These kinds of evidence should meet certain criteria.

- **Accuracy:** Facts, examples, and opinions should be taken from reliable sources and presented without error or distortion.

- **Representation:** The evidence should reflect reality, neither slanting nor exaggerating it.

- **Relevance:** All evidence should apply directly to the claims, reflecting current thinking by recognized experts.

- **Adequacy:** The evidence should be sufficient to support the claims entirely, not just in part.

Appeals

To strengthen the support for your claims, you can also make APPEALS to readers either directly or indirectly, in the way you present your evidence. In classical argument these appeals are often referred to as *logos, ethos,* and *pathos;* we refer to them as RATIONAL APPEALS, ETHICAL APPEALS, and EMOTIONAL APPEALS, respectively.

- **Rational appeals** rely on sound reasoning (*logos*) and marshal evidence that meets the criteria above. See the following pages for more on reasoning.

- **Ethical appeals** show readers that you are a well-informed person of goodwill, good sense, and good moral character — and, therefore, to be believed (*ethos*). Strengthen your ethical appeal by collecting ample evidence, reasoning carefully, demonstrating respect for opposing views, using an appropriate emotional appeal (see below), and minding your TONE (see the next page).

- **Emotional appeals** acknowledge what you know of readers' sympathies and beliefs and show how your argument relates to them (*pathos*). An example in this chapter appears in Linda Chavez's "Supporting Family Values": The author argues for immigration reform by appealing to readers' respect for intact families and fear of cultural disintegration. Carefully used, an emotional appeal can stir readers to constructive belief and action by engaging their feelings as well as their minds, as long as the appeal is appropriate for the audience and the argument.

FOCUS ON TONE

Readers are most likely to be persuaded by an argument when they sense that the writer is reasonable, trustworthy, and sincere. Sound reasoning, strong evidence, and acknowledgment of opposing views do much to convey these attributes, but so does tone, the attitude implied by choice of words and sentence structures.

Generally, you should try for a tone of moderation in your view of your subject and a tone of respectfulness and goodwill toward readers and opponents.

- **State opinions and facts calmly:**

  OVEREXCITED   One clueless administrator was quoted in the newspaper as saying she thought many students who claim learning disabilities are "faking" their difficulties to obtain special treatment! Has she never heard of dyslexia, attention deficit disorders, and other well-established disabilities?

  CALM   Particularly worrisome was one administrator's statement, quoted in the newspaper, that many students who claim learning disabilities may be "faking" their difficulties to obtain special treatment.

- **Replace arrogance with deference:**

  ARROGANT   I happen to know that many students would rather party or just bury their heads in the sand than get involved in a serious, worthy campaign against the school's unjust learning-disabled policies.

  DEFERENTIAL   Time pressures and lack of information about the issues may be what prevent students from joining the campaign against the school's unjust learning-disabled policies.

- **Replace sarcasm with plain speaking:**

  SARCASTIC   Of course, the administration knows even without meeting students what is best for every one of them.

  PLAIN   The administration should agree to meet with each learning-disabled student to learn about his or her needs.

- **Choose words whose CONNOTATIONS convey reasonableness** rather than anger, hostility, or another negative emotion:

  HOSTILE   The administration coerced some students into dropping their lawsuits. [*Coerced* implies the use of threats or even violence.]

  REASONABLE   The administration convinced some students to drop their lawsuits. [*Convinced* implies the use of reason.]

  (For more on connotations and tone in general, refer to the Glossary and to pp. 56–57 in Chapter 4.)

Assumptions

Another element of argument, the ASSUMPTION, is in Toulmin's conception the connective tissue between grounds, or evidence, and claims: An assumption explains why the evidence leads to and justifies a claim. Called a *warrant* by Toulmin, an assumption is usually a belief, a principle, or an inference whose truth the writer takes for granted. Here is how an assumption might figure in an argument for one of the claims given earlier:

CLAIM   The United States must intensify its efforts to reduce the production of heroin in Afghanistan.

EVIDENCE   Afghanistan is the world's largest heroin producer and a major supplier to the United States.

ASSUMPTION   The United States can and should reduce the production of heroin in other countries when its own citizens are affected.

As important as they are, the assumptions underlying an argument are not always stated. As we will see in the discussion of deductive reasoning, which begins on the next page, unstated assumptions can sometimes pitch an argument into trouble.

Reasoning

When we argue rationally, we reason—that is, we make statements that lead to a conclusion. Two reliable methods of rational argument date back to the classical Greek philosopher Aristotle, who identified the complementary processes of inductive and deductive reasoning.

Inductive Reasoning

In INDUCTIVE REASONING, the method of the sciences, we collect bits of evidence on which to base a GENERALIZATION, the claim of the argument. The assumption linking evidence and claim is that what is true for some circumstances is true for others as well. For instance, you might interview a hundred representative students about their attitudes toward changing your school's honor code. You find that 65 percent of the interviewees believe that the code should remain as it is, 15 percent believe that the code should be toughened, 10 percent believe that it should be loosened, and 10 percent have no opinion. You then assume that these statistics can be applied to the student body as a whole and make a claim against changing the code because 65 percent of students don't want change.

The more evidence you have, the more trustworthy your claim will be, but it would never be airtight unless you interviewed every student on campus. Since such thoroughness is almost always impractical if not impossible, you assume in an *inductive leap* that the results can be generalized. The smaller the leap—the more evidence you have—the better.

Deductive Reasoning

DEDUCTIVE REASONING works the opposite way of inductive reasoning: It moves from a general statement to particular cases. The basis of deduction is the SYLLOGISM, a three-step form of reasoning practiced by Aristotle:

All men are mortal.

Socrates is a man.

Therefore, Socrates is mortal.

The first statement, called a *major premise*, is an assumption: a fact, principle, or inference that you believe to be true. The second statement, or *minor premise*, is the evidence—the new information about a particular member of the larger group named in the major premise. The third statement, or *conclusion*, is the claim that follows inevitably from the premises. If the premises are true, then the conclusion must be true. Following is another example of a syllogism. You may recognize it from the discussion of assumptions on page 497, only here the statements are simplified and arranged differently:

MAJOR PREMISE (ASSUMPTION)   The United States can and should reduce heroin production when its own citizens are affected.

MINOR PREMISE (EVIDENCE)   A major producer of heroin for the US market is Afghanistan.

CONCLUSION (THESIS)   The United States can and should reduce heroin production in Afghanistan.

Problems with deductive reasoning start in the premises. Consider this untrustworthy syllogism: "To do well in school, students must cheat a little. Jolene wants to do well in school. Therefore, she must cheat." This is bad deductive reasoning, and its flaw is in its major premise, which is demonstrably untrue: Plenty of students do well without cheating. Because the premise is false, the conclusion is necessarily false as well.

When they're spelled out neatly, bad syllogisms are pretty easy to spot. But many deductive arguments are not spelled out. Instead, one of the premises goes unstated, as in this statement: "Mayor Perkins was humiliated in his recent bid for reelection, winning only 2,000 out of 5,000 votes." The unstated assumption here, the major premise, is "Winning only two-fifths of the votes humiliates a candidate." (The rest of the syllogism: "Mayor Perkins received only two-fifths of the votes. Thus, Mayor Perkins was humiliated.")

The unstated premise isn't necessarily a problem in argument — in fact, it's quite common. But it *is* a problem when it's wrong or unfounded. For instance, in the statement "She shouldn't be elected mayor because her husband has bad ideas on how to run the city," the unstated assumption is that the candidate cannot form ideas independently of her husband. This is a possibility, perhaps, but it requires its own discussion and proof, not concealment behind other assertions.

Logical Fallacies

In arguments we read and hear, we often meet logical FALLACIES: errors in reasoning that lead to wrong conclusions. From the time you start thinking about your thesis and claims and begin planning your paper, you'll need to watch out for them. To help you recognize logical fallacies when you see them or hear them, and so guard against them when you write, here is a list of the most common.

- **Non *sequitur*** (from the Latin, "it does not follow"): stating a conclusion that doesn't follow from one or both premises.

  I've lived in this town a long time — why, my great-grandfather was one of the first settlers — so I'm against putting fluoride in the drinking water.

- **Oversimplification:** supplying neat and easy explanations for large and complicated phenomena.

  No wonder drug abuse is out of control. Look at how the courts have hobbled police officers.

  Oversimplified solutions are also popular:

  All these teenage kids that get in trouble with the law — why, they ought to put them in work camps. That would straighten them out!

- **Post *hoc*, *ergo propter hoc*** (from the Latin, "after this, therefore because of this"), or *post hoc* for short: a form of oversimplification assuming that because B follows A, B was caused by A.

  Ever since the city suspended height restrictions on skyscrapers, the city budget has been balanced.

  (For more on *post hoc* and oversimplification, see "Causal Relations," pp. 402–3.)

- **Either/or reasoning:** assuming that a reality may be divided into only two parts or extremes or assuming that a given problem has only one of two possible solutions.

  What's to be done about the trade imbalance with Asia? Either we ban all Asian imports, or American industry will collapse.

Obviously, either/or reasoning is a kind of extreme oversimplification.

- **Hasty generalization:** leaping to a generalization from inadequate or faulty evidence. The most familiar hasty generalization is the stereotype.

  Men aren't sensitive enough to be day-care providers.

  Women are too emotional to fight in combat.

- **Argument from doubtful or unidentified authority:** citing an unreliable source.

  Uncle Oswald says that we ought to imprison all sex offenders for life.

  According to an anonymous informant, my opponent is lying.

- **Argument *ad hominem*** (from the Latin, "to the man"): attacking a person's views by attacking his or her character.

  Mayor Burns is divorced and estranged from his family. How can we listen to his pleas for a city nursing home?

- **Begging the question:** taking for granted from the start what you set out to demonstrate. When you reason in a *logical* way, you state that because something is true, then, as a result, some other truth follows. When you beg the question, however, you repeat that what is true is true.

  Dogs are a menace to people because they are dangerous.

  This statement proves nothing, because the idea that dogs are dangerous is already assumed in the statement that they are a menace. Beggars of questions often just repeat what they already believe, only in different words. This fallacy sometimes takes the form of arguing in a circle, or demonstrating a premise by a conclusion and a conclusion by a premise.

  I am in college because that is the right thing to do. Going to college is the right thing to do because it is expected of me.

- **False analogy:** the claim of persuasive likeness when no significant likeness exists. An ANALOGY asserts that because two things are comparable in some respects, they are comparable in other respects as well. Analogies cannot serve as evidence in rational arguments because the differences always outweigh the similarities; but analogies can reinforce such arguments *if* the subjects are indeed similar in some ways. If they aren't, the analogy is false. Many observers see the "war on drugs" as a false and damaging analogy because warfare aims for clear victory over a specific, organized enemy, whereas the complete eradication of illegal drugs is probably unrealistic and, in any event, the "enemy" isn't well defined: the drugs themselves? users? sellers? producers? the producing nations? (These critics urge approaching drugs as a social problem to be skillfully managed and reduced.)

THE PROCESS

Finding a Subject

Your way into a subject will probably vary depending on whether you're writing an argument that supports an opinion or one that proposes a change. In stating an opinion, you set forth and support a claim—a truth you believe. You may find such a truth by thinking and feeling, by reading, by talking to your instructors or fellow students, by listening to a discussion of some problem or controversy. Before you run with a subject, take a minute to weigh it: Is this something about which reasonable people disagree? Arguments go nowhere when they start with ideas that are generally accepted (pets should not have to endure physical abuse from their owners) or are beyond the pale (pet owners should be able to hurt their animals if they want).

In stating a proposal, you already have an opinion in mind, and from there, you go on to urge an action or a solution to a problem. Usually, these two statements will take place within the same piece of writing: You will first set forth a view ("The campus honor code is unfair to first offenders"), provide the evidence to support it, and then present your proposal as a remedy ("The campus honor code should be revised to give more latitude to first offenders").

Whatever your subject, resist the temptation to make it big. If you have two weeks to prepare, an argument about the litter problem in your town is probably manageable: In that time you could conduct your own visual research and talk to town officials. But an argument about the litter problem in your town compared with that in similar-sized towns across the state would surely demand more time than you have.

Organizing

There's no one right way to organize an argument because so much depends on how your readers will greet your claim and your evidence. Below we give some ideas for different situations.

Introduction

In your opening paragraph or two, draw readers in by connecting them to your subject if possible, showing its significance, and providing any needed background. End the INTRODUCTION with your thesis statement if you think readers will entertain it before they've seen the evidence. Put the thesis statement later, in the middle or even at the end of the essay, if you think readers need to see some or all of the evidence in order to be open to the idea.

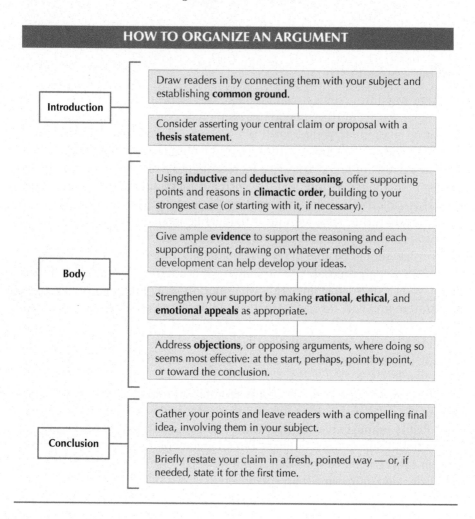

HOW TO ORGANIZE AN ARGUMENT

Introduction
- Draw readers in by connecting them with your subject and establishing **common ground**.
- Consider asserting your central claim or proposal with a **thesis statement**.

Body
- Using **inductive** and **deductive reasoning**, offer supporting points and reasons in **climactic order**, building to your strongest case (or starting with it, if necessary).
- Give ample **evidence** to support the reasoning and each supporting point, drawing on whatever methods of development can help develop your ideas.
- Strengthen your support by making **rational**, **ethical**, and **emotional appeals** as appropriate.
- Address **objections**, or opposing arguments, where doing so seems most effective: at the start, perhaps, point by point, or toward the conclusion.

Conclusion
- Gather your points and leave readers with a compelling final idea, involving them in your subject.
- Briefly restate your claim in a fresh, pointed way — or, if needed, state it for the first time.

Body

The BODY of the essay develops and defends the points that support your thesis. Generally, follow a CLIMACTIC ORDER, starting with your least important point and building in a crescendo to your strongest point. However, if you think readers may resist your ideas, consider starting strong and then offering the more minor points as reinforcement.

For every point you make, give the evidence that supports it. The methods of development can help here, providing many options for injecting evidence. Say you were arguing for or against further reductions in welfare funding. You might give EXAMPLES of wasteful spending, or of neighborhoods where welfare funds are still needed. You might spell out the CAUSES of social problems that call for welfare funds, or foresee the likely EFFECTS of cutting welfare programs or of keeping them. You could use NARRATION to tell a pointed story; you could use DESCRIPTION to portray certain welfare recipients and their neighborhoods.

Response to Objections

Part of the body of the essay, but separated here for emphasis, a response to probable objections is crucial to effective argument. If you are arguing fairly, you should be able to face potential criticisms fairly and give your critics due credit, reasoning with them, not dismissing them. This is the strategy Linda Chavez uses later in this chapter in "Supporting Family Values" (p. 506) by conceding, more than once, that arguments against immigration have some merit ("But the greater concern for some opponents," "It is true that," and so on) before she points out what she sees as their logical flaws. As Chavez does, you can tackle possible objections throughout your essay, as they pertain to your points. You can also field objections near the end of the essay, an approach that allows you to draw on all of your evidence. But if you think that readers' own opposing views may stiffen their resistance to your argument, you may want to address those views very early, before developing your own points.

Conclusion

The CONCLUSION gives you a chance to gather your points, restate your thesis in a fresh way, and leave readers with a compelling final idea. In an essay with a strong emotional component, you may want to end with an appeal to readers' feelings. But even in a mostly rational argument, try to involve readers in some way, showing why they should care or what they can do.

CHECKLIST FOR REVIEWING AND REVISING AN ARGUMENT

✔ **Audience.** Have you taken account of your readers' probable views and feelings? Have you reasoned with readers, seeking common ground? Are any emotional appeals appropriate? Are opposing views acknowledged and addressed?

✔ **Thesis.** Does your argument have a thesis, a claim about how the subject is or should be? Is the thesis narrow enough to argue convincingly in the space and time available? Is it stated clearly? Is it reasonable?

✔ **Evidence.** Is the thesis well supported with facts, statistics, expert opinions, and examples? Is the evidence accurate, representative, relevant, and adequate?

✔ **Assumptions.** Have you made sound connections between the evidence and the thesis and other claims?

✔ **Logical fallacies.** Have you made any common errors in reasoning, such as oversimplifying or begging the question? (See pp. 499–500 for a list of fallacies.)

✔ **Structure.** Does the organization lead readers through your argument step by step, building to the strongest ideas and frequently connecting the evidence to your central claim?

✔ **Tone.** Is the tone of your argument reasonable and respectful?

STUDENT CASE STUDY: A PROPOSAL

In many courses and occupations, you'll be expected to write proposals that identify specific problems or related sets of problems and argue for reasonable solutions. A proposal usually addresses clearly defined readers who are in a position to take action or approve an action. It addresses those readers' unique needs and concerns, anticipating objections and offering evidence to demonstrate the benefits of the solution.

As a nursing student in California as well as a mother, Adrianne Silver knew that school districts across the nation had been struggling with an escalating problem of bullying and that many states had recently instituted new laws to address the issue. Eager to see her own state government improve its response, she researched possible changes and also attitudes toward change on the part of schoolteachers and administrators. The following paragraphs come from her longer proposal for a law mandating prosecution and counseling for bullies. Before this section, Silver opened with an overview of the problem and of recent laws that had been passed in response to bullied students' suicides. After this section, Silver explained her solution in greater detail, suggested steps for implementing it, and addressed objections more fully.

Yet with all the anti-bullying policies, procedures, and training being implemented nationwide, not much is being done to address the behavior before it reaches the level of violence. Unfortunately, many teachers have the opinion that teasing and taunting is just "kids being kids" and that nothing needs to be done. But these kids grow up to become teenagers with destructive behaviors. If we are to reduce aggression, we must understand the cause and deal with the offender while the behavior can still be corrected.

Transition from discussion of problem

Acknowledgment of objections

In order to reduce the problem of school bullying, I propose to establish a new law . . . to make bullying or discrimination and harassment a summary offense, which does not require a jury trial. Unlike existing laws that provide only guidelines to protect students from acts of bullying, this new law will take the course of action one step further: If a student is accused of bullying, it will be mandatory for the incident to be reported to the police. The student will be charged and must appear in juvenile court for disciplinary action.

Solution: new law making bullying a "summary offense"

The penalty for this offense will include court-mandated counseling to determine the severity of the student's behavior. In accordance with the California Education Code, suspension from school may be recommended, and family counseling may also be imposed. The student's parents or guardians will be responsible for adhering to all treatment(s) as recommended by the court counselor. . . . If the student commits a second offense, he or she will receive a one-week suspension and family counseling will be required as a condition of returning to school. A third offense will result in mandatory expulsion. Each incident and court ruling will be noted in the student's permanent school records and police record.

Elements of the solution:
• Criminal charges

• Court-mandated counseling

• Consequences (suspension, expulsion) for additional offenses

Enforcement of this new anti-bullying law will be the key to its success. It will be the responsibility of the teachers, school counselors, school administrators, and parents or guardians of each student to ensure that all claims of discrimination and harassment are reported and investigated. Failure of a school administrator to investigate any complaint can be reported to the school board, and the school board will be obligated to compel an immediate investigation.

• Enforcement

Once a student is found guilty of discrimination and harassment, the police and juvenile court will enforce the penalty. The court will monitor the individual's progress through family counseling, and the school administrator will be advised of the student's status.

Each day another bully becomes empowered when his or her actions are dismissed and the victim's cries are ignored. We must be more proactive in dealing with these offenders before more young lives are needlessly lost.

Response to objections

LINDA CHAVEZ

An outspoken commentator on issues of civil rights and affirmative action, Linda Chavez was born in 1947 in Albuquerque, New Mexico, to a Spanish American family long established in the Southwest. She graduated from the University of Colorado (BA, 1970) and did graduate work at the University of California at Los Angeles and at the University of Maryland. She has held a number of government positions, including director of the White House Office of Public Liaison under President Ronald Reagan and chair of the National Commission on Migrant Education under President George H. W. Bush. She has published three books: *Out of the Barrio: Toward a New Politics of Hispanic Assimilation* (1991), which argues against affirmative action and bilingual education; *An Unlikely Conservative: The Transformation of an Ex-Liberal (Or How I Became the Most Hated Hispanic in America)* (2002); and *Betrayal: How Union Bosses Shake Down Their Members and Corrupt American Politics* (with Daniel Gray, 2004). In 2000 the Library of Congress named Chavez a "Living Legend" in recognition of her ongoing contributions to American politics and culture. She currently chairs the Center for Equal Opportunity, a nonprofit public policy organization. Chavez also writes a syndicated newspaper column and is a political analyst for Fox News. She lives in Purcellville, Virginia.

Supporting Family Values

In this piece written in 2009 for *townhall.com*, a conservative news and information site, Chavez makes an unusual case in favor of immigration, legal or not. Presenting evidence that challenges the stereotype of immigrants as unstable and unable to adapt to life in the United States, she argues that established American citizens should be taking life lessons from their newest neighbors. We annotate the essay to illustrate how the author applies the elements of argument and structures her points to support her claims.

It is worth noting that even ten years after Chavez first made this argument, family migration, from Mexico and Central America especially, continues to be the subject of much heated debate in the legislature. The numbers cited in the essay also continue to hold steady. As of early 2019 the Pew Hispanic Center estimates that nearly 11 million unauthorized immigrants reside in the United States, and 5 million American-born children live with parents who are in the country illegally. Overall immigration rates continue to decline as well, despite public perceptions to the contrary. The issue of illegal immigration and its effects on children continues to play out and will not likely be resolved on the national level any time soon.

"Supporting Family Values" from *townhall.com*, Friday, April 17, 2009. Reprinted by permission of Linda Chavez and Creators Syndicate, Inc.

A new report out this week from the Pew Hispanic Center   1   Rational appeal
confirms what many observers already suspected about the ille-   Issue introduced
gal immigrant population in the United States: It is made up
increasingly of intact families and their American-born chil-
dren. Nearly half of illegal immigrant households consist of   Context provided with
two-parent families with children, and 73 percent of these chil-   evidence from source
dren were born here and are therefore US citizens.

The hard-line immigration restrictionists will, no doubt, find   2   Ethical appeal
more cause for alarm in these numbers. But they should represent
hope to the rest of us. One of the chief social problems afflict-   Common ground
ing this country is the breakdown in the traditional family. But   established
among immigrants, the two-parent household is alive and well.

Only 21 percent of native households are made up of two   3   Rational appeal
parents living with their own children. Among legal immi-   Supporting idea
grants, the percentage of such households jumps to 35 percent.   Evidence from source
But among the illegal population, 47 percent of households con-
sist of a mother, a father and their children.

Age accounts for the major difference in household compo-   4   Emotional appeal
sition between the native and foreign-born populations: Immi-
grants, especially illegal immigrants, tend to be younger, while   Interpretation of
the native population includes large numbers of older Americans   evidence
whose children have already left home. But out-of-wedlock births
and divorce, which are more common among the native born—
especially blacks, but also Hispanics and whites—also mean
that even young native households with children are more likely
to be headed by single women than immigrant households are.

But the greater concern for some opponents of immigration—   5   Opposing viewpoint
legal and illegal—is the fear that these newcomers will never   acknowledged
fully adapt, won't learn English, will remain poor and unedu-
cated, and transform the United States into a replica of Mexico
or some other Latin American country. The same fears led
Americans of the mid-nineteenth century to fear German and
Irish immigrants, and in the early twentieth century to fear
Italians, Jews, Poles and others from Eastern and Southern
Europe.

Such worries are no more rational today—or born out of   6   Rational appeal
actual evidence—than they were a hundred years ago. It is   Common ground
true that Hispanic immigrants today take a while to catch up   established
with the native born just as their European predecessors did,
and illegal immigrants never fully do so in terms of education
or earnings. But there is still some room for optimism in the Pew
Hispanic report. Nearly half of illegal immigrants between the

ages of 18 and 24 who have graduated from high school attend college. A surprising 25 percent of illegal immigrant adults have at least some college, with 15 percent having completed college.

Opposing viewpoint refuted with evidence from source

And although earnings among illegal immigrants are lower 7 than among either the native population or legal immigrants, they are far from destitute. The median household income for illegal immigrants was $36,000 in 2007 compared with $50,000 for native-born households. And illegal immigrant males have much higher labor force participation rates than the native born, 94 percent compared with 83 percent for US-born males.

Rational appeal

Supporting idea

Evidence from source

The inflow of illegal immigrants has slowed substantially 8 since the peak, which occurred during the economic boom of the late 1990s, not in recent years, contrary to popular but unin-formed opinion. The Pew Hispanic Center estimates there are nearly 12 million illegal immigrants living in the United States now, a number that has stabilized over the last few years as a result both of better border enforcement and the declining job market. As a result, there might never be a better time to grap-ple with what to do about this population than right now.

Supporting idea

Evidence from source

The fact that so many illegal immigrants are intertwined 9 with American citizens or legal residents, either as spouses or parents, should give pause to those who'd like to see all ille-gal immigrants rounded up and deported or their lives made so miserable they leave on their own. A better approach would allow those who have made their lives here, established families, bought homes, worked continuously and paid taxes to remain after paying fines, demonstrating English fluency and proving they have no criminal record. Such an approach is as much about supporting family values as it is granting amnesty.

Thesis

Proposed solution

Journal Writing

How do you feel about illegal immigrants? Are they criminals who should be punished? victims of circumstance who should be helped? something in between? In your jour-nal, explore your thoughts on illegal immigration. Why do you feel as you do?

Questions on Meaning

1. What seems to have prompted Chavez's essay? How can you tell?

2. What distinctions, if any, does Chavez make between legal and illegal immigrants? Are such distinctions important to her?

3. What is Chavez's point in paragraphs 5 and 6, and how does this point fit into her larger argument?

4. Where does Chavez reveal her PURPOSE in writing? Why do you suppose she chose not to state her THESIS in the introduction?

Questions on Writing Strategy

1. How does Chavez characterize those who hold opposing views? What does this characterization suggest about how she imagines her AUDIENCE?

2. On what underlying ASSUMPTION does Chavez base her argument? Is that assumption reasonable?

3. As a whole, is Chavez's essay an appeal to emotion or a reasoned argument, or both? Give EVIDENCE to support your answer.

4. **OTHER METHODS**   Where and how does Chavez use CLASSIFICATION to support her argument?

Questions on Language

1. Consult a dictionary if you are unsure of the meaning of any of the following: restrictionists (par. 2); wedlock (4); replica (5); predecessors (6); destitute, median (7); stabilized, grapple (8); intertwined, amnesty (9).

2. What does Chavez mean by "native" households and populations? Do you detect any IRONY in her use of the word?

3. How would you describe Chavez's TONE in this essay?

Suggestions for Writing

1. **FROM JOURNAL TO ESSAY**   Based on your journal entry, draft an essay in which you respond directly to Chavez, explaining why you agree or disagree with her position. If you wish, write your essay as a letter to the editor of *townhall.com*, the online journal in which Chavez's essay was published. (See p. 407 for an example of a letter to the editor.)

2. Write an essay in which you present your view on an aspect of US immigration policy or practice that you have strong opinions about — for example, amnesty for illegal immigrants, treatment of asylum seekers, border control, or restrictions on immigration. Before beginning your draft, do some research to support your position and also to explore opposing views so that you answer them squarely and fairly.

3. Identify a current controversy over national policy — raising taxes for the wealthy, the right to carry a concealed weapon, government funding for private schools, and so on. Read newspaper and weekly magazine editorials, letters to

the editor, and other statements on the subject of the controversy. You could also discuss the issue with your friends and family. Based on your research, write a classification essay in which you group people according to their stand on the issue. Try to be as objective as possible.

4. **CRITICAL WRITING**   Write an essay in which you ANALYZE the main CLAIMS of Chavez's argument. What evidence does she provide to back up these claims? Do you find the evidence adequate? (You may wish to track down and examine the source Chavez cites in her introduction: Published by the Pew Hispanic Center on April 14, 2009, its title is *A Portrait of Unauthorized Immigrants in the United States*.)

5. **CONNECTIONS**   While defending the status of some illegal immigrants, Chavez stresses the need for all immigrants to "fully adapt," or assimilate, to American culture. Read Tal Fortgang's "Checking My Privilege" (p. 460), which touches on the author's grandparents' experiences as Polish refugees during World War II. What does it mean to be "American" in a country as diverse as the United States? In an essay, define, defend, or dispute the concept of assimilation. To what extent should recent immigrants be expected to trade ethnic or national identity for a new American identity? What might such an identity encompass, and how could it be obtained? What is gained, or lost, when immigrants become "Americanized"?

Linda Chavez on Writing

To Linda Chavez, telling writers they don't need to know the rules of grammar is like "telling aerospace engineers they don't need to learn the laws of physics." In a 2002 article for *The Enterprise*, Chavez writes about her affection for the lost art of diagramming sentences — using a branching structure to identify sentence parts and map their relationships. She fondly recalls her years in elementary school, then called "grammar school," when learning "where to place a modifier and whether to use an adverb or adjective" was an essential part of the curriculum. Abandoning grammar instruction, she writes, is leaving students scrambled.

Chavez criticizes recent classroom practices of emphasizing creativity over accuracy in composition: "For years now, schools have been teaching students to 'express' themselves, without worrying about transmitting the finer points of grammar and syntax. . . . But effective communication always entails understanding the rules. There are no short-cuts to good writing." According to Chavez, self-expression and grammar are not at odds with each other at all. As she sees it, a solid grasp of grammar is what allows a writer to clearly communicate meaning. In her own writing, Chavez follows the adage of her childhood teacher: "If you can't diagram it, don't write it."

The Bedford Reader on Writing

Like many of the educators Chavez criticizes, we, too, suggest setting sentence-level concerns aside when you begin to write, because doing so is an important tool in getting that first draft done (see p. 31). A finished essay needs a different set of tools, however, and we have to agree with Chavez that grammar is a useful one. For a rundown of ways to bring polish to your writing, and to correct common grammatical errors in particular, check out Chapter 4 on Editing (pp. 55–64).

CHUCK DIXON AND PAUL RIVOCHE

Born in Philadelphia in 1954, comics legend Chuck Dixon has written graphic novels—most notably an adaption of J. R. R. Tolkien's *The Hobbit* (1990)—and several installations of *The Punisher*, *The Green Lantern*, and *Superman*, among other titles, but he is best known for his long run at DC Comics with *Batman*, which included cocreating the villain Bane and the series *Nightwing*. Toronto native Paul Rivoche was born in 1959 and studied at the Ontario College of Art and Design. He began his career as one of the developers of *Mister X* and has since done graphic work for advertising agencies and magazines; illustrated covers and stories for DC Comics, Marvel, and Boom Studios; and created design for several Warner Brothers animated series, including *Batman*, *Superman*, *Justice League*, and *X-Men*. Together, the writer and the illustrator are coauthors of *The Forgotten Man* (2014), a best-selling graphic novel adapted from a conservative history of the Great Depression.

How Liberalism Became Kryptonite for Superman

In this essay published in the *Wall Street Journal* in 2014, Dixon and Rivoche set forth their reasons for creating *The Forgotten Man*. A culture of political correctness in the comics industry, they claim, has corrupted our heroes—and therefore threatens to corrupt our children. Conservatives, they say, need to make their voices heard if they hope to protect "truth, justice, and the American way."

The selection that follows this one offers a (liberal) comic-book editor's direct response to Dixon and Rivoche's argument.

In the nine-hundredth issue of *Action Comics*, Superman decides to go 1
before the United Nations and renounce his US citizenship. "'Truth, justice and the American way'—it's not enough anymore," he despairs. That issue, published in April 2011, is perhaps the most dramatic example of modern comics' descent into political correctness, moral ambiguity and leftist ideology.

We are comic-book artists and comics are our passion. But more important, 2
they've inspired and shaped many millions of young Americans. Our fear is that today's young comic-book readers are being ill-served by a medium that often presents heroes as morally compromised or no different from the criminals they battle. With the rise of moral relativism, "truth, justice and the American way" have lost their meaning.

This story commences way back in the 1930s. Superman, as he first   3
appeared in early comics and later on radio and TV, was not only "able to leap
tall buildings in a single bound," he was also good, just and wonderfully American. Superman and other "superheroes" like Batman went out of their way to
distinguish themselves from villains like Lex Luthor or the Joker. Superman
even battled Nazi Germany and Imperial Japan during World War II.

Cover illustration for *World's Finest Comics*, with Superman, Batman and Robin selling US War Bonds to sink the
"Japanazis." —Hulton Archive/Getty Images

Superman also led domestic crusades, the most famous against the   4
Ku Klux Klan. A man familiar with the Klan, Stetson Kennedy, approached
radio show producers in the mid-1940s with some of the Klan's secret codes
and rituals. The radio producers developed more than ten anti-Klan episodes
of *The Clan of the Fiery Cross*, which aired in June 1946. The radio show's
unmistakable opposition to bigotry sharply reduced respect of young white
Americans for the Klan.

The family of one of us, Paul Rivoche, fled Soviet Russia. The fact that   5
Superman's creators, Jerry Siegel and Joe Shuster, were themselves immigrants, inspired Paul. Superman was a kind of immigrant, having come to
Earth from Krypton, a planet "far far away." Paul grew up in Canada, but
he wanted to depict through his art and illustrations appreciation for both
North America and the United States. Similar idealism drew Chuck, the
writer in our team, into comics.

In the 1950s, the great publishers, including DC and what later became   6
Marvel, created the Comics Code Authority, a guild regulator that issued
rules such as "Crimes shall never be presented in such a way as to create
sympathy for the criminal." The idea behind the CCA, which had a stamp
of approval on the cover of all comics, was to protect the industry's main
audience—kids—from story lines that might glorify violent crime, drug use
or other illicit behavior.

In the 1970s, our first years in the trade, nobody really altered the   7
superhero formula. The CCA did change its code to allow for "sympathetic
depiction of criminal behavior . . . [and] corruption among public officials"
but only "as long as it is portrayed as exceptional and the culprit is punished."
In other words, there were still good guys and bad guys. Nobody cared what
an artist's politics were if you could draw or write and hand work in on schedule. Comics were a brotherhood beyond politics.

The 1990s brought a change. The industry weakened and eventually   8
threw out the CCA, and editors began to resist hiring conservative artists.
One of us, Chuck, expressed the opinion that a frank story line about AIDS
was not right for comics marketed to children. His editors rejected the idea
and asked him to apologize to colleagues for even expressing it. Soon enough,
Chuck got less work.

The superheroes also changed. Batman became dark and ambiguous, a   9
kind of brooding monster. Superman became less patriotic, culminating in his
decision to renounce his citizenship so he wouldn't be seen as an extension
of US foreign policy. A new code, less explicit but far stronger, replaced the
old: a code of political correctness and moral ambiguity. If you disagreed with
mostly left-leaning editors, you stayed silent.

The political-correctness problem stretches beyond traditional comics   10
into graphic novels. These works, despite the genre title, are not all fiction.
For years a graphic novel of *A People's History of American Empire* by Howard Zinn has been taught in US schools. There's even a cartoon version of
Working by Studs Terkel. Che Guevara, the Marxist Cuban revolutionary, is
the subject of several graphic novels, as is the anarchist Emma Goldman.

Yet not all comics and graphic novels parrot the progressive line. *Maus*   11
and *Persepolis* have both sold many hundreds of thousands of copies, and are
taught in schools. Neither of these two mega-successes can be called left-
or right-wing. Pixar's *The Incredibles* is a parable about the evils of bringing
down great people merely because they feature special talents. You can, if
you choose, find libertarian content in *X-Men*. Still the general message
most modern comics send is—in a morally ambiguous world largely created
by American empire—head left.

This would matter less if comics were fading away. But comics are more 12 popular than ever, as evidenced by Hollywood megahits like *X-Men*. One third of English-as-a-second-language teachers in the US use comics. If you doubt the future of this medium, look to Amazon, which bought comiXology, a company that translates comics to e-books. Or try getting a booth this July at Comic-Con, the mob scene that is the annual comics convention.

As a peer of ours recently wrote on *comicsbeat.com*, when it comes to 13 catching up to the left in modern comics, "Conservatives are taking the remedial course." As our contribution to that course, the two of us poured years into a graphic novel of *The Forgotten Man*, conservative writer Amity Shlaes's new history of the Great Depression. But ours is one book. We hope conservatives, free-marketeers and, yes, free-speech liberals will join us. It's time to take back comics.

Journal Writing

Do you agree with Dixon and Rivoche that children are strongly influenced by the comics they read? In your journal, list particular books and magazines from your childhood that stand out in your memory. What made these works come alive so that you still remember them today — the stories, the characters, the illustrations, the language?

Questions on Meaning

1. What do you take to be the authors' PURPOSE in writing this essay? Of what major claim, or THESIS, do they attempt to convince readers?

2. What do Dixon and Rivoche mean by "political correctness" (pars. 1, 9) and "moral relativism" (2)? How are these concepts central to their point?

3. Why do the authors focus their criticism of modern comics on Superman? What other works do they cite, and to what end? How effective do you find their EXAMPLES?

4. Why do Dixon and Rivoche bemoan the switch to "dark and ambiguous" (par. 9) characters that began in the 1990s? What ASSUMPTIONS about the function of comics in popular culture are evident in their preference for earlier superheroes?

Questions on Writing Strategy

1. For whom do Dixon and Rivoche seem to be writing? Liberals, conservatives, historians, comic book fans, editors, another group? How can you tell?

2. Identify the primary APPEALS Dixon and Rivoche make in the essay. Do you find them effective?

3. What kinds of EVIDENCE do the authors provide to support their claims, and how do they ORGANIZE it? Is their evidence convincing? Why, or why not?

4. Take a close look at the visual image that appears with this essay. Why do the authors include it? What does the illustration contribute to their meaning?

5. **OTHER METHODS**   Much of the authors' argument is developed by CAUSE-AND-EFFECT analysis. What do they say has been the result of liberal politics in the comics industry? Who is affected?

Questions on Language

1. How do Dixon and Rivoche characterize conservative and liberal values? Point to a few words that SUMMARIZE their attitude toward adherents of their own political ideology and toward their opponents.

2. How would you describe the writers' TONE in this essay — for instance, worried, condescending, frustrated, dismissive, optimistic, angry, defensive, reassuring, serious, irritated? Is the tone appropriate, given their audience and purpose?

3. Consult a dictionary if you are unsure of the meanings of any of the following: ambiguity, ideology (par. 1); compromised (2); commences, Imperial (3); domestic (4); guild (6); culminating, renounce (9); Marxist, anarchist (10); progressive, libertarian (11).

Suggestions for Writing

1. **FROM JOURNAL TO ESSAY**   Working from your journal entry (p. 515), write a brief essay that explores the messages sent by one of your childhood books or magazines. Did it contain positive role models? negative ones? moral messages? values that you now embrace or reject? Did you learn anything in particular from this text? Based on your recollections, come to your own conclusions about what's appropriate or not in children's literature, comics especially.

2. At a library or online, locate a sampling of Superman comics from the original *Action Comics #1* (1938) through the current day. Write an essay that traces the evolution of Superman's personality and behavior over the years. You might also consider his stature as the anchor character of multiple television and film franchises, or his position as a SYMBOL of American values. For more information on Superman and a selection of recent comics and graphic novels, visit his character page, *www.dccomics.com/characters/superman*, maintained by DC Comics.

3. Dixon and Rivoche suggest that, for a variety of reasons, comics have been ruined — they're no longer as good as they once were. Write an essay in which you offer your view of this idea, arguing for or against some recent change in a particular realm of popular culture. If you generally support the change, offer specific examples and speculate about the benefits. If you generally disapprove, challenge supporters with examples that counter their arguments.

4. **CRITICAL WRITING**   Based on this essay, ANALYZE Dixon and Rivoche's view of the state of national politics. In what ways has the political climate changed in recent decades, according to the writers? How do they portray conservative and liberal philosophies, as well as disagreements among political parties? How meaningful do they find "political correctness," for instance, or the distinction between "immigrants" and "aliens"? Which groups do Dixon and Rivoche consider most powerful and which most disadvantaged? Why? What problems do they identify, and what solutions, if any, do they propose?

5. **CONNECTIONS**   In the next essay, "Superhuman Error: What Dixon and Rivoche Get Wrong," Janelle Asselin analyzes the authors' argument and finds that it comes up short. Before you read her response, EVALUATE the success of Dixon and Rivoche's essay for yourself, considering especially how well their evidence supports their GENERALIZATIONS. Are there important examples they overlook, exceptions they do not account for, gaps in definitions? Offer specific evidence for your own view, whether positive or negative.

JANELLE ASSELIN

A self-described geek and feminist, Janelle Asselin is a freelance writer and editor. She has also worked as the publisher of *Fresh Romance* comics, as an editor for the *Batman* franchise at DC Comics, and for Disney Publishing Worldwide, whose subsidiaries include Marvel. Asselin was born in 1983, grew up in the Midwest, and earned a BA in English from Southern New Hampshire University (2009) and an MA in publishing from Pace University (2011). A life-long fan of comics, Asselin has devoted her "entire career," she has said, to "the study of broadening . . . readership to wider, more diverse demographics," particularly girls and young women. Her essays, reviews, and criticism have appeared in *Shotgun Reviews*, *Newsarama*, *xoJane*, *Bitch*, *The Mary Sue*, and *ComicsAlliance*, the last "an online community of comic book fans" where Asselin worked as a senior editor. She has also published several comics of her own, including strips for *Mickey Mouse Mickey Shorts* (2013) and *Don't Be a Dick* with the Ladydrawers Comics Collective (2014). In addition to writing, Asselin has contributed her editorial talents to humanitarian efforts, among them the Homeless Shift Project and Architecture for Humanity in New York City. She lives in Madison, Wisconsin.

Superhuman Error:
What Dixon and Rivoche Get Wrong

As a working comics editor, Janelle Asselin wrote "Superhuman Error" in heated response to Chuck Dixon and Paul Rivoche's "How Liberalism Became Kryptonite for Superman" (p. 512) and posted it to *ComicsAlliance* two days after their article appeared in the *Wall Street Journal*. In her essay, which she revised for print publication in *The Bedford Reader*, Asselin methodically analyzes Dixon and Rivoche's claims, questioning in particular their assumptions and their evidence.

Asselin's argument is based on her interpretation of multiple texts, so she acknowledges those sources in the body of her essay and in a works-cited list at the end. In accordance with MLA style, she includes page numbers for the one source that has them but not for unpaginated online documents, films, or references to entire works.

Comics creators Chuck Dixon and Paul Rivoche have written a frus- 1
trating piece for the *Wall Street Journal* titled "How Liberalism Became

Kryptonite for Superman." Beating familiar conservative pundit drums like jingoistic nostalgia and referencing a lot of demonstrably incorrect information, these two experienced pros manage to paint a picture of an industry tottering on the edge of moral collapse to an audience that knows little about what's actually going on in cape comics and the American comics industry in general.

The goal here, of course, is to sell comics. By complaining to the *Wall* 2 *Street Journal's* ostensibly conservative audience about how liberals have taken over the American medium, conservatives Dixon and Rivoche attempt to persuade non-comics readers to buy their new book, an adaptation of Amity Shlaes's *The Forgotten Man*, as an exercise in political activism.

For those unfamiliar with their accomplishments, Dixon and Rivoche 3 have created great and enduring work in comics. While writing one of the most popular and fan-favorite eras of Batman comics in the 1990s (including *Detective Comics, Robin, Birds of Prey,* and *Nightwing*), Dixon and artist Graham Nolan cocreated the villain Bane, now a household name. Working with Dean Motter, artist Rivoche developed the hugely influential *Mister X,* whose creative progeny includes, most notably, *Batman: The Animated Series.* Both have numerous other credits to their names.

Like many conservative comics fans, Dixon and Rivoche bemoan the 4 lack of conservative comics being published today, and a perceived liberal bent of the industry, while limiting their definition of comics primarily to superhero books published by Marvel and DC Comics. The problem is not with their politics; it's with their misrepresentation of the industry and its history.

To begin, Dixon and Rivoche start their piece by citing *Action Comics* 5 #900, in which "Superman decides to go before the United Nations and renounce his US citizenship," explaining, "'Truth, justice and the American way [is] not enough anymore. . . .'" They go on to claim that "[w]ith the rise of moral relativism, 'truth, justice and the American way' have lost their meaning." Dixon and Rivoche have drawn their line in the sand, then, by characterizing *conservative* as American with a sense of right and wrong and *liberal* as morally ambiguous. The charge of "moral relativism" is beloved by conservatives when talking about liberals. The term is often used incorrectly, however, or misunderstood.

There are different kinds of moral relativism, including descriptive moral 6 relativism—the idea that there are widespread moral disagreements across different societies as a fact, and that those disagreements are more significant than agreements—and meta-ethical moral relativism—the idea that moral judgments are not absolute, but instead relative to individual groups. Just using the term "moral relativism" is actually not all that helpful or accurate.

The way this idea gets tied into liberalism for conservatives seems to be   7
twofold. One: Many liberals preach tolerance and acceptance for cultures and
people whose ideals differ from our own. This is often assumed to be related
to moral relativism, but is not in fact considered such by actual philosophers
who write about these things. Two: Moral relativism leads to moral ambiguity.
Accepting the morals of other cultures will lead to the downfall of American
society, which has for hundreds of years been primarily Judeo-Christian in its
moral view. In other words: dogs and cats living together—mass hysteria.

Now, to be fair, the issue of *Action Comics* that Dixon and Rivoche cite *is*   8
a particularly political one, but since when has it been okay to claim that only
conservatives are patriotic? Or that it's "politically correct" for someone to
care about what happens beyond the boundaries of their own country? Why
wouldn't an alien from another planet want to help his entire adopted home
planet, versus just his home country? You could argue, as this issue of *Action*
does implicitly, that limiting Superman to just America is like limiting Green
Lantern to one half of a planet in his sector (Goyer and Sepulveda 77).

But the merits of David S. Goyer and Miguel Sepulveda's comic are a   9
discussion for another time, really. The problem here is that Dixon and Rivoche
are pretending before an ignorant audience that within the story, Superman
has forsworn his home country because of those darn liberals—and in a particularly dramatic way. The truth is that this was one short story in an anniversary
issue filled with them, and a story that really didn't matter in the long run. Was
it a political story? Yes. Did it ultimately impact the tone of other Superman
stories? Not at all. Indeed, Goyer's own *Man of Steel* movie script goes out of its
way to identify Superman as a firmly American character when he tells a military commander, "I'm from Kansas; I'm as American as it gets."

Superman is "wonderfully American," say Dixon and Rivoche, but their   10
criteria for that judgment ignore other pieces of the Superman mythos that
would seem to be at odds with contemporary conservative values. Is Superman not the ultimate "illegal alien"? He wasn't born in the United States, his
biological parents weren't born in the United States, and he didn't enter the
country in any state-approved way—plus he's literally an alien. Yet he's built
his life in the US, continues to work in the country, and, one short story notwithstanding, identifies as a proud American. Real-life humans whose stories
reflect that dimension of Superman are as a group frequently targeted by conservative politics, so it's interesting that the Man of Steel is the figure being
upheld by Dixon and Rivoche as the conservative ideal.

The greater and more damaging implication in Dixon and Rivoche's piece   11
is that only American conservatives can perceive right and wrong. The two
authors attempt to draw a correlation between the idea of accepting or even
just respecting other viewpoints and understanding right and wrong at all.

This position is limiting both to our society and to our entertainment, and it is incredibly flawed. People who tolerate other folks with different opinions do not, as a rule, lack a moral compass—they simply are willing to listen to others. It's not as if tolerance is a solely liberal trait, either. Why draw that comparison? When America entered World War II and "Superman even battled Nazi Germany and Imperial Japan," were all of our soldiers conservatives? Or is the rise of what the authors call moral relativism (again, most likely meaning "tolerance") only a recent phenomenon, and prior to that, liberals were okay? There are a lot of people in this country today who are "good, just and wonderfully American" and plenty of those people are not conservatives. Or even citizens.

As well as hailing Superman as a (fictional) war hero, Dixon and Rivoche   12 cite some radio episodes in which Superman led a crusade against the Ku Klux Klan, which they reference in the context of conservatives' allegedly stronger understanding of justice. To be fair, the KKK did in its earliest incarnation target Republicans, and Southern Democrats had plenty of racists and bigots among them. But it seems odd to bring up race in regards to liberals versus conservatives, as Republicans consistently tolerate racism within their party and block legislation meant to address racial injustice. It's a very cool thing that Superman was employed as anti-racist propaganda, but it would seem, based on their own track record on civil rights for minorities, that contemporary conservative politicians have more to learn from the Man of Steel's example than modern-day liberals do.

"How Liberalism Became Kryptonite for Superman" transcends mere   13 wrongness into weirdness when the authors write about comics from the 1950s to the 1970s. In that section of their argument, they speak of the loathsome Comics Code Authority (CCA) with what sounds like teary-eyed nostalgia.

That's right. In an article bemoaning the lack of free speech in comics   14 because of oppressive liberal values, two men who presumably share a political ideology that believes in minimizing government manage to talk with admiration about a literally oppressive set of censoring regulations that the comics industry imposed on itself following actual government hearings about whether comics—even superhero comics—were corrupting children. When Dixon and Rivoche say of one of the CCA's rules that "there were still good guys and bad guys," it's like they're pointing to the Code as a kind of proper morality that they wish comics still had. This is not longing for free speech. This is longing for a limited kind of morality that matches the authors' own particular set of morals.

Dixon and Rivoche also bemoan the dark and gritty turn superheroes   15 have taken, and a new "code of political correctness and moral ambiguity."

Again, this is just factually inaccurate. The tonal shift from black-and-white morality of older comics to the pervasive "grim and gritty" aesthetic of the 1990s was not ushered in solely by liberal creators. It's true that Alan Moore and Frank Miller[1] (now an outspoken right-winger) wrote popular works in this vein (Ronald Reagan was actually a villain in Miller's *Batman: The Dark Knight Returns*), but then again, so did Chuck Dixon, whose *Punisher* comics — where the protagonist circumvents the law to murder anyone he thinks deserves it — are remembered as some of the most intensely dark and violent anti-hero comics of the era. The shift had less to do with politics and more to do with fashion and an aging audience. To assign a political bent towards these changes because of "political correctness and moral ambiguity" is like accusing anyone who believes in tolerance of actively encouraging crime. Tolerating other viewpoints does not equal anarchy or a lack of morals.

Later in their piece, Dixon and Rivoche hold up the graphic novels *Perse-* 16 *polis* and *Maus* as examples of popular comic books that do not fall on either side of the political divide. This is just completely incorrect. The story of author Marjane Satrapi's growing up in Iran during the Islamic Revolution, *Persepolis* is a manifestly anti-fascist work. Likewise, Art Spiegelman's *Maus* dramatized his father's ordeal during the Holocaust. These comics may not, in Dixon and Rivoche's minds, "parrot the progressive line," but the truth is that these are political comics that Dixon and Rivoche happen accidentally to have enjoyed.

There are a lot of other issues in the phrasing chosen by Dixon and 17 Rivoche that help spread incorrect facts to newspaper readers who likely wouldn't know any better. Simple things like saying comics are for kids, referring to comiXology as a company that "translates comics to e-books," or describing San Diego Comic-Con International as "the annual comics convention" are misleading at best. Perhaps most crucially, Dixon and Rivoche's pretending that American comics are made up entirely of superhero comics, rather than discussing the wide range of work that exists and is successful today, ignores the fact that there *is* room in the comics market for a book like the one they have produced. If the only comics that existed were the superhero books and graphic novels they discuss, they would never have had the chance to create *The Forgotten Man*.

Dixon and Rivoche are right that there should be more conservative 18 comics. They're both talented creators who have written some amazing and

---

[1] English writer Alan Moore (born 1953) is best known for the graphic novels *Watchmen*, *V for Vendetta*, and *From Hell*. American writer, artist, and director Frank Miller (born 1957) has written episodes of *Daredevil*, *Sin City*, *300*, *Batman: The Dark Knight Returns*, and *Batman: The Dark Knight Strikes Again*. —Eds.

influential comics and created some important characters, and they deserve the opportunity to produce work that accurately represents their world view. It's good that they've taken the advice so many Internet commenters are eager to throw at feminist fans: "If you don't like what's being made, make your own comics." However, two accomplished pros should know the facts about their industry and be able to speak to an audience beyond that industry in an accurate way. The authors' use of rose-colored glasses of nostalgia and political fallacies may help them sell books to readers inclined to accept such notions without further investigation; it won't do the industry any good. In the end, that is the issue — Dixon and Rivoche have misrepresented American comics to an audience that probably doesn't care in the first place, but now will be kept away from any future contemplation of the work and medium and community we all love.

Works Cited

Dixon, Chuck, and Paul Rivoche. "How Liberalism Became Kryptonite for Superman." *The Wall Street Journal*, 8 June 2014, www.wsj.com/articles/dixon-and-rivoche-how-liberalism-became-kryptonite-for-superman-1402265792.

Goyer, David S., writer. *Man of Steel.* Directed by Zack Snyder, performance by Henry Cavill, Warner Brothers, 2013.

Goyer, David S., and Miguel Sepulveda. "The Incident." *Action Comics*, no. 900, DC Comics, 2011, pp. 70–78.

Miller, Frank. *Batman: The Dark Night Returns.* DC Comics, 1996.

Satrapi, Marjane. *Persepolis.* Pantheon Books, 2003.

Spiegelman, Art. *Maus: A Survivor's Tale.* Penguin Books, 2003.

Journal Writing

How do you access various kinds of popular culture, and what GENRES do you like the most? Make a list of what you've read, seen, or heard over the past month or so and what the medium was — whether the Internet or more traditional channels such as magazines, books, TV, radio, or theaters.

Questions on Meaning

1. What does Asselin claim is the PURPOSE of Dixon and Rivoche's essay? What seems to be hers? Why, that is, do you think she was compelled to write "Superhuman Error"?

2. What is Asselin's THESIS? Where does she state it directly?

3. Why does Asselin dwell on the meanings of "moral relativism" and "moral ambiguity" (pars. 5–7, 11)? What is her point?

4. In what sense, according to Asselin, can Superman be considered both "the ultimate 'illegal alien'" and a "proud American" (par. 10)? Why is this SYMBOLISM important to her?

5. How does Asselin explain the "dark and gritty turn superheroes have taken" (par. 15)? What general ASSUMPTION about comics is she disputing here?

Questions on Writing Strategy

1. Does Asselin seem to be writing mainly for readers familiar with the comics industry or for a wider AUDIENCE? Cite passages from the essay to support your answer.

2. From where does Asselin draw her EVIDENCE? What strategies does she use to SYNTHESIZE information and ideas from multiple sources?

3. Why does Asselin highlight Dixon's and Rivoche's accomplishments in paragraph 3 and admit in paragraphs 8, 12, and 18 that they are correct on some points? How do these concessions affect her argument?

4. In her conclusion, Asselin accuses Dixon and Rivoche of using "fallacies" (par. 18) but doesn't specify which logical errors she has in mind. What do you think she means? Does Asselin slip into any fallacies herself? (For an overview, refer to pp. 499–500 and to FALLACIES in the Glossary.)

5. **OTHER METHODS**   Asselin's essay is also a model of DIVISION or ANALYSIS, in that she picks apart the elements of another essay. What principle of analysis does she use to ORGANIZE her argument?

Questions on Language

1. Asselin says that Dixon and Rivoche define "*conservative* as American with a sense of right and wrong and *liberal* as morally ambiguous" (5). How does *she* characterize liberal and conservative values? In a few words, SUMMARIZE her depictions.

2. At what points in her essay, and how, does Asselin adopt a sarcastic TONE? What does her use of sarcasm contribute to (or take away from) her argument? (For a definition of *sarcasm*, see IRONY in the Glossary.)

3. Consult a dictionary if you are unsure of the meanings of any of the following: pundit, jingoistic (par. 1); ostensibly (2); progeny (3); bemoan, bent (4); renounce, ambiguous (5); meta-ethical, absolute (6); Judeo-Christian (7); implicitly (8); forsworn (9); mythos (10); correlation (11); incarnation, propaganda (12); transcends, loathsome (13); aesthetic, circumvents, anti-hero, anarchy (15); manifestly, fascist (16).

4. How would you describe Asselin's DICTION? Is it appropriate, given her purpose and audience? Is it effective? Why, or why not?

Suggestions for Writing

1. **FROM JOURNAL TO ESSAY**   Write an essay in which you explain and defend your own relationship with one medium of popular culture — Internet, TV, books, radio, and so on. Which genres do you prefer, and why? Have your preferences changed over time? Give specific examples to support your explanation.

2. Asselin notes that "feminist fans" are often told, "If you don't like what's being made, make your own comics" (par. 18). Why should that be? Although the entertainment media have come a long way in the portrayal of female characters in recent decades, some critics complain that there is still much progress to be made. Write an essay in which you EVALUATE the depictions of women in comics today. Base your analysis on your own experiences with graphic novels or with franchises such as *Superman, Supergirl, Batman, The Avengers, Wonder Woman, Jessica Jones,* and the like — whether online or in magazines, books, TV, or film. Overall, do you find the portrayals to be negative or positive? What messages do these portrayals send to audiences? How might the portrayals be improved?

3. Censorship is a controversial issue with arguments and strong feelings on both sides. In a page or so of preliminary writing, respond to Asselin's remarks on the Comics Code Authority (pars. 13–14) with your own gut feelings on the issue. Then do some library research to extend, support, or refute your views. In a well-reasoned and well-supported essay, give your opinion on whether or not the media and publishing industries should censor themselves to avoid "corrupting children" or for any other reasons.

4. **CRITICAL WRITING**   Select any essay in *The Bedford Reader* that inspires a strong response for you. Using Asselin's argument as a model, write a rhetorical analysis of the essay you have chosen, breaking down what makes it effective or ineffective or why you agree or disagree with the author (or authors) in some fundamental way. As Asselin did, be sure to carefully examine the author's claims and evidence and to include citations for any summaries, paraphrases, and quotations you decide to integrate into your essay. (See the Appendix for more on citing sources in MLA or APA style.)

5. **CONNECTIONS**   In "How Liberalism Became Kryptonite for Superman" (p. 512), Chuck Dixon and Paul Rivoche use a method similar to that taken by Janelle Asselin in "Superhuman Error," synthesizing ideas from popular culture and academics to develop an argument, but the two essays' approaches are markedly different and their conclusions are squarely opposed. Write an essay of your own in which you analyze how these writers adapt their evidence and tone for their audience and purpose, using quotations from both essays to support your analysis. Which essay, in your opinion, is more successful? Why?

DAVID B. MUHLHAUSEN

David B. Muhlhausen is the director of the National Institute for Justice, the research agency of the US Department of Justice. Born in Colorado and raised in Ellicot City, Maryland, Muhlhausen studied political science and justice studies at Frostburg State University (BA, 1993) and completed a PhD in public policy at the University of Maryland, Baltimore County (2004). A former research fellow in empirical policy analysis for the Heritage Foundation in Washington, DC (1999–2017), Muhlhausen has also served on the staff of the Senate Judiciary Committee, worked as the manager of a juvenile corrections facility, and taught program evaluation and statistical methods to graduate students at George Mason University's Schar School of Policy and Government. His research and articles have appeared in the *Washington Post*, *Forbes*, *USA Today*, and other publications, and his commentary and analyses have been featured on news programming for CNN, Fox News, MSNBC, and PBS. As an expert in the effectiveness of federal social programs and criminal justice policies, Muhlhausen has frequently been called to testify at congressional hearings before the House and the Senate. He lives in Falls Church, Virginia.

How the Death Penalty Saves Lives

Muhlhausen is a proponent of the death penalty and often writes about its benefits to society. In this September 2014 op-ed essay for *US News and World Report*, the policy expert cites opinion polls and academic studies to demonstrate his point that capital punishment results in reduced murder rates and is therefore morally acceptable. The essay following this one—Semon Frank Thompson's "What I Learned from Executing Two Men" (p. 530)—argues the opposite.

On September 10, Earl Ringo, Jr., was executed in Missouri. Before you   1
decide whether or not this is right, consider what Ringo did.

In July 1998, Ringo and an accomplice planned to rob a restaurant where   2
Ringo had previously worked. Early one morning, they followed delivery truck driver Dennis Poyser and manager-in-training Joanna Baysinger into the building before shooting Poyser to death and forcing Baysinger to hand over $1,400. Then, Ringo encouraged his partner to kill her. A jury convicted Ringo of two first-degree murders.

Some crimes are so heinous and inherently wrong that they demand strict   3
penalties—up to and including life sentences or even death. Most Americans
recognize this principle as just. A Gallup poll from May on the topic found
that 61 percent of Americans view the death penalty as morally acceptable,
and only 30 percent disagreed. Even though foes of capital punishment have
for years been increasingly vocal in their opposition to the death penalty,
Americans have consistently supported capital punishment by a 2-to-1 ratio
in murder cases. They are wise to do so.

Studies of the death penalty have reached various conclusions about its   4
effectiveness in deterring crime. But a 2008 comprehensive review of capital
punishment research since 1975 by Drexel University economist Bijou Yang
and psychologist David Lester of Richard Stockton College of New Jersey
concluded that the majority of studies that track effects over many years and
across states or counties find a deterrent effect.

Indeed, other recent investigations, using a variety of samples and statis-   5
tical methods, consistently demonstrate a strong link between executions and
reduced murder rates. For instance, a 2003 study by Emory University researchers of data from more than 3,000 counties from 1977 through 1996 found
that each execution, on average, resulted in 18 fewer murders per county. In
another examination, based on data from all 50 states from 1978 to 1997,
Federal Communications Commission economist Paul Zimmerman demonstrated that each state execution deters an average of 14 murders annually.

A more recent study by Kenneth Land of Duke University and others   6
concluded that, from 1994 through 2005, each execution in Texas was associated with "modest, short-term reductions" in homicides, a decrease of up to
2.5 murders. And in 2009, researchers found that adopting state laws allowing defendants in child murder cases to be eligible for the death penalty was
associated with an almost 20 percent reduction in rates of these crimes.

In short, capital punishment does, in fact, save lives. That's certainly not   7
to say that it should be exercised with wild abandon. Federal, state and local
officials must continually ensure that its implementation rigorously upholds
constitutional protections, such as due process and equal protection of the
law. However, the criminal process should not be abused to prevent the
lawful imposition of the death penalty in capital cases.

Moral indignation is an appropriate response to inherently wrongful   8
conduct, such as that carried out by Earl Ringo, Jr. While the goal of lower
crime through deterrence is worthwhile, lawmakers need to place special
emphasis on the moral gravity of offenses in determining the proportionality
of punishment.

The execution of Ringo was morally just. And it may just save the lives   9
of several innocents.

Journal Writing

Muhlhausen objects to the "abuse" of "the criminal process" by those attempting to "prevent the lawful imposition of the death penalty in capital cases" (par. 7). What does he mean? And do you agree with his position? In your journal, write down your own opinions about American methods of trying the accused, sentencing the convicted, or appealing the sentences of convicted criminals in the United States. Does the justice system seem fair to you?

Questions on Meaning

1. What seems to be Muhlhausen's PURPOSE? Is he writing to express indignation, offer a solution, influence government regulations, change attitudes, or do something else? What details from the essay support your answer?

2. What two main reasons does Muhlhausen offer to persuade readers to support capital punishment? Do you find these reasons persuasive? Why, or why not?

3. For what types of crimes does Muhlhausen advocate the death penalty?

4. In which sentence or sentences does Muhlhausen state his THESIS most directly?

Questions on Writing Strategy

1. What does Muhlhausen accomplish by opening with a discussion of Earl Ringo, Jr., and the crime he was executed for?

2. As a whole, is this essay an appeal to emotion or a reasoned argument, or both? What ASSUMPTIONS does Muhlhausen make about his readers? Give evidence for your answer.

3. Examine Muhlhausen's TRANSITIONS between paragraph 2 and 3, 4 and 5, and 7 and 8. How do they work?

4. Where, if at all, does Muhlhausen address opposing points of view? How effective do you find his treatment of counterarguments?

5. **OTHER METHODS**   Much of Muhlhausen's argument is developed by CAUSE-AND-EFFECT analysis. What does he claim is the link between capital executions and murder rates? How convincing do you find his EVIDENCE?

Questions on Language

1. What is the TONE of the essay? How does it contribute to Muhlhausen's ETHICAL APPEAL?

2. Be sure you are familiar with the following words, checking a dictionary if necessary: accomplice (par. 2); heinous, inherently (3); deterring, comprehensive (5); associated, homicides (6); implementation, due process, imposition, capital (7); gravity, proportionality (8); just (9).

Suggestions for Writing

1. **FROM JOURNAL TO ESSAY**   Develop a focused and persuasive thesis from the opinion you expressed in your journal entry, and support it with evidence from your reading and observations. (You may also wish to do research among the many books and articles written on the criminal justice system.) Rather than take on the entire administration of justice, follow Muhlhausen's model and narrow your thesis to one aspect of the system.

2. Use the library to investigate the status of the death penalty in your state, and report your findings in an essay. In your research, consider these questions: Is there a death-penalty law on the books? If so, who may be executed and under what conditions? What appeals are available to the defendant? How many people have been executed under the law, and how many more await execution? If there is no death-penalty law, has such legislation been proposed? What is its current status? Have views on capital punishment changed in recent years? In your essay, avoid taking sides on the issue. View your task as fact gathering for the purpose of providing yourself and others with objective background information.

3. **CRITICAL WRITING**   Write an essay refuting Muhlhausen's argument; or take Muhlhausen's side but supply additional reasons you can think of. In either case, begin your argument with an ANALYSIS of Muhlhausen's claims, and use examples (real or hypothetical) to support your view.

4. **CONNECTIONS**   Compare this essay with the following one by Semon Frank Thompson, "What I Learned from Executing Two Men." Imagine a debate between the two writers. How would Thompson respond to Muhlhausen's argument that capital punishment is "morally just" (par. 9) in some circumstances? How might Muhlhausen answer Thompson's charge that implementing the death penalty traumatizes the executioners? On what points do they seem to agree?

SEMON FRANK THOMPSON

Semon Frank Thompson is a career corrections professional and an advocate for criminal justice reform. Having grown up in Little Rock, Arkansas, in the midst of the civil rights movement, he started at the University of Arkansas at Fayetteville in 1961 with the intention of becoming a doctor but left after two years to enlist with the military; he later returned and earned a BA in social welfare in 1969. While continuing his studies at the University of Arkansas School of Law, Thompson worked on the campus police force, first as a patrolling officer and then as the department's first black criminal investigator; he also served as assistant dean of minority affairs and associate dean of students. After graduating from the Arkansas Law Enforcement Training Academy, Thompson worked as a warden and superintendent with the Arkansas Department of Corrections before accepting the position of superintendent at the Oregon State Penitentiary in 1994; he continued with the Oregon Department of Corrections in various prison leadership capacities until his retirement in 2010. He lives in Salem, Oregon, and now travels the country speaking against the death penalty.

What I Learned from Executing Two Men

For Semon Frank Thompson, the issue of capital punishment is unexpectedly personal. At one time agreeing with policymakers like David B. Muhlhausen (p. 526) that the death penalty was fair and just punishment for especially violent crimes, his experience at the Oregon State Penitentiary changed his mind. In this essay written for the *New York Times* in September 2016, the former prison superintendent and reluctant executioner tells his story.

As superintendent of the Oregon State Penitentiary, I planned and 1 carried out that state's only two executions in the last fifty-four years. I used to support the death penalty. I don't anymore.

I was born and raised in the segregated South. I was thirteen when 2 Emmett Till was lynched for "flirting" with a white woman. I can remember upstanding black Christians expressing hope that his murderers would be caught and hanged. It seemed quite reasonable to me then that death was the only proportionate response for people who would so egregiously violate the norms of a society.

Years later, as a young law enforcement officer, I lost a close friend, John 3 Tillman Hussey, and a cousin, Louis Perry Bryant—both law enforcement officers themselves — to execution-style murders at the hands of felons who were attempting to avoid arrest. I remember feeling that justice had been served when one of their killers was executed.

In 1994, during my interview for the superintendent job, I was asked ⁤4 if I would be willing to conduct an execution. I said yes. Oregon had not executed anyone in decades, but the death penalty was part of the criminal justice system, and I had to be prepared for all of the duties that a superintendent could be called upon to perform.

Shortly afterward, I was charged with executing two inmates on the ⁤5 penitentiary's death row, Douglas Franklin Wright and Harry Charles Moore. Moore had been convicted of killing his half sister and her former husband, and he said he'd take legal action against anyone who tried to stop his execution. Wright was sentenced to death for killing three homeless men. He later admitted to killing a ten-year-old boy. He, too, had given up his appeals.

Regardless of their crimes, the fact that I was now to be personally ⁤6 involved in their executions forced me into a deeper reckoning with my feelings about capital punishment. After much contemplation, I became convinced that, on a moral level, life was either hallowed or it wasn't. And I wanted it to be.

I could not see that execution did anything to enhance public safety. ⁤7 While death penalty supporters suggest that capital punishment has the power of deterrence, a 2012 report by the National Research Council found that research "is not informative about whether capital punishment decreases, increases or has no effect on homicide rates."

I now believed that capital punishment was a dismal failure as a policy, ⁤8 but I was still expected to do my job. So I met with my staff and explained my position. I made it known that anyone who felt similarly opposed could back out of our assignment. According to state policy, assisting in the executions was voluntary for everyone but the superintendent. And yet each of those asked to serve chose to stay to ensure that the job was done professionally.

I'm a Vietnam-era veteran, and a law enforcement professional who has ⁤9 been trained to deal with life-or-death situations, as were many of my colleagues. We focused on carrying out our responsibilities and leaving everyone involved with as much dignity as possible.

I began to feel the weight of this undertaking while practicing for the ⁤10 executions. Teams rehearsed for more than a month. There was a full "run through" of the execution every week.

The weight intensified during the executions, which took place eight ⁤11 months apart, and it didn't subside until well after they were completed. I cannot put into words the anxiety I felt about the possibility of a botched procedure. I wasn't certain how my staff would fare. These were the first executions in Oregon in over three decades. These were the first executions in Oregon to be administered by use of lethal injections. I was the first black superintendent of the Oregon State Penitentiary. All of these firsts had the potential to come together in a very negative way if my team made a single mistake.

Planning an execution is a surreal business. During a prisoner's final days, 12 staff members keep the condemned person under twenty-four-hour surveillance to, among other things, ensure that he doesn't harm or kill himself, thus depriving the people of Oregon of the right to do the same. I can understand the administrative logic for this reality, but it doesn't make this experience any less strange.

During the execution itself, correctional officers are responsible for every- 13 thing, from strapping the prisoner's ankles and wrists to a gurney to administering the lethal chemicals. One of the condemned men asked to have his wrist straps adjusted because they were hurting him. After the adjustment was made, he looked me in the eye and said: "Yes. Thanks, boss."

After each execution, I had staff members who decided they did not want 14 to be asked to serve in that capacity again. Others quietly sought employment elsewhere. A few told me they were having trouble sleeping, and I worried they would develop post-traumatic stress disorder if they had to go through it another time.

Together, we had spent many hours planning and carrying out the deaths 15 of two people. The state-ordered killing of a person is premeditated and calculated, and inevitably some of those involved incur collateral damage. I have seen it. It's hard to avoid giving up some of your empathy and humanity to aid in the killing of another human being. The effects can lead to all the places you'd expect: drug use, alcohol abuse, depression and suicide.

But the job gets done — despite the qualms and the cost. That's the way 16 it's supposed to work. Capital punishment keeps grinding on, out of sight of society.

The average citizen will never find himself looking a death row prisoner 17 in the eye, administering a lethal injection and stating the time of death in front of observers and reporters. But we all share the burden of a policy that has not been shown to make the public any safer, and that endures despite the availability of reasonable alternatives.

I am encouraged that Oregon now has a moratorium on executions, and 18 there have not been any in the state since the ones I oversaw. Nationwide, in the past few decades, executions have also been declining, from a high of ninety-eight in 1999 to fifteen so far this year. But people continue to be sentenced to death.

Since I retired from corrections in 2010, my mission has been to persuade 19 people that capital punishment is a failed policy. America should no longer accept the myth that capital punishment plays any constructive role in our criminal justice system. It will be hard to bring an end to the death penalty, but we will be a healthier society as a result.

Journal Writing

Thompson calls the state-sanctioned executions of Douglas Franklin Wright and Harry Charles Moore "a dismal failure as a policy" (par. 8) and "a surreal business" (12). How do you respond to this characterization of capital punishment? In your journal write down as many reasons as you can think of both for and against capital punishment. The reasons may be moral, emotional, or purely pragmatic. Write down whatever comes to mind.

Questions on Meaning

1. What seems to be the author's primary PURPOSE in this essay? Where does he make that purpose most clear to readers?

2. In paragraph 6 Thompson writes, "I became convinced that, on a moral level, life was either hallowed or it wasn't. And I wanted it to be." What does he mean? What point is he making here?

3. Thompson refers to the "availability of reasonable alternatives" (par. 17) to the death penalty, but he doesn't indicate what they might be. Why not? What alternatives can you think of?

4. What connection does the author make between executing prisoners and the "collateral damage" (par. 15) inflicted by the practice? Who else is harmed by capital punishment? Express Thompson's THESIS in a sentence or two of your own.

Questions on Writing Strategy

1. What reasons does Thompson give for opposing capital punishment? What does he offer as EVIDENCE for his claims?

2. Who is Emmett Till (par. 2)? John Tillman Hussey and Louis Perry Bryant (3)? What does Thompson achieve by remarking on their deaths in his opening paragraphs?

3. Is this essay an appeal to emotion, a reasoned argument, or both? Give evidence for your answer.

4. Do you think the author expects his AUDIENCE to agree with him? At what points does he seem to recognize that some readers may see things differently?

5. **OTHER METHODS**   This essay is a good example of NARRATION being used in the service of an argument. What advantage does Thompson gain by presenting his argument in the form of a personal account?

Questions on Language

1. Check a dictionary if you are unfamiliar with the meanings of any of the following words: segregated, proportionate, egregiously (par. 2); felons (3); reckoning, hallowed (6); deterrence (7); subside (11); surreal (12); gurney (13); capacity (14); premeditated, calculated, collateral, empathy (15); qualms (16); moratorium (18).

2. How would you describe the TONE of this essay? How well is it suited to Thompson's purpose?

Suggestions for Writing

1. **FROM JOURNAL TO ESSAY**   Write an essay in which you argue either for or against the death penalty. Support your argument with the evidence in favor of your position that you developed in your journal writing (p. 533). As for the evidence that contradicts your opinion, use it to try to anticipate — and respond to — readers' likely objection to your view.

2. Expand your knowledge about post-traumatic stress disorder (PTSD) by researching the condition. You might start with its definition in the *Diagnostic and Statistical Manual of Mental Disorders*, Fifth Edition, published by the American Psychiatric Association and available in most college libraries. Look also for scholarly articles in a periodical database, and perhaps some personal accounts by people who have the condition. What causes PTSD, and what are some of its symptoms? How is it treated? In an essay, SYNTHESIZE what you discover.

3. **CRITICAL WRITING**   In an essay, examine the organization of Thompson's argument. What does Thompson accomplish in each paragraph or groups of related paragraphs? How effectively does he use TRANSITIONS to move from one idea to the next?

4. **CONNECTIONS**   In "How the Death Penalty Saves Lives" (p. 526), David B. Muhlhausen approaches the death penalty quite differently from Thompson. Not only do their opinions differ fundamentally, but Muhlhausen's view is broad and ABSTRACT, while Thompson's is intensely personal; and Muhlhausen's appeal is largely rational, while Thompson's is largely emotional. In an essay, discuss the effectiveness of these two essays apart from the opinions they support — that is, focus on the authors' strategies of argument rather than on the arguments themselves. What are the advantages and disadvantages of each strategy?

JESSICA BLANK AND ERIK JENSEN

Jessica Blank and Erik Jensen are actors, writers, and collaborators, married since 2002 and known for their shared interest in social justice issues. Born in New Haven, Connecticut, in 1975, Blank grew up there and in Washington, DC, attended Macalester College in St. Paul for two years, and graduated from the University of Minnesota. She debuted as an actress with *One Life to Live* (2004) and has since appeared on several other programs. She regularly writes for and occasionally produces television and film projects, freelances as a writing coach, and has published three novels: *Almost Home* (2007), *Karma for Beginners* (2009), and *Legacy* (2018). Jensen, by contrast, is a Minnesota native, born in 1970 and educated at Carnegie Mellon University in Pittsburgh, Pennsylvania. An author and cocreator of the graphic novel *The Reconcilers* (2010), he is best known as an actor and has performed in more than a hundred television, movie, and stage productions—notably *Black Knight* (2001), *The Bronx Is Burning* (2007), *Gravity* (2010), *The Walking Dead* (2014), and *Mr. Robot* (2016–17). Together Blank and Jensen have written the award-winning documentary plays *The Exonerated* (2002), excerpted here; *Aftermath* (2009), based on interviews with Iraqi refugees; and *How to Be a Rock Critic* (2015), about music journalist Lester Bangs. They are also the coauthors of *Living Justice: Love, Freedom, and the Making of* The Exonerated (2005), a memoir of their first collaboration and the work that changed their lives.

from *The Exonerated*

Newly dating at the time, Blank and Jensen were inspired to research and write *The Exonerated* after attending a 2000 seminar on capital punishment at Columbia University, where they were shocked to learn that dozens of death-row inmates had been released or were pending release after proof of their innocence had surfaced. The documentary play tells the true stories of six of those exonerees: Delbert Tibbs, whose description fit that of a man suspected of violent crimes; Robert Earl Hayes, accused of raping and murdering a coworker; Gary Gauger, arrested after having reported finding his parents killed in their home; Kerry Max Cook, whose fingerprints allegedly tied him to the death of a woman he had seen once, months earlier; David Keaton, arrested for involvement in a deadly robbery he had no knowledge of; and Sunny Jacobs, a helpless bystander to a police shooting whose husband Jesse, also present and also absolved, was nonetheless executed by the state.

As a whole, *The Exonerated* weaves together the stories of each person's experience, from the crimes for which they were accused to their ultimate releases and struggles to adjust to life after prison. The excerpts we present here are passages from two key episodes: conviction and imprisonment, followed by new evidence, retrial, and exoneration. As Blank and Jensen explain in their comments on writing (p. 546), the dialog is taken directly from interviews conducted by the playwrights and from the archived court transcripts and case files they scoured afterward. Although this is a play, none of it is fiction.

Poster advertising the 2018 revival of *The Exonerated*, at the Secret Theater in Queens, New York.

Characters

DELBERT, African-American, sixty. A seminary dropout, radical, and poet. His whole personality is like an old soul song: smooth, mellow, and with an underlying rhythm that never lets up. Actors playing DELBERT should take care to find his substantial sense of humor, in addition to his obvious depth.

SUNNY, white, fifty. A bright, pixieish yoga teacher from California; her lightness and positivity contrast with moments of great depth and clarity.

ROBERT, African-American, thirties. A former horse groomer from the Deep South; hardened but not lacking a sense of humor. Deep rural Mississippi accent.

. . . .

GARY, white, forty-five. A midwestern hippie and an organic farmer. Clearly was in his element in the late 1960s and early 1970s. He is generally good-natured, friendly, and quite smart.

KERRY, white, forty-five. A nineteen-year-old trapped in a forty-five-year-old's body, born and bred in Texas. KERRY was imprisoned for twenty-two of his forty-five years and is eager to rediscover the world. Always wants to make sure he connects with whomever he is talking to. Strong Texas accent.

DAVID, African-American, forty. A gentle, sad man, born and raised in northern Florida (otherwise known as southern Alabama). Has a very strong spiritual sense and had aspirations to the ministry before being put on death row at eighteen. He is continually engaged in a battle between resignation and hope.

. . . .

OPEN *on a stage, bare except for ten plain armless chairs. These chairs can be used variously to set up scenes throughout the piece. The entire play can be performed using only these chairs. No further set pieces are necessary, although tables and other set pieces might work, too. The play is seamless: There are no blackouts during the performance, and no intermission. Unless otherwise noted, the exonerated people deliver their monologues to the audience.* DELBERT *can see the other exonerated people; unless otherwise noted, none of the other exonerated people see one another or* DELBERT. *At various points in the play, we see "scenes" illustrating the stories being told by the exonerated. These scenes exist in the exonerated people's memories, and unless otherwise noted, they should take place behind or beside the character telling the story.*

DELBERT *functions as a sort of Chorus, fading in and out of the action.*

. . . .

Lights up on SUNNY.

SUNNY: They tell you exactly how they're gonna do it. They're gonna send 1
twenty-two hundred volts of electricity through your body until you're dead.
And then they ask you if you have anything to say to that, and really it's kind
of dumbfounding. So after the judge read the sentence, I just said, "Are you
finished?" I didn't have anything to say. What do you say? How can you say
anything to that?

Sound of a cell door slamming shut. Lights up on DELBERT, *down on* SUNNY.

DELBERT: I don't remember any of my dreams from when I was on death 2
row. I almost never recall my dreams, which I am absolutely fascinated by.
   When I was at the University of Chicago, I took part in a laboratory 3
experiment. They were running a test to see if creative people's dreams differ
from those who are less creative. And so of course, it appealed to the ego in
me, thinking somebody thought I was creative.
   So you go to bed in the lab and they are monitoring your respiration 4
and your REM and so forth. And they would wake me up over the microphone, and it always sounded to me like one of the Nazi doctors 'cause he
had an accent, you know, he would be like, "MISTA TIBBS, YOU VERE
DREAMINK." And I wanted to say, No shit.
   But the fascinating thing was, when the [mother%+*!ers] hooked me up, 5
they put the receptors by your ears, right exactly at the same place they do
when they're getting ready to execute your ass.

Lights down on DELBERT, *up on* SUNNY.

SUNNY: Instead of sending me to be Jesse's cellmate, they decided to clear 6
out an entire disciplinary unit at the women's prison. It's a very old prison,
it's like a dungeon-type place. It was six steps from the door to the toilet
bowl — you could stretch out your arms and touch both walls. They take your
clothes; they give you a number, so basically they're taking . . . who you *are*
from you. You no longer have a name, you're a number. You're locked inside
this *tomb*. It's like you're thrown to the bottom of the well.

Lights down on SUNNY, *up on* DAVID.

DAVID: There was one woman, lived across the street when I was a little 7
boy, she had a goiter on her neck. And I was sayin', "Lord, if I only had the

power of the Spirit, I would go lay my hands on her and her illness would disappear." And that's all I want, just to let the Spirit be operatin' through me, whether it be knowledge, discernment, speak the Word, or whatever. [*to God*] I would love to just do that before I die.

I had a relationship to God when I got in here, but somehow I've lost it. 8 I guess I'm still reachin' out to find it— you know, I said some nights now I wanna light me a couple candles, lay back and just meditate, 'cause they say the kingdom of God is within you, isn't it? You know, everybody lookin' for something outward, but then, that light's *within* you, that voice we speak to . . . [*whispering God's voice*] "C'mon, boy."

Give you the chills when I say that, right?   9

Lights down on DAVID, *up on* KERRY.

KERRY: You know, when I was in there, I saw a hundred and forty-one 10 guys go down. All's I got to do is pick up the newspaper, turn on the news, "such and such becomes the two hundred and twenty-second inmate executed resulting from capital punishment," and I hear the name and I say, "Oh my God," 'cause I know him. I mean, I don't just *know* him, I *ate* with him, I *cried* with him, we used to play basketball and talk about "Man, you're gonna go free."

You know, I got a book, a book about Texas death row, and seriously, this 11 book is what, five years old, and everyone in here has been executed. I can go through that book, one by one, and point out every face in here that's gone.

INMATE: Executed.   12

Sound of a switch being thrown.

INMATE: Executed.   13

Sound of a switch being thrown.

INMATE: Executed.   14

Sound of a switch being thrown.

KERRY: And you know, at a capital trial, the prosecutors always say, "He's 15 dangerous, he's a maniac, the sick, twisted murderer." But I'm no different from you—I mean, I wasn't a street thug, I wasn't trash, I came from a good family—if it happened to me, man, it can happen to anyone.

Lights down on KERRY, *up on* GARY.

GARY: I was in X house—the execution house. That place was like somethin' 16
out of a movie. There were no guards. They would just open your cell door and
let you run around. I guess they figured you were gonna die anyway, so why not.

So you can walk around through this dimly lit series of corridors, and 17
through the observation room, into the execution room. That's where the
phone was that all of us used. Which was also the phone that the governor
would use to call in and stop an execution.

The whole place was run by gangs, you know, there was ongoing warfare 18
between the different factions. And the only gang open to white guys was
the Northsiders—which is basically made up of the Aryan Nation and the
Skinheads. So I had no gang protection. So I kept to myself a lot. Killed a lot
of time on my own.

One way I killed time, was I found a sewing needle stuck in a concrete 19
wall. Somebody had smuggled it in. So I taught myself embroidery.

You'd take extra clothing—the blue jeans made real good blue thread. 20
And I was lucky—I had kept my old yellow jumpsuit that they gave me to
wear when I first went in. So that gave me yellow. You take your sheet apart,
that gives you white. So I had three colors of thread, just from unraveling
cloth. I made myself a tote bag I'd take to chow hall, and I embroidered flowers on it. I put bell-bottoms on a couple of my prison blues, made a Calvin
and Hobbes patch I put on my hat. They confiscated that one.

Lights down on GARY, *up on* ROBERT.

ROBERT: The electric chair was downstairs and I was upstairs, and every 21
Wednesday morning they cranked that electric chair up and you could hear
it buzz.

And when they served breakfast, you gotta have sharp ears to hear that 22
front door open, 'cause if you oversleep, the roaches and the rats come and
eat your breakfast, and that's the God's honest truth.

And the guards—I think nine times out of ten, the average person that 23
became a guard, the only way I can see it, when he grew up he was a little
runt and then the bigger guy would mess with him and all of that. And then
they grow up and they wanna do that too.

When I was in there, one day, this officer was harassing my neighbor and 24
I was a witness. And the other inmate, he wanted to write the officer up, he
asked me—[1]

---

[1]The scene here cuts to a drawn-out legal confrontation between Robert, another inmate,
and a guard, followed by additional incarceration experiences as recounted by Kerry, Delbert,
David, and Sunny. For the sake of brevity in these excerpts we jump forward to Robert's new
trial. —EDS.

. . . .

ROBERT: Well, see, before I went to prison, I had a dream about   25
prison—and I seen death row, I seen the inside, and I seen myself get out.
And 'cause a that dream, I always said, I'm gonna get a new trial. And sure
enough, one day, I get awakened by all this commotion. All the inmates, they
get up in the vents, hollerin' —

Lights up on MEN.

ALL MEN [*ad lib*]: Man, you got a new trial! Damn, Robert, you gonna go   26
free! You on the radio! Turn on the radio! [*etc.*]
CELLMATE: Put the radio on!   27
ROBERT: Well, I put the radio on.   28
And later that day, my lawyer came, and she said to me—   29

Lights down on INMATES, *up on* FEMALE LAWYER.

FEMALE LAWYER: Now, you know, Robert, if you lose, you can go back   30
to death row.
ROBERT: And I said [*to lawyer*], "Well, now, accordin' to that dream,   31
I'm gonna go free."
And she said—   32
FEMALE LAWYER [*to* ROBERT]: You gonna put all your trust in a dream?   33
ROBERT: And I said, "Yep" [*small beat*]   34

Lights up on PROSECUTOR, GEORGIA, *and* EX-BOYFRIEND.[2]

FEMALE LAWYER: Back in 1990, what color was your hair, and how long   35
was it?
ROBERT: And by then he had short hair, salt-and-pepper, you know, and   36
he said—
EX-BOYFRIEND [*on the stand*]: My hair was the same color and length back   37
then as it is now.
ROBERT: And my lawyer said—   38
FEMALE LAWYER: Are you sure?   39
EX-BOYFRIEND: Of course I'm sure.   40
ROBERT: So my lawyer pulls out this envelope. And she said —   41
FEMALE LAWYER: Again in 1990, do you remember having your picture   42
taken near the racetrack?
EX-BOYFRIEND: Uh, yeah.   43

---

[2]Georgia is Robert's wife. The ex-boyfriend in this scene is a man who was known to have
been involved with his alleged murder victim at the time of her death. —EDS.

ROBERT: And then she pulled that big ol' photograph picture out and   44
showed it to him. And there he was, his hair red and brown and sixteen
inches long on the picture.

ROBERT *looks to* GEORGIA.   45

ROBERT *and* GEORGIA: *Okay?!*   46

Lights down on ROBERT, GEORGIA, EX-BOYFRIEND, PROSECUTOR, *and* FEMALE LAWYER,
up on KERRY.

KERRY: So then after I've been on death row for twenty-two years, they   47
find this DNA evidence, you know, and the prosecution says that this will
be the final nail in Kerry Max Cook's coffin: "We'll show the world once and
for all that he committed that murder." And then the results come in and it
did just the opposite; it finally took the nail out of my coffin, told the world
the truth—that that was Professor Whitfield's DNA they found on that girl.
And he's still out. They never even went after him. He's been walking around
a free man, laughing at the system for twenty-two years.

Twenty-two years.   48

Lights down on KERRY, *up on* GARY.

GARY: About halfway through my time on death row, a lawyer named   49
Larry Marshall took on my case. He's at Northwestern; he works with a
bunch of law students on wrongful convictions. My twin sister found out
about him and went down there literally through a blinding snowstorm to see
if he would take me on. And he said yes.

Man, that was like the cavalry coming.   50

Once he started working on it, Larry found out about this motorcycle   51
gang called the Outlaws. Guys gained entrance into the gang by performing
violent acts: They killed a bunch of people, they'd bomb the Hell's Angels—
they just did a lot of stuff. And the federal government, the ATF, was running
wiretaps on them. Well, in 1995, the ATF got a videotaped confession from
an Outlaw guy saying he killed my parents. But I wasn't released until 1996.
And that whole year in between, they were fighting my appeal. They fought
it all the way to the Illinois Supreme Court.

The two guys who killed my parents were just found guilty last year.   52

But I've been adamant that those guys not get the death penalty. Some   53
people think that's stupid, but why would I want them to die? It's not gonna
bring my parents back. No good's gonna come from it.

Lights down on GARY; *up on* SUNNY *and* RHODES.

SUNNY [*to audience*]: In 1979, Walter Rhodes wrote the following letter   54
to the judge.

RHODES: I, Walter Norman Rhodes, hereby depose and say that I am under   55
no duress nor coercion to execute this affidavit. This statement is made freely
and voluntarily, and to purge myself before my Creator.

Briefly. On February 20, 1976, at approximately 7:15 a.m., I did, in fact,   56
shoot to death two law-enforcement officers with a nine-millimeter Brown-
ing pistol.

I state emphatically and unequivocally that my previous testimony   57
against Jesse Tafero and Sonia Jacobs was *false* and part of the statements
I was instructed to make by the assistant state attorney, who did coerce me
into lying.

I took a polygraph examination relative to this case, but owing to the fact   58
that I am a student of Yoga and karate, and have been for the last ten years, I
passed it. And can pass any such test, in my opinion.

The foregoing statements are true and correct to the best of my knowl-   59
edge and belief. I so swear.

Walter Norman Rhodes, Jr., 9 November 1979.   60

Lights down on RHODES.

SUNNY: Keep in mind that I wasn't released until 1992.   61

So I'll just give you a moment to reflect: From 1976 to 1992, just remove   62
that entire chunk from your life, and that's what happened. [*long pause, the
length of a count of six*]

But after all that, one day, the guard came into my cell and told me I was   63
getting out. I thought he was trying to trick me.

Sound of cell door opening; SUNNY *takes it in.*

SUNNY: And it was just so *joyous.* I mean, I know a lot of people are angry,   64
and I was angry some, but I didn't want to waste my time being mad.

Journal Writing

Of the six characters represented in these excerpts from *The Exonerated*, whose story
most affected you, and why? (If you weren't moved by any of their stories, why not?)
Make note of your reactions to the play in your journal.

Questions on Meaning

1. What do you take to be Blank and Jensen's PURPOSE in researching, writing, and staging this play? What implicit argument against capital punishment do they make with it?

2. Kerry says that during his time on death row he "saw a hundred and forty-one guys go down" to their executions (par. 10). Can he be right, or is he exaggerating? Why do you think so?

3. What is it like to be on death row, according to the characters in *The Exonerated*? What DOMINANT IMPRESSION of the experience do they create?

4. Why did it take so long for Sunny to be released after Walter Rhodes admitted to committing the crime and giving false testimony? What might have been taking place behind the scenes? Why isn't she angry?

5. What role do dreams play in Delbert's and Robert's experiences? How do Blank and Jensen transform these dreams into SYMBOLS?

Questions on Writing Strategy

1. *The Exonerated* is meant to be performed before a live AUDIENCE. Whom do you think Blank and Jensen hoped to reach with this play? How well do their stage directions (in *italics*) help readers imagine seeing the play in person?

2. What reason does Gary give for not wanting his parents' killers to receive the death penalty?

3. How does Kerry characterize lawyers' arguments in favor of the death penalty? How does he respond to these opposing points of view?

4. **OTHER METHODS**   Blank and Jensen use EXAMPLES and NARRATION to build their argument. Why? How persuasive do you find this EVIDENCE?

Questions on Language

1. Some of the characters in this play use vulgar, explicit language. Why do you suppose that is? What is the EFFECT?

2. Other characters seem naturally to use metaphors and similes to relate their experiences. Find a few examples and comment on their meanings. (If necessary, see FIGURES OF SPEECH in the Glossary for definitions of *metaphor* and *simile*.)

3. Use a dictionary if necessary to help you define any of the following words: REM (par. 4); goiter (7); factions (18); confiscated (20); commotion (25); adamant (52); depose, affidavit (54); unequivocally (56); polygraph (57).

Suggestions for Writing

1. **FROM JOURNAL TO ESSAY**   Based on your personal response to the stories in *The Exonerated* that you recorded in your journal (p. 543), ANALYZE Blank and Jensen's uses of rational, ethical, and emotional appeals to structure their argument. Consider these questions as you develop your analysis: To what extent

do the playwrights attempt to reason with their audience? How do they enlist empathy for their characters? Are they respectable authorities on the issue, in your estimation? Why, or why not? What, if anything, could the authors have done to make the play more persuasive?

2. Laws reflect and reinforce basic social values: What behaviors are acceptable? What transgressions are punishable? How far should we go to enforce social norms? Although incarceration practices might seem reasonable in a contemporary cultural context, viewed from an outsider's perspective they can often be quite surprising. For much of American history, for instance, whole families—including dependent infants—were routinely placed in debtors' prisons for a father's failure to provide for them. And in the early twentieth century, unmarried women could be jailed for pregnancy. Think of a past or current law that strikes you as absurd or extreme, and look for the underlying social value that it's meant to enforce. Then write an essay that explains the law to somebody from another culture or another time who might have trouble understanding it. You may be ironic or satiric, if you wish, or you may prefer a more straightforward informative approach.

3. **CRITICAL WRITING**   Prison is a perennially popular subject in fiction. Pick a novel, film, or television show that takes prison, or something related to prison (such as involuntary commitment to a mental hospital), as its subject. (For novels, you might consider Charles Dickens's *Little Dorrit*, Malcolm Braly's *On the Yard*, or Kurt Vonnegut's *Hocus Pocus*. Films touching on this subject include *Cool Hand Luke*, *Escape from Alcatraz*, *Bad Boys*, *The Green Mile*, and *The Shawshank Redemption*, the last two based on stories by Stephen King. Popular television programs include *The Wire*, *Prison Break*, *Orange Is the New Black*, and *Proven Innocent*.) Write an essay comparing and contrasting the novel, film, or show with *The Exonerated*. Are the criticisms the same? Where do they differ?

4. **CONNECTIONS**   Proponents and opponents of the death penalty—such as David B. Muhlhausen and Semon Frank Thompson in the preceding two essays (pp. 526 and 530)—use statistics, expert opinions, and other evidence to support their arguments. But for many people the issue is a matter only of morality: It is right to execute convicted murderers, or it is not right. What are your moral views on this issue? Write a brief essay in which you defend or oppose capital punishment on moral grounds, explaining as best you can the sources of your views (family, religion, experience, and so on).

Jessica Blank and Erik Jensen on Writing

In their introduction to the 2004 print book of the script of *The Exonerated*, Jessica Blank and Erik Jensen do readers the service of explaining where the idea for the play came from—and outlining how they researched, drafted, and revised the show for a live audience.

Over the summer of 2000, we traveled across the United States, sat in people's living rooms, and listened as they told us what it was like to be innocent and on death row. They were from vastly different ethnic, religious and educational backgrounds. Their views on the world varied greatly. The only thing they held in common was that they had each been sentenced to die, spent anywhere from two to twenty-two years on death row, and had subsequently been found innocent and freed by the state. We interviewed forty people on the phone and twenty in person. Six of these interviews form the core of *The Exonerated*.

The previous spring, we had gotten the idea for the play at a conference on the death penalty at Columbia University. We took the idea to producer Allan Buchman, a friend of ours from the downtown theater community in New York who ran the Culture Project.

Governor George Ryan of Illinois had just declared a moratorium on the death penalty in his state, and another George[1] was running for high office — with more executions carried out under his watch as governor of Texas than in any other state since the reinstatement of the death penalty in 1976. The issue was very much in the news. Allan told us we could have his theater for three nights in the fall if we could have something up before the elections. So we hit the road. We went as far north and west as Chicago, as far south as Texas and Miami, and just about everywhere in between to meet the people whose stories appear in this play.

We returned from the interviews with hours and hours of tape, which became several hundred pages of transcripts. We're both primarily actors, which means we have lots of talented and underemployed friends. We enlisted them to come workshop the transcripts with us, and began the process of shaping hundreds of pages of everyday speech into a play. At the same time, we called director Bob Balaban and asked him to direct three readings of the play at Allan's theater that fall. Bob brought his highly trained eye to the material we were developing, while also helping us assemble a cast for the readings. That cast included Gabriel Byrne, Ossie Davis, Vincent D'Onofrio, Charles Dutton, Cherry Jones, David Morse, Susan Sarandon, Tim Robbins, Debra Winger, and many other extraordinary actors. They performed an initial version of the play, which then consisted of the stories of twelve exonerated people, taken entirely from the interviews we had conducted.

After three readings at the Culture Project and a performance at the United Nations, we hit the road again. It was clear to us, Bob, and our audiences how the exonerated people felt about what had happened to them;

---

[1] George W. Bush (born 1946) served as governor of Texas from 1995 to 2000 and president of the United States from 2001 to 2009. — Eds.

what was still unclear was how it could've happened in the first place. So we went through the extremely difficult process of paring down the number of stories in the play in order to tell each one more fully. Additionally, we dug into the court transcripts and case files of the people whose stories we were telling. We spent countless hours in dusty courthouse record rooms, pawing through thousands of microfiche files and cardboard boxes full of affidavits, depositions, police interrogations, and courtroom testimony. The court employees assumed we were law students—and we did nothing to discourage that belief. With a few exceptions, each word spoken in this play comes from the public record—legal documents, court transcripts, letters—or from an interview with an exonerated person. The names of the exonerated people are their own; some names of auxiliary characters have been fictionalized for legal reasons.

The vast majority of the piece is as it was said, two, five, ten, and twenty years ago by the actual participants. At the time we conducted these interviews, there were eighty-nine people who had been exonerated from death row. As of this writing, there are now 102. We consider every one of their stories to be part of this play.

The Bedford Reader on Writing

Determined to faithfully tell the stories of real people, Blank and Jensen conducted grueling research to gather strong, relevant EVIDENCE and then collaborated with their colleagues to produce an engaging and powerful work of art. Yet when they realized that the original draft of their play had failed to fulfill the specific PURPOSE they had in mind for it, they undertook the demanding work of gathering even more evidence and REVISING the script extensively. For our tips on conducting research, see the Appendix (pp. 648–51). And for help working with peers to review and revise a work of your own, turn to pages 50–51 of Chapter 3 and the revision checklists in the introductions to Chapters 5–14.

DAWN LUNDY MARTIN

Dawn Lundy Martin is a professor of English and the director of the Center for African American Poetry and Poetics at the University of Pittsburgh. Born in 1969, she grew up in a small working-class family in Hartford, Connecticut, and earned a BA from the University of Connecticut, an MA in creative writing from San Francisco State University, and a PhD in literature from the University of Massachusetts Amherst. She has published four books of poetry: *A Gathering of Matter / A Matter of Gathering* (2007), *Discipline* (2011), *Life in a Box Is a Pretty Life* (2015), and *Good Stock, Strange Blood* (2017). Martin is also a coeditor of *The Fire This Time: Young Activists and the New Feminism* (2004) and a cofounder of the Third Wave Foundation, a feminist and transgender youth activism organization in New York. Her creative nonfiction has appeared in several publications, including *The New Yorker*, *Harper's*, and *n+1*. An experimental performance artist as well, Martin has displayed video installations at the Museum of Contemporary Art in Detroit and the Whitney Biennial and is a member of the Black Took Collective, a multimedia artist trio. In 2018 she won a grant from the National Endowment for the Arts to support her memoir, a work in progress.

Weary Oracle

"Weary Oracle" first appeared in *Harper's* magazine in 2016, part of a group of essays commissioned to debate the issue of safe spaces on college campuses, responding to recent demands by activists that their schools offer protective environments where minority students can interact without fear of judgment or hostility. Showing empathy toward students who may be suffering from "race trauma," Martin urges her readers to be supportive of their needs.

In the essay following this one, "Blanket Security," fellow *Harper's* contributor Thomas Chatterton Williams shares Martin's concerns for students of color but argues against seeking safe spaces on campus.

My mother, who was born more than eighty years ago, deep in the Jim Crow[1] South, insists that she has never experienced a single moment of racism. I have never heard her say a derogatory word about white people as a race or use the word "white" as an insult. When she calls people "black," she does not do so affectionately, to suggest kinship, community, or belonging. And she gets

[1] A name taken from the title of a nineteenth-century minstrel song, Jim Crow refers to the systematic discrimination and legalized segregation practiced against African Americans in the southern states throughout the first half of the twentieth century. —EDS.

visibly annoyed when black people organize around black*ness*, as though claiming the category that is also used to disparage them were a criminal act. Why excite the ghost? Why call its hideous name? Yet when I ask her whether she remembers black people getting lynched, she says, "Yeah, they did sometimes."

That is what race trauma looks like—although it is not reducible to that.   2

At Claremont McKenna College, a young woman's voice cracks as she   3
speaks into a megaphone handed to her by protesters who seek redress for the racial slights that they believe have been encouraged by the culture of the campus. Instead of talking about her own experiences of racism, the woman testifies to the more generalized experiences of others. She weeps; her whole body vibrates. Against my mother's stoicism, the weeping almost reads as performance. It has the texture of a sleeve pulled up to reveal a sore and disgust the viewer. *Put it away.*

But the pitch of the reactions on campuses is not a display of "excessive   4
vulnerability" resulting in "self-diminishment," as some critics of student tactics claim. Something is pressing on these students, making them burst at the seams, and it's not imaginary. They are like oracles whose bodies bear the collective weight of what others do not—or will not—see: the lynchings my mother cannot incorporate into her worldview, the black boy the police shot down in the street just yesterday. They feel all of it when, for example, a white person mistakes them for another brown person who looks nothing like them.

It is not unreasonable for college students to desire to be carefully held by   5
the universities that courted them. In fact, universities and colleges imply a promise, in their mottoes of "Light and Truth," in their ivy-encrusted buildings, in the serenity around their lakes and on their manicured greens, and especially in their invitations for students to engage in the leisure of intellectual work. That's one place where I think students of color hurt: right where leisurely study becomes labor. As a professor who has spent more than half my life on college campuses, I know this labor intimately—the labor of having to name racism when it is already nakedly visible; the labor of being perpetually suspect, never afforded the possibility of neutral innocence; the labor of negotiating others' racially offensive speech; or the very special labor of pretending (because you are tired) that everything is fine. Instead of being protected by the institution that you see your white counterparts inhabiting so casually, you find the institution protected from you. That it is guarded by historical figures such as Woodrow Wilson,[2] a KKK sympathizer whose name is emblazoned on a campus building, is not lost on you. Still, folks want to know, why are you so enraged, what is causing your pain, why do you act so insane?

[2] Woodrow Wilson (1856–1924) was the twenty-eighth president of the United States, in office from 1913 to 1921 and notorious today for his racist positions and policies, including his vocal support of the Ku Klux Klan, a secret society formed after the Civil War to assert white supremacy through intimidation, harassment, and violence. —Eds.

Journal Writing

As a student yourself, you're probably had at least one experience with the sort of uncomfortable public displays of vulnerability Martin describes, whether as the person upset or as a witness to someone else's negative reaction. Do you agree with Martin that students should be "carefully held by the universities that courted them" (par. 5), or do you think it's more beneficial to confront disturbing emotions directly? Or are your feelings mixed? In your journal, explore your thoughts on some students' demands for "safe spaces" on college campuses.

Questions on Meaning

1. What is Martin's PURPOSE for writing? What problem does she identify, and what solution does she propose?

2. What is "race trauma," as Martin explains it? How does she describe its causes and effects?

3. What do you make of Martin's title? What is an oracle, and why would one be weary?

4. Does Martin's argument have a THESIS? Where is this thesis stated most clearly, if at all?

Questions on Writing Strategy

1. "Weary Oracle" was directed at a very specific AUDIENCE. Who were Martin's intended readers? What ASSUMPTIONS does she make about them?

2. Where and how does Martin address opposing points of view? Do her concessions seem adequate to you? Why, or why not?

3. Clearly Martin's argument relies on EMOTIONAL APPEAL, but it is nonetheless based on an implied SYLLOGISM. Tease out her major claim, minor claim, and conclusion, and express them in your own words. (For help, refer to pp. 498–99 on deductive reasoning.)

4. Take note of the final sentence of this essay. What strategy is Martin using for her CONCLUSION? What is the effect?

5. **OTHER METHODS**   Discuss how Martin uses EXAMPLES to explain the labor required of students of color. Why do you suppose she highlights just a few potential burdens?

Questions on Language

1. Find some FIGURES OF SPEECH in Martin's essay. What is the effect of the author's metaphors and similes in particular? Do they strike you as appropriate for an academic argument?

2. Be sure you are familiar with the following words, checking a dictionary if necessary: derogatory, disparage, lynched (par. 1); redress, stoicism (3); perpetually, emblazoned (5).

3. Examine the language Martin uses to describe people who suffer from race trauma. Is it OBJECTIVE? sympathetic? negative?

Suggestions for Writing

1. **FROM JOURNAL TO ESSAY**   Working from your journal entry, write an essay that responds to Martin's argument, putting forth your own position on calls for safe spaces on college campuses. Under what circumstances (if any) is it advisable, or even necessary, to shield students from racism? Are some students more susceptible to discrimination than others? Do the benefits of preventing discomfort indeed outweigh the drawbacks? Why do you think so? Like Martin, you may arrange your thoughts into an argument for or against safe spaces, or you may prefer to structure your essay as a personal NARRATIVE focused on your own experiences.

2. Enhance your understanding of race trauma through research. You might start with a quick online search to get an overview of how psychiatrists view the problem. But look also for scholarly articles in a periodical database, and seek out some descriptions by people who, like Martin, have experienced such emotions themselves. Is race trauma formally recognized as a psychiatric diagnosis? What causes it, what are some of its symptoms, and how can it be mitigated? How do "microaggressions" come into play? In an essay, SYNTHESIZE what you discover.

3. **CRITICAL WRITING**   In a brief essay, analyze Martin's use of ETHICAL APPEALS in making her argument. What qualifications does she claim to write on the subject of safe spaces on college campuses? How does she present herself to readers? What attempts, if any, does she make to establish common ground? How would you characterize her tone? How persuasive does she seem to you, and why?

4. **CONNECTIONS**   In the next essay, Thomas Chatterton Williams writes about what he sees as the problem with college students calling for safe spaces on campus. Write an essay in which you COMPARE AND CONTRAST the ways Martin and Williams present their cases. Which argument do you find more effective? Why?

Dawn Lundy Martin on Writing

"I'm really attempting to push myself to be able to write a stable speaking *I* that is a black subjectivity without it feeling in some ways overly constructed," poet Dawn Lundy Martin tells Abigail Meinen in a 2017 interview for *Sampsonia Way*, an online literary journal. Reflecting on the nature of that subjectivity, she continues: "I think that one of my core beliefs about what it means to *be* is that if you experience trauma — and I think that in some ways, the black experience is a kind of trauma — that it's difficult to be cohesive. That impossibility of being cohesive makes it hard for me to re-write that *I* over and over and over again. It's a very slippery thing. If I write it in one moment, it slips away in the next and it becomes something else. Sometimes *I* can become *you*, sometimes it can become *she*, sometimes it can become *it*, even. I'm wondering if there's language that I can write around it, that I can reconfigure, so that I can use it more persistently, without it feeling constructed, or slightly fake, like an artifice that I don't necessarily want in a poem."

Martin doesn't necessarily want that artifice to affect her prose, either. "Weary Oracle," she suggests to Meinen, was one of several essays she wrote in the service of drafting a memoir, a process that Martin has found daunting. "I was trying to publish the essays in mainstream publications" like *Harper's* magazine, she explains. "But what I found out, actually, is that the big famous magazines have certain conventions for editing — and your work starts to look less like your work." So the poet has turned back to her own voice, the one she's still working out how to construct. "I'm learning how to write auto-biographical prose," she says. "I'm really trying to teach myself. And I'm also trying to figure out what that kind of writing means for me."

The Bedford Reader on Writing

Martin constantly works to find and refine her VOICE by playing with POINT OF VIEW in her writing. And as she struggles to establish a SUBJECTIVE view that feels honest to her, she sometimes finds herself slipping between first-, second-, and third-PERSON — from *I* to *you* to *she* — a problem many writers face in their drafts. For help addressing such unnecessary shifts as you edit, see "Shifts" in Chapter 4 (p. 61) and "Focus on Consistency" in Chapter 9 (p. 259).

THOMAS CHATTERTON WILLIAMS

Thomas Chatterton Williams was born in Newark, New Jersey, in 1981. The son of a black sociologist with an extensive library and a white stay-at-home mother, he grew up in the suburbs negotiating a balance between his attraction to the "thug life" promoted by rap artists and Black Entertainment Television (BET) and his parents' insistence on education and self-discipline. Williams received a BA in philosophy from Georgetown University and an MA in cultural reporting and criticism from New York University and is now a contributing writer at the *New York Times Magazine*, a contributing editor at the *American Scholar*, a National Fellow at *New America*, and the recipient of a Berlin Prize. His first book, *Losing My Cool: How a Father's Love and 15,000 Books Beat Hip-Hop Culture* (2010), which originated as a graduate school op-ed assignment, serves as both a criticism of hip-hop's damaging influences on African American society and a tribute to his father. His *Virginia Quarterly Review* essay "Black and Blue and Blonde" was collected in *Best American Essays 2016* and is being expanded into a forthcoming book that will tackle the definition of race and identity. Williams currently resides in Paris, France, with his wife and their "half-French" daughter.

Blanket Security

Williams first published "Blanket Security" in *Harper's* magazine, immediately following Dawn Lundy Martin's argument (p. 548). Responding indirectly to her claims, Williams counters that seeking safe spaces on college campuses threatens to intensify the very inequalities such spaces seek to overcome.

A few days ago, I went to the grocery store near my apartment, in Paris. The weather was cold, and I was bundled up, a beanie low over my forehead and the large hood of my parka over the beanie. The moment I entered the store, a security guard — almost certainly assuming I was a young Arab — was on me, gruffly demanding that I lower my hood. I was cold and refused. We argued, and the man ended up shadowing me, perhaps out of spite, for the duration of my shopping. It was the kind of ambiguous, unimportant, but frankly unpleasant experience that I can't help imagining wouldn't happen if I were white. And it would qualify as what many Americans, particularly on college campuses, have increasingly come to interpret and describe as a form of "microaggression."

In this instance, my options were limited. I insisted on my right to pres- 2
ent myself as I wanted, and finally ignored the man. I left the store irritated
but in no way damaged. I am still not positive that what transpired was racism. Were I on an American college campus, however, it would be easier now
than ever before to seek refuge in a "safe space." There, I could recount the
affront to others who looked like me and to sympathetic allies, without fear
of judgment, contradiction, or even skeptical questioning. This would likely
make me feel better in the short term, but it is also entirely plausible that I
would emerge from a vague and trivial situation having decided to unequivocally assume the role of the victim.

And that would be a Pyrrhic satisfaction. Such reflexive thinking com- 3
pounds rather than alleviates whatever residual injuries come with membership in a historically oppressed group. It's a strange and ironic double
diminishment: first to feel oneself aggrieved, and then to conclude that the
best response is to bask in fragility and retreat into an artificially indulgent
social context. There is something utterly dehumanizing about being fit to a
demographic profile, reduced to the sex or color of a body. While I may not
be able to control how I look or how others perceive me, I control absolutely
the ways I perceive myself. The idea that minorities need bubbles betrays an
internalized sense of inferiority. When we concede public space as inherently
hostile instead of deliberately claiming it as our own—as Martin Luther
King, Jr., and so many others did in the Sixties, as the gay-rights movement
did more recently—we perpetuate and reinforce some of the very biases we
seek to counteract.

Just as troubling, the growing power and influence of the appeal to vul- 4
nerability transforms it from a strictly defensive (if ineffective) tool into an
increasingly potent method of intimidation that can silence even meaningful
disagreement. If the point is for everybody to be treated equally and with
dignity, it should cause alarm when we watch a seething crowd shout down
a lone professor at Yale, or physically repel a photographer at the University
of Missouri. In such situations, the victim has not been redeemed—she has
swapped places with her tormentor.

Ultimately, the quest for guaranteed emotional security and a coerced or 5
rigged affirmation in conditions of real or imagined oppression, while understandable, does little to alter the status quo. On the contrary, that quest
painfully concedes the point that inequality is permanent. Real safety and
freedom—which is to say, full participation in a society in which one has
an equal stake, and not merely a symbolic shelter—requires systemic support, but it also needs personal imagination and courage. At the very least,
it requires the courage to be uncomfortable and the imagination to see ourselves as strong.

Journal Writing

Have you ever been subjected to the sort of encounter Williams experienced in the grocery — or perhaps been an unwitting offender in such an incident? (If not, have you seen someone else treated poorly on the basis of their appearance?) What happened, and how did you respond? How did the incident affect you? Were you hurt, for instance, or frightened, or angry? Why? Recall one such moment and write about it in your journal.

Questions on Meaning

1. What do you take to be Williams's main PURPOSE in writing? What is his THESIS, and where does he state it?

2. Why, according to Williams, are safe spaces a bad idea? What are "microaggressions," as he understands them? What's wrong with seeking protection from racism?

3. What alternative solution to the problem of racist encounters does Williams propose?

4. What does Williams believe to be the purpose of a college education? Where does he reveal the primary ASSUMPTION behind his argument?

Questions on Writing Strategy

1. Why does Williams open his essay with an ANECDOTE from his own experience? What is the effect of telling a personal story in his INTRODUCTION?

2. To what extent does Williams use rational, emotional, and ethical APPEALS in his argument? Identify examples of each kind of appeal in your answer.

3. Does Williams seem to expect his AUDIENCE to agree or disagree with his position? In answering this question, consider his TONE and his use of pronouns (*I* and *we* especially). What audience reaction does he seem to be seeking?

4. **OTHER METHODS**   Examine the way Williams uses CAUSE AND EFFECT to develop his argument in paragraph 4. From where does he draw his EXAMPLES? How persuasive are they as EVIDENCE for his claim that "the appeal to vulnerability" is itself turning into a "method of intimidation that can silence even meaningful disagreement"?

Questions on Language

1. Check a dictionary if you are unfamiliar with the meanings of any of the following words: gruffly, ambiguous (par. 1); affront, allies, plausible, unequivocally (2); compounds, alleviates, residual, aggrieved, demographic, inherently, perpetuate, counteract (3); status quo (5).

2. How would you characterize Williams's DICTION? Explain the overall EFFECT of his word choices.

3. What does Williams mean by "Pyrrhic satisfaction" (par. 3)? Do you notice any other FIGURES OF SPEECH or ALLUSIONS that underscore his attitude toward students demanding safe spaces?

Suggestions for Writing

1. **FROM JOURNAL TO ESSAY**   Based on your journal entry, write an essay in which you narrate your experience (or, perhaps, experiences) with microaggression. As you plan and draft your essay, try to draw a larger point about the results of the experience(s) on your sense of fairness. What did you learn about yourself and the world around you?

2. Do some research on another issue related to free speech on campus. For example: Should schools adopt codes banning speech that might offend any group based on race, gender, ethnicity, religion, or sexual orientation? Should administrators have control over what students publish in school newspapers? Should instructors include "trigger warnings," or advance notice of potentially upsetting content, in their syllabi? What is the proposed Academic Bill of Rights, and how would its enactment affect the exchange of ideas on campus? Write an essay in which you give background information on the issue and support your own view in a well-reasoned argument.

3. **CRITICAL WRITING**   In an essay, EVALUATE Williams's argument. How truly does it resonate with your own experience? How persuasive do you find his reasoning? How well does he convince you of the threats posed by safe spaces? How well do you think he develops his proposed solution?

4. **CONNECTIONS**   On what points does Williams seem to agree with *Harper's* contributor Dawn Lundy Martin (p. 548)? On what points does he disagree? To what extent do the two writers' perspectives explain their difference of opinion? What are *your* thoughts on the issue they debate, and how does your own perspective influence your opinion? Answer these questions in an essay.

Thomas Chatterton Williams on Writing

Williams writes a weekly blog about living as an expatriate in Paris for *The American Scholar*. "Window Gazing," reprinted here, is his post from June 7, 2017. Sometimes, he suggests, the work of writing, and of reading, is best put aside for the sake of living.

Boarding the TGV[1] last Sunday in Nimes, I intended to spend the three-and-a-half-hour journey to Barcelona working — with any luck writing, or at the very least making progress on a slow-going book I've been reading.

[1] France's high-speed train service. —EDS.

Through a dry, sun-soaked landscape that turned overcast and wet, and rolling past a patchwork of vineyards in towns whose names seemed to belong more on a wine list than a map, I felt the familiar resistance. There is a short passage in [Jorge Luis] Borges's 1953 story "The South" that I often remember in such moments, whether in southern France or on an Amtrak wending up the Hudson Valley. In the story, Borges's protagonist, Dahlmann, leaves Buenos Aires for the pampas:

> When the train started off, he took down his valise and extracted, after some hesitation, the first volume of *The Thousand and One Nights*. . . . Along both sides of the train the city dissipated into suburbs; this sight, and then a view of the gardens and villas, delayed the beginning of his reading. The truth was that Dahlmann read very little. The magnetized mountain and the genie who swore to kill his benefactor are—who would deny it?—marvelous, but not so much more than the morning itself and the mere fact of being. The joy of life distracted him from paying attention to Scheherazade[2] and her superfluous miracles. Dahlmann closed his book and allowed himself to live.

There is so much to read and learn and *do*—and this will always be the case. We should welcome, then, a reminder that even the most ingenious thought and the most pressing questions fall apart in the face of the simple splendors unfurling outside our windows.

The Bedford Reader on Writing

As Williams attests, if our heads are always buried in a book or hidden behind a screen, we'll miss what's going on around us. Though of course it's important to read as a writer (see pp. 9–12), you can also DISCOVER great ideas for writing simply by living your life (see pp. 30–32). Don't forget to gaze out the window once in a while.

---

[2] Borges (1899–1986) was an Argentinian poet, novelist, and short-story writer. The title he refers to is a medieval collection of Middle Eastern and Indian folktales narrated by Scheherazade, a bride whose new husband (a king) has had each of his previous wives killed on their wedding night. She staves off her own execution by telling him stories but withholding their endings for a thousand and one nights, until he spares her life for good. —EDS.

SARAH HEMPHILL

Born in Rancho Mirage, California, in 1998, Sarah Hemphill grew up in nearby Desert Hot Springs, graduating from Palm Springs High School in 2016. As a student at California State University, Northridge, she studies speech-language pathology and serves as president of a campus libertarian club while working part time. Her interests include animals and the outdoors, history, politics, and travel.

What Happened to Free Speech on College Campuses?

Why are students seeking protections from "race trauma" and "microaggressions" in the first place? In this essay written in her first year of college and selected for *Waves*, CSU Northridge's annual collection of excellent student work, Hemphill challenges the notion that anyone should be shielded from potentially troubling or offensive speech. Looking past the question of "safe spaces" debated by Dawn Lundy Martin (p. 548) and Thomas Chatterton Williams (p. 553) in the previous two essays, she examines instead several related—and to her mind, disturbing—trends involving her peers' demands for safety.

Notice that Hemphill bases her argument on information and opinions gleaned from research, and so she cites her sources in the text of her essay and in a works-cited list at the end, following MLA style (see pp. 656–70 of the Appendix). Because her online sources have no page numbers to cite, she includes none in her citations.

Universities used to be bastions of free speech and the flow of ideas. 1 Students passionately fought for their right to not be silenced in regards to the most controversial of issues. Now, it seems as if the opposite is occurring: Students in general are in favor of limiting speech and establishing safe spaces on campuses, and many universities are actively discouraging free speech through their policies. This isn't progressive; this is regressive and isn't suitable at the university level, where students are supposed to be challenged by different views and ideas to foster critical thinking.

In 1964, the Free Speech Movement was founded at the University of 2 California, Berkeley. Students protested a ban on on-campus political activities, such as campaigning, gathering signatures, and handing out literature.

They also demanded that their rights to free speech and academic freedom be recognized. Thousands of students had witnessed Jack Weinberg being arrested for passing out civil rights literature on campus. As they "spontaneously chanted 'let him go,'" reports NPR correspondent Richard Gonzales, "the Free Speech Movement was ignited." That December, "a massive sit-in" resulted in the arrest of eight hundred students: Students were "pushed down the stairs, beat and kicked" by police (Gonzales). Several sit-ins and protests followed, with thousands of students from different political backgrounds, socialist to republican, participating with the unified goal of forever changing student activism on college campuses. Thanks to these passionate students, the movement was victorious and the university consequently ended all bans on political activity and free speech.

Today, however, many colleges and universities are once again barring   3 students from exercising free speech rights through policies that require permission to use them, in forms such as tabling or distributing literature on campus. Sometimes those rights are limited to "free speech zones," which are designated areas on campuses where students don't need permission to exercise their First Amendment rights. Cliff Maroney, Jr., a student activist and the director of Young Americans for Liberty, offers several examples:

> When rolling an inflated free-speech ball around campus, students at the University of Delaware were halted by campus police for their activities. A Young Americans for Liberty leader at Fairmont State University in West Virginia was confronted by security when he was attempting to speak with other students about his beliefs. A man at Clemson University was stopped from praying on campus because he was outside of the free-speech zone. And a student at Blinn College . . . [was told to] seek special permission to advocate for self-defense.

Universities have also instituted policies that ban certain types of speech, such as language that can be deemed discriminatory or offensive. However, these policies are often vague about what exactly falls under those categories. Anything a person might say can be taken as offensive by some, therefore making it dangerous for students to say anything controversial or of bad taste in the slightest.

Unfortunately, it seems that most college students aren't exactly opposed   4 to these anti-speech policies. In fact, "a large percentage of millennials . . . want the government to restrict certain types of speech that is protected by the First Amendment [and a] whopping forty percent of millennials think the government should be able to punish speech that is offensive to minority groups" (Barrows). Why have students, who once largely supported their right to speak about the most controversial topics, changed their minds?

A new culture of hypersensitivity to anything deemed offensive — whether it be a joke taken out of context; clothing, hair, or costumes that may not be from a student's own culture; or views that are not part of the mainstream — is to blame for students allowing these policies to take place. Anti-free speech policies have further inhibited students from hearing points of view that are different from their own. They have helped make students more sensitive, feeling "triggered" when they simply hear something they don't like or agree with. They have made students oppose free speech and demand further protections and safe spaces from words or behaviors they feel are offensive. As journalist Susan Milligan describes it, "the buzzwords of the antiwar students of the '60s — free speech, free love, and down with the 'Establishment' — have been replaced by phrases that make contemporary college life sound like a war zone. Safe spaces. Trigger warnings. Cultural appropriation."

Don't believe it? "Then why," as the *San Diego Union-Tribune* editorial 5 board asks,

> . . . did a feminist professor's essay about campus hypersensitivity lead to Northwestern graduate students trying to get the university punished . . .? Why are the University of California faculty told that statements such as "I believe the most qualified person should get the job" is a potentially traumatizing microaggression? Why are students on college campuses across America complaining about having to read novels with themes that "trigger" student discomfort — such as the violence and misogyny in F. Scott Fitzgerald's *The Great Gatsby*? Why are Harvard law students urging professors not to teach about laws relating to sexual violence and to not even use the word "violate"? ("Why")

This is all strong evidence of a culture in which students expect to be coddled and protected instead of exposed to different ideas or views, or even to things that may make them uncomfortable — which used to be an important part of education and personal growth at the university level.

Although this is a trend among most universities across the nation, not 6 all are conforming to the banning of speech and the establishment of safe spaces and trigger warnings. John Ellison, dean of students at The University of Chicago, wrote a welcome letter to members of the class of 2020 that went against college political correctness: "Our commitment to academic freedom means that we do not support so-called trigger warnings, we do not cancel invited speakers because their topics might prove controversial, and we do not condone the creation of intellectual 'safe spaces' where individuals can retreat from ideas and perspectives at odds with their own," he explained (qtd. in Pérez-Peña). Even President Obama did not condone this supposedly "progressive" movement. In a 2016 commencement speech he gave at Howard University, he condemned students trying to get universities to disinvite speakers with different views, advising them not to shut people out no matter how much they may disagree with them: "There's been a trend around the country of trying to get colleges to disinvite speakers with a different point of view, or disrupt a politician's rally," he commented. "Don't do that — no matter how ridiculous or offensive you might find the things that come out of their mouths" (qtd. in Pérez-Peña).

Because of anti-speech policies, safe spaces, and trigger warnings, college   7 students are not being prepared for the rigors and realities of the real world. The real world doesn't provide safe spaces or protections against offense. Universities are supposed to foster an environment that accepts the diversity of ideas and views so that students can become more aware of, not more sensitive to, different beliefs and so that they can understand why others hold them. Students should be able to engage in respectful discussion about controversial topics, instead of thinking they have the right to silence others if they don't agree with them. Students need to be able to question their own beliefs as well. All of this can sometimes lead to discomfort or anger, but in the end it fosters critical thinking and understanding.

Universities, especially public, taxpayer-funded ones, should have no   8 right to limit free speech or discourage ways of thinking that are not in line with the "status quo." They also should not be establishing safe spaces and trigger warnings to keep students "safe" from ideas that offend them. Doing so not only deprives students of the well-rounded education they deserve, but it also lets the future leaders of our nation think that it is acceptable to censor speech they don't like and, ultimately, to infringe on the Constitution and the core values our country was founded on. Continuing this way is not only a threat to the First Amendment, but to democracy itself.

Works Cited

Barrows, Katie. "Pew Report: Of All Age Groups, Millennials Most Favor Speech Restrictions." *FIRE*, Foundation for Individual Rights in Education, 25 Nov. 2015, www.thefire.org/pew-report-of-all-age-groups-millenials-most-favor-speech-restrictions/.

Gonzales, Richard. "Berkeley's Fight for Free Speech Fired Up Student Protest Movement." *Weekend Edition Sunday*, National Public Radio, 5 Oct. 2014, www.npr.org/2014/10/05/353849567/when-political-speech-was-banned-at-berkeley. Transcript.

Maloney, Cliff, Jr. "Colleges Have No Right to Limit Students' Free
    Speech." *Time*, 13 Oct. 2016, www.time.com/4530197/college-free-
    speech-zone/.

Milligan, Susan. "From Megaphones to Muzzles." *US News and World Report*,
    15 Nov. 2015, www.usnews.com/news/the-report/articles/2015/11/25/
    from-megaphones-to-muzzles-free-speech-safe-spaces-and-college-
    campuses.

Pérez-Peña, Richard. "University of Chicago Strikes Back Against Campus
    Political Correctness." *The New York Times*, 27 Aug. 2016, www.nytimes
    .com/2016/08/27/us/university-of-chicago-strikes-back-against-campus-
    political-correctness.html.

"Why 'Safe Spaces' Are Dangerous on College Campuses." *San Diego
    Union-Tribune*, 1 Sept. 2016, www.sandiegouniontribune.com/opinion/
    editorials/sdut-obama-college-campuses-and-free-speech-2016sep01-
    story.html. Editorial.

Journal Writing

"This is all strong evidence of a culture in which students expect to be coddled and protected instead of exposed to different ideas or views, or even to things that may make them uncomfortable—which used to be an important part of education and personal growth at the university level," Hemphill writes in paragraph 5. How do you respond to this characterization? Write in your journal about your thoughts on higher education—not necessarily what you see as the ideal learning environment, but rather why you think people go to college in the first place. What is the purpose of a college education? What do students hope to gain? What do they give up? What kinds of risks are they taking? To what extent is a college degree necessary for a happy, successful life? Base your entry on your observations and experiences.

Questions on Meaning

1. What seems to have prompted Hemphill to compose this essay? What does her opening paragraph reveal about her PURPOSE for writing?

2. What, according to Hemphill, is the common attitude among college students toward freedom of speech? What is Hemphill's own understanding of the First Amendment? What is yours?

3. How does Hemphill explain students' acceptance of, even demand for, policies limiting free speech on campus?

4. What is Hemphill's THESIS? Does she state her main idea anywhere, or is it implied?

Questions on Writing Strategy

1. What AUDIENCE probably would not like this essay? Why would they not like it?

2. Notice that Hemphill quotes several news articles as she makes her case for free speech. How does she use SOURCES to support her argument? What is the effect?

3. Where and how does Hemphill address objections or opposing arguments? Do you find her strategy of counterargument effective? Why, or why not?

4. Hemphill's overall argument relies on a SYLLOGISM. Express the author's major premise, minor premise, and conclusion in your own words. Is her reasoning valid, in your opinion?

5. **OTHER METHODS**   What role does CAUSE-AND-EFFECT analysis play in the essay?

Questions on Language

1. What are free-speech zones (par. 3)? safe spaces (4)? trigger warnings (4)? cultural appropriations (4)? microaggressions (5)? From what discipline or disciplines does Hemphill seem to pick up this JARGON? Is it necessary to understand the meaning of such phrases to follow her point?

2. How would you characterize Hemphill's DICTION? What does it contribute to (or take away from) her TONE?

3. Use a dictionary if necessary to help you define any of the following words: bastions, progressive, regressive, foster (par. 1); consequently (2); hypersensitivity, inhibited (4); misogyny, coddled (5); condone, disinvite (6); rigors (7); status quo, infringe (8).

Suggestions for Writing

1. **FROM JOURNAL TO ESSAY**   Using your journal writing as a starting point, write an essay that presents a detailed view of the function of a college education in contemporary society. Refer to specific examples from your experience as appropriate. If you wish, use your observations and reflections to make a point about who should (or should not) go to college, and why.

2. Does your school provide "safe spaces" (par. 1) or limit political discourse on campus to "free speech zones" (3)? Are such policies as common as Hemphill suggests? Using the Internet, research the current state of speech codes on campus, both at your current institution and at a small sampling of other colleges and universities in the United States. In an essay, summarize the content of such codes, which may include definitions of offensive language, harassment policies, or lists of penalties for noncompliance. Then discuss whether you approve or disapprove of the implementation of speech codes in college settings. Do you feel they infringe on individuals' First Amendment rights, for instance, or do you think they're a necessary tool in protecting the rights of minority students? Or perhaps your opinion lies somewhere in between the two extremes. (You may need to narrow your discussion to a particular aspect of the codes you investigate.)

3. **CRITICAL WRITING**   Respond to Hemphill's argument. How sufficient do you find her evidence? How persuaded are you by her reasoning? Do you agree with her that campus policies allowing for sites such as safe spaces and free-speech zones rob students of their First Amendment rights, or do you believe that putting restrictions on potentially upsetting or offensive speech brings positive effects for students and society? Why? Begin your response by ANALYZING Hemphill's argument, and then present your own.

4. **CONNECTIONS**   In the previous two essays, "Weary Oracle" (p. 548) and "Blanket Security" (p. 553), Dawn Lundy Martin and Thomas Chatterton Williams debate the need for safe spaces, one particular form of the college protections Sarah Hemphill opposes. How might Martin and Williams respond to Hemphill's attitude toward other students and their embrace of "anti-speech policies" (par. 4)? How do you respond? In an essay, bring these three writers together, considering what they have in common as well as what they do not.

Sarah Hemphill on Writing

We asked Sarah Hemphill what advice she would offer to other college writers. In comments prepared especially for *The Bedford Reader,* she stresses the importance of taking your time and keeping an open mind as you write.

While it may be common for students to write a paper a few days or even the night before it is due, a speedily written paper will never be as great as one that has more time devoted to it. It has been my experience that a writer's best work will often entail weeks or even months of researching, drafting, writing, and revising.

In addition to giving yourself ample time to write, drafting in an outline form can be helpful. After I have thought about and researched a subject, I produce an outline with a bullet point for each paragraph's topic and subpoints for items or arguments I will address in support. I also include notes on works I found while researching that I may want to cite to support my thesis. Such an outline can be used as a tool to guide you when you start writing, and is usually not set in stone. During the writing process, I have found, you will add new ideas and more supporting evidence as you go. This is why it can be good to not limit yourself to a thesis before writing, but instead to finalize your thesis after you finish.

For revision, I always seek others to read my work and offer their advice, whether it be writing tutors at my university, my professors, or other students. Other readers can catch mistakes or make observations about your paper you may not have noticed. For instance, I tend to write sentences that sound good to me but that readers will say are too long and wordy. Getting feedback will give you an audience's perspective and immensely improve the way you write.

My last piece of advice is to choose a subject you're passionate about, if possible. It makes the writing process much easier and more enjoyable. All of my best works have been about subjects I am interested in or have strong opinions about. Even if the focus is controversial, like it was for my essay about free speech on campus, don't be afraid to put your thoughts on paper. The result may turn out to be your best work, and it might even be featured in a publication like *The Bedford Reader.*

The Bedford Reader on Writing

Hemphill echoes our own advice to student writers, especially about taking the time to research (pp. 648–51), organize (pp. 36–38), and revise (pp. 41–45) a draft "as you go," and saving the thesis (pp. 34–35 and 43) for last when it makes sense to do so. For guidelines on how to seek and use the help of reviewers, especially to catch problems with your writing, refer to pages 50–51 of Chapter 3.

ADDITIONAL WRITING TOPICS

Argument and Persuasion

1. Write a persuasive essay in which you express a deeply felt opinion. In it, address a particular person or audience. For instance, you might direct your essay to any of the following readers:

   A friend unwilling to attend a ballet performance (or a car race) with you on the grounds that such an event is a waste of time

   A teacher who asserts that the prevalence of texting has led to a decline in students' writing skills

   A developer who plans to tear down a historic building

   Someone who sees no purpose in studying a foreign language

   A high-school class whose members don't want to commit to public service

   An older generation insistent on the value of home ownership

   A skeptic who asserts that religion is a leading cause of violence

   The members of a community organization who want to ban pit bulls or another breed of dog

2. Write a letter to your campus newspaper or a city newspaper in which you argue for or against a certain cause or view. You may wish to object to a particular feature or editorial in the paper. Send your letter and see if it is published.

3. Write a short letter to your congressional or state representative, arguing in favor of (or against) the passage of some pending legislation. Look in a news magazine or a newspaper for a worthwhile bill to write about. Or else write in favor of some continuing cause: for instance, requiring (or not requiring) cities to provide shelter for homeless people, reducing (or increasing) military spending, providing (or refusing) aid to the arts, solving (or ignoring) income inequality.

4. Write an essay arguing that something you feel strongly about should be changed, removed, abolished, enforced, repealed, revised, reinstated, or reconsidered. Be sure to propose some plan for carrying out whatever suggestions you make. Possible topics, listed to start you thinking, are these:

   Drug laws
   Unpaid internships
   Women in combat
   Police brutality
   Graffiti
   Fraternities and sororities
   Genetically modified organisms (GMOs) in food
   Public transportation

PART THREE

MIXING THE METHODS

Throughout this book, we have tried to prove how flexible the methods of development are. All the preceding selections offer superb examples of DEFINITION or CLASSIFICATION or ARGUMENT, but every one illustrates other methods, too — DESCRIPTION in PROCESS ANALYSIS, NARRATION in COMPARISON, ANALYSIS and EXAMPLES in CAUSE AND EFFECT.

In this part of the book, we take this point even further by presenting a collection of readings that share a significant feature: All the authors draw on whatever methods of development, at whatever length, will help them achieve their PURPOSES. To show how the writers combine methods, we highlight the most significant ones in the notes preceding each essay.

You have already begun to command the methods by focusing on them individually, making each a part of your kit of writing tools. Now, when you face a writing assignment, you can consider whether and how each method may help you sharpen your focus, develop your ideas, and achieve your aim. Indeed, one way to approach a subject is to apply each method to it, one by one. The following list offers a set of questions that you can ask about any subject.

- **Narration:** Can you tell a story about the subject?
- **Description:** Can you use your senses to illuminate the subject?
- **Example:** Can you point to instances that will make the subject concrete and specific?
- **Comparison and contrast:** Will setting the subject alongside another one generate useful information?
- **Process analysis:** Will a step-by-step explanation of how the subject works add to readers' understanding?
- **Division or analysis:** Can slicing the subject into parts produce a clearer vision of it?
- **Classification:** Is it worthwhile to sort the subject into kinds or groups?
- **Cause and effect:** Does it help to ask why something happened or what its results are?
- **Definition:** Can you trace boundaries that will clarify the meaning of the subject?
- **Argument and persuasion:** Can you back up an opinion or make a proposal about the subject?

Rarely will every one of these questions produce fruit for a given essay, but inevitably some will. Try the whole list when you're stuck at the beginning of an assignment or when you're snagged in the middle of a draft. You'll find the questions are as good at removing obstacles as they are at generating ideas.

JOAN DIDION

A legendary writer whose fame is fourfold—as novelist, essayist, journalist, and screenwriter—Joan Didion was born in 1934 in California, where her family had lived for five generations. After graduating from the University of California, Berkeley, she spent a few years in New York, working as a feature editor for the fashion magazine *Vogue*. Didion gained wide notice in the 1960s and 1970s with the publication of the essay collections *Slouching towards Bethlehem* (1968) and *The White Album* (1979), followed by several additional collections, most recently *We Tell Ourselves Stories in Order to Live* (2006). *Salvador* (1983), her book-length reporting on a visit to war-torn El Salvador, and *Miami* (1987), a study of Cuban exiles in Florida, also received close attention. Didion has published five novels: *Run River* (1963), *Play It as It Lays* (1971), *A Book of Common Prayer* (1977), *Democracy* (1984), and *The Last Thing He Wanted* (1996). With her late husband, John Gregory Dunne, she coauthored a number of screenplays, notably for *A Star Is Born* (1976), *True Confessions* (1981), and *Up Close and Personal* (1996). Her latest books are *The Year of Magical Thinking* (2005), an examination of her reactions to Dunne's sudden death; *Blue Nights* (2011), an emotional memoir of losing their adult daughter after an extended illness; and *South and West* (2017), selected excerpts from two of her travel notebooks. Over the span of her career Didion has been recognized with several major awards, among them the National Book Award (2005) and the National Book Foundation's Medal for Distinguished Contribution to American Letters (2007). In 2013 she was honored with the National Medal of Arts and the PEN Center USA's Lifetime Achievement Award.

Earthquakes

Long a resident of California, Didion knows firsthand the experience of earthquakes and the peculiar blend of dread and denial with which most Californians view seismic catastrophe. This piece is a self-contained excerpt from a longer essay, "Los Angeles Days," that appeared first in 1988 in *The New Yorker* and then in Didion's collection *After Henry* (1992).

"Earthquakes" relies on a range of methods to depict the attitudes of Didion herself and of her fellow Californians toward "the Big One":

Narration (Chap. 5): paragraphs 1, 2–7, 8, 9
Description (Chap. 6): paragraphs 1, 2–7, 9
Example (Chap. 7): paragraphs 1, 2–7, 8, 9
Process analysis (Chap. 9): paragraph 2
Cause and effect (Chap. 12): paragraphs 1, 7, 8, 9
Definition (Chap. 13): paragraphs 1, 8, 9

We have annotated the essay to map out Didion's masterful mix of these methods.

During one of the summer weeks I spent in Los Angeles in
1988 there was a cluster of small earthquakes, the most noticeable of which, on the Garlock Fault, a major lateral-slip fracture
that intersects the San Andreas in the Tehachapi range north
of Los Angeles, occurred at six minutes after four on a Friday
afternoon when I happened to be driving in Wilshire Boulevard
from the beach. People brought up to believe that the phrase
terra firma[1] has real meaning often find it hard to understand
the apparent equanimity with which earthquakes are accom-
modated in California, and tend to write it off as regional
spaciness. In fact it is less equanimity than protective detachment, the useful adjustment commonly made in circumstances
so unthinkable that psychic survival precludes preparation.
I know very few people in California who actually set aside, as
instructed, a week's supply of water and food. I know fewer still
who could actually lay hands on the wrench required to turn
off, as instructed, the main gas valve; the scenario in which this
wrench will be needed is a catastrophe, and something in the
human spirit rejects planning on a daily basis for catastrophe.
I once interviewed, in the late sixties, someone who did prepare:
a Pentecostal minister who had received a kind of heavenly
earthquake advisory, and on its quite specific instructions was
moving his congregation from Port Hueneme, north of Los
Angeles, to Murfreesboro, Tennessee. A few months later, when
a small earthquake was felt not in Port Hueneme but in Murfreesboro, an event so novel that it was reported nationally, I
was, I recall, mildly gratified.

A certain fatalism comes into play. When the ground starts
moving all bets are off. Quantification, which in this case takes
the form of guessing where the movement at hand will rank on
the Richter scale, remains a favored way of regaining the illusion of personal control, and people still crouched in the nearest
doorjamb will reach for a telephone and try to call Caltech, in
Pasadena, for a Richter reading. "Rock and roll," the DJ said
on my car radio that Friday afternoon at six minutes past four.
"This console is definitely shaking . . . no word from Pasadena
yet, is there?"

"I would say this is a three," the DJ's colleague said.

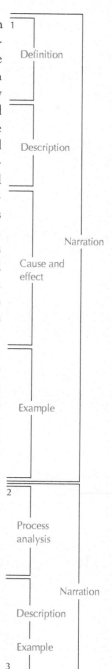

Definition

Description

Narration

Cause and
effect

Example

1

2

Process
analysis

Narration

Description

Example

3

---

[1] Latin, "solid earth." —EDS.

"Definitely a three, maybe I would say a little higher than 4
a three."

"Say an eight . . . just joking." 5

"It felt like a six where I was." 6

What it turned out to be was a five-two, followed by a 7
dozen smaller after-shocks, and it had knocked out four of the
six circuit breakers at the A. D. Edmonston pumping plant on
the California Aqueduct, temporarily shutting down the flow of
Northern California water over the Tehachapi range and cutting off half of Southern California's water supply for the weekend. This was all within the range not only of the predictable
but of the normal. No one had been killed or seriously injured.
There was plenty of water for the weekend in the system's four
southern reservoirs, Pyramid, Castaic, Silverwood, and Perris
lakes. A five-two earthquake is not, in California, where the
movements people remember tend to have Richter numbers well
over six, a major event, and the probability of earthquakes like
this one had in fact been built into the aqueduct: The decision
to pump the water nineteen hundred feet over the Tehachapi
was made precisely because the aqueduct's engineers rejected
the idea of tunneling through an area so geologically complex,
periodically wrenched by opposing displacements along the San
Andreas and the Garlock, that it has been called California's
structural knot.

Still, this particular five-two, coming as it did when what 8
Californians call "the Big One" was pretty much overdue (the
Big One is the eight, the Big One is the seven in the wrong
place or at the wrong time, the Big One could even be the
six-five centered near downtown Los Angeles at nine on a
weekday morning), made people a little uneasy. There was
some concern through the weekend that this was not merely
an ordinary five-two but a "foreshock," an earthquake prefig-
uring a larger event (the chances of this, according to Caltech
seismologists, run about one in twenty), and by Sunday there
was what seemed to many people a sinister amount of activity
on other faults: a three-four just east of Ontario at twenty-two
minutes past two in the afternoon, a three-six twenty-two
minutes later at Lake Berryessa, and, four hours and one minute later, northeast of San Jose, a five-five on the Calaveras
Fault. On Monday, there was a two-three in Playa del Rey and
a three in Santa Barbara.

Description

Example

Narration

Cause and
effect

Definition

Narration

Cause and
effect

Example

Had it not been for the five-two on Friday, very few peo- 9
ple would have registered these little quakes (the Caltech
seismological monitors in Southern California normally
record from twenty to thirty earthquakes a day with magnitudes below three), and in the end nothing came of them,
but this time people did register them, and they lent a certain moral gravity to the way the city happened to look that
weekend, a temporal dimension to the hard white edges and
empty golden light. At odd moments during the next few
days people would suddenly clutch at tables, or walls. "Is it
going," they would say, or "I think it's moving." They almost
always said *it*, and what they meant by *it* was not just the
ground but the world as they knew it. I have lived all my life
with the promise of the Big One, but when it starts going
now even I get the jitters.

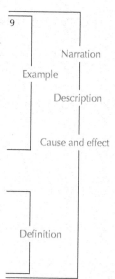

Narration

Example

Description

Cause and effect

Definition

Journal Writing

What potential threat or threats in your life most give you "the jitters"? Write a journal entry exploring your specific worries.

Questions on Meaning

1. What does Didion mean by "protective detachment" in referring to Californians'
   attitude toward earthquakes (par. 1)?

2. How, according to Didion, do Californians maintain the illusion of personal
   control during earthquakes?

3. Why was the earthquake Didion writes about a cause of special concern, even
   though it was not a major disturbance?

4. What is the ultimate threat of "the Big One"? Why does its possibility give
   Didion "the jitters" (par. 9)?

Questions on Writing Strategy

1. Why in paragraphs 1 and 8 is Didion so specific about the times of the earthquakes?

2. How does Didion use IRONY in paragraph 1?

3. Why do you suppose Didion quotes the on-air conversation between the radio DJ and his associate in paragraphs 2–6?

4. **MIXED METHODS**   What other method does Didion use in paragraph 8 to DEFINE "the Big One"?

5. **MIXED METHODS**   What CAUSE-AND-EFFECT relationship does Didion explore in paragraph 9?

Questions on Language

1. What is the effect of Didion's use of "as instructed" twice in the middle of paragraph 1?

2. Throughout the essay Didion refers to specific Richter-scale numbers when describing earthquakes. Why does she do so?

3. What does Didion mean by the phrase "temporal dimension" in paragraph 9? What does *temporal* mean?

4. Check a dictionary if any of the following are unfamiliar to you: equanimity, precludes, scenario (par. 1); fatalism (2); displacements (7); seismologists (8); magnitudes (9).

Suggestions for Writing

1. **FROM JOURNAL TO ESSAY**   Expand your journal entry into an essay in which you explore your concerns about a potential threat in your life. What has led you to feel the way you do? Do you think many other people share your concern? How do you cope with your feelings? What might you do if the threat became real?

2. Do some research about the incidence and probability of earthquakes in the United States. (A good starting point would be the Geologic Hazards Team of the US Geological Survey: *geohazards.usgs.gov*.) Is California the only state vulnerable to earthquakes? (The answer may surprise you.) What kinds of damage and loss of life have been caused by earthquakes in this country? Write a report about earthquakes in which you answer these questions and others that interest you.

3. **CRITICAL WRITING**   Didion is noted for a distinctive STYLE of writing. In an essay, ANALYZE her style in "Earthquakes." What seems notable about the words Didion chooses and the ways she structures her sentences? What is her TONE? What does her style say about her? How do you respond to it?

4. **CONNECTIONS**   In "At Risk" (p. 212), Jourdan Imani Keith also considers dangers along the north Pacific coastline. Write an essay that COMPARES AND CONTRASTS Didion's and Keith's essays. How are the authors' assumptions, conclusions, self-presentations, and attitudes toward natural catastrophe similar and different?

5. **CONNECTIONS**   Like that in "Earthquakes," Didion's reporting often involves herself as part of the story. In "Live Free and Starve" (p. 437) Chitra Divakaruni is also involved in the situation she reports. Write an essay that considers how the presence of the writer affects each essay. How would the essays be different if they had been written from a completely OBJECTIVE perspective?

Joan Didion on Writing

In "Why I Write," an essay published by the *New York Times Book Review,* adapted from her Regents' Lecture at the University of California at Berkeley, Joan Didion writes, "I stole the title for this talk, from George Orwell. One reason I stole it was that I like the sound of the words: Why I Write. There you have three short unambiguous words that share a sound, and the sound they share is this:

I

I

I

In many ways writing is the act of saying *I*, of imposing oneself upon other people, of saying *listen to me, see it my way, change your mind.* . . ."

Didion's "way," though, comes not from notions of how the world works or should work but from its observable details. She writes, "I am not in the least an intellectual, which is not to say that when I hear the word 'intellectual' I reach for my gun, but only to say that I do not think in abstracts. During the years when I was an undergraduate at Berkeley I tried, with a kind of hopeless late-adolescent energy, to buy some temporary visa into the world of ideas, to forge for myself a mind that could deal with the abstract. . . . In short, I tried to think. I failed. My attention veered inexorably back to the specific, to the tangible, to what was generally considered, by everyone I knew then and for that matter have known since, the peripheral. I would try to contemplate the Hegelian dialectic and would find myself concentrating instead on the flowering pear tree outside my window and the particular way the petals fell on my floor."

Later in the essay, Didion writes, "During those years I was traveling on what I knew to be a very shaky passport, forged papers: I knew that I was no legitimate resident in any world of ideas. I knew I couldn't think. All I knew then was what I wasn't, and it took me some years to discover what I was.

"Which was a writer.

"By which I mean not a 'good' writer or a 'bad' writer but simply a writer, a person whose most absorbed and passionate hours are spent arranging words on pieces of paper. Had my credentials been in order I would never have become a writer. Had I been blessed with even limited access to my own mind there would have been no reason to write. I write entirely to find out what I'm thinking, what I'm looking at, what I see, and what it means. What I want and what I fear. . . . *What is going on in these pictures in my mind?*"

In the essay, Didion emphasizes that these mental pictures have a grammar. "Grammar is a piano I play by ear, since I seem to have been out of school the year the rules were mentioned. All I know about grammar is its infinite power. To shift the structure of a sentence alters the meaning of that sentence, as definitely and inflexibly as the position of a camera alters the meaning of the object photographed. Many people know about camera angles now, but not so many know about sentences. The arrangement of the words matters, and the arrangement you want can be found in the picture in your mind. The picture dictates the arrangement. The picture dictates whether this will be a sentence with or without clauses, a sentence that ends hard or a dying-fall sentence, long or short, active or passive. The picture tells you how to arrange the words and the arrangement of the words tells you, or tells me, what's going on in the picture."

The Bedford Reader on Writing

Didion writes, she says, to make sense of her observations and to learn what she thinks. That is, she doesn't start with a THESIS but works her way into it, as we suggest you try when you draft your own essays (see pp. 30–36). For quick guidelines on how to harness the "infinite power" of grammar and sentences for yourself, turn to Chapter 4 on Editing (pp. 55–64).

LOUISE ERDRICH

Known mainly for her fiction, Louise Erdrich has been called "a sorceress with language" for her unusual, lyrical prose. Part Chippewa Indian and part German American, she was born in 1954 and raised in North Dakota. Her parents worked at the Bureau of Indian Affairs boarding school that she attended. Erdrich graduated from Dartmouth College (BA, 1976) and in 1979 received an MA degree in creative writing from Johns Hopkins University. Beginning in 1984 with the hugely successful *Love Medicine,* she wrote a series of intercon-nected novels that follow generations of Chippewa families in North Dakota; the other volumes are *The Beet Queen* (1986), *Tracks* (1988), and *The Bingo Palace* (1994). An avalanche of best-selling and award-winning novels has followed, among them *The Plague of Doves* (2008), nominated for a Pulitzer Prize; *The Round House* (2012), winner of the National Book Award; *LaRose* (2016), winner of the National Book Critic's Circle Award; and *Future Home of the Living God* (2017), a *New York Times* Notable Book. Her publications also include three volumes of poetry, a collection of short stories, a memoir, a nonfiction study of Ojibwe history and culture, and a series of children's books. A mother of six, Erdrich lives with her daughters in Minneapolis, Minnesota, where she owns Birchbark Books, an independent bookstore featuring native arts and jewelry.

The Crest

Erdrich structures many of her novels by stitching together a series of stand-alone stories told from multiple points of view into a coherent whole, a tech-nique that has earned the author praise from critics and fans alike. The tale we present here originally appeared, in slightly different form, in Erdrich's novel *Tales of Burning Love* (1996), a study of the fictional contractor Jack Mauser and his five failed marriages; it was later presented as a short story collected in *The Red Convertible: Selected and New Stories* (2009).

On the whole a narrative, "The Crest" draws on every other method of development to reveal the depths of its protagonist's character and pull readers through a destructive episode of his third divorce:

Narration (Chap. 5): throughout
Description (Chap. 6): paragraphs 1–3, 5, 10, 49, 53–54, 58
Example (Chap. 7): paragraphs 20–25, 55, 58
Comparison and contrast (Chap. 8): paragraphs 11–19
Process analysis (Chap. 9): paragraphs 8, 19, 29–36
Division or analysis (Chap. 10): paragraphs 9, 55
Cause and effect (Chap. 12): paragraphs 4–5, 7, 9, 49–57

Definition (Chap. 13): paragraph 58
Argument and persuasion (Chap. 14): paragraphs 20–29, 37–50

Jack's hands were deep in the oiled workings of his uncle's planting attach- 1
ment, a piece of farm equipment they were fixing together, as they always
fixed things, with bread ties and duct tape and spit and sometimes the right
bolt or screw. It was August, not the dog days of heat, but clear and cool. Jack
was now on his third wife and although he was losing Candice—at that very
moment probably, she was with a lawyer, his lawyer, he didn't tend to think
about her at all. *She thinks enough about herself for the two of us,* he'd told his
uncle Chuck, weary. Soon, she'd be gone. He couldn't seem to keep a woman.

"The hell!" Chuck delicately fiddled with some flattened threads he'd 2
forced. "I don't think this is gonna work."

The two men were lying on purple plastic toboggans from Kmart, sliding 3
themselves up and down underneath the bellies of various machines in a hot
orange quonset garage. Sweat and grease coated Jack's neck, plus a dusting of
grit, but it all felt good. He had always liked the fixing and the tinkering, but
not the winter paperwork, the sowing, frantic harvesting, the dependence on
weather. He hadn't liked the money, either. Lousy once the payments on the
big equipment were made. Farming made him think of getting away from it.
He thought he should return to the construction site. Just wanted to see his
uncle. As usual he'd come to visit and got caught up in a small endless job the
way he always did with Chuck.

Chuck stared at him with a pulled-long expression, but then sighed and 4
said so long. *Get the hell out of here. Go play trucks.* Jack wanted to tell him
that moment, right there, about the development and the land, but he just
couldn't. A few years back when dirt was still cheap and Chuck had got in
over his means, Jack had bought out his quarter section just west of Fargo.
He'd leased it back, and Chuck Mauser had put all that acreage into flowers.
Sunflowers. They were now in bloom. Tomorrow, Jack would draw his first
payment on the line of credit he'd been finessing and politicking and begging
after for so many years. The bank had come through. He would have to tell
Chuck that those fields would soon be a subdivision—a good one, *unique and
high quality,* he thought of saying, as though that would matter.

The next morning, early, Jack accepted the bank check, stiff and clean 5
in its plain white envelope. He pinched it in his fingers, lifted it to his face,
and inhaled the sharp odor of the ink and paper. But then—and this offhand
decision was the one that affected his life for the next two years—he did
not deposit the check. No, instead of securing it immediately, Jack kept the

envelope in his hands and walked out the doors of heavy glass and polished steel. He went to his car. He put the envelope on the dashboard and laid his fingers on the cool paper.

Jack drove back out to Chuck's place with the white rectangle of the 6 envelope reflecting into the windshield. As he drove along, houses popping up to either side, new ones, his beliefs were easy, his thoughts simple: *I am the luckiest of lucky sons of bitches.* He had formed an idea, a plan, and he saw now that it was going to work. Jack Mauser was going to put something big into operation.

Mauser & Mauser, Construction. Jack twice. He had doubled his name 7 because he thought it looked more stable, as though there were generations involved. But there was no other Mauser, no partner, just him. Over the years, he had built up the cash, crews, and equipment, by himself, from noth-ing, from a secondhand Cat and a couple of boys who couldn't get their high school diplomas. He'd had luck, but his main secret was he worked everybody just as brutally as he worked himself. Plus, he could crawl and connive with the best and worst. Jack had patched together his own company by scraping money off the cash edifice, the limestone façades of banks. He knew how to wear a suit jacket and a tie, how to shake hands and look a banker in the eye and promise on a schedule he had no hope of meeting, but did anyway, or almost, by killing his crews. And the very last secret of his success — he always paid his best subcontractors just enough of what he owed to keep them working for him on the next job. Keep them hooked in, keep them work-ing alongside him, but never let them get too far away. He never paid any-one entirely, never evened up his accounts. Contractors didn't do that sort of thing, Jack's thought was, while they were alive at least. He kept a keen balance of debt and walked the knife's edge. Of course, he was running low now. Some, the best, wouldn't work with him. Still there were always others to take their places, always would be.

Jack had barged through doors of black glass, through the tinted lobbies, 8 over wheat rich carpet, over sugar-beet wealth and desks of polished oak bought off the interest on loans to sunflower farmers like Chuck. He went in with the grit of digging septic systems under his nails and he came out, time after time, with that dirt turned miraculously paper crisp and green. Every day was a ground-floor day for Jack. The local boom was just beginning. There was an interstate to build. Local crews got hired on by the government. Jack didn't bid too high and didn't bid too low, and he held where proper, a knack he had learned at the keno tables.

All that hustling, and now he had this. Too much, almost. In the middle 9 of his biggest road construction project to date, a highway by-pass, his loan came through. Huge draw, first draw on the biggest sum of money he'd ever landed. The check. More zeros in a string than he'd ever seen. *And here he was*, Jack faltered. *Here I am.* He was about to think *in Fargo*, but instead he thought an *Indian*. That part of his background was like a secret joke he had on everyone. His crews. His banker. Asshole clients. Even his own wives. He'd thought, strangely sometimes, when walking through those bank lobby doors, *the hell with all of you. Your doors would swing the other way if you knew who I was!* But who did? He was a mixed-blood with dark eyes and dark hair and a big father and a crazy mother. He never thought of her. Or him, either. Both eaten up by time.

Jack turned down a dirt road between two of his fields, parked, opened the 10 car's windows, and let in the day of perfect sunflowers. Their leaves brushed in the still air, dollar bills in a vault of blue sky. Their fat chock-full faces, surrounded by petals, reminded Jack of legions of rich women in fancy hats. He sank back in the warm seat, let the sun shine hard, stretched, and yawned until his nerves hummed. Cannons popped, set to go off on small timers so the ravenous swirls of blackbirds wouldn't land. Chuck Mauser had tied balloons to his fences, too, and painted them with eyes to look like owls. The fields looked jolly, circus bright, and of course the blackbirds weren't the least afraid. Jack could hear them pecking, flapping, talking, feeding noisily and full of joy.

Chuck Mauser happened by, stopped his truck when he saw Jack. Jack 11 stepped out of the car, walked with his uncle into the field, and then the two men stood together moving clods of dirt back and forth with the toes of their boots. Jack was uncomfortable. His face burned. There was a buzzing in his ears. He thought about getting underneath the seeder again, trying to fix that fuel pump in the old John Deere or goof with the new Steiger, figure it out a little, but more than that he wanted a drink. So Jack and his uncle talked about the crop, the value, weather, and then Jack told Chuck that his first draw was through, showed him the check.

Chuck did not look pleased. He did not in fact look at Jack at all. He just 12 stared over the bright blank flowers. Jack hadn't thought exactly what his good fortune meant for his uncle, but now he grew irritated at Chuck's lack of interest. The truth was, Chuck Mauser only had those fields on a lease which was up four months ago. Chuck knew and had agreed on what was coming. Naturally, Jack intended to let him work the fields until he broke ground next month. A farmer had to obtain his yield, of course. But those fields were the first open land past the last mall, between the DollarSave and Nowhere. Any fool could have figured.

Jack's uncle narrowed his gaze and screwed his mouth sour, scratched his 13 chin. He had a bad shave, all nicked. But he had the guts to bring up the subject.

"So, you're putting in what, a new development?" 14

Jack nodded. Chuck nodded. The two men stood at the edge of the field 15
nodding with the nodding heads of sunflowers. They were posed in a vast
surround of serene and unthinking agreement, but each harbored different
thoughts. The farmer looked keenly into his own distance and said:

"These are good fields. Rich dirt. Too bad." 16

Jack took a step back, swayed, put his thumbs in his belt. 17

"Location, location, location," he mumbled. 18

Looking down at the ground, they both saw money. But Chuck thought 19
of rain, too. He looked up the way a farmer looks into the sky—not to see the
weekend ahead but to see his whole future. Just a slow rain, a soaking rain,
a careful rain, no hail. Please no hail to beat the flowers flat. All right? Just
water. Jack thought of water, too. Well water, for instance. However, it did
not occur to Jack that just to drill his wells through that lush crust of black
dirt, to suck the sinking aquifer into his faucets and underground sprinkling
systems and to pipe it through his showerheads and into his dishwashers, was
a temporary luxury that would last only as long as the water down there did.
Water dries up. Topsoil blows off. Trees topple. Land lasts, but of the two only
the farmer knew how easily it can turn against you. Since the Ojibwe part of
Jack was inaccessible, he was a German with a trapdoor in his soul, an inner
life still hidden to him. Both men saw money when they looked at land. It
was just that they saw the fields delivering the wealth in different ways. As
dead, as alive, as more and as less autonomous or powerful.

"You'll get a lot of money from this crop," Jack went on, "it's a bumper. 20
You'll buy a big damn house right at the end of this cul-de-sac." He smashed
his foot against a chunk of topsoil. "We'll build it here. Every one of your
grandkids will have their own room. Your wife will have a dream kitchen."

"I don't have a wife," Chuck reminded Jack. "Your aunt won't come back. 21
Women ditch us."

There was an underlying implication. *They ditch us the way you ditched* 22
me, Jack. But Jack felt no guilt toward his uncle. Only irritation. He never
said he'd be a dirt farmer, had he? Never so much as hinted!

"Your grandkids will cook, then," Jack laughed, shrugging off Chuck's 23
malice and loss. "We'll make everything the right height, their bathrooms,
the dish sink, whatever, so they won't have to always stand on stools."

"Kids grow," Chuck said. 24

"Bless 'em," Jack agreed, but there was a note in his voice, a mean little 25
edge, and Chuck stopped talking, shifted nervously. They stood in silence
and then Chuck Mauser, the dirt farmer, gathered himself. His voice grated,
almost shaking in low rage at the sky, at the horizon, at the creeping façades
of the edge of Fargo.

"The more you fill it up the emptier it gets." 26

Jack stepped back another foot or so.   27

"People have to live somewhere," Jack said, and he managed to keep his 28
voice mild enough, but inside he was setting to boil. He and his uncle were
too much alike, maybe. Candice, deep into the pop psychology she used on
her patients, had counseled Jack to memorize a trick that would help him
keep his temper when he was in that no-man's-land between feeling normal
and letting go. She told Jack to mentally image a wire cage, to visualize himself putting up the chain-link, and then to get right inside the damn thing
like an animal. She told him that he could pace inside the cage, he could
go wild, he could let off his steam as though he had just been captured in a
jungle. The only thing was he had to stay in the cage, not jump the fence, not
ever let himself out.

Jack was not ready to do that. He got into his car, backed out and drove 29
away without saying good-bye. His stomach was turning over with the frustration of it all, because he wanted to celebrate, to raise the roof with someone, not deal with a farmer's problems, a farm boy's mistakes. He tried to
step back, unheat, look at life through his uncle's glasses. The man probably
needed those fields to get himself over the edge, he probably felt like shit
when he thought of a new house that he never could afford in this life anyway, in this world, and Jack had pushed it in his face. He didn't look back.
He drove to town and wished he could get Candy and go to their favorite
bar, which was called The Library, but Candy had probably by now left the
lawyer's office and was in a real library. She was back in school taking another
class on some new dental technique that she said would stop pain with little
electric jolts.

I want some of those, thought Jack, or maybe that drink.   30

Jack drove past the bar, then doubled back, pulled into the lot, went in, 31
and sat down. The room was dim and calm, the talk quiet. No music played,
no pool balls clicked, the television was a muted natter. It was only eleven
o'clock.

He ordered and drank two beers. Ate a hamburger. Two beers more. He 32
considered what next — go back to the office, the bank, or the current work
site. There was plenty of work pending, pressure, hordes of details, but he felt
that this day should be experienced differently, out of time, out of his regular life's routine. The more he thought about it in the quiet of the morning
tavern the more it seemed unfair. He recalled the hard work he'd done and
anticipated all of the work that was in store, and with that in mind he felt
righteous about enjoying the zeros on the first draw check he held against his
chest within his inside pocket. He thought of driving to the lakes, fishing, eating out, taking simple enjoyment in the cash, the fat roll he'd taken out of his
account against the big deposit he would feed it later on.

"I should I should," he muttered to himself, tapping the ashtray with 33 the plastic rapier that had held his hamburger together. "I should go back to work," he said decisively, and then instead, as the waitress approached, he ordered his fifth beer.

The fifth was the one that always sent Jack. He weighed 210. He could 34 handle four and then he'd skate in the sky. He promised, as he poured the Blue Ribbon, that this was his last little gesture.

35

One afternoon passed. An evening. He slept. He woke. Needed a jump start. Raw egg in a glass of cold Pilsener. More of latter. Morning flowed into another afternoon. A night. The winnowing sky, wild dark and some girl, too young. A long trip to South Dakota. He was as good as divorced. Morning fell. Again the need clamped down but Jack was broke and stank and couldn't find his check.

He decided to go home. 36

He'd had his car keys all along, but couldn't recall where the car was 37 parked. Now he walked over to The Library lot to see if it was there. It was. Plus Candy, sitting in the front seat, reading a book. She had figured Jack would have to come back there before he came home.

Jack leaned over beside her, at the open window. 38

"I'm sorry," he said. 39

She waved his breath away. 40

"Get in." 41

"Where are you going?" he asked. His voice was so small, so unnoticeable, 42 so guilty, that she was able to brush it away the same as she had his apology.

"I'm driving you out to the construction site," she said. "Your stuff is 43 already out there in the accounts trailer."

"Oh come on, Candy," he was hurting. "It was just a onetime thing." Or 44 was it? He was lost, could not remember.

She turned on him, her face fierce. 45

"So is this," she answered. "This is the one time I'm getting rid of you." 46

He needed her right now, addled and in awe of his stupidity, but still 47 he could understand the reasoning. Her self-assurance suddenly made him desperate.

"Tell me, just tell me! I'd do anything for you, baby!" 48

For some reason this just made her laugh, and her laugh was surprising, 49 free, as though she enjoyed his wit. She hummed a little tune to herself, and it occurred to Jack to tell her it bothered him, to stop, but he didn't. He fantasized that if he kept his mouth shut she'd turn the car around and bring him home, make some lunch. She pulled up into the construction yard. Her car was already parked there alongside the bulldozer and a couple of tractors, so he guessed she had a friend in on this scheme. He felt it coming on then, as she indicated with a neutral wave that he should go. He felt the hot place in his stomach, the empty place that sent the anger up his arms like cold jelly, the rage into his head. The sudden feeling was so blinding and futile that it scared even Jack. He tried to stop it from happening, and he put himself into the cage like Candy herself had always advised. As soon as he was in the wire enclosure, in his mind, Candy walked away and got into her car. Before he could jump out of the cage and catch her, he was alone in the dirt lot. Her car was already raising dust on the road to town.

And she took his car keys. Maybe by mistake, but they weren't there in 50 the ignition.

He stumbled out of the car, wheeled around, went looking in the win- 51 dows of the other cars, the equipment, finally climbed up on the bulldozer. He was in luck. The silver key was in the ignition, he turned it, started the thing up and went bouncing after Candy at full throttle thinking he would catch her somehow, cut her off before she took the turn to town. He would yell at her, reason with her, weep, pull his hair, and throw himself down at her feet or beneath the black treads of the dozer. He'd humble himself and start all over just as soon as he stopped being mad, which he was as he moved, as the thing got going. It was as though the power of the machine, the throb and heft of it, the things he could do with a lever and a switch, were part of his anger then.

It got too big for him, too big for the wire net he put up to contain it, too 52 big for anything. It roared over him and he grappled with it weakly for one moment and then he was out of the cage, bigger than life, rattling iron on iron down the road with his blade in the air and looking for he didn't know what, until he saw it — fields.

His fields. The flowers looked at Jack, all fat and frowsy, full of light.   53

"Harvest time," he shouted, sweeping in with the blade lowered, and he 54 kept on shouting, he didn't know what, as he cleared swathe after swathe, as the air above him filled with swirling petals and excited birds, as the seeds rang down on the hot metal, as the seeds poured down his neck and shirt, as the heads of sunflowers bounced off the fenders and rolled under the cleated treads and the dust flew everywhere, a great cloud that hung around him in the air of a cool and dry September.

I'm not a truly destructive man. I've built about anything that you could name. 55 *You look around Fargo — banks, half the hospital complex, the highway, Vistawood Views, the nursing home, most of the mall, house upon house — you'll see it's set up and hooked in and put there to stay by Jack Mauser. I do things from plans. I make them real. I could do it for myself if I could get a guy that could design me. But since that's not possible, I've always relied on women. Somewhere inside I think—they're women, they should know. Like if they make kids then by god they should be able to make me too.*

And that's how trouble starts—you plant all your hopes in another heart.   56

Jack stripped most of a field down before that cold strength stopped flow- 57
ing through his arms. He was breathing hard and his eyes were fixed upon the gauges and dials of the machine's control panel. He couldn't hear anything around him, anything outside himself, and then gradually his heart slowed and the adrenaline that had flooded him turned so mellow he lay back in his seat limp with self pity. He surveyed the crushed welter of stalks and plants on which the birds were already lighting with starved cries. In the distance, he could see people, his construction crew, coming at him. Candy's car wasn't in sight.

The heat of noon lifted off the fields like a gleaming veil. He'd always 58
intended to build the best house in the whole development for Candice. She wouldn't want one, now, he thought. But as he sat there, he saw them rising anyway. He saw stone trim with clerestory windows, the Gothic look, or colonial homes with shutters, plantationlike spreads with columns to either side of the front door. He would set the mailboxes into little brick hutches that could not be knocked over by a teenager with a baseball bat. He would sod in big lawns, plant seven-year-old maples. The garages would be double, triple, some with arches, and all would open automatically to accept their owners. Executives would buy these places, school principals, the owners of local businesses, wealthy farmers who wanted a town home in the winter. He would name the place The Crest. Just The Crest. Not Crest Park, Crest Acres, Crest Ridge, Crest Wood, or Crest Go Fuck Yourself. His development would speak class through simplicity, like it just meant the top of something, the place we all want to get.

Journal Writing

How do you respond to Jack Mauser's impulse to mow down his uncle's sunflowers even though he knew Chuck was depending on the harvest? Do you have any sympa-thy for his action? Recall a time when you acted against your better judgement in the face of strong emotion. Write as honestly as you can about what motivated you and what mistakes you made.

Questions on Meaning

1. How does Jack Mauser see himself? How do you suppose others see him? Sum up his character as Erdrich's narrator portrays him.

2. Why do you suppose Candice is divorcing Jack? How does Jack understand her decision to leave?

3. "The more you fill it up the emptier it gets," Chuck says of Jack's housing development in paragraph 26. What does he mean? Explain the PARADOX of his remark.

4. Why does Jack plow the sunflower field? Does he show any remorse for his actions?

5. What is the TONE of this story? What seems to be Erdrich's PURPOSE in telling it?

Questions on Writing Strategy

1. What ASSUMPTIONS does Erdrich seem to make about her AUDIENCE? Are those assumptions reasonable, in your case?

2. Why are the narrator's portrayals of the sunflower fields as striking as they are? What DOMINANT IMPRESSION does the author create? Point to any other IMAGES that appeal to you and explain their effect.

3. Consider how Erdrich uses the literary technique of *foreshadowing*, or hinting at future events, in paragraph 5. What happens to the check? How does the writer build suspense through the story?

4. Comment on the IRONY of the story's conclusion. What EFFECT does Erdrich achieve with it?

5. **OTHER METHODS**   Evaluate the ARGUMENT that takes place in paragraphs 20–28. What are Chuck's objections to Jack's proposal? Why does it upset Jack that his uncle doesn't want to buy one of his houses?

6. **OTHER METHODS**   On what points does Erdrich's short story COMPARE AND CONTRAST Jack and Chuck? What larger themes might the two men be said to represent?

Questions on Language

1. Why does Jack intend to name his development "The Crest"? What is a crest? Why is the word particularly suited to the plot of land on which he will build it?

2. What is the effect of Erdrich's use of DIALOG in this story? Why does the author places quotation marks around some words but italicizes others?

3. Be sure you know how to define the following words as Erdrich uses them: quonset (par. 3); draw, finessing (4); connive, edifice, facades, keen (7); knack (8); faltered (9); legions, ravenous (10); clods (11); yield (12); harbored (15); aquifer

(19); cul-de-sac (20); malice (23); natter (31); hordes, righteous (32); rapier (33); Pilsener, latter, winnowing (35); addled (47); frowsy (53); swathe, cleated (54); welter (57); clerestory, Gothic, hutches (58).

4. Identify some FIGURES OF SPEECH in Erdrich's story and explain their effects. Why do some of the metaphors Jack uses to describe himself, in particular, come off as slightly funny?

Suggestions for Writing

1. **FROM JOURNAL TO ESSAY**   Write a narrative essay — or if you like, a short story — that expands on your journal entry (p. 584). Tell the story of your action, and consider what the results were, what you might have done differently, and what you learned from the experience.

2. According to the National Institute of Food and Agriculture, seventeen percent of Americans live in rural areas and fewer than two percent farm for a living. Research a current issue with small farms in the United States: Timely topics include real-estate development, competition with agribusiness, federal regulations and subsidies, financial stability, and opportunities. Then write an essay that presents your findings.

3. **CRITICAL WRITING**   Erdrich has a talent for injecting humor, sometimes very dark humor, into tales that might otherwise be unrelievedly bleak. Where do you see humor in "The Crest"? How does the author achieve it? How effective do you find it? Write an essay analyzing Erdrich's use of humor, focusing your analysis on a single central idea of your own and supporting it with examples from this story.

4. **CONNECTIONS**   In her essay "Shitty First Drafts" (p. 262) Anne Lamott imagines placing critics in a jar and sealing it off so she can't hear them, an image similar to Jack's angry monster in a cage (pars. 28, 49–52). Why do you imagine that is? What might be the origins of this kind of mental trick, and who might benefit from it? What do writers and builders have in common, and how are they different? What are some likely causes of frustration and irritation for each, for instance? In an essay of your own, COMPARE AND CONTRAST Lamott's and Erdrich's imagery, commenting on the effects of each writer's vision.

5. **CONNECTIONS**   "Location, location, location," Jack Mauser mutters to his farmer uncle (par. 18). . . . "People have to live somewhere" (28). How do you feel about the real-estate and economic issues Erdrich addresses in this story, such as housing encroaching on farmland, or rich homeowners crowding out less affluent residents in urban settings? Before you answer, read Rebecca Solnit's "Division Street" (p. 602) and take into consideration her analysis of economic pressures on housing and land use in a climate of income inequality. How does business growth contribute to the problem of homelessness, for instance? What are the best uses of land in a crowded environment? What can be done to ensure fair distribution of limited resources, and why does it matter?

Louise Erdrich on Writing

In a 2010 interview for his PBS series *Journal*, Bill Moyers marveled at Louise Erdrich's ability to produce as much fiction and poetry as she has while raising six children, for a long stretch as a single mother. On behalf of other writing parents, he asked her, "How can [you] be so prolific? How can [you] find time?" Erdrich's response: "How do I do—I don't know. I've—my sisters have seen me. . . . My kids have seen me every day, and they don't know how it happens, but I suspect it has to do with a small, incremental persistent insect-like devotion to putting one word next to the other word. It's a very dogged process. I make myself go upstairs, where I write, whenever I can, no matter how—one thing is I never have writer's block, because I—if I went up there and had writer's block, I think I'd lose my mind. You know, I have to get up to my papers and my books and my notebooks. I jot things down all the time. I just keep going."

In another interview, *TeachingBooks.net* asked Erdrich how a "typical workday" goes for her. She had a similar response. "I bring my youngest daughter to school," she began. "Then I come back and drink tea. I walk around the lakes here in Minneapolis with my dog and sometimes with a friend or with my husband, and (if I'm alone) I think about what I'm going to do. Then I go upstairs. I have a special chair that I have sat in ever since I started writing. So, I sit down in my chair that is stuffed with old, tired-out sentences. And it's my 'sentence' to sit in that chair until I stop writing, which will never happen until I'm gone. It's my chair. I work as long as I can."

The Bedford Reader on Writing

Louise Erdrich's writing process seems simple enough: She makes herself sit down to write and keeps at it. But notice that she follows many of our suggestions for DRAFTING—giving herself long stretches of time to write, working in her own quiet space where she can write undisturbed, and letting herself write freely without focusing on mistakes (see pp. 33–34). Erdrich is lucky, though, if she never has writer's block. Should you ever find yourself stuck when you sit down to draft, revisit our advice under "Discovering Ideas" (pp. 30–33).

MAXINE HONG KINGSTON

Maxine Hong Kingston grew up caught between two complex and very different cultures: the China of her parents and the America of her surroundings. In her first two books, *The Woman Warrior: Memoirs of a Girlhood among Ghosts* (1976) and *China Men* (1980), winners of the National Book Critics Circle Award and the National Book Award respectively, Kingston combines Chinese myth and history with family tales to create a dreamlike world that shifts between reality and fantasy. Born in 1940 in Stockton, California, Kingston was the first American-born child of a scholar and a medical practitioner who became laundry workers in this country. After graduating from the University of California, Berkeley (BA, 1962), Kingston taught English at high schools in California and Hawaii, at the University of Hawaii, and for many years at UC Berkeley. She has contributed essays, poems, and stories to many periodicals, including *The New Yorker*, the *New York Times Magazine*, and *Ms.* Other books by Kingston include a collection of essays, *Hawaii One Summer* (1987); a novel, *Tripmaster Monkey: His Fake Book* (1989); a blend of fiction and nonfiction, *The Fifth Book of Peace* (2003); and a memoir in verse, *I Love a Broad Margin to My Life* (2011). She also edited *Veterans of War, Veterans of Peace* (2006), a collection of essays written in workshops she holds for military veterans. For her lifelong contributions to the written word, Kingston was honored with the National Medal of Arts in 2014 and the Museum of Chinese in America's Legacy Award in 2018. She lives in Oakland, California.

No Name Woman

"No Name Woman" is part of *The Woman Warrior*. Like much of Kingston's writing, it blends the "talk-stories" of Kingston's elders, her own vivid imaginings, and the reality of her experience—this time to discover why her Chinese aunt drowned herself in the family well.

Kingston develops "No Name Woman" with four main methods, all intertwined: In the context of narrating her own experiences, she seeks the causes of her aunt's suicide by comparing various narratives of it, and she employs description to make the narratives concrete and vivid. The main uses of these methods appear below:

Narration (Chap. 5): paragraphs 1–8, 14, 16–20, 23, 28–30, 34–35, 37–46
Description (Chap. 6): paragraphs 4–8, 21, 23–27, 31, 37, 40–46
Comparison and contrast (Chap. 8): paragraphs 15–18, 20–24, 27–28, 31
Cause and effect (Chap. 12): paragraphs 10–11, 15–18, 21–25, 29–31, 33–39, 44–48

"You must not tell anyone," my mother said, "what I am about to tell   1
you. In China your father had a sister who killed herself. She jumped into the
family well. We say that your father has all brothers because it is as if she had
never been born.

"In 1924 just a few days after our village celebrated seventeen hurry-   2
up weddings — to make sure that every young man who went 'out on the
road' would responsibly come home — your father and his brothers and
your grandfather and his brothers and your aunt's new husband sailed for
America, the Gold Mountain. It was your grandfather's last trip. Those
lucky enough to get contracts waved good-bye from the decks. They fed
and guarded the stowaways and helped them off in Cuba, New York, Bali,
Hawaii. 'We'll meet in California next year,' they said. All of them sent
money home.

"I remember looking at your aunt one day when she and I were dressing;   3
I had not noticed before that she had such a protruding melon of a stomach.
But I did not think, 'She's pregnant,' until she began to look like other pregnant women, her shirt pulling and the white tops of her black pants showing.
She could not have been pregnant, you see, because her husband had been
gone for years. No one said anything. We did not discuss it. In early summer
she was ready to have the child, long after the time when it could have been
possible.

"The village had also been counting. On the night the baby was to be   4
born the villagers raided our house. Some were crying. Like a great saw, teeth
strung with lights, files of people walked zigzag across our land, tearing the
rice. Their lanterns doubled in the disturbed black water, which drained away
through the broken bunds. As the villagers closed in, we could see that some
of them, probably men and women we knew well, wore white masks. The
people with long hair hung it over their faces. Women with short hair made
it stand up on end. Some had tied white bands around their foreheads, arms,
and legs.

"At first they threw mud and rocks at the house. Then they threw eggs   5
and began slaughtering our stock. We could hear the animals scream their
deaths — the roosters, the pigs, a last great roar from the ox. Familiar wild
heads flared in our night windows; the villagers encircled us. Some of the
faces stopped to peer at us, their eyes rushing like searchlights. The hands
flattened against the panes, framed heads, and left red prints.

"The villagers broke in the front and the back doors at the same time,   6
even though we had not locked the doors against them. Their knives dripped
with the blood of our animals. They smeared blood on the doors and walls.

One woman swung a chicken, whose throat she had slit, splattering blood in red arcs about her. We stood together in the middle of our house, in the family hall with the pictures and tables of the ancestors around us, and looked straight ahead.

"At that time the house had only two wings. When the men came 7 back, we would build two more to enclose our courtyard and a third one to begin a second courtyard. The villagers pushed through both wings, even your grandparents' rooms, to find your aunt's, which was also mine until the men returned. From this room a new wing for one of the younger families would grow. They ripped up her clothes and shoes and broke her combs, grinding them underfoot. They tore her work from the loom. They scattered the cooking fire and rolled the new weaving in it. We could hear them in the kitchen breaking our bowls and banging the pots. They overturned the great waist-high earthenware jugs; duck eggs, pickled fruits, vegetables burst out and mixed in acrid torrents. The old woman from the next field swept a broom through the air and loosed the spirits-of-the-broom over our heads. 'Pig.' 'Ghost.' 'Pig,' they sobbed and scolded while they ruined our house.

"When they left, they took sugar and oranges to bless themselves. They 8 cut pieces from the dead animals. Some of them took bowls that were not broken and clothes that were not torn. Afterward we swept up the rice and sewed it back up into sacks. But the smells from the spilled preserves lasted. Your aunt gave birth in the pigsty that night. The next morning when I went up for the water, I found her and the baby plugging up the family well.

"Don't let your father know that I told you. He denies her. Now that 9 you have started to menstruate, what happened to her could happen to you. Don't humiliate us. You wouldn't like to be forgotten as if you had never been born. The villagers are watchful."

Whenever she had to warn us about life, my mother told stories that ran 10 like this one, a story to grow up on. She tested our strength to establish realities. Those in the emigrant generations who could not reassert brute survival died young and far from home. Those of us in the first American generations have had to figure out how the invisible world the emigrants built around our childhoods fit in solid America.

The emigrants confused the gods by diverting their curses, misleading 11 them with crooked streets and false names. They must try to confuse their offspring as well, who, I suppose, threaten them in similar ways — always trying to get things straight, always trying to name the unspeakable. The Chinese I know hide their names; sojourners take new names when their lives change and guard their real names with silence.

Chinese-Americans, when you try to understand what things in you 12
are Chinese, how do you separate what is peculiar to childhood, to poverty,
insanities, one family, your mother who marked your growing with stories,
from what is Chinese? What is Chinese tradition and what is the movies?

If I want to learn what clothes my aunt wore, whether flashy or ordinary, 13
I would have to begin, "Remember Father's drowned-in-the-well sister?"
I cannot ask that. My mother has told me once and for all the useful parts. She
will add nothing unless powered by Necessity, a riverbank that guides her life.
She plants vegetable gardens rather than lawns; she carries the odd-shaped
tomatoes home from the fields and eats food left for the gods.

Whenever we did frivolous things, we used up energy; we flew high kites. 14
We children came up off the ground over the melting cones our parents
brought home from work and the American movie on New Year's Day—*Oh,
You Beautiful Doll* with Betty Grable one year, and *She Wore a Yellow Ribbon*
with John Wayne another year. After the one carnival ride each, we paid in
guilt; our tired father counted his change on the dark walk home.

Adultery is extravagance. Could people who hatch their own chicks and 15
eat the embryos and the heads for delicacies and boil the feet in vinegar for
party food, leaving only the gravel, eating even the gizzard lining—could
such people engender a prodigal aunt? To be a woman, to have a daughter in
starvation time was a waste enough. My aunt could not have been the lone
romantic who gave up everything for sex. Women in the old China did not
choose. Some man had commanded her to lie with him and be his secret evil.
I wonder whether he masked himself when he joined the raid on her family.

Perhaps she encountered him in the fields or on the mountain where 16
the daughters-in-law collected fuel. Or perhaps he first noticed her in the
marketplace. He was not a stranger because the village housed no strangers.
She had to have dealings with him other than sex. Perhaps he worked an
adjoining field, or he sold her the cloth for the dress she sewed and wore. His
demand must have surprised, then terrified her. She obeyed him; she always
did as she was told.

When the family found a young man in the next village to be her hus- 17
band, she stood tractably beside the best rooster, his proxy, and promised
before they met that she would be his forever. She was lucky that he was her
age and she would be the first wife, an advantage secure now. The night she
first saw him, he had sex with her. Then he left for America. She had almost
forgotten what he looked like. When she tried to envision him, she only saw
the black and white face in the group photograph the men had had taken
before leaving.

The other man was not, after all, much different from her husband. They 18
both gave orders: She followed. "If you tell your family, I'll beat you. I'll kill

you. Be here again next week." No one talked sex, ever. And she might have separated the rapes from the rest of living if only she did not have to buy her oil from him or gather wood in the same forest. I want her fear to have lasted just as long as rape lasted so that the fear could have been contained. No drawn-out fear. But women at sex hazarded birth and hence lifetimes. The fear did not stop but permeated everywhere. She told the man, "I think I'm pregnant." He organized the raid against her.

On nights when my mother and father talked about their life back home, sometimes they mentioned an "outcast table" whose business they still seemed to be settling, their voices tight. In a commensal tradition, where food is precious, the powerful older people made wrongdoers eat alone. Instead of letting them start separate new lives like the Japanese, who could become samurais and geishas, the Chinese family, faces averted but eyes glowering sideways, hung on to the offenders and fed them leftovers. My aunt must have lived in the same house as my parents and eaten at an outcast table. My mother spoke about the raid as if she had seen it, when she and my aunt, a daughter-in-law to a different household, should not have been living together at all. Daughters-in-law lived with their husbands' parents, not their own; a synonym for marriage in Chinese is "taking a daughter-in-law." Her husband's parents could have sold her, mortgaged her, stoned her. But they had sent her back to her own mother and father, a mysterious act hinting at disgraces not told me. Perhaps they had thrown her out to deflect the avengers. 19

She was the only daughter; her four brothers went with her father, husband, and uncles "out on the road" and for some years became western men. When the goods were divided among the family, three of the brothers took land, and the youngest, my father, chose an education. After my grandparents gave their daughter away to her husband's family, they had dispensed all the adventure and all the property. They expected her alone to keep the traditional ways, which her brothers, now among the barbarians, could fumble without detection. The heavy, deep-rooted women were to maintain the past against the flood, safe for returning. But the rare urge west had fixed upon our family, and so my aunt crossed boundaries not delineated in space. 20

The work of preservation demands that the feelings playing about in one's guts not be turned into action. Just watch their passing like cherry blossoms. But perhaps my aunt, my forerunner, caught in a slow life, let dreams grow and fade and after some months or years went toward what persisted. Fear at the enormities of the forbidden kept her desires delicate, wire and bone. She looked at a man because she liked the way the hair was tucked behind his ears, or she liked the question-mark line of a long torso curving at the shoulder and straight at the hip. For warm eyes or a soft voice or a slow 21 walk — that's all — a few hairs, a line, a brightness, a sound, a pace, she gave up family. She offered us up for a charm that vanished with tiredness, a pigtail that didn't toss when the wind died. Why, the wrong lighting could erase the dearest thing about him.

It could very well have been, however, that my aunt did not take subtle 22 enjoyment of her friend, but, a wild woman, kept rollicking company. Imagining her free with sex doesn't fit, though. I don't know any women like that, or men either. Unless I see her life branching into mine, she gives me no ancestral help.

To sustain her being in love, she often worked at herself in the mirror, 23 guessing at the colors and shapes that would interest him, changing them frequently in order to hit on the right combination. She wanted him to look back.

On a farm near the sea, a woman who tended her appearance reaped a 24 reputation for eccentricity. All the married women blunt-cut their hair in flaps about their ears or pulled it back in tight buns. No nonsense. Neither style blew easily into heart-catching tangles. And at their weddings they displayed themselves in their long hair for the last time. "It brushed the backs of my knees," my mother tells me. "It was braided, and even so, it brushed the backs of my knees."

At the mirror my aunt combed individuality into her bob. A bun could 25 have been contrived to escape into black streamers blowing in the wind or in quiet wisps about her face, but only the older women in our picture album wear buns. She brushed her hair back from her forehead, tucking the flaps behind her ears. She looped a piece of thread, knotted into a circle between her index fingers and thumbs, and ran the double strand across her forehead. When she closed her fingers as if she were making a pair of shadow geese bite, the string twisted together catching the little hairs. Then she pulled the thread away from her skin, ripping the hairs out neatly, her eyes watering from the needles of pain. Opening her fingers, she cleaned the thread, then rolled it along her hairline and the tops of her eyebrows. My mother did the same to me and my sisters and herself. I used to believe that the expression "caught by the short hairs" meant a captive held with a depilatory string. It especially hurt at the temples, but my mother said we were lucky we didn't have to have our feet bound when we were seven. Sisters used to sit on their beds and cry together, she said, as their mothers or their slaves removed the bandages for a few minutes each night and let the blood gush back into their veins. I hope that the man my aunt loved appreciated a smooth brow, that he wasn't just a tits-and-ass man.

Once my aunt found a freckle on her chin, at a spot that the almanac said 26 predestined her for unhappiness. She dug it out with a hot needle and washed the wound with peroxide.

More attention to her looks than these pullings of hairs and pickings at   27
spots would have caused gossip among the villagers. They owned work clothes
and good clothes, and they wore good clothes for feasting the new seasons.
But since a woman combing her hair hexes beginnings, my aunt rarely found
an occasion to look her best. Women looked like great sea snails — the corded
wood, babies, and laundry they carried were the whorls on their backs. The
Chinese did not admire a bent back; goddesses and warriors stood straight.
Still there must have been a marvelous freeing of beauty when a worker laid
down her burden and stretched and arched.

Such commonplace loveliness, however, was not enough for my aunt.   28
She dreamed of a lover for the fifteen days of New Year's, the time for families
to exchange visits, money, and food. She plied her secret comb. And sure
enough she cursed the year, the family, the village, and herself.

Even as her hair lured her imminent lover, many other men looked at   29
her. Uncles, cousins, nephews, brothers would have looked, too, had they
been home between journeys. Perhaps they had already been restraining their
curiosity, and they left, fearful that their glances, like a field of nesting birds,
might be startled and caught. Poverty hurt, and that was their first reason
for leaving. But another, final reason for leaving the crowded house was the
never-said.

She may have been unusually beloved, the precious only daughter,   30
spoiled and mirror gazing because of the affection the family lavished on her.
When her husband left, they welcomed the chance to take her back from the
in-laws; she could live like the little daughter for just a while longer. There
are stories that my grandfather was different from other people, "crazy ever
since the little Jap bayoneted him in the head." He used to put his naked
penis on the dinner table, laughing. And one day he brought home a baby
girl, wrapped up inside his brown western-style greatcoat. He had traded one
of his sons, probably my father, the youngest, for her. My grandmother made
him trade back. When he finally got a daughter of his own, he doted on her.
They must have all loved her, except perhaps my father, the only brother who
never went back to China, having once been traded for a girl.

Brothers and sisters, newly men and women, had to efface their sexual   31
color and present plain miens. Disturbing hair and eyes, a smile like no other,
threatened the ideal of five generations living under one roof. To focus blurs,
people shouted face to face and yelled from room to room. The immigrants
I know have loud voices, unmodulated to American tones even after years
away from the village where they called their friendships out across the fields.
I have not been able to stop my mother's screams in public libraries or over
telephones. Walking erect (knees straight, toes pointed forward, not pigeon-
toed, which is Chinese-feminine) and speaking in an inaudible voice, I have

tried to turn myself American-feminine. Chinese communication was loud, public. Only sick people had to whisper. But at the dinner table, where the family members came nearest one another, no one could talk, not the outcasts nor any eaters. Every word that falls from the mouth is a coin lost. Silently they gave and accepted food with both hands. A preoccupied child who took his bowl with one hand got a sideways glare. A complete moment of total attention is due everyone alike. Children and lovers have no singularity here, but my aunt used a secret voice, a separate attentiveness.

She kept the man's name to herself throughout her labor and dying; she 32 did not accuse him that he be punished with her. To save her inseminator's name she gave silent birth.

He may have been somebody in her own household, but intercourse with 33 a man outside the family would have been no less abhorrent. All the village were kinsmen, and the titles shouted in loud country voices never let kinship be forgotten. Any man within visiting distance would have been neutralized as a lover — "brother," "younger brother," "older brother" — one hundred and fifteen relationship titles. Parents researched birth charts probably not so much to assure good fortune as to circumvent incest in a population that has but one hundred surnames. Everybody has eight million relatives. How useless then sexual mannerisms, how dangerous.

As if it came from an atavism deeper than fear, I used to add "brother" 34 silently to boys' names. It hexed the boys, who would or would not ask me to dance, and made them less scary and as familiar and deserving of benevolence as girls.

But, of course, I hexed myself also — no dates. I should have stood up, 35 both arms waving, and shouted out across libraries, "Hey, you! Love me back." I had no idea, though, how to make attraction selective, how to control its direction and magnitude. If I made myself American-pretty so that the five or six Chinese boys in the class fell in love with me, everyone else — the Caucasian, Negro, and Japanese boys — would too. Sisterliness, dignified and honorable, made much more sense.

Attraction eludes control so stubbornly that whole societies designed to 36 organize relationships among people cannot keep order, not even when they bind people to one another from childhood and raise them together. Among the very poor and the wealthy, brothers married their adopted sisters, like doves. Our family allowed some romance, paying adult brides' prices and providing dowries so that their sons and daughters could marry strangers. Marriage promises to turn strangers into friendly relatives — a nation of siblings.

In the village structure, spirits shimmered among the live creatures, 37 balanced and held in equilibrium by time and land. But one human being flaring up into violence could open up a black hole, a maelstrom that pulled in the sky. The frightened villagers, who depended on one another to maintain the real, went to my aunt to show her a personal, physical representation of the break she made in the "roundness." Misallying couples snapped off the future, which was to be embodied in true offspring. The villagers punished her for acting as if she could have a private life, secret and apart from them.

If my aunt had betrayed the family at a time of large grain yields and   38
peace, when many boys were born, and wings were being built on many houses, perhaps she might have escaped such severe punishment. But the men — hungry, greedy, tired of planting in dry soil, cuckolded — had been forced to leave the village in order to send food-money home. There were ghost plagues, bandit plagues, wars with the Japanese, floods. My Chinese brother and sister had died of an unknown sickness. Adultery, perhaps only a mistake during good times, became a crime when the village needed food.

The round moon cakes and round doorways, the round tables of grad-   39
uated size that fit one roundness inside another, round windows and rice bowls — these talismans had lost their power to warn this family of the law: A family must be whole, faithfully keeping the descent line by having sons to feed the old and the dead who in turn look after the family. The villagers came to show my aunt and lover-in-hiding a broken house. The villagers were speeding up the circling of events because she was too shortsighted to see that her infidelity had already harmed the village, that waves of consequences would return unpredictably, sometimes in disguise, as now, to hurt her. This roundness had to be made coin-sized so that she would see its circumference: punish her at the birth of her baby. Awaken her to the inexorable. People who refused fatalism because they could invent small resources insisted on culpability. Deny accidents and wrest fault from the stars.

After the villagers left, their lanterns now scattering in various direc-   40
tions toward home, the family broke their silence and cursed her. "Aiaa, we're going to die. Death is coming. Death is coming. Look what you've done. You've killed us. Ghost! Dead Ghost! Ghost! You've never been born." She ran out into the fields, far enough from the house so that she could no longer hear their voices, and pressed herself against the earth, her own land no more. When she felt the birth coming, she thought that she had been hurt. Her body seized together. "They've hurt me too much," she thought. "This is gall, and it will kill me." With forehead and knees against the earth, her body convulsed and then relaxed. She turned on her back, lay on the ground. The black well of sky and stars went out and out and out

forever; her body and her complexity seemed to disappear. She was one of the stars, a bright dot in blackness, without home, without a companion, in eternal cold and silence. An agoraphobia rose in her, speeding higher and higher, bigger and bigger; she would not be able to contain it; there would be no end to fear.

Flayed, unprotected against space, she felt pain return, focusing her body. 41 This pain chilled her — a cold, steady kind of surface pain. Inside, spasmodically, the other pain, the pain of the child, heated her. For hours she lay on the ground, alternately body and space. Sometimes a vision of normal comfort obliterated reality: She saw the family in the evening gambling at the dinner table, the young people massaging their elders' backs. She saw them congratulating one another, high joy on the mornings the rice shoots came up. When these pictures burst, the stars drew out further apart. Black space opened.

She got to her feet to fight better and remembered that old-fashioned 42 women gave birth in their pigsties to fool the jealous, pain-dealing gods, who do not snatch piglets. Before the next spasms could stop her, she ran to the pigsty, each step a rushing out into emptiness. She climbed over the fence and knelt in the dirt. It was good to have a fence enclosing her, a tribal person alone.

Laboring, this woman who had carried her child as a foreign growth that 43 sickened her every day, expelled it at last. She reached down to touch the hot, wet, moving mass, surely smaller than anything human, and could feel that it was human after all — fingers, toes, nails, nose. She pulled it up onto her belly, and it lay curled there, butt in the air, feet precisely tucked one under the other. She opened her loose shirt and buttoned the child inside. After resting, it squirmed and thrashed and she pushed it up to her breast. It turned its head this way and that until it found her nipple. There, it made little snuffling noises. She clenched her teeth at its preciousness, lovely as a young calf, a piglet, a little dog.

She may have gone to the pigsty as a last act of responsibility: She 44 would protect this child as she had protected its father. It would look after her soul, leaving supplies on her grave. But how would this tiny child without family find her grave when there would be no marker for her anywhere, neither in the earth nor the family hall? No one would give her a family hall name. She had taken the child with her into the wastes. At its birth the two of them had felt the same raw pain of separation, a wound that only the family pressing tight could close. A child with no descent line would not soften her life but only trail after her, ghostlike, begging her to give it purpose. At dawn the villagers on their way to the fields would stand around the fence and look.

Full of milk, the little ghost slept. When it awoke, she hardened her   45
breasts against the milk that crying loosens. Toward morning she picked up
the baby and walked to the well.

Carrying the baby to the well shows loving. Otherwise abandon it. Turn   46
its face into the mud. Mothers who love their children take them along. It
was probably a girl; there is some hope of forgiveness for boys.

"Don't tell anyone you had an aunt. Your father does not want to hear   47
her name. She has never been born." I have believed that sex was unspeakable and words so strong and fathers so frail that "aunt" would do my father
mysterious harm. I have thought that my family, having settled among immigrants who had also been their neighbors in the ancestral land, needed to
clean their name, and a wrong word would incite the kinspeople even here.
But there is more to this silence: They want me to participate in her punishment. And I have.

In the twenty years since I heard this story I have not asked for details   48
nor said my aunt's name; I do not know it. People who comfort the dead
can also chase after them to hurt them further—a reverse ancestor worship. The real punishment was not the raid swiftly inflicted by the villagers, but the family's deliberately forgetting her. Her betrayal so maddened
them, they saw to it that she would suffer forever, even after death. Always
hungry, always needing, she would have to beg food from other ghosts,
snatch and steal it from those whose living descendants give them gifts.
She would have to fight the ghosts massed at crossroads for the buns a few
thoughtful citizens leave to decoy her away from village and home so that
the ancestral spirits could feast unharassed. At peace, they could act like
gods, not ghosts, their descent lines providing them with paper suits and
dresses, spirit money, paper houses, paper automobiles, chicken, meat,
and rice into eternity—essences delivered up in smoke and flames, steam
and incense rising from each rice bowl. In an attempt to make the Chinese
care for people outside the family, Chairman Mao encourages us now to
give our paper replicas to the spirits of outstanding soldiers and workers,
no matter whose ancestors they may be. My aunt remains forever hungry.
Goods are not distributed evenly among the dead.

My aunt haunts me—her ghost drawn to me because now, after fifty   49
years of neglect, I alone devote pages of paper to her, though not origamied
into houses and clothes. I do not think she always means me well. I am telling
on her, and she was a spite suicide, drowning herself in the drinking water.
The Chinese are always very frightened of the drowned one, whose weeping
ghost, wet hair hanging and skin bloated, waits silently by the water to pull
down a substitute.

Journal Writing

Most of us have heard family stories that left lasting impressions — ghost stories like Kingston's, biographies of ancestors, explanations for traditions, family superstitions, and so on. Write in your journal about a family story you remember vividly from your childhood.

Questions on Meaning

1. What PURPOSE does Kingston have in telling her aunt's story? How does this differ from her mother's purpose in relating the tale?

2. According to Kingston, who could have been the father of her aunt's child? Who could not?

3. Kingston says that her mother told stories "to warn us about life" (par. 10). What warning does this story provide?

4. Why is Kingston so fascinated by her aunt's life and death?

Questions on Writing Strategy

1. Whom does Kingston seem to include in her AUDIENCE: her family and other older Chinese? second-generation Chinese Americans like herself? other Americans? How might she expect each of these groups to respond to her essay?

2. Why is Kingston's opening line — her mother's "You must not tell anyone" — especially fitting for this essay? What secrets are being told? Why does Kingston divulge them?

3. As Kingston tells her tale of her aunt, some events are based on her mother's story or her knowledge of Chinese customs, while others are wholly imaginary. What is the EFFECT of blending these several threads of reality, perception, and imagination?

4. **MIXED METHODS**   Examine the details in the two contrasting NARRATIVES of how Kingston's aunt became pregnant: one in paragraphs 15–18 and the other in paragraphs 21–28. How do the details create different realities? Which version does Kingston seem more committed to? Why?

5. **MIXED METHODS**   Kingston COMPARES AND CONTRASTS various versions of her aunt's story, trying to find the CAUSES that led her aunt to drown in the well. In the end, what causes does Kingston seem to accept?

Questions on Language

1. How does Kingston's language — lyrical, poetic, full of FIGURES OF SPEECH and other IMAGES — reveal her relationship to her Chinese heritage? Find phrases that are especially striking.

2. Look up any of these words you do not know: bunds (par. 4); acrid (7); frivolous (14); tractably, proxy (17); hazarded (18); commensal (19); delineated
   (20); depilatory (25); plied (28); miens (31); abhorrent, circumvent (33); atavism (34); maelstrom (37); talismans, inexorable, fatalism, culpability (39); gall,
   agoraphobia (40); spasmodically (41).

3. Sometimes Kingston indicates that she is reconstructing or imagining events
   through verbs like "would have" and words like "maybe" and "perhaps" ("Perhaps
   she encountered him in the fields," par. 16). Other times she presents obviously
   imaginary events as if they actually happened ("Once my aunt found a freckle
   on her chin," 26). What effect does Kingston achieve with these apparent
   inconsistencies?

Suggestions for Writing

1. **FROM JOURNAL TO ESSAY**   Develop the family story from your journal (p. 599)
   into a narrative essay. Build in the context of the story as well: Who told it to
   you? What purpose did he or she have in telling it to you? How does it illustrate
   your family's beliefs and values?

2. Write an essay explaining the role of ancestors in Chinese family and religious life,
   supplementing what Kingston says with research in the library or on the Web or
   (if you are Chinese or Chinese American) drawing on your own experiences.

3. **CRITICAL WRITING**   ANALYZE the ideas about gender roles revealed in "No Name
   Woman," both in China and in the Chinese American culture Kingston grew up
   in. How have these ideas affected Kingston? Do you perceive any semblance of
   them in contemporary American culture?

4. **CONNECTIONS**   Both Maxine Hong Kingston and Brad Manning, in "Arm
   Wrestling with My Father" (p. 125), examine communication within their families. Relate an incident or incidents from your own childhood that portray something about communication within your family. You might want to focus on the
   language of communication, such as the words used to discuss (or not discuss) a
   taboo topic, the special family meanings for familiar words, a misunderstanding
   between you and an adult about something the adult said. Use dialog and as
   much CONCRETE detail as you can to clarify your experience and its significance.

5. **CONNECTIONS**   Several other authors in this book also write about relationships between immigrants and their American- or Canadian-raised children.
   These include Amy Tan in "Fish Cheeks" (p. 77), Scaachi Koul in "Impatiently
   Waiting for the Horror of Death" (p. 133), Firoozeh Dumas in "Sweet, Sour,
   and Resentful" (p. 275), Sandra Cisneros in "And Some More" (p. 361), Tal
   Fortgang in "Checking My Privilege" (p. 460), Roxane Gay in "Peculiar Benefits" (p. 467), and Linda Chavez in "Supporting Family Values" (p. 506). Select
   two or three of these essays and read or reread them. Then, in an essay of your
   own, analyze what the authors you have chosen suggest about the experiences of
   the children of immigrants to North America. Do any expectations, supports, or
   conflicts strike you as common, even universal? How do your own experiences
   with your parents (or grandparents) compare? Do particular cultures seem to
   influence family relationships in particular ways? Why do you think so?

Maxine Hong Kingston on Writing

In an interview with Jean W. Ross published in *Contemporary Authors* in 1984, Maxine Hong Kingston discusses the writing and revising of *The Woman Warrior*. Ross asks Kingston to clarify an earlier statement that she had "no idea how people who don't write endure their lives." Kingston replies: "When I said that, I was thinking about how words and stories create order. Some of the things that happen to us in life seem to have no meaning, but when you write them down you find the meanings for them; or, as you translate life into words, you force a meaning. Meaning is intrinsic in words and stories."

Ross then asks if Kingston used an outline and planned to blend fact with legend in *The Woman Warrior*. "Oh no, no," Kingston answers. "What I have at the beginning of a book is not an outline. I have no idea of how stories will end or where the beginning will lead. Sometimes I draw pictures. I draw a blob and then I have a little arrow and it goes to this other blob, if you want to call that an outline. It's hardly even words; it's like a doodle. Then when it turns into words, I find the words lead me to various scenes and stories which I don't know about until I get there. I don't see the order until very late in the writing and sometimes the ending just comes. I just run up against it. All of a sudden the book's over and I didn't know it would be over."

A question from Ross about whether her emotions enter her writing leads Kingston to talk about revision. "Well, when I first set something down I feel the emotions I write about. But when I do a second draft, third draft, ninth draft, then I don't feel very emotional. The rewriting is very intellectual; all my education and reading and intellect are involved. The mechanics of sentences, how one phrase or word goes with another one—all that happens in later drafts. There's a very emotional first draft and a very technical last draft."

The Bedford Reader on Writing

Blending memory with fiction, as Kingston did, can be similar to drawing outside research into your writing. In the beginning, you might work with general ideas similar to Kingston's doodles, and then refine them as you go. As Kingston notes, it's important to pay close attention to how you weave in the details. After getting everything down on the page, don't forget to check back and make sure everything works in the way you intended, revising as necessary. For more advice on integrating source material, see pages 45–50 in Chapter 3 and 653–56 in the Appendix.

REBECCA SOLNIT

Rebecca Solnit was born in 1961 in Bridgeport, Connecticut, and as a child moved with her parents to greater San Francisco, where she still lives. After passing the GED exam in the tenth grade she left to study abroad in Paris before completing a BA in English language and literature from San Francisco State University (1981) and earning a master's degree in journalism from the University of California, Berkeley (1984). An influential essayist, critic, and activist, Solnit has published more than twenty books in a wide span of genres. They include histories such as *Savage Dreams: A Journey into the Hidden Wars of the American West* (1994) and *Wanderlust: A History of Walking* (2000); art criticism in *As Eve Said to the Serpent: On Landscape, Gender, and Art* (2001); *River of Shadows* (2003), a biography of photographer Eadweard Muybridge and winner of a Guggenheim, the National Book Critics' Circle Award, and the Lannan Literary Award; *Infinite City: A San Francisco Atlas* (2010), a political and cultural map of her longtime home; and several collections of academic essays focused on issues of feminism, politics, and culture, most recently *Call Them by Their True Names* (2018), longlisted for the National Book Award. Her explosive 2008 *Los Angeles Times* essay "Men Explain Things to Me," which opens with Solnit's recollection of being forced to listen to someone inform her about a critically acclaimed book she had herself written, is largely credited as the inspiration for the term *mansplaining*. Active in several environmental and human rights campaigns, including #YesAllWomen and the Western Shoshone Defense Project, Solnit is also a contributing editor for *Harper's* and writes the magazine's "Easy Chair" column every other month.

Division Street

A former museum researcher, Solnit often contributes essays and text to accompany visual works. "Division Street" was first published in *Harper's* magazine in 2016 as the introduction to a photo essay by Robert Gumpert; we include three of the photographer's images here.

Primarily an argument (Chap. 14) based on cause-and-effect analysis (Chap. 12), Solnit's essay mixes in several other methods of development to examine the problem of homelessness in San Francisco:

Description (Chap. 6): paragraph 6
Example (Chap. 7): paragraphs 6–8, 10
Comparison and contrast (Chap. 8): paragraphs 2–3, 8, 11
Process analysis (Chap. 9): paragraph 11
Division or analysis (Chap. 10): paragraph 9
Definition (Chap. 13): paragraph 1

Chances are that you are living the good life, at least in the most fun- 1
damental sense. You have the liberty to leave your home and the security of a home you can return to; privacy and protection on the one hand
and work, pleasure, social encounter, exploration, and engagement on the
other. This is almost a definition of quality of life, the balance of public
and private, the confidence that you have a place in the world—or a place
and the world.

In the years since the Reagan[1] revolution, this basic condition of well- 2
being has become unavailable to millions in the United States: the unhoused
and the imprisoned. The former live in an outside without access to the inside
that is shelter, home, and stability; the latter live in an inside without access
to the outside that is liberty. Both suffer a chronic lack of privacy and agency.

Their ranks are vast, including 2.2 million prisoners and, at any given 3
time, about half a million people without homes. These people are regarded
as disposable; prison and the streets are the places to which they've been
disposed. Prison and the streets. The two are closely related, and they feed
each other in the general manner of vicious circles, as the photographer
Robert Gumpert knows from shooting in both arenas. Prisoners exit with
few resources to integrate themselves back into the world of work and housing, which sometimes leads them straight onto the street. People living on
the street are often criminalized for their everyday activities, which can
put them in prison. In San Francisco, local laws ban sitting or lying down
on sidewalks and sleeping in public parks, as well as public urination and
defecation—doing the things you do inside your house, the things biology
requires that we all do. Many people who lack homes of their own are invisible, living in vehicles, staying overnight in workplaces, riding the night bus,
couch-surfing, and looking like everyone else. The most devastated and marginalized are the most visible. Even they try to keep a low profile: I walk past
the unhoused daily, seeing how they seek to disappear, situating themselves
behind big-box stores and alongside industrial sites, where they are less likely
to inspire the housed to call for their removal.

The young can't remember (and many of their elders hardly recall) how 4
few people were homeless before the 1980s. They don't grasp that this problem doesn't have to exist, that we could largely end it, as we could many other
social problems, with little more radical a solution than a return to the buffered capitalism of forty years ago, when real wages were higher, responsibility

---

[1] Ronald Reagan (1911–2004), a Republican politician and former Hollywood actor, was
the thirty-third governor of California (1967–75) and the fortieth president of the United
States (1981–89). —EDS.

Police officers help Baby Face get rid of some of his belongings, a process the female officer called "downsizing," after ordering him to leave their patrol area in the Design Center, a few blocks east of Division Street, March 1. Robert Gumpert/Redux

for taxes more equitably distributed, and a far stronger safety net caught more of those who fell. Homelessness has been created by federal, state, and local policies—not just by defunding mental-health programs, which is too often cited as the cause. Perfectly sane people lose access to housing every day, though the resultant ordeal may undermine some of that sanity, as it might yours and mine.

In our antitax era, many cities fish for revenue by taxing homelessness, 5 turning the police into de facto bill collectors. Those unable to pay the fines and warrants for panhandling, loitering, or sleeping outdoors—meaning most people forced to panhandle, loiter, or sleep outdoors in the first place—can be hauled into court at any time. As Astra Taylor[2] put it recently, "Municipal budgets are overly reliant on petty infraction penalties because affluent, mostly white citizens have been engaged in a 'tax revolt' for decades, lobbying for lower rates and special treatment." Black Lives Matter has in part been a revolt against this criminalization of poverty and in particular the police persecution of African Americans for minor infractions.

Two homeless people have already been killed by the police in San 6 Francisco this year. On April 7, in front of the encampment where he had

_____

[2] Born in 1979, Taylor is a Canadian American documentary filmmaker. —EDS.

lived for several months, officers shot Luis Gongora within thirty seconds of getting out of their cars. They said Gongora, a forty-five-year-old indigenous man from the Yucatán, was menacing them; several witnesses said he was cowering on the ground. The police chief made a big show of a photographic blowup of Gongora's thirteen-inch kitchen knife, and suggested that owning such an item was sinister. (Many unhoused people own knives for protection.) I went home from the police meeting and measured my largest kitchen knife: thirteen inches, the same length. Owning a kitchen knife without owning a kitchen can be considered criminal.

Six weeks later, on May 19, a single bullet killed Jessica Williams, a 7 pregnant, African-American mother of five who was unarmed and posed no threat to anyone at the time of her execution. She was in a stolen car, though who stole it was never made clear, and she was trying to flee the police out of what proved to be justified fear.

The situation is particularly bitter in San Francisco, now annexed as part of 8 Silicon Valley, since the tech industry created a gigantic bubble of wealth that puts economic inequality in much sharper relief. Here is Mark Zuckerberg,[3]

An encampment at the eastern edge of Division Street, February 14. Robert Gumpert/Redux

[3] Zuckerberg (born 1984) is the cofounder and chairman of Facebook, the multibillion-dollar social media company headquartered in Menlo Park, California, on the outskirts of San Francisco. —Eds.

the sixth-richest person in the world, in his house on the western edge of the historically Latino and working-class Mission District. Here is Division Street, on the northern edge of that neighborhood, where more than 250 housing-deprived people settled in tents early in 2016, seeking shelter from both the rain and the mayor's sweeps of the homeless as he primped the city for Super Bowl visitors.

The tech boom has also brought an influx of highly paid employees to the 9 city. They have precipitated a housing crisis, marked by skyrocketing rents, evictions, displacement, and the transformation of single-room-occupancy hotels — traditionally the last refuge of the indigent — into tech dorms. (Thousands of other former long-term residences — houses and apartments — have been converted into short-term rentals for Airbnb, a corporation founded in San Francisco whose impact has been bitterly denounced from Venice to New Orleans to Vancouver.) One of the common narratives about the homeless is that they came here to reap the social services of San Francisco: that they are intruders, outsiders, freeloaders, and that we can therefore justify their expulsion. But a recent survey of people living on San Francisco's streets concluded that seventy-one percent had already been in

Kelly, thirty-four, on Brannan Street, less than a block from Airbnb, February 16, 2015.
Robert Gumpert/Redux

the city before becoming homeless, and most of the rest were from the region or the state.

Silicon Valley also leads the way in creating technologies that elimi-   10 nate a plethora of jobs—toll-takers, sales clerks, inventory and warehouse workers, and (if Google, Tesla, and Uber have their way) taxi drivers and truckers—that might once have been filled by our current homeless population.

Of course, being homeless is itself hard work—over the thirty-six years   11 that I've observed the indigent in San Francisco, they have often made me think of hunter-gatherers. These people forage for survival, eluding attack, roaming, watching, maybe making the rounds of social services and soup kitchens, trying to protect what possessions they have, starting over from nothing when medications, phones, and identities are stolen by compatriots or seized by police. The city is a wilderness to them; that they now live in tents designed for recreational camping is all the more ironic. Gumpert notes that some feel they cannot leave their tents for even short lengths of time, for fear of losing their belongings. Others suffer from sleep deprivation, since they can find no safe place to rest.

Those without houses are too often considered to be problems to peo-   12 ple rather than people with problems. No wonder the means for addressing them is often that used to address litter, dirt, and contamination: removal. "If you're trying to prevent the undesirables from using park bathrooms, adding porta potties seems like a pretty decent solution," said a Mission resident named Branden on an online neighborhood forum. "If you're try-ing to keep the dirty undesirables away forever, you'll need constant police presence with a mandate to use violence to enforce whatever law prohibits their existence."

Journal Writing

Solnit notes that some new technologies, such as "Google, Tesla, and Uber" (par. 10), have exacerbated problems of poverty and homelessness in Silicon Valley, the very region where such technologies are being developed. Think of a technology or development that some people view positively but that you view differently because of its risks, unintended consequences, or ethical implications: space travel? stem-cell research? wind farms? an everyday convenience such as Bitcoin or Airbnb? In your journal, explore your thoughts about this technology or development.

Questions on Meaning

1. What do you take to be Solnit's PURPOSE in writing this piece? How well does she accomplish it?
2. When, according to Solnit, did homelessness first become a problem in America? Who or what does she implicitly blame for the phenomenon, and why?
3. What does Solnit identify as the causes of homelessness, in the United States in general and in San Francisco in particular?
4. What would you say is Solnit's THESIS? What solution to the problem of homelessness does she propose?

Questions on Writing Strategy

1. Who does Solnit imagine as her AUDIENCE? Why do you suppose she addresses readers directly, as *you*, in the essay's INTRODUCTION? What is the effect?
2. Where in the essay does Solnit address opposing viewpoints? What possible causes of homelessness does she dismiss, and why? What solutions does she reject?
3. Take a close look at the photographs sampled from Robert Gumpert's photo essay. How would you characterize these images? What do they contribute to Solnit's main idea?
4. **MIXED METHODS**   What point does Solnit make in COMPARING AND CONTRASTING "prison and the streets" in paragraphs 2–3? What stylistic techniques does she use to help drive that point home?
5. **MIXED METHODS**   How does Solnit use EXAMPLES to develop her argument? What is the effect of the particular examples she provides?

Questions on Language

1. How would you characterize Solnit's relationship to her subject? What POINT OF VIEW does she take in writing about it?
2. What is the TONE of this essay? Is the tone appropriate, given the author's subject, audience, and purpose?
3. Define fundamental (par. 1); former, latter (2); defecation, marginalized (3); buffered (4); de facto, infraction (5); indigenous, cowering (6); annexed (8); influx, precipitated, indigent, denounced, expulsion (9); plethora (10); compatriots, deprivation (11); mandate (12).

Suggestions for Writing

1. **FROM JOURNAL TO ESSAY**   Compose an essay in which you explain why you believe that the technology or development you wrote about in your journal has or may have negative consequences ignored by others. Be sure to acknowledge

what others see as the benefits. Also keep in mind that some readers may not immediately agree with you, so you will need to defend your views carefully and fully.

2. Consider a personal experience that involved misfortune. Have you ever needed to beg on the street, been evicted from an apartment, or had to scrounge for food? Have you ever been asked for money by beggars, worked in a soup kitchen, or volunteered at a shelter or public hospital? Write an essay about one such experience, using narration and examples to convey the causes of the misfortune and the effects the experience had on you.

3. Estimates of the number of homeless people in the United States vary widely. Research the numbers, and then write an essay in which you present your findings and propose reasons for the variations. Consider, for instance, how different organizations DEFINE homelessness and what distinctions they use to CLASSIFY homeless populations. Who counts as homeless, and who doesn't? Why do you think that is?

4. In paragraphs 3 and 5 Solnit refers to the imprisonment of homeless people and the concerns such government action raises among supporters of individual rights, such as the Black Lives Matter movement. What is your opinion of the rights of homeless people to live on the streets? How do you distinguish among the individual's rights, the community's responsibilities to the individual, and the community's rights? (For instance, what if a homeless person seems sick? What if he or she seems unstable, if not violent?) You may work solo on this assignment — stating your ideas and supporting them with evidence from your own observations and experience — or you may conduct research to discover legal and other arguments and data to support your ideas.

5. **CRITICAL WRITING** Take a close look at the nature of Solnit's SOURCES and her use of SUMMARY, PARAPHRASE, and direct QUOTATION. In an essay, analyze the way she SYNTHESIZES and integrates information and ideas. Why does she quote directly where she does? How effective are her summaries and paraphrases? How does she combine source materials to develop a thesis of her own?

6. **CONNECTIONS**   COMPARE AND CONTRAST the views of homelessness and its solutions in Solnit's "Division Street" and Anna Quindlen's "Homeless" (p. 181), written some thirty years earlier in 1987. Use specific passages from each essay to support your comparison.

7. **CONNECTIONS**   In "The Capricious Camera" (p. 342), Laila Ayad describes a photograph of a young girl and attempts to interpret its historical meanings. Using Solnit's and Ayad's essays for examples, write an essay of your own in which you discuss how writers can create meaning through description and analysis of visual images, particularly as they pertain to photojournalism.

JONATHAN SWIFT

Jonathan Swift (1667–1745), the son of English parents who had settled in Ireland, divided his energies among literature, politics, and the church. He was educated at Trinity College in Dublin (BA, 1686) and Oxford University (MA, 1692). In 1695 he was ordained a priest in the Church of Ireland. Dissatisfied with the quiet life of a parish priest, Swift spent much of his time in London hobnobbing with writers and producing pamphlets in support of the Tory Party. In 1713 Queen Anne rewarded his political services with an assignment the London-loving Swift didn't want: to supervise St. Patrick's Cathedral in Dublin. There, as Dean Swift, he ended his days—beloved by the Irish, whose interests he defended against the English government. Although Swift's chief works include the remarkable satires *The Battle of the Books* and *A Tale of a Tub* (both 1704) and scores of fine poems, he is best remembered for *Gulliver's Travels* (1726), an account of four imaginary voyages. This classic is abridged when it is given to children because of its frank descriptions of human filth and viciousness. In *Gulliver's Travels*, Swift pays tribute to the reasoning portion of "that animal called man," and delivers a stinging rebuke to the rest of him.

A Modest Proposal

Three consecutive years of drought and sparse crops had worked hardship upon the Irish when Swift wrote this ferocious essay in the summer of 1729. At the time, there were said to be thirty-five thousand wandering beggars in the country: Whole families had quit their farms and had taken to the roads. Large landowners, of English ancestry, preferred to ignore their tenants' sufferings and lived abroad to dodge taxes and payment of church duties. Swift had no special fondness for the Irish, but he hated the inhumanity he witnessed.

Although printed as a pamphlet in Dublin, Swift's essay is clearly meant for English readers as well as Irish ones. When circulated, the pamphlet caused a sensation in both Ireland and England and had to be reprinted seven times in the same year. Swift is an expert with plain, vigorous English prose, and "A Modest Proposal" is a masterpiece of SATIRE and IRONY. (If you are uncertain what Swift argues for, see the discussion of these devices in the Glossary.)

"A Modest Proposal" is an argument developed chiefly by process analysis and cause and effect, with notable uses of description, example, and comparison.

Description (Chap. 6): paragraphs 1–2, 19
Example (Chap. 7): paragraphs 1–2, 6, 10, 14, 18, 32
Comparison and contrast (Chap. 8): paragraph 17
Process analysis (Chap. 9): paragraphs 4, 6–7, 10–17
Cause and effect (Chap. 12): paragraphs 4–5, 13, 21–29, 31, 33
Argument and persuasion (Chap. 14): throughout

*For Preventing the Children of Poor People in Ireland from Being a Burden
to Their Parents or Country, and for Making Them Beneficial to the Public*

It is a melancholy object to those who walk through this great town[1] or
travel in the country, when they see the streets, the roads, and cabin doors,
crowded with beggars of the female sex, followed by three, four, or six children,
all in rags and importuning every passenger for an alms. These mothers, instead
of being able to work for their honest livelihood, are forced to employ all their
time in strolling to beg sustenance for their helpless infants, who, as they grow
up, either turn thieves for want of work, or leave their dear native country to
fight for the Pretender in Spain, or sell themselves to the Barbados.[2]

I think it is agreed by all parties that this prodigious number of children
in the arms, or on the backs, or at the heels of their mothers, and frequently
of their fathers, is in the present deplorable state of the kingdom a very great
additional grievance; and therefore whoever could find out a fair, cheap, and
easy method of making these children sound, useful members of the commonwealth would deserve so well of the public as to have his statue set up for
a preserver of the nation.

But my intention is very far from being confined to provide only for the
children of professed beggars; it is of a much greater extent, and shall take in
the whole number of infants at a certain age who are born of parents in effect
as little able to support them as those who demand our charity in the streets.

As to my own part, having turned my thoughts for many years upon this
important subject, and maturely weighed the several schemes of other pro-
jectors,[3] I have always found them grossly mistaken in their computation. It
is true, a child just dropped from its dam may be supported by her milk for a
solar year, with little other nourishment; at most not above the value of two
shillings, which the mother may certainly get, or the value in scraps, by her
lawful occupation of begging; and it is exactly at one year that I propose to
provide for them in such a manner as instead of being a charge upon their
parents or the parish, or wanting food and raiment for the rest of their lives,
they shall on the contrary contribute to the feeding, and partly to the clothing, of many thousands.

There is likewise another great advantage in my scheme, that it will prevent those voluntary abortions, and that horrid practice of women murdering

---

[1] Dublin. —EDS.

[2] The Pretender was James Stuart, exiled in Spain; in 1718 many Irishmen had joined
an army seeking to restore him to the English throne. Others wishing to emigrate had signed
papers as indentured servants, agreeing to work for a number of years in the Barbados or other
British colonies in exchange for their ocean passage. —EDS.

[3] Planners. —EDS.

their bastard children, alas, too frequent among us, sacrificing the poor innocent babes, I doubt, more to avoid the expense than the shame, which would
move tears and pity in the most savage and inhuman breast.

The number of souls in this kingdom being usually reckoned one million   6
and a half, of these I calculate there may be about two hundred thousand
couples whose wives are breeders; from which number I subtract thirty thousand couples who are able to maintain their own children, although I apprehend there cannot be so many under the present distress of the kingdom;
but this being granted, there will remain an hundred and seventy thousand
breeders. I again subtract fifty thousand for those women who miscarry, or
whose children die by accident or disease within the year. There only remain
an hundred and twenty thousand children of poor parents annually born.
The question therefore is, how this number shall be reared and provided for,
which, as I have already said, under the present situation of affairs, is utterly
impossible by all the methods hitherto proposed. For we can neither employ
them in handicraft or agriculture; we neither build houses (I mean in the
country) nor cultivate land. They can very seldom pick up a livelihood stealing till they arrive at six years old, except where they are of towardly parts;[4]
although I confess they learn the rudiments much earlier, during which
time they can however be looked upon only as probationers, as I have been
informed by a principal gentleman in the country of Cavan, who protested to
me that he never knew above one or two instances under the age of six, even
in a part of the kingdom so renowned for the quickest proficiency in that art.

I am assured by our merchants that a boy or a girl before twelve years old   7
is no salable commodity; and even when they come to this age they will not
yield above three pounds, or three pounds and half a crown at most on the
Exchange; which cannot turn to account either to the parents or the kingdom,
the charge of nutriment and rags having been at least four times that value.

I shall now therefore humbly propose my own thoughts, which I hope   8
will not be liable to the least objection.

I have been assured by a very knowing American of my acquaintance   9
in London, that a young healthy child well nursed is at a year old a most
delicious, nourishing, and wholesome food, whether stewed, roasted, baked,
or boiled; and I make no doubt that it will equally serve in a fricassee or a
ragout.[5]

I do therefore humbly offer it to public consideration that of the hundred   10
and twenty thousand children, already computed, twenty thousand may be
reserved for breed, whereof only one fourth part to be males, which is more
than we allow to sheep, black cattle, or swine; and my reason is that these

[4] Teachable wits, innate abilities. —Eds.
[5] Stew. —Eds.

children are seldom the fruits of marriage, a circumstance not much regarded by our savages, therefore one male will be sufficient to serve four females. That the remaining hundred thousand may at a year old be offered in sale to the persons of quality and fortune through the kingdom, always advising the mother to let them suck plentifully in the last month, so as to render them plump and fat for a good table. A child will make two dishes at an entertainment for friends; and when the family dines alone, the fore or hind quarter will make a reasonable dish, and seasoned with a little pepper or salt will be very good boiled on the fourth day, especially in winter.

I have reckoned upon a medium that a child just born will weigh twelve   11
pounds, and in a solar year if tolerably nursed increaseth to twenty-eight pounds.

I grant this food will be somewhat dear, and therefore very proper for   12
landlords, who, as they have already devoured most of the parents, seem to have the best title to the children.

Infant's flesh will be in season throughout the year, but more plentiful in   13
March, and a little before and after. For we are told by a grave author, an eminent French physician,[6] that fish being a prolific diet, there are more children born in Roman Catholic countries about nine months after Lent than at any other season; therefore, reckoning a year after Lent, the markets will be more glutted than usual, because the number of popish infants is at least three to one in this kingdom; and therefore it will have one other collateral advantage, by lessening the number of Papists among us.

I have already computed the charge of nursing a beggar's child (in which list   14
I reckon all cottagers, laborers, and four-fifths of the farmers) to be about two shillings per annum, rags included; and I believe no gentleman would repine to give ten shillings for the carcass of a good fat child, which, as I have said, will make four dishes of excellent nutritive meat, when he hath only some particular friend or his own family to dine with him. Thus the squire will learn to be a good landlord, and grow people among the tenants; the mother will have eight shillings net profit, and be fit for work till she produces another child.

Those who are more thrifty (as I must confess the times require) may flay   15
the carcass; the skin of which artificially[7] dressed will make admirable gloves for ladies, and summer boots for fine gentlemen.

As to our city of Dublin, shambles[8] may be appointed for this purpose   16
in the most convenient parts of it, and butchers we may be assured will not be wanting; although I rather recommend buying the children alive, and dressing them hot from the knife as we do roasting pigs.

---

[6] Swift's favorite French writer, François Rabelais, sixteenth-century author; not "grave" at all, but a broad humorist. —EDS.

[7] With art or craft. —EDS.

[8] Butcher shops or slaughterhouses. —EDS.

A very worthy person, a true lover of his country, and whose virtues I highly   17
esteem, was lately pleased in discoursing on this matter to offer a refinement
upon my scheme. He said that many gentlemen of his kingdom, having of late
destroyed their deer, he conceived that the want of venison might be well supplied by the bodies of young lads and maidens, not exceeding fourteen years of
age nor under twelve, so great a number of both sexes in every county being
now ready to starve for want of work and service; and these to be disposed of by
their parents, if alive, or otherwise by their nearest relations. But with due deference to so excellent a friend and so deserving a patriot, I cannot be altogether
in his sentiments; for as to the males, my American acquaintance assured me
from frequent experience that their flesh was generally tough and lean, like
that of our schoolboys, by continual exercise, and their taste disagreeable; and
to fatten them would not answer the charge. Then as to the females, it would, I
think with humble submission, be a loss to the public, because they soon would
become breeders themselves; and besides, it is not improbable that some scrupulous people might be apt to censure such a practice (although indeed very
unjustly) as a little bordering upon cruelty; which, I confess, hath always been
with me the strongest objection against any project, how well soever intended.

But in order to justify my friend, he confessed that this expedient was   18
put into his head by the famous Psalmanazar,[9] a native of the island Formosa,
who came from thence to London above twenty years ago, and in conversation told my friend that in his country when any young person happened
to be put to death, the executioner sold the carcass to persons of quality as
a prime dainty; and that in his time the body of a plump girl of fifteen, who
was crucified for an attempt to poison the emperor, was sold to his Imperial
Majesty's prime minister of state, and other great mandarins of the court, in
joints from the gibbet, at four hundred crowns. Neither indeed can I deny
that if the same use were made of several plump young girls in this town, who
without one single groat to their fortunes cannot stir abroad without a chair,
and appear at the playhouse and assemblies in foreign fineries which they
never will pay for, the kingdom would not be the worse.

Some persons of a desponding spirit are in great concern about that   19
vast number of poor people who are aged, diseased, or maimed, and I have
been desired to employ my thoughts what course may be taken to ease the
nation of so grievous an encumbrance. But I am not in the least pain upon
that matter, because it is very well known that they are every day dying and
rotting by cold and famine, and filth and vermin, as fast as can be reasonably
expected. And as to the younger laborers, they are now in almost as hopeful

---

[9] Georges Psalmanazar—a Frenchman who pretended to be Japanese, the author of a
completely imaginary *Description of the Isle Formosa* (1705)—had become a well-known figure
in gullible London society. —EDS.

a condition. They cannot get work, and consequently pine away for want of nourishment to a degree that if any time they are accidentally hired to common labor, they have not strength to perform it; and thus the country and themselves are happily delivered from the evils to come.

I have too long digressed, and therefore shall return to my subject. I think 20 the advantages by the proposal which I have made are obvious and many, as well as of the highest importance.

For first, as I have already observed, it would greatly lessen the number of 21 Papists, with whom we are yearly overrun, being the principal breeders of the nation as well as our most dangerous enemies; and who stay at home on purpose to deliver the kingdom to the Pretender, hoping to take their advantage by the absence of so many good Protestants, who have chosen rather to leave their country than to stay at home and pay tithes against their conscience to an Episcopal curate.

Secondly, the poorer tenants will have something valuable of their own, 22 which by law may be made liable to distress,[10] and help to pay their landlord's rent, their corn and cattle being already seized and money a thing unknown.

Thirdly, whereas the maintenance of an hundred thousand children, from 23 two years old and upwards, cannot be computed at less than ten shillings a piece per annum, the nation's stock will be thereby increased fifty thousand pounds per annum, besides the profit of a new dish introduced to the tables of all gentlemen of fortune in the kingdom who have any refinement in taste. And the money will circulate among ourselves, the goods being entirely of our own growth and manufacture.

Fourthly, the constant breeders, besides the gain of eight shillings 24 sterling per annum by the sale of their children, will be rid of the charge of maintaining them after the first year.

Fifthly, this food would likewise bring great custom to taverns, where the 25 vintners will certainly be so prudent as to procure the best receipts for dressing it to perfection, and consequently have their houses frequented by all the fine gentlemen, who justly value themselves upon their knowledge in good eating; and a skillful cook, who understands how to oblige his guests, will contrive to make it as expensive as they please.

Sixthly, this would be a great inducement to marriage, which all wise 26 nations have either encouraged by rewards or enforced by laws and penalties. It would increase the care and tenderness of mothers toward their children, when they were sure of a settlement for life to the poor babes, provided in some sort by the public, to their annual profit instead of expense. We should see an honest emulation among the married women, which of them could

---

[10] Subject to seizure by creditors. —Eds.

bring the fattest child to the market. Men would become as fond of their wives during the time of their pregnancy as they are now of their mares in foal, their cows in calf, or sows when they are ready to farrow; nor offer to beat or kick them (as is too frequent a practice) for fear of a miscarriage.

Many other advantages might be enumerated. For instance, the addition 27 of some thousand carcasses in our exportation of barreled beef, the propagation of swine's flesh, and improvements in the art of making good bacon, so much wanted among us by the great destruction of pigs, too frequent at our tables, which are no way comparable in taste or magnificence to a well-grown, fat, yearling child, which roasted whole will make a considerable figure at a lord mayor's feast or any other public entertainment. But this and many others I omit, being studious of brevity.

Supposing that one thousand families in this city would be constant 28 customers for infants' flesh, besides others who might have it at merry meetings, particularly weddings and christenings, I compute that Dublin would take off annually about twenty thousand carcasses, and the rest of the kingdom (where probably they will be sold somewhat cheaper) the remaining eighty thousand.

I can think of no one objection that will possibly be raised against this 29 proposal, unless it should be urged that the number of people will be thereby much lessened in the kingdom. This I freely own, and it was indeed one principal design in offering it to the world. I desire the reader will observe, that I calculate my remedy for this one individual kingdom of Ireland and for no other that ever was, is, or I think ever can be upon earth. Therefore let no man talk to me of other expedients: of taxing our absentees at five shillings a pound: of using neither clothes nor household furniture except what is of our own growth and manufacture: of utterly rejecting the materials and instruments that promote foreign luxury: of curing the expensiveness of pride, vanity, idleness, and gaming in our women: of introducing a vein of parsimony, prudence, and temperance: of learning to love our country, in the want of which we differ even from Laplanders and the inhabitants of Topinamboo:[11] of quitting our animosities and factions, nor acting any longer like the Jews, who were murdering one another at the very moment their city was taken:[12] of being a little cautious not to sell our country and conscience for nothing: of teaching landlords to have at least one degree of mercy toward their tenants: lastly, of putting a spirit of honesty, industry, and skill into our shopkeepers; who, if a resolution could now be taken to buy only our native

---

[11] A district of Brazil. —EDS.

[12] During the Roman siege of Jerusalem (AD 70), prominent Jews were executed on the charge of being in league with the enemy. —EDS.

goods, would immediately unite to cheat and exact upon us in the price, the measure, and the goodness, nor could ever yet be brought to make one fair proposal of just dealing, though often and earnestly invited to it.

Therefore I repeat, let no man talk to me of these and the like expedients, 30 till he hath at least some glimpse of hope that there will ever be some hearty and sincere attempt to put them in practice.

But as to myself, having been wearied out for many years with offering 31 vain, idle, visionary thoughts, and at length utterly despairing of success, I fortunately fell upon this proposal, which, as it is wholly new, so it hath something solid and real, of no expense and little trouble, full in our own power, and whereby we can incur no danger in disobliging England. For this kind of commodity will not bear exportation, the flesh being of too tender a consistence to admit a long continuance in salt, although perhaps I could name a country which would be glad to eat up our whole nation without it.

After all, I am not so violently bent upon my own opinion as to reject any 32 offer proposed by wise men, which shall be found equally innocent, cheap, easy, and effectual. But before something of that kind shall be advanced in contradiction to my scheme, and offering a better, I desire the author or authors will be pleased maturely to consider two points. First, as things now stand, how they will be able to find food and raiment for an hundred thousand useless mouths and backs. And secondly, there being a round million of creatures in human figure throughout this kingdom, whose sole subsistence put into a common stock would leave them in debt two millions of pounds sterling, adding those who are beggars by profession to the bulk of farmers, cottagers, and laborers, with their wives and children who are beggars in effect; I desire those politicians who dislike my overture, and may perhaps be so bold to attempt an answer, that they will first ask the parents of these mortals whether they would not at this day think it a great happiness to have been sold for food at a year old in this manner I prescribe, and thereby have avoided such a perpetual scene of misfortunes as they have since gone through by the oppression of landlords, the impossibility of paying rent without money or trade, the want of common sustenance, with neither house nor clothes to cover them from the inclemencies of the weather, and the most inevitable prospect of entailing the like or greater miseries upon their breed forever.

I profess, in the sincerity of my heart, that I have not the least personal 33 interest in endeavoring to promote this necessary work, having no other motive than the public good of my country, by advancing our trade, providing for infants, relieving the poor, and giving some pleasure to the rich. I have no children by which I can propose to get a single penny; the youngest being nine years old, and my wife past childbearing.

Journal Writing

Swift's proposal is aimed at a serious social problem of his day. In your journal, consider a contemporary problem that — like the poverty and starvation Swift describes — seems to require drastic action. For instance, do you believe that a particular group of people is neglected, mistreated, or victimized? Turn to the news media for ideas if no problem comes immediately to mind.

Questions on Meaning

1. On the surface, what is Swift proposing?
2. Beneath his IRONY, what is Swift's argument?
3. What do you take to be the PURPOSE of Swift's essay?
4. How does the introductory paragraph serve Swift's purpose?
5. Comment on the statement "I can think of no one objection that will possibly be raised against this proposal" (par. 29). What objections can you think of?

Questions on Writing Strategy

1. Describe the mask of the personage through whom Swift writes.
2. By what means does the writer attest to his reasonableness?
3. At what point in the essay did it become clear to you that the proposal isn't modest but horrible?
4. **MIXED METHODS**　As an ARGUMENT, does "A Modest Proposal" appeal primarily to reason or to emotion? (See p. 495 for a discussion of the distinction.)
5. **MIXED METHODS**　What does Swift's argument gain by his careful attention to PROCESS ANALYSIS and to CAUSE AND EFFECT?

Questions on Language

1. How does Swift's choice of words enforce the monstrousness of his proposal? Note especially words from the vocabulary of breeding and butchery.
2. Consult your dictionary for the meanings of any of the following words not yet in your vocabulary: importuning, sustenance (par. 1); prodigious, commonwealth (2); computation, raiment (4); apprehend, rudiments, probationers (6); nutriment (7); fricassee (9); repine (14); flay (15); scrupulous, censure (17); mandarins (18); desponding, encumbrance (19); per annum (23); vintners (25); emulation, foal, farrow (26); expedients, parsimony, animosities (29); disobliging, consistence (31); overture, inclemencies (32).

Suggestions for Writing

1. **FROM JOURNAL TO ESSAY**   Write an essay in which you propose a solution to the problem raised in your journal. Your essay may be either of the following:

   a. A straight argument, giving EVIDENCE, in which you set forth possible solutions to the problem.

   b. An ironic proposal in the manner of Swift. If you do this one, find a device other than cannibalism to eliminate the victims or their problems. You don't want to imitate Swift too closely; he is probably inimitable.

2. In an encyclopedia, look into what has happened in Ireland since Swift wrote. Choose a specific contemporary aspect of Irish-English relations, research it in books and periodicals, and write a report on it.

3. **CRITICAL WRITING**   Choose several examples of irony in "A Modest Proposal" that you find particularly effective. In a brief essay, ANALYZE Swift's use of irony. Do your examples of irony depend on understating, overstating, or saying the opposite of what is meant? How do they improve on literal statements? What is the value of irony in argument?

4. **CONNECTIONS**   Read Jessica Mitford's "Behind the Formaldehyde Curtain" (p. 289) alongside "A Modest Proposal," and analyze the use of irony and humor in these two essays. How heavily does each author depend on irony and humor to make his or her argument? Do these elements strengthen both authors' arguments? What evidence does each offer that would also work in a more straightforward argument?

5. **CONNECTIONS**   Analyze the strategies that Jonathan Swift and N. Scott Momaday, in "The Way to Rainy Mountain" (p. 144), use to create sympathy for the oppressed groups they are concerned about. Concentrate not only on what they say but also on the words they use and their TONE. Then write a process analysis explaining techniques for portraying oppression so as to win the reader's sympathy. Use quotations or PARAPHRASES from Swift's and Momaday's essays as EXAMPLES. If you can think of other techniques that neither author uses, by all means include and illustrate them as well.

HENRY DAVID THOREAU

Henry David Thoreau (1817–62) was born in Concord, Massachusetts, where, excerpt for short excursions, he remained for the whole of his life. After his graduation from Harvard College, he taught school briefly, worked irregularly as a surveyor and house painter, and for a time labored in his father's pencil factory. The small sales of his first, self-published book, *A Week on the Concord and Merrimac Rivers* (1849), led him to remark, "I have now a library of nearly nine hundred volumes, over seven hundred of which I wrote myself." The lecturer Ralph Waldo Emerson befriended his neighbor Thoreau; but although these leading figures of Transcendentalism shared a faith in instinct and agreed that a unity exists between humankind and nature, they did not always see eye to eye on matters of politics. Unlike Emerson, Thoreau was an activist. He helped escaped slaves flee to Canada; he publicly renounced the church; he went to jail rather than pay his poll tax to a government that made war against Mexico. He recounts these brushes with the law in his essay "Civil Disobedience" (1849), in which later readers (including Mahatma Gandhi and Martin Luther King, Jr.) have found encouragement for their own nonviolent resistance. One other book appeared in Thoreau's lifetime: *Walden* (1854), a searching account of his time in (and around, and beyond) the one-room cabin he built for himself on the edges of Concord. When the famously solitary Thoreau lay dying, an aunt asked whether he had made his peace with God. "I did not know we had quarreled," he replied.

What I Lived For

At Walden Pond, Thoreau mercilessly scaled back his existence. Making himself almost fully self-reliant, he proved to his own satisfaction that he could build a home, grow beans, read classics in the original Greek and Latin, indulge the occasional visitor, and observe in minute detail the glories of the natural world.

Thoreau wrote with equal attentiveness: To revise *Walden*, a relatively short book, took him seven years. The following excerpt—the second half of the second chapter—is foremost an earnest argument for simplicity, but the poet-philosopher relies on multiple methods to develop and give significance to his artful commentary:

Narration (Chap. 5): paragraphs 4, 6
Description (Chap. 6): paragraphs 6, 7–8
Example (Chap. 7): paragraphs 3, 4, 5

I went to the woods because I wished to live deliberately, to front only 1
the essential facts of life, and see if I could not learn what it had to teach,
and not, when I came to die, discover that I had not lived. I did not wish
to live what was not life, living is so dear; nor did I wish to practice resignation, unless it was quite necessary. I wanted to live deep and suck out all the
marrow of life, to live so sturdily and Spartan-like as to put to rout all that
was not life, to cut a broad swath and shave close, to drive life into a corner,
and reduce it to its lowest terms, and, if it proved to be mean, why then to get
the whole and genuine meanness of it, and publish its meanness to the world;
or if it were sublime, to know it by experience, and be able to give a true
account of it in my next excursion. For most men, it appears to me, are in a
strange uncertainty about it, whether it is of the devil or of God, and have
somewhat hastily concluded that it is the chief end of man here to "glorify
God and enjoy him forever."

Still we live meanly, like ants; though the fable tells us that we were long 2
ago changed into men; like pygmies we fight with cranes; it is error upon error,
and clout upon clout, and our best virtue has for its occasion a superfluous and
evitable wretchedness. Our life is frittered away by detail. An honest man has
hardly need to count more than his ten fingers, or in extreme cases he may
add his ten toes, and lump the rest. Simplicity, simplicity, simplicity! I say, let
your affairs be as two or three, and not a hundred or a thousand; instead of a
million count half a dozen, and keep your accounts on your thumb nail. In
the midst of this chopping sea of civilized life, such are the clouds and storms
and quicksands and thousand-and-one items to be allowed for, that a man
has to live, if he would not founder and go to the bottom and not make his
port at all, by dead reckoning, and he must be a great calculator indeed who
succeeds. Simplify, simplify. Instead of three meals a day, if it be necessary eat
but one; instead of a hundred dishes, five; and reduce other things in proportion. Our life is like a German Confederacy, made up of petty states, with its
boundary forever fluctuating, so that even a German cannot tell you how
it is bounded at any moment. The nation itself, with all its so-called internal improvements, which, by the way are all external and superficial, is just
such an unwieldy and overgrown establishment, cluttered with furniture and
tripped up by its own traps, ruined by luxury and heedless expense, by want
of calculation and a worthy aim, as the million households in the land; and

the only cure for it as for them is in a rigid economy, a stern and more than Spartan simplicity of life and elevation of purpose. It lives too fast. Men think that it is essential that the *Nation* have commerce, and export ice, and talk through a telegraph, and ride thirty miles an hour, without a doubt, whether *they* do or not; but whether we should live like baboons or like men, is a little uncertain. If we do not get out sleepers,[1] and forge rails, and devote days and nights to the work, but go to tinkering upon our *lives* to improve *them*, who will build railroads? And if railroads are not built, how shall we get to heaven in season? But if we stay at home and mind our business, who will want railroads? We do not ride on the railroad; it rides upon us. Did you ever think what those sleepers are that underlie the railroad? Each one is a man, an Irishman, or a Yankee man. The rails are laid on them, and they are covered with sand, and the cars run smoothly over them. They are sound sleepers, I assure you. And every few years a new lot is laid down and run over; so that, if some have the pleasure of riding on a rail, others have the misfortune to be ridden upon. And when they run over a man that is walking in his sleep, a supernumerary sleeper in the wrong position, and wake him up, they suddenly stop the cars, and make a hue and cry about it, as if this were an exception. I am glad to know that it takes a gang of men for every five miles to keep the sleepers down and level in their beds as it is, for this is a sign that they may sometime get up again.

Why should we live with such hurry and waste of life? We are determined to be starved before we are hungry. Men say that a stitch in time saves nine, and so they take a thousand stitches today to save nine tomorrow. As for *work*, we haven't any of any consequence. We have the Saint Vitus's dance,[2] and cannot possibly keep our heads still. If I should only give a few pulls at the parish bell-rope, as for a fire, that is, without setting the bell, there is hardly a man on his farm in the outskirts of Concord, notwithstanding that press of engagements which was his excuse so many times this morning, nor a boy, nor a woman, I might almost say, but would forsake all and follow that sound, not mainly to save property from the flames, but, if we will confess the truth, much more to see it burn, since burn it must, and we, be it known, did not set it on fire—or to see it put out, and have a hand in it, if that is done as handsomely; yes, even if it were the parish church itself. Hardly a man takes a half hour's nap after dinner, but when he wakes he holds up his head and asks, "What's the news?" as if the rest of mankind had stood his sentinels. Some give directions to be waked every half hour, doubtless for no other

---

[1] Railroad ties. —Eds.
[2] Colloquial term for Sydenham's chorea, an acute neurological condition often preceded by rheumatic fever and characterized by uncontrolled jerking movements. —Eds.

purpose; and then, to pay for it, they tell what they have dreamed. After a night's sleep the news is as indispensable as the breakfast. "Pray tell me anything new that has happened to a man anywhere on this globe" — and he reads it over his coffee and rolls, that a man has had his eyes gouged out this morning on the Wachito River; never dreaming the while that he lives in the dark unfathomed mammoth cave of this world, and has but the rudiment of an eye himself.

For my part, I could easily do without the post-office. I think that there are very few important communications made through it. To speak critically, I never received more than one or two letters in my life — I wrote this some years ago — that were worth the postage. The penny-post is, commonly, an institution through which you seriously offer a man that penny for his thoughts which is so often safely offered in jest. And I am sure that I never read any memorable news in a newspaper. If we read of one man robbed, or murdered, or killed by accident, or one house burned, or one vessel wrecked, or one steamboat blown up, or one cow run over on the Western Railroad, or one mad dog killed, or one lot of grasshoppers in the winter — we never need read of another. One is enough. If you are acquainted with the principle, what do you care for a myriad instances and applications? To a philosopher all *news*, as it is called, is gossip, and they who edit and read it are old women over their tea. Yet not a few are greedy after this gossip. There was such a rush, as I hear, the other day at one of the offices to learn the foreign news by the last arrival, that several large squares of plate glass belonging to the establishment were broken by the pressure — news which I seriously think a ready wit might write a twelvemonth or twelve years beforehand with sufficient accuracy. As for Spain, for instance, if you know how to throw in Don Carlos and the Infanta, and Don Pedro and Seville and Granada, from time to time in the right proportions — they may have changed the names a little since I saw the papers — and serve up a bull-fight when other entertainments fail, it will be true to the letter, and give us as good an idea of the exact state or ruin of things in Spain as the most succinct and lucid reports under this head in the newspapers: and as for England, almost the last significant scrap of news from that quarter was the revolution of 1649; and if you have learned the history of her crops for an average year, you never need attend to that thing again, unless your speculations are of a merely pecuniary character. If one may judge who rarely looks into the newspapers, nothing new does ever happen in foreign parts, a French revolution not excepted.

What news! how much more important to know what that is which was never old! "Kieou-he-yu (great dignitary of the state of Wei) sent a man to Khoung-tseu to know his news. Khoung-tseu caused the messenger to be seated near him, and questioned him in these terms: What is your master doing? The messenger answered with respect: My master desires to diminish the number of his faults, but he cannot come to the end of them. The messenger being gone, the philosopher remarked: What a worthy messenger! What a worthy messenger!" The preacher, instead of vexing the ears of drowsy farmers on their day of rest at the end of the week — for Sunday is the fit conclusion of an ill-spent week, and not the fresh and brave beginning of a new one — with this one other draggle-tail of a sermon, should shout with thundering voice — "Pause! Avast! Why so seeming fast, but deadly slow?"

Shams and delusions are esteemed for soundest truths, while reality is fabulous. If men would steadily observe realities only, and not allow themselves to be deluded, life, to compare it with such things as we know, would be like a fairy tale and the Arabian Nights' Entertainments.[3] If we respected only what is inevitable and has a right to be, music and poetry would resound along the streets. When we are unhurried and wise, we perceive that only great and worthy things have any permanent and absolute existence — that petty fears and petty pleasures are but the shadow of the reality. This is always exhilarating and sublime. By closing the eyes and slumbering, and consenting to be deceived by shows, men establish and confirm their daily life of routine and habit everywhere, which still is built on purely illusory foundations. Children, who play life, discern its true law and relations more clearly than men, who fail to live it worthily, but who think that they are wiser by experience, that is, by failure. I have read in a Hindu book that "there was a king's son, who, being expelled in infancy from his native city, was brought up by a forester, and, growing up to maturity in that state, imagined himself to belong to the barbarous race with which he lived. One of his father's ministers, having discovered him, revealed to him what he was, and the misconception of his character was removed, and he knew himself to be a prince. So soul," continues the Hindu philosopher, "from the circumstances in which it is placed, mistakes its own character, until the truth is revealed to it by some holy teacher, and then it knows itself to be *Brahme*." I perceive that we inhabitants of New England live this mean life that we do because our vision does not penetrate the surface of things. We think that that *is* which *appears* to be. If a man should walk through this town and see only the reality, where, think you, would the "Mill-dam" go to? If he should give us an account of the realities he beheld there, we should not recognize the place in his description. Look at a meeting-house, or a courthouse, or a jail, or a shop, or a dwelling-house,

6

[3] Thoreau is referring to *One Thousand and One Nights*, a medieval collection of Middle Eastern and Indian folktales narrated by a bride whose new husband (a king) has had each of his previous wives killed on their wedding night. Scheherazade staves off her own execution by telling him stories but withholding their endings to the next evening, until he spares her life for good. — EDS.

and say what that thing really is before a true gaze, and they would all go to pieces in your account of them. Men esteem truth remote, in the outskirts of the system, behind the farthest star, before Adam and after the last man. In eternity there is indeed something true and sublime. But all these times and places and occasions are now and here. God himself culminates in the present moment, and will never be more divine in the lapse of all the ages. And we are enabled to apprehend at all what is sublime and noble only by the perpetual instilling and drenching of the reality that surrounds us. The universe constantly and obediently answers to our conceptions; whether we travel fast or slow, the track is laid for us. Let us spend our lives in conceiving then. The poet or the artist never yet had so fair and noble a design but some of his posterity at least could accomplish it.

Let us spend one day as deliberately as Nature, and not be thrown off the track by every nutshell and mosquito's wing that falls on the rails. Let us rise early and fast, or break fast, gently and without perturbation; let company come and let company go, let the bells ring and the children cry—determined to make a day of it. Why should we knock under and go with the stream? Let us not be upset and overwhelmed in that terrible rapid and whirlpool called a dinner, situated in the meridian shallows. Weather this danger and you are safe, for the rest of the way is down hill. With unrelaxed nerves, with morning vigor, sail by it, looking another way, tied to the mast like Ulysses.[4] If the engine whistles, let it whistle till it is hoarse for its pains. If the bell rings, why should we run? We will consider what kind of music they are like. Let us settle ourselves, and work and wedge our feet downward through the mud and slush of opinion, and prejudice, and tradition, and delusion, and appearance, that alluvion which covers the globe, through Paris and London, through New York and Boston and Concord, through church and state, through poetry and philosophy and religion, till we come to a hard bottom and rocks in place, which we can call *reality*, and say, This is, and no mistake; and then begin, having a *point d'appui*,[5] below freshet and frost and fire, a place where you might found a wall or a state, or set a lamppost safely, or perhaps a gauge, not a Nilometer,[6] but a Realometer, that future ages might know how deep a freshet of shams and appearances had gathered from time to time. If you stand right fronting and face to face to a fact, you will see the sun glimmer on both its surfaces, as if it were a cimeter, and feel its sweet edge dividing you

[4] In a memorable scene from the ancient Greek epic poem *The Odyssey* by Homer, Ulysses must pass his ship through a strait populated by sirens, whose songs were known to lure sailors and cause them to crash into the rocky shore. Ulysses asks his crew to restrain him to save them all from a deadly fate. —EDS.

[5] French, "point of support," or foundation. —EDS.

[6] An ancient Egyptian device for measuring the depth and clarity of the Nile River. —EDS.

through the heart and marrow, and so you will happily conclude your mortal career. Be it life or death, we crave only reality. If we are really dying, let us hear the rattle in our throats and feel cold in the extremities; if we are alive, let us go about our business.

Time is but the stream I go a-fishing in. I drink at it; but while I drink   8 I see the sandy bottom and detect how shallow it is. Its thin current slides away, but eternity remains. I would drink deeper; fish in the sky, whose bottom is pebbly with stars. I cannot count one. I know not the first letter of the alphabet. I have always been regretting that I was not as wise as the day I was born. The intellect is a cleaver; it discerns and rifts its way into the secret of things. I do not wish to be any more busy with my hands than is necessary. My head is hands and feet. I feel all my best faculties concentrated in it. My instinct tells me that my head is an organ for burrowing, as some creatures use their snout and forepaws, and with it I would mine and burrow my way through these hills. I think that the richest vein is somewhere hereabouts; so by the divining rod and thin rising vapors I judge; and here I will begin to mine.

Journal Writing

In your journal, respond to Thoreau's contention that we should all simplify our existence and become attuned to nature for the sake of leading more purposeful lives. How persuaded are you by his argument? Do you agree that forsaking the world of business and commerce, for instance, could make you a happier person, or do you think meaningful work (or religion, or building relationships, or something else) is the purpose of living? Why do you feel the way you do?

Questions on Meaning

1. Notice the first sentence of this excerpt from *Walden*: "I went to the woods because I wished to live deliberately," Thoreau writes. What does he mean by "live deliberately"? What does this statement reveal about his PURPOSE for writing?

2. Why did Thoreau choose to live in isolation? What, to his mind, were the major problems with society at the time? Do his criticisms still apply?

3. In two or three words, what would you say is Thoreau's THESIS?

4. What can you INFER from this piece about Thoreau's attitude toward organized religion? Does he seem to believe in God or some other divinity?

5. How does Thoreau explain the relationship between perception and reality? Does he think it's possible to know truth?

6. "I have always been regretting that I was not as wise as the day I was born," Thoreau writes in his conclusion (par. 8). How do you account for this PARADOX?

Questions on Writing Strategy

1. For whom does Thoreau seem to be writing: general readers? politicians? business owners? religious leaders? some other group? What influence does he apparently hope to have on his readers' behavior? To what extent did he influence your opinion about simple living?

2. Thoreau's writing feels impressionistic — even transcendent, one might say. What strategies does he use to give his musings UNITY and COHERENCE?

3. **MIXED METHODS**   How does Thoreau use EXAMPLES to DEFINE *news* (par. 4)? How does the news COMPARE to gossip, as far as he's concerned?

4. **MIXED METHODS**   What role does NARRATION play in Thoreau's ARGUMENT? What do the ANECDOTES in paragraphs 5 and 6 contribute to his point? To what other works of literature does Thoreau ALLUDE? Must readers be familiar with these stories to appreciate his meaning?

Questions on Language

1. Thoreau was a poet as well as a philosopher, and his writing is, accordingly, rich in FIGURES OF SPEECH. Point to the two or three metaphors or similes you find most lyrical or compelling (or confounding) and explain their meaning.

2. Explain how and why Thoreau gives human qualities to railroads. What is the effect of these uses of PERSONIFICATION?

3. What is the TONE of this selection? In his chosen solitude does Thoreau seem grim, pleased, appalled, disgusted, mocking, or what? How can you tell?

4. You may find Thoreau's vocabulary more difficult than that of some other writers in this book. Look up, as necessary, definitions for any of these words you aren't sure of: dear, Spartan, rout, mean, sublime (par. 1); superfluous, founder, heedless, forge, supernumerary (2); forsake, unfathomed, rudiment (3); jest, myriad, lucid, pecuniary (4); vexing, avast (5); barbarous, Brahme, culminates, lapse, posterity (6); perturbation, meridian, alluvion, freshet, cimeter (7); rifts, faculties (8).

Suggestions for Writing

1. **FROM JOURNAL TO ESSAY**   Expand your journal writing into an essay in which you respond personally to Thoreau's plea: "Simplify, simplify" (par. 2). What do you think is the purpose of life? If you generally agree with Thoreau's assessment, what can you add to convince others who do not? If you generally disagree, how do you counter his argument?

2. Are your thoughts and actions a matter of habit or of deliberate choice? Write an essay about the importance (or unimportance) of self-awareness and conscious decision making, using several concrete examples or a single extended example to support your point. You may refer to some of Thoreau's ideas if you wish, but be sure to develop a unique thesis of your own.

3. If Thoreau objected so strongly to the rapid growth of the newspaper business enabled by the telegraph and the construction of railroads in the mid-nineteenth

century, what do you think he would make of today's online news feeds and twenty-four-hour broadcast cycles? What do *you* make of them? Do new technologies necessarily advance civilization, or might they also hinder it? Why do you think so? Can you think of other recent technologies that might be said to do more harm than good? Ponder these questions in a short essay.

4. **CRITICAL WRITING**   When Thoreau decamped to the woods to write *Walden* in 1845, the United States (and indeed much of the world) was experiencing a period of immense social, cultural, and political upheaval. The economy was shifting from one of home-based subsistence and informal trade to paid labor in structured workplaces. Abolitionists were pushing for an end to slavery, and women's rights activists were demanding equal protection under the law. The church was losing its influence and its place in local government. Social workers were seeking reforms in charitable, penal, and psychiatric institutions; others were calling for universal education and a new approach to schooling. Even Transcendentalism was a reform movement of sorts. Choose any one of these developments that interests you and do some research to learn more about it. Then, in an essay, explain how and why Thoreau incorporates critiques of that change into his argument in "What I Lived For."

5. **CONNECTIONS**   Zadie Smith, in "Find Your Beach" (p. 319), uses division or analysis to explore her own conceptions of the meaning of life. In an essay, COMPARE AND CONTRAST Smith's purpose and method with Thoreau's. What similarities and differences do you find in the two writers' approaches to the subject of deliberate living? To what extent do Smith's conclusions fit with Thoreau's ideas about simplicity?

6. **CONNECTIONS**   Recalling his own pilgrimage to Walden Pond, the author of the next essay, Luis Alberto Urrea, comments that as a teenager he had thought he understood what Thoreau meant when he wrote "Time is but the stream I go a-fishing in" (Thoreau, par. 8), but suggests that he didn't, really. What is your understanding of this famous line? In a paragraph or two, PARAPHRASE Thoreau's extended metaphor in plain language. What exactly is Thoreau saying here?

Henry David Thoreau on Writing

"Keep a journal," Emerson had urged Thoreau, and in 1837 the younger writer began making entries. For the rest of his life, he continued to be a faithful journal keeper. Into this intimate volume, kept only for his own eyes, Thoreau poured ideas, opinions, impressions, poems, meditations, passages from his reading that he wished to remember. Much of this raw material found its way into *Walden* and other published works. From Thoreau's *Journal*, here is a provocative sampling of his thoughts about writing. (To help identify each, we have given them subject headings.)

Physical Exercise. "How vain it is to sit down to write when you have not stood up to live! Methinks that the moment my legs begin to move, my thoughts begin to flow, as if I had given vent to the stream at the lower end and consequently new fountains flowed into it at the upper. A thousand rills which have their rise in the sources of thought burst forth and fertilize my brain. . . . The writing which consists with habitual sitting is mechanical, wooden, dull to read." (August 19, 1851)

Not Saying Everything. "It is the fault of some excellent writers — De Quincey's first impressions on seeing London suggest it to me — that they express themselves with too great fullness and detail. They give the most faithful, natural, and lifelike account of their sensations, mental and physical, but they lack moderation and sententiousness. They do not affect us by an intellectual earnestness and a reserve of meaning, like a stutterer; they say all they mean. Their sentences are not concentrated and nutty. Sentences which suggest far more than they say, which have an atmosphere about them, which do not merely report an old, but make a new impression; sentences which suggest as many things and are as durable as a Roman aqueduct: to frame these, that is the *art* of writing. Sentences which are expensive, towards which so many volumes, so much life, went; which lie like boulders on the page, up and down or across; which contain the seed of other sentences, not mere repetition, but creation: which a man might sell his grounds and castles to build." (August 22, 1851)

Writing with Body and Senses. "We cannot write well or truly but what we write with gusto. The body, the senses, must conspire with the mind. Expression is the act of the whole man, that our speech may be vascular. The intellect is powerless to express thought without the aid of the heart and liver and of every member. Often I feel that my head stands out too dry, when it should be immersed. A writer, a man writing, is the scribe of all nature; he is the corn and the grass and the atmosphere of writing. It is always essential that we love what we are doing, do it with a heart." (September 2, 1851)

Thought and Style. "Shall I not have words as fresh as my thoughts? Shall I use any other man's words? A genuine thought or feeling can find expression for itself, if it have to invent hieroglyphics. It has the universe for type-metal. It is for want of original thought that one man's style is like another's." (September 8, 1851)

Revision. "In correcting my manuscripts, which I do with sufficient phlegm, I find that I invariably turn out much that is good along with the bad, which it is then impossible for me to distinguish — so much for keeping bad company; but after the lapse of time, having purified the main body and thus created a distinct standard for comparison, I can review the rejected sentences and easily detect those which deserve to be readmitted." (March 1, 1854)

The Value of Lapsed Time. "Often I can give the truest and most interesting account of any adventure I have had after years have elapsed, for then I am not confused, only the most significant facts surviving in my memory. Indeed, all that continues to interest me after such a lapse of time is sure to be pertinent, and I may safely record all that I remember." (March 28, 1857)

Self-Inspiration. "The writer must to some extent inspire himself. Most of his sentences may at first lie dead in his essay, but when all are arranged, some life and color will be reflected on them from the mature and successful lines; they will appear to pulsate with fresh life, and he will be enabled to eke out their slumbering sense, and make them worthy of their neighborhood. . . . Most that is first written on any subject is a mere groping after it, mere rubble-stone and foundation." (February 3, 1859)

Thought Breeds Thought. "The Scripture rule, 'Unto him that hath shall be given,' is true of composition. The more you have thought and written on a given theme, the more you can still write. Thought breeds thought. It grows under your hands." (February 13, 1860)

The Bedford Reader on Writing

Thoreau's JOURNAL entries afford useful insight into a master craftsman's approach to writing. Especially noteworthy are his views on revision: Thoreau's suggestion to let some time pass between DRAFTING and REVISING echoes our own advice in Chapter 3 (p. 42). Let your draft sit for a while; after a "lapse of time" you can review it with fresh eyes and a refreshed mind, better able to see what could be improved. For more help, you can turn to "Questions for Peer Review and Revision" on page 42 and the individual revision checklists in the introductions to the methods (Chaps. 5–14).

LUIS ALBERTO URREA

Often praised as a significant "voice of the border," writer Luis Alberto Urrea has explained the reason for his persistent focus on life at the edge: "The border runs down the middle of me," he says. "I have a barbed-wire fence neatly bisecting my heart." He was born in Tijuana in 1955 and raised in San Diego, torn between the conflicting cultures of his father's Mexico and his mother's America. Urrea earned writing degrees from the University of California, San Diego (BA, 1977), and the University of Colorado Boulder (MA, 1994), and for a decade he pursued a dual career as a relief worker and investigative journalist in the slums surrounding Tijuana. He wrote four books exposing the horrors of extreme poverty that he encountered, all of them acclaimed for their combination of stark realism and lyrical voice: *Across the Wire* (1993); *By the Lake of Sleeping Children* (1996); *Nobody's Son* (1998), winner of the American Book Award; and *The Devil's Highway* (2004), nominated for a Pulitzer Prize. A popular fiction writer as well, Urrea has published multiple collections of short stories and poems, most recently *The Water Museum* and *The Tijuana Book of the Dead* (both 2015) and many novels, including *The Hummingbird's Daughter* (2005) and *The House of Broken Angels* (2018). Currently a professor at the University of Illinois at Chicago, he has taught expository and creative writing at Harvard University, Massachusetts Bay Community College, and the University of Colorado. He was inducted into the Latino Literature Hall of Fame in 2000.

Barrio Walden

Growing up, Urrea witnessed the effects of involuntary poverty in the neighborhoods of San Diego and Tijuana both. In this 2013 essay for *Orion* magazine, he recounts, with a mix of mirth and embarrassment, a youthful pilgrimage to the site of Henry David Thoreau's famous experiment in self-imposed simplicity (p. 620) in Concord, Massachusetts.

"Barrio Walden" is foremost a narrative, but Urrea also uses description, example, comparison and contrast, and definition to develop and give significance to his story.

Narration (Chap. 5): throughout
Description (Chap. 6): paragraphs 4–5, 9–12, 27–35
Example (Chap. 7): paragraphs 1, 3
Comparison and contrast (Chap. 8): paragraphs 10–26, 27–35
Definition (Chap. 13): paragraphs 3, 9

Imagine my shock. I was living in Massachusetts for the first time. 1
Adjusting. The first time I saw snow falling past my Somerville[1] apartment
window, I told a woman on the phone that a neighbor was on the roof shaking
out a pillow. Not many snowstorms in my desertified homeland. The first
time I saw ice on the sidewalk, I thought a prankster had smeared Vaseline on
the bricks to watch businessmen fall down.

This old world was all new to me. I was manhandled by quotidian revela- 2
tions, wrenched by the duende of Yankee cultural hoodoo. So when I realized
I could walk over to Porter Square[2] (where the porterhouse steak was first
hacked out of some Bostonian cow) and catch a commuter train to Concord,
to Walden freakin' Pond, I was off and running.

Perhaps I was a barrio Transcendentalist. Well, I was certainly one by 3
the time I hit the San Diego 'burbs in my tweens. I loved me some Thoreau.
"Civil Disobedience," right? What Doors fan couldn't get behind that? I also
had copied passages of "Self Reliance" by Emerson and pasted them to my
walls amid posters of hot rods and King Kong and John Lennon and trees.
Even in the '70s, I was deeply worried about trees.

So I trudged to the T stop and went down to the suburban rail level and 4
caught the Purple Line.[3] I, and all the rambunctious Concord high school
kids, were deeply plugged into our Walkmans.[4] I was all Screaming Blue
Messiahs and class rage, scribbling in my notebooks about rich bastards gig-
gling self-indulgently and shrieking "Eau my GWOD!" at each other as they
ignored the woods and the mangy deer outside. For me, it was a Disneyland
train ride, all this stuff I had only experienced robotically before. I was imagining the ditch diggers from my old neighborhood tripping out over all this
water. These damned New Englanders had water everywhere. And deer.

We pulled into Concord as if it were a normal thing, and I detrained 5
and stepped into the Friendly's.[5] At the time, if I could have had deep-tissue
grafts of Americana I would have, and a striped-awning ice cream place
where the happy lady called me "Deah" was just about the shiniest moment
of my Americanness to date.

"I'm looking for Walden," I announced. "Pond." Helpful-like, as if she 6
didn't know.

"Right out the door." Doah. "Go out and walk about a mile." 7

---

[1] A small city adjacent to Boston and Cambridge, Somerville has a large population
of college students and recent graduates. —Eds.

[2] A section of Cambridge less than a mile north of Harvard University. —Eds.

[3] The "T" is local shorthand for the MBTA, or the Massachusetts Bay Transportation
Authority. —Eds.

[4] Portable cassette players. —Eds.

[5] A chain of family restaurants in the eastern United States. —Eds.

I drank some soda. She called it "tonic." And I was off. She didn't tell me   8
I had to turn south. I turned north. And walked away.

Before we proceed much farther on our first New England early autumn   9
country walk, before we grow dizzy with red maples actually turning red in
a natural psychedelic blowmind, we might consider the dearth of what you
might call "ponds" where I come from. To me, a pond was a muddy hole you
could jump across, and it housed six or seven crawdads and some tadpoles.
(My friend Mark put dead polliwogs in a jar with hand lotion and charged kids
a nickel to look at "elephant sperm." We were guttersnipe naturalists.) When
Thoreau said, "Time is but the stream I go a-fishing in," I thought I knew what
he was talking about, though my stream was rain-shower runoff in an alley.
I had been fishing exactly once in my life, and I felt guilt about the poor worm
that came out of the water not only impaled on the hook but stiff as a twig.

So there I was, marching at a splendid pace! Away to Walden Pond! Or,   10
as my homeboys would have spelled it, GUALDENG! Delighted by every
tree! White fences! Orange and yellow and scarlet leaves! Concord thinned
and vanished and I was suddenly among farms! Huzzah! Well-met, shrieking
farm dogs threatening me! Bonjour, paranoiac farm wives hanging laundry
and glaring at me from fields of golden, uh, barley! Eau my gwod! I saw stacks
of lobster pots. I saw pumpkins. It was a shock to me that pumpkins grew
somewhere. Next to lobster pots! And a red tractor to boot.

Behold the festive black-and-white New England moo-cow. Scenes   11
bucolic and poetic — scenes the Alcotts[6] might have penned. Sad autumn
light, what a hipster pal in Harvard Square had called "Irish light," slanted
through the trees to make everything tremble with the most delicious melancholy I have yet to see again. I was bellowing along to Sisters of Mercy:
"Oh Marian, this world is killing me." Cows regarded me. Goths in paradise.

Right about then, I beheld it. In a field of mown hay. Next to a small   12
house and a slanty barn. Walden Pond. It was about twenty feet across and
surrounded by meditative heifers. I removed my headphones and went to the
fence and leaned upon the topmost rail and communed with the transcendent.
I wrestled with man's fate and the epic movements of the universe and the
natural splendour of the Creator's delight in the temple of His Creation.

The farmer came out of his house and stared at me. I waved. He jumped   13
in his truck and banged over ruts in his field. He wasn't smiling.

"I help you?" he shouted.   14

---

[6] Bronson Alcott (1799–1888) and his daughter Louisa May Alcott (1832–88) were both
writers and Transcendentalists friendly with Henry David Thoreau. For a short time in 1843
the Alcotts hosted an experimental utopian community in Concord called Fruitlands. —Eds.

"Just looking at the pond," said I.   15

"What pond?"   16

"Walden Pond!"   17

"Jesus Christ!" he reasoned. He looked back at his cows. He looked at   18
me. He looked at the cows. He said, "You're not from around here, are ya?"

"California," I said.   19

"That explains it."   20

What ho, my good fellow!   21

"You walked the wrong damned direction. It's about four mile that way."   22

I looked back, as though the great pond would reveal itself in the autum-   23
nal haze.

"Could you give me a ride?" I asked.   24

"Hell no!"   25

He smoked as he watched me trudge back toward Concord with a slightly   26
less splendid cadence.

Yeah, whatever. Barking dogs. Screw you. Farm wives gawking. What's   27
your problem? My feet hurt. Past Friendly's. Don't do me any favors, Deah.
And south, out of town again, across the crazed traffic on the highway, and
past a tumbledown trailer park and a garbage dump. What is this? Tijuana?

Gradually, I became aware of a bright blue mass to my right. A sea. A   28
Great Lake. This deal wasn't a pond, man. Are you kidding? Who called this
Sea of Cortez[7] a pond?

Down to the water. A crust of harlequin leaves lay along the shore. It   29
was dead silent. Thin wisps of steam rode the far shoreline. I squatted and
watched and fancied myself living in a shack, smoking my pipe, scratching
out one-liners with a quill, changing the world.

An ancient Dalmatian came along. He was stiff and arthritic, walking   30
at an angle, grinning and making horking sounds. His tag said his name was
Jason.

"Jason," I said. "I'm looking for Thoreau."   31

"Snork," he said, and headed out. I followed. We walked past cove and   32
bog and found ourselves at Henry's stone floor. The cairn of stones left by
travelers. I was glad my homeys did not see me cry over mere rocks.

The shack was about the size of my small bedroom back home in   33
San Diego. I put my hand on the old pines and felt Henry's bark against my
palm. Jason sneezed and thumped along to his own meditations. The pond
moved in slow motion before us, Henry and me. A train rolled past the far
trees like some strange dream.

---

[7] The Gulf of California, in the northwest of Mexico. —Eds.

Crows went from shadow to shadow, arguing.   34

Was it just me, or did I smell pipe tobacco burning?   35

I placed my stone on the cairn. I tipped my collar to my chin. Fall turned   36
cold fast in those days. "Adios, Enrique," I said. Then I headed back to town
for a hot cup of coffee and a ride home on a dark train.

Journal Writing

What works of literature hold a special place in your memory? In your journal, recall
as much as you can about a text or a writer that had a strong influence on you.

Questions on Meaning

1. Why is Urrea drawn to Walden Pond? What does it represent to him?

2. What one sentence best SUMMARIZES Urrea's understanding of Thoreau's Transcendentalist philosophy?

3. What does Urrea mean by "guttersnipe naturalists" (par. 9)? In what ways does this term seem to encapsulate his own philosophy?

4. Why does Urrea cry over the pile of rocks at Thoreau's cabin?

5. What would you say is Urrea's PURPOSE in this piece? How would you express his unstated THESIS?

Questions on Writing Strategy

1. Why might Urrea have chosen to open his NARRATIVE as he does? What is the function of his first three paragraphs?

2. For whom does Urrea seem to be writing? (Hint: Look up *Orion* magazine's mission and history online.) What ASSUMPTIONS does the author make about his readers' knowledge and interests? Does one need to be familiar with the works of Henry David Thoreau or Ralph Waldo Emerson to understand Urrea's meaning?

3. Most of Urrea's essay moves in SPATIAL ORDER, from the streets of Somerville to the center of Concord to an outlying farm and then to Walden Pond. Paragraph 9, however, jumps back to San Diego, as Urrea explains what "ponds" were like in the neighborhood where he grew up. Why do you think Urrea places this paragraph in the middle of his essay, instead of at the beginning?

4. What is the EFFECT of the last sentence of the essay?

5. **MIXED METHODS**   Which of the five senses does Urrea mainly appeal to in his DESCRIPTIONS? Point to some sensory IMAGES that seem especially concrete. What DOMINANT IMPRESSION does the author create?

6. **MIXED METHODS**   Where does Urrea use COMPARISON AND CONTRAST? What do these passages contribute to the essay?

Questions on Language

1. Notice that Urrea mixes urban slang, teenage colloquialisms, academic vocabulary, regional pronunciations, and a few words and phrases that sound as though he transported them from the nineteenth century. What does this DICTION contribute to the author's TONE?

2. "Barrio Walden" is riddled with sentence fragments (see p. 59 if you need an explanation). Identify four or five of them. Does Urrea need a better copy editor, or does he use sentence fragments for a reason? If so, what is it?

3. Contrast Urrea's DIALOG with the farmer (pars. 13–26) with his conversation with Jason the dog (30–33). What FIGURE OF SPEECH is he using here, and does he use it anywhere else? What point is he getting at, do you think?

4. How does Urrea seem to define *barrio* as it's used in his title and paragraph 3? What CONNOTATIONS can the word have?

5. Define any of these other words you may have doubts about: quotidian, duende (par. 2); Transcendentalist (3); rambunctious, mangy (4); grafts, Americana (5); psychedelic, dearth, polliwogs, impaled (9); paranoiac (10); bucolic, melancholy (11); heifers, communed, transcendent (12); harlequin, quill (29); cairn (32).

Suggestions for Writing

1. **FROM JOURNAL TO ESSAY**   In an essay, describe the effect one of the written works you discussed in your journal (p. 635) has had on you, but also do more: Like Urrea, focus not just on the text itself but also on its larger context. Why is it so special? What does it represent to you? How has it influenced your take on the world and the way you live your life? Be sure to infuse your writing with vivid IMAGES evoking concrete sensory experiences.

2. Have you ever had the experience of feeling caught between two worlds, whether because of region or culture or "class rage" (par. 4) or because of some other sense of disconnection—being new in town, struggling with neighbors, feeling friendless, or returning home after being away? Describe the experience in an essay to be read out loud, using plenty of details to help your listeners understand your feelings.

3. **CRITICAL WRITING**   In an essay, ANALYZE the image that Urrea presents of himself. Consider in particular his language and tone, as well as how thoroughly he develops his narrative with details, images, and dialog. How seriously does he take himself and his subject?

4. **CONNECTIONS**   Closely read or reread Henry David Thoreau's "What I Lived For" (p. 620), which is excerpted from *Walden*. What similarities do you notice between it and Urrea's essay? Why is it significant, for instance, that Urrea takes

a commuter train to visit Thoreau's cabin? Do you notice any other themes in common? In an essay, explain how and why Urrea incorporates Thoreau's Transcendentalist philosophy into his own writing.

5. **CONNECTIONS**   Urrea writes of feeling "dizzy" from "a natural psychedelic blowmind" (par. 9) when he walks the New England countryside in the fall. Similarly, Joan Didion, in "Earthquakes" (p. 569), expresses a growing sense of anxiety over the possibility of "the Big One" violently destroying her home of northern California. What else do these two writers' experiences have in common? How are they different? In an essay that combines narration and description, write about a time when observing your environment filled you with emotion and made you feel connected to the natural world.

Luis Alberto Urrea on Writing

Luis Alberto Urrea is a prolific and diverse writer: Even while teaching he has published volumes of poetry, short stories, novels, investigative journalism, and essays, and he promises to "write a bunch more." In a 2011 interview for the journal *Bookslut*, reviewer Terry Hong asked him, "When you get stuck—do you get stuck?—what do you do for inspiration?" Here we give you Urrea's ebullient answer.

I do get stuck! I think everyone gets stuck! Here's the thing, and this is a part of my belief system that continues to grow over the years: I have to thank the ancient Chinese poets and writers, and especially the Japanese haiku poets. Through them, I've come to realize that writing is not a product, but a process. Writing is a life style, a life choice, a path. Writing is part of my process of sacredness and prayer even. What I do is writing; that's how I've chosen to understand and process the world, as a writer.

When I feel stuck, then that season has taken a bit of a pause. The garden has already grown many different blossoms, and my task is to know when not to force something more. It would be a mistake to do battle with the writing spirit. Writer's block is like a stop sign; it's a warning. So sometimes I just think for a while, sometimes I drive cross-country, sometimes I read something. That's the time to do something fascinating that's outside of myself, and there's *always* something fascinating going on. If I get all wrapped up in myself, I'll grind to a halt eventually. If nothing else, I'm just not that interesting.

The world is full of hilarious, upsetting, entertaining, disturbing stuff out there—that well just never runs dry. That's a great gift for all of us. We just have to go out and look.

The Bedford Reader on Writing

We have to agree with Urrea that the world around you can be fascinating and inspiring. And as he suggests, looking with a critical eye can help you turn such inspiration into concrete ideas for writing. For help with delving into the meanings of the images you encounter—online, on television, in advertisements and the movies—see pages 22–26 of Chapter 1. For additional inspiration, you might also heed Urrea's advice to "read something," such as one of the other essays in this book. Any of them might spark fresh ideas for you.

E. B. WHITE

For half a century Elwyn Brooks White (1899–1985) was a regular contributor to *The New Yorker*, and his essays, editorials, anonymous features for "The Talk of the Town," and fillers helped build the magazine a reputation for wit and good writing. If as a child you read *Charlotte's Web* (1952), you have met E. B. White before. The book reflects some of his own life on a farm in North Brooklin, Maine. White wrote other children's books, including *Stuart Little* (1945), and in 1970 he received the Laura Ingalls Wilder Award for his "substantial and lasting contribution to literature for children." He is also widely known for revising and expanding *The Elements of Style* (50th anniversary edition, 2008), a writer's guide by his college professor William Strunk, Jr. White's *Letters* were collected in 1976, his *Essays* in 1977, and his *Poems and Sketches* in 1981. On July 4, 1963, President Kennedy named White in the first group of Americans to receive the Presidential Medal of Freedom, with a citation that called him "an essayist whose concise comment . . . has revealed to yet another age the vigor of the English sentence."

Once More to the Lake

"Once More to the Lake" first appeared in *Harper's* magazine in 1941. Perhaps if a duller writer had written the essay, or an essay with the same title, we wouldn't much care about it, for at first its subject seems as personal and ordinary as a letter home. White's loving and exact portrayal, however, brings this lakeside camp to life for us. In the end, the writer arrives at an awareness that shocks him — shocks us, too, with a familiar sensory detail.

"Once More to the Lake" is a stunning mixture of description and narration, but it is also more. To make his observations and emotions clear and immediate, White relies extensively on several methods of development.

Narration (Chap. 5): throughout
Description (Chap. 6): throughout
Example (Chap. 7): paragraphs 2, 7–8, 11, 12
Comparison and contrast (Chap. 8): paragraphs 4–7, 9–10, 11–12
Process analysis (Chap. 9): paragraphs 9, 10, 12

August 1941

One summer, along about 1904, my father rented a camp on a lake in 1 Maine and took us all there for the month of August. We all got ringworm from some kittens and had to rub Pond's Extract on our arms and legs night and morning, and my father rolled over in a canoe with all his clothes on; but outside of that the vacation was a success and from then on none of us ever thought there was any place in the world like that lake in Maine.

We returned summer after summer — always on August 1 for one month. I have since become a salt-water man, but sometimes in summer there are days when the restlessness of the tides and the fearful cold of the sea water and the incessant wind that blows across the afternoon and into the evening make me wish for the placidity of a lake in the woods. A few weeks ago this feeling got so strong I bought myself a couple of bass hooks and a spinner and returned to the lake where we used to go, for a week's fishing and to revisit old haunts.

I took along my son, who had never had any fresh water up his nose and 2 who had seen lily pads only from train windows. On the journey over to the lake I began to wonder what it would be like. I wondered how time would have marred this unique, this holy spot — the coves and streams, the hills that the sun set behind, the camps and the paths behind the camps. I was sure that the tarred road would have found it out, and I wondered in what other ways it would be desolated. It is strange how much you can remember about places like that once you allow your mind to return into the grooves that lead back. You remember one thing, and that suddenly reminds you of another thing. I guess I remembered clearest of all the early mornings, when the lake was cool and motionless, remembered how the bedroom smelled of the lumber it was made of and of the wet woods whose scent entered through the screen. The partitions in the camp were thin and did not extend clear to the top of the rooms, and as I was always the first up I would dress softly so as not to wake the others, and sneak out into the sweet outdoors and start out in the canoe, keeping close along the shore in the long shadows of the pines. I remembered being very careful never to rub my paddle against the gunwale for fear of disturbing the stillness of the cathedral.

The lake had never been what you would call a wild lake. There were 3 cottages sprinkled around the shores, and it was in farming country although the shores of the lake were quite heavily wooded. Some of the cottages were owned by nearby farmers, and you would live at the shore and eat your meals at the farmhouse. That's what our family did. But although it wasn't wild, it was a fairly large and undisturbed lake and there were places in it that, to a child at least, seemed infinitely remote and primeval.

I was right about the tar: It led to within half a mile of the shore. But 4 when I got back there, with my boy, and we settled into a camp near a farmhouse and into the kind of summertime I had known, I could tell that it was going to be pretty much the same as it had been before — I knew it, lying in bed the first morning smelling the bedroom and hearing the boy sneak quietly out and go off along the shore in a boat. I began to sustain the illusion that he was I, and therefore, by simple transposition, that I was my father. This sensation persisted, kept cropping up all the time we were there. It was not an entirely new feeling, but in this setting it grew much stronger. I seemed to be living a dual existence. I would be in the middle of some simple act, I would be picking up a bait box or laying down a table fork, or I would be saying something and suddenly it would be not I but my father who was saying the words or making the gesture. It gave me a creepy sensation.

We went fishing the first morning. I felt the same damp moss covering 5 the worms in the bait can, and saw the dragonfly alight on the tip of my rod as it hovered a few inches from the surface of the water. It was the arrival of this fly that convinced me beyond any doubt that everything was as it always had been, that the years were a mirage and that there had been no years. The small waves were the same, chucking the rowboat under the chin as we fished at anchor, and the boat was the same boat, the same color green and the ribs broken in the same places, and under the floorboards the same fresh water leavings and debris—the dead hellgrammite, the wisps of moss, the rusty discarded fishhook, the dried blood from yesterday's catch. We stared silently at the tips of our rods, at the dragonflies that came and went. I lowered the tip of mine into the water, tentatively, pensively dislodging the fly, which darted two feet away, poised, darted two feet back, and came to rest again a little farther up the rod. There had been no years between the ducking of this dragon-fly and the other one—the one that was part of memory. I looked at the boy, who was silently watching his fly, and it was my hands that held his rod, my eyes watching. I felt dizzy and didn't know which rod I was at the end of.

We caught two bass, hauling them in briskly as though they were mack- 6 erel, pulling them over the side of the boat in a businesslike manner without any landing net, and stunning them with a blow on the back of the head. When we got back for a swim before lunch, the lake was exactly where we had left it, the same number of inches from the dock, and there was only the merest suggestion of a breeze. This seemed an utterly enchanted sea, this lake you could leave to its own devices for a few hours and come back to, and find that it had not stirred, this constant and trustworthy body of water. In the shallows, the dark, water-soaked sticks and twigs, smooth and old, were undulating in clusters on the bottom against the clean ribbed sand, and the track of the mussel was plain. A school of minnows swam by, each minnow with its small individual shadow, doubling the attendance, so clear and sharp in the sunlight. Some of the other campers were in swimming, along the shore, one of them with a cake of soap, and the water felt thin and clear and unsubstantial. Over the years there had been this person with the cake of soap, this cultist, and here he was. There had been no years.

Up to the farmhouse to dinner through the teeming dusty field, the road 7 under our sneakers was only a two-track road. The middle track was missing, the one with the marks of the hooves and the splotches of dried, flaky manure. There had always been three tracks to choose from in choosing which track to walk in; now the choice was narrowed down to two. For a moment I missed terribly the middle alternative. But the way led past the tennis court, and something about the way it lay there in the sun reassured me; the tape had loosened along the backline, the alleys were green with plantains and other weeds, and the net (installed in June and removed in September) sagged in the dry noon, and the whole place steamed with midday heat and hunger and emptiness. There was a choice of pie for dessert, and one was blueberry and one was apple, and the waitresses were the same country girls, there having been no passage of time, only the illusion of it as in a dropped curtain—the waitresses were still fifteen; their hair had been washed, that was the only difference—they had been to the movies and seen the pretty girls with the clean hair.

Summertime, oh, summertime, pattern of life indelible, the fade-proof 8 lake, the woods unshatterable, the pasture with the sweetfern and the juniper forever and ever, summer without end; this was the background, and the life along the shore was the design, the cottages with their innocent and tranquil design, their tiny docks with the flagpole and the American flag floating against the white clouds in the blue sky, the little paths over the roots of the trees leading from camp to camp and the paths leading back to the outhouses and the can of lime for sprinkling, and at the souvenir counters at the store the miniature birchbark canoes and the postcards that showed things looking a little better than they looked. This was the American family at play, escaping the city heat, wondering whether the newcomers in the camp at the head of the cove were "common" or "nice," wondering whether it was true that the people who drove up for Sunday dinner at the farmhouse were turned away because there wasn't enough chicken.

It seemed to me, as I kept remembering all this, that those times and those 9 summers had been infinitely precious and worth saving. There had been jollity and peace and goodness. The arriving (at the beginning of August) had been so big a business in itself, at the railway station the farm wagon drawn up, the first smell of the pine-laden air, the first glimpse of the smiling farmer, and the great importance of the trunks and your father's enormous authority in such matters, and the feel of the wagon under you for the long ten-mile haul, and at the top of the last long hill catching the first view of the lake after eleven months of not seeing this cherished body of water. The shouts and cries of the other campers when they saw you, and the trunks to be unpacked, to give up their rich burden. (Arriving was less exciting nowadays, when you sneaked up in your car and parked it under a tree near the camp and took out the bags and in five minutes it was all over, no fuss, no loud wonderful fuss about trunks.)

Peace and goodness and jollity. The only thing that was wrong now, really, 10 was the sound of the place, an unfamiliar nervous sound of the outboard motors. This was the note that jarred, the one thing that would sometimes break the illusion and set the years moving. In those other summertimes all motors were inboard; and when they were at a little distance, the noise they made was a sedative, an ingredient of summer sleep. They were one-cylinder and two-cylinder engines, and some were make-and-break and some were jump-spark, but they all made a sleepy sound across the lake. The one-lungers throbbed and fluttered, and the twin-cylinder ones purred and purred, and that was a quiet sound, too. But now the campers all had outboards. In the daytime, in the hot mornings, these motors made a petulant irritable sound; at night in the still evening when the afterglow lit the water, they whined about one's ears like mosquitoes. My boy loved our rented outboard, and his great desire was to achieve single-handed mastery over it, and authority, and he soon learned the trick of choking it a little (but not too much), and the adjustment of the needle valve. Watching him I would remember the things you could do with the old one-cylinder engine with the heavy flywheel, how you could have it eating out of your hand if you got really close to it spiritually. Motorboats in those days didn't have clutches, and you would make a landing by shutting off the motor at the proper time and coasting in with a dead rudder. But there was a way of reversing them, if you learned the trick, by cutting the switch and putting it on again exactly on the final dying revolution of the flywheel, so that it would kick back against compression and begin reversing. Approaching a dock in a strong following breeze, it was difficult to slow up sufficiently by the ordinary coasting method, and if a boy felt he had complete mastery over his motor, he was tempted to keep it running beyond its time and then reverse it a few feet from the dock. It took a cool nerve, because if you threw the switch a twentieth of a second too soon you would catch the flywheel when it still had speed enough to go up past center, and the boat would leap ahead, charging bull-fashion at the dock.

We had a good week at the camp. The bass were biting well and the sun 11 shone endlessly, day after day. We would be tired at night and lie down in the accumulated heat of the little bedrooms after the long hot day and the breeze would stir almost imperceptibly outside and the smell of the swamp drift in through the rusty screens. Sleep would come easily and in the morning the red squirrel would be on the roof, tapping out his gay routine. I kept remembering everything, lying in bed in the mornings — the small steamboat that had a long rounded stern like the lip of a Ubangi, and how quietly she ran on the moonlight sails, when the older boys played their mandolins and the girls sang and we ate doughnuts dipped in sugar, and how sweet the music was on the water in the shining night, and what it had felt like to think about girls then. After breakfast we would go up to the store and the things were in the same place — the minnows in a bottle, the plugs and spinners disarranged and pawed over by the youngsters from the boys' camp, the Fig

Newtons and the Beeman's gum. Outside, the road was tarred and cars stood in front of the store. Inside, all was just as it had always been, except there was more Coca-Cola and not so much Moxie and root beer and birch beer and sarsaparilla. We would walk out with a bottle of pop apiece and sometimes the pop would backfire up our noses and hurt. We explored the streams, quietly, where the turtles slid off the sunny logs and dug their way into the soft bottom; and we lay on the town wharf and fed worms to the tame bass. Everywhere we went I had trouble making out which was I, the one walking at my side, the one walking in my pants.

One afternoon while we were at the lake a thunderstorm came up. It was   12
like the revival of an old melodrama that I had seen long ago with childish awe. The second-act climax of the drama of the electrical disturbance over a lake in America had not changed in any important respect. This was the big scene, still the big scene. The whole thing was so familiar, the first feeling of oppression and heat and a general air around camp of not wanting to go very far away. In midafternoon (it was all the same) a curious darkening of the sky, and a lull in everything that had made life tick; and then the way the boats suddenly swung the other way at their moorings with the coming of a breeze out of the new quarter, and the premonitory rumble. Then the kettle drum, then the snare, then the bass drum and cymbals, then crackling light against the dark, and the gods grinning and licking their chops in the hills. Afterward the calm, the rain steadily rustling in the calm lake, the return of light and hope and spirits, and the campers running out in joy and relief to go swimming in the rain, their bright cries perpetuating the deathless joke about how they were getting simply drenched, and the children screaming with delight at the new sensation of bathing in the rain, and the joke about getting drenched linking the generations in a strong indestructible chain. And the comedian who waded in carrying an umbrella.

When the others went swimming my son said he was going in, too. He   13
pulled his dripping trunks from the line where they had hung all through the shower and wrung them out. Languidly, and with no thought of going in, I watched him, his hard little body, skinny and bare, saw him wince slightly as he pulled up around his vitals the small, soggy, icy garment. As he buckled the swollen belt, suddenly my groin felt the chill of death.

Journal Writing

White strongly evokes the lake camp as a place that was important to him as a child. What place or places were most important to you as a child? In your journal, jot down some memories.

Questions on Meaning

1. How do you account for the distortions that creep into the author's sense of time?
2. What does the discussion of inboard and outboard motors (par. 10) have to do with the author's divided sense of time?
3. To what degree does White make us aware of his son's impression of this trip to the lake?
4. What do you take to be White's main PURPOSE in the essay? At what point do you become aware of it?

Questions on Writing Strategy

1. In paragraph 4 the author first introduces his confused feeling that he has gone back in time to his own childhood, an idea that he repeats and expands throughout his account. What is the function of these repetitions?
2. Try to describe the impact of the essay's final paragraph. By what means is it achieved?
3. To what extent is this essay written to appeal to any but middle-aged readers? Is it comprehensible to anyone whose vacations were never spent at a Maine summer cottage?
4. What is the TONE of White's essay?
5. **MIXED METHODS** White's DESCRIPTION depends on many IMAGES that are not FIGURES OF SPEECH but literal translations of sensory impressions. Locate four such images.
6. **MIXED METHODS** Within White's description and NARRATION of his visit to the lake, what purpose is served by the COMPARISON AND CONTRAST between the lake now and when he was a boy?

Questions on Language

1. Be sure you know the meanings of the following words: incessant, placidity (par. 1); gunwale (2); primeval (3); transposition (4); hellgrammite (5); undulating, cultist (6); indelible, tranquil (8); petulant (10); imperceptibly (11); premonitory (12); languidly (13).
2. Comment on White's DICTION in his reference to the lake as "this unique, this holy spot" (par. 2).
3. Explain what White is describing in the sentence that begins, "Then the kettle drum . . ." (par. 12). Where else does the author use figures of speech?

Suggestions for Writing

1. **FROM JOURNAL TO ESSAY** Choose one of the places suggested by your journal entry (p. 644), and write an essay describing the place now, revisiting it as an adult. (If you haven't visited the place since childhood, you can imagine what

seeing it now would be like.) Your description should draw on your childhood memories, making them as vivid as possible for the reader, but you should also consider how your POINT OF VIEW toward the place differs now.

2. In a descriptive paragraph about a real or imagined place, try to appeal to each of your reader's five senses.

3. **CRITICAL WRITING**   While on the vacation he describes, White wrote to his wife, "This place is as American as a drink of Coca-Cola. The white collar family having its annual liberty." Obviously, not everyone has a chance at the lakeside summers White enjoyed. To what extent, if at all, does White's privileged point of view deprive his essay of universal meaning and significance? Write an essay answering this question. Back up your ideas with EVIDENCE from White's essay.

4. **CONNECTIONS**   In White's "Once More to the Lake" and Brad Manning's "Arm Wrestling with My Father" (p. 125), the writers reveal a changing sense of what it means to be a father. Write an essay that examines the similarities and differences in their definitions of fatherhood. How does a changing idea of what it means to be a son connect with this redefinition of fatherhood?

5. **CONNECTIONS**   White's essay is full of images that place readers in an important setting of his childhood. David Sedaris, in "Remembering My Childhood on the Continent of Africa" (p. 235), also uses vivid images to evoke childhood, both his own and that of his partner. After reading these two essays, write an essay of your own ANALYZING four or five images from each that strike you as especially evocative. What sense impression does each image draw on? What does each one tell you about the author's feelings?

APPENDIX

RESEARCH AND DOCUMENTATION

Responding to the readings in this book—thinking critically about them and synthesizing the writers' ideas with your own—prepares you for the researched writing that will occupy you for much of your college career. The academic disciplines—history, psychology, chemistry, and the like—examine different subjects and take different approaches, but they share the common goal of using reading and writing to build and exchange knowledge.

Reading critically and writing effectively are both key skills for this kind of ACADEMIC WRITING, which calls on your ability to think critically about what you read. Part One of this book shows you how to read and write in response to a single SOURCE, such as any of the selections in Part Two. This appendix covers the essentials of using multiple sources in your writing: finding and evaluating them (below), synthesizing source material without plagiarizing (p. 652), and documenting sources using the styles of the Modern Language Association (MLA) for papers in English and most humanities (p. 656) or the

American Psychological Association (APA) for papers in the social sciences and business (p. 677).

CONDUCTING RESEARCH

Research is a process of inquiry, driven by curiosity. Whatever discipline you are working in, the process is most productive when you start with a specific question that interests you enough to spend some time investigating. Often such questions will be provided for you, as is the case with many of the writing suggestions that accompany the reading selections in this book. Other times, you will need to come up with intriguing questions for yourself. In either case, try to focus on a question you care about, because you will put a good deal of effort into finding and examining sources that can help you answer it.

Using the Library

You have two paths to sources for a research project: your school's library and a public search engine such as *Google* or *Bing*. Although it may seem easier to turn to the open Internet first, always start with the library: Its Web portal will lead you to books, scholarly journals, reputable newspapers, and other quality sources that information professionals have deemed worthwhile. Furthermore, some of the most useful source material is not freely available or online at all. Your library can link you to online resources that are accessible only to paid subscribers, and it can provide periodicals and specialized reference works in both print and digital formats.

The Internet is home to many valuable sources as well, but finding them requires ingenuity and an extra degree of caution. Tapping a question into a search engine will not lead you to the best materials as if by magic. A quick keyword search can give you an overview of your subject and generate ideas, but it can just as easily direct you to the rantings of extremists, advertisements posing as science, and dubious claims in anonymous posts. It will also generally bring up an unwieldy number of hits, with little indication of which ones are worthy of your attention. Most of the quality material you can find on the Web is indexed on your library's home page; searching from there will save you time and trouble in the long run.

Evaluating Sources

When examining multiple works for possible use in your paper, you of course want each one to be relevant to your subject and to your question. But you also want it to be reliable — that is, based on good evidence and carefully reasoned. To evaluate relevance and reliability, you'll depend on your critical-reading skills of analysis, inference, and synthesis (see pp. 16–18). Use the questions for evaluating sources in the box below and the following discussion of the criteria. Take extra care when evaluating Internet sources you have reached directly, for those materials have not been filtered and are therefore inherently less reliable.

QUESTIONS FOR EVALUATING SOURCES

ALL SOURCES

✔ What is the PURPOSE of the source?

✔ Who is the intended AUDIENCE?

✔ Is the material a primary or a secondary source?

✔ Is the author an expert? What are his or her credentials?

✔ Does the author's bias affect his or her argument?

✔ Is the argument supported with EVIDENCE that is complete and up to date?

✔ How current is the source?

INTERNET SOURCES

✔ What is the origin of the source? Can you identify the author?

✔ Who created the Web site? Does the sponsor have any biases or agendas?

✔ Does the site contain links to sources used as evidence? Is the evidence credible?

Purpose and Audience

The potential sources you find may have been written for a variety of reasons — for instance, to inform the public, to publish new research, to promote a product or service, to influence readers' opinions about a particular issue. The first two of these purposes might lead to a balanced approach to the subject, one that treats all sides fairly. The second two are likely to be biased toward one view, and you'll need to weigh what they say accordingly.

A source's intended audience can suggest relevance. Was the work written for general readers? Then it may provide a helpful overview but not much detail. Was the work written for specialists? Then it will probably cover the topic in depth, but understanding it may require careful reading or consulting additional sources for clarification.

Primary versus Secondary Sources

Primary sources are works by people who conducted or saw events firsthand. They include research reports, eyewitness accounts, diaries, and personal essays as well as novels, poems, and other works of literature. *Secondary sources*, in contrast, present and analyze the information in primary sources and include histories, reviews, and surveys of a field. Both types of sources can be useful in research writing. For example, if you were writing about the debate over the assassination of President John F. Kennedy, you might seek an overview in books that discuss the evidence and propose theories about what happened— secondary sources. But you would be remiss if you did not also consult eyewitness accounts and law-enforcement documents—the primary sources.

Author's Credentials and Bias

Before you use a source to support your ideas, investigate the author's background to be sure that he or she is trustworthy. Look for biographical information in the introduction or preface of a book or in a note at the beginning or end of an article. Is the author an expert on the topic? Do other writers cite the author of your source in their work?

Often you won't be able to tell easily, or at all, who put a potential source on the Internet and thus whether that author is credible and reliable. Specific background may require digging. On Web sites, look for pages that have information about the author or sponsor or links to such information on other sites. On blogs and social media, ask anonymous writers for information about themselves. If you can't identify an author or a sponsor at all, you probably should not use the source.

Investigating an author's background and credentials will likely also uncover any bias—that is, the author's preference for a particular view of an issue. Bias itself is not a problem: Everyone has a unique outlook created by experience, training, and even research techniques. What does matter is whether the author deals frankly with his or her bias and argues reasonably despite it. (See Chap. 14, pp. 497–500, for a discussion of reasoning.)

Evidence

Look for strong and convincing EVIDENCE to support the ideas in a source: facts, examples, reported experience, expert opinions. A source that doesn't muster convincing evidence, or much evidence at all, is not a reliable source. For very current topics, such as in medicine or technology, the source's ideas and evidence should be as up to date as possible.

The most reliable sources acknowledge borrowed evidence and ideas and tell you where they came from, whether with general mentions in the case of journalism, with formal references in scholarly works, or (sometimes online) with links to the borrowed material. Check out references or links to be sure they represent a range of views. Be suspicious of any work that doesn't acknowledge sources at all.

Currency

If you are writing about a current topic, you want your sources to be up to date. Online sources tend to be more current than print sources, but they also have some potential disadvantages. Very current information may not have been tested by others and therefore may not be reliable. And because Web sites change constantly, information you locate one day could be missing or altered the next. Finally, sites that seem current may actually be dated because their authors or sponsors have not tended them. Look for a date of copyright, publication, or last revision to gauge currency. If you don't find a date (and you may not), compare the source with others you know to be recent before using its information.

Preparing an Annotated Bibliography

Whether for your own use or as part of an assignment, preparing an annotated bibliography during research can help you keep track of your sources and your evaluation of them, ensuring that you use them effectively.

A common form of annotated bibliography contains a two-part entry for every potential source: (1) full publication information for the source, so that you can find it again and cite it accurately in your paper; and (2) your own comments on the source, including an overview and a brief ANALYSIS that identifies its contents, addresses its value in its field, and considers its usefulness to you. One student, for instance, researched and wrote a literary analysis about revenge in the works of Edgar Allan Poe, focusing on the parallels in Poe's life and fiction. She read and reread several of Poe's short stories and then searched her school's library and the Internet for critical analyses of the author's work. At her instructor's request, she compiled an annotated bibliography that listed and commented on the sources she thought would be most helpful in writing her paper, using MLA style (p. 656) to format the publication information. Here are two of her entries:

Allen, Brooke. "The Tell-Tale Artist: Edgar Allan Poe Turns 200." *The Weekly Standard*, 28 Sept. 2009, pp. 28–31.   *Source: magazine article*

A literary critic's view of Poe's place in literary history and popular culture on the 200th anniversary of his birth. Allen claims that Poe essentially invented horror fiction, science   *Contents of article*

      1. Poe's influence

fiction, and the detective story. She also sees parallels between
Poe himself and the characters in his fiction. Allen's focus
on Poe's mental instability and its effects on his creativity is
helpful in understanding some themes in his work, particularly
revenge. Poe's sensitivity to insults, for example, connects to
Montressor in "The Cask of Amontillado," who kills to avenge
an unnamed slight.

2. Parallels between
   Poe's life and work

Potential use of source

The Edgar Allan Poe Society of Baltimore. 1997–2016, www
.eapoe.org/. Accessed 4 Feb. 2019.
A comprehensive online collection of all of Poe's works,
including letters and other documents, as well as links to critical articles from the journal *Poe Studies/Dark Romanticism.* The
site's most useful features are essays by scholars that address
common misconceptions about Poe, particularly that his
poems and stories about anger, loss, fear, and vengeance mirror events and relationships in his own life. This perspective is
valuable to balance Allen and other writers who make a great
deal of the connections between Poe's life and work. At the
same time, the site seems somewhat defensive about Poe and
protective of him, so information about Poe and his life needs
to be verified in other sources.

Source: Web site

Contents of Web site
1. Collection of Poe's
   works
2. Scholarly criticism

3. Balancing
   perspectives

Potential use of source

You may or may not be required to include an annotated bibliography
with the final draft of a research paper. But if you do, the annotations along
with the publication information can help readers locate and assess your
sources for themselves.

WRITING WITH SOURCES

In researched writing, you test and support a THESIS by exploring and
orchestrating a range of opinions and evidence found in multiple sources.
The writing is source *based* but not source *dominated:* As when responding
to a single work, your critical reading and your views set the direction and
govern the final presentation.

Building Knowledge

In college you will read and write in many disciplines, each with its own
subjects, approaches, and GENRES for shaping ideas and information. As varied as your research assignments may be, however, they will all share the
goals and requirements of academic writing: They will ask you to build and

exchange knowledge by thinking critically and writing effectively about what you read, see, hear, or do.

For a taste of such academic knowledge building, you can take a look at any of the selections in this book that synthesize information and ideas gleaned from sources—such as Rosie Anaya's look at portrayals of disability on television (p. 62), Laila Ayad's examination of a historical photograph (p. 342), Ben Healy's review of the literature on gossip (p. 411), Marie Javdani's study of the global effects of the drug trade (p. 442), Sarah Hemphill's defense of free speech on campus (p. 558), Margaret Lundberg's environmental argument for vegetarianism (p. 671), or Eric Kim's overview of recent developments in neuroscience (p. 687).

When called upon to create academic writing of your own, you will be expected to follow certain conventions:

- **Present a clearly stated thesis**—a debatable idea about a subject—and attempt to gain readers' agreement with it.

- **Provide evidence to support the thesis,** drawing on one or more TEXTS, or works that can be examined or interpreted.

- ANALYZE **meaning, infer** ASSUMPTIONS, **and** SYNTHESIZE **texts with your own views.** Academic writers do not merely summarize sources; they grapple with them—in short, they read and write critically.

- **Assume an educated audience**—one that can be counted on to read critically in turn. Express your ideas clearly, provide the information readers need to analyze those ideas, and organize points and evidence effectively. Further, approach your subject seriously and discuss evidence and opposing views fairly.

- **Acknowledge the use of sources,** using in-text citations and a bibliography in a format appropriate for the discipline.

Knowledge builds as you bring your own perspectives to bear on what others have written, making your own contributions to what has come before. By locating sources, reading them carefully, and writing thoughtfully in response, you're well on your way to becoming an academic writer yourself.

Integrating Source Material

Writing with sources, you have an opportunity and an obligation to think critically—to analyze, infer, evaluate, and synthesize as described on pages 16–19. Key to SYNTHESIS is first deciding how to present evidence from your research and then working the evidence into your paper smoothly and informatively so it flows with your own ideas.

Depending on what the source material contributes to your thesis, you might use summary, paraphrase, or quotation to integrate it with your text. When you SUMMARIZE or PARAPHRASE a source, you express its ideas in your own words; when you QUOTE, you use the source's exact words, in quotation marks. See pages 45–48 in Chapter 3 for guidelines and examples. And remember that *all summaries, paraphrases, and quotations must be acknowledged with source citations*, as modeled in the sections on MLA and APA documentation later in this appendix (pp. 656–86).

Synthesizing Multiple Sources

In research writing as in response writing, your views should predominate over those of others. You decide which sources to use, how to treat them, and what conclusions to draw from them in order to test and support your thesis. In your writing, this thinking about sources' merits and relevance should be evident to readers. Here, for example, is a paragraph from a student writer's research paper about the problem of mental illness in college. Notice how the writer states her idea at the outset, guides us through the presentation of evidence from three sources, and finally concludes by tying the evidence back to her idea.

> Despite the prevalence of depression and related disorders on campus, however, most students avoid seeking help when they need it. The American Psychiatric Association maintains that most mental-health issues can be managed or overcome with treatment by therapy and/or medication. But among students with a history of depression, according to the American College Health Association, a mere ten percent currently receive any kind of treatment (35). One reason for such low numbers can be found in a study published in *Journal of Mental Health Counseling:* Four in five American students are unwilling to ask for help even when they are certain they need it, because they perceive mental illness as embarrassing or shameful (Aegisdóttir et al. 327–28). Thus students who need help suffer additional pain — and no treatment — because they fear the stigma of mental illness.

Margin annotations:
- Writer's idea
- Evidence from a Web site
- Evidence from a survey
- Evidence from a scholarly journal
- Writer's interpretation of the evidence

This paragraph illustrates the techniques of synthesis detailed in pages 48–50 of Chapter 3:

- **Summarize and paraphrase data and ideas from sources,** stressing your own voice and your mastery of the source material.

- **Integrate each summary or paraphrase into your sentences.** Use SIGNAL PHRASES that name the source authors, and tell readers how the borrowed material relates to your idea.
- **Clearly indicate what material is borrowed and where it is borrowed from.** Such source citation is crucial to avoid plagiarism, discussed in the next section.

Avoiding Plagiarism

Academic knowledge building depends on the integrity and trust of its participants. PLAGIARISM — the theft of someone's ideas or written work — violates that trust. Most students know that passing off another writer's work as their own, or copying long passages from published texts, are unacceptable practices that can bring severe punishments. Such intentional plagiarism is obviously cheating and is easily detected.

But plagiarism is often more subtle, the result of carelessness or misunderstanding. Writers of researched papers must be cautious in their use of sources to avoid instances of unintentional plagiarism, such as poorly handled paraphrases or missing quotation marks. As you synthesize the information and ideas gathered through research in your writing, it is essential that you make clear to readers what ideas are your own and what ones are borrowed, *always citing the sources of borrowed material.* Avoid plagiarism by following these guidelines:

- **Identify the sources of all borrowed information and ideas.** Introduce every summary, paraphrase, or quotation and name the author in a signal phrase or a parenthetical citation. See pages 45–50 on integrating source material.
- **Indicate where the material can be found.** Follow any information or idea taken from a source with a parenthetical citation that provides the name of the author (if not mentioned in a signal phrase) and the page number(s), if available. (If you are using APA style, give the year of publication as well.) See pages 657–60 on MLA parenthetical citations and pages 677–80 on APA parenthetical text citations.
- **Mark direct quotations.** Whether sentences, phrases, or distinctive words, another writer's language must be clearly distinguished from your own. (See p. 47.) Enclose brief quotations in quotation marks. Set off longer quotations with an indentation. See page 672 for an example in MLA style.
- **Take care to express all paraphrases and summaries in your own words.** Check your sentences against the original sources, making sure that you

haven't picked up any of the writers' phrasings or sentence structures. For examples of acceptable and unacceptable summary and paraphrase, see pages 45–47.

- **Include a list of sources.** On a separate page (or pages) at the end, provide a complete list of the sources cited within your paper, with full publication information for each. See pages 660–70 for guidelines on creating an MLA list of works cited and see pages 680–86 for guidelines on creating an APA references list.

- **Recognize common knowledge.** Not all information from sources must be cited. Some falls under the category of common knowledge — facts so widely known or agreed upon that they are not attributable to a specific source. You may not know that President Dwight Eisenhower coined the term *military-industrial complex* during his 1961 farewell address, for example, but because anyone can easily find that fact in encyclopedias, in books, and in articles about Eisenhower, it requires no citation (as long as you express it in your own words). In contrast, a scholar's argument that Eisenhower waited too long to criticize the defense industry, or the president's own comments, would need to be credited because each remains the property of its author.

Be especially cautious about plagiarism when you are working online. Whether accidentally or deliberately, you can download source material directly into your own document with a few clicks. And you might be tempted to buy complete papers from term-paper sites. Don't. *It is plagiarism to use downloaded material without credit, even accidentally, and it is plagiarism to submit someone else's work as your own, even if you paid for it.* Getting caught is more than likely, too, because anything from the Internet is easy to trace.

SOURCE CITATION USING MLA STYLE

In this section we explain the documentation style of the Modern Language Association, as described in the *MLA Handbook*, 8th edition (2016). This style — used in English, foreign languages, and some other humanities — involves providing a citation in your text that names the author of borrowed material and gives the page number(s) in the source where the material appears. Readers can use the name to locate the full source information in a list of works cited at the end of your text, and they can find the location of the borrowed material in the source itself.

In your text, the author's name may appear in a SIGNAL PHRASE, or it may appear in parentheses. In either case, put any page numbers in parentheses:

TEXT CITATION, AUTHOR NAMED IN SIGNAL PHRASE

As Quindlen suggests, people's dwellings seem to have lost their emotional hold and to have become just investments (182).

TEXT CITATION, AUTHOR NAMED IN PARENTHESES

People's dwellings seem to have lost their emotional hold and to have become just investments (Quindlen 182).

ENTRY IN LIST OF WORKS CITED

Quindlen, Anna. "Homeless." *The Bedford Reader*, edited by X. J. Kennedy et al., 14th ed., Bedford/St. Martin's, 2020, pp. 181-83.

MLA Parenthetical Citations

The following examples of MLA text citations show the author named in a signal phrase or named in parentheses.

MLA Parenthetical Citations

A work with two authors

By shortening the time to product-in-hand, 3D printing enables designers and engineers to create prototypes quickly and cheaply (Lipson and Kurman 30).

A work with three or more authors

With three or more authors, name only the first author followed by et al. (*et alii*, "and others").

Gilman herself created the misconception that doctors tried to ban her story "The Yellow Wallpaper" when it appeared in 1892 (Dock et al. 61).

A work with a group author

For a work that lists an organization as author—for instance, a government agency or a corporation—treat the group's name as the author name.

> In a tongue-in-cheek graphic novel, the Centers for Disease Control and Prevention invokes the threat of a zombie apocalypse to encourage Americans to gather materials for an all-purpose emergency kit and keep them readily at hand (United States 5).

If the group author is also the publisher of the work, however, you will need to alphabetize it by title in your works-cited list (see pp. 660–70), so provide the title in a parenthetical citation.

> According to the National Coalition for the Homeless, several city governments have passed legislation meant to discourage individuals and charitable organizations from providing food to homeless people (*Share No More* 4).

A work with no identified author

Cite an unsigned work by its title. In a signal phrase, use the full title. In a parenthetical citation, shorten a long title to the first one, two, or three main words.

> A growing number of national chain hotels allow guests to bring dogs and cats with them—a welcome relief for travelers whose pets require specialized care ("Rooming" 10).

Two or more works by the same author(s)

If you cite more than one work by the same author or authors, include a short version of each work's title. The full titles for the citations below are "The Case for Reparations" and "The Black Family in the Age of Mass Incarceration."

> Ta-Nehisi Coates argues that a long history of systemic oppression, discrimination, and racial injustice has inflicted "practical damage" that can only be repaired with government payments of cash to African Americans ("Case" 55).

> One example of such oppression can be found in contemporary imprisonment rates: At least twenty-five percent of black men living in America today have been jailed, affecting not only those incarcerated but also their families and their larger communities (Coates, "Black Family" 66).

A source without page numbers

Cite an unpaginated source, such as an HTML document, a sound recording, or a DVD, as you would any printed source: by author's name or, if there is no author specified, by title. If a source numbers paragraphs instead of pages, give the reference number after par. (one paragraph) or pars. (more than one paragraph). If a source's numbering system is unstable, as is often the case with e-books, refer to section or chapter numbers (sec., secs.; ch., chs.) instead of page numbers. For a source with no reference numbers at all, use the model for an entire work below.

> One nurse questions whether doctors are adequately trained in tending patients' feelings (Van Eijk, pars. 6–7).

> Kozol believes that most people do not understand the effect that tax and revenue policies have on the quality of urban public schools (ch. 2).

An entire work or a work with no reference numbers

Omit page numbers when you cite an entire work or cite a work that does not number pages, paragraphs, or other parts.

> Vogel recommends that new entrants into the job market strive to create their own professional roles, rather than search for existing positions.

A work in more than one volume

If you cite two or more volumes of a multivolume work, identify the volume number before the page number. Separate volume number and page number with a colon and a space.

> According to Gibbon, during the reign of Gallienus "every province of the Roman world was afflicted by barbarous invaders and military tyrants" (1: 133).

An indirect source

Use qtd. in ("quoted in") to indicate that you found the source you quote within another source.

> Despite his tendency to view human existence as an unfulfilling struggle, Schopenhauer disparaged suicide as "a vain and foolish act" (qtd. in Durant 248).

A literary work

Because novels, poems, and plays may be published in various editions, the page number may not be enough to lead readers to the quoted line or passage. For a novel, specify the chapter number after the page number and a semicolon.

Among South Pacific islanders, the hero of Conrad's *Lord Jim* found "a
totally new set of conditions for his imaginative faculty to work upon"
(160; ch. 21).

For a verse play or a poem, omit the page number in favor of line numbers.

In "Dulce et Decorum Est," Wilfred Owen undercuts the heroic image of
warfare by comparing suffering soldiers to "beggars" and "hags" (lines 1-2)
and describing a man dying in a poison-gas attack as "guttering, choking,
drowning" (17).

If the work has parts, acts, or scenes, cite those as well (below: act 1, scene 5,
lines 16–17).

Lady Macbeth worries about her husband's ambition: "Yet I do fear thy
nature; / It is too full o' the milk of human kindness" (1.5.16-17).

More than one work in the same citation

In the post-Watergate era, some journalists have been accused of employing
aggressive reporting techniques not for the good of the public but more to
advance their careers (Fallows 64; Gopnik 92).

MLA List of Works Cited

Your list of works cited is a complete record of your sources. Follow these
guidelines for the list:

- **Title the list** Works Cited.
- **Double-space the entire list.**
- **Arrange the sources alphabetically** by the last name of the first author or
  by the first main word of the title if the source has no named author.
- **Begin the first line of each entry at the left margin,** and indent subse-
  quent lines one-half inch.

Following are the essentials of a works-cited entry:

- **Reverse the names of the author,** last name first, with a comma between.
  (If there are two authors, give the second name in normal order.)
  Conclude the author name(s) with a period.
- **Give the full title of the work,** capitalizing the first, last, and all important words. Italicize the titles of books, periodicals, and Web sites; use
  quotation marks for the titles of parts of books, articles in periodicals, and
  pages on Web sites. Place a period after the title.

- **Give publication information.** For this information, MLA style operates on a principle of nested "containers." For a scholarly article, for instance, the journal that published it is the primary container; if you accessed the article through a periodicals database, the database is a second container. In each container, list as many of the following elements that apply to the source, in the order listed: Title of the container, names and functions of additional contributors, version of the material (a revised edition of a book, for example), sequence numbers (such as volumes and issues for journals), publisher or sponsor, date of publication, and location details (typically page numbers or a URL). Separate the elements within a container with commas, and separate each container with a period.

- **Include any additional information that might help clarify the nature of the source.** Optional elements include descriptive labels such as Review, Letter, or Address; access dates for some online sources; and original publication information for republished works.

In the pages that follow, we demonstrate how the MLA system works when applied to several common types of sources. You may need to combine the following models for a given source—for instance, combine "Three or more authors," "An article in a scholarly journal," and "A short work on a Web site" for an online journal article with five authors.

Authors

One author

Olson, W. Scott. "Nine Variations on the Idea of Street Music." *Utne Reader*, Winter 2015, pp. 80-83.

Two authors

Mullally, Megan, and Nick Offerman. *The Greatest Love Story Ever Told: An Oral History*. Penguin Random House, 2018.

Three or more authors

List only the first author followed by et al. (*et alii*, "and others").

Platt, Spencer, et al. "Eyes of the Storm." *Newsweek*, 1 Feb. 2019, pp. 28-35.

A group author

For a publication by an organization, corporation, or government agency, use the group name as the author name. If the group is also the publisher, omit the author name and start with the title of the work.

Associated Press. "Concussion Lawsuit Deadline Extended for Players."
Sports Illustrated, 18 Jan. 2019, www.si.com/nhl/2019/01/18/
concussion-lawsuit-settlement-deadline-extended-players.

Share No More: The Criminalization of Efforts to Feed People in Need.
National Coalition for the Homeless, 2014, nationalhomeless.org/
wp-content/uploads/2014/10/Food-Sharing2014.pdf. Accessed
5 Apr. 2019.

MLA List of Works Cited

No identified author

"Go Fish." *Outside*, Mar. 2018, p. 38.

More than one work by the same author(s)

Coates, Ta-Nehisi. "The Black Family in the Age of Mass Incarceration." *The Atlantic*, Oct. 2015, pp. 60-84.

---. "The Case for Reparations." *The Atlantic*, June 2014, www.theatlantic .com/magazine/archive/2014/06/the-case-for-reparations/361631/.

Periodicals: Journals, Magazines, and Newspapers

An article in a scholarly journal

After the journal title, give the volume and issue numbers, the date of publication, and the page numbers of the article. If the journal numbers issues but not annual volumes, give just the issue number after the title.

Rogoss, Jay. "The Paris Diet." *Able Muse*, no. 19, 2015, pp. 24-25.

Wan, Neng, et al. "The Association of Point-of-Sale E-cigarette Advertising with Socio-Demographic Characteristics of Neighborhoods." *The Journal of Primary Prevention*, vol. 39, no. 3, June 2018, pp. 191-203.

For journals published online, provide a location where the article can be accessed. If the article has been assigned a DOI (digital object identifier), use that as its locator; if there is no DOI, provide the URL.

Barringer, Tim. "Landscape Then and Now." *British Art Studies*, no. 10, Autumn 2018, doi:10.17658.

Zhou, Coco. "Magical Girl as a Shōjo: Genre and the Male Gaze." *Flow*, vol. 22, no. 4, Feb. 2016, www.flowjournal.org/2016/02/magical-girl-as-a-shojo-genre/.

An article in a magazine

Chabon, Michael. "The Recipe for Life." *The New Yorker*, 5 Feb. 2018, pp. 20-24.

Keating, Joshua. "Today's Threats to Global Democracies Are Coming from Democracies Themselves." *Slate*, 4 Feb. 2019, slate.com/news-and-politics/2019/02/freedom-house-democracy.html.

Starr, Alexandra. "Pushing the Limit: What the US Olympic Committee Can—and Can't—Do about Sexual Abuse." *Harper's Magazine*, Nov. 2017, pp. 47-55.

An article in a newspaper

Fox, Jeremy C. "State Police to Wear Body Cameras." *The Boston Globe*, greater Boston ed., 5 Feb. 2019, pp. B1+.

Will, George F. "What's Next, a Tariff on Peanut Butter?" *The Washington Post*, 8 Feb. 2019, www.washingtonpost.com/opinions/whats-next-a-tariff-on-peanut-butter/.

The page number B1+ in the first example means that the article begins on page 1 of section B and continues on a later page. If the newspaper has an edition, such as greater Boston ed. in the example, it will be labeled at the top of the first page.

A review

Tóibín, Colm. "She Played Hard with Happiness." Review of *The Complete Stories*, by Clarice Lispector. *The New York Review of Books*, 17 Dec. 2015, pp. 61-63.

A periodical article from a database

For an article that you obtain from a library or online database, provide publication information using the models above. Add the database title and the DOI (if available) or URL.

Layne, Bethany. "The Turn of the Century: Henry James in Millennial Fiction." *Henry James Review*, vol. 39, no. 2, Spring 2018, pp. 178-94. *Academic Search Premier*, doi:10.1353/hjr.2018.0013.

Wortham, Stanton, et al. "Scattered Challenges, Singular Solutions: The New Latino Diaspora." *The Phi Delta Kappan*, vol. 94, no. 6, Mar. 2013, pp. 14-19. *JSTOR*, www.jstor.org/stable/23611744.

Books

A book with an author

Mailhot, Terese Marie. *Heart Berries: A Memoir*. Counterpoint, 2018.

A book with an editor or editors

Burnes, Catherine, editor. *All These Wonders: True Stories about Facing the Unknown*. Crown Publishing Group, 2017.

Gessen, Keith, and Stephen Squibb, editors. *City by City: Dispatches from the American Metropolis*. N+1 / Farrar, Straus and Giroux, 2015.

A book with an author and an editor

Austen, Jane. *Northanger Abbey: An Annotated Edition*. Edited by Susan J.
Wolfson, Harvard UP, 2014.

A later edition

Friedan, Betty. *The Feminine Mystique*. 50th anniversary ed., W. W. Norton,
2015.

A work in a series

Carey, Chris. *Thermopylae*. Oxford UP, 2019. Great Battles.

An anthology or collection

Kennedy, X. J., et al., editors. *The Bedford Reader*. 14th ed., Bedford/St.
Martin's, 2020.

Cite an entire anthology only when you are citing the work of the editor(s)
or you are cross-referencing it, as in the Hemphill and Lutz models below.

A selection from an anthology or collection

The numbers at the end of the following entry identify the pages on
which the entire cited selection appears.

Hemphill, Sarah. "What Happened to Free Speech on College Campuses?" *The
Bedford Reader*, edited by X. J. Kennedy et al., 14th ed., Bedford/St.
Martin's, 2020, pp. 558-62.

If you cite more than one selection from the same anthology, you may
give the anthology as a separate entry and cross-reference it by the editor's or
editors' last name(s) in the entries for the selections. Place each entry in its
proper alphabetical place in the list of works cited.

Hemphill, Sarah. "What Happened to Free Speech on College Campuses?"
Kennedy et al., pp. 558-62.
Kennedy, X. J., et al., editors. *The Bedford Reader*. 14th ed., Bedford/St.
Martin's, 2020.
Lutz, William. "The World of Doublespeak." Kennedy et al., pp. 387-93.

A reference work

Myhrvold, Nathan. "Coffee." *Encyclopaedia Brittanica*, 2019.
"Seagrass Beds." *Ocean: A Visual Encyclopedia*, Dorling Kindersley, 2015.

A book on the Web

Addington, H. Bruce. *Historic Ghosts and Ghost Hunters*. Moffat, Yard,
    1908. *Project Gutenberg*, www.gutenberg.org/files/28699/28699-h/
    28699-h.htm. Accessed 6 Apr. 2019.

Visual, Audio, and Multimedia Sources

A photograph, painting, sculpture, or other work of art

For a work of art that you see in the original, follow this format:

van Gogh, Vincent. *The Starry Night*. 1889, Museum of Modern Art,
    New York.

For a work of art that you see online or in a reproduction, provide the
publication information for the source you used:

Doble, Rick. *Spring Rain Abstraction*. 2009. *Digital Art Photography*, 2019,
    www.rickdoble.net/. Accessed 18 Apr. 2019.

Hockney, David. *Nichols Canyon*. 1980. *David Hockney: A Retrospective*, edited
    by Maurice Tuchman and Stephanie Barron, Los Angeles County Museum
    of Art, 1988, p. 205.

If the image originally or simultaneously appeared in another medium, you
may provide the information for the other medium before the publication
information:

Matisse, Henri. *La Musique*. 1939, Albright-Knox Gallery, Buffalo. *WebMuseum*,
    www.ibiblio.org/wm/paint/auth/matisse/matisse.musique.jpg. Accessed
    3 Mar. 2019.

A map, graph, or chart

If the title doesn't make the type of visual clear, provide a label describing
it at the end of the entry.

Fisk, Charles. "Las Vegas Annual Precipitation, 1949-2018." *Climate Stations*,
    20 Jan. 2019, www.climatestations.com/wp-content/uploads/2019/01/
    lvprcp.gif. Graph.

An advertisement

American Spirit. Advertisement. *Rolling Stone*, Jan. 2019, p. 21.

A television or radio broadcast

What information you provide, and in what order, depends on your focus in using the source. If your emphasis is on a particular contributor, start with that person's name and function:

Shteyngart, Gary, performer. "The Devil You Know." *This American Life*, hosted
by Ira Glass, episode 666, Chicago Public Media, 11 Jan. 2019.

If your focus is on an episode or the series as a whole, start with the relevant title and list any significant contributors:

"The Theme That Shall Not Be Named." *This American Life*, hosted by Ira Glass,
performances by Kelefa Sanneh and Gary Shteyngart, episode 666,
Chicago Public Media, 11 Jan. 2019.

This American Life. Hosted by Ira Glass, Chicago Public Media, 1995-2019.

A television program on the Web

Cite the program using one of the models above, followed with information about the Web source.

"Breath Play." *Criminal Minds*, season 10, episode 17, CBS, 11 Mar. 2015.
Netflix, www.netflix.com/search/criminalminds. Accessed 19 Feb. 2018.

Joubert, Beverly, and Dereck Joubert, narrators. "Soul of the Elephant."
Nature, season 34, episode 4, WNET, 14 Oct. 2015. *PBS*, www.pbs.org/
wnet/nature/soul-elephant-full-episode/12956/.

A podcast or sound recording

"The Arrival." *Caliphate*, narrated by Rukmini Callimachi, season 1, episode 3,
The New York Times, 3 May 2018. *iTunes*, itunes.apple.com/us/podcast/
caliphate/id1357657583?mt=2.

Mendelssohn, Felix. *A Midsummer Night's Dream*. Conducted by Erich Leinsdorf,
Boston Symphony Orchestra. RCA, 1982.

Roosevelt, Franklin D. Inaugural address. 20 Jan. 1941. *Vincent Voice Library*,
Michigan State University, 2015, www.lib.msu.edu/cs/branches/vvl/
presidents/fdr.html.

A film or video

For untitled works, provide a generic description of the content. If a video recording originally or simultaneously appeared in another medium, you may provide the information for the other medium before the publication information:

> Edison, Thomas A. Gordon sisters boxing. Edison Manufacturing, 1901. *American Memory*, Library of Congress, NCN046321, memory.loc.gov/ mbrs/varsmp/1628.mpg.
>
> *Manufacturing Consent: Noam Chomsky and the Media*. Directed by Mark Achbar and Peter Wintonick, Humanist Broadcasting Foundation, 1992. Zeitgeist Video, 2002. *Prime Video*, amazon.com. Accessed 4 Nov. 2018.
>
> vlogbrothers. *We Have Destroyed Copyright. YouTube*, 1 Feb. 2019, www .youtube.com/vlogbrothers.

Other Online Sources

Online sources vary greatly, and they may be and often are updated. Your aim in citing such a source should be to tell what version you used and how readers can find it for themselves. If you don't see a model for the type of source you used, follow a model that comes close. If you can't find all the information shown in a model, give what you can find.

A short work on a Web site

The following example shows the basic elements to include when citing a source from the Web: (1) author's name, (2) title of the work, (3) title of the site, (4) sponsor or publisher of the site, (5) date of the online publication or last update, (6) URL (omitting "http://"), and (7) date you consulted the source (optional).

>   ①   ②   ③   ④
> Speer, Cindy Lynn. "Neil Gaiman's Film Work." *Neil Gaiman*, Harper Collins
>   ⑤   ⑥
> Publishers, Aug. 2007, www.neilgaiman.com/Cool_Stuff/Essays/Essays
>   ⑦
> _About_Neil/Neil_Gaiman's_Film_Work. Accessed 28 Apr. 2019.

An entire Web site

> *Civic Engagement*. University of Chicago, civicengagement.uchicago.edu/. Accessed 10 Feb. 2019.

A government publication on the Web

> United States, Department of Education. "Preventing Dropout in Secondary Schools." *What Works Clearinghouse*, Institute of Education Sciences, Sept. 2017, ies.ed.gov/ncee/wwc/PracticeGuide/24. Accessed 2 Mar. 2019.

A wiki

"Carnival." *Wikipedia*, 3 Feb. 2019, en.wikipedia.org/wiki/Carnival. Accessed
    26 Feb. 2019.

A blog post or comment

Allan, Patrick. "The Power of Going It Alone." *LifeHacker*, Gawker
    Media, 16 May 2016, lifehacker.com/the-power-of-going-it-alone-
    1776843438.
EasyBakeGirl. Comment on "The Power of Going It Alone," by Patrick
    Allen. *LifeHacker*, Gawker Media, 17 May 2016, lifehacker.com/
    the-power-of-going-it-alone-1776843438.
Skenazy, Lenore. "Let's Hear it for Boredom!" *Free-Range Kids*, 5 Feb.
    2019, freerangekids.com.

A posting to a discussion group

aja675. "How do I regain my confidence in speaking English?" *ESL Forums*,
    English Club, 8 Apr. 2013, www.englishclub.com/esl-forums/viewtopic
    .php?f=125&t=71310#p412546.
Sinha, Sanjay. "RE: How do I regain my confidence in speaking English?" *ESL
    Forums*, English Club, 28 Dec. 2017, www.englishclub.com/esl-forums/
    viewtopic.php?f=125&t=71310#p427630.

If the posting has no title, use the label Online posting in the place of a
title.

Twitter and social media

Provide the user name or pseudonym as the author name; you may follow
it with the writer's real name (if known) in parentheses. If a posting has a
title, use it. Otherwise, quote the entire content of a tweet or a short message
or use Post for anything else, citing the date and time. End with the URL.

@NASA (United States, National Aeronautics and Space Administration).
    "Listening for #marsquakes is serious business! Now with its cover in
    place, our @NASAInSight lander will collect accurate data despite wind
    and temperature changes on the Red Planet." *Twitter*, 4 Feb. 2019, 2:32
    p.m., twitter.com/NASA/status/1092551373844033542.
Rainbow, Randy. "There Is Nothin' Like a Wall." *Instagram*, 14 Jan. 2019,
    www.instagram.com/p/BsnpyROIWLn/.
Rather, Dan. Post. *Facebook*, 2 Feb. 2019, 12:23 p.m., www.facebook.com/pg/
    theDanRather/.

Personal Communications

E-mail

Dove, Chris. "Re: Elizabeth Bishop's Poems." Received by Rhonda Blake,
    7 May 2018.

A letter

For a letter that you receive, list the source under the writer's name, use
the label Letter to the author, and provide the date of the correspondence.

Dove, Chris. Letter to the author. 14 May 2018.

List a published letter under the author's name, and provide full publication information.

Stetson, James A. Letter to Dolly W. Stetson. 8 Feb. 1845. *Letters from an*
    American Utopia: The Stetson Family and the Northampton Association,
    1843-1847, edited by Christopher Clark and Kerry W. Buckley, U of
    Massachusetts P, 2004, pp. 133-34.

An interview

Arnaldo, Donald. Personal interview. 13 May 2019.

Brownstein, Carrie. Interview by Rachel Brodsky. *Spin,* 27 Oct. 2015,
    www.spin.com/2015/10/carrie-brownstein-hunger-makes-me-a-modern-
    girl-memoir-interview/.

A SAMPLE RESEARCH PAPER IN MLA STYLE

Margaret Lundberg wrote the following research paper for a first-year
writing course at Tacoma Community College in Washington State and
revised and updated it for *The Bedford Reader.* We present Lundberg's paper
for three reasons: It illustrates many techniques of using and documenting
sources, which are highlighted in the marginal comments; it demonstrates
elements of effective ARGUMENT, also noted in the margins; and it shows a
writer working with a topic that interests her in a way that arouses the readers' interest as well.

Lundberg's advice to other writers is straightforward: "Keep a notebook
handy at all times," she says. "You never know when that 'perfect' idea will
show up."

Margaret Lundberg
Professor Fox
English 101
12 April 2016

Eating Green

When I was a child, our family's diet was important to
my mother. We had two vegetables with every meal, ate plain
yogurt for breakfast, and exercised with Jack LaLanne. Later, as
a young mom myself, I learned to cook meals from scratch, froze
and canned fresh produce, and did aerobics with Jane Fonda.
I was concerned with my sons' nutrition, having learned early
that good health didn't just happen—you had to work for it.
Now that my family circle has widened to include grandchildren,
I find that my concerns go beyond just the health of my own
family, to the health of the planet we live on. I believe that our
personal and global health is tightly interconnected, and what
benefits one will benefit the other.

I became a vegetarian about three years ago, and "went
vegan" last spring. I could tout all sorts of reasons, but suffice
it to say that I look and feel better at fifty-two than I did five
years ago. For *my* health and well-being, becoming a vegetarian
was the best thing I could have done. Which got me thinking—
what if we could establish that a vegetarian diet would benefit
not only our personal health, but the health of the planet as
well? Between pollution, greenhouse gases, and dependence on
a dwindling supply of fossil fuels, our little blue planet isn't feeling too well. If all of us adopting a vegetarian diet could slow
or stop all of these ills, shouldn't we consider it? The idea is not
as far-fetched as it might sound: A vegetarian diet could be just
what the doctor ordered for our global health.

Eating meat is such a big part of the American way of life
that it almost feels unpatriotic to spurn it. Would it still be
Thanksgiving without the turkey, the Fourth of July without the
hamburgers, a baseball game without the hotdogs? All of these
things seem to be permanently interwoven into our culture.
But the great American love affair with burgers and fries also
has a dark side. Just as the standard American diet is killing us

Title arouses readers' curiosity.

Introduction provides context and establishes Lundberg's purpose.

Evidence from personal experience. No source citation needed for Lundberg's generalizations.

Thesis statement.

Acknowledgment of opposing viewpoint (see p. 503).

Refutation of opposing viewpoint.

individually—with skyrocketing rates of obesity, diabetes, heart disease, and a host of other ills—it is also having devastating effects on our planet. Pollution, global warming, and an alarming dependence on fossil fuels can all be traced back, in large part, to the agricultural practices that are required to feed our ever-growing craving for meat. Dietician Kate Geagan compares the environmental impact of the American diet with that of "our love affair with SUVs," warning that the energy use involved in the "production, transport, processing, packaging, storing, and preparation [of food] is now the single largest contributor to global warming" (x).

Livestock production in this country and throughout the Western world has come a long way from the era of the American cowboy. The days of cattle grazing serenely on huge expanses of prairie pasture land are pretty much over. As journalist Michael Pollan points out in his book *The Omnivore's Dilemma*, raising cattle and other livestock is a multi-billion dollar operation that is now more manufacturing plant than traditional ranching. Cows no longer spend their lives grazing the hillsides until they are ready for slaughter. They are warehoused and fed a diet that is contrary to their very physiology—intended to eat grass, they are now fattened on corn, in as short a time as possible. In the early 1900s it took four to five years to ready a steer for slaughter; it now takes fourteen to sixteen months (ch. 4).

The corn-based diet they are fed leads to a variety of health issues for the cattle. In his article "The Ecology of Eating: The Power of the Fork," Mark Hyman offers an example:

> Of the 24 million pounds of antibiotics produced each year in this country, 19 million are put in the factory-farmed animals' feed to prevent infection, which results from overcrowding, and to prevent the cow's stomach from exploding with gas from the fermentation of the corn. (15)

As a result of what is basically indigestion, Hyman explains, cattle belch vast amounts of methane, which is twenty-three times more potent at trapping heat than carbon dioxide. Livestock manure is the source of two-thirds of the man-made

---

Quotation integrated into Lundberg's text. Brackets indicate change to original wording (see p. 48).

Citation includes page number only because author (Geagan) is named in the text.

Citation for summary uses a chapter number because the source, an e-book, does not have stable page numbers.

Quotation of more than four lines is indented one-half inch.

Parenthetical citation for set-off quotation falls outside final period.

nitrous oxide now circulating in our atmosphere—a green-house gas that is three hundred times more potent than carbon dioxide (14).

Other statistics are equally grim. Kate Geagan reports that livestock raised for meat production are responsible for 18 percent of greenhouse gas emissions—more than the cars we drive. The food sector is responsible for 20 percent of the total energy use in the United States every year, and most of that comes from the raising and packaging of livestock animals (30). The average household could make a bigger impact on greenhouse gas emissions by cutting their meat consumption in half than by cutting their driving in half!

A nonvegetarian diet requires 2.9 times more water, 2.5 times more energy, 13 times more fertilizer (also made from petroleum products), and 1.4 times more pesticides than does a vegetarian diet—and the greatest difference comes from beef consumption (Marlow et al. 1699). Less than half of the harvested acreage in the United States is used to grow food for people, and it takes sixteen pounds of grain and soybeans fed to cattle to get one pound of meat ready for us to eat. Ten times as much land is required for meat-protein production than is required for plant-protein production, and producing one pound of animal protein uses almost a hundred times more water than it takes to produce one pound of plant protein ("Land").

As a population's income rises, its people have traditionally eaten more meat and dairy foods, replacing wheat and rice in their diets—exactly what we have been experiencing over the last fifty years (Bittman). Nevertheless, between global warming and decreased natural resources such as farmable land and water, the earth simply can't support any greater increase in meat production. In my lifetime, the world population has doubled, and it is still growing exponentially. Yet, with finite resources, how will we continue to feed us all? Factory farming is simply unsustainable. Even Dennis Avery, director of the Centre for Global Food Issues (a very pro-livestock organization), has

---

Citation of a paraphrase includes only page number because author is named in the text.

Statistics provided as evidence.

Author's name above and parenthetical page number clearly indicate the beginning and end of paraphrased material.

Lundberg's interpretation of the evidence.

Paragraph synthesizes information from two sources to support Lundberg's argument (see pp. 48–50).

Citation includes author's name and page number; "et al." ("and others") indicates more than two authors.

Citation includes title of source published by a group author. Online source has no page or reference numbers.

Paragraph synthesizes information from two sources to support Lundberg's argument.

Lundberg's interpretation of the evidence.

Expert opinion offered as evidence.

Lundberg 4

commented that "[t]he world must create 5 billion vegans in the next several decades, or triple its total farm output without using more land" (qtd. in "Land"). If *he* thinks so, it *must* be time to rethink our diet!

But what about our burgers? For far too many of us, giving up meat seems like an unreasonable thing to ask. Meat is good for us, isn't it? Maybe. But the average American consumes nearly 200 pounds of meat a year—33 percent more than five decades ago. We eat about 110 grams of protein a day (more than three-quarters of which is animal protein), while the USDA's Food Pyramid recommends less than half that—an amount still nearly twice the 30 grams most other experts say we actually *need* (Bittman). Since the advent of products like McDonald's Quarter Pounder with Cheese (30 grams of protein all by itself!), it has become entirely too easy to eat much more meat than any of us could ever need ("USA Nutrition"). Our expanding waist-lines and rising levels of diabetes and heart disease prove that any benefit we might gain from a modest amount of meat in our diet is being overcome by the sheer amount we are eating on a daily basis.

With growing evidence that human activities in general—and livestock production in particular—are causing large-scale environmental effects, many major corporations are attempting to make changes and "do their part" for the environment. A group of dairy farmers in New York State, for example, is team-ing with General Electric to produce renewable energy from cow manure. Apparently manure from 2,500 cows can generate enough electricity for 200 homes. In a state with over 600,000 dairy cows, that's a lot of potential kilowatts. "We've estimated that this could generate $38 million in new revenue for dairy farmers around the country and offset 2 million tons of carbon dioxide equivalents annually by 2020," says Rick Naczi, execu-tive vice president at Dairy Management Inc., in a press release ("GE"). Naczi reports that the dairy industry has committed to reducing greenhouse gas emissions by 25 percent by 2020—the

Brackets indicate change to original passage (see p. 48). Source quoted in another source.

Acknowledgment of opposing viewpoint.

Refutation of opposing viewpoint.

Citation uses shortened version of title for work with corporate author and no page numbers.

Lundberg's interpreta-tion of the evidence.

Acknowledgment of opposing viewpoint.

Citation uses shortened version of title for work with no named author. Online source has no page numbers.

equivalent of getting "1.25 million passenger cars off the road
every year." That's a lot of gas.

    But even if we *can* make electricity from "cow pies," does
that make up for the fact that we in the Western world are using
far more than our fair share of the earth's limited resources? We
use substantial amounts of fossil fuels and other nonrenewable
resources to grow a "crop" that many in our global population
cannot access; one that pollutes and sickens the planet—and its
inhabitants—in ways we are only beginning to comprehend.
In the face of a looming worldwide crisis where food prices are
rising and nearly 3 billion people earn less than two dollars a
day, two of every three people in the world already subsist on
a vegetarian diet (Clemmit 1). Yet in the industrialized world over
50 percent of the grain that we grow is used to fatten livestock
(Hyman 14). Peter Timmer, a fellow at the Washington-based
Center for Global Development, states, "There's still plenty
of food for everyone, but only if everyone eats a grain and
legume-based diet. If the diet includes large . . . amounts of
animal protein . . . , food demand is running ahead of global
production" (qtd. in Clemmit 3).

    With finite resources already being stretched thin by a
growing global population, is it rational for us to continue on as
we are? Our food systems are not sustainable, and today's livestock production methods make potential food crises more likely
every day. If greenhouse gases continue to build as they have
over the last fifty years, the effects on today's farmlands may
be irreversible. As global temperatures continue to rise, Alaska
may become the new "Corn Belt" and the Midwest could become
a desert. How much of the land we now depend on to feed us
could be lost to agriculture? A vegetarian diet would enable us
to healthfully feed many more people, and make much better use
of the resources we have. Do we really want to wait until it's too
late to change our way of eating?

Lundberg's comment
on the evidence.

Refutation of opposing
viewpoint.

No source citation for
common knowledge.

Citation of a quotation
from an indirect
source. Ellipses
indicate omission from
quotation (see p. 48).

Conclusion summarizes
Lundberg's main points
and restates her thesis.

Paper ends with a
provocative question.

Works Cited

Bittman, Mark. "Rethinking the Meat-Guzzler." *The New York Times*, 27 Jan. 2008, www.nytimes.com/2008/01/27/weekinreview/27bittman.html?_r=0. Accessed 2 Apr. 2016.

Clemmit, Marcia. "Global Food Crisis: What's Causing the Rising Prices?" *Social Problems: Selections from* CQ *Researcher*, Sage, 2010, pp. 1-24.

Geagan, Kate. *Go Green Get Lean: Trim Your Waistline with the Ultimate Low-Carbon Footprint Diet*. Rodale, 2009.

"GE, US Dairy Industry Shine Light on Potential of 'Cow Power' in New York." *Business Wire*, 29 Oct. 2009, www.businesswire.com/news/home/20091029006166/en/GE-U.S.-Dairy-Industry-Shine-Light-Potential. Accessed 4 Apr. 2016.

Hyman, Mark. "The Ecology of Eating: The Power of the Fork." *Alternative Therapies in Health and Medicine*, vol. 15, no. 4, July/Aug. 2009, pp. 14-15.

"Land." *Information Resources*, The Vegan Society, www.vegansociety.com/resources. Accessed 18 Mar. 2016.

Marlow, Harold J., et al. "Diet and the Environment: Does What You Eat Matter?" *American Journal of Clinical Nutrition*, vol. 89, no. 5, May 2009, pp. 1699-1703. *General One File*, doi:10.3945/.

Pollan, Michael. *The Omnivore's Dilemma: A Natural History of Four Meals*. Penguin Books, 2006.

"USA Nutrition Facts for Popular Menu Items." *Nutrition Choices*, McDonald's, nutrition.mcdonalds.com/getnutrition/nutritionfacts.pdf. Accessed 25 Mar. 2016.

List of works cited begins on a new page.

An article in the Web version of a newspaper.

A selection in an anthology.

A print book.

A newspaper article posted on the Web.

An article from a print journal.

A short work from a Web site published by a group author.

Journal article from a database. "Et al." ("and others") indicates more than two authors.

An e-book.

A short work from a Web site published by a corporate author.

SOURCE CITATION USING APA STYLE

In this section we explain the documentation style of the American Psychological Association, as described in the *Publication Manual of the American Psychological Association*, 6th edition (2010). This style—used in psychology, sociology, business, education, economics, and other social sciences—involves a citation within the text that identifies the author and date of a source, as well as the page number(s) for a quotation or paraphrase (page numbers are not required for a summary).

In your text, the author's name may appear in a SIGNAL PHRASE, or it may appear in parentheses along with the date and any page numbers. Either way, the citation information directs readers to the source's full publication information in a list of references at the end of the text:

TEXT CITATION, AUTHOR NAMED IN SIGNAL PHRASE

As Quindlen (2020) has suggested, people's dwellings seem to have lost their emotional hold and to have become just investments (p. 182).

TEXT CITATION, AUTHOR NAMED IN PARENTHESES

One observer has suggested that people's dwellings seem to have lost their emotional hold and to have become just investments (Quindlen, 2020, p. 182).

ENTRY IN REFERENCE LIST

Quindlen, A. (2020). Homeless. In X. J. Kennedy, D. M. Kennedy, J. E. Aaron, & E. K. Repetto (Eds.), *The Bedford Reader* (14th ed., pp. 181-83). Boston: Bedford.

APA Parenthetical Citations

The following examples of APA text citations show the author named in a signal phrase or named in parentheses.

APA Parenthetical Citations

A work with two authors

Comer and White (2016) reported that a mere 1.5% of writing students enrolled in their Massive Open Online Course earned a certificate of accomplishment, presumably because only a small number of enrollees intended to complete the work in the first place (p. 320).

A work with three to five authors

With more than two but fewer than six authors, list all of the authors in the first parenthetical citation. Separate the names with commas, and precede the final name with &.

Emergency room visitors over 65 years old are twice as likely as younger patients to be admitted for a hospital stay (Murdoch, Turpin, Johnston, MacLullich, & Losman, 2015, p. 1).

In later references to the same source, shorten the citation to the first author's name followed by et al. (*et alii*, "and others").

Murdoch et al. (2015) have suggested that all medical personnel need to be better trained in recognizing and addressing the unique needs of a growing elderly population (p. 6).

A work with six or more authors

Name only the first author followed by et al. (*et alii*, "and others").

In the midst of global political turmoil in the early twenty-first century, some activists believe that turning to the fine arts can bring a sense of peace, even optimism (DuVernay et al., 2019).

A work with a group author

For a work published under the name of an organization, such as a government agency or a corporation, use the name of the group as the author.

The United States Conference of Mayors (2018) reported that most American cities run youth council programs to get students directly involved in local government (p. vi).

A work with no identified author

Cite an unsigned work by using the first one or two main words of the title (excluding any initial "A," "An," or "The").

Researchers have found that taking pictures daily and posting them online yields unexpected health benefits for amateur photographers ("Photo," 2019, p. 36).

Two or more works by exactly the same author(s)

If you cite more than one work by the same author or authors, in most cases the year of publication will indicate which work you're referring to. If two or more works were published in the same year, assign lowercase letters to the years in your list of references (see p. 682) and include the same letters in your parenthetical citations.

> Gladwell (2011a) has argued that although popular wisdom held that Apple founder "[Steve] Jobs stole the personal computer from Xerox," the reality was that he refined ideas that Xerox showed little interest in pursuing (p. 48).

> According to Gladwell (2011b), Jobs's most significant personality trait—more so than his perfectionism, his aggressiveness, or his resilience—was his preference to "tweak" other people's inventions instead of innovate from scratch.

A source without page numbers

Cite an unpaginated source, such as an HTML document, a sound recording, or a DVD, as you would any print source: by author's name or, if there is no author indicated, by title. If a source numbers paragraphs instead of pages, give the appropriate number(s) as in the following model, after para. (one paragraph) or paras. (more than one paragraph).

> For several years in the 1970s, folk singer Joni Mitchell occasionally appeared on stage disguised as a black man, a deviant practice that Grier (2019) has claimed gave her "authority and prestige" among rock musicians (para. 2).

For a source with no page or paragraph numbers, provide a heading for the section in which the cited material appears (abbreviated if it is long), followed by the paragraph number within the section, as determined by your own count.

> One patient developed a painful, swollen rash that dermatologists attributed to an exclusive diet of fast food; in the months he abstained from such meals, his condition improved (Sundhar et al., 2012, Case section, para. 1).

An indirect source

Use as cited in to indicate that you found the source you quote within another source.

> Of the many difficulties of living in space, astronaut Norm Thagard felt that "boredom was the most common problem" (as cited in Roach, 2010, p. 28).

More than one work in the same citation

List the names in alphabetical order and separate the entries with a semicolon.

Moving welfare recipients out of blighted neighborhoods has been shown to increase their happiness, if not their earning potential (Rothwell, 2015; Sard, 2016).

Personal communications

Interviews you conduct and letters, e-mails, and messages you receive should be cited in your text with the correspondent's initials and last name, the words personal communication, and the full date. Because readers cannot retrieve such materials, they are not included in the list of references.

A county health inspector explained that meat must be shelved at the bottom of refrigeration units to reduce the risk of contaminating vegetables and dairy products with bacteria (M. K. Edwards, personal communication, May 30, 2019).

APA Reference List

Your reference list is a complete record of your sources. Follow these guidelines for the list:

- **Title the list** References.
- **Double-space the entire list.**
- **Arrange the sources alphabetically** by the last name of the first author or by the first main word of the title if the source has no named author.
- **Begin the first line of each entry at the left margin.** Indent the subsequent lines of the entry one-half inch or five spaces.

Following are the essentials of a reference-list entry:

- **Reverse the names of the authors,** last name first, followed by a comma and initials for first and middle names (even if the names are given in full on the source), with another comma after the initials.
- **Provide a publication date** in parentheses after the name or names.
- **Give the full title of the work.** For titles of books, use italics and capitalize only the first word of the title and subtitle and any proper nouns. Use the same capitalization style for titles of articles, but don't italicize them or enclose them in quotation marks. For titles of periodicals, capitalize all major words and italicize the title.
- **Give publication information.** For books, include the city and state of publication and the publisher's name. For periodicals, include the volume number and sometimes the issue number along with the page numbers for the article you cite. For print periodical articles, also include a digital object identifier (DOI) if one is available. Always include the DOI or a URL for online periodical articles. (See pp. 682–84 for more on DOIs and URLs.)

- **Use periods between parts of each entry,** but do not include a period at the end of a DOI or URL.

You may need to combine some of the following models to document a particular source—for instance, combine "Eight or more authors" and "A periodical article from a database" for an online database article with twelve listed authors.

APA Reference List

Authors

One author 681
Two to seven authors 681
Eight or more authors 681
A group author 682
No identified author 682
More than one work by exactly the
  same author(s) 682

*Periodicals: Journals, Magazines,
and Newspapers*

An article in a journal 682
An article in a magazine 683
An article in a newspaper 683
A periodical article from a
  database 684

Books

A book with an author 684
A book with an editor or
  editors 684
A later edition 684
A selection from an anthology 684
A book on the Web 685
A book on an e-reader 685

*Other Online and Multimedia
Sources*

A document from a Web site 685
A video or audio recording 686
A podcast 686
A posting to a blog or discussion
  group 686

Authors

One author

Pollan, M. (2018). *How to change your mind: What the new science of psychedelics teaches us about consciousness, dying, addiction, depression, and transcendence.* New York, NY: Penguin Press.

Two to seven authors

McFadden, J., & Al-Khalili, J. (2014). *Life on the edge: The coming of age of quantum biology.* New York, NY: Crown.

Murdoch, I., Turpin, S., Johnston, B., Maclullich, A., & Losman, E. (2015). *Geriatric emergencies.* Malden, MA: Wiley-Blackwell.

Eight or more authors

Name the first six authors, insert ellipses, and end with the name of the last listed author.

Weatherburn, S., Zapata, A., Tsatie, S., Laiteyse, M., O'Grady, S., Reyes, V., . . . Martinez, R. (2018). Tai chi, wu chi, and learning spaces: A brief proposal for doing nothing in the classroom. *Council Chronicle, 28*(2), 30-31.

A group author

U.S. Department of Justice, Cybersecurity Unit. (2018). *Best practices for victim response and reporting of cyber incidents.* Retrieved from https://www.justice.gov/criminal-ccips/file/1096971/download

No identified author

Start the entry with the title of the work, followed by the date and publication information.

Modern-day alchemy. (2018, September 29). *The Economist, 428*(9111), 8-11.

More than one work by exactly the same author(s)

When you cite two or more works by the same author that were published in *different* years, include the author's name in each entry and list the entries in chronological order by publication date.

Ehrenreich, B. (2014). *Living with a wild god: A nonbeliever's search for the truth about everything.* New York, NY: Hatchette Book Group.

Ehrenreich, B. (2018). *Natural causes: An epidemic of wellness, the certainty of dying, and killing ourselves to live longer.* New York, NY: Hatchette Book Group.

When you cite two or more works by the same author that were published in the *same* year, list the works in alphabetical order by title and add lowercase letters (a, b, c, etc.) to the date. Use the same letters with the date in the corresponding parenthetical citations (see p. 679).

Gladwell, M. (2011a, May 16). Creation myth: Xerox PARC, Apple, and the truth about innovation. *The New Yorker, 87*(13), 44-53.

Gladwell, M. (2011b, November 14). The tweaker: The real genius of Steve Jobs. *The New Yorker, 87*(36), 32-35.

Periodicals: Journals, Magazines, and Newspapers

An article in a journal

Most journals number issues consecutively throughout the year, so that the first page of issue 3, for instance, might begin on page 409. In such cases, follow the journal title with the volume number (italicized), a comma, the inclusive page numbers of the article, and a period. If a journal starts each issue with page 1, include the issue number in parentheses (not italicized) after the volume number. APA strongly recommends listing the digital object identifier (DOI) for any article that has one assigned to it.

Conti, R. (2015). Compassionate parenting as a key to satisfaction, efficacy and
meaning among mothers of children with autism. *Journal of Autism and
Developmental Disorders, 45*, 2008-2018. doi:10.1007/s10803-015-2360-6

Richter, Uwe, Ng, K. Y., Marttinen, P., Turunen, T., Jackson, C., Soumalainen,
A., . . . Battersby, B. J. (2019). Mitochondrial translation stress
response. *Life Science Alliance, 2*(1), 1-17. doi:10.26508/lsa.201800219

Base an entry for an online journal article on one of the above models for print journals. Include the DOI if one is provided.

Lawindi, M. E., Salem, M., Razik, M., & Balas, E. (2019). Socioeconomic
predictors of morbidity in a rural setting: A community based study.
Internet Journal of Epidemiology, 15(1). doi:10.5580/IJE.53712

If no DOI is provided, give the URL of the journal's home page after Retrieved from.

Peel, M. (2015). Assessing fitness to detain in police custody. *Nursing
Standard, 30*(11), 43-49. Retrieved from http://nursingstandard
.rcnpublishing.co.uk

(If you must break a DOI or URL, do it after the two slashes following http:// or before a single slash, a period, or another punctuation mark. Do not add a hyphen.)

An article in a magazine

Include the complete date in parentheses and provide volume and issue numbers.

Brown, D. (2017, Autumn). Opioids and paternalism: To help end the crisis,
both doctors and patients need to find a new way to think about pain.
The American Scholar, 86(4), 22-35.

Chua, A., & Rubenfeld, J. (2018, October). The threat of tribalism. *The
Atlantic, 322*(3). Retrieved from http://www.theatlantic.com

McNamee, R. (2019, January 28). How to fix social media before it's too late.
Time, 193(3), 22-28.

An article in a newspaper

Include the year, month, and day in the date. List all page numbers, preceded by p. (for one page) or pp. (for multiple pages).

Singer, N. (2019, January 24). "Hard part of computer science class? Getting
in." *The New York Times*, pp. A1, A16.

For an article from the Web version of a newspaper, replace page numbers with the URL for the full site.

Ferdman, R. A. (2016, March 4). The magical thing eating chocolate does to your brain. *The Washington Post.* Retrieved from https://www .washingtonpost.com/

A periodical article from a database

For an article that you obtain from a library or online database, provide print publication information using the models for journals, magazines, and newspapers above. Add the DOI or, if there is none, the URL of the periodical's home page. Do not include the name of the database.

McDonald, Y. J., & Jones, N. E. (2018). Drinking water violations and environmental justice in the United States. *American Journal of Public Health, 108*(10), 1401-1407. doi:10.2105/AJPH.2018.304621

Scudellari, M. (2015, July 31). The kids aren't all right. *Newsweek, 165*(5), 44-47. Retrieved from http://www.newsweek.com

Books

A book with an author

Gregory, A. (2018). *Nodding off: The science of sleep from cradle to grave.* London, England: Bloomsbury.

A book with an editor or editors

Masih, T. L. (Ed.). (2012). *The chalk circle: Intercultural prizewinning essays.* Deadwood, OR: Wyatt-MacKenzie.

Zeigler-Hill, V., & Marcus, D. K. (Eds.). (2016). *The dark side of personality: Science and practice in social, personality, and clinical psychology.* Washington, DC: American Psychological Association.

A later edition

Coleman, E. (2018). *The new organic grower: A master's manual of tools and techniques for the home and market gardener* (30th anniv. ed.). White River Junction, VT: Chelsea Green.

A selection from an anthology

Use the anthology's publication year after the author's name, even if the selection was originally published earlier. In the page numbers in parentheses, give the location of the cited selection within the anthology.

Mohabir, R. (2018). Pygmy right whale. In R. H. Buchanan (Ed.), *Go home!* (pp. 102-103). New York, NY: Feminist Press.

A book on the Web

Instead of print publication information, provide the URL you used to retrieve the book. In this example, the final parenthesis provides the date of the book's original publication:

Barker, C. H. (2004). *Wanted, a young woman to do housework: Business principles applied to housework.* Retrieved from http://www.gutenberg .org/files/14117/14117-h/14117-h.htm (Original work published 1915)

A book on an e-reader

For an electronic book on an e-reader such as a Kindle, Nook, or an iPad, add the type of file in brackets after the title, followed by the URL where you retrieved the book.

Cohen, A. (2016). *Imbeciles: The Supreme Court, American eugenics, and the sterilization of Carrie Buck* [Apple Books version]. Retrieved from http://www.itunes.apple.com

Smith, J. N. (2019). *Breaking and entering: The extraordinary story of a hacker called "Alien"* [Kindle version]. Retrieved from http://www.amazon.com

Other Online and Multimedia Sources

Online sources vary greatly, and they may be and often are updated. Your aim in citing such a source should be to tell what version you used and how readers can find it for themselves. Include the date on which you accessed the source only if the source is likely to change or if it lacks a publication date or version number (see the first model below for an example). Substitute n.d. (for "no date") in parentheses if a source is undated. If you don't see a model for the type of source you used, follow a model that comes close. If you can't find all the information shown in a model, give what you can find.

A document from a Web site

Include as much of the following information as you can find: author's name, date of publication or last update, title, and URL.

Rosen, H., Ciecinski, S., Saucedo, M., & Shah, R. (2018). *Aerobotics.* Retrieved from https://www.gsb.stanford.edu/faculty-research/ case-studies/aerobotics

If no author is listed, begin the entry with the title followed by the date in parentheses. The following example also includes the date of retrieval because the source has no publication date and is likely to change.

Lyme disease. (n.d.). Retrieved March 1, 2019, from http://www.webmd .com/rheumatoid-arthritis/arthritis-lyme-disease

A video or audio recording

Include a description of the medium or file type in brackets after the title of the work.

Scott, R. (Producer), & Villenueve, D. (Director). (2017). *Blade runner 2049* [DVD]. Burbank, CA: Warner Bros.

Peterson, B. (2017, March/April). Wolf music [Audio file]. Retrieved from https://orionmagazine.org/article/brenda-peterson-reads-wolf-music/

Waits, T. (1976). The piano has been drinking (not me). On *Small change* [CD]. New York, NY: Elektra/Asylum Records.

A podcast

Crespi, S., & Grimm, D. (Hosts). (2016, January 8). Dancing dinosaurs, naked black holes, and more [Audio podcast]. *Science podcasts*. Retrieved from http://www.sciencemag.org/podcasts

A posting to a blog or discussion group

HypnoToad72. (16 July 2018). Re: Go mobile or go home: From augmented reality to language learning to virtual classrooms, the word is mobile [Blog comment]. Retrieved from http://www.zdnet.com/article/go-mobile-or-go-home

Northrup, L. (2016, February 16). Our growing e-commerce addiction means mountains of cardboard [Blog post]. Retrieved from http://consumerist.com

A SAMPLE RESEARCH PAPER IN APA STYLE

As a bioengineering major and pre-med student at the University of Pennsylvania in Philadelphia, Eric Kim enrolled in the sophomore-level composition seminar "The Novelist and the Neuroscientist" to fulfill a critical writing requirement. "Writing has always been difficult" for him, Kim says, but he enjoyed the course because "it was nice to write on a topic he is interested in." The paper we present on the following pages explores Kim's interest in one recently discovered aspect of the human brain; it also demonstrates the uses of APA documentation style in a brief yet thoroughly developed sample of researched writing. Kim revised and updated the essay for *The Bedford Reader*.

Notice that in accordance with APA style, the writer provides a title page with an (optional) author note and a running head that continues through the paper; he also follows the American Psychological Association's convention of using past tense or past perfect tense in signal phrases that introduce the findings of other researchers.

Running head: BRAIN 1

Title page provides a shortened version of title used as a running head throughout paper.

The Brain That Changes

Eric Kim

University of Pennsylvania

Title, author name, and school are centered on page.

Optional author note provides additional information about course and lists any acknowledgments.

Author Note: This paper was prepared for *Critical Writing Seminar in Psychology: The Novelist and the Neuroscientist*, taught by Professor Charbonnier.

Until recently, neuroscientists held the notion that the structure of the brain was fixed after infancy; neurons could never regenerate or form new networks. Less than two decades ago, however, researchers documented neural cell division in adult primates (Gould, Tanapat, McEwen, Flügge, & Fuchs, 1998). A flurry of subsequent experiments illustrated that the brain continuously changes throughout life. This property has been termed *neuroplasticity* and it involves modifying neural connections, building new neural networks, destroying old neurons, and generating new neurons. Through neuroplasticity, everything from experiences, injuries, and even thoughts can change the fabric of the brain (Carr, 2011, p. 27). In fact, if this concept is new to you, your brain is undergoing reorganization as you read. For some, this might be a startling notion: Are these structural changes in the brain taking place for better or worse? After all, in a system as complex as the brain, any changes might disrupt a natural balance. On the other hand, neuroplasticity implies an opportunity to improve the brain. Human experience shows both results can occur. For the most part, however, neuroplasticity is beneficial.

It would be wrong to ignore that, in some cases, neuroplasticity can lead to harmful conditions. For example, neuroplasticity may malfunction in response to injury. Normal injuries rearrange nerve cells to help enforce a feeling of pain. These neural changes eventually revert, and the pain subsides. With severe injuries, however, the neural changes may become irreversible, leading to many cases of chronic pain. Amputees often develop this problem in their severed limbs, a disorder known as "phantom limb" pain (Carr, 2011, p. 30). Many other harmful results of neuroplasticity have been documented. For example, writers who used hand muscles frequently strengthened corresponding networks in the motor cortex. In some cases, this development led to a hyperactive motor cortex that caused painful, involuntary contractions of hand muscles (Johnston, 2009, p. 99). Likewise, drug use can overstimulate and change neural pathways, ultimately leading to addiction (Rácz, 2014). While

---

Citation of a source with five authors not named in the text. No page number required for a summary.

Citation of a source with one author not named in the text. Page number provided for paraphrase.

Introduction engages readers' interest and identifies Kim's research question.

Thesis statement answers research question.

Acknowledgment of opposing viewpoint (see p. 503).

Paragraph synthesizes information from four sources (see pp. 48–50).

Page numbers provided for quotations (Carr) and paraphrases (Johnston), but not for summaries (Rácz and Wilson & Hunt [on next page]).

neuroplasticity can have harmful results, virtually all biological functions have some negative effects. Errors in nuclear division, for example, can lead to Down syndrome; likewise, faulty protein synthesis can result in diabetes, cystic fibrosis, cancer—the list goes on (Wilson & Hunt, 2015). However, normal functioning of nuclear division and protein synthesis are both critical for human life. Similarly, while neuroplasticity can have some problems, it still plays an overall positive role in our biology.

For one, neuroplasticity allows the brain to improve useful mental functions. When the brain engages in a challenging mental task, it structures a network of neurons to perform the task. With repetition, the neurons thicken, and new connections are added to the network to make it more advanced. To study this role of neuroplasticity, a research team at the University of Dokuz Eylül in Turkey examined the parietal lobes of mathematicians; this part of the brain helps process the abstract creativity used in advanced mathematics. The results showed that the density of neurons and neural connections in the parietal lobes "were strongly correlated with the time spent [training] as an academician" (Aydin et al., 2007, p. 1859). Other studies found similar correlations between violinists and the motor and auditory cortexes, as well as taxi cab drivers and brain regions that store spatial information (Wilson, Conyers, & Rose, 2015, Redefining section, para. 2). In other words, practicing a skill, such as mathematicians do when repeatedly solving difficult problems, leads to lasting changes in the brain that make a person better at that skill. Just like physical exercises that can strengthen specific body parts, mental exercises can literally reshape the brain to suit different functions as needed. Without neuroplasticity, the brain would be a fixed structure and any improvements would be impossible.

Beyond improving the usual roles of brain regions, neuroplasticity allows brain regions to adopt radically new functions. This mechanism plays a critical role in compensating for the disruption or loss of a function. The first experiment to illustrate this notion was conducted by MIT neuroscientists von Melchner,

Refutation of opposing viewpoint.

Paragraph synthesizes information from two sources.

Quotation integrated into Kim's text. Brackets indicate word added for clarity (see p. 48).
Citation of a source with eight authors not named in the text; page number required for quotation.

Citation of source with three authors not named in the text; abbreviated section heading and paragraph number for paraphrase from an unpaged document.

Kim's interpretation of the evidence.

BRAIN   4

Pallas, and Sur (2000), who disturbed retinal connections in newborn ferrets by redirecting them to the auditory cortex. Because the structure of the auditory cortex cannot process light, the ferrets should have been completely blind. Remarkably, the ferrets still responded to light stimuli. Brain imaging showed that neurons in the auditory cortex had reorganized to resemble networks normally present in the visual cortex (pp. 874-875). Thus, neuroplasticity can adapt brain regions to suit new needs. Later studies have found numerous parallels in humans. Deaf subjects, for instance, can use the auditory cortex to interpret sign language, while blind people can use the visual cortex to read Braille; if a finger is lost, its brain area can be taken over by the remaining fingers to make them more efficient (Carr, 2011, p. 29; Johnston, 2009, pp. 96-97). These studies have shown that when regions of the brain can no longer be used for their normal functions, they are adapted for other purposes. In this context, neuroplasticity operates to constantly make the most of the brain's neural real estate. This efficiency cushions the impact when normal processes are compromised.

      Moreover, neuroplasticity helps patients recover from physical brain injuries. Because the brain is such an integral part of normal functioning, brain injuries often have devastating consequences. Strokes, for example, can destroy an entire hemisphere of the brain, leading to paralysis in half of the body. Other brain injuries can occur from surgeries, tumors, and blood vessel disorders; these commonly result in severe speech impairments, disrupted vision, and memory problems. Luckily, neuroplasticity acts as a built-in healing mechanism. When the brain senses injury, it forms new neurons and synapses to repair the damaged networks, often leading to dramatic improvements. Stroke patients, for example, can recover almost full speech and motor function (Johnston, 2009). In this way, neuroplasticity prevents brain damage from leading to permanent disability.

      In a related manner, neuroplasticity assists in recovery from psychological disorders. Insight into this process was first gained by studying the brains of Buddhist monks after

---

Margin notes:

Names and date here and page number later in the paragraph frame evidence paraphrased from a source.

Two sources cited in a single citation.

Kim's interpretation of the evidence.

No citation needed for common knowledge, or generally accepted information that cannot be traced to any single source.

No page numbers for a summary.

meditation (Kaufman, 2005). The results indicated that brain regions associated with positive attitudes and happiness underwent lasting changes during meditation that made them more active. In other words, conscious thoughts (such as the positive ones common during meditation) can fundamentally alter the brain, and these thoughts can be controlled. Thus, it is not surprising that in many cases of depression and anxiety, patients reported marked improvements by simply thinking positive thoughts (Marx, 2013). In this context, neuroplasticity allows us to actively improve our mental health. When something goes wrong, we have the power to fix it.

> Paragraph synthesizes information from two sources.

> Kim's interpretation of the evidence.

Neuroplasticity has shattered the concept of a static brain. Within less than twenty years of its discovery, numerous benefits of neuroplasticity have been identified. Such broad implications are beginning to change old notions. In education, for example, neuroplasticity has strongly swung the nature-nurture debate in favor of the nurturists; educators are helping children overcome learning difficulties and actually improve their intelligence through training programs that restructure the brain (Wilson, Conyers, & Rose, 2015). Neuroplasticity is impacting the adult population as well. As news of a malleable brain spreads, people are engaging in mental exercises to proactively improve themselves (Marx, 2013). Meditation, anyone?

> Conclusion considers implications of the research.

> Citation for a source with three authors not named in the text; no page numbers for a summary.

BRAIN   6

References

Aydin, K., Ucar, A., Oguz, K. K., Okur, O. O., Agayev, A.,
      Unal, Z., . . . Ozturk, C. (2007). Increased gray matter
      density in the parietal cortex of mathematicians: A voxel-
      based morphometry study. *Neuroradiology, 28*, 1859-64.
      Retrieved from http://link.springer.com/journal/234

Carr, N. (2011). *The shallows: What the Internet is doing to our
      brains.* New York, NY: Norton.

Gould, E., Tanapat, P., McEwen, B. S., Flügge, G., & Fuchs, E.
      (1998). Proliferation of granule cell precursors in the
      dentate gyrus of adult monkeys is diminished by stress.
      *Proceedings of the National Academy of Sciences of the
      United States of America, 95*, 3168-71.

Johnston, M. V. (2009). Plasticity in the developing brain:
      Implications for rehabilitation. *Developmental Disabilities
      Research Reviews, 15*(2), 94-101. doi:10.1002/ddrr.64

Kaufman, M. (2005, January 3). Meditation gives brain a charge,
      study finds. *The Washington Post*. Retrieved from http://
      www.washingtonpost.com

Marx, P. (2013, July 29.) Mentally fit: Workouts at the brain
      gym. *The New Yorker, 89*(22), 24-28.

Rácz, I. (2014). Neuroplastic changes in addiction. *Frontiers in
      Molecular Neuroscience, 6*(56). doi:10.3389/fnmol2013.00056

von Melchner, L., Pallas, S. L., & Sur, M. (2000). Visual behavior
      mediated by retinal projections directed to the auditory
      pathway. *Nature, 404*, 871-75.

Wilson, D., Conyers, M., & Rose, K. (2015). Rethinking learning
      potential. *Independent School, 75*(1). Retrieved from
      https://www.nais.org

Wilson, J. H., & Hunt, T. (2015). *Molecular biology of the cell*
      (6th ed.). New York, NY: Garland Science.

Reference list begins on a new page.

An article with eight authors and no DOI from a database.

A print book with one author.

An article with five authors from a print journal.

A journal article with a DOI from a database.

A newspaper article on the Web.

A print article from a weekly magazine.

An online scholarly journal without page numbers.

An article with three authors from a print journal.

A journal article without page numbers or a DOI from a database.

A print book with two authors in a later edition.

GLOSSARY OF
USEFUL TERMS

Abstract and concrete Two kinds of language. *Abstract* words refer to ideas, conditions, and qualities we cannot directly perceive: *truth, love, happiness, courage, evil, poverty, progressive. Concrete* words indicate things we can know with our senses: *tree, chair, bird, pen, courthouse, motorcycle, perfume, thunderclap.* Concrete words lend vigor and clarity to writing, for they help a reader to picture things. See IMAGE.

Writers of expository and argumentative essays tend to shift back and forth from one kind of language to the other. They often begin a paragraph with a general statement full of abstract words ("There is *hope* for the *future* of *driving*"). Then they usually go on to give examples and present evidence in sentences full of concrete words ("Inventor *Jones* claims his *car* will go from *Fresno* to *Los Angeles* on a *gallon* of *peanut oil*"). Inexperienced writers often use too many abstract words and not enough concrete ones. See also pages 56–57 and 122.

Academic writing The kind of writing generally undertaken by scholars and students, in which a writer responds to another's work or uses multiple SOURCES to develop and support an original idea. Typically based on one or more TEXTS, all academic writing calls on a writer's CRITICAL THINKING, READING, AND WRITING abilities and shares the common goal of using reading and writing to build and exchange knowledge. See Chapter 3, pages 45–50, and the Appendix, pages 652–56.

Active voice   The form of the verb when the sentence subject is the actor: *Trees* [subject] *shed* [active verb] *their leaves in autumn.* Contrast PASSIVE VOICE.

Allude, allusion   To refer to a person, place, or thing believed to be common knowledge (*allude*), or the act or result of doing so (*allusion*). An allusion may point to a famous event, a familiar saying, a noted personality, or a well-known story or song. Usually brief, an allusion is a space-saving way to convey much meaning. For example, the statement "The game was Coach Johnson's Waterloo" informs the reader that, like Napoleon meeting defeat in a celebrated battle, the coach led a confrontation resulting in his downfall and that of his team. If the writer is also showing Johnson's character, the allusion might further tell us that the coach is a man of Napoleonic ambition and pride. To make an effective allusion, you have to ensure that it will be clear to your audience. Not every reader, for example, would understand an allusion to a neighbor, to a seventeenth-century Russian harpsichordist, or to a little-known stock-car driver.

Analogy   An extended comparison based on the like features of two unlike things: one familiar or easily understood, the other unfamiliar, abstract, or complicated. For instance, most people know at least vaguely how the human eye works: The pupil adjusts to admit light, which registers as an image on the retina at the back of the eye. You might use this familiar information to explain something less familiar to many people, such as how a camera works: The aperture (like the pupil) adjusts to admit light, which registers as an image on a sensor (like the retina) at the back of the camera. Analogies are especially helpful for explaining technical information in a way that is nontechnical, more easily grasped. For example, the spacecraft *Voyager 2* transmitted spectacular pictures of Saturn to Earth. To explain the difficulty of their achievement, NASA scientists compared their feat to a golfer sinking a putt from five hundred miles away. Because it can make abstract ideas vivid and memorable, analogy is also a favorite device of philosophers, politicians, and preachers.

    Analogy is similar to the method of COMPARISON AND CONTRAST. Both identify the distinctive features of two things and then set the features side by side. But a comparison explains two obviously similar things — two jobs for actors, two responses to a mess — and considers both their differences and their similarities. An analogy yokes together two apparently unlike things (eye and camera, spaceflight and golf) and focuses only on their major similarities. Analogy is thus an extended *metaphor*, the FIGURE OF SPEECH that declares one thing to be another — even though it isn't, in a strictly literal sense — for the purpose of making us aware of similarity: "Hope," writes the poet Emily Dickinson in the poem on page 474, "is the thing with feathers / That perches in the soul."

    In an ARGUMENT, analogy can make readers more receptive to a point or inspire them, but it can't prove anything because in the end the subjects are dissimilar. A false analogy is a logical FALLACY that claims a fundamental likeness when none exists. See page 500.

Analyze, analysis   To separate a subject into its parts (*analyze*), or the act or result of doing so (*analysis*, also called *division*). Analysis is a key skill in CRITICAL THINKING, READING, AND WRITING; see pages 16, 18–22, and 25. It is also considered a method of development; see Chapter 10.

Anecdote   A brief NARRATIVE, or retelling of a story or event. Anecdotes have many uses: as essay openers or closers, as examples, as sheer entertainment. See Chapter 5.

Appeals   Resources writers draw on to connect with and persuade readers:

- A **rational appeal (*logos*)** asks readers to use their intellects and their powers of reasoning. It relies on established conventions of logic and evidence.
- An **emotional appeal (*pathos*)** asks readers to respond out of their beliefs, values, or feelings. It inspires, affirms, frightens, angers.
- An **ethical appeal (*ethos*)** asks readers to look favorably on the writer. It stresses the writer's intelligence, competence, fairness, morality, and other qualities desirable in a trustworthy debater or teacher.

See also page 495.

Argument   A mode of writing intended to win readers' agreement with an assertion by engaging their powers of reasoning. Argument often overlaps PERSUASION. See Chapter 14.

Assume, assumption   To take something for granted (*assume*), or a belief or opinion taken for granted (*assumption*). Whether stated or unstated, assumptions influence a writer's choices of subject, viewpoint, EVIDENCE, and even language. See also pages 17 and 497.

Audience   A writer's readers. Having in mind a particular audience helps the writer in choosing strategies, such as which method(s) to use, what details to include, and how to shape an ARGUMENT. You can increase your awareness of your audience by asking yourself a few questions before you begin to write. Who are to be your readers? What is their age level? background? education? Where do they live? What are their beliefs and attitudes? What interests them? What, if anything, sets them apart from most people? How familiar are they with your subject? Knowing your audience can help you write so that your readers will not only understand you better but care more deeply about what you say. See also pages 20, 28–29, 119, and 493.

Body   The part of an essay, usually several PARAGRAPHS, that develops the writer's main idea. See pages 35–36.

Cause and effect   A method of development in which a writer ANALYZES reasons for an action, event, or decision, or analyzes its consequences. See Chapter 12. See also EFFECT.

Chronological order   The arrangement of events as they occurred or occur in time, first to last. Most NARRATIVES and PROCESS ANALYSES use chronological order.

Claim   The proposition that an ARGUMENT demonstrates, generally expressed in a THESIS STATEMENT. See pages 493–94.

Classification   A method of development in which a writer sorts out multiple things (contact sports, college students, kinds of music) into categories. See Chapter 11.

Cliché   A worn-out, trite expression that a writer employs thoughtlessly. Although at one time the expression may have been colorful, from heavy use it has lost its luster. It is now "old as the hills." In conversation, most of us sometimes use clichés, but in writing they "stick out like sore thumbs." Alert writers, when they revise, replace a cliché with a fresh, CONCRETE expression. Writers who have trouble recognizing clichés should be suspicious of any phrase they've heard before and should try to read more widely. Their problem is that, because so many expressions are new to them, they do not know which ones are full of moths.

Climactic order   The arrangement of points from least to most important, weakest to strongest. Essays organized by EXAMPLE and CAUSE AND EFFECT often use climactic order, as do many ARGUMENTS.

Coherence   The clear connection of the parts in effective writing so that the reader can easily follow the flow of ideas between sentences, paragraphs, and larger divisions, and can see how they relate successively to one another.

   In making an essay coherent, you may find certain devices useful. TRANSITIONS, for instance, can bridge ideas. Reminders of points you have stated earlier are helpful to a reader who may have forgotten them—as readers tend to do sometimes, particularly if an essay is long. However, a coherent essay is not one merely pasted together with transitions and reminders. It derives its coherence from the clear relationship between its THESIS (or central idea) and all its parts. See also pages 44–45 and 308.

Colloquial expressions   Words and phrases occurring primarily in speech and in informal writing that seeks a relaxed, conversational tone. "I need a burger and a shake" or "This mess is making me twitchy" may be acceptable in talking to a roommate, in corresponding with a friend, or in writing a humorous essay for general readers. Such choices of words, however, would be out of place in formal writing—in, say, a laboratory report or a letter to your senator. Contractions (*let's, don't, we'll*) and abbreviated words (*pic, sales rep, ad*) are the shorthand of spoken language. Good writers use such expressions with an awareness that they produce an effect of casualness.

Common ground   One or more aspects of an ARGUMENT on which both writer and reader can agree. A writer arguing in favor of raising highway speed limits might, for example, start by acknowledging the importance of safe driving before citing evidence showing that higher average speeds would have little effect on accident rates. By conceding the validity of opposing points or identifying ASSUMPTIONS shared by people on both sides of an issue, the writer establishes the fairness of his or her position and helps to win over readers who may otherwise be inclined to reject the argument outright. See page 493.

Comparison and contrast   Two methods of development usually found together. Using them, a writer examines the similarities and differences between two things to reveal their natures. See Chapter 8.

Conclusion   The sentences or paragraphs that bring an essay to a satisfying and logical end. See pages 37–38.

Concrete   See ABSTRACT AND CONCRETE.

Connotation and denotation   Two types of meanings most words have. *Denotation* is the explicit, literal, dictionary definition of a word. *Connotation* refers to a word's implied meaning, resonant with associations. The denotation of *blood* is "the fluid that circulates in the vascular system." The connotations of *blood* range from *life force* to *gore* to *family bond*. A doctor might use the word *blood* for its denotation, and a mystery writer might rely on the word's connotations to heighten a scene.

   Because people have different experiences, they bring to the same word different associations. A conservative's emotional response to the word *welfare* is not likely to be the same as a liberal's. And referring to your senator as a *diplomat* evokes a different response, from the senator and from others, than would *baby-kisser, political hack,* or even *politician.* The effective use of words involves knowing both what they mean literally and what they are likely to suggest.

Critical thinking, reading, and writing   A group of interlocking skills that are essential for college work and beyond. Each seeks the meaning beneath the surface of a statement, poem, editorial, picture, advertisement, Web site, or other TEXT. Using ANALYSIS, INFERENCE, SYNTHESIS, and often EVALUATION, the critical thinker, reader, and writer separates a text into its elements in order to see and judge meanings, relations, and ASSUMPTIONS that might otherwise remain buried. See also pages 10–12, 15–26, 305, and 492–93.

Data   A name for EVIDENCE favored by philosopher Stephen Toulmin in his conception of ARGUMENT. See pages 494–95.

Deductive reasoning, deduction   The method of reasoning from the general to the particular: From information about what we already know, we deduce what we need or want to know. See Chapter 14, pages 498–99.

Definition   A statement of the literal and specific meaning or meanings of a word or a method of developing an essay. In the latter, the writer usually explains the nature of a word, a thing, a concept, or a phenomenon. Such a definition may employ NARRATION, DESCRIPTION, or any other method. See Chapter 13.

Denotation   See CONNOTATION AND DENOTATION.

Description   A mode of writing that conveys the evidence of the senses: sight, hearing, touch, taste, smell. See Chapter 6.

Dialog   The quoted speech of participants in a story. Dialog is commonly included in a NARRATIVE, especially fiction, but it can also be useful in bringing any form of reported writing to life. See page 72.

Diction   The choice of words. Every written or spoken statement uses diction of some kind. To describe certain aspects of diction, the following terms may be useful:

- **Standard English:** the formal language, words, and grammatical forms that are commonly used and expected in North American schools, businesses, and professions.
- **Nonstandard English:** words and grammatical forms such as *theirselves* and *ain't* that are used mainly by people who speak a dialect other than standard English.
- **Dialect:** a variety of English based on differences in geography, education, or social background. Dialect is usually spoken but may be written. Maya Angelou's essay in Chapter 5 (p. 98) transcribes the words of dialect speakers ("'He gone whip him till that white boy call him Momma.'").
- **Slang:** certain words in highly informal speech or writing, or in the speech of a particular group—for example, *yas, dweeb, woke.*
- **Colloquial expressions:** words and phrases from conversation. See COLLOQUIAL EXPRESSIONS for examples.
- **Regional terms:** words heard in a certain locality, such as *spritzing* for "raining" in Pennsylvania Dutch country.
- **Technical terms:** words and phrases that form the vocabulary of a particular discipline (*monocotyledon* from botany), occupation (*drawplate* from die-making), or avocation (*interval training* from running). See also JARGON.
- **Archaisms:** old-fashioned expressions, once common but now used to suggest an earlier style, such as *ere* and *forsooth.*
- **Obsolete diction:** words that have passed out of use (such as the verb *werien,* "to protect or defend," and the noun *isetnesses,* "agreements"). *Obsolete* may

also refer to certain meanings of words no longer current (*fond* for foolish, *clipping* for hugging or embracing).

- **Pretentious diction:** use of words more numerous and elaborate than necessary, such as *institution of higher learning* for "college," and *partake of solid nourishment* for "eat."

Archaic, obsolete, and pretentious diction usually have no place in good writing unless for ironic or humorous effect: The journalist and critic H. L. Mencken delighted in the hifalutin use of *tonsorial studio* instead of barber shop. Still, any diction may be the right diction for a certain occasion: The choice of words depends on a writer's PURPOSE and AUDIENCE.

Discovery   The stage of the writing process before the first draft. It may include deciding on a topic, narrowing the topic, creating or finding ideas, doing reading and other research, defining PURPOSE and AUDIENCE, or planning and arranging material. Discovery may follow from daydreaming or meditation, reading, or perhaps carefully ransacking memory. In practice, though, it usually involves considerable writing and is aided by the act of writing. The operations of discovery — reading, research, further idea creation, and refinement of subject, purpose, and audience — may all continue well into drafting. See also pages 30–33.

Division   See ANALYZE, ANALYSIS.

Dominant impression   The main idea a writer conveys about a subject through DESCRIPTION — that an elephant is gigantic, for example, or an experience scary. See Chapter 6.

Drafting   The stage of the writing process during which a writer expresses ideas in complete sentences, links them, and arranges them in a sequence. See also pages 33–38 and 39–40.

Editing   The final stage of the writing process, during which a writer corrects errors and improves stylistic matters by, for example, using the ACTIVE VOICE and reworking sentences to achieve PARALLEL STRUCTURE. Contrast with REVISION. And see Chapter 4.

Effect   The result of an event or action, usually considered together with CAUSE as a method of development. See the discussion of cause and effect in Chapter 12. In discussing writing, the term *effect* also refers to the impression a word, a sentence, a paragraph, or an entire work makes on the reader: how convincing it is, whether it elicits an emotional response, what associations it conjures up, and so on.

Emotional appeal (*pathos*)   See APPEALS.

Emphasis   The stress or special importance given to a certain point or element to make it stand out. A skillful writer draws attention to what is most important in a sentence, a paragraph, or an essay by controlling emphasis in any of the following ways:

- **Proportion:** Important ideas are given greater coverage than minor points.
- **Position:** The beginnings and ends of sentences, paragraphs, and larger divisions are the strongest positions. Placing key ideas in these spots helps draw attention to their importance. The end is the stronger position, for what stands last stands out. A sentence in which less important details precede the main point is called a **periodic sentence:** "Having disguised himself as a guard and walked through the courtyard to the side gate, the prisoner made his escape."

A sentence in which the main point precedes less important details is a **loose sentence**: "Autumn is orange: gourds in baskets at roadside stands, the harvest moon hanging like a pumpkin, and oak leaves flashing like goldfish."
- **Repetition:** Careful repetition of key words or phrases can give them greater importance. (Careless repetition, however, can cause boredom.)
- **Mechanical devices:** Italics (underlining), capital letters, and exclamation points can make words or sentences stand out. Writers sometimes fall back on these devices, however, after failing to show significance by other means. Italics and exclamation points can be useful in reporting speech, but excessive use makes writing sound exaggerated or bombastic.

For additional ways to emphasize ideas at the sentence level, see pages 57–58.

Essay   A short nonfiction composition on one central theme or subject in which the writer may offer personal views. Essays are sometimes classified as either formal or informal. In general, a **formal essay** is one whose DICTION is that of the written language (not colloquial speech), whose TONE is serious, and whose focus is on a subject the writer believes is important. (For example, see Zadie Smith's "Find Your Beach," p. 319.) An **informal essay**, in contrast, is more likely to admit COLLOQUIAL EXPRESSIONS; the writer's tone tends to be lighter, perhaps humorous, and the subject is likely to be personal, sometimes even trivial. (See Naomi Shihab Nye's "Museum," p. 81.) These distinctions, however, are rough ones: An essay such as Augusten Burroughs's "How to Identify Love by Knowing What It's Not" (p. 482) uses colloquial language and speaks of personal experience, but its tone is serious and its subject important. See also EXPOSITION.

Ethical appeal (*ethos*)   See APPEALS.

Euphemism   The use of inoffensive language in place of language that readers or listeners may find hurtful, distasteful, frightening, or otherwise objectionable—for instance, a police officer's announcing that someone *passed on* rather than *died*, or a politician's calling for *revenue enhancement* rather than *taxation*. Writers sometimes use euphemism out of consideration for readers' feelings, but just as often they use it to deceive readers or shirk responsibility. (For more on euphemism, see William Lutz's "The World of Doublespeak," p. 387.)

Evaluate, evaluation   To judge the merits of something (*evaluate*) or the act or result of doing so (*evaluation*). Evaluation is often part of CRITICAL THINKING, READING, AND WRITING. In evaluating a work of writing, you base your judgment on your ANALYSIS of it and your sense of its quality or value. See also pages 18, 23, 26, and 648–51.

Evidence   The details that support an argument or an explanation, including facts, examples, and expert opinions. A writer's opinions and GENERALIZATIONS must rest upon evidence. See pages 494–95.

Example   Also called **exemplification** or **illustration**, a method of development in which the writer provides instances of a general idea. See Chapter 7. An *example* is a verbal illustration.

Exposition   The mode of prose writing that explains (or exposes) its subject. Its function is to inform, to instruct, or to set forth ideas: the major trade routes in the Middle East, how to make a dulcimer, why the United States consumes more energy than it needs. Exposition may call various methods to its service: EXAMPLE, COMPARISON AND CONTRAST, PROCESS ANALYSIS, and so on. Most college writing is at least partly exposition, and so are most of the ESSAYS in this book.

Fallacies Errors in reasoning. See pages 499–500 for a list and examples.

Figures of speech Expressions that depart from the literal meanings of words for the sake of emphasis or vividness. To say "She's a jewel" doesn't mean that the subject of praise is literally a kind of shining stone; the statement makes sense because the CONNOTATIONS of *jewel* come to mind: rare, priceless, worth cherishing. Some figures of speech involve comparisons of two objects apparently unlike:

- A **simile** (from the Latin, "likeness") states the comparison directly, usually connecting the two things using *like, as,* or *than*: "The moon is like a snow-ball"; "He's as lazy as a cat full of cream"; "My feet are flatter than flyswatters."
- A **metaphor** (from the Greek, "transfer") declares one thing to *be* another: "A mighty fortress is our God"; "The sheep were bolls of cotton on the hill." (A **dead metaphor** is a word or phrase that, originally a figure of speech, has come to be literal through common usage: "the *hands* of a clock.")
- **Personification** is a simile or metaphor that assigns human traits to inanimate objects or abstractions: "A stoop-shouldered refrigerator hummed quietly to itself"; "The solution to the math problem sat there winking at me."

Other figures of speech consist of deliberate misrepresentations:

- **Hyperbole** (from the Greek, "throwing beyond") is a conscious exaggeration: "I'm so hungry I could eat a saddle"; "I'd wait for you a thousand years."
- The opposite of hyperbole, **understatement**, creates an ironic or humorous effect: "I accepted the ride. At the moment, I didn't feel like walking across the Mojave Desert."
- A **paradox** (from the Greek, "conflicting with expectation") is a seemingly self-contradictory statement that, on reflection, makes sense: "Children are the poor person's wealth" (wealth can be monetary, or it can be spiritual). *Paradox* may also refer to a situation that is inexplicable or contradictory, such as the restriction of one group's rights in order to secure the rights of another group.

Flashback A technique of NARRATION in which the sequence of events is inter-rupted to recall an earlier period.

Focus The narrowing of a SUBJECT to make it manageable. Beginning with a general subject, you concentrate on a certain aspect of it. For instance, you may select crafts as a general subject, then decide your main interest lies in weaving. You could focus your essay still further by narrowing it to operating a hand loom. You also focus your writing according to who will read it (AUDIENCE) or what you want it to achieve (PURPOSE).

General and specific Terms that describe the relative number of instances or objects included in the group signified by a word. *General* words name a group or class (*flowers*); *specific* words limit the class by naming its individual members (*rose, violet, dahlia, marigold*). Words may be arranged in a series from more general to more specific: *clothes, pants, jeans, Levis.* The word *cat* is more specific than *animal*, but less specific than *tiger*, or *Garfield*. See also ABSTRACT AND CONCRETE and pages 56–57 and 122.

Generalization A statement about a class based on an examination of some of its members: "Lions are fierce." The more members examined and the more rep-resentative they are of the class, the sturdier the generalization. The statement

"Solar panels saves home owners money" would be challenged by home owners who have yet to recover their installation costs. "Solar panels can save home owners money in the long run" would be a sounder generalization. Insufficient or nonrepresentative EVIDENCE often leads to a hasty generalization, such as "All freshmen hate their roommates" or "Men never express their feelings." Words such as *all, every, only, never,* and *always* have to be used with care: "Some men don't express their feelings" is more credible. Making a trustworthy generalization involves the use of INDUCTIVE REASONING (discussed on pp. 497–98).

Genre The category into which a piece of writing fits. Shaped by PURPOSE, AUDIENCE, and context, genres range from broad types (such as fiction and non-fiction) to general groups (novel, essay) to narrower groups (science fiction novel, personal narrative) to specific document formats (steampunk graphic novel, post on a retail workers' forum)—and they tend to overlap. The genres of college writing vary widely. Examples appear on pages 74 (police log), 123 (field observation), 167 (job-application letter), 210 (review), 260 (lab report), 309 (critical analysis), 359 (résumé), 406 (letter to the editor), 458 (essay exam), and 504 (proposal).

Most readers are instinctively aware of individual genres and the characteristics that distinguish them, and they expect writers to follow the genre's conventions for POINT OF VIEW, structure and organization, types of EVIDENCE, language, TONE, length, appearance, and so forth. Consider, for instance, a daily newspaper: Readers expect the news articles to be objective statements of fact, with none of the reporters' personal thoughts and little rhetorical flourish; but when they turn to the op-ed page or their favorite columnists, such opinions and clever turns of phrase are precisely what they're looking for. Similar expectations exist for every kind of writing, and good writers make a point of knowing what they are. See also pages 10, 30, and 43 and the individual chapter introductions in Part Two.

Grounds A name for EVIDENCE favored by philosopher Stephen Toulmin in his conception of ARGUMENT. See pages 494–95.

Hyperbole See FIGURES OF SPEECH.

Illustration Another name for EXAMPLE. See Chapter 7.

Image A word or word sequence that evokes a sensory experience. Whether literal ("We picked two red apples") or figurative ("His cheeks looked like two red apples, buffed and shining"), an image appeals to the reader's memory of seeing, hearing, smelling, touching, or tasting. Images add concreteness to fiction—"The farm looked as tiny and still as a seashell, with the little knob of a house surrounded by its curved furrows of tomato plants" (Eudora Welty in a short story, "The Whistle")—and are an important element in poetry. But writers of essays, too, use images to bring ideas down to earth. See also FIGURES OF SPEECH.

Inductive reasoning, induction The method of reasoning from the particular to the general: We reach a conclusion about an entire class by examining some of its members. See pages 497–98.

Infer, inference To draw a conclusion (*infer*), or the act or result of doing so (*inference*). In CRITICAL THINKING, READING, AND WRITING, inference is the means to understanding a writer's meaning, ASSUMPTIONS, PURPOSE, fairness, and other attributes. See also pages 17, 23, and 25.

Introduction   The opening of a written work. Often it states the writer's subject, narrows it, and communicates the writer's main idea (THESIS). See page 37.

Irony   A manner of speaking or writing that does not directly state a discrepancy, but implies one. **Verbal irony** is the intentional use of words to suggest a meaning other than literal: "What a mansion!" (said of a shack); "There's nothing like sunshine" (said on a foggy morning). (For more examples, see the essays by David Sedaris, p. 235, and Jessica Mitford, p. 289.) If irony is delivered contemptuously with an intent to hurt, we call it **sarcasm**: "Oh, you're a real friend!" (said to someone who refuses to lend the coins to operate a clothes dryer). With **situational irony**, the circumstances themselves are incongruous, run contrary to expectations, or twist fate: Juliet regains consciousness only to find that Romeo, believing her dead, has stabbed himself. See also SATIRE.

Jargon   Strictly speaking, the special vocabulary of a trade or profession. The term has also come to mean inflated, vague, meaningless language of any kind. It is characterized by wordiness, ABSTRACT terms galore, pretentious DICTION, and needlessly complicated word order. Whenever you meet a sentence that obviously could express its idea in fewer words and shorter ones, chances are that it is jargon. For instance: "The motivating force compelling her to opt continually for the most labor-intensive mode of operation in performing her functions was consistently observed to be the single constant and regular factor in her behavior patterns." Translation: "She did everything the hard way." (For more on such jargon, see William Lutz's "The World of Doublespeak," p. 387.)

Journal   A record of one's thoughts, kept daily or at least regularly. Keeping a journal faithfully can help a writer gain confidence and develop ideas. See also page 31.

Logos   See APPEALS.

Metaphor   See FIGURES OF SPEECH.

Narration, narrative   The mode of writing (*narration*) that tells a story (*narrative*). See Chapter 5.

Narrator   The teller of a story, usually either in the first PERSON (*I*) or in the third (*he, she, it, they*). See pages 69–70.

Nonstandard English   See DICTION.

Objective and subjective   Kinds of writing that differ in emphasis. In *objective* writing the emphasis falls on the topic; in *subjective* writing it falls on the writer's view of the topic. Objective writing occurs in factual journalism, science reports, certain PROCESS ANALYSES (such as recipes, directions, and instructions), and logical arguments in which the writer attempts to downplay personal feelings and opinions. Subjective writing sets forth the writer's feelings, opinions, and interpretations. It occurs in friendly letters, journals, bylined feature stories and columns in periodicals, personal essays, and ARGUMENTS that appeal to emotion. Few essays, however, contain one kind of writing exclusive of the other.

Organization   The way ideas and supporting evidence are structured in the BODY of an essay. The methods of development typically lend themselves to different approaches, discussed in the introductions to Chapters 5–14. Independent of the methods, a successful writer orders subpoints and details in whatever way will best get the main idea across. While a NARRATIVE or a PROCESS ANALYSIS typically follows a CHRONOLOGICAL ORDER, for instance, the writer may need to step back to relate previous or concurrent events. DESCRIPTION often uses a SPATIAL ORDER, arranging details the way one's eyes might take them in. And the writer of an essay that presents EXAMPLES or an ARGUMENT may choose to move from most compelling points to least, or vice versa with a CLIMACTIC ORDER, depending on the desired EFFECT. See pages 21 and 36 and the graphic organizers on pages 73 (narration), 121 (description), 166 (example), 208 (COMPARISON AND CONTRAST), 257 (process analysis), 307 (DIVISION OR ANALYSIS), 358 (CLASSIFICATION), 403 (CAUSE AND EFFECT), 455 (DEFINITION), and 502 (argument or persuasion).

Paradox   See FIGURES OF SPEECH.

Paragraph   A group of closely related sentences that develop a central idea. In an essay, a paragraph is the most important unit of thought because it is both self-contained and part of the larger whole. Paragraphs separate long and involved ideas into smaller parts that are more manageable for the writer and easier for the reader to take in. Good paragraphs, like good essays, possess UNITY and COHERENCE. The central idea is usually stated in a TOPIC SENTENCE, often found at the beginning of the paragraph and related directly to the essay's THESIS. All other sentences in the paragraph relate to this topic sentence, defining it, explaining it, illustrating it, providing it with evidence and support. If you come across a unified and coherent paragraph that has no topic sentence, it will contain a central idea that no sentence in it explicitly states, but that every sentence in it clearly implies. See also pages 44–45, 308 (coherence); 44, 356 (development); and 44, 457 (unity).

Parallelism, parallel structure   A habit of good writers: keeping related ideas of equal importance in similar grammatical form. A writer may place nouns side by side ("*Trees* and *streams* are my weekend tonic") or in a series ("Give me *wind, sea,* and *stars*"). Phrases, too, may be arranged in parallel structure ("*Out of my bed, into my shoes, up to my classroom*—that's my life"), as may clauses ("Ask not what your country can do for you; ask what you can do for your country").

Parallelism may be found not only in single sentences but in larger units as well. A paragraph might read: "Rhythm is everywhere. It throbs in the rain forests of Brazil. It vibrates ballroom floors in Vienna. It snaps its fingers on street corners in Chicago." In a whole essay, parallelism may be the principle used to arrange ideas in a balanced or harmonious structure. See the essay "Checking My Privilege" by Tal Fortgang (p. 460), in which paragraphs 4–7, 10–12, and 15 all begin with some variation of the words "maybe it's the privilege" and examine the author's perceived advantages in life. Not only does such a parallel structure organize ideas, but it also lends them force. See also pages 58 and 210.

Paraphrase   Putting another writer's thoughts into your own words. In writing a research paper or an essay containing EVIDENCE gathered from your reading, you will find it necessary to paraphrase—unless you are using another writer's very words with quotation marks around them—and to acknowledge your sources. Contrast SUMMARY. And see pages 46–47.

Passive voice   The form of the verb when the sentence subject is acted upon: *The report* [subject] *was published* [passive verb] *anonymously.* Contrast ACTIVE VOICE.

Pathos   See APPEALS.

Person   A grammatical distinction made between the speaker, the one spoken to, and the one spoken about. In the first person (*I, we*), the subject is speaking. In the second person (*you*), the subject is being spoken to. In the third person (*he, she, it*), the subject is being spoken about. The point of view of an essay or work of literature is often specified according to person: "This short story is told from a first-person point of view." See also POINT OF VIEW.

Personification   See FIGURES OF SPEECH.

Persuasion   A mode of writing intended to influence people's actions by engaging their beliefs and feelings. Persuasion often overlaps ARGUMENT. See Chapter 14.

Plagiarism   The offense of using someone else's ideas or words as if they were your own, without acknowledging the original author. See pages 45–48 and 655–56.

Point of view   In an essay, the physical position or the mental angle from which a writer beholds a SUBJECT. On the subject of starlings, the following three writers would likely have different points of view: An ornithologist might write OBJEC-TIVELY about the introduction of these birds into North America, a farmer might advise others how to prevent the birds from eating seed, and a bird watcher might SUBJECTIVELY describe a first glad sighting of the species. Whether objective or subjective, point of view also encompasses a writer's biases and ASSUMPTIONS. For instance, the scientist, farmer, and bird watcher would likely all have different perspectives on starlings' reputation as nuisances: Although such perspectives may or may not be expressed directly, they would likely influence each writer's approach to the subject. See also PERSON.

Premise   A proposition or ASSUMPTION that leads to a conclusion. See pages 498–99 for examples.

Process analysis   A method of development that most often explains step by step how something is done or how to do something. See Chapter 9.

Purpose   A writer's reason for trying to convey a particular idea (THESIS) about a particular subject to a particular AUDIENCE of readers. Though it may emerge gradually during the writing process, in the end, purpose should govern every element of a piece of writing.

   In trying to define the purpose of an essay you read, ask yourself, "Why did the writer write this?" or "What was this writer trying to achieve?" Even though you cannot know the writer's intentions with absolute certainty, an effective essay will make some purpose clear. See also pages 19–20, 29–30, and 43.

Rational appeal   See APPEALS.

Revision   The stage of the writing process during which a writer "re-sees" a draft from the viewpoint of a reader. Revision usually involves rethinking fundamental matters such as PURPOSE and organization as well as rewriting to ensure COHER-ENCE and UNITY. Contrast with EDITING. And see Chapter 3.

Rhetoric   The study (and the art) of using language effectively. *Rhetoric* also has a negative CONNOTATION of empty or pretentious language meant to waffle, stall, or even deceive: This is the meaning in "The senator had nothing substantial to say about taxes, just the usual rhetoric."

Rhetorical question   A question posed for effect, one that requires no answer. Instead, it often provokes thought, lends emphasis to a point, asserts or denies something without making a direct statement, launches further dis-cussion, introduces an opinion, or leads the reader where the writer intends. Sometimes a writer throws one in to introduce variety in a paragraph full of declarative sentences. The following questions are rhetorical: "When will we learn that sending people into space does not feed them on the earth?" "Shall I compare thee to a summer's day?" "What is the point of making money if you've no one but yourself to spend it on?" Both reader and writer know what the answers are supposed to be: (1) Someday, if we ever wise up. (2) Yes. (3) None.

Sarcasm   See IRONY.

Satire   A form of writing that employs wit to attack folly. Unlike most comedy, the purpose of satire is not merely to entertain, but to bring about enlightenment—even reform. Usually, satire employs irony—as in Koji Frahm's "How to Write an A Paper" (p. 268) and Jonathan Swift's "A Modest Proposal" (p. 610). See also IRONY.

Scene   In a NARRATION, an event retold in detail to re-create an experience. See Chapter 5.

Signal phrase   Words used to introduce a quotation, PARAPHRASE, or SUMMARY, often including the source author's name and generally telling readers how the source material should be interpreted: "Nelson argues that the legislation will backfire." See also pages 50, 655, 657, and 677.

Simile   See FIGURES OF SPEECH.

Slang   See DICTION.

Source   Any outside TEXT or material that a writer uses to develop and support ideas. Often found through the process of researching a subject, a single source might be the focus of an essay (as when you write about a selection in this book), or a writer might SYNTHESIZE multiple sources as EVIDENCE for one or more points. Any source referred to in an essay must be documented with an in-text citation and an entry in a works-cited or references list. See pages 32–33 on responding to a text, 45–50 on integrating evidence, and the Appendix on research and documentation.

Spatial order   An organizational technique in which a writer DESCRIBES an object or scene by presenting details parallel to the way people normally view them—for instance, near to far, top to bottom, left to right. See also pages 120–21.

Specific   See GENERAL AND SPECIFIC.

Standard English   See DICTION.

Strategy   Whatever means a writer employs to write effectively. The methods set forth in this book are strategies; but so are narrowing a SUBJECT, organizing ideas clearly, using TRANSITIONS, writing with an awareness of your AUDIENCE, and other effective writing practices.

Style   The distinctive manner in which a writer writes. Style may be seen especially in the writer's choice of words and sentence structures. Two writers may write on the same subject, even express similar ideas, but it is style that gives each writer's work a personality.

Subject   What a piece of a writing is about. The subject of an essay starts with a general topic, but because writers narrow their FOCUS on a subject until they have a specific point to make about it, multiple works on the same topic will typically be very different from one another. See also page 28, PURPOSE, and THESIS.

Subjective   See OBJECTIVE AND SUBJECTIVE.

Summarize, summary   To condense a work (essay, movie, news story) to its essence (*summarize*), or the act or result of doing so (*summary*). Summarizing a piece of writing in one's own words is an effective way to come to understand it. (See pp. 15–16.) Summarizing (and acknowledging) others' writing in your own text is a good way to support your ideas. (See pp. 46 and 49.) Contrast PARAPHRASE.

Suspense   Often an element in NARRATION: the pleasurable expectation or anxiety we feel that keeps us reading a story. In an exciting mystery story, suspense is constant: How will it all turn out? Will the detective get to the scene in time to prevent another murder? But there can be suspense in less melodramatic accounts as well. See, for instance, Maya Angelou's gripping essay "Champion of the World" (p. 98).

Syllogism   A three-step form of reasoning that employs DEDUCTION. See pages 498–99 for illustrations.

Symbol   A visible object or action that suggests further meaning. The flag suggests country; the crown suggests royalty — these are conventional symbols familiar to us. Life abounds in such clear-cut symbols. Football teams use dolphins and rams for easy identification; married couples symbolize their union with a ring.

In writing, symbols usually do not have such a one-to-one correspondence, but evoke a whole constellation of associations. In Herman Melville's *Moby-Dick*, the whale suggests more than the large mammal it is. It hints at evil, obsession, and the untamable forces of nature. Such a symbol carries meanings too complex or elusive to be neatly defined.

Although more common in fiction and poetry, symbols can be used to good purpose in nonfiction because they often communicate an idea in a compact and concrete way.

Synthesize, synthesis   To link elements into a whole (*synthesize*), or the act or result of doing so (*synthesis*). In CRITICAL THINKING, READING, AND WRITING, synthesis is the key step during which you use your own perspective to reassemble a work you have ANALYZED or to connect the work with others. (See pp. 17–18 and 25.) Synthesis is a hallmark of ACADEMIC WRITING in which you respond to others' work or use multiple sources to support your ideas. (See pp. 48–50 and 654–55.)

Text   Any creation — written, visual, auditory, physical, or experiential — that can be interpreted or used as a SOURCE for writing. The starting point for most ACADEMIC WRITING, texts include written documents such as essays, articles, and books, of course, but also photographs, paintings, advertisements, Web sites, performances, musical scores, experiments, conversations, lectures, field observations, interviews, dreams, jokes — anything that invites a response, sparks an idea, or lends itself to CRITICAL THINKING, READING, AND WRITING. See pages 652–56.

Thesis, thesis statement   The central idea in a work of writing (*thesis*), to which everything else in the work refers; one or more sentences that express that central idea (*thesis statement*). In some way, each sentence and PARAGRAPH in an effective essay serves to support the thesis and to make it clear and explicit to readers. Good writers, while writing, often set down a thesis statement to help them define their purpose. They also often include this statement in their essay as a promise and a guide to readers. See pages 18–19, 34–35, 43, and the introductions to Chapters 5–14.

Tone   The way a writer expresses his or her regard for subject, AUDIENCE, or self. Through word choice, sentence structures, and what is actually said, the writer conveys an attitude and sets a prevailing spirit. Tone in writing varies as greatly as tone of voice varies in conversation. It can be serious, distant, flippant, angry, enthusiastic, sincere, sympathetic. Whatever tone a writer chooses, usually it informs an entire essay and helps a reader decide how to respond. For examples of strong tone, see the essays by Scaachi Koul (p. 133), Jessica Mitford (p. 289), David Sedaris (p. 235), Ben Healy (p. 411), Chitra Divakaruni (p. 437), Tal Fortgang (p. 460), Sarah Hemphill (p. 558), and Luis Alberto Urrea (p. 631). See also "Focus on Tone," page 496.

Topic sentence   The statement of the central idea in a PARAGRAPH, usually asserting one aspect of an essay's THESIS. Often the topic sentence will appear at (or near) the beginning of the paragraph, announcing the idea and beginning its development. Because all other sentences in the paragraph explain and support this central idea, the topic sentence is a way to create UNITY.

Transitions   Words, phrases, sentences, or even paragraphs that relate ideas. In moving from one topic to the next, a writer must bring the reader along by showing how the ideas are developing, what bearing a new thought or detail has on an earlier discussion, or why a new topic is being introduced. A clear purpose, strong ideas, and logical development certainly aid COHERENCE, but to ensure that the reader is following along, good writers provide signals, or transitions.

To bridge sentences or paragraphs and to point out relationships within them, you can use some of the following devices of transition:

- Repeat or restate words or phrases to produce an echo in the reader's mind.
- Use PARALLEL STRUCTURES to produce a rhythm that moves the reader forward.
- Use pronouns to refer back to nouns in earlier passages.
- Use transitional words and phrases. These may indicate a relationship of time (*right away, later, soon, meanwhile, in a few minutes, that night*), proximity (*beside, close to, distant from, nearby, facing*), effect (*therefore, for this reason, as a result, consequently*), comparison (*similarly, in the same way, likewise*), or contrast (*yet, but, nevertheless, however, despite*). Some words and phrases of transition simply add on: *besides, too, also, moreover, in addition to, second, last, in the end*.

Understatement   See FIGURES OF SPEECH.

Unity   The quality of good writing in which all parts relate to the THESIS. In a unified essay, all words, sentences, and PARAGRAPHS support the single central idea. Your first step in achieving unity is to state your thesis; your next step is to organize your thoughts so that they make your thesis clear. See also pages 44 and 457.

Voice   In writing, the sense of the author's character, personality, and attitude that comes through the words. See TONE.

Warrant   The name for ASSUMPTION favored by philosopher Stephen Toulmin in his conception of ARGUMENT. See page 497.

DIRECTORY TO THE WRITERS ON WRITING

DISCOVERING IDEAS

DRAFTING

EDITING

ORGANIZATION

PLANNING

POETRY

POINT OF VIEW

PROCRASTINATION

PURPOSE

READING

RESEARCH

REVIEW

REVISION

SELF-DISCOVERY

SENTENCES

STYLE

SUBJECT

SYNTHESIS

THESIS

UNITY AND COHERENCE

VOICE

WORD CHOICE

WRITER'S BLOCK

Acknowledgments

Angelou, Maya. Chapter 19 ("Champion of the World") from *I Know Why the Caged Bird Sings* by Maya Angelou. Copyright © 1969 and renewed 1997 by Maya Angelou. Used by permission of Random House, an imprint and division of Penguin Random House LLC. All rights reserved.

Angelou, Maya. "On Writing" excerpted from "Work in Progress/Maya Angelou" by Sheila Weller, *Intellectual Digest*, June 1973. Reprinted with the permission of Sheila Weller.

Asselin, Janelle. "Superhuman Error: What Dixon and Rivoche Get Wrong." *Comics Alliance*, June 10, 2014. Reprinted by permission of the author.

Blank, Jessica, and Erik Jensen. Excerpts from *The Exonerated* by Jessica Blank and Erik Jensen. Copyright © 2004 by Jumpydance, Inc. Reprinted by permission of Farrar, Straus and Giroux and The Gersh Agency.

Blank, Jessica, and Erik Jensen. "Introduction" from *The Exonerated* by Jessica Blank and Erik Jensen. Copyright © 2004 by Jumpydance, Inc. Reprinted by permission of Farrar, Straus and Giroux and The Gersh Agency.

Braudy, Leo. "Where Our Monsters Come From," *The Wall Street Journal*, October 28, 2016. Copyright © 2016 Dow Jones & Company, Inc. All rights reserved worldwide. Reprinted by permission.

Britt, Suzanne. "Neat People vs. Sloppy People" from *Show and Tell* (1982). Reprinted by permission of the author.

Britt, Suzanne. "On Writing." Reprinted by permission of the author.

Burroughs, Augusten. "How to Identify Love by Knowing What It's Not" from *This Is How: Surviving What You Think You Can't*. Copyright © 2012 by Augusten, Inc., published by permission of Augusten Burroughs c/o Selectric Artists LLC.

Chavez, Linda. "Supporting Family Values," *townhall.com*, Friday, April 17, 2009. By permission of Linda Chavez and Creators Syndicate, Inc.

Chiang, Ted. "The Great Silence," from *Exhalation: Stories* by Ted Chiang, compilation copyright © 2019 by Ted Chiang. Used by permission of Alfred A. Knopf, an imprint of the Knopf Doubleday Publishing Group, a division of Penguin Random House LLC. All rights reserved.

Churchill, Susan. "E-mail to Exeter Hospital." Reprinted by permission of the author.

Churchill, Susan. "Résumé." Reprinted by permission of the author.

Cisneros, Sandra. "And Some More," from *The House on Mango Street*. Copyright © 1984 by Sandra Cisneros. Published by Vintage Books, a division of Penguin Random House, and in hardcover by Alfred A. Knopf in 1994. Reprinted by permission of Susan Bergholz Literary Services, New York, NY, and Lamy, NM. All rights reserved.

Cisneros, Sandra. "On Writing," excerpted from *Interviews with Writers of the Post-Colonial World*, edited by Feroza Jussawalla and Reed Way Dasenbrock. Copyright © 1992 by the University Press of Mississippi. Reprinted by permission.

Didion, Joan. Excerpt from *After Henry*, copyright © 1992 by Joan Didion. Reprinted by permission of the author.

Didion, Joan. "On Writing" excerpted from "Why I Write." Originally published in the *New York Times Book Review*, December 5, 1976. Copyright © 1976 by Joan Didion. Reprinted by permission of the author.

Divakaruni, Chitra. "Live Free and Starve." Copyright © 2009 by Chitra Divakaruni. This article first appeared in *Salon.com*, at *http://www.salon.com*. Reprinted by permission of the author and the Sandra Dijkstra Literary Agency.

Dixon, Chuck, and Paul Rivoche. "How Liberalism Became Kryptonite for Superman." *The Wall Street Journal Commentary*, June 8, 2014. Copyright © 2014 Dow Jones & Company, Inc. All rights reserved worldwide.

Doyle, Brian. "Three Basketball Stories," from *Bin Laden's Bald Spot & Other Stories*, by Brian Doyle. (Red Hen Press, 2011.) Reprinted by permission of Red Hen Press.

Doyle, Brian. "On Writing" from "How Did You Become a Writer?" Reprinted from *The American Scholar* online, August 23, 2013. Copyright © 2013 by Brian Doyle. Reprinted by permission of *The American Scholar*.

Dumas, Firoozeh. "Sweet, Sour, and Resentful." Copyright © 2009 Condé Nast. All rights reserved. Originally printed in *Gourmet*. Reprinted by permission.

Dumas, Firoozeh. "A Reader's Guide," from *Funny in Farsi: A Memoir of Growing Up Iranian in America* by Firoozeh Dumas. Copyright © 2006 by Random House LLC. Used by permission of Villard Books, an imprint of Random House, a division of Penguin Random House LLC. All rights reserved.

Erdrich, Louise. "The Crest" from *The Red Convertible: Selected and New Stories, 1978–2008* by Louise Erdrich. Copyright © 2009 by Louise Erdrich. Reprinted by permission of HarperCollins Publishers.

Fortgang, Tal. "Checking My Privilege." *The Princeton Tory*, April 2, 2014. Reprinted by permission of the author.

Frahm, Koji. "How to Write an A Paper." *Prized Writing* 2005–2006. UC Davis. Reprinted by permission of the author.

Frahm, Koji. "On Writing." Reprinted by permission of the author.

Gay, Roxane. "Peculiar Benefits" from *Bad Feminist* by Roxane Gay. Copyright © 2014 by Roxane Gay. Reprinted by permission of HarperCollins Publishers.

Gilb, Dagoberto. "Pride." Reprinted by permission of the author.

Gladwell, Malcolm. "Little Fish in a Big Pond" from *David and Goliath*. Copyright © 2015 by Malcolm Gladwell. Reprinted by permission of the author.

Healy, Ben. "Gossip Is Good," *The Atlantic*, July/August 2018. Copyright © 2018 The Atlantic Media Company, as first published in *The Atlantic* magazine. All rights reserved. Distributed by Tribune Content Agency, LLC.

Hemphill, Sarah. "Whatever Happened to Free Speech on College Campuses?" from *Waves*, August 2017, California State University, Northridge. Copyright © 2017. Reprinted by permission of the author.

Hughes, Langston. "Harlem (2)" from *The Collected Poems of Langston Hughes* by Langston Hughes, edited by Arnold Rampersad with David Roessel, Associate Editor. Copyright © 1994 by the Estate of Langston Hughes. Used by permission of Alfred A. Knopf, an imprint of the Knopf Doubleday Publishing Group, a division of Penguin Random House LLC, and Harold Ober Associates Incorporated. All rights reserved.

Jackson, Shirley. "The Lottery" from *The Lottery and Other Stories*. Copyright © 1948, 1949 by Shirley Jackson, renewed © 1976, 1977 by Laurence Hyman, Barry Hyman, Mrs. Sarah Webster, and Mrs. Joanne Schnurer. Reprinted with the permission of Farrar, Straus and Giroux.

Keith, Jourdan Imani. "At Risk." First published in *Orion*, January/February 2014. Copyright © 2014 by Jourdan Imani Keith. Reprinted by permission of the author.

Keith, Jourdan Imani. "On Writing," excerpted from Demetria Haigh, "Interview with Poet Jourdan Keith," *The Cub*, the student news site of Sedro-Wooley High School, May 6, 2016. Reprinted by permission.

Kim, Eric. "The Brain That Changes." *3808: A Journal of Critical Writing*, Spring 2012. Reprinted by permission of the author.

Kingston, Maxine Hong. "No Name Woman" from *The Woman Warrior: Memoirs of a Girlhood among Ghosts*. Copyright © 1975, 1976 by Maxine Hong Kingston. Used by permission of Alfred A. Knopf, an imprint of the Knopf Doubleday Publishing Group, a division of Penguin Random House LLC. All rights reserved.

Koul, Scaachi. "Impatiently Waiting for the Horror of Death," *Hazlitt Magazine*, January 9, 2015. Reprinted by permission of the author.

Koul, Scaachi. From "Mute" by Scaachi Koul, from *One Day We'll All Be Dead and None of This Will Matter: Essays*. Copyright © 2017 by Scaachi Koul. Reprinted by permission of Picador, an imprint of St. Martin's Press. All Rights Reserved.

Lamott, Anne. "Shitty First Drafts," from *Bird by Bird: Some Instructions on Writing and Life*. Copyright © 1994 by Anne Lamott. Used by permission of Pantheon Books, an imprint of the Knopf Doubleday Publishing Group, a division of Penguin Random House LLC. All rights reserved.

Lundberg, Margaret. "Eating Green." Reprinted by permission of the author.

INDEX

Page numbers in boldface refer to definitions in the Glossary of Useful Terms.